KU-168-685

ART

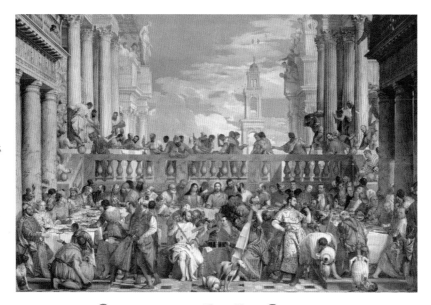

a visual history

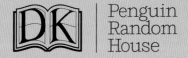

DK UK

Senior editors Angela Wilkes, Hannah Bowen
Senior art editor Helen Spencer
Editorial assistant Stuart Neilson
Jacket designer Laura Brim, Natalie Godwin
Jacket editor Claire Gell
Jacket design development manager Sophia MTT
Producer, pre-production Gillian Reid
Producer Mandy Inness
Managing editors Stephanie Farrow, Gareth Jones
Managing art editor Lee Griffiths
Publisher Liz Wheeler
Art director Karen Self
Publishing director Jonathan Metcalf

DK DELHI

Senior editor Anita Kakar
Senior art editor Mahua Mandal
Editors Arpita Dasgupta, Sonia Yooshing
Art editors Shreya Anand, Upasana Sharma
Jacket designer Suhita Dharamjit
Managing jackets editor Saloni Singh
Senior DTP designer Harish Aggarwal, Neeraj Bhatia
DTP designer Jaypal Singh Chauhan,
Rajesh Singh, Mohammad Usman
Picture researcher Aditya Katyal
Managing editor Rohan Sinha
Managing art editor Sudakshina Basu
Production manager Pankaj Sharma
Pre-production manager Balwant Singh

First published in Great Britain in 2005 as *Art*
This revised edition published in 2015 by
Dorling Kindersley Limited
80 Strand, London WC2R 0RL

Copyright © 2005, 2015 Dorling Kindersley Limited

A Penguin Random House Company

2 4 6 8 10 9 7 5 3 1
001–274825–September/2015

A CIP catalogue record for this
book is available from the British Library.

ISBN 978-0-2411-8610-7

Printed in China

A WORLD OF IDEAS:
SEE ALL THERE IS TO KNOW

www.dk.com

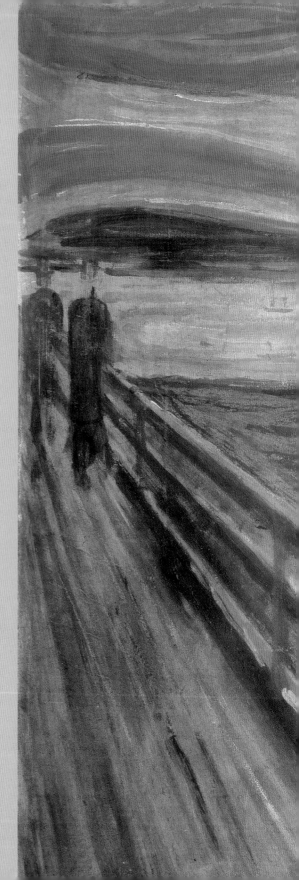

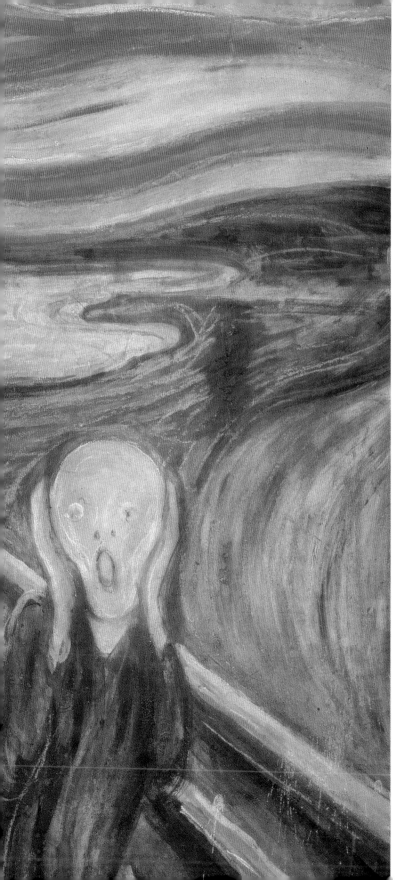

CONTENTS

Robert Cumming is a bestselling writer and art critic whose books have won several international awards. The founder and former Chairman of Christie's Education, he is currently an Adjunct Professor of Art History at Boston University. His previous books for DK include *Annotated Art* and *Great Artists*.

This book has evolved over many years of looking at works of art, often on my own, but preferably in the company of others. The eye is the sovereign of the senses, and to share looking is one of life's great pleasures – it increases with age and is not confined to works of art.

My first job in the art world was at the Tate Gallery, as a new member of a small team whose task was to stand in front of the works on display and explain them to the public. I soon learned that three questions were asked over and over again:
1 What should I look for? What are the key features in a Picasso, a Rembrandt, a Raphael, a Turner?
2 What is going on? What is the story? Who is Hercules? What is the Nativity? Who is that girl with a broken wheel? Who is the man abducting the woman who looks like a tree? Does that big red square mean anything?
3 How was it made? Why was it made? Is it any good?

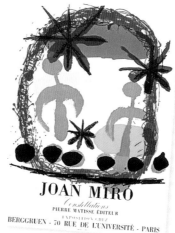

⌃ *Poster for Miró exhibition*

I also found that most of my audience seemed to enjoy getting involved in an informed discussion or exchange of opinions about a particular work of art, or about specific issues (especially provocative or controversial ones) and about what they saw, thought, and felt.

In this book, I have tried to capture that sort of involvement and to address the three basic questions I listed earlier. Also, I have been part of the art world long enough to know that when those of us who work in it are "off duty", looking at art purely for pleasure, uninhibited by the need to maintain professional credibility, we often voice different – and sometimes much more interesting – opinions than we do when "on duty".

» *Hidden treasures, the Hermitage, St Petersburg*
This photograph, taken in 1994, gives some idea of the vast quantities of works of art that are not on display but are held in museum archives around the world.

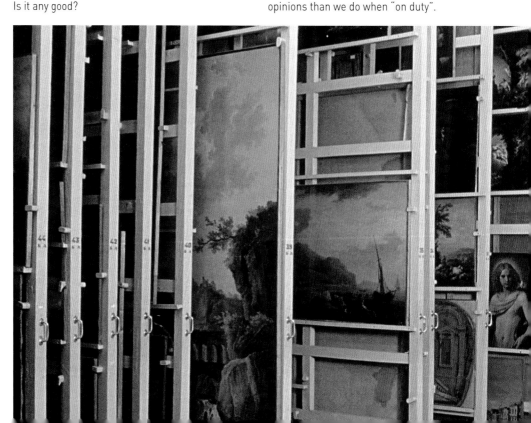

The present-day art world is a huge industry of museums, teaching institutions, commercial operations, and official bodies, all with reputations and postures to maintain. They are often desperate to convince us of the validity of their official messages.

I understand the pressures that impel all these official art institutions to maintain a party line, but in the face of all that vested self-interest there is a need for alternative voices.

In the main section of the book, The History of Art (pages 6–401), you will find painters and sculptors, from the early Renaissance onwards, arranged as separate entries. In these I have indicated characteristics to serve as a guideline when looking at their works. My observations are entirely personal, but I have tried to pick out qualities that anyone with a pair of eyes can see and have pleasure in searching for. Most of the entries were written, at least in note form, while looking at the works of art. In fact, nearly everything I have written in this book is what I would say if we were standing in front of a work of art. In such a situation it is, I think, better to say too little rather than too much, so as to allow those who are with me to make their own discoveries and connections.

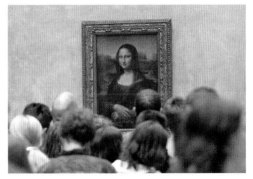
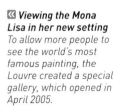

« Viewing the Mona Lisa in her new setting
To allow more people to see the world's most famous painting, the Louvre created a special gallery, which opened in April 2005.

I hope this book will prove to be a friendly companion, as well as an entertaining and practical aid for looking at art. If it fulfils its aims, it will provoke you, make you query your own opinions, cause you to stop, think, and, I hope, smile, too. It should also encourage you to believe what you see, rather than what you are told, and make you go back to a painting or sculpture and see aspects of it you had not perceived before. My first wish is to increase the pleasure you get when looking at a work of art.

Robert Cumming
London

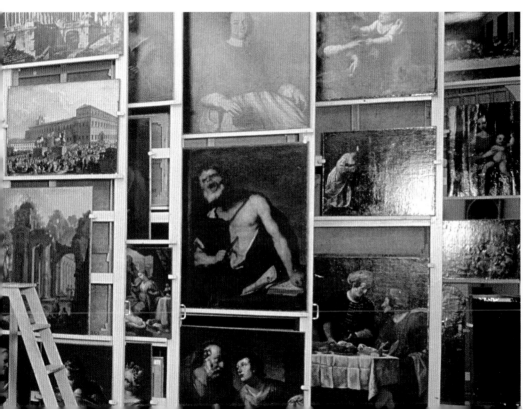

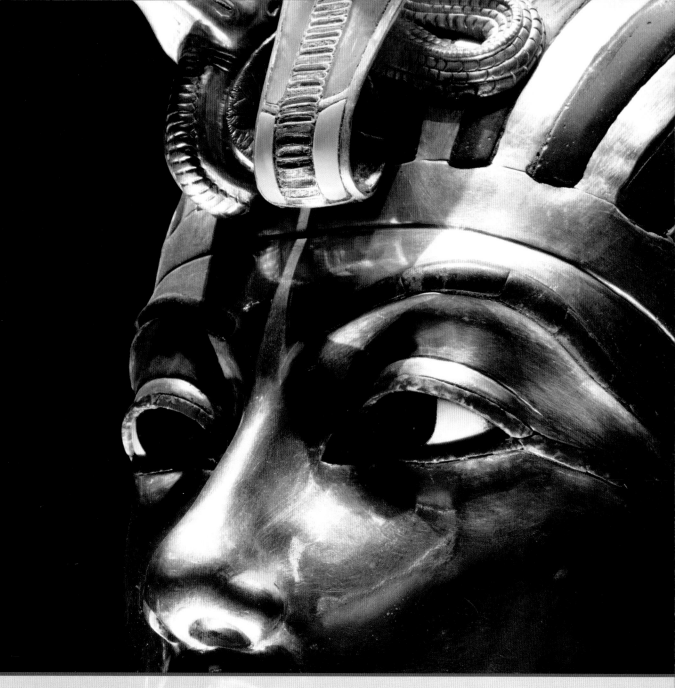

Early Art
c.30,000BCE—1300CE

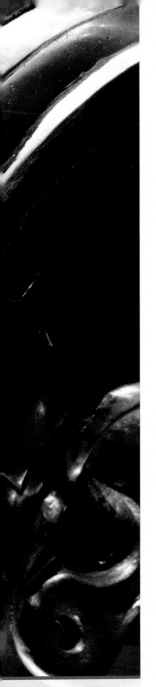

Artists, like children, are great borrowers and imitators and take delight in what they see in the world around them. However, curiosity and a desire to create do not in themselves produce works of art. So how do we identify that moment when what we choose to call "art" first appeared as a significant activity?

The oldest known works of art to have been discovered in Europe are stone carvings, dating from perhaps 32,000 years ago. Found across Europe and Russia, they are rare survivals. It is no accident that carvings, inherently durable, should be the oldest surviving examples of human art. They are inevitably few in number, their survival almost entirely a matter of chance. The clues they offer as to the nature of the hunter-gatherer societies that produced them are tantalizing at best. But their claims to be considered art are undoubted. They satisfy the innate human need for aesthetic appeal, whether by means of craftsmanship, colour, or form. As important, they almost uniformly seem to have had a mystical, probably religious, purpose. They make clear the enduring human need to understand – perhaps to appease – an uncertain and frequently hostile world by means of deliberately contrived objects.

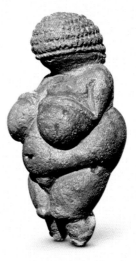

◀◀ *Venus of Willendorf*
c.30,000BCE, limestone, height 11.5 cm (4½ in), Vienna: Naturhistorisches Museum. The carving's swelling limbs and breasts invest it with a strong sexual quality.

Stone-age sculpture

The best-known of these chance survivals is a tiny limestone figure of a woman. It was found in Austria and dates from between 32,000 and 27,000 years ago. The *Venus of Willendorf*, as this oddly misshapen figure is known, was almost certainly a fertility offering. At first sight, she appears to be just a crude caricature of the female form. Closer inspection reveals a remarkably rhythmic treatment allied to considerable technical sophistication on the part of her unknown creator. The taut curls that hug her head are not just closely observed but precisely rendered.

◀◀ **Mask from the mummy-case of Tutankhamun**
c.1340BCE, height 54 cm (21¼ in), gold, enamel and semi-precious stones, Cairo: Egyptian Museum. The artists of early civilizations, such as ancient Egypt, used the most precious materials to produce stylized depictions of rulers and their families.

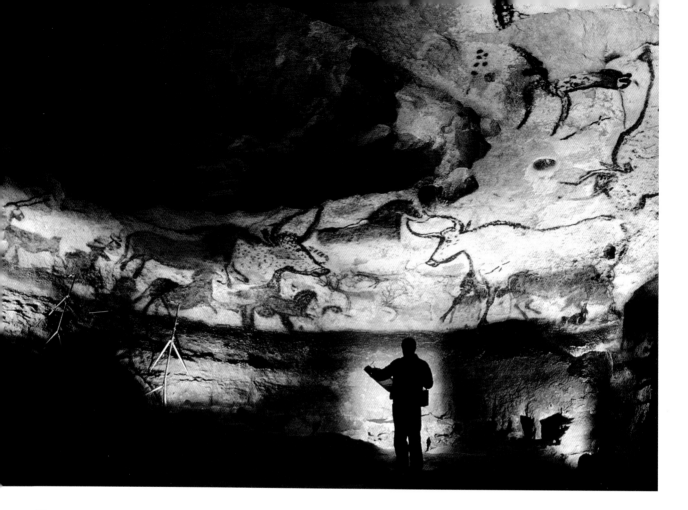

▲ **The Great Hall, Lascaux** *c.15,000BCE.* Like the other Stone Age cave paintings in Europe, those at Lascaux survived because, once abandoned, they were then completely forgotten until rediscovered by chance.

Cave painting

More spectacular by far are the cave paintings of southwest France and northern Spain. It is no surprise that when the first was discovered, in 1879, it was widely assumed to be a fake. Virtuosity on such an epic scale was hard to reconcile with current beliefs about

Stone Age man. Between about 25,000 and 12,000 years ago, during the peak of the last Ice Age, an astonishingly vigorous tradition of cave painting developed in which acutely observed and brilliantly depicted animals – mammoths, bison, hyenas, and horses – were painted onto cave walls. A variety of

TIMELINE: EARLY ART

c.25,000 Stylized female figurines made throughout Europe; first cave paintings (France and Spain)

c.10,000 Retreat of glaciers; larger mammals extinct

c.7000 Pigs domesticated (Anatolia); farming spreads to SE Europe

c.5000 Cereal-farming villages in western Europe; copper first used (Mesopotamia)

35,000BCE	25,000BCE	10,000BCE	5000BCE

c.35,000 Homo sapiens established in Europe; Neanderthals extinct

c.20,000 Peak of last Ice Age

c.9000 Earliest evidence of wheat cultivation (Syria)

c.5500 Bandkeramik pottery produced (C Europe); metallurgy discovered (SE Europe)

c.4500 Megalithic tombs built in western Europe

materials, chiefly red ochre and charcoal, were used. These were applied by sticks, feathers, or moss, sometimes by hand. In almost every case the most spectacular images were created deep inside the caves. That their purpose was religious – part fearful, part celebratory – can scarcely be doubted. That they constitute everything that we understand today as art is no more in question. Curiously, there are almost no representations of humans: those that do appear, in contrast to the immediately recognizable animals, are schematic and crude, more like a child's attempt to draw a person.

Cities and civilization

Perhaps 5,000 years ago, the world's first civilizations were forming in the Near East. As settled agriculture began, reinforced by the domestication of goats and sheep, so surplus food production permitted the development of divisions of labour and the emergence of ruling classes, often priestly. At the same time, cities began to appear. These were organized societies, self-aware, technically sophisticated, and literate, that recognized how artistic images could be pressed into service on their behalf. Impelled by a need to justify themselves to their gods or to assert

their dominance over their subjects, a series of rulers commissioned images that would underline their status and their right to rule.

The earliest of these civilizations was Sumer, in what is today Iraq. What has survived – fragments of pottery, a handful of battered marble figures – shows this to have been a society with a well-developed sense of the power of visual images. Yet more remarkable is a product of Sumer's successors, the Akkadians, who from about 2300BCE united much of Mesopotamia in a single empire. The bronze head of an Akkadian ruler, cast between 2300 and 2200BCE, is not just a technical triumph but a defining image of a hierarchical ruler: remote and magnificent.

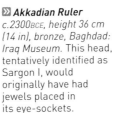

» *Akkadian Ruler*
c.2300BCE, height 36 cm (14 in), bronze, Baghdad: Iraq Museum. This head, tentatively identified as Sargon I, would originally have had jewels placed in its eye-sockets.

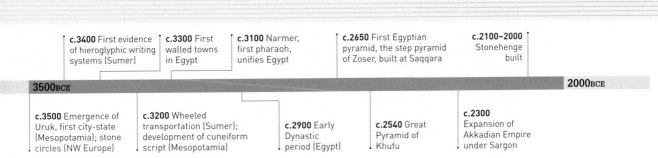

c.3400 First evidence of hieroglyphic writing systems (Sumer)

c.3300 First walled towns in Egypt

c.3100 Narmer, first pharaoh, unifies Egypt

c.2650 First Egyptian pyramid, the step pyramid of Zoser, built at Saqqara

c.2100–2000 Stonehenge built

3500BCE

2000BCE

c.3500 Emergence of Uruk, first city-state (Mesopotamia); stone circles (NW Europe)

c.3200 Wheeled transportation (Sumer); development of cuneiform script (Mesopotamia)

c.2900 Early Dynastic period (Egypt)

c.2540 Great Pyramid of Khufu

c.2300 Expansion of Akkadian Empire under Sargon

ANCIENT EGYPT

c.3000–300BCE

Ancient Egyptian art reflected the rigidly hierarchical society from which it developed. It placed a premium on lavish materials and epic scale and, above all, it echoed ancient Egypt's obsession with death and the afterlife. Once established, its forms hardly changed for almost 3,000 years. Such tenacious conservatism was matched only by the similarly inward-looking civilization of China.

Writing in the 4th century BCE, Plato claimed there had been no change in Egyptian art for 10,000 years. If his chronology was faulty, he nonetheless touched on a central truth: that the art of ancient Egypt has a near-unique continuity.

The *Palette of Narmer*, which celebrates the first pharaoh, Narmer, who unified Egypt around 3100BCE, already contains many of the essential elements of this fixed tradition. Perhaps the most striking is the pose in which Narmer is depicted. Head, arms, and legs are in profile, with legs characteristically splayed. Yet, in an obvious anatomical distortion, his chest faces directly outwards. Exactly the same pose can be found in works produced 2,500 years later. Although individual details are rendered with great precision, the overall effect is anything but naturalistic. Egyptian art was almost entirely symbolic, intended to convey precise meanings, in this case the triumph of Narmer over his enemies. The sizes of the figures denote status: the larger the figure, the greater its importance (nakedness also indicated inferiority). Though the figures stand on a common ground, there is no attempt to represent the space they occupy naturalistically.

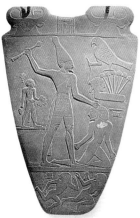

⬆ **Palette of Narmer** *c.3000BCE, schist carved in low relief, Cairo: Egyptian National Museum.*

⏩ **Weighing of the Heart against the Feather of Truth** *c.1250BCE, painted papyrus, London: British Museum.* This scene is found in every *Book of the Dead*.

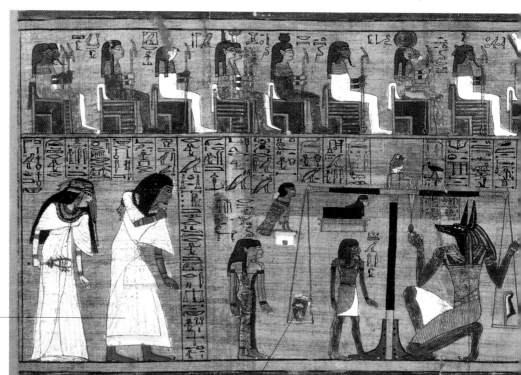

The deceased is ushered into the hall of judgement

The heart is weighed against a feather in the other scale

Anubis, the jackal-headed god, supervises the weighing of the heart

Hierarchy and symbolism

Because its rulers were considered gods, their "eternal wellbeing" was dependent on preserving their mortal remains with as much splendour as possible. Hence the deliberate grandeur of the pyramids and, later, the vast tombs at Thebes. Complex and absolute rules governed how the pharaohs should be represented in art. The imperturbably blank features of the four giant seated statues of Ramses II guarding the entrance to his temple at Abu Simbel express this formal monumentality just as the gold head of Tutenkhamun underlines the premium placed on precious metals and craftsmanship.

There were exceptions. The less important the subject – slaves, dancing girls, or musicians, for example – the more naturalistically they could be depicted. Further, for a brief period in New Kingdom Egypt, above all during the reign of Akhenaten (1364–1347BCE), who shocked the priesthood by banishing all gods other than Aten (the "disc of the sun"), a slight relaxation of this otherwise absolute formality is evident. In the tomb of Akhenaten's chief minister, Ramose, is a relief of the brother of Ramose and his wife carved not just with extraordinary delicacy and skill but also with a hint, if nothing more, of genuine humanity.

More typical of the Egyptian attitude to art are the many surviving examples of the parchment known as the *Book of the Dead*. This was a book of spells, placed in a tomb to guide the dead through the afterworld. Not only are the figures – gods and humans – depicted following exact conventions, but the hieroglyphs inserted above and between them, themselves essentially pictorial, contain equally precise and detailed instructions.

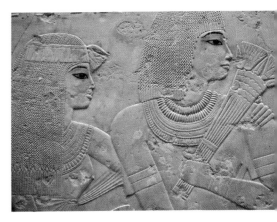

▲ **Relief from tomb of Ramose** *c.1350BCE, limestone, Thebes. Originally, when painted, its impact would have been still more remarkable.*

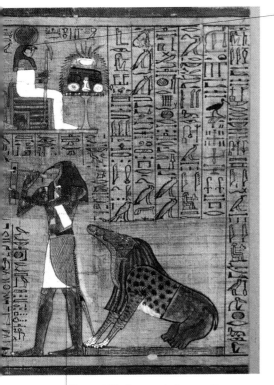

Pantheon of Egyptian gods headed by Horus

The god Thoth records the result of the weighing of the heart

KEY EVENTS

c.3100BCE	Early Dynastic period (to 2686BCE): Egypt unified under Narmer; Memphis made capital; hieroglyphic writing developed
2686BCE	Old Kingdom (to 2181BCE)
c.2540BCE	Construction of the Great Pyramid of Khufu
2180BCE	First Intermediate Period (to 2040BCE): centralized rule dissolves
2040BCE	Middle Kingdom (to 1730BCE)
1730BCE	Second Intermediate Period (to 1552BCE): much of Egypt ruled by Hyksos, an Asiatic people
1552BCE	New Kingdom (to 1069BCE): Egyptian power at its height: new capital founded at Thebes
1166BCE	Death of Ramses III, last great pharaoh
1069BCE	Third Intermediate Period (to 664BCE)
664BCE	Late Period (to 30BCE)
332BCE	Egypt conquered by Alexander the Great

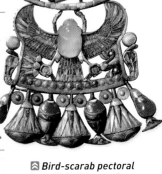

▲ **Bird-scarab pectoral from Tutankhamun's tomb** *c.1352BCE, gold, semi-precious stones, and glass paste, Cairo: Egyptian National Museum.*

THE EARLY AEGEAN WORLD

c.2000–500BCE

Between about 2000 and 1150BCE, two distinctive though related early Greek civilizations were established in the eastern Mediterranean: by the Minoans on the island of Crete and, perhaps 400 years later, by the more warlike Mycenaeans on the Greek mainland. The reasons for their later disappearance remain unclear, but by the beginning of the first millennium a new fully Greek culture was emerging.

Both Minoan Crete and Mycenae were stratified, literate societies, presided over by elites. They appear to have enjoyed substantial agricultural surpluses and to have had extensive trading links. What was originally assumed to be the labyrinth at the palace of Knossos, the principal centre of power in Crete (although nothing is known of its rulers), was in fact a huge storage area for wine, grain, and oil.

That Minoan Crete was a society with a taste for luxury and a highly developed visual sense is clear from the decoration of its palaces and villas. Frescoes of ships, landscapes, animals, and cavorting dolphins convey an expressive delight in the natural world. The best-known are those of youths and girls bull-leaping. Though this practice may have had a religious significance – bulls are a

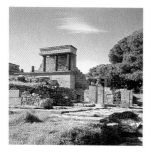

⚄ ⏩ **Bull-leaping fresco** *c.1500BCE, Athens: National Archaeological Museum.* One of the prize discoveries when the palace of Knossos (above) was excavated in the early 1900s.

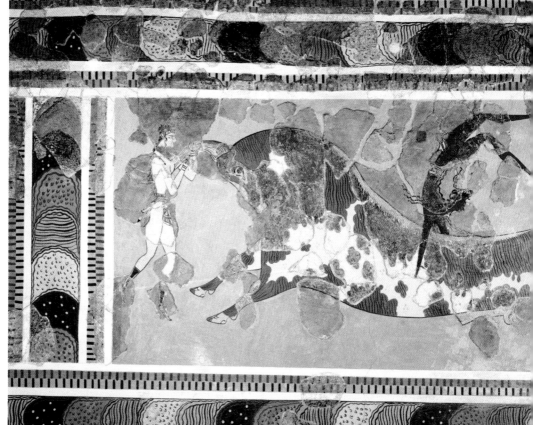

recurring theme in Minoan art – overridingly these images suggest an exuberant pleasure in physicality.

The palaces and villas of Minoan Crete were successively rebuilt, perhaps following natural disasters such as the volcanic eruption that wiped out the Minoan colony on the island of Thera in the mid-17th century BCE. But this apparently unwarlike world was also threatened from outside. Around 1450BCE, Minoan Crete fell victim to the Mycenaeans from mainland Greece.

Mycenaean culture

The heavily fortified remains at Mycenae itself underline just how much this was a society presided over by an aggressive warrior elite. Yet, as the remarkable gold death mask of a Mycenaean ruler demonstrates, theirs was a world that was not just materially rich but capable of great technical sophistication.

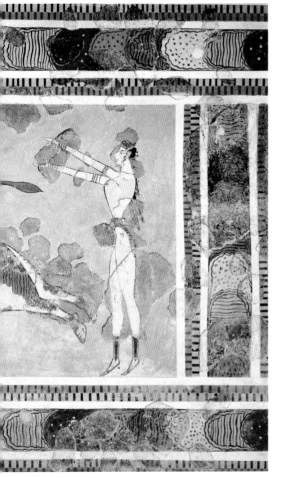

With the collapse of these first Aegean civilizations, probably in the face of invasions from the north, Greek culture effectively disappeared for over 400 years. Almost nothing is known of this "Dark Age". Yet, by about 800BCE, a new, very different Greek world was emerging. Although politically fragmented, it came to enjoy an exceptionally strong sense not just of its identity but also of its intellectual superiority.

In the visual arts, there were two key developments: a trend towards an idealized naturalism and the adoption of the male nude as its chief subject. It is a measure of the dominance of Greek cultural values that, to Western eyes at least, these have come to seem obviously desirable goals. In fact, they express values no culture outside the West has ever particularly esteemed. To most societies, for example, nakedness was a clear indication of servility.

The Greek obsession with the male nude began in the 7th century BCE. Over 100 life-size statues known as *kouroi* (youths) have survived. Though formalized – all face rigidly forwards, with hands clenched and one foot in front of the other (evidence of Egyptian influences) – they demonstrate a new interest in naturally rendered anatomical detail. By the 5th century BCE, they would give rise to a naturalism unprecedented in the history of art.

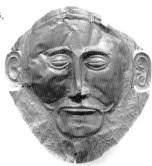

⌃ **Mycenaean death mask from royal tomb** *c.1550BCE, gold, Athens: National Archaeological Museum.*

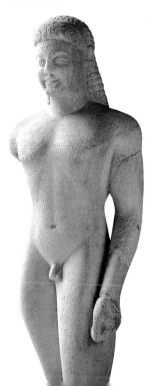

⌄ **Kouros** *c.540BCE, height 105 cm (41 in), marble, Paris: Musée du Louvre.*

KEY EVENTS

c.2000BCE	Minoan civilization established on Crete; palace of Knossos built
c.1600BCE	Linear B script comes into use on Crete
c.1500BCE	Mycenaeans become dominant power on Greek mainland
c.1450BCE	Collapse of Minoans; Mycenaeans take control of island
c.1150BCE	Collapse of Mycenaean Greece
c.1000BCE	Greek colonists migrate to Asia Minor and eastern Aegean
776BCE	First pan-Hellenic athletics festival, Olympics, Olympia
c.750BCE	First evidence of use of Greek alphabet; Homer's *Iliad* first written down
c.700BCE	Beginning of Archaic period; emergence of city-states

CLASSICAL GREECE

c.500–300BCE

Between the 5th century and 197BCE, when it was absorbed by Rome, Greece evolved ideals in art, philosophy, mathematics, literature, and politics that would exercise an extraordinary hold on subsequent Western beliefs. That it did so in the face of external threats and internal turmoil makes this achievement all the more remarkable.

Victory over the Persians in 490BCE and again in 480BCE left Athens clearly the strongest of the Greek city-states. Despite the debilitating and eventually disastrous Peloponnesian War against rivals Sparta between 431 and 404BCE, culturally at least the city would retain its leading role even after the rise of Macedonia in the following century. Fifth-century BCE Athens saw an astonishingly fertile burst of artistic creation, establishing an artistic canon that would not only dominate the Roman world but, when rediscovered by

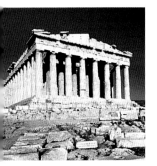

⏫⏩ *Centaur Triumphing over a Lapith* 447–432BCE, marble, London: British Museum. The relief (right) was part of the frieze on the south side of the Parthenon (above). It was removed by Lord Elgin in the early 1800s.

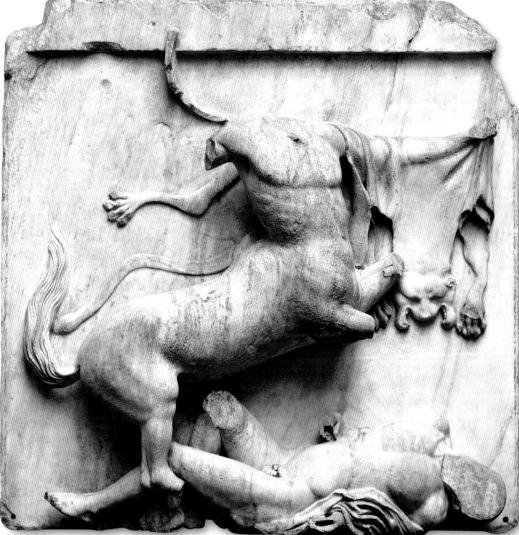

Renaissance Europe, would constitute an absolute artistic standard for a further 400 years.

Only a handful of fragments of Greek paintings have survived; many Greek sculptures are known only from Roman copies or written descriptions; and what architecture still exists is extensively ruined. But enough remains to make clear the extraordinary artistic impact of Classical Greece.

The Parthenon, begun in 447BCE, is the supreme example. Today, even stripped of its sculpture, its crumbling grandeur constitutes an emphatic statement of the lucid priorities that drove the Classical Greek world. Originally, brilliantly painted and embellished with statuary, its impact would have been more remarkable still.

Greek sculpture

The Parthenon's sculptures fall into three groups. On the triangular pediments at either end of the building were large-scale free-standing groups

◀◀ **Red-figure vase** c.450BCE, height 48 cm (18 ⅞ in), ceramic, Paris: Musée du Louvre. The vase shows a Hoplite (citizen soldier) returning from war.

containing numerous figures showing the birth of Athena and her struggles with Poseidon for control of Attica; below these as well as along both sides were nearly 100 individual reliefs of struggling figures (men and centaurs; Greeks and Amazons; gods and giants); behind the outer colonnade and running around the entire building was a relief, 160 m (525 ft) long, depicting the Great Panathenaia, a religious festival held every four years in honour of Athena.

Even badly damaged, the Parthenon sculptures reveal the confidence and technical mastery of their creators. These are wholly convincing figures, dramatically grouped and heroically conceived. Other examples of Classical Greek sculpture are better preserved. The slightly more than life-size bronze Boy from Antikythera combines calm elegance with technical sophistication in ways that were genuinely new, infusing the naturalistic with the ideal to produce a supremely self-confident image of a god-like youth. The sculpture manages the rare feat of being both supremely rational and yet at the same time extraordinarily sensual.

Descriptions of Greek painting suggest it, too, reached comparable levels of technical achievement. The Roman frescoes at Pompeii were almost certainly heavily influenced by Greek originals. Perspective, foreshortening, and the naturalistic representation of figures all seem to have been mastered in ways that would not reappear until Renaissance Italy. Greek vases reinforce the point. Although painted on curved and small-scale surfaces, their decoration contains complex and ambitious groups of figures in settings that have a real sense of space and depth.

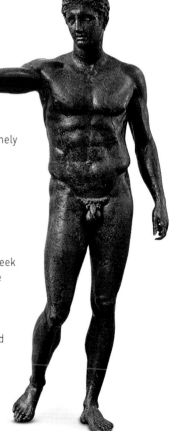

▼ **Boy from Antikythera** c.340BCE, height 194 cm (76 in), bronze, Athens: National Archaeological Museum.

KEY EVENTS

505BCE	Democracy established in Athens
490BCE	Greeks defeat Persians in battle at Marathon
480BCE	Greeks defeat Persians at Salamis and Plataea
478BCE	Confederation of Delos founded; later transformed into Athenian empire
461BCE	Beginning of domination of Athenian political life by Pericles
447BCE	Parthenon begun (completed 432BCE)
431BCE	Peloponnesian Wars between Athens and Sparta (to 404BCE)
399BCE	Athenian philosopher Socrates condemned to death for corrupting youth
385BCE	Plato returns to Athens; opens Academy
384BCE	Birth of Aristotle

HELLENISTIC GREEK ART

c.300–1BCE

In 336BCE, Alexander the Great began his blaze of conquest across the Middle East and Egypt. His empire fragmented after his death, but the cultural impact of Greece on these vast territories proved enduring. The progress of "Hellenization" was encouraged by the Romans, who, by the 1st century BCE, had exported Greek artistic traditions across the whole Mediterranean.

Alexander and his successors implanted Greek cultural values across a vast swathe of the ancient world. Rather like the city states of 5th-century Greece, these new Greek kingdoms were political rivals but shared a common cultural inheritance. A huge programme of new city building began in Asia Minor, the Near East, Mesopotamia, and North Africa. Alexandria, Antioch, and Pergamum for instance are all Hellenic cities.

Greek prestige was also enhanced by learning. The library at Alexandria was the most famous in the ancient world. The influence of Aristotle, who died in 322 and had been Alexander's tutor, extended over the entire period and beyond. In the face of this huge expansion of the Greek world, the original city-states of Greece were overshadowed politically, but they retained much of their cultural status.

Though Hellenistic art continues as a clear line of development from the Classical period, with naturalism again the chief concern, there are important differences. The most obvious is that the restraint of Classical Greek art gives way to a sense of movement and drama. One reason may have been that increasing technical mastery led artists to set themselves harder problems to solve. But there is a sense, too, that the Hellenistic world needed a more emphatic style of art to underline the fact of its conquests. Whereas on the Parthenon, for example, civic piety set the tone, on the Alexander Sarcophagus, a sumptuous marble tomb carved probably in 310BCE for the ruler of Sidon, not only is there a sense that technical mastery is being celebrated for its own sake, a clear note of triumphalism creeps in. One side of the sarcophagus is a battle scene in which

◢ **The Battle of Issus**
(detail), 1st century BCE, mosaic, Naples: Museo Archeologico Nazionale. This mosaic from Pompeii is a Roman copy of a Greek original. The young Alexander (left) defeats Persian King Darius (centre).

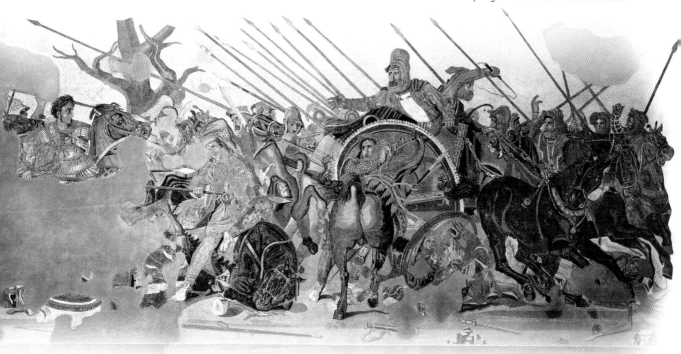

the figure of Alexander, clad in a lion-skin, is accorded the sort of heroic treatment previously reserved only for gods.

A new trend in sculpture

The Altar of Zeus at Pergamum, perhaps the most famous work from the entire period, embodies another key characteristic: scale. The base of the

platform on which the altar stands contains a frieze 2.3 m (7½ ft) high and fully 90 m (295 ft) long. On the upper level is a second frieze 1.5 m (5 ft) high and 73 m (240 ft) long. The vigour of the carvings, with their writhing, interlocking figures, is far removed from the placid assurance of the Classical period.

The expressiveness of heroic figures such as these found a different outlet in the almost equally well-known *Dying Gaul*. The stoic dignity with which he accepts his fate makes clear an interest in the individual that was reflected in the development of lifelike portraiture. This was partly prompted by the teachings of Aristotle. Whereas in Classical Greece individual worth was automatically equated with physical perfection, now personality was judged at least as important. The mid-3rd-century bronze statue of a philosopher, possibly Hermarchus, portrays an ageing and crumpled figure. But his obvious nobility of spirit makes it clear that the sculpture is intended as a sympathetic portrayal, a point that is emphasized by his physical frailty and decrepitude.

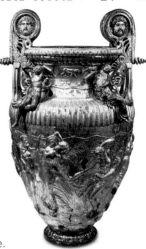

⌃ **Derveni krater** *late 4th-century BCE, height 86 cm (34 in), gilded bronze, Thessaloníki: Archaeological Museum.* This enormous vessel is a technical tour de force, decorated with statuettes and repoussé reliefs of Dionysus, Ariadne, and other mythological figures.

» LAOCOÖN

The Laocoön was carved at the very end of the Hellenistic period. Stylistically, it derives from the Altar of Zeus at Pergamum of around 150 years before. It is an astonishingly accomplished work, acutely observed and highly finished. Its impact stems from the heightened and tragic emotion generated by its contorted, writhing figures.

The statue illustrates an incident in Virgil's account of the Trojan Wars, *The Aeneid*. Laocoön was a Trojan priest who had urged his countrymen to reject the apparent Greek peace offering of a wooden horse. As punishment, the gods sent two snakes to kill him and his sons. Despite its technical sophistication, the work is only intended to be viewed from the front. As with all Antique statues, it would originally have been painted.

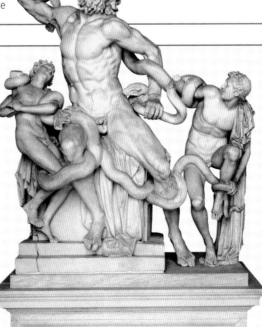

« **Laocoön** *Hagesandrus, Polydorus, and Athendorus, c.42–20BCE, marble, Rome: Vatican Museums.* The Laocoön had a great hold on the Renaissance imagination. This was partly due to its discovery in Rome in 1506, when interest in Greek statuary was reaching a peak, and partly due to the nobility of its struggling figures. This kind of dramatic large-scale treatment had a significant impact on Michaelangelo and the later artists of the Roman Baroque.

IMPERIAL ROME

c.27BCE–c.300CE

Uniquely among the leading powers of the ancient world, Rome developed only a limited artistic language of its own. Roman architecture, like Roman engineering, was never less than bold, but Roman painting and sculpture were derived largely from Greek models. However potently Rome projected images of its political power, the visual means it used to do so were second-hand.

Roman art was largely imitative and utilitarian. Greece provided Rome with a huge range of models to adapt to its own ends. Yet rather than acting as a stimulus, the result was an apparently permanent Roman inferiority complex in the face of Greek artistic achievement and the stifling of independent Roman schools of art. Hence the lifelessness traditionally and, on balance, rightly attributed to Roman art.

The 1st-century CE Medici Venus, for example, is just one of 33 surviving Roman copies of the Hellenistic original. Greek sculptures were not just copied by the Romans, they were actively recycled. Greek poses recast in Roman garb were pressed into service to reinforce Roman power. At its most extreme, this practice allowed a kind of off-the-peg shopping whereby heroic Greek figures, available in a variety of sizes, could be supplied headless, the buyer supplying his own, easily installed, portrait head.

This kind of pragmatism is illustrated by the celebrated late-2nd-century CE equestrian statue of Marcus Aurelius. Arm outstretched and his head turned slightly to the side, his pose is just one of numerous Roman reworkings of the 5th-century BCE statue of Doryphorus, itself known only from Roman copies. What was originally an idealized image of male beauty has been slightly clumsily converted into a vehicle stressing Roman imperial might and the god-like person of the emperor.

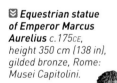

Equestrian statue of Emperor Marcus Aurelius c.175CE, height 350 cm (138 in), gilded bronze, Rome: Musei Capitolini.

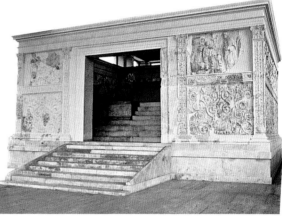

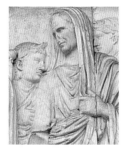

Ara Pacis 13–9BCE, marble, Rome. The frieze shows members of Augustus's family and state officials. The man in the detail (left) is Marcus Agrippa, the emperor's son-in-law.

Even the much earlier Ara Pacis Augustae (Altar of Augustan Peace), whilst seeking to stress the continuity between the rule of the Emperor Augustus and the earlier Roman Republic, is obviously dependent on Greek models, above all in its use of a continuous large-scale frieze of figures. The virtues they seek to embody may be Roman; the manner in which they do so is unambiguously Greek.

Roman painting

In Imperial Rome, the love of luxury, severely disapproved of by those seeking a return to the stern values of the republic, tended to equate opulence with quality. This was a world in which more almost always meant better. Most of the surviving examples of Roman painting are from Pompeii (they were preserved thanks to the volcanic eruption that obliterated the city in 79CE). These offer crucial clues to the earlier Greek painting on which they were modelled.

In contrast to what is known of these Greek originals, the paintings at Pompeii seem to have been almost exclusively decorative murals for expensive villas. Landscapes and seascapes augmented by complex architectural settings using sophisticated illusionistic devices seem to have been the preferred subjects. As ever in the imperial Roman world, there was a premium on presentation over content. The surviving murals were clearly painted by journeymen, in most cases Greeks – superior interior decorators rather than artists as the Greeks would have understood the term.

KEY EVENTS

264BCE	Rome completes conquest of Italy; first Punic War (to 241BCE)
218BCE	Second Punic War (to 201BCE): Hannibal invades Italy
149BCE	Third Punic War (to 146BCE): Carthage destroyed by Roman army
46BCE	Julius Caesar appointed dictator (assassinated 44BCE)
27BCE	Octavian becomes first Roman emperor (as Augustus); dies 14CE
13–9BCE	Ara Pacis Augustae created, Rome
79CE	Pompeii and Herculaneum destroyed after eruption of Vesuvius
113CE	Trajan's Column built, Rome
117CE	Death of Emperor Trajan; Roman empire at its greatest extent
161–180CE	Equestrian statue of Emperor Marcus Aurelius cast, Rome

Nile in Flood (detail), c.80BCE, mosaic, Palestrina: Museo Archeologico Prenestino. The Romans followed Greek models to produce magnificent floor mosaics.

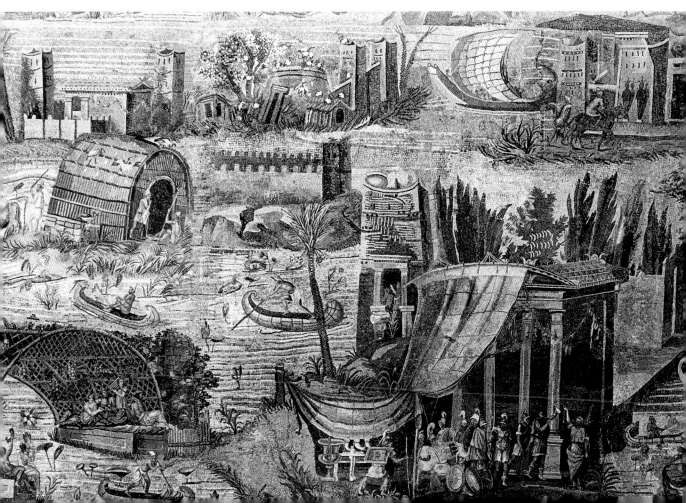

LATE ROMAN AND EARLY CHRISTIAN ART

c.300–450ce

As Rome's empire was eroded, Roman art increasingly departed from the naturalistic ideals it had inherited from the Greeks. In turn, these vigorous but less sophisticated artistic models were adapted by the early Christian Church in the search for a visual language appropriate to its theological needs.

The Arch of Constantine in Rome, built by the Emperor Constantine early in the 4th century, neatly encapsulates the move away from the rationalism of Greece. As well as reliefs carved in the reign of Constantine himself, the arch incorporates a series of sculptured reliefs from earlier periods. The choice of these was deliberate: all come from the reigns of well-loved emperors with whom Constantine wished to identify, so as to legitimize his rule. The early reliefs are all carved in the fully naturalistic tradition inherited from Greece. The later reliefs, by contrast, contain figures that almost deliberately seem to caricature their more elegant predecessors: stumpy and badly proportioned, almost all shown in profile. In the same way, foreshortening and other devices to

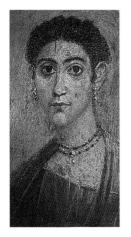

⌃ *Mummy-case portrait from Fayum* encaustic on wood, *London: British Museum.* A tradition of Roman-style portrait painting continued in Egypt through the 2nd and 3rd centuries ce.

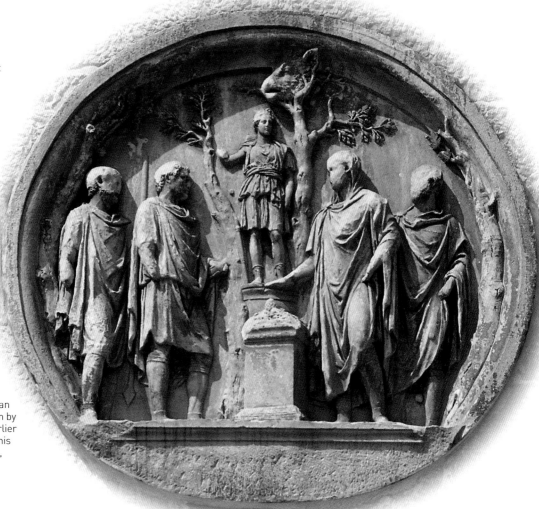

≫ *Roundel from the Arch of Constantine* This medallion, which shows a sacrifice being made to Apollo, dates from the reign of Hadrian (117–138ce). It was taken by Constantine from an earlier monument to decorate his triumphal arch in Rome, erected c.315ce.

create a sense of space are totally ignored. The contrast is so great there is a sense that these reliefs are almost flaunting their deliberate abandonment of the Greek visual tradition.

Radical change

Constantine's reign marked a crucial moment for Rome. His decision in 330CE to move the capital of the empire from Rome to Constantinople (modern Istanbul) confirmed an existing shift of political and economic power to the east. His legitimization of Christianity in 313CE had consequences that were equally momentous. What had been a minor sect, frequently persecuted, now enjoyed the full weight of imperial patronage. Constantine's decision was overridingly political: he used the Church as a central point around which the empire could regroup, hence the urgency with which he set out to reconcile rival Christian sects. The challenge thereafter was to find visual means to express the Christian message. Inevitably, Roman, which is to say pagan, prototypes were used. The basic form of churches themselves came from secular Roman buildings known as basilicas, large oblong halls, often arcaded with aisles and an apse at the far end.

Christianity and art

There was a long-running controversy as to whether God the Father could be represented or whether this would constitute idolatry. No such strictures applied to the figure of Christ himself, it being a central tenet of Christianity that Christ had been made man. However, there was little agreement as to how he should be shown: young, old, stern, benign, even bearded or beardless. Although many scenes from the life of Christ were depicted quite early on, these never included the Crucifixion, a form of death reserved for the lowest class of criminals. Even the cross itself was only slowly adopted as a universal symbol. In the absence of surviving paintings, early Christian statuary and mosaics provide the only clues as to how these questions were resolved. The sumptuous mid-4th-century CE sarcophagus of Junius Bassus, for example, has two tiers, each containing five scenes of sharply carved if crudely realized figures. In both, a youthful Christ occupies the central scene. His pose in the upper tier, seated with arms outstretched in benediction, derives directly from an imperial Roman tradition.

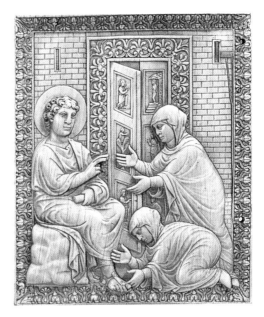

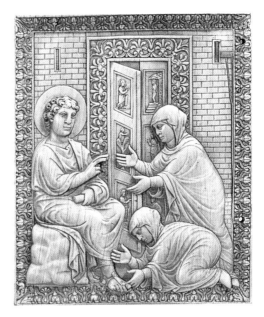 *Holy Women at the Tomb of Christ* c.400CE, ivory, Milan: Castello Sforzesco. Mary, the mother of Jesus, and Mary Magdalene worship the risen Christ, who is portrayed as a young, beardless man in Roman dress.

A similar fusion of pagan forms and Christian subject matter is evident in an ivory of around 400CE depicting the *Holy Women at the Tomb of Christ*. Again, if the figures are slightly awkwardly rendered, they clearly stem from the earlier Greek tradition.

KEY EVENTS

312CE	Constantine confirmed as emperor
313	Edict of Milan: Constantine legitimizes Christianity in Roman Empire
325	Council of Nicaea called by Constantine to resolve theological differences within Church
329	St Peter's Basilica, Rome, completed
330	Constantine dedicates Constantinople as new capital of Roman Empire
391	Emperor Theodosius imposes Christianity on Roman Empire as sole religion
395	Death of Theodosius: Roman Empire definitively split into East and West
410	Visigoths under Alaric sack Rome
455	Vandals under Gaiseric sack Rome
476	Deposition of Romulus Augustulus, last Roman emperor in the West

BYZANTINE ART

c.500–1200

Vastly richer than the beleaguered Western Empire and increasingly drawn towards the East, the Byzantine Empire evolved a new and elaborate visual language dominated by complex religious imagery. It marked a near absolute break with the Classical Greek inheritance that had driven earlier Roman art.

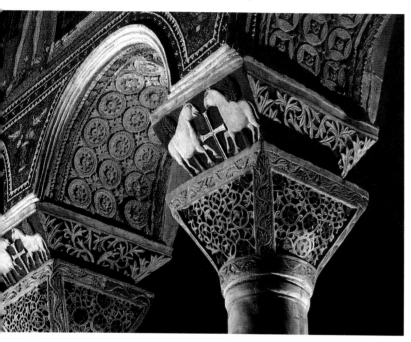

⚑ *Byzantine capitals in the Church of San Vitale, Ravenna* 6th century. The interiors of Byzantine churches were richly decorated with mosaics, gilding, and reliefs, but not statues, which were not venerated as icons.

The most important subject of Byzantine art was Christianity. As the teachings of the Church were codified, precise rules came to govern how they could be depicted. Gestures and even colours came to acquire precise and unvariable meanings.

Among the earliest examples of Byzantine art are the glittering, near otherworldly mosaics in the Church of San Vitale in Ravenna in Italy. They are important not just as an emphatic assertion of the vigorous (if short-lived) Justinian reconquest – the attempt by the Eastern Emperor Justinian

to recreate a unified Roman Empire in the face of the barbarian conquests in the West – but as a supreme example of the new sensibilities of the Byzantine world. The dominant image, over the altar, is of a luminous, seated Christ, flanked by angels and donors. But hardly less remarkable is that of Justinian and his retinue. This portrait of the splay-footed emperor, part gangster, part man of destiny, is one of the most compelling images in Western art. Justinian's Church of Hagia Sophia in Constantinople projects this mood of fierce piety even more strikingly. Even today – almost 600 years after the Ottoman conquest of Byzantium in 1453, when what was then still the largest church in Christendom became a mosque – its glinting mosaics and vast, shadowy recesses evoke an astonishing sense of the grandeur and mystery at the heart of imperial Byzantium.

The later formality of the Byzantine tradition belies how inventive it originally was. The mosaic figure of Christ Pantocrator, "Christ the ruler of all", staring down from the dome of the monastery church of Daphni in Greece, is an extremely potent image of an implacable God. It was in Byzantium, too, that the Virgin Mary was developed as one of the key icons of Christian art. In part this was a matter of doctrine. Yet once established in the

⚑ *Emperor Justinian I and his Retinue* c.547CE, mosaic, Ravenna: Church of San Vitale. Flanked by imperial officials, generals, and high-ranking members of the clergy, Justinian is portrayed as the political, military, and religious leader of the Byzantine Empire.

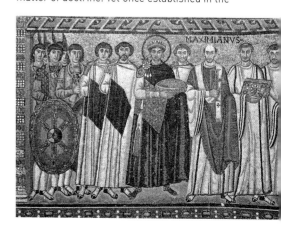

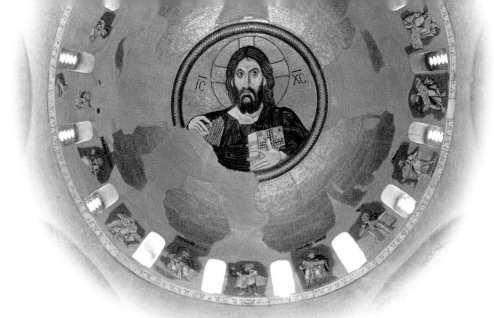

Christ Pantocrator
*late 11th century,
mosaic, Daphni (Greece):
monastery church.*
The figure of "Christ the
ruler of all", his left hand
holding the Bible, his
right hand raised in
blessing, remains a
ubiquitous icon of the
Orthodox Church.

5th century that it was precisely her virginity that made her "the Mother of God" – a central figure of Byzantine, and later of Western, Christian art.

Far-reaching influence

An image such as the 6th-century panel painting of the Virgin and Child from the Monastery of St Catherine in the Sinai Peninsula, Egypt,

highlights a further, central fact of Byzantine art: that religious "icons" (literally "images") were increasingly valued as aids to contemplation. Small and often portable, they would exercise a profound influence on the spreading world of "orthodox" Christianity ("orthodox" because sanctioned by the Byzantine Church). The conversions of Bulgaria in 864 and Kievan Rus in 988 to this distinctive brand of Christianity were crucial in expanding its reach and in implanting it in new lands.

KEY EVENTS

532	Hagia Sophia begun in Constantinople (consecrated 537)
533	Justinian launches reconquest of Western Roman Empire
c.547	Mosaics created in San Vitale, Ravenna
555	Byzantine conquest of Italy and southern Iberia complete
558	Dome of Hagia Sophia collapses (rebuilt by 563)
692	Trullan Council sanctions use of figures of Christ in art
726	Emperor Leo III bans worship of religious images, provoking "iconoclast" crisis
751	Ravenna, last Byzantine possession in Italy, falls to Lombards
843	Triumph of Orthodoxy: religious images officially promoted
864	Mission of Cyril and Methodius begins spread of Orthodoxy in eastern Europe
1054	Final schism between Roman and Orthodox churches

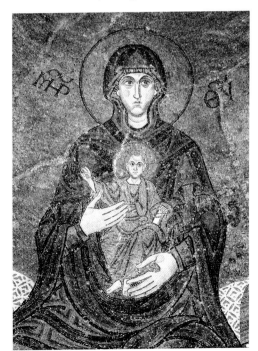

Madonna and Child
*12th century, mosaic
in vault of apse (detail),
Trieste: Cathedral of
St Just.* The Byzantine
tradition that Mary
should be depicted
wearing a blue robe
was carried over
into Western art.

CELTIC, SAXON, AND VIKING ART

c.600–900

Northern Europe after the collapse of the Roman Empire has traditionally been seen as entering a "dark age" lost in impenetrable obscurity: marginal, shadowy, and violent. Yet drawing on earlier Celtic traditions and increasingly becoming part of the Christian world, it produced exceptionally vivid and sophisticated works of art.

The discovery at Sutton Hoo in 1939 of the burial goods of an early Anglo-Saxon king, generally agreed to be Raewald, ruler of East Anglia, transformed people's understanding of emerging Anglo-Saxon England. Raewald died around 625, not much more than 200 years after the Romans had abandoned Britain. Yet among the objects found in his grave were a Byzantine bowl and gold coins from Gaul, evidence of long-range trading contacts. At the same time, the treasure highlights a world poised between a pagan past and a Christian future. Already Christianity was penetrating Britain, from Ireland and from the Continent. Once these rival traditions had been reconciled in 664 by the Synod of Whitby, Britain came firmly within the orbit of the Roman Church.

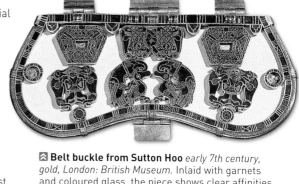

⬆ **Belt buckle from Sutton Hoo** *early 7th century, gold, London: British Museum.* Inlaid with garnets and coloured glass, the piece shows clear affinities with the intricately intertwined patterns of Celtic jewellery and illuminated manuscripts.

The Vikings

By contrast, the Viking world as it emerged over the next 200 years was at first genuinely beyond Rome's reach. Nonetheless, drawing on the same Celtic roots that are obvious at Sutton Hoo, it, too, produced works of art of a remarkable and immediately recognizable potency. The 9th-century carved dragon ship's figurehead, found in a burial mound at Oseberg in Norway, is evidence of a warrior society capable of exceptional craftsmanship.

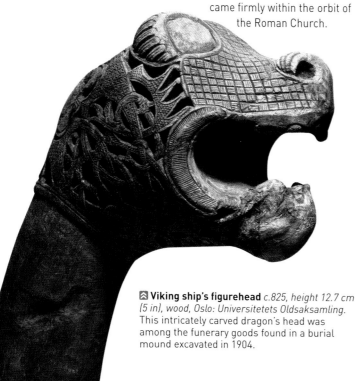

⬆ **Viking ship's figurehead** *c.825, height 12.7 cm (5 in), wood, Oslo: Universitetets Oldsaksamling.* This intricately carved dragon's head was among the funerary goods found in a burial mound excavated in 1904.

KEY EVENTS

563	Irish monastery established at Iona
597	Mission of papal emissary St Augustine to England
c.650	Lindisfarne Gospels made
664	Synod of Whitby: Roman Christianity adopted in England
731	Bede completes his *Ecclesiastical History of England*
c.790	First Viking raids on western Europe
c.800	*Book of Kells* made

The *Book of Kells*

The monastery established in 563 on the remote island of Iona off the west coast of Scotland was one of a handful of isolated Dark Age Irish Christian communities that were responsible for an extraordinary outpouring of Celtic Christian art, above all a series of sumptuous illuminated manuscripts.

The *Book of Kells*, produced at Iona in about 800 and taken to Ireland for safekeeping when the Viking raids began, is the most famous product of the fusion of Celtic art and Christian subject matter. It is a book of verses, interspersed with extracts from the Gospels. The thousands of hours of patient labour lavished on it represented an act of worship just as much as the examination of it was intended to induce a mood of contemplation.

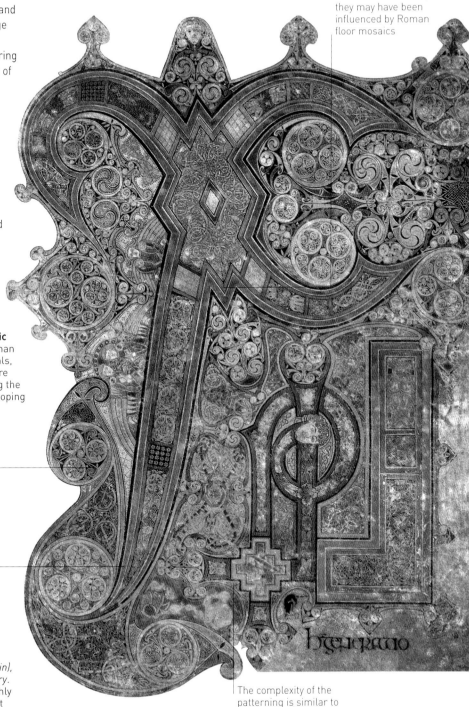

Interlaced patterns are a key characteristic of Celtic decorative art; they may have been influenced by Roman floor mosaics

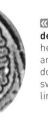

◀ **Naturalistic details** – human heads, animals, and birds – are dotted among the swirling, swooping line work.

Triskele – three legs radiating from a central point – are a recurring motif in Celtic art

The capitals – Chi and Rho – are the first two letters of the Greek word for Christ and are one of the oldest Christian symbols

▶ **Book of Kells** *c.800, 33 x 25 cm (13 x 10 in), ink on vellum, Dublin: Trinity College Library.* Among its innovations was the use of richly decorated and elaborate capital letters at the start of each passage.

The complexity of the patterning is similar to contemporary Celtic jewellery

MEDIEVAL ART OF NORTHERN EUROPE

c.800–1000

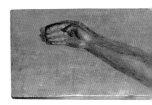

By the 8th century, the Frankish Empire had become the most successful of the new states formed after the collapse of Rome. It reached its largest extent under Charlemagne in the early 9th century, when it covered France, Germany, the Low Countries, and most of Italy. Charlemagne also sparked a cultural revival that decisively influenced the development of later medieval art.

On Christmas day 800, Charlemagne, king of the Franks, was crowned emperor of a new Roman empire by Pope Leo III in St Peter's in Rome.

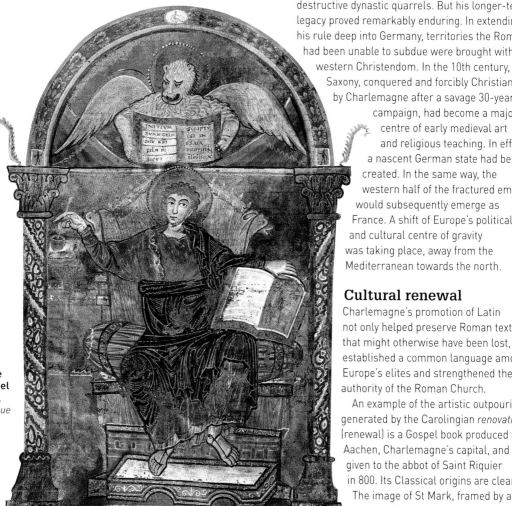

▶ St Mark from the Saint-Riquier Gospel
c.800, purple vellum, Abbeville: Bibliothèque Municipale. The strange-looking creature framed by the arch is the winged lion, symbol of St Mark the Evangelist.

It was a deliberate assertion of Rome reborn. In the event, Charlemagne's empire would prove vulnerable, its unity sundered after his death in destructive dynastic quarrels. But his longer-term legacy proved remarkably enduring. In extending his rule deep into Germany, territories the Romans had been unable to subdue were brought within western Christendom. In the 10th century, Saxony, conquered and forcibly Christianized by Charlemagne after a savage 30-year campaign, had become a major centre of early medieval art and religious teaching. In effect, a nascent German state had been created. In the same way, the western half of the fractured empire would subsequently emerge as France. A shift of Europe's political and cultural centre of gravity was taking place, away from the Mediterranean towards the north.

Cultural renewal

Charlemagne's promotion of Latin not only helped preserve Roman texts that might otherwise have been lost, it established a common language among Europe's elites and strengthened the authority of the Roman Church.

An example of the artistic outpouring generated by the Carolingian *renovatio* (renewal) is a Gospel book produced at Aachen, Charlemagne's capital, and given to the abbot of Saint Riquier in 800. Its Classical origins are clear. The image of St Mark, framed by a triumphal arch, is not just an obvious

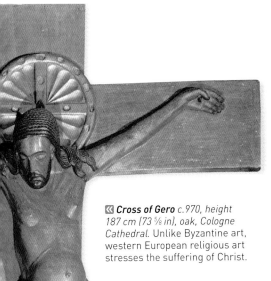

◀◀ *Cross of Gero* c.970, height 187 cm (73 ⅝ in), oak, Cologne Cathedral. Unlike Byzantine art, western European religious art stresses the suffering of Christ.

KEY EVENTS

771	Charlemagne sole ruler of Frankish Empire
772	Conquest of Saxony begun; complete 802
774	Lombardy brought within Charlemagne's empire
792	Imperial (Palatine) Chapel begun at Aachen; completed 805
800	Coronation of Charlemagne in Rome
814	Death of Charlemagne
843	Treaty of Verdun divides Carolingian Empire into three
845	Paris sacked by Vikings
875	Charles the Bald crowned first Holy Roman Emperor
910	Foundation of Benedictine abbey at Cluny, France
936	Accession of Otto I as Holy Roman Emperor

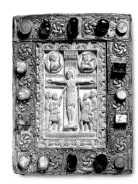

🔺 **Book cover** *8th century, silver gilt and ivory, Cividale del Friuli: Museo Archeologico.* The carving of the Crucifixion shows Longinus thrusting his spear into the dead Christ's side.

celebration of the Evangelist, it is a clear attempt to imitate the richness of the late Roman world. In reality, however, it looks forward to the Middle Ages rather than back to Rome. There is no Roman precedent for the double-jointed twist of the Evangelist's right wrist any more than there is for his oddly angled feet.

As important was the development of a narrative tradition in religious art that would endure throughout the Middle Ages. As early as the 6th century, Pope Gregory I had affirmed the didactic purpose of religious imagery: "What scripture is to the educated, images are to the ignorant." Under Charlemagne, narrative images of this kind became a fixed part of the Western tradition. An early 9th-century ivory panel, which was subsequently used as the cover of a devotional volume known as the Pericopes (meaning simply "extracts") of Henry II, set within an elaborately jewelled frame, contains three scenes, dominated by the Crucifixion, in an obvious narrative sequence. Similar painted scenes, only faded fragments of which survive, are known to have decorated Carolingian churches.

This depiction of the Crucifixion is an early example, its provenance hard to unravel, of what would become almost the single most important

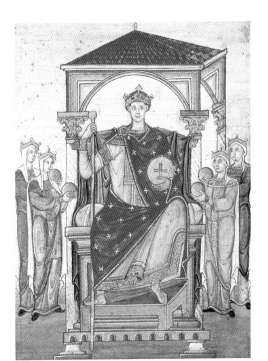

◀◀ *Otto II, Holy Roman Emperor* c.985, illumination on vellum, Chantilly: Musée Condé. Otto, the second Saxon Emperor, ruled 967–983. He married a Byzantine princess. The four women offering homage to the emperor represent the four parts of his empire.

Christian image in medieval Europe: Christ not just on the cross but clearly human, suffering unbearable agonies. The so-called Cross of Gero, carved around 970 and now in Cologne Cathedral, encapsulates this new, tortured sensibility.

ROMANESQUE AND EARLY GOTHIC ART

c.1000–1300

Despite external threats, whether Viking, Magyar, or Muslim, by about 1000 the Christian states of Europe had begun a slow process of recovery. At the heart of their regeneration was the Church, the only pan-European body in Christendom. Early medieval art, increasingly lavish, in architecture above all, was almost exclusively religious.

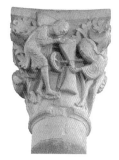

⬈ *Romanesque capital* c.1135. The pilgrimage church of Ste. Madeleine in Vézelay in the Burgundy region of France has many fine examples of Romanesque carving.

⬇ *Nave of Pisa Cathedral* 1094. Pisa was one of the powerful maritime republics of medieval Italy. Wealth from trade funded the city's beautiful Romanesque cathedral.

The foundation of a new monastery at Cluny in central France in 910 sparked a hugely important reform of the Western Church. Under its second abbot, St Odo, Cluny extended its control over a number of other monastic foundations. In the process, they were not merely reinvigorated themselves but the Church as a whole became much more expansive and assertive. One consequence was a programme of new church building across much of western Europe.

Romanesque architecture

Quite rapidly, a new architectural language, the Romanesque, came into being. As a reflection of the new power of the Church, these were buildings that were deliberately magnificent and, in many cases, much larger than anything yet seen in Europe. The cathedral of Santiago de Compostela, for example, built around 1120, possesses this austere gravity in abundance. There is a heaviness to its massive walls and immense tunnel vaults

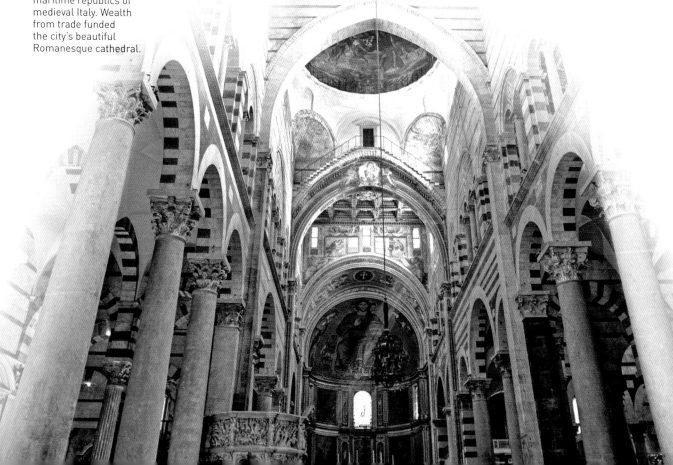

that emphatically projects the new self-assurance of the Church. At much the same time, in France, a new manner of sculptural decoration was created. At Autun Cathedral, for example, the tympanum (the area immediately above the main entrance) is crowded with figures dominated by Christ in the centre. The subject depicted, as it is on almost all later such carvings, is the Last Judgement, a reminder to worshippers entering the building of their mortality. The vigour and elegance of this teeming scene – filled with demons, angels, the damned, and the saved, the whole presided over by the serene figure of Christ – makes clear the revitalization of European sculpture, an art form almost abandoned after the fall of Rome. As with all medieval sculpture, it would originally have been painted.

The Gothic

In 1144, Abbot Suger, abbot of the monastery of St Denis just outside Paris, presided over the consecration of the rebuilt choir of the abbey church. That this is a radically different type of structure is obvious. Structurally, there is nothing new – its ribbed vaults and pointed arches had appeared in a number of earlier buildings – yet St Denis has a unity, the whole lit by what Suger memorably called "the liquid light of heaven", that is quite different. Gothic art was more than just an extension of the Romanesque. It was different in every important sense, a visual language expressly designed to celebrate the central place of the Church in an increasingly confident European society. This was not a world looking back to Rome. Self-aware and increasingly self-assured, it sought to create its own towering monuments to God. The early Gothic cathedrals, with their soaring verticals reaching up to pointed arches, were triumphant assertions of a new sensibility that equated massive building projects with personal piety. It was a style that reached maturity at Chartres, begun in 1194, and climaxed at

KEY EVENTS

1031	Beginning of Christian reconquest of Spain
1065	Earliest known stained glass in Europe, at Augsburg Cathedral, Germany
1066	Norman conquest of England
1077	Emperor Henry IV forced to seek absolution from Gregory VII, reinforcing papal authority
1085	Third abbey church at Cluny, the largest in the world, begun
1088	First university in Europe established, at Padua, Italy
1096	First Crusade (to 1099)
1098	Foundation of Cistercian order in France
1137	Rebuilding of St Denis: first properly Gothic building
1147	Second Crusade (to 1149)
1154	Accession of Angevin King Henry II unites much of France and England

⚅ *Rose window* c.1224, stained glass, south wall of Chartres Cathedral.

Amiens, begun in 1220, and the Sainte-Chapelle in Paris (1243–48), where the floor-to-ceiling stained-glass windows are both a technical tour de force and an exultant celebration of a new monarchy certain of its own power.

The self-confidence of this world found other outlets. The mid-12th-century illustration of St John from the *Gospel of Liessies,* for example, probably painted by an English illustrator in the Low Countries, projects a similar certainty of its own worth: stylized, lavish, and elegant. It is a compelling example of the self-belief that underpinned the art of medieval Europe.

⚅ **Gothic carvings, Chartres Cathedral** These Old Testament figures, flanking the central door of the west façade, date from the late 12th century.

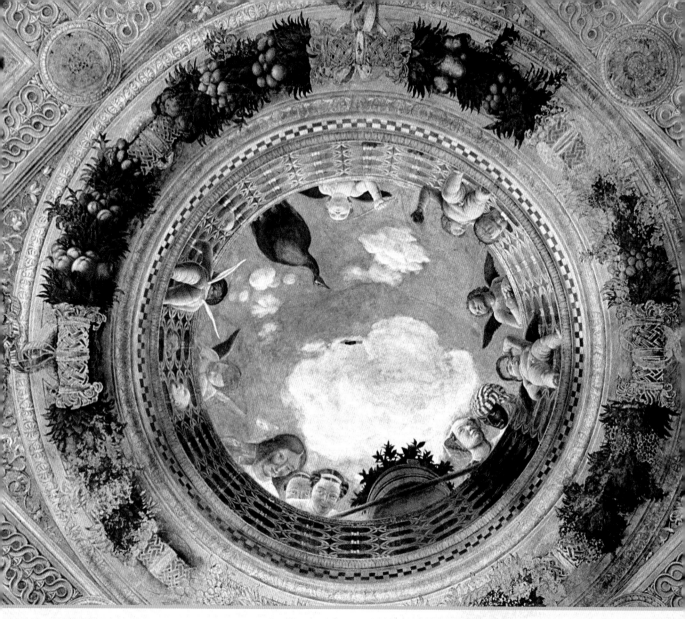

Gothic and Early Renaissance
c.1300–1500

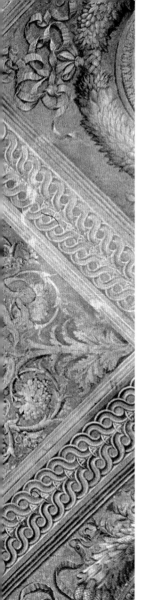

The word "Renaissance" (meaning "rebirth") was first used in the 15th century to describe a revival in Classical learning. At the same time, "Gothic" was used to describe a style of architecture regarded as barbaric, the creation of the Goths who had destroyed the glories of art and architecture in the Roman Empire.

It was only in the 19th century that "Renaissance" was used to explain the cultural flowering of the 14th and 15th centuries that launched the intellectual framework and artistic traditions of the modern world. Yet politically, socially, and economically the soil from which the Renaissance grew could hardly have seemed more barren.

When in 1346, the Black Death, carried by ship-borne rats from the Orient, began to wipe out one third of Europe's population, it seemed just the latest in a series of traumatic events. In the previous century, huge areas of eastern Europe had been seized by the Mongols. Between 1315 and 1319, there had been a run of catastrophic harvests. At the same time, the southeast of the continent was being menaced by the aggressively expanding Ottomans.

Europe looked ill equipped to deal with these threats. Technologically inferior and politically fragmented, it appeared destined to remain at the mercy of more powerful neighbours. In addition, it was wracked by periodic bouts of savage internal warfare. Edward III's attempted conquest of France in 1339 began over 100 years of brutal conflict between England and France. Meanwhile, the Catholic Church was divided by a period of schism.

Recovery through trade

Yet in the face of these enormous handicaps Europe staged a comeback. A sense of pan-European identity began to emerge, principally as the result of commerce. Throughout the Middle Ages, trade routes had been consolidated. By the end of the 14th century, a network of sea and land routes linked much of the continent. Money and goods were exchanged, but so were ideas, and together these led to a general rise in prosperity. Venice and Genoa, city-states grown rich on trade with the Orient, led the way, but others were quick to imitate them. For example, the establishment of the Hanseatic League in 1360 created a series of northern European cities that could rival the traditionally dominant Mediterranean. Equally important was the establishment, by Hans Fugger in Bavaria in 1380, of a banking network that in time would make the Fuggers the richest family in Europe.

◀ **Camera degli Sposi** *Andrea Mantegna, fresco, 1465–74, Mantua: Palazzo Ducale.* The virtuoso use of perspective, combined with Classical motifs, demonstrates the enthusiasm with which the Gonzaga family, the rulers of Mantua, embraced the new art and learning.

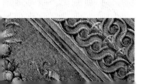

Italy

Nevertheless it was in Italy that the Renaissance achieved its fullest flowering. It was here that the physical remains of the ancient world – notably sculpture and architecture – were most numerous and so most easily studied. Also the newly rich city-states believed that they needed to embody the spirit of the Roman Empire itself. Florence, by the early 15th century the most powerful of these city-states, consciously chose to see itself as the direct heir of Rome. Financed by its own indigenous banking dynasty, the Medici, Florentine artists not only proclaimed the superiority of Classical antiquity but asserted that it represented a golden age of creativity whose spirit needed to be revived in the present, and they condemned the recent past as a dark age. At the same time, European thought was becoming more questioning and freethinking. People began to look for rational explanations of the physical environment and human behaviour, and were ready to reject the dogmatic propositions and blind faith that controlled the elaborately complex medieval world. Painters, sculptors, and architects were at the forefront in instigating these fundamental changes. When Brunelleschi demonstrated how perspective could be represented schematically on a flat surface, he was conscious that he was unifying science, philosophy, and art, and was thus looking ahead to a world in which all three would be, and would look, permanently different.

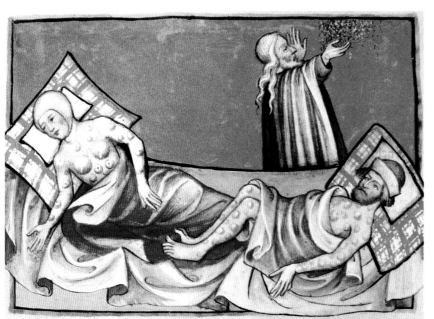

◄ *Illustration of plague victims*
from the Toggenburg Bible, Swizerland, 1411. The frequent ravages of plagues such as the Black Death or smallpox were visited indiscriminately on all ranks of society.

TIMELINE: c.1300–1500

c.1300 Venetians improve Brenner Pass, facilitating trade with northern Europe

1337 Start of 100 Years' War between England and France

1380 Foundation of international banking system by Hans Fugger in Augsburg, Germany

1389 Battle of Kosovo: Ottomans gain control of Balkans

1300

1350

1304–12 Scrovegni Chapel, Padua, painted by Giotto

1346 First occurrence of Black Death; in three years reduces Europe's population by one third

1356 Hanseatic League Parliament founded

1378 The Great Schism: rival popes in Rome and Avignon (to 1417)

1387 Medici bank founded, Florence

Poised for expansion

The most decisive contribution to this new spirit of enquiry was the invention of moveable type by Johannes Gutenberg in Germany in the 1450s. This sparked an unprecedented revolution in the speed, ease, and cost of the spread of information and ideas. When Christopher Columbus crossed the Atlantic in 1492 he opened new horizons and at the same time confirmed that Europe had moved from the shadowy margins of the world to occupy centre stage.

⟫ GOTHIC ART

"Gothic" describes principally a style of architecture common in Northern Europe between 1100 and 1500. It also includes the decorative art of the period, which was usually highly ornamental with realistic detail, but without any overall scheme of representation. In its later years Gothic art became increasingly decorative and elegant with sophisticated patterns and rhythms, and the fusion between Italian and Northern European styles is known as "International Gothic".

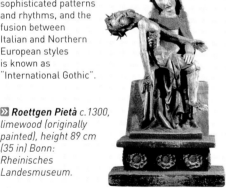

⟫ **Roettgen Pietà** c.1300, limewood (originally painted), height 89 cm (35 in) Bonn: Rheinisches Landesmuseum.

⟫ **Dome of Florence Cathedral**
Completed by Filippo Brunelleschi in 1436, the dome of Florence Cathedral was an emphatic statement of civic pride in which science was used to produce architecture of outstanding beauty.

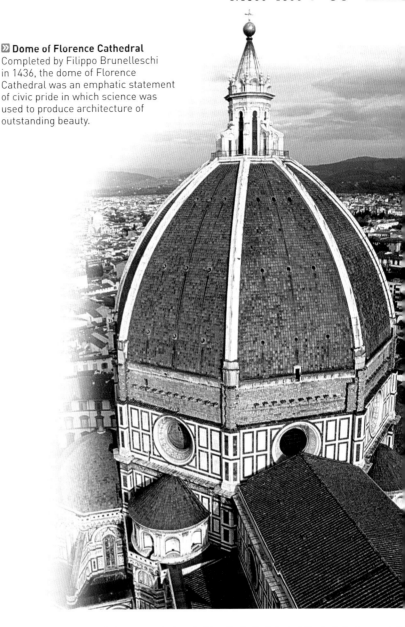

1419–24 Brunelleschi's Foundling Hospital, Florence, first properly classical building of the Renaissance

1425 Masaccio's *Holy Trinity*, Santa Maria Novella, Florence

1453 Constantinople falls to Ottomans; fall of Bordeaux to France ends 100 Years' War

1454 Gutenberg Bible, oldest known book printed with moveable type

1492 Muslim Granada falls to Spain; Columbus's first Atlantic crossing

1400

1450

1415 Burning of Jan Hus for heresy provokes religious wars in Bohemia

1429 Joan of Arc sparks French revival in 100 Years' War

1436 Dome of Florence cathedral completed

1450 Alliance of Florence, Naples, and Milan dominates north and central Italy

1469 Lorenzo de' Medici (the Magnificent) assumes control of republic of Florence

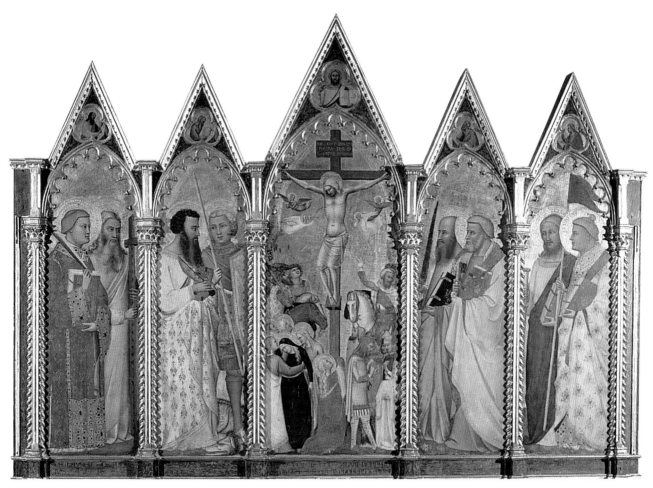

⌂ Polyptych with the Crucifixion and Saints
Bernardo Daddi, c.1348, approx. 155 x 217 cm (61 x 85 ⅜ in), tempera and gold leaf on panel, London: Courtauld Institute of Art.

Nicola and Giovanni **Pisano**

● 13TH–14TH CENTURIES ⵍ ITALIAN
⚏ SCULPTURE

Nicola (c.1220–c.1284) and Giovanni (c.1245–c.1314/19) were father and son. Nicola (also called Niccolò) founded a workshop, at which Giovanni was a pupil. They worked together, but each retained a distinct individual style and they were pioneers of the Gothic style. They were renowned for their religious stonework, such as altars and pulpits. The Fontana Maggiore in Perugia is the most famous of their joint works. They are credited with bringing naturalism to stone sculpture.

KEY WORKS: *Nativity* (pulpit), 1265–68 (Siena Cathedral); *Madonna and Child*, c.1305 (Padua: Cappella degli Scrovegni); *Madonna*, c.1315 (Prato Cathedral)

Bernardo **Daddi**

● c.1290–c.1349 ⵍ ITALIAN ⚏ OILS, FRESCO

Daddi was a younger contemporary of Giotto, who was possibly his teacher. He blended Giotto's tough realism with the sweetly lyrical qualities of Sienese artists (such as Ambrogio Lorenzetti). Look for smiling Madonnas, cute children, flowers, and draperies. He was the creator of popular, easy-to-look-at, small-scale portable altarpieces. Then, as now, art that is kind to the eye and mind tends to have a wide following.

KEY WORKS: *Arrival of St Ursula at Cologne*, 1330 (Los Angeles: J. Paul Getty Museum); *The Coronation of the Virgin*, c.1330–40 (London: National Gallery); *Martyrdoms of Sts Lawrence and Stephen*, c.1330 (Florence: Santa Croce)

Jean **Pucelle**

● 1300–c.1350 🏴 FRENCH ✍ ILLUMINATION

Pucelle was an eminent illuminator of manuscripts and a master miniaturist; recognized as such in his lifetime. He owned an influential workshop in Paris at the start of the 14th century and travelled to Italy and Belgium to learn new techniques.

A favourite of the French court, his works were expensive and purchased by nobility and royalty. Pucelle's works are renowned for being more realistic in their depiction of human features than those of the traditional, "flat" icon painters.

KEY WORKS: *Belleville Breviary*, 1323–26 (Paris: Bibliothèque Nationale); *Hours of Jeanne d'Evreux*, 1325–28 (New York: Metropolitan Museum of Art)

Limbourg brothers

● ACTIVE 1390s–c.1416 🏴 NETHERLANDISH ✍ ILLUMINATION

Paul (or Pol), Herman, and Jean were pioneering illuminators who trained as goldsmiths and then worked for the great French patron of the period, Jean, Duc de Berry, at a time of great political turmoil. They were born in the Netherlands, where their father was a woodcarver. Through the influence of an uncle, who was a painter, they were sent to train in Paris. Paul was probably the head of the workshop, but it is not possible to distinguish his hand from his brothers.

They used old forms (illustrated *Books of Hours* – personal prayer books) with fresh and stunningly innovative illustrations – scenes of everyday life, unusual biblical events, observation from life, and landscapes (such as the Duc's châteaux). Their brilliant colours and meticulous technique marry perfectly with their subjects.

Their best-known work is the "Months" from *Les Très Riches Heures* – the most accessible to a secular society and looks wonderful in reproduction. Note how they used contemporary advanced Italian ideas such as landscape background (one of the brothers went to Italy); and anticipated Netherlandish art – storytelling, fine detail, and observation. Their work and patronage reflect the notion that, for the wealthy, commissioning and collecting art was a celebration of God's glory and an act of true devotion.

KEY WORKS: *The Nativity*, c.1385–90 (Paris: Bibliothèque Nationale); *Les Très Riches Heures*, 1413–16 (Chantilly, France: Musée Condé); *The Anatomy of Man and Woman*, c.1416 (Chantilly, France: Musée Condé)

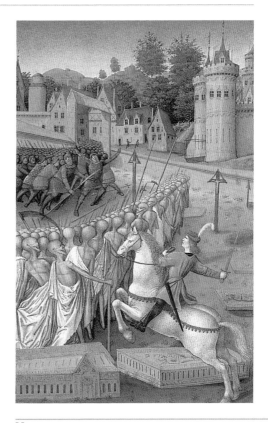

◩ *Death, One of the Four Riders of the Apocalypse* Paul (or Pol) Limbourg, c.1413–16, illumination on vellum, Chantilly (France): Musée Condé. Note the fine detail – an obsession of the brothers.

›› ILLUMINATION 7TH–15TH CENTURIES

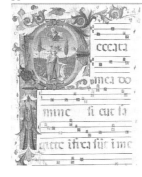

"Illumination" is the term used to describe the hand-painting and handwriting of books decorated with motifs in rich colours. Characteristically, the initial letter of a page is much larger than the others and furnished with images and bold colours. Gold is often used along with vivid hues of red, blue, and green. Other styles may include elaborate borders around the text or small pictorial scenes. The medium is often associated with religious books.

◩ **Illuminated "P"** by Bartolomeo di Fruosino, 1421

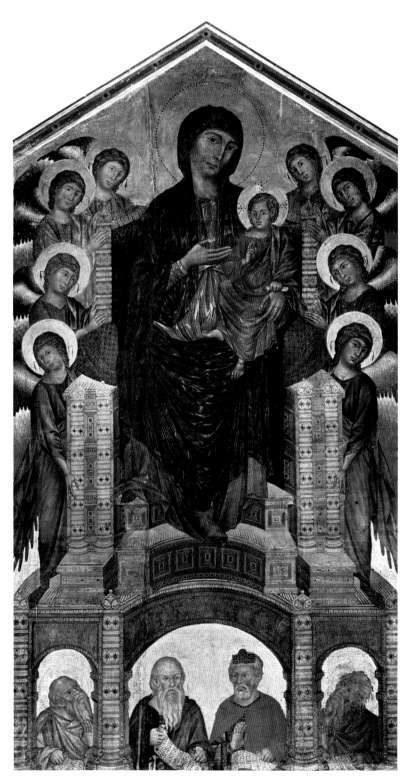

Madonna and Child Enthroned with Eight Angels and Four Prophets (or Maestà) Cimabue, c.1280, 385 x 223 cm (151 ½ x 87 ¾ in), tempera on wood, Florence: Galleria degli Uffizi.

Taddeo **Gaddi**

⬤ c.1300–c.1366 📖 ITALIAN ✍ OILS; FRESCO

Gaddi was Giotto's principal follower (and possibly his godson). He popularized Giotto's tough realism by making it decorative, adding anecdotal details and emphasizing the storytelling side of picture making.

KEY WORKS: *Annunciation to the Shepherds*, c.1328 (Florence: Santa Croce); *Madonna and Child Enthroned*, 1355 (Florence: Galleria degli Uffizi); *The Entombment of Christ*, c.1360–66 (New Haven: Yale University Art Gallery)

Cimabue (Cenni di Peppi)

⬤ c.1240–1302 📖 ITALIAN ✍ OILS; TEMPERA; FRESCO; MOSAIC

The most prominent artist working in Florence at the end of the 13th century, Cimabue was a contemporary of Dante. He is traditionally said to be Giotto's teacher – it is claimed that he initiated the move from the static "old" and "unreal" Byzantine style to the "modern" and "realistic" style, with more credible 3-D space, human form, and emotion. So many works have been attributed to him that his name has almost come to represent a group of like-minded artists rather than an individual, though we know he existed.

KEY WORKS: *Maestà*, 1280–85 (Florence: Galleria degli Uffizi); *Madonna and Child Enthroned with Two Angels and Saints Francis and Dominic*, c.1300 (Florence: Palazzo Pitti); *Christ Enthroned between the Virgin and St John the Evangelist*, 1301–1302 (Pisa Cathedral)

Duccio di Buoninsegna

● ACTIVE 1278–1319 ⫶ ITALIAN ✎ OILS

A key early Sienese painter, Duccio influenced all those artists that followed (just as Giotto influenced Florentine artists).

He tells a story with tenderness and humanity. Duccio is not as innovative in style or technique as Giotto, who was his contemporary, but he is a better narrator of events. Look at the way the people act and react together, and the way he uses the setting as part of the narrative. The perspective and scale may be haywire, but the buildings still look real and lived-in, and may be arranged so as to divide up the constituent parts of the story.

Duccio paints no-nonsense (slightly sceptical?) faces with long, straight noses, small mouths, and almond-shaped eyes, which can seem rather sly. His hand gestures help tell the story. He makes decorative use of colour, notably blue, red, and pale green. Some of the oddities or quirkiness can be explained because his style is not actually characteristic of the early Renaissance: it is essentially Byzantine and Gothic – that is, old-fashioned, but with a new twist, rather than completely new like Giotto's.

KEY WORKS: *Maestà*, c.1308 (Siena: Museo dell'Opera Metropolitana); *Nativity*, c.1308–11 (Washington DC: National Gallery of Art); *The Apostles Peter and Andrew*, c.1308–11 (Siena: Museo dell'Opera Metropolitana); *The Holy Women at the Sepulchre*, c.1308–11 (Washington DC: National Gallery of Art)

Lorenzetti brothers

● ACTIVE c.1319–48 ⫶ ITALIAN
✎ FRESCO; OILS

Sienese brothers Pietro (1320–c.1348) and Ambrogio Lorenzetti (1319–c.1348) followed in the steps of Duccio di Buoninsegna, but with more realism and expression. Both brothers had shadowy lives (there is a difficult chronology for extant works) and both died of plague. Ambrogio's work is warmer and less solemn than that of his brother: his most important works are the frescoes of *Good and Bad Government* (Palazzo Pubblico, Siena), which were the first Italian paintings where landscape was used as background.

KEY WORKS: *Charity of St Nicholas of Bari*, Ambrogio Lorenzetti, 1335–40 (Paris: Musée du Louvre); *Scenes from the Life of Blessed Humility*, Pietro Lorenzetti, c.1341 (Florence: Galleria degli Uffizi)

☒ *Allegory of Good Government: Effects of Good Government in the City* (detail), Ambrogio Lorenzetti, c.1338–39, 296 x 1398 cm (116 ½ x 550 ⅜ in), fresco, Siena: Palazzo Pubblico.

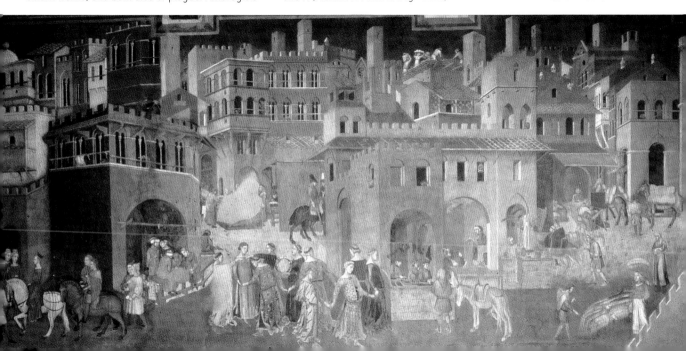

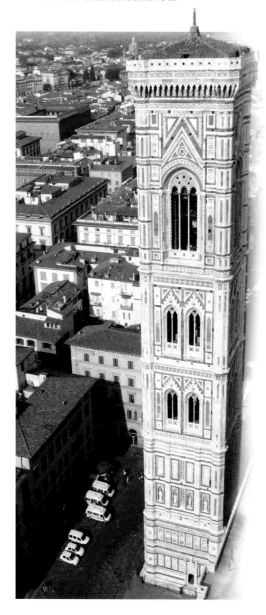

» *Campanile of the Duomo, Florence*
Giotto designed the Campanile in 1334, and construction was finished in 1359, 22 years after his death. Here, it is viewed from the top of the Duomo.

Giotto di Bondone

c.1267–1337 **ITALIAN** **FRESCO; OILS**

The painter who brought a new level of realism to art, which would establish the framework for Western art until 20th-century Modernism changed the rules.

Despite humble beginnings as the son of a farmer, Giotto became an educated and cultivated man, who grew rich and important in Florentine society. An unsubstantiated story tells how he was discovered by chance by the great painter Cimabue, who saw the boy Giotto sketching his father's sheep. Giotto then became Cimabue's apprentice, and lived through a period when Florence was becoming one of Europe's most important and influential cities.

What to look for

Giotto's innovation was in the way he portrayed supposedly real-life events to appear as though enacted by lifelike people expressing believable emotions and occupying recognizable settings and spaces. He looked, painted what he saw, and then opened up a "window on the world". The impact, even now, is one of directness, simplicity, accessibility, and believability. In other words, his paintings are about *life*.

Look for his outstanding features: faces expressing genuine emotion; meaningful gestures; strong, self-explanatory storylines (as in early silent movies, you only have to look to know exactly what is going on); the sense of space around and between the figures; how shape and movement of incidentals, such as trees and rocks, support the

> When I see the **Giotto frescoes at Padua** I do not trouble myself to recognize which scene of the life of Christ I have before me, but I **immediately understand the sentiment** which emerges from it. For it is in the **lines**, the **composition**, the **colour**.

Henri Matisse

main action or emotion; large-boned, well-built, solid figures. But notice also where he finds problems that are difficult for him to resolve; for example, he had no knowledge of perspective or anatomy, and a convincing sense of weightlessness (such as flying angels) eluded him.

Giotto's key monument is the Capella degli Scrovegni in Padua (c.1304–13), which is decorated from floor to ceiling with a complex arrangement of self-contained scenes, most memorable for their emotional and spiritual impact.

KEY WORKS: *Stigmata of St Francis*, c.1295–1300 (Paris: Musée du Louvre); *The Lamentation of Christ*, c.1305 (Padua: Cappella degli Scrovegni); *The Virgin and Child*, c.1305–06 (Oxford: Ashmolean Museum); *Enthroned Madonna with Saints and Angels*, c.1305–10 (Florence: Galleria degli Uffizi)

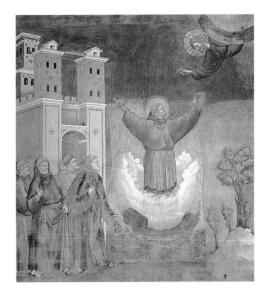

◀ *The Ecstasy of St Francis* 1297–99, 270 x 230 cm (106 ⅜ x 90 ½ in), fresco, Assisi: Church of San Francesco. One of the frescoes depicting "The Legend of St Francis", who had died less than 80 years earlier.

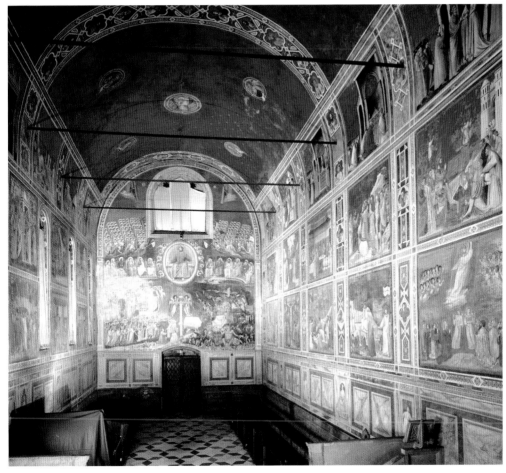

◀ *Cappella degli Scrovegni* c.1305, fresco, Padua. The climax of the chapel's glorious decoration is the large fresco of the *Last Judgement* on the west wall.

Simone **Martini**

● c.1285–1344 ▣ ITALIAN ✍ TEMPERA; FRESCO; OILS; ILLUMINATION

Simone was one of the leading painters from Siena and a follower of Duccio. Although he experimented with new ideas (such as perspective), he was essentially a large-scale, decorative illustrator, not least of illuminated manuscripts.

Look for the qualities you might see in illuminated manuscripts (despite the difference in scale): glowing colour; lively drawing; a precise, closely worked line; meticulous observation of detail; rhythmic, flowing, golden draperies. Simone's all-consuming emphasis was on decoration for sumptuous overall effect.

It is interesting to compare his work with that of his exact contemporary, Giotto, because, lovely as it is, it lacks everything that is in Giotto's: Simone's figures are artificial, with convoluted poses and gestures; their faces are stylized and without genuine emotion; the story-telling lacks deep meaning; everything is arranged decoratively, not to create ideas of space, form, and movement. Simone's work was a final chapter of the past – Giotto's was the future.

KEY WORKS: *Maestà*, 1315 (Siena: Palazzo Pubblico); *Death of St Martin*, c.1326 (Assisi: Lower Church); *The Angel and the Annunciation*, 1333 (Florence: Galleria degli Uffizi); *Apotheosis of Virgil*, 1340–44 (Milan: Biblioteca Ambrosiana); *Christ Discovered in the Temple*, 1342 (Liverpool: Walker Art Gallery)

Lorenzo **Monaco**

● c.1370–1425 ▣ ITALIAN ✍ OILS; FRESCO; ILLUMINATION

Lorenzo was born in Siena, but seems to have spent all his professional life in Florence. A highly gifted monk (*monaco* is Italian for "monk") he created

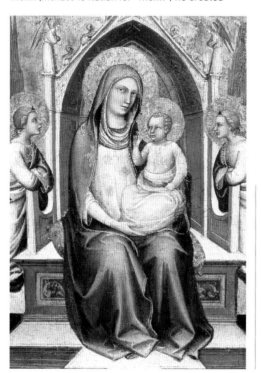

altarpieces and illuminated manuscripts (look for a love of detail; fine technique; luminous blues, reds, golds; rhythmical, decorative lines). His poetic imagination strove to unite the natural with the supernatural, and decorative Gothic with Giotto's realism. He was happiest when working on a small scale – predella panels and manuscripts.

KEY WORKS: *The Nativity*, 1409 (New York: Metropolitan Museum of Art); *Madonna and Child*, 1413 (Washington DC: National Gallery of Art); *The Adoration of the Magi*, c.1422 (Florence: Galleria degli Uffizi)

◀ *Madonna Enthroned between Adoring Angels*
Lorenzo Monaco, c.1400, 32.4 x 21.2 cm (12 ¾ x 8 ⅜ in), panel, Cambridge: Fitzwilliam Museum.

Ugolino di Nerio

● ACTIVE 1317–27 ▣ ITALIAN ✍ OILS

A Sienese painter who was also known as Ugolino da Siena. A close follower of Duccio and with a similar style, but the narrative is less well focused, the colours are less clear, and the faces and gestures lack Duccio's precision.

KEY WORKS: *St Mary Magdalene*, c.1320 (Boston: Museum of Fine Arts); *The Betrayal of Christ*, c.1324–25 (London: National Gallery)

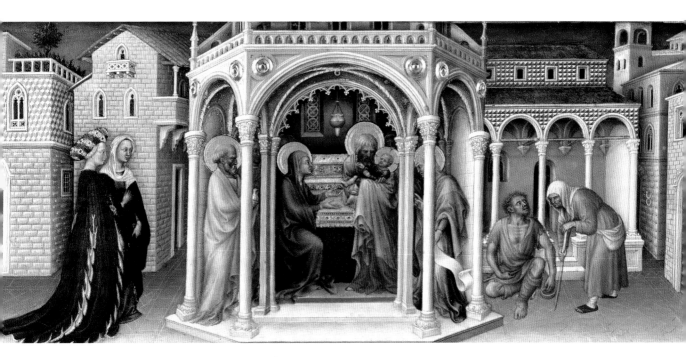

Gentile da **Fabriano**

● 1370–1427 🏴 ITALIAN ✍ OILS; FRESCO

Fabriano was an Italian painter, named after his birthplace, Fabriano in the Marches. One of the foremost artists of his day, he was the most accomplished exponent of the International Gothic style and worked all over Italy. Most of his work is lost or destroyed. His preference was to turn a work of art into a highly luxurious object (a characteristic of the International Gothic style) rather than provide a window on the world (Renaissance). His works could almost be fabulous textiles woven with gold thread.

As well as using traditional techniques, such as tooled gold, and with a liking for patterned textiles and static figures, Fabriano also experimented with light, space, and narrative. He created delicate, unreal figures with pink cheeks, and paid great attention to natural detail – animals, birds, plants – which he recorded with delicacy and sympathy.

KEY WORKS: *Virgin and Child Enthroned*, c.1395 (Berlin: Staatliche Museum); *Coronation of the Virgin*, 1420 (Los Angeles: J. Paul Getty Museum); *Adoration of the Magi*, 1423 (Florence: Galleria degli Uffizi)

Stefano di Giovanni **Sassetta**

● 1392–1450 🏴 ITALIAN ✍ OILS

The best painter of early Renaissance Siena, Sassetta effectively combined the old decorative style of the International Gothic with the new ideas from Florence.

In his works look for his charming, uninhibited qualities – the kind that children show when making a picture. His art reflects a delight in storytelling; lots of physical activity; spaces and perspective that don't quite work; sudden attention to unexplained detail; unsophisticated, decorative colours.

The characters in a Sassetta painting have bright little eyes with prominent whites and, sometimes, faces with wide-eyed expressions. They also have somewhat prissy, bow-shaped lips, and curious harp-shaped ears. Look, too, for the stylized crow's-feet on older male faces.

KEY WORKS: *St Margaret*, c.1435 (Washington DC: National Gallery of Art); *The Madonna and Child Surrounded by Six Angels*, c.1437–44 (Paris: Musée du Louvre); *The Meeting of St Anthony and St Paul*, c.1440 (Washington DC: National Gallery of Art)

⌃ *The Presentation in the Temple (from the Altarpiece of the Adoration of the Magi)*
Gentile da Fabriano, 1423, 26.5 x 66 cm (10 ½ x 30 in), oil on panel, Paris: Musée du Louvre.

Pisanello (Antonio Pisano)

◉ c.1395–1455 🇮🇹 ITALIAN ✍ OILS; ENGRAVINGS; FRESCO

Pisanello was very popular with princely courts as a painter, decorator, portraitist, and medallist, but few of his works now survive.

His work has qualities similar to those of illuminated manuscripts. It is good for an inconclusive art-historical debate: is he the late flowering of the International Gothic style or the pioneer of early Renaissance? (It is more profitable to forget the debate and just enjoy what you can, when you can.)

Notice his fascinating direct observation from life, and meticulous, fresh draughtsmanship, especially of animals, birds, and costumes. He painted flat, decorative backgrounds like tapestries, using fresh colours. His portraits have distinctive profiles, which relate to his pioneering of the art of the portrait medal – a medium at which he excelled.

KEY WORKS: *The Annunciation*, 1423–24 (Verona: San Fermo); *St George and the Princess of Trebizond*, 1437–38 (Verona: Santa Anastasia)

⬆ *Portrait of a Princess*
Antonio Pisano Pisanello, c.1436–38, 43 x 30 cm (17 x 11 ¾ in), tempera on wood, Paris: Musée du Louvre. Although unidentified, she is probably a member of the d'Este family.

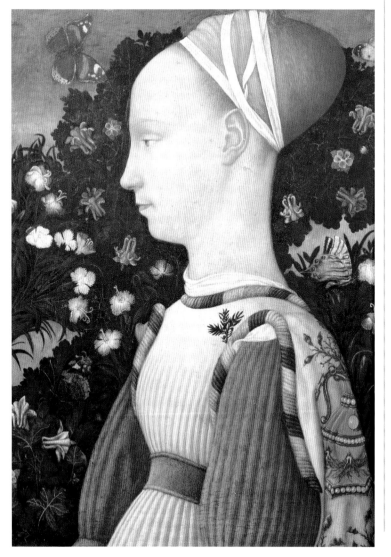

Masolino da Panicale

◉ c.1383–1447 🇮🇹 ITALIAN ✍ OILS; FRESCO

Best remembered as a collaborator of Masaccio, Masolino was recognized as a painter of great distinction. He had a graceful figure style, learned by working with the sculptor Lorenzo Ghiberti, and made skilful use of perspective. An accomplished modeller of flesh and hair, with an interest in everyday details.

KEY WORKS: *Madonna of Humility*, c.1415–20 (Florence: Galleria degli Uffizi); *St John the Evangelist and St Martin of Tours*, c.1423 (Philadelphia: Museum of Art); *St Liberius and St Matthias*, c.1428 (London: National Gallery)

Giovanni di Paolo

◉ ACTIVE 1420–82 🇮🇹 ITALIAN ✍ OILS

"The El Greco of the Quattrocento." A Sienese painter who adopted a deliberately old-fashioned style, in reply to the influential "modern" style of Duccio. He developed a charming, decorative, and convincing narrative style, in which the spaces, perspective, scale, emotions, and logic of the "real" world are deliberately ignored.

KEY WORKS: *St John the Baptist Retiring into the Wilderness*, c.1453 (London: National Gallery); *The Feast of Herod*, c.1453 (London: National Gallery); *The Nativity and the Adoration of the Magi*, c.1455–59 (Paris: Musée du Louvre)

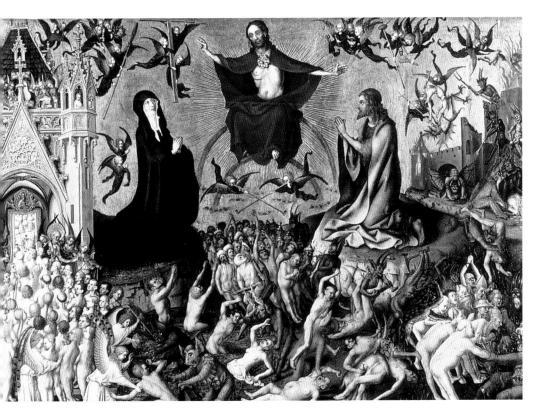

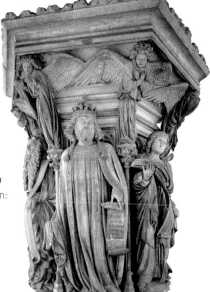

⊠ *The Moses Well*
Claus Sluter, late 14th century, height of figures 180 cm (70 ⅘ in), stone, Dijon: Chartreuse de Champmol. This symbolic well is surrounded by statues of Moses and other Old Testament prophets.

⊠ *The Last Judgment* Stefan Lochner, 1440s, 122 x 171 cm (48 x 67 ⅓ in), oil on wood, Cologne: Wallraf-Richartz-Museum. Central panel from an altarpiece made for the church of St Laurenz, Cologne.

Stefan **Lochner**

⊖ c.1400–51 | GERMAN ✍ OILS

A shadowy early German painter about whom little is known and to whom few works are attributed for certain. Lochner was the leading master of his time in Cologne, where he worked from 1442 until his death. He authored religious works of soft, rounded figures with slightly silly, chubby faces; glowing colours; rich, gold backgrounds; somewhat fussy, natural, and anecdotal detail.

KEY WORKS: *The Virgin in the Rose Bush*, c.1440 (Cologne: Wallraf-Richartz-Museum); *Annunciation*, c.1440–45 (Cologne Cathedral); *Sts Matthew, Catherine of Alexandria, and John the Evangelist*, c.1445 (London: National Gallery); *The Adoration of Christ*, c. 1445 (Munich: Alte Pinakothek)

Claus **Sluter**

⊖ c.1350–c.1405 | DUTCH ✍ SCULPTURE

A sculptor and a founder of the Burgundian School, Sluter was hugely influential on the development of northern European sculpture. He was born in Haarlem and worked in Brussels before moving to France. For 21 years, he lived in Dijon as chief sculptor of Philip the Bold, Duke of Burgundy. His work is characterized by fine draperies, silken-looking hair, and realistic human figures. Look for ordinary mortals introduced into religious works, standing alongside divine figures.

KEY WORKS: *Portal of the Chartreuse de Champmol*, 1385–93 (Dijon); *Arms of a Virgin or a Magdalene*, 14th century (Dijon: Musée Archéologique); *Fragment of Crucified Christ*, 14th century (Dijon: Musée Archéologique)

The Early Renaissance

15TH CENTURY

Three major principles underlined the Renaissance (literally, rebirth) in early 15th-century Italy: a renewed, more systematic study of Classical Antiquity in the belief that it constituted an absolute standard of artistic worth; a faith in the nobility of man (Humanism); and the discovery and mastery of linear perspective. Together, they made up a revolution in Western art.

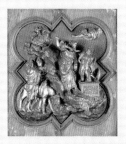

⌃ *The Sacrifice of Isaac* Lorenzo Ghiberti, 1402, 53.3 x 43.4 cm (21 x 17 in), bronze, Florence: Museo Nazionale del Bargello. The frame may still be Gothic, but the key elements of the Renaissance are unmistakably present e.g. the muscular Isaac derived from Classical originals.

From the start, Renaissance artists, especially those based in its birthplace, Florence, were conscious that their work represented a decisive break with the immediate past. The change came first – and most obviously – in sculpture. Ghiberti's panel for a new set of bronze doors for the Florence Baptistery owes a direct and immediate debt to Roman models. The figures are modelled naturalistically and the sense of space is equally marked.

Subjects

Though religious subjects continued to predominate, there was an increasing interest in secular subjects. Gozzoli's mid-century *Procession of the Magi* artfully combined the two. His Magi are portraits of his patrons, the Medici, surrounded by numerous retainers, on a procession that is more regal than religious. If the shimmering, jewel-like picture surface harks back to the

International Gothic style, the figures and landscape are just as clearly products of the Renaissance.

What to look for

The two most obvious technical triumphs of Renaissance painting were the ability to portray convincingly naturalistic figures in illusionistic spaces that were equally convincingly realized. Piero della Francesca, an artist, and the author of three mathematical treatises, epitomized both developments. He constructed exceptionally elaborate perspective schemes, while his figures have an overwhelming sense of assured monumentality. Yet however rational his paintings may be, what ultimately marks them is a distinctively haunting sense of serene detachment.

KEY EVENTS	
1424	Ghiberti completes the first set of Florence Baptistery bronze doors; more commissioned
c.1427	Masaccio completes the frescoes in Brancacci Chapel, Santa Maria del Carmine, Florence, the first great Renaissance fresco cycle
1434–64	Florence ruled by Cosimo de' Medici
1452-55	Johannes Gutenberg's Bible, the first printed book in Europe (Germany)
1452	Publication of Alberti's *De Re Aedificatoria*, the first comprehensive treatise to set out the principles of Classical architecture
1469–92	Lorenzo (the "Magnificent") de' Medici rules Florence

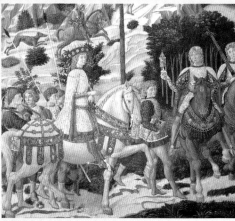

» *The Procession of the Magi* (detail), Benozzo Gozzoli, 1459, fresco, Florence: Palazzo Medici-Riccardi. The richly garbed figure on the white horse is Lorenzo de' Medici, commandingly certain of his worth in every sense.

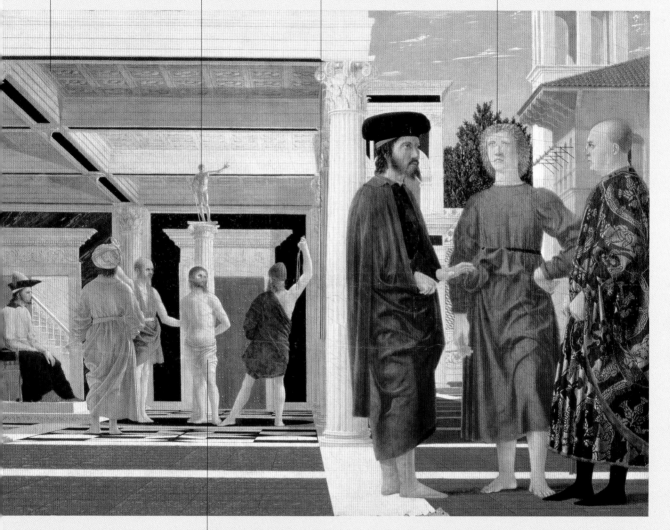

The architectural structure – the ceiling of the semi open-air loggia and the rich floor tiles – is mathematically exact

A guilded antique statue symbolically tops the classical pillar to which Christ is bound

The vanishing point is precisely calculated: exactly on the centre line of the painting, dividing it in two, a quarter of the way up

The significance of the three figures in the foreground has been endlessly questioned. Who are they, and why are they so detached from the flagellation?

⚠ **The Flagellation of Christ**
Piero della Francesca, c.1470, 58.4 x 81.5 cm (23 x 32 in), oil and tempera, Urbino: Galleria Nazionale delle Marche. The art historian Kenneth Clark called this "the greatest small painting in the world".

The flagellation is carried out with hardly any animation. On the left, the seated figure of Pontius Pilate gazes impassively at Christ's punishment

⟫ TECHNIQUES

Piero's palette, consistently cool and clear, is a key element in the curious air of mystery that pervades his work. Flesh tones (which use a base of green paint), no less than limpid skies, are realized with remarkable economy.

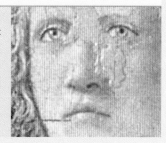

Lorenzo **Ghiberti**

● c.1378–1455 Ⓜ ITALIAN ✍ SCULPTURE; GLASS

Ghiberti was a sculptor, goldsmith, designer, and writer. He was born and worked in Florence, but also worked in Siena. Renowned in his lifetime as the best bronze-caster in Florence, he was famous for the bronze doors of the Baptistery in Florence and also produced stained glass and sculptures. Ghiberti opened a large influential workshop, and his pupils included Donatello. He married a young woman, Marsilia, around 1415 and had two sons, Tommaso and Vittorio, both of whom worked in the studio.

Look for rich decoration and elegance of sculpting. His relief work is defined by clean lines and activity, with the eye drawn by fluid drapery, movement in the landscape, and ornate carving – a fusion of classical artistic style with realism.

KEY WORKS: *The Sacrifice of Isaac*, 1402 (Florence: Museo Nazionale del Bargello); *Joseph in Egypt*, 1425–52 (Porta del Paradiso)

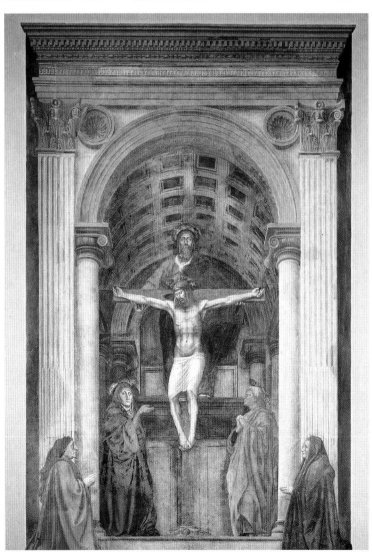

◪ *The Trinity* Tommaso Masaccio, 1425, 670 x 315 cm (263 ¾ x 124 in), fresco (post-restoration), Florence: Santa Maria Novella. This piece was covered over in 1570 with a panel painting by Vasari, and only rediscovered in 1861.

Masaccio (Tommaso Giovanni di Mone)

● 1401–28 Ⓜ ITALIAN ✍ FRESCO; TEMPERA

The greatest of the early-Renaissance Florentines, Masaccio revolutionized the art of painting during his short lifetime and was the bridge between Giotto and Michelangelo. Masaccio means "big ugly Tom". He left very few known works, yet his deeply moving pictures can plumb the most basic and profound of human emotions. Masaccio painted believable and dignified human figures, expressing qualities of feeling, emotion, and intellectual curiosity that are as relevant today as they were 600 years ago. His simple, well-ordered compositions, in which the human figure is the central feature, accord with the Renaissance principle that human beings are the measure of all things.

The individual expressions on the faces show minds and emotions at work – enquiring, doubting, suffering – that are also expressed simultaneously through gestures and hands (but why are the hands so small?). Masaccio created believable spaces, which human figures dominate with authority. He used light to model draperies and figures which, instead of outlining, helps them to look real. Masaccio was the first painter to understand and use scientific perspective; the same is true of foreshortening.

KEY WORKS: *Crucifixion*, 1426 (Naples: Museo di Capodimonte); *The Expulsion from Paradise*, c.1427 (Florence: Santa Maria del Carmine)

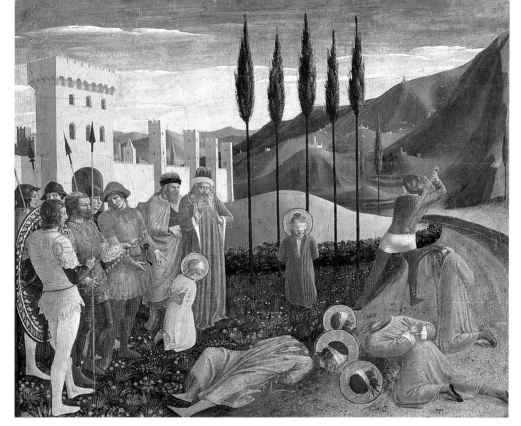

◀ *The Beheading of St Cosmas and St Damian* Fra Angelico, c.1438–40, 37 x 46 cm (14 ½ x 18 in), tempera on panel, Paris: Musée du Louvre. After previous failed attempts on their lives, the twin martyrs were finally killed.

Fra **Filippo Lippi**

⬤ c.1406–69 ▥ ITALIAN ✍ FRESCO; TEMPERA; OILS

Lippi was an important early-Renaissance Florentine whose work forms a bridge between Masaccio and Botticelli.

His sincerely-felt religious works expressed his worship of God by sensitive interpretation of the New Testament and by mastery of all the chief technical interests and developments of the period (all of them, including the artist's skill, being a gift from God): perspective; landscape; proportion; communication between human figures; finely painted decorative detail; and carefully drawn drapery folds.

Look for the chubby figures with slightly glum, youthful faces, and eyes that look as though they never blink. Note, too, his love of rich detail – marble floors, gold grounds, and decorated costumes.

KEY WORKS: *Virgin and Child*, c.1440–45 (Paris: Musée du Louvre); *The Annunciation*, c.1450–53 (London: National Gallery); *Madonna and Child with Stories of the Life of St Anne*, c.1452 (Florence: Palazzo Pitti)

Fra **Angelico**

⬤ c.1395–1455 ▥ ITALIAN ✍ FRESCO; TEMPERA; OILS

Fra Angelico was a Dominican friar whose work combines old-fashioned (Gothic) and progressive (Renaissance) ideas.

His paintings interpret the Christian message with directness, enthusiastically telling the story of God's goodness. They are delightfully happy, attractive, and holy, and have great innocent purity – as though he saw no evil in the world (perhaps he didn't).

There is disarming and childlike innocence in the detail: youthful, happy faces with peaches and cream complexions and pink cheeks; everyone is busy doing something. Angelico takes evident pleasure in colours (especially pink and blue) and things that he has observed closely, such as flowers. He uses old-fashioned gold embellishments and modern perspective with equal enthusiasm; his soft draperies have highly detailed borders.

KEY WORKS: *Noli me Tangere*, 1425–30 (Florence: Convent of San Marco); *The Annunciation*, 1435–45 (Madrid: Museo del Prado)

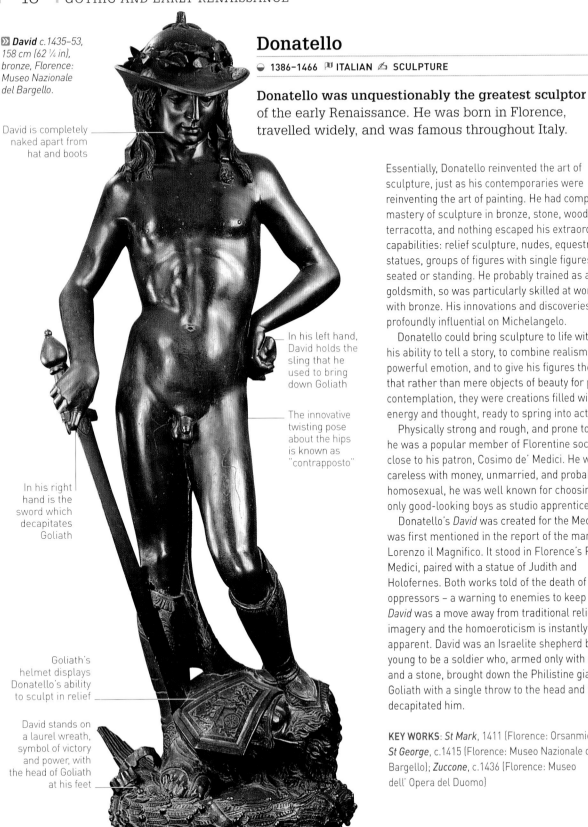

⟫ *David* c.1435–53, 158 cm (62 ¼ in), bronze, Florence: Museo Nazionale del Bargello.

David is completely naked apart from hat and boots

In his left hand, David holds the sling that he used to bring down Goliath

The innovative twisting pose about the hips is known as "contrapposto"

In his right hand is the sword which decapitates Goliath

Goliath's helmet displays Donatello's ability to sculpt in relief

David stands on a laurel wreath, symbol of victory and power, with the head of Goliath at his feet

Donatello

● 1386–1466 ▥ ITALIAN ✍ SCULPTURE

Donatello was unquestionably the greatest sculptor of the early Renaissance. He was born in Florence, travelled widely, and was famous throughout Italy.

Essentially, Donatello reinvented the art of sculpture, just as his contemporaries were reinventing the art of painting. He had complete mastery of sculpture in bronze, stone, wood, and terracotta, and nothing escaped his extraordinary capabilities: relief sculpture, nudes, equestrian statues, groups of figures with single figures seated or standing. He probably trained as a goldsmith, so was particularly skilled at working with bronze. His innovations and discoveries were profoundly influential on Michelangelo.

Donatello could bring sculpture to life with his ability to tell a story, to combine realism and powerful emotion, and to give his figures the sense that rather than mere objects of beauty for passive contemplation, they were creations filled with energy and thought, ready to spring into action.

Physically strong and rough, and prone to anger, he was a popular member of Florentine society and close to his patron, Cosimo de' Medici. He was careless with money, unmarried, and probably homosexual, he was well known for choosing only good-looking boys as studio apprentices.

Donatello's *David* was created for the Medici, and was first mentioned in the report of the marriage of Lorenzo il Magnifico. It stood in Florence's Palazzo Medici, paired with a statue of Judith and Holofernes. Both works told of the death of oppressors – a warning to enemies to keep away. *David* was a move away from traditional religious imagery and the homoeroticism is instantly apparent. David was an Israelite shepherd boy, too young to be a soldier who, armed only with a sling and a stone, brought down the Philistine giant Goliath with a single throw to the head and then decapitated him.

KEY WORKS: *St Mark*, 1411 (Florence: Orsanmichele); *St George*, c.1415 (Florence: Museo Nazionale del Bargello); *Zuccone*, c.1436 (Florence: Museo dell' Opera del Duomo)

Luca **della Robbia**

◔ c.1399–1482 ▥ ITALIAN ✍ SCULPTURE; CERAMICS

Luca di Simone della Robbia came from a family of artists and artisans. He was a prolific sculptor and a warm personality, who gave practical help to struggling artisans. Trained in textiles and as a goldsmith, he worked in stone and terracotta.

Della Robbia was patronized by the Medici and had patrons in Naples, Portugal, and Spain. He achieved fame and wealth with glazed terracotta artworks, setting up a successful studio in Florence and keeping the formula of his tin glazes a secret. He worked closely with his nephew Andrea.

Look for rich colour and luminous tin glazes, strict attention to detail, and an awareness of the properties of draperies and metalwork reflected in his sculpture. His scenes are dense with symbolism, and the faces expressive.

KEY WORKS: *The Resurrection*, c.1442–45 (Florence: Museo Nazionale del Bargello); *Roundels of the Apostles*, c.1444 (Florence: Pazzi Chapel)

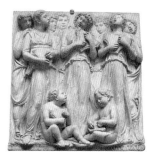

▣ **Cantoria (Choir Gallery,** detail) Luca della Robbia, c.1432–38, 100 x 94 cm (39 ³/₈ x 37 in), marble, Florence: Museo dell'Opera del Duomo. The carvings illustrate the 150th Psalm and depict angels, boys, and girls in song.

Domenico **Veneziano**

◔ c.1410–61 ▥ ITALIAN ✍ TEMPERA; FRESCO

Veneziano was an important and very influential Venetian who worked in Florence. He is considered a founding member of the 15th-century Florentine School. Almost nothing is known about him now, and few known works survive. He was more interested in constructing with light and colour than with modelled form and perspective.

KEY WORKS: *The Annunciation*, c.1442–48 (Cambridge: Fitzwilliam Museum); *Santa Lucia dei Magnoli altarpiece* c.1445–47 (Florence: Galleria degli Uffizi)

Paolo **Uccello**

◔ 1397–1475 ▥ ITALIAN ✍ TEMPERA; OILS; FRESCO

Paolo di Dono was a Florentine painter nicknamed *Uccello* (the bird). His works are recognizable for the schematic use of perspective. His over-theoretical application of it tends to swamp all other considerations and can make his work look wooden and the figures toy-like, but the sheer gusto with which he used it stops his pictures from becoming boring. Did he use a single viewpoint or are there several? Forget about it, and enjoy his strong sense of design and attention to decorative detail. Sadly, many of his works are in poor condition. They are also often hung at the wrong height so that his perspective effects are ruined. (If necessary, sit or lie on the floor to work out the proper viewpoint.)

KEY WORKS: *Battle of San Romano*, c.1455 (Florence: Galleria degli Uffizi); *St George and the Dragon*, c.1470 (London: National Gallery)

▣ **The Hunt in the Forest** Paolo Uccello, c.1465–70, 75 x 178 cm (29 ½ x 70 in), oil on canvas, Oxford: Ashmolean Museum. One of Uccello's greatest works, this demonstrates his fascination with perspective. The leading stag (centre) is the focus of the vanishing point.

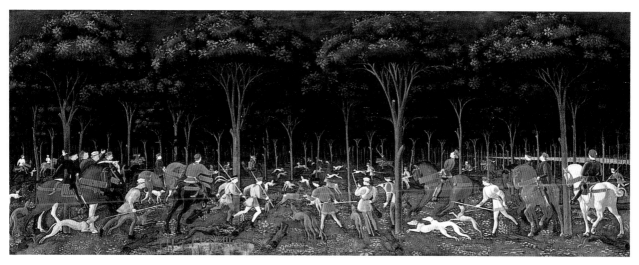

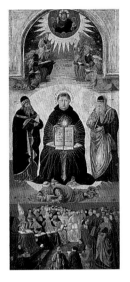

⌃ The Triumph of St Thomas Aquinas
Benozzo di Lese Gozzoli, c.1470–75, 230 x 102 cm (90 ½ x 40 ¼ in), tempera on panel, Paris: Musée du Louvre. The saint is enthroned between Aristotle and Plato.

Benozzo di Lese **Gozzoli**

◔ c.1421–97 ⚲ ITALIAN ✍ FRESCO; TEMPERA

A down-to-earth, early-Renaissance Florentine, Gozzoli was a good craftsman. Originally trained as a goldsmith, he worked in his early years with Ghiberti on the doors of the Baptistry in Florence.

He was a painter of high-quality altarpieces and predella panels. His crowded scenes have brilliant, decorative qualities, and carefully observed solid figures, with no-nonsense faces and expressions.

Gozzoli's figures have good hands (with long fingers) and feet, and are firmly placed on the ground. Note how well he arranges crowds, and has a propensity to paint the tops of heads, particularly if bald, or with a hat or helmet.

KEY WORKS: *Procession of the Magi*, 1459–61 (Florence: Palazzo Medici-Riccardi); *The Dance of Salome*, 1461–62 (Washington DC: National Gallery of Art); *Madonna and Child with Saints*, 1461–62 (London: National Gallery)

Andrea del **Verrocchio**

◔ c.1435–88 ⚲ ITALIAN
✍ SCULPTURE; TEMPERA; OILS

The son of a brickmaker, Verrocchio trained with a goldsmith, whose name he took. He became a leading Florentine painter, goldsmith, and (principally) sculptor. Verrocchio had a workshop where Leonardo da Vinci trained. Authentic paintings by him are very rare.

His altarpieces show an overall mood and style of refinement, grace,

《 Equestrian Monument to Bartolomeo Colleoni
Andrea del Verrocchio, 1480s, height 395 cm (155 ½ in), bronze, Venice: Campo Santi Giovanni e Paolo. The work was a competitive challenge to Donatello.

freshness, and delicate idealism. They have a dreamy, faraway atmosphere, which is reflected in the eyes and expressions on the faces. He portrayed two types of face or body: epicene youth and craggy, tough warrior. He also painted similarly fresh, delicate landscapes and skies that contrast with craggy outcrops and rocks. Look for clear, sharp outlines and bright colours.

Note his love of fine detail, displayed in expensive fabrics decorated with gold thread and jewellery. Notice the bow-shaped lips pressed together; the stylized curly, wiry hair; the refined hands touching each other or others; poses that imply movement through weight being placed on one foot or leg. His figures seem modelled and conceived as sculpture.

KEY WORKS: *Putto with Dolphin*, c.1470 (Florence: Palazzo Vecchio); *Tobias and the Angel*, 1470–80 (London: National Gallery); *The Baptism of Christ*, c.1475–75 (Florence: Galleria degli Uffizi)

Piero di Cosimo

◔ c.1462–c.1521 ⚲ ITALIAN ✍ OILS

Cosimo was an out-of-the-ordinary, early-Renaissance Florentine with a bohemian lifestyle and a fascination with primitive life. He was a prime example of artist as craftsman.

He painted portraits, altarpieces, and mythologies. Especially endearing and memorable are his love of animals and birds, his observations of nature, and his storytelling. His strange, mythological fantasy pictures are unique; they are entirely fanciful and can have disturbing suggestions of struggle and violence. Nobody knows what they mean or why they were painted, so we are free to interpret them as we like.

How do you interpret the strangely ambivalent role played by the animals in his pictures? Note the charming landscape details that look as though they have come out of a woven medieval tapestry. Many of his works were done as decorative panels for furniture (such as *cassoni*) or rooms, hence their elongated shape.

KEY WORKS: *The Visitation with St Nicholas and St Anthony Abbot*, c.1490 (Washington DC: National Gallery of Art); *A Satyr Mourning over a Nymph*, c.1495 (London: National Gallery)

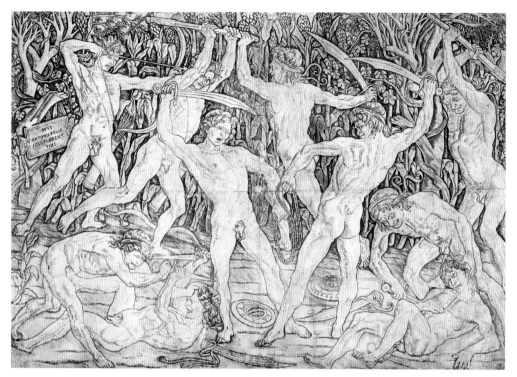

◀◀ **Battle of the Ten Naked Men** Antonio Pollaiuolo, c.1470–75, 38.3 x 59 cm (15 ⅛ x 23 ¼ in), engraving, Florence: Galleria degli Uffizi. This work shows the artist's mastery of depicting the human body in motion.

Pollaiuolo brothers

● c.1432–98 🏳 ITALIAN ✍ OILS; SCULPTURE; ENGRAVINGS

Antonio (c.1432–98) was a shadowy figure who, with his brother Piero (c.1441–96) ran one of the most successful workshops in Florence.

The Pollaiuolo brothers had a pioneering interest in anatomy and landscape, choosing subjects to display these interests and skills to the full, notably anatomy – the male, nude or semi-naked, doing something that shows straining muscles and sinews. Their works show front, side, and back views in the manner of an anatomical analysis (they are said to have dissected corpses to study anatomy which would have been a daring and risky venture at the time).

The brothers also painted detailed landscapes and had an interest in spatial recession, but their work jumps abruptly from foreground to background. They never worked out how to use the middleground.

KEY WORKS: *Hercules and the Hydra*, c.1470 (Florence: Galleria degli Uffizi); *Portrait of a Woman*, c.1470 (Milan: Museo Poldi Pezzoli); *Apollo and Daphne*, c.1470–80 (London: National Gallery)

Luca **Signorelli**

● c.1450–1523 🏳 ITALIAN ✍ FRESCO; OILS; TEMPERA

Signorelli was an intense and gifted artist, but outclassed by Raphael and Michelangelo. His religious and secular subjects were chosen to make the most of his interest in dramatic compositions. Observe the movement, muscles, and gestures in his figures – but sometimes there is too much of this and the paintings can seem overcrowded. His draughtsmanship was good. Signorelli emphasized the sculptural quality of the figures to the point where they sometimes look as though they have been carved out of wood. (Michelangelo always showed flesh and blood.) He painted hands that look distorted by arthritis and mouths with set expressions.

KEY WORKS: *The Holy Family*, 1486–90 (London: National Gallery); *The End of the World*, 1499–1502 (Frescoes, Orvieto Cathedral); *The Circumcision*, c.1491 (London: National Gallery); *St Agostino Altarpiece*, 1498 (Berlin: Staatliche Museen)

Alessandro ("Sandro") **Botticelli**

● 1445–1510 ◫ ITALIAN ✎ TEMPERA; FRESCO

Alessandro di Mariano Filipepe Botticelli was the principle Florentine artist of the later 15th century. He was highly strung and inclined to laziness. His principal patrons were members of the Medici dynasty.

Botticelli painted deeply-felt religious pictures and pioneering large-scale mythologies. Note the way he portrays the human figure (on its own, in relationship to others, or in crowd scenes) – always with great dignity, strange and distant, with dream-like unreality and distortions. One of the greatest draughtsmen of all time. His later work is odd and retrogressive because he retreated into the past, unable to cope with Florence's turbulent descent into social and political turmoil.

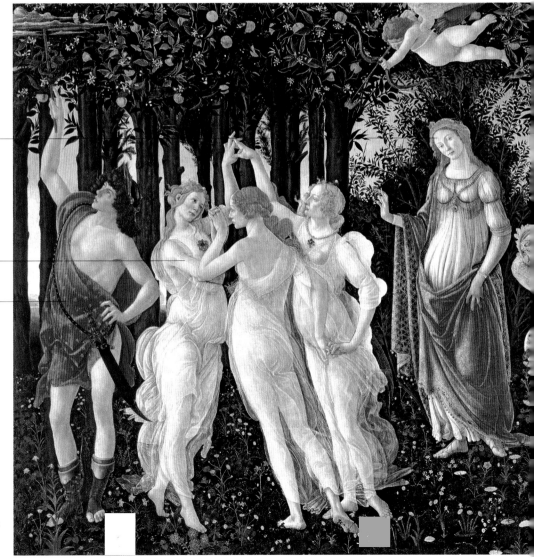

Venus wears the characteristic headdress of a Florentine wife

The three Graces – with their long necks, sloping shoulders, curving bellies, and slender ankles – embody the ideal of feminine beauty in Renaissance Florence

Mercury, the messenger of the gods, uses his caduceus – a wand entwined with snakes – to hold back the clouds

» La Primavera (Spring)
c.1482, 203 x 314 cm (80 x 123 in), tempera on panel, Florence: Galleria degli Uffizi. This painting shows the garden of Venus, the Goddess of Love. It was probably commissioned by Lorenzo di Pierfrancesco de' Medici (1463–1503).

Botticelli's refined, feminine style found favour with the Florentine intelligentsia in the troubled times in which they lived. His masterpieces were his large mythological paintings, which promoted a particular type of divinely inspired beauty, combined with complex literary references.

His figures have wonderful bone structure – especially in their cheeks and noses, long and refined hands, wrists, feet, and ankles – as well as beautifully manicured nails; they have fine and crisply drawn outlines like tense wires. Notice his fascination with pattern – in elaborate materials, hair, and crowds, which he turns into designs of shape or colour, or both. He found ideas like scientific perspective of no interest; instead, he combined old Gothic decorative styles with new, classical, and humanist ideals.

KEY WORKS: *The Madonna of the Magnificat*, c.1480–81 (Florence: Galleria degli Uffizi); *Virgin and Child with Eight Angels*, c.1481–83 (Berlin: Staatliche Museen); *The Birth of Venus*, c.1484 (Florence: Galleria degli Uffizi)

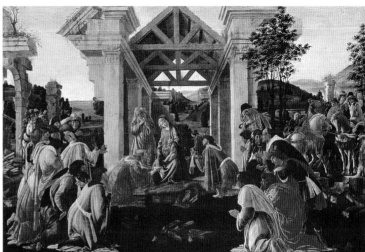

⊠ *The Adoration of the Magi* 1481, 70 x 104 cm (27 ½ x 41 in), tempera and oil on panel, Washington DC: National Gallery of Art. Botticelli may have painted this while in Rome working on the Sistine Chapel.

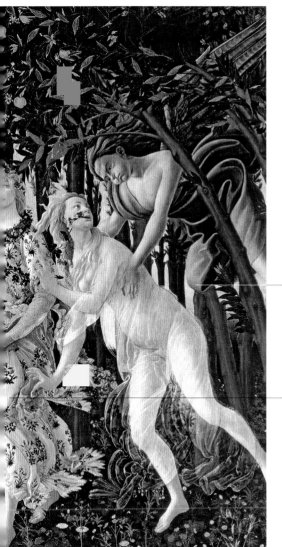

Zephyrus, god of the West Wind and herald of Venus, pursues his lover, Chloris, whom he transforms into Flora

Flora, the goddess of flowers, tiptoes across the meadow, strewing blossoms around her. She has particular significance for Florence – the city of flowers

》 TECHNIQUES

Flora's gown is decorated with flowers that are slightly raised to imitate embroidery. Botticelli was fascinated by decoration and stylized pattern. Other examples are the "halo" of foliage that is silhouetted against the sky around Venus, and the carpet of flowers.

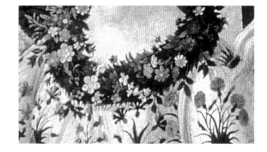

Domenico **Ghirlandaio**

● 1449–94 🏛 ITALIAN ✍ FRESCO; OILS; TEMPERA

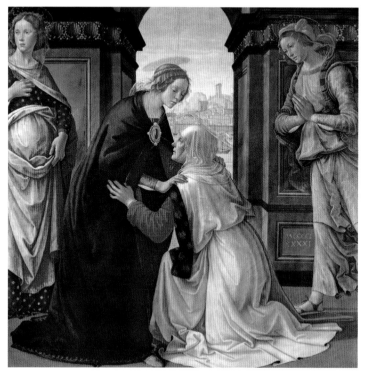

🔼 **The Visitation**
Domenico Ghirlandaio, 1491, 172 x 165 cm (67 ⅝ x 65 in), tempera on panel, Paris: Musée du Louvre. Mary, pregnant with Jesus, visits her cousin Elizabeth who is pregnant with St John the Baptist.

Ghirlandaio was a Florentine painter who achieved success with a solid, old-fashioned yet realistic storytelling style. His most famous pupil was Michelangelo.

His frescoes were commissioned as decoration for important public buildings. Consequently, many are still *in situ*. He used contemporary settings, dress, manners, faces, and portraits to illustrate religious subjects. Look for homely, domestic pictures, which could be illustrations to a story – a forerunner of Dutch and 19th-century genre.

He painted serious, well-fed, middle-class people, like the patrons who commissioned these works. His figures have long hands, wrists, and legs. In tempera he used long, widely spaced strokes that follow the main curves and contours. Do not confuse him with his brother David (1452–1525), who was left-handed so used hatching that goes from top left to bottom right.

KEY WORKS: *A Legend of Sts Justus and Clement of Volterra*, c.1479 (London: National Gallery); *Birth of John the Baptist*, 1479–85 (Florence: Santa Maria Novella); *Birth of the Virgin*, 1486–90 (Florence: Santa Maria Novella); *Portrait of an Old Man and a Boy*, c.1490 (Paris: Musée du Louvre)

Filippino **Lippi**

● c.1457–1504 🏛 ITALIAN ✍ FRESCO; OILS; TEMPERA

The son of Filippo Lippi, Filippino was successful, but stylistically outdated in his later years.

His religious subjects show all the standard technical qualities of early-Renaissance Florentine painting (see Filippo Lippi). He painted important fresco series and a few portraits.

Look out for sweet, young faces with soft eyes, good male bone structure, and forward inclination of heads. Note also the wonderful hands and fingers, which look as though they really touch, feel, and grasp.

KEY WORKS: *The Adoration of the Kings*, c.1480 (London: National Gallery); *The Vision of St Bernard*, c.1486 (Florence: Badia Fiorentina)

Lorenzo di **Credi**

● c.1458–1537 🏛 ITALIAN ✍ OILS; TEMPERA

A minor Florentine, Lorenzo had a similar style to the early works of fellow pupil, Leonardo da Vinci (they attended Verrocchio's workshop together). He was a painter of altarpieces and portraits and was technically competent, but his style was lifeless and lacked individuality. He used an intense, high-key palette with orange/gingery tones and his draperies and flesh both have the same squashy appearance. He painted odd, upturned thumbs and toes. The story goes that in 1497, influenced by the fanatical friar Savonarola, Lorenzo destroyed many of his works featuring profane subjects.

KEY WORKS: *The Annunciation*, c.1480–85 (Florence: Galleria degli Uffizi); *Venus*, c.1490 (Florence: Galleria degli Uffizi)

Pietro **Perugino**

◔ c.1445–1523 🏛 ITALIAN ✍ FRESCO;
OILS; TEMPERA

A hardworking, prolific, middle-ranking painter
from Perugia, Umbria (hence the nickname).
Perugino's real name was Pietro Vannucci.
He trained in Florence. Raphael was also
trained in his workshop.

His religious pictures are painted in a soft, pretty,
simplified, sentimental style that tends to become
routine – he reused figures from other compositions.

Look for slender figures with gently tilting
heads, weight on one foot; oval-faced Madonnas;
delicate fingers and a genteelly crooked little
finger; pressed lips, the bottom one fleshy;
feathery trees and milky
horizons, graduating to
deep blue at the zenith.
While his portraits can be
very good and direct, his
work declined in quality
in later years.

KEY WORKS: *Crucifixion
with the Virgin, St John,
St Jerome, and Mary
Magdalene*, c.1485
(Washington DC: National
Gallery of Art); *Mary
Magdalene*, 1490s
(Florence: Palazzo Pitti)

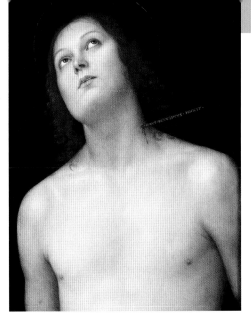

⌃ *St Sebastian Pietro
Perugino, c.1495, 53 x
39 cm (21 x 15 in),
tempera and oil on
panel, St Petersburg:
Hermitage Museum.
The artist's name
is painted in gold on
the arrow embedded
in the saint's neck.*

Bernardino di Betto
Pinturicchio

◔ c.1454–1513 🏛 ITALIAN ✍ FRESCO;
OILS; TEMPERA

The last serious artist from Perugia and Umbria,
Pinturicchio was probably a pupil of Perugino. He
was highly skilled, prolific, ambitious, but not at the
forefront of new ideas and ultimately second rank.
A master of fresco painting and supremely skilled
at fitting his decorative scheme to the space of the
room, he gives a particularly vivid sense of looking
through the wall at a busy, bustling scene, full of
incident. Enjoy his intense and childlike realism,
attention to detail, and love of storytelling; you
will feel as if you have walked into the daily life
of Umbria in the 15th or 16th century.

Notice his carefully planned and executed
perspectives (geometric and aerial); his ability
to record almost microscopic details in nature;
and his uninhibited love of colour. His lavish and
brilliant decorative borders influenced Raphael.

KEY WORKS: Borgia Rooms frescoes, 1492–95
(Rome: Vatican); *Virgin and Child between
St Jerome and St Gregory the Great*, c.1502–08
(Paris: Musée du Louvre)

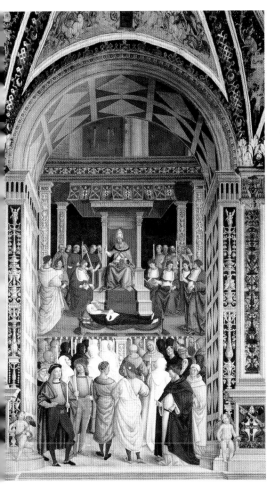

◅ **Pope Pius II Canonizes St Catherine of Siena**
*Bernardino di Betto Pinturicchio, 1503–08,
fresco, Siena: Cathedral. From a series of frescoes
illustrating the life of the pope, who was Sienese.*

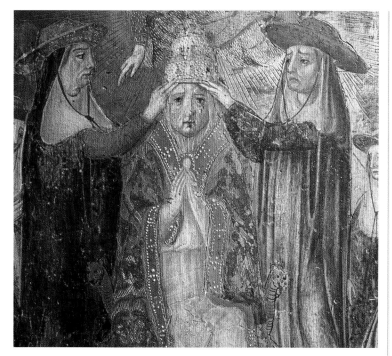

⌂ Pope Pius II (1405–64) Crowned by Two Cardinals
Vecchietta, 1458–64, tempera on panel, Siena: Palazzo Piccolomini. The use of foreshortening suggests the influence of Florentine art.

Vecchietta

◑ 1410–80   🏴 ITALIAN   ✍ TEMPERA; FRESCO; ILLUMINATION; SCULPTURE

Vecchietta was an architect, painter, sculptor, goldsmith, and engineer, who was also called by his birth-name, Lorenzo di Pietro (although known by his nickname "Vecchietta" from c.1442 onwards). He was born and worked in Siena, but was influenced by the Florentine art world. Far ahead of his peers in Siena, in terms of understanding lighting and its painterly properties, he was adept at working both in miniature and on a large scale. He also produced illuminated manuscripts, including the illuminations for Dante's *Divine Comedy*. In the 1430s Vecchietta was commissioned by Cardinal Branda Castiglione to paint a series of frescoes in Lombardy; he continued to paint frescoes for the rest of his career. In the 1450s he met Donatello, who had a strong influence on his sculptural techniques. Towards the end of his life, Vecchietta designed, built, and decorated an ornate burial chapel for himself and his wife, Francesca, inside Santa Maria della Scala, in Siena.

Look for Vecchietta's precise brushwork, the densely populated scenes in his frescoes, his understanding of foreshortening, and his

forward-thinking lighting techniques. His figures are always realistically portrayed, with faces recreated without idealism; sometimes he includes his self-portrait as one of the figures. His works also demonstrate his architectural training: look for intricately detailed buildings and architectural details in his paintings and sculptures.

KEY WORKS: *Madonna and Child Enthroned with Saints*, 1457 (Florence: Galleria degli Uffizi); *Assumption of the Virgin*, c.1461–62 (Pienza Cathedral); *St Catherine*, c.1461–62 (Siena: Palazzo Pubblico); *The Resurrection*, 1472 (New York: Frick Collection); *The Risen Christ*, 1476 (Siena: Santa Maria della Scala)

Piero della Francesca

◑ 1420–92   🏴 ITALIAN   ✍ FRESCO; TEMPERA; OILS

Piero della Francesca was one of the greatest masters of the early Renaissance, and currently very much in fashion. However, few of his works remain and many are severely damaged.

His religious works and portraits have special qualities of stillness and a dignified serenity – a result of deep Christian belief, and humanist interest in man's independence and observation of the world. He had a passionate fascination with mathematics and perspective, which he used to construct geometrically exact spaces and strictly proportioned compositions. He had a loving, instinctive feel for light and colour.

Piero's figures and faces are reserved, aloof, and self-absorbed (a reflection of his own slow, hard-working, intellectual character?). The works show an interest in new ideas and experiments as a means of reaching greater spiritual and scientific truths. Look for his ability to fill mathematical spaces with light; his mastery of technique (fresco, tempera, oil, and precise line). Nothing was left to chance – he recorded everything with certainty and care.

KEY WORKS: *Madonna della Misericordia*, c.1445 (Borgo Sansepolcro: Museo Civico); *The Story of the True Cross*, c.1452–57 (Arezzo: San Francesco); *The Baptism of Christ*, 1450s (London: National Gallery); *The Flagellation of Christ*, c.1460s (Urbino: Galleria Nazionale delle Marche)

Matteo di Giovanni

● 1435–95 ⚐ ITALIAN ✍ TEMPERA; OILS

Matteo was one of the most prolific and popular painters of the Sienese School. In contrast to contemporary Florentines, he had a rather awkward and traditional style. His work shows the influence of modern ideas (perspective, foreshortening, movement, and expression) uncomfortably combined with old-fashioned ones (gold grounds, figures placed one above the other, and elaborate decoration). In Matteo's work, look out for open mouths, flowing draperies, and experiments with foreshortening.

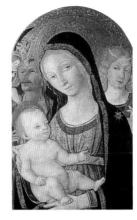

《 Madonna and Child with Saints Catherine and Christopher
Matteo di Giovanni, 1470, 62 x 44 cm (23 ⅜ x 17 ⅜ in), panel, Moscow: Pushkin Museum. The artist's style is elegant, decorative, and linear.

KEY WORKS: *Christ Crowned*, c.1480–95 (London: National Gallery); *Saint Sebastian*, c.1480–95 (London: National Gallery); *The Crucifixion*, c.1490 (San Francisco: De Young Museum)

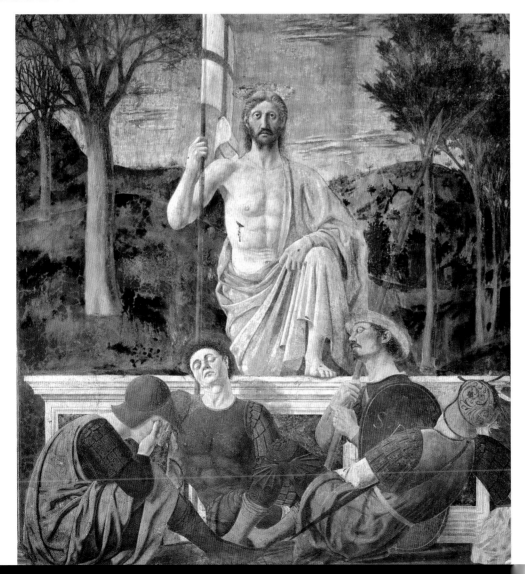

《 Resurrection of Christ
Piero della Francesca, c.1463, 225 x 205 cm (89 x 81 in), fresco, Borgo Sansepolcro: Museo Civico. The painting was commissioned for a place in Italy called the "Town of the Holy Sepulchre".

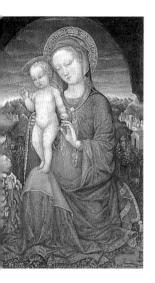

⌃ *The Madonna of Humility adored by Leonello d'Este* Jacopo Bellini, c.1440, 60 x 40 cm (23 ⅝ x 15 ¾ in), oil on panel, Paris: Musée du Louvre. The figure on the left is the donor who commissioned the painting.

Jacopo **Bellini**

◔ c.1400–70 ⚑ ITALIAN ✍ TEMPERA; OILS

Jacopo Bellini was Giovanni Bellini's father. Not much is known about him. Very little of his work survives other than sketchbooks. A progressive artist, he was interested in the latest artistic developments, such as perspective, landscape, and architecture.

KEY WORKS: *Madonna and Child*, 1448 (Milan: Pinacoteca di Brera); **Sketchbooks**, c.1450 (London: British Museum/Paris: Musée du Louvre); *Madonna and Child Blessing*, 1455 (Venice: Gallerie dell'Accademia); *Saint Anthony Abbot and Saint Bernardino of Siena*, 1459–60 (Washington DC: National Gallery of Art)

Giovanni **Bellini**

◔ c.1430–1516 ⚑ ITALIAN ✍ OILS; TEMPERA

One of the supreme masters of the early Renaissance and the Father of Venetian painting, Giovanni was the best known of a distinguished family of painters. He was among the first to exploit oil-painting technique in Venice.

Bellini was known for his altarpieces, portraits, and, above all, his depiction of light – beautifully and carefully observed, lovingly and accurately recorded, and always warm. His work sings of the harmonious relationship that should exist between man, nature, and God. The profound mood and spirituality of his religious pictures results from his belief in God's presence in light and nature.

His figures respond to light and often turn their faces and bodies towards it, in order to enjoy its physical and spiritual benefits. Was he the first

Gentile **Bellini**

◔ c.1429–1507 ⚑ ITALIAN ✍ OILS; TEMPERA

Gentile Bellini was Giovanni's brother. A Venetian artist, he made a significant contribution to oil-paintings. Much respected in his own lifetime, he was noted especially for panoramic views of his native Venice, peopled with crowds and processions. He thus established a subject and tradition that reached its apogee in Canaletto. Many of his works have perished.

KEY WORKS: *Portrait of Doge Giovanni Mocenigo*, c.1480 (Venice: Museo Correr); *Sultan Mohammed II*, c.1480 (London: National Gallery); *Miracle at Ponte di Lorenzo*, 1500 (Venice: Gallerie dell'Accademia)

⏵ *Procession in St Mark's Square* Gentile Bellini, 1496, 367 x 745 cm (144 ½ x 293 ⅜ in), oil on canvas, Venice: Gallerie dell' Accademia. This is one of a series of nine Venetian paintings showing the Miracles of the Cross.

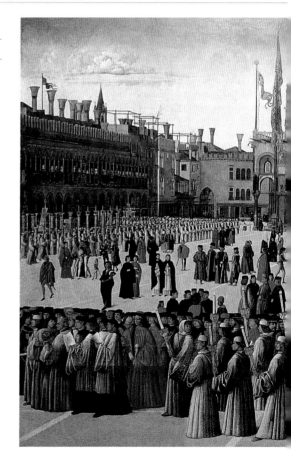

painter who really looked at clouds and studied their structure and formation? Notice his love of detail in rocks, leaves, architecture, and rich materials, such as silks. Note how his style became softer as he grew older (a natural trait in most humans?). There are no outlines, just gradations of tone.

Bellini's influence on Venetian painting was enormous. He was appointed offical painter to the republic in 1483, and almost all of Venice's eminent painters during the next generation are believed to have trained in his workshop.

KEY WORKS: *St Francis in the Wilderness*, c.1480 (New York: Frick Collection); *Barbarigo Altarpiece*, 1488 (Murano: San Pietro Martire); *The Madonna of the Meadow*, c.1501 (London: National Gallery); *The Doge Leonardo Loredan*, 1501–04 (London: National Gallery); *San Zaccaria Altarpiece*, 1505 (Venice: San Zaccaria)

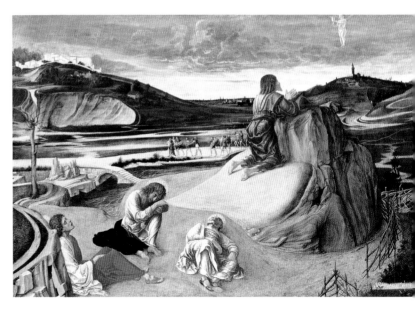

⌃ *Agony in the Garden*
Giovanni Bellini, c.1460,
81 x 127 cm (32 x 50 in),
tempera on wood,
London: National Gallery.
The painting shows Bellini's sensitive gift for understanding and representing light, as well as a keen awareness of figures in space.

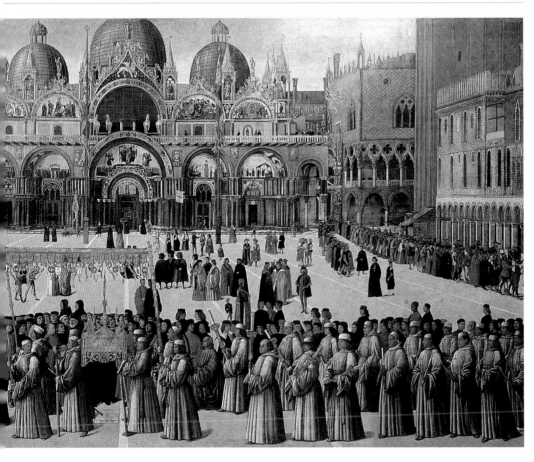

Antonello da Messina

⬥ c.1430–79 🏛 **ITALIAN** ✍ **OILS; TEMPERA**

Antonello was from Messina, Sicily, but made a key visit to Venice in 1475 until 1476. He was one of the pioneers of oil painting in Italy.

Antonello combined Italian interests (sculptural modelling, rational space, and man-the-measure-of-all-things characterization) with northern European obsessions (minute detail and unadorned reality). He had a marvellous ability to observe and paint light, and created wonderful portraits and faces that seem to live and breathe, showing bones under the skin and an intelligence behind the eyes that looks and answers back. He shone both an intellectual and a physical spotlight on his subjects.

He had the ability to recreate the appearance and feel of skin – differentiating between lips, a stubbly or shaven chin, a hairless cheek – eyebrows, hair, the liquid surface of an eye (this can only be done with oil paint and requires supreme technical mastery). He learned the equation for mixing oil paint from northern artists in Naples and handed it on to clever Venetians, such as Giovanni Bellini. It is very likely that he used a magnifying glass – and it is worth using one when looking at his paintings.

KEY WORKS: *Christ Blessing*, 1465 (London: National Gallery); *Virgin Annunciate*, c.1465 (Palermo: Galleria Nazionale); *Portrait of a Man*, c.1475 (London: National Gallery); *St Jerome in his Study*, c.1475 (London: National Gallery)

Vivarini family

⬥ ACTIVE 15TH CENTURY 🏛 **ITALIAN** ✍ **OILS; TEMPERA**

Two members of a Venetian family, Antonio Vivarini (c.1415–84) and his younger brother, Bartolomeo, Vivarini (c.1432–c.1499) created old-fashioned, large polyptych altarpieces with stiff figures and elaborate carved frames. Antonio's son, Alvise (c.1445–1505) produced more modern work in the style of Giovanni Bellini. A good example of a traditional craftsmen's business producing work to please a conservative clientele.

KEY WORKS: *The Madonna with the Blessed Child*, 1465 (Venice: Gallerie dell'Accademia); *Saints Francis and Mark*, 1440–46 (London: National Gallery)

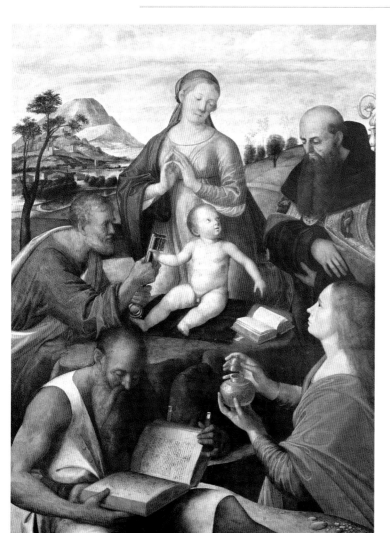

◀ **Madonna and Child with Saints Peter, Jerome, and Mary Magdalene with a Bishop** *Alvise Vivarini, 1500, oil on panel, Amiens (France): Musée de Picardie*. Notice the way in which the baby Jesus is set in the absolute centre of the painting, his pale skin drawing the eye towards him.

Lombardo family

🌐 15TH–16TH CENTURIES 🏛 ITALIAN
✍ SCULPTURE

Pietro Lombardo (c.1435–1515), an architect
and sculptor, worked in several Italian cities
before moving to Venice around 1467. He set
up a workshop employing large numbers of
apprentices. His sculptor sons, Tullio (c.1455–
1532) and Antonio (c.1458–1516) were among
his pupils. Pietro was instrumental in bringing the
Renaissance to Venice, reworking Florentine ideas
about Classical antiquity into a Venetian ideal. His
most famous work was rebuilding the Doge's
palace (1498). By the 1480s, Tullio and Antonio
were recognized as sculptors in their own right,
often commissioned for tomb sculptures and
religious pieces. Tullio collected Classical
statues and is noted for poetic portraits, such as
reliefs inspired by Roman grave portraits. Both
of them worked for the courts of Northern Italy
(see page 62). Pietro's grandsons continued as
architects and sculptors well into the 16th century.

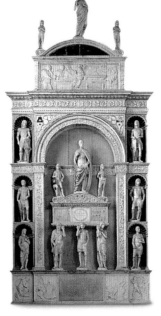

◀ **Monument
to Doge Pietro
Mocenigo** *Pietro
Lombardo, 1476–81,
Istrian stone and
marble, Venice:
Basilica dei Santi
Giovanni e Paolo.*
As part of the
tomb of Pietro
Mocenigo, this
intricate monument
features 15 life-size
marble figures.

KEY WORKS: *Adam and Tullio Lombardo*, c.1493
(New York: Metropolitan Museum); *Monument
to Andrea Vendramin, Pietro and Tullio Lombardo*,
c.1493 (Venice: Santi Giovanni e Paolo)

Carlo **Crivelli**

🌐 ACTIVE 1457–93 🏛 ITALIAN ✍ TEMPERA

Crivelli was an average Venetian artist with a
rather self-conscious, old-fashioned style.

Crivelli's work shows an extraordinary and
obsessive attention to detail, a system that virtually
overwhelms everything else. His strange, hard, dry,
linear style makes the figures look real but unreal
(a bit like biological specimens). Similarly with the
architecture: his buildings look like painted stage
sets rather than the real thing.

Note the lined faces with bags under the eyes
and bulging veins on hands and feet. The real yet
unreal-looking fruit and garlands, which have
complicated symbolic meanings, resemble
marzipan cake decorations.

KEY WORKS: *Madonna and Child Enthroned with Donor*,
c.1470 (Washington DC: National Gallery of Art);
St Michael, c.1476 (London: National Gallery)

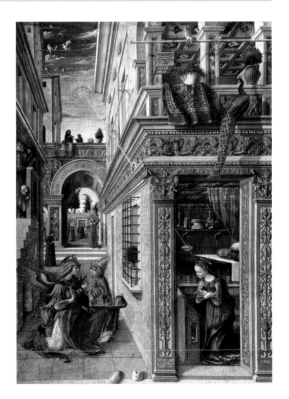

◀ *The Annunciation
with St Emidius*
*Carlo Crivelli, 1486,
207 x 146.5 cm (81 ½
x 57 ⅝ in), tempera
and oil on canvas,
London: National
Gallery.* Painted for
the Annunciation
Church at Ascoli
Piceno, Italy.

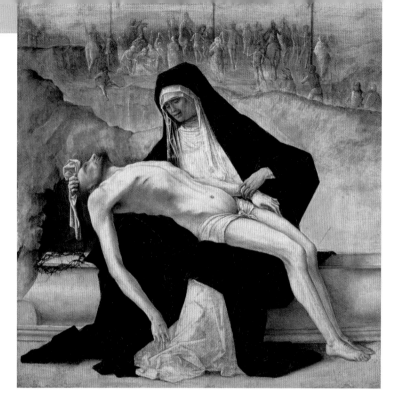

Ercole de' **Roberti**

⬤ c.1450–96   🏴 ITALIAN   ✍ TEMPERA

Roberti's most famous post was as court painter to the d'Este family in Ferrara. He was a shadowy figure, with very few works firmly attributed to him.

Look for meticulous, fine detail and poetic sensibility; the careful placing of figures in space – well-proportioned with good movement. He was interested in perspective, architectural details, and the way buildings are constructed.

KEY WORKS: *St Jerome in the Wilderness*, c.1470 (Los Angeles: J. Paul Getty Museum); *The Wife of Hasdrubal and Her Children*, c.1490–93 (Washington DC: National Gallery of Art)

⬈ *Pietà* Ercole de' Roberti, c.1490–96, 34.4 x 31.3 cm (13 ½ x 12 ⅖ in), oil and tempera on panel, Liverpool: Walker Art Gallery. An altarpiece predella.

Cima da Conegliano

⬤ c.1459–c.1517   🏴 ITALIAN   ✍ OILS

He was a successful but minor Venetian, content just to follow others. Often referred to as "The poor man's Bellini", he made similar use of light, but harder and less subtle. He worked best on a small scale, when his crispness came to the fore.

Characteristics of his works include: good light, satisfying blue mountains, intense faces, a general air of busyness, and slightly comical, frozen poses (as when a photographer says "hold it").

KEY WORKS: *Madonna with the Orange Tree*, 1487–88 (Venice: Gallerie dell'Accademia); *Virgin and Child*, c.1505 (London: National Gallery)

》 THE COURTS OF NORTHERN ITALY

During the Renaissance, being an artist could be a lucrative career. Most artists worked solely for commission and survived through patronage of the aristocratic courts. Italy was divided into city-states or principalities, and almost every city, large or small, had a system of artistic patronage. Among the most important of the large cities north of Florence were Mantua and Urbino.

In Mantua, the ruling family were called Gonzaga (prominent from the 14th to 17th centuries). Their court artists included Andrea Mantegna and the Lombardi. Urbino came to artistic prominence in the 15th and 16th centuries, soon outshining the earlier established courts. With the naming of Federigo da Montefeltro (1422–82) as the 1st Duke of Urbino, the region became a centre for artistic excellence. The Duke showed a partiality for Flemish art, but his most famous court painter was a fellow Italian, Piero della Francesca.

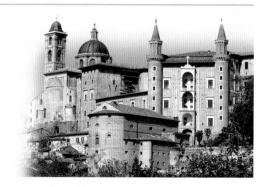

⬈ **It has been** suggested that Piero della Francesca, court painter to the 1st Duke of Urbino, partially designed the palace at Urbino.

Andrea **Mantegna**

1431–1506 ◎ ITALIAN ✎ ENGRAVINGS; OILS; FRESCO; TEMPERA

He was a precocious, highly individual master of the early Renaissance and an austere intellectual who worked for the dukes of Gonzaga at Mantua.

Mantegna's panel paintings are highly individual interpretations of standard Renaissance subjects such as altarpieces and portraits. He had a dry, scholarly style, and became obsessed with detail, especially when it came to the archaeology of classical antiquity and geology. His frescoes are wonderful large-scale schemes for churches and villas. He was a pioneering printmaker and had a superb engraving technique, which suited his style.

Notice the extraordinary outcrops of rock and the way he could make everything (even human flesh) look like carved stone (late monochrome works consciously look like bas-relief sculpture). He had stunning mastery of scientific perspective and foreshortening – seen at its most impressive (in situ) in his large, decorative schemes, which are more relaxed than the panel paintings.

KEY WORKS: *St James Led to His Execution*, c.1455 (Padua: Ovetari Chapel, Church of the Eremitani); *St Sebastian*, c.1455–60 (Vienna: Kunsthistorisches Museum)

▣ ***The Dead Christ***
Andrea Mantegna, 1480s, 68 x 81 cm (26 ¾ x 31 ⅘ in), oil on canvas, Milan: Pinacoteca di Brera. Mantegna's first teacher (Squarcione) criticized his work for "resembling ancient statues... rather than living creatures". The just reply is that his figures resemble both.

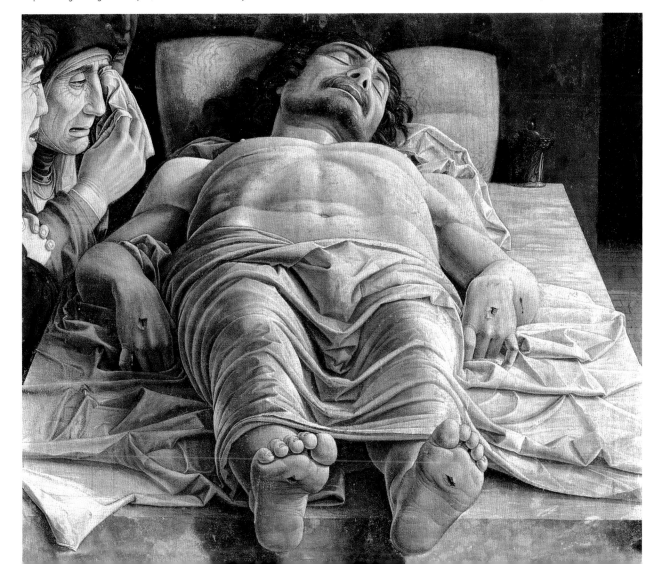

The Northern Renaissance

⬤ c.1420–1520

At the same time that the Renaissance was emerging in Italy, an equally significant artistic flowering was occurring in the Low Countries. Art in northern Europe was not "re-born" in the sense of rediscovering an antique past. But it was crucially reinvigorated, above all by the development and almost immediate maturity of a new medium: oil painting.

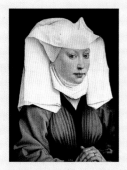

⌃ *Portrait of a Young Woman in a Pinned Hat*
Rogier van der Weyden, c.1435, 47 x 32 cm (18 ½ x 12 ⅗ in), oil on oak, Berlin: Gemäldegalerie.

Oil painting was not the only important innovation introduced in the Low Countries. Of almost equal significance was easel painting. The notion, still prevalent today, of paintings as self-contained and independent of their settings, was being born. The combination was revolutionary. Unlike tempera and fresco, oil dries slowly, allowing precise reworkings; it can be applied in tiny increments before drying to a hard, brilliant finish. Painted onto durable and largely non-absorbent woods such as oak, the result is highly detailed and lustrously jewel-like. As early as the 1430s, painters such as Jan van Eyck had developed a form of linear perspective the equal of that devised in Italy, but arrived at pragmatically rather than theoretically. It was augmented by aerial perspective – the gradual softening of colours to create the illusion that the background is receding.

Religious subjects dominate the art of the period, but they are always given an earthly, hard-edged precision. There is no lack of opulence – in draperies, settings, or landscapes – but where the Italian Renaissance is characterized by unworldly idealism, northern European painting of the same date has an almost unnervingly clear-eyed and dispassionate directness.

What to look for

Figures seem always to have been painted from life. There is a growing stress on domestic detail. This may frequently be loaded with allegorical or other allusive meanings, but the sense that everyday objects – and by extension everyday life – are worthy of being precisely rendered for their own sake is central. In *The Arnolfini Portrait*, van Eyck piles detail upon detail to create an entirely believable world.

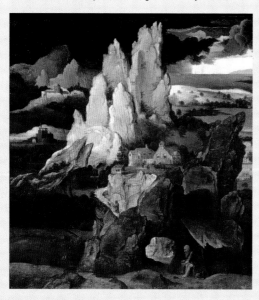

⏩ *St Jerome in a Rocky Landscape*
Joachim Patenier, 1515–24, 36 x 34 cm (14 ⅕ x 13 ⅖ in), oil on oak, London: National Gallery. Patenier, later widely imitated, was the first painter to make landscapes his principal subject.

KEY EVENTS	
1432	Completion of van Eyck's monumental *Ghent Altarpiece*
1450	Presumed visit by Rogier van der Weyden to Rome and Florence
1456	Van Eyck's spreading fame is confirmed by a Neapolitan account of his achievements
1475	Hugo van der Goes's *Portinari Altarpiece* (see page 71) dispatched to Florence

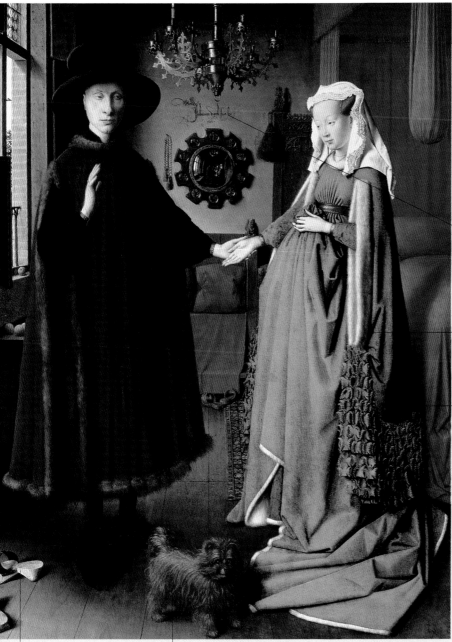

◀ The Arnolfini Portrait Jan van Eyck, 1434, 82 x 60 cm (32 x 23 in), oil on oak, London: National Gallery. The work's exact subject, although it clearly concerns a wedding or betrothal, is unknown.

The Latin text reads: "Van Eyck was here." It may mean he was a witness or he was "here" in the sense of creating the painting. Either way, it underlines the new status claimed by artists

Both figures are very richly dressed, a statement of wealth and social status

The bride is in green, the colour of fertility. Is she pregnant or merely fashionably attired?

⟫ TECHNIQUES

Van Eyck's use of oil paint allowed him to achieve an extraordinary level of detail. Every object in the painting is depicted with the same concentrated clarity.

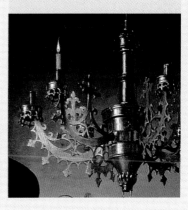

Neither figure wears shoes, an indication that they are on sacred ground

The dog may symbolize fidelity or lust. The bed is similarly suggestive

⟫ The convex mirror is a technical triumph. Window, bed, ceiling, and the two principals are shown from new angles, and two other figures are visible. The border shows 10 scenes from the life of Christ.

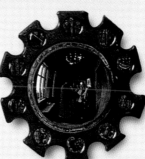

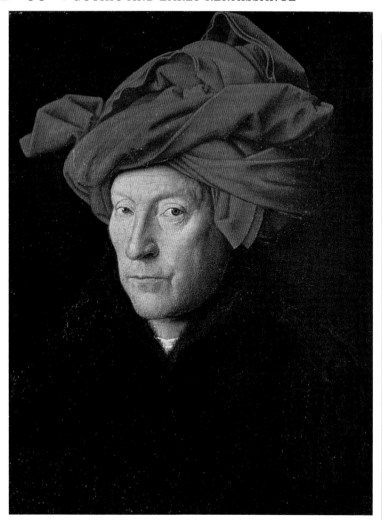

His three-quarter pose of a face brought new realism to portraiture. He painted Madonnas that look like housewives, and saints that look like businessmen. Note his precise delineation of facial features, especially the eyes. He was fascinated with ears (they are miniature portraits) and by folds and creases in cloth. Also note the fall of light that unifies and models the objects. He used convincing but empirical perspective and his paintings contain rich symbolism and occasional inscriptions.

KEY WORKS: *Ghent Altarpiece (The Adoration of the Lamb)*, 1432 (Ghent: St Bavo's Cathedral); *The Arnolfini Marriage*, 1434 (London: National Gallery)

Robert **Campin** (Master of Flemalle)

● **c.1378-1444** 🏳 **NETHERLANDISH** ✍ **OILS**

One of the founders of the Netherlandish School, Campin was a shadowy figure whose identity is difficult to pin down. Attributions to him are rare and speculative.

His devotional altarpieces and portraits are painted with the concentrated intensity that you get in a diminishing mirror (does his visual intensity and detail equate to his spiritual intensity and commitment?). Virgin and Christ child are shown as down-to-earth people in everyday settings – not idealized, but presented in a way that creates a fascinating three-way tension between realism, symbolism, and distortion, which Campin is able to manipulate with the greatest subtlety.

Notice his acute powers of observation, especially in the way things (such as window shutters) are made, how light catches a corner, how drapery falls, or flames look. He used light to isolate objects. The odd perspective is worked out experimentally, not scientifically. Use a magnifying glass to examine the extraordinarily fine detail; don't forget to look out of his windows at what is happening in the street. Objects and details usually contain or imply much complex symbolism.

KEY WORKS: *Entombment*, c.1420 (Private Collection); *A Woman*, c.1430 (London: National Gallery); *St Barbara*, 1438 (Madrid: Museo del Prado)

⌃ *A Man in a Turban*
Jan van Eyck, 1433, 25.5 x 19 cm (10 x 7 ½ in), oil on oak, London: National Gallery. The detailed depiction of the headdress and the uneasy way it sits on the head suggest that it may have been studied separately.

Jan **van Eyck**

● **c.1390-1441** 🏳 **NETHERLANDISH** ✍ **OILS**

An artist-cum-diplomat in the service of Philip the Good, Duke of Burgundy, van Eyck was a key exponent of Netherlandish art and oil painting. His only known works date from 1430s onwards.

He was the first painter to portray the merchant class and bourgeoisie. His work reflects their priorities – having their portraits painted; taking themselves seriously (as donors of altarpieces, for example); art as the imitation of nature; art as evidence of painstaking work and of craftsmanship; prosperity and tidiness; wariness; and restrained emotion. He had a brilliant oil-painting technique, which he was the first to perfect. Look for luminous, glowing colours, and minute detail.

Dieric **Bouts (the elder)**

● c.1415–75 🏴 NETHERLANDISH ✍ OILS

Also known as Dirk Bouts, Dieric was possibly a pupil of Rogier van der Weyden. Very little is known about Bouts and few attributable works exist. He created altarpieces, narrative scenes, and portraits. He made solemn, restrained paintings with beautifully observed detail and painstaking craftsmanship. His static figures are exaggeratedly slender and graceful, and often set in landscapes of exquisite beauty. His works have lovely details of rocky backgrounds and shimmering light.

KEY WORKS: *The Annunciation*, 1445 (Madrid: Museo del Prado); *Portrait of a Man*, 1462 (London: National Gallery); *Justice of the Emperor Otto*, 1470–75 (Brussels: Musées Royaux des Beaux-Arts)

✉ **Hell** *Dieric Bouts, 1450, 115 x 69.5 cm (45 ¼ x 27 ⅜ in), oil on wood, Lille: Musée des Beaux-Arts.* Bouts created two separate paintings that depict the tortures of the damned (*Hell*) and the *Way to Paradise*. In *Hell* the eyes of some of the humans and also of the demons, deliberately catch those of the spectator.

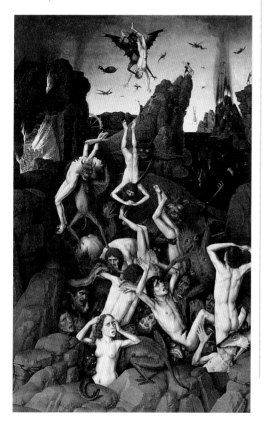

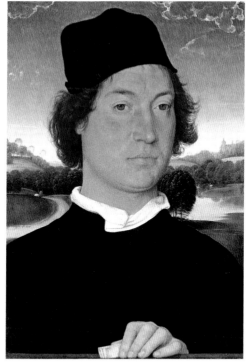

🎨 *Portrait of a Man*
Hans Memling, 1480s, 33 x 25 cm (13 x 9 ¾ in), oil on wood, Florence: Galleria degli Uffizi. Memling's gentle and occasionally sentimental style made him a popular acquisition for 19th-century collectors.

Hans **Memling**

● c.1430–94 🏴 FLEMISH ✍ OILS

Also known as Hans Memlinc, Memling was a prolific, Bruges-based successor to van der Weyden, from whom he borrowed motifs and compositions.

His large altarpieces are rather too rigid, with stiff figures like statues. He was better at small devotional pictures (full of life, with good space) and small portraits (he learned from manuscript illuminations). He liked soft textures (his drapery has soft, not crisp, folds); soft hair; soft landscapes and smooth, rounded, demure, idealized faces. He had a decorative, rather than intense, style.

Look out for his interesting skies of intense blue, melting to white on the horizon; clouds like chiffon veils; small, almost unnoticeable birds; pronounced eyelids. His motifs, such as garlands of fruit and flowers held by putti, are borrowed from the Italian Renaissance (from Mantegna?).

KEY WORKS. *Portrait of a Man with an Arrow*, c.1470–75 (Washington DC: National Gallery of Art); *The Virgin and Child with an Angel*, c.1470–80 (London: National Gallery); *Bathsheba*, c.1485 (Stuttgart: Staatsgalerie)

Rogier **van der Weyden**

◑ c.1399–1464 ⋈ NETHERLANDISH ✎ OILS

The greatest and most influential northern painter of his day, van der Weyden set a standard by which the rest are judged. Based in Brussels, he worked for the dukes of Burgundy. He had a large workshop, and was much imitated.

This altarpiece is one of the outstanding masterpieces of early Netherlandish painting. Northern European artists brought an intensity of emotional expression and a minuteness of realistic detail to their work, which gives it a quite different character and appearance to that of their Italian counterparts. This is the central panel of a three-part altarpiece (called a "triptych"). The two side panels became detached at some time and, sadly, are now lost. Many northern altarpieces in van der Weyden's time were made with carved wooden figures set in shallow boxlike spaces. He seems to have accepted this convention, but through the new medium and technique of oil painting he has brought the figures to life.?

In *Descent from the Cross*, van der Weyden heightens the sense of tension by forcing the eye and mind to reconcile conflicting qualities. Much of the painting detail is intensely realistic, such as red-rimmed eyes and tears on faces. This conflicts with the highly unnatural composition in which the almost life-size figures are hunched and packed into a narrow space beneath a tiny crucifix.

Set against a plain gold background, *Descent from the Cross* has an overriding sense of dramatic power about it. The shrine-like background concentrates the viewer's attention on the figures and avoids the distractions of a true-to-life setting. Van der Weyden was a master of depicting human emotion, and his religious painting reflects the strength of his personal conviction. His work had a profound effect on the course of art throughout Europe.

Note also his superb portraits, each with minute, natural individuality – especially the fingernails, knuckles, eyes, and stitches on clothing. He was also fascinated by architectural and sculptural detail. See how he uses facial expression and poses that are appropriate to the emotion expressed. Observe how one figure often echoes the poses and gestures of another, as if

in emotional sympathy. He adopted a softer, more relaxed style after 1450, under Italian influence, following a visit to Rome.

KEY WORKS: *St Luke Drawing the Virgin*, 15th century (St Petersburg: Hermitage Museum); *Descent from the Cross*, c.1435 (Madrid: Museo del Prado); *Triptych: The Crucifixion*, c.1440 (Vienna: Kunsthistorisches Museum); *Francesco d'Este*, c.1455 (New York: Metropolitan Museum of Art); *Portrait of a Lady*, c.1455 (Washington DC: National Gallery of Art)

Mary, wife of the disciple Cleopas, who was supposedly present at the Crucifixion

》 *Descent from the Cross* c.1435, *220 x 262 cm (86 ³/₈ x 103 ¹/₄ in), oil on panel, Madrid: Museo del Prado.* Van der Weyden was a celebrated portrait painter; and the individuality of the faces shows that the figures here are taken from life. The expressions of grief are highly individual. The face of St John, for example, is grave yet restrained as he struggles to control his emotions.

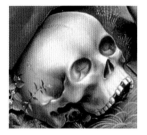

The skull represents Adam, who was cast out of Paradise after eating the forbidden fruit. Christ sacrificed himself on the cross to redeem the world from Adam's original sin.

Joseph of Arimathea was permitted to take the body down from the Cross

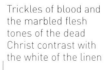

Trickles of blood and the marbled flesh tones of the dead Christ contrast with the white of the linen

St John the Evangelist stoops to comfort Mary, Christ's Mother, who swoons with grief

Nicodemos holds the feet of Christ. He will wrap his body in the linen cloth.

TECHNIQUES

Notice the intriguing conflict between the deep emotion of the picture and the artist's ability to look at an area such as the cloak of Nicodemus and record every detail with dispassionate objectivity.

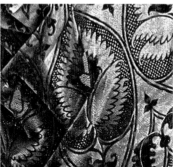

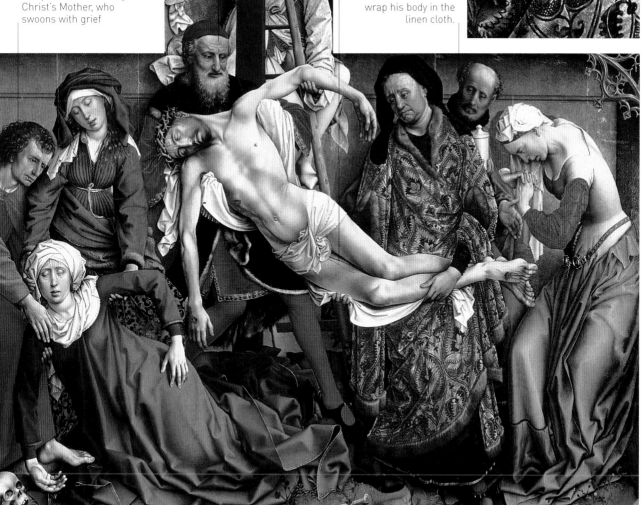

Petrus **Christus**

⊖ **ACTIVE 1444-72/3** 🏳 **FLEMISH** ✐ **OILS**

Christus was a major painter from Bruges, a follower of van Eyck, and influenced by van der Weyden. He was an underrated artist.

His intimate, small-scale religious works and portraits are highly organized and have meticulous detail. Note especially his interest in space and light: Christus liked deep space and placed figures in the corners of rooms to suggest both space and intimacy. He was the first northern painter to understand and use Italian single-point perspective.

Robes have elaborate, crisp drapery, with folds arranged decoratively, often flipped back to show a lining or undergarment in contrasting colour, sometimes brightly outlined. Note how Christus uses brownish rather than pink flesh tones, and favours red and green colour schemes. He organized broad areas of tone, filled in on top with meticulous detail, which makes cleaning and restoration especially risky.

KEY WORKS: *Edward Grimston*, 1446 (London: National Gallery); *The Last Judgement*, 1452 (Berlin: Staatliche Museum); *Virgin and Child with Saints Jerome and Francis*,1457 (Frankfurt: Städelsches Kunstinstitut); *A Young Lady,* c.1470 (Berlin: Staatliche Museen)

☑ *The Money Lender and his Wife* Quentin Massys, 1514, 74 x 68 cm (29 ¼ x 26 ¾ in), oil on panel, Paris: Musée du Louvre. The painting's attention to meticulous detail forms a clear and satisfying artistic parallel with the couple's evident obsession with material possessions.

Jan **Provost**

⊖ **c.1465-1529** 🏳 **FLEMISH** ✐ **OILS**

A major original early-northern Renaissance painter, with pre-Italian influences, Provost met Dürer in 1521 and was a follower of Massys. He painted altarpieces with figures that are lifelike (for the time). Note his precise drawing (he trained as a miniaturist); delicate modelling; good colour; long fingers bent at the second joint; faces with wide cheeks and prominent lower lip; and airy landscapes.

KEY WORKS: *The Crucifixion*, c.1495 (New York: Metropolitan Museum of Art); *A Christian Allegory*, c.1500 (Paris: Musée du Louvre); *The Last Judgement*, 1525 (Bruges: Municipal Museums)

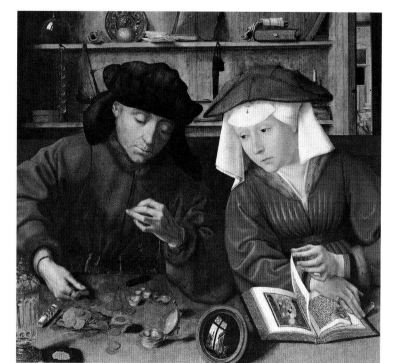

Quentin **Massys**

⊖ **c.1466-1530** 🏳 **FLEMISH** ✐ **OILS**

Massys was also known as Quentin Metsys. An important painter of unknown origins, he brought Italian refinement to the northern realist tradition (he visited Italy; admired Leonardo's way with soft light and his interest in the contrast between ugliness and beauty). Massys is best known for animated portraits of tax collectors, bankers, merchants, and wives, with understated satire (perhaps showing the influence of Erasmus, whom he met). Note the opulent details of his works.

KEY WORKS: *St Anne*, 1507-09 (Bruges: Musées Royaux des Beaux-Arts); *Portrait of a Canon*, c.1515 (Private Collection); *The Adoration of the Magi*, 1526 (New York: Metropolitan Museum of Art)

Hugo van der **Goes**

◉ ACTIVE 1467–82 ◫ NETHERLANDISH ✍ OILS

An obscure genius about whom little is known, van der Goes spent his last years in a monastery, going mad. The only work known for certain by him is the *Portinari Altarpiece* (c.1474–76), which was commissioned for a chapel in Florence. He introduced Italian artists to new ideas and techniques: oil paint, fine natural detail, and different symbolism.

The *Portinari Altarpiece* is of an unusually large scale for a Netherlandish painting (commissioned to be the standard size of Italian triptych); there are Portinari men (from a prosperous Florentine mercantile family) in the left panel, women in the right (each with patron saints); the central panel has Virgin and Child (a naked child on the floor is a northern idea), Joseph, and shepherds (an Italian idea); the Magi are at the back of the right panel.

The kneeling man (left panel) is Tommasso Portinari (agent in Bruges for the Medici bank – he was reckless and the bank was closed). The kneeling woman (right panel) is his wife, Maria. The men look troubled and the women have fashionably high foreheads and pale faces. The very wobbly space and odd changes of scale in

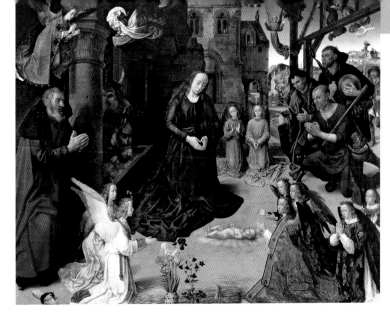

the central panel perhaps suggest the artist was in difficulty with such a large-scale work? There is much symbolism: a scarlet lily as the blood and passion of Christ; a discarded shoe as holy ground; purple columbine as the Virgin's sorrow, and so on.

KEY WORKS: *Death of our Lady*, c.1470 (Bruges: Municipal Museums); *The Fall of Man*, c.1475 (Vienna: Kunsthistorisches Museum); *Portrait of a Man*, c.1475 (New York: Metropolitan Museum of Art); *The Adoration of the Magi*, 1470s (Bath, UK: Victoria Art Gallery)

⊼ *The Adoration of the Shepherds* Hugo van der Goes, c.1476, 254 x 305 cm (100 x 120 in), oil on panel, Florence: Galleria degli Uffizi. This is the centre panel from the *Portinari Altarpiece*.

Jan **Gossaert**

◉ c.1478–c.1532 ◫ FLEMISH ✍ OILS

Also called Jan Mabuse, Gossaert played a crucial role in the development of Netherlandish painting by introducing (albeit derivative) Italianate ideas.

His work is a fascinating although (sometimes uncomfortable) synthesis of northern skills and vision – acute observation; fine oil technique; clear, precise draughtsmanship à la Dürer; and, after visit to Rome in 1508–9, Italian aspirations – idealization of figures and faces; perspective; classical architecture and details; firm modelling; and subtle shading with light. He had a more conservative portrait style.

KEY WORKS: *Neptune and Amphitrite*, 1516 (Berlin: Staatliche Museum); *Adam and Eve*, c.1520 (London: National Gallery); *A Nobleman*, c.1525–28 (Berlin: Staatliche Museum)

Joachim **Patenier**

◉ c.1480–c.1525 ◫ FLEMISH ✍ OILS

Patenier was also known as Joachim Patinir. He was the first painter to make landscape the principal theme. His works have a bird's-eye viewpoint, with improbably craggy inhabited mountains, blue distances with heavy clouds and cold seas, and tiny-scale hermits and holy families, sometimes with Christ tucked in somewhere – fantasy at its most endearing. His paintings display a high-quality, detailed technique. There are few attributed works, but he had many imitators.

KEY WORKS: *Rest on the Flight to Egypt*, c.1515 (Minnesota: Minneapolis Institute of Arts); *The Baptism of Christ*, c.1515 (Vienna: Kunsthistorisches Museum); *The Penitence of St Jerome*, c.1518 (New York: Metropolitan Museum of Art)

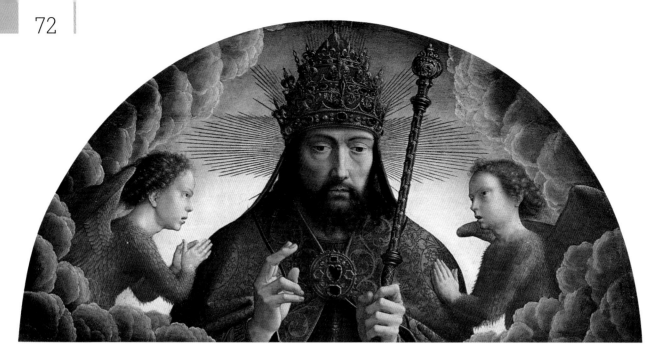

Gerrit **David**

● 1460–1523 🗺 NETHERLANDISH ✍ OILS;

Also known as Gerard David, he was the last great Netherlandish painter in the tradition of van Eyck's and van der Weyden's meticulous realism.

A painter of altarpieces and portraits, David loved exact details of objects and faces. He was aware of and acknowledged the Netherlandish tradition that he followed, and that was coming to an end). He was fascinated with landscape and townscape, placing figures naturally within them. His landscapes are especially fine; the spaces are open and relaxed, not crowded, which creates a feeling of calm, poise, and harmony with nature and God.

The Italian influence on his work increased over time but never took over completely; he moved from love of detail to more general storytelling. Note the individualism of each tree with detailed leaves. His characters have modest, solemn, seemingly expressionless, faces. Splendid, subtle, rich colours are harmoniously woven together. His paintings remind us that fine craftsmanship and skill are God-given talents, and that he worshipped God by exercising his.

KEY WORKS: *Christ Nailed to the Cross*, c.1481 (London: National Gallery); *A Rest during the Flight to Egypt*, c.1510 (Madrid: Museo del Prado)

Joos **van Cleve**

● c.1490–1540 🗺 NETHERLANDISH ✍ OILS

A popular, Antwerp-based painter of altarpieces and portraits, Cleve combined tradition (detailed northern technique, overloaded symbolism, and stiffly posed figures and draperies) with progressive ideas (landscapes and rocky formations, Italian-style modelling with light, extravagant costumes, and detailed surfaces). Note the cosy, homely details.

KEY WORKS: *Joris Vezeleer*, c.1518 (Washington DC: National Gallery of Art); *The Annunciation,* c.1525 (New York: Metropolitan Museum of Art)

Fernando **Gallego**

● c.1440–c.1507/10 🗺 SPANISH ✍ OILS; FRESCO

Gallego's birth and death dates are shrouded in mystery – surprising for an artist whose importance was recognized in his own lifetime. Credited as the master of Castilian painting, he was at the centre of the Hispano–Flemish movement. He spent 14 years (1479–93) painting the ceiling in the Old Library at Salamanca University. Towards the end of his life, Gallego's palette changed from bright tones to muted shades, such as a flat yellow instead of gold.

Look for paintings thick with symbols, figures with obviously Spanish features, and Gallego's realism, which is often uncomfortable. He made much use of gold and sumptuous draperies and jewellery. The paintings are markedly northern European in contrast to Italian ones of the same era.

KEY WORKS: *The Virgin, St Andrew, and St Christopher*, c.1470 (Spain: Salamanca Cathedral); *Epiphany*, c.1480–90 (Barcelona: Museu Nacional d'Art de Catalunya)

Pedro **Berruguete**

● c.1455–1504 ⚑ SPANISH ✍ OILS; FRESCO

Berruguete was court painter to King Ferdinand and Queen Isabella. He was strongly influenced by Italian Renaissance and Flemish art. His works include the decoration of the palace at Urbino. His art greatly influenced the Castilian style, even after his death. He taught his son, Alonso (c.1488–1561), who went on to become court painter to Charles V.

KEY WORKS: *Virgin of the Milk*, c.1465 (Museo de Bellas Artes de Valencia); *St Peter the Martyr*, c.1494 (Madrid: Museo del Prado)

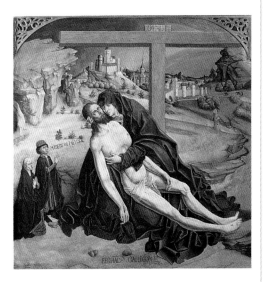

⬆ *Pietà with Two Donors* Fernando Gallego, c.1470, 118 x 122 cm (46 ½ x 48 in), tempera on panel, Madrid: Museo del Prado. Note the Northern influences: rigid poses, sorrowful expressions, and a carefully depicted landscape.

Jean **Fouquet**

● c.1415–c.1481 ⚑ FRANCE ✍ OILS; ILLUMINATION; CHALKS

A master painter and illuminator allied to the royal court in Tours, Fouquet was an important French painter of his time, although little survives as testimony. Influenced by the Italian Renaissance, he was famed for bringing the Renaissance to France. He travelled to Italy c.1446–48 and lived and worked in Tours for the rest of his life. Fouquet married and had at least two sons. He was appointed *Peintre du Roi* in 1475, a post he held until death. His illuminations drew on his Italian experiences; the surroundings of Tours were inspiration.

KEY WORKS: *Portrait of the Ferrara Court Jester Gonella*, c.1442 (Vienna: Kunsthistorisches Museum); *Self-Portrait*, 1450 (Paris: Musée du Louvre); *Hours of Simon de Varie*, 1455 (Los Angeles: J. Paul Getty Museum)

Jean **Bourdichon**

● 1457–1521 ⚑ FRENCH ✍ ILLUMINATION; SCULPTURE; OILS

Bourdichon was a prolific illuminator, painter, gold- and silversmith, and designer. He lived and worked in Tours and appears never to have travelled abroad. He was a great favourite with French royalty, from Louis XI to Francis I and was appointed *Peintre du Roi* in 1481. His wages from the royal court allowed him to become a wealthy landowner. Little of his work is documented. He is most renowned for illuminated manuscripts, of which his most famous work is the illuminated *Grandes Heures* (*Book of Hours*) for Queen Anne of Brittany.

KEY WORKS: *Book of Hours*, 1480 (Los Angeles: J. Paul Getty Museum)

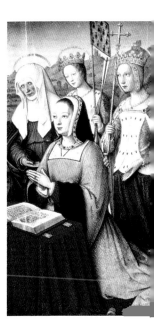

⏩ *Anne of Brittany with St Anne, St Ursula, and St Helen (Book of Hours)* Jean Bourdichon c.1503–08, illumination on vellum, Paris: Bibliothèque Nationale. From the *Grandes Heures* of Anne of Brittany. Bourdichon's close-up technique placed large figures in the foreground.

Jean **Hey**

⬤ 15TH–16TH CENTURIES ⵊ UNKNOWN ✍ OILS

He was also known as Hay. His birth and death dates are a mystery, but he is known to have lived and worked in France around the last quarter of the 15th century. His name suggests he or his parents originated from the Netherlands or Belgium; his art was greatly influenced by the Netherlandish style. In his lifetime he was respected and appears in the 1504 list of "Greatest Living Painters", compiled by Jean Lemaire de Belge. Another artist about whom very little is known today was nicknamed the "Master of Moulins"; some believe Hey and the Master were the same person, others are sceptical.

KEY WORKS: *Margaret of Austria*, c.1490 (New York: Metropolitan Museum of Art); *Portrait presumed of Madeleine de Bourgogne presented by St Madeleine*, c.1490–95 (Paris: Musée du Louvre); *Madonna with Saints and Donors*, c.1498 (Moulins Cathedral); *Charlemagne and the Meeting at the Golden Gate*, c.1500 (London: National Gallery)

Hieronymus **Bosch**

⬤ c.1450–1516 ⵊ NETHERLANDISH ✍ OILS

Bosch was the last, and perhaps the greatest, of the medieval painters. He was much admired in his lifetime, especially by ardent Catholics such as Philip II of Spain, who was an avid collector.

He is best known for his complex, moralizing works, of which the central themes are the sinful depravity of man, human folly, deadly sin (notably lust), the seductive temptations of the flesh, and the almost inevitable fate of eternal damnation (salvation is possible but only with the greatest difficulty). Like hellfire sermons, they are a complete contrast to the Renaissance view of man controlling a rational world. He also produced more conventional religious works. Probably the greatest fantasy artist ever, his works show bewildering detail and unique imagery of part-animal, part-human creatures, and visions of depraved activity and torture. His work was not drug-induced but illustrations of ideas and images in wide circulation at the time. He had a brilliant rapid technique and applied luminous colour:

◩ *Triptych of the Temptation of St Anthony* Hieronymus Bosch, c.1505, 132 x 120 cm (52 x 47 in), oil on panel, Brussels: Musées Royaux. St Anthony of Egypt was tempted by demons and erotic visions.

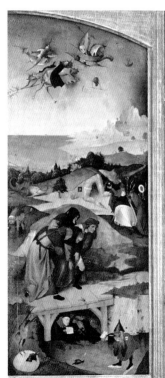
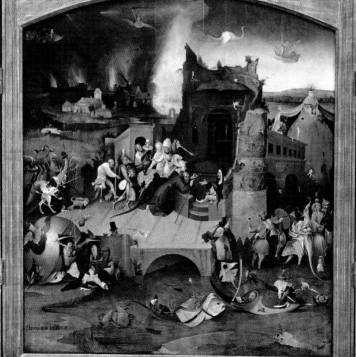
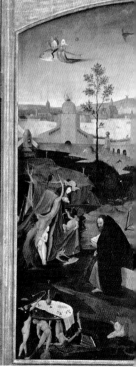

flecked highlights and chalk underdrawing can be seen in his works. He was influenced by ornate manuscript illumination. His acute, intricate intensity reflects his belief that he was depicting certainty and reality. Bosch had no real successor until Bruegel (see page 109).

KEY WORKS: *Death and the Miser*, c.1485–90 (Washington DC: National Gallery of Art); *The Garden of Earthly Delights*, c.1500 (Madrid: Museo del Prado)

Tilman **Riemenschneider**

◉ 1460–1531 🏴 GERMAN ✍ SCULPTURE

Riemenschneider was a major figure in German art history. He was the first sculptor to produce limewood altarpieces finished in a monochrome brown glaze rather than multicoloured polychrome. His works are mainly religious: altarpieces, reliefs, busts, and life-size statues, characterized by strong Gothic symbolism and realistic carving. Successful in his own time, he became very wealthy, owning land and vineyards. He married three times and had five children. He lost his fortune in 1525 after backing the wrong side in a peasants' revolt against the Prince Bishop.

KEY WORKS: *St Jerome and the Lion*, c.1490 (Ohio: Cleveland Museum of Art); *Seated Bishop*, 1495 (New York: Metropolitan Museum of Art); *Virgin of the Annunciation*, late 15th century (Paris: Musée du Louvre); *Holy Blood Altarpiece*, c.1501 (Rothenburg: St Jacob's Church)

Veit **Stoss**

◉ c.1445–1533 🏴 GERMAN ✍ SCULPTURE

Stoss was a prominent German sculptor, painter, and engraver. He was renowned for his wood sculptures – with Riemenschneider, he was the greatest woodcarver of his age – executed in a unique, truly expressive style. He had a modest workshop in which he trained his apprentices – among them his sons – to a high standard. He produced few paintings and engravings, and none are as noteworthy as his sculpture. His rare paintings (only four are known) are characterized

by a tame palette of muted colours. His most famous piece of stone sculpture is the altarpiece at Bamberg Cathedral.

KEY WORKS: *Mourning Virgin*, c.1500–10 (New York: Metropolitan Museum of Art); *The Annunciation*, 1518 (Nuremberg: Parish Church of St Lorenz)

Michael **Pacher**

◉ ACTIVE 1462–98 🏴 UNKNOWN ✍ OILS; SCULPTURE

Pacher was a panel-painter and woodcarver, although nothing is known of his training. He is believed to have been German or Austrian. His work was strongly influenced by Italian art, suggesting he may have travelled to Italy. He is credited with melding Germanic and Italian techniques, and thus influencing the future of Northern European art. He died at Salzburg, but most of his career was spent at Bruneck (Brunico) in the South Tyrol.

KEY WORKS: *St Anne with the Virgin and Child*, 15th century (Barcelona: Museu Nacional d'Art de Catalunya); *Altarpiece of the Four Latin Fathers*, c.1483 (Munich: Alte Pinakothek)

Martin **Schongauer**

◉ c.1430–91 🏴 GERMAN ✍ TEMPERA; OILS; ENGRAVINGS

Schongauer was the son of a goldsmith who settled in Colmar, Alsace. In his day, he was probably the most famous artist in Germany. He was especially well known in his lifetime for his engravings, with precise lines and convincing forms. He borrowed from Flemish techniques and ideas (especially from van der Weyden). He was much admired by Dürer. He concentrated on religious subjects and about 115 plates by him are known. His later work has a more delicate, soft touch – his gracefulness became the stuff of legend.

KEY WORKS: *Madonna in the Rose Garden/Madonna of the Rose Bower*, 1473 (Colmar: St Martin's); *The Large Carrying of the Cross*, c.1474 (St Petersburg: Hermitage Museum)

Mathis **Grünewald**

🌐 c.1470–1528 🗣 GERMAN 🎨 OILS

Grünewald was an obscure, austere, religious fanatic about whom little is certain, and very few of whose works survive. It is known that he worked for the archbishop of Mainz and was well regarded in his day, but subsequently he was ignored until the 20th century. He is now revered above all for his great masterpiece – the Isenheim Altarpiece – which is in Colmar, near Strasbourg.

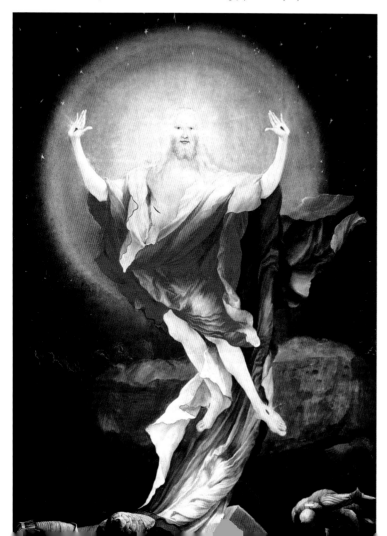

The Resurrection of Christ (detail) c.1512–16, oil on panel, Colmar (France): Musée d'Unterlinden. From a right wing of the many-panelled Isenheim Altarpiece, Christ overcomes death as he soars from the grave in a blaze of ethereal light.

The Isenheim Altarpiece was commissioned as the focus of the high altar of the chapel in the monastery of St Anthony at Isenheim. The monks there specialized in the treatment of ergotism, a gangrenous poisoning known as "Saint Anthony's Fire" from which there was no hope of recovery. It was caused by ingesting fungus-infected cereals, and the excruciatingly painful symptoms included shedding of the outer layers of the skin, body tissues becoming black and putrefying, distorted joints, and hallucinations. The monks attempted to offer physical comfort though herbal remedies and ointments, and spiritual comfort. Grünewald's Altarpiece shows Christ suffering on the Cross with the same symptoms as those with ergotism.

Although the central panel representing the Crucifixion is most usually illustrated, the altarpiece is, in fact, an elaborate construction with two sets of wings, and complex imagery that includes the Annunciation and the Resurrection, the 12 Apostles, and St Anthony tormented by horrific creatures sent by the Devil. Several different configurations are possible, and taken together the different panels show Grünewald's art to be a unique and personal combination of the intensely real and the fantastical, the earthly and the Divine. He displays a highly accomplished technique, and an ability to draw on a wide range of well-assimilated influences such as Northern Gothic art and the Italian Renaissance. He also demonstrates a deep knowledge of Church liturgy and the Bible, and he uses symbolism to convey his message and sentiments, sometimes obscurely, but sometimes directly - for example, beside Mary Magdalene is the pot of ointment with which she had once anointed Christ's feet. He uses changes of scale to convey emotion or significance, and intense colours, ranging from pitch black to bright yellow, to express states of mind. His settings range from the bare and almost abstract to the highly detailed. It is difficult to point to any precedent for Grunewald's art, or to any subsequent influence until the 20th century.

KEY WORKS: *The Mocking of Christ*, c.1503–05 (Munich: Alte Pinakothek); *Saints Erasmus and Maurice*, c.1520–24 (Munich: Alte Pinakothek)

⊠ Crucifixion
(from the Isenheim Altarpiece) c.1510–15, 500 x 800 cm (198 x 312 in), oil on panel, Colmar (France): Musée d'Unterlinden.

The background of the painting is dark and threatening. Darkness has fallen onto the earth as described in the Gospels

The size of the figures reflects their importance – Christ is the largest and Mary Magdelene is the smallest

›› GESTURES

Christ's hands express his intense physical pain and spiritual reaching out. The other figures have equally expressive hand gestures. The crown of thorns is placed on the head of Christ not as an adornment but as an instrument of torture.

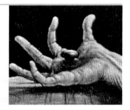

The wooden Cross bends to bear the weight of Christ, adding to the emotional tension and anguish of the scene

The words above the hand of St John the Baptist are "He must increase but I must diminish".

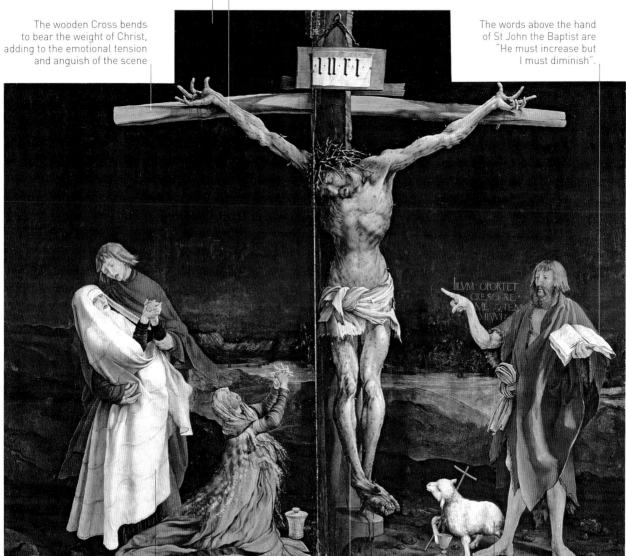

St John the Evangelist comforts Mary, the Mother of Christ. All the figures are lit by a strange unworldly light

Mary Magdalene was the first person to whom Christ appeared after his Resurrection

Christ's agony is depicted by his broken feet, his pierced skin, and his unbearably stretched arms

The lamb of God represents Christ's sacrifice in shedding his blood for the salvation of mankind

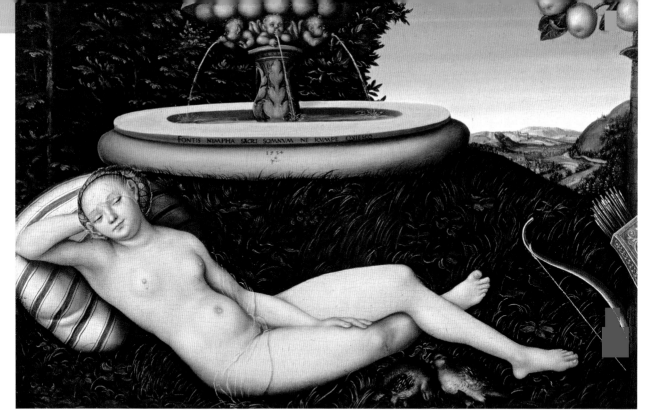

⌃ The Nymph of the Fountain Lucas Cranach (the elder), 1534, 51.3 x 76.8 cm (20 ⅕ x 30 ¼ in), oil on panel, Liverpool: Walker Art Gallery. A teasing, diaphanous wisp of silk simultaneously covers and reveals the nymph's loins.

Lucas **Cranach** (the elder)

⊖ 1472–1553　🏳 GERMAN　✍ OILS

A leading figure of the German Renaissance, Cranach worked for the Electors of Saxony in Wittenberg, although his style remained essentially provincial rather than international (Italian). A staunch Protestant, he had a large, active studio.

He painted impressive, solid court portraits and was especially good at old men's faces. However, he is most notable for strange, unique, and capricious pictures of female mythological subjects. These women are curiously reminiscent of the brittle, present-day fashion models. Both wear outrageous creations, and have hard little faces and faraway looks. Cranach makes us adopt the role of a voyeur.

Note the sloping shoulders; small, round breasts; feet turned out; long arms and legs; one leg twisted over another; prominent navels; crazy hats and clothes; rings on fingers; feathers; jewelled collars; rocky landscapes, and armour. Note too the hard, glassy eyes with strange highlights; manipulative hands, and greedy, calculating facial expressions.

KEY WORKS: *A Princess of Saxony*, c.1517 (Washington DC: National Gallery of Art); *Judith with the Head of Holofernes*, c.1530 (Vienna: Kunsthistorisches Museum); *Cupid Complaining to Venus*, 1525 (London: National Gallery)

Hans **Baldung Grien**

⊖ c.1484–1545　🏳 GERMAN　✍ OILS; WOODCUTS

A painter and engraver from Strasbourg, Grien may have trained with Dürer. He was especially gifted at visionary themes which incorporate the elemental and supernatural, and sometimes the gruesome and macabre. His early subjects tended to be religious, while his later work was secular. A good draughtsman, he also made high-quality woodcuts with strong *chiaroscuro*.

KEY WORKS: *The Three Ages of Man and Death*, c.1510 (Madrid: Museo del Prado); *Coronation of the Virgin*, c.1512 (Freiburg, Germany: Freiburg Cathedral); *Girl and Death*, 1517 (Basel, Switzerland: Kunstmuseum)

Albrecht **Dürer**

● 1471–1528　〽 GERMAN　✍ OILS; WOODCUTS; ENGRAVINGS

The greatest northern artist of the Renaissance, Dürer was born in Nuremberg, four years before Michelangelo. Prolific, tenacious, immensely ambitious, and very successful, he travelled widely in Europe and went on key visits to Italy in 1494 and 1505. He fused northern European and Italian styles, and had a profound influence on art, both north and south of the Alps. Many thousands of his works survive to this day. He was a follower of Martin Luther's Reformation.

Dürer's goldsmith father, who came from Hungary and trained in the Netherlands, taught him the technique of engraving and an admiration for van Eyck and van der Weyden. He had rich, patrician patrons who encouraged him to travel, and he established his own busy workshop in Nuremberg. His marriage was unhappy and childless. His social pretensions, artistic ambitions, and unusual degree of self-consciousness are revealed in his numerous self-portraits.

Highly gifted but self-conscious as a painter, Dürer was greater, more at ease, and more innovative as a printmaker: he produced powerful woodcuts and pioneering engravings. He was a brilliant draughtsman and painted exquisite watercolours. His portraits have strong lines; curious, lopsided faces with enlarged eyes that have liquid surfaces; and beautiful, strong hands and feet. He was fascinated by landscape, plants, and animals, and anything unusual. Also look for objects as symbols.

Dürer uniquely and subtly synthesized (often in the same work) characteristics of the old northern or medieval tradition and the new Italian and humanist discoveries. Look for northern features – apocalyptic imagery; emotional expression; complexity of design; crisp, angular line; and minute observation of detail. Note also the Italian features – strong, dignified, composed, assured figures and faces; soft, rounded modelling; classical architecture; perspective and foreshortening; New Testament subjects; and nudes.

KEY WORKS: *The Great Piece of Turf – Study of Weeds*, 1503 (Austria: Albertina Museum); *Melancolia I*, 1514 (London: British Museum); *Rhinoceros*, 1515 (London: British Museum)

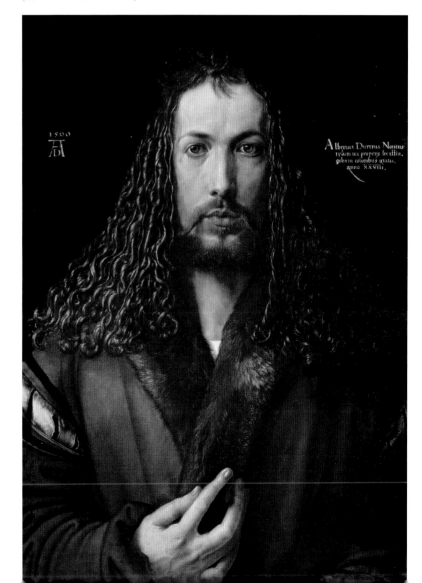

》 *Self-Portrait at the Age of Twenty-eight*
1500, 67.1 x 48.7 cm (26 ⅖ x 19 ⅖ in), oil on panel, Munich: Alte Pinakothek. Dürer portrays himself in an image reminiscent of Christ.

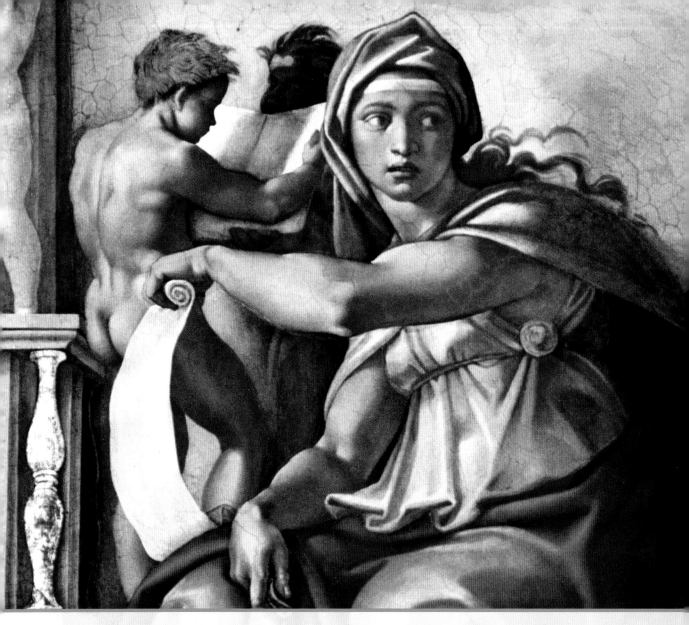

High Renaissance and Mannerism
c.1500–1600

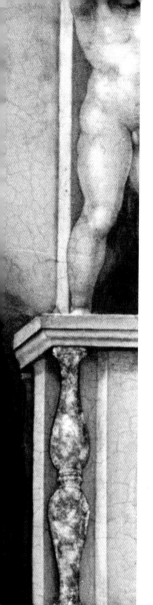

The 16th century saw the establishment of an ideal that would be followed by all self-respecting European rulers until the 20th century, and accounts in no small measure for the great flowering of European art. It was twofold: be strong and fearless in battle, and a generous and knowledgeable patron and protector of the arts.

These principles were set out in one of the best-selling books of the 16th century, *Il Cortegiano* ("The Book of the Courtier") by Baldassare Castiglione, a diplomat from Urbino, Italy. Written in 1514 and first published in 1528, it summarized what had already been established as an ideal of behaviour for monarchs, nobles, and ladies.

Established powers

By 1511, Europe had four major powers, each led by strong-willed men who did indeed fight hard and use art to display and reinforce their power and ambition. The fall of Constantinople in 1453 effectively left the Roman Church as the sole defender of Christendom. A succession of energetic popes made Rome an artistic showpiece that proclaimed their spiritual and political might. Europe's most powerful temporal ruler was the Habsburg Holy Roman Emperor, Charles V, who controlled Spain, Austria, the Low Countries, and southern Italy. Francis I of France was determined that

◄◄ *The Delphic Sibyl* (detail from Sistine Chapel ceiling) Michelangelo, 1508–12, fresco, Rome: Vatican Museums. The Papacy cleverly combined Classical and Biblical learning to affirm its political and spiritual leadership.

his country should compete with both these powers, while Henry VIII of England also wanted his nation, with its new ruling dynasty, to be a major player on the European stage.

At first there was a certain equilibrium between these rival power blocks, and their wish to outdo each other culturally, with virtually no limit on expense, was profoundly beneficial for the arts. Indeed, the achievements of the artists of the High Renaissance marked the pinnacle that subsequent generations constantly revered and tried to emulate. But by the late 1520s warfare engulfed Europe, the Church began to fragment, and the intellectual certainties predicated on the perception of a universe in which the Earth was at the very centre, and the Mediterranean at the centre of the world, also fractured.

Disintegration

What had started as cultural rivalry degenerated into destructive warfare. In 1525, Francis I invaded Italy. In the course of the ensuing conflict, Charles V's army sacked Rome in 1527, burning and destroying what had become the finest city in the world. Meanwhile, the Catholic Church was severely

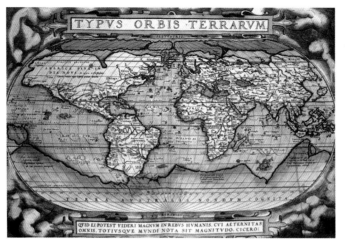

TYPVS ORBIS TERRARVM

QVID EI POTEST VIDERI MAGNVM IN REBVS HVMANIS, CVI AETERNITAS
OMNIS, TOTIVSQVE MVNDI NOTA SIT MAGNITVDO. CICERO:

>> *Theatrum Orbis Terrarum:* Map of the World by Abraham Ortelius, 1574. The pace of European exploration after the 1490s was exceptionally rapid. Even in the first decade of the 16th century, the African coastline was accurately known. By the second half of the century, the outline of the American continent was assuming recognizable shape.

>> REFORMATION

When in 1517 Martin Luther nailed his *95 Theses* to a church door in Wittenberg, his aim was simply to protest against the corruption of the Church, especially in the sale of indulgences. But his further writings struck such a chord with anti-papal feeling and the pope's authority was rejected across much of northern Europe. Many German princes, as well as the kings of Denmark and Sweden, were rapidly won over to the Lutheran doctrine; then Henry VIII of England – albeit for political rather than theological reasons – broke with Rome in 1534.

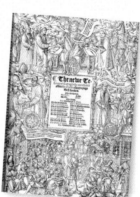

>> *Title Page, the Great Bible,* 1539. Printing was crucial in spreading the Reformation, as the Bible became available in vernacular languages, in this case English, instead of Latin.

weakened by the crisis sparked by Martin Luther in 1517. His supporters had intended to strengthen the Church by stamping out corruption. Instead they created a permanent split between an emerging Protestant north and a Catholic south, and unleashed a campaign to destroy art treasures with Catholic connections. This north-south divide gave a savage twist to the rivalries between the continent's leading powers. In 1565, a vicious, protracted conflict began in the Low Countries, where the Habsburgs were determined to crush an anti-Catholic revolt and reimpose their own rule.

With the Council of Trent, summoned in 1545, the Catholic Church committed itself to restoring its former supremacy, but in reality power was shifting away from Italy. By the mid-16th century, after an audacious act of conquest, Spain found itself in control of much of South America, and the staggering wealth gained as a result made it the richest country in Europe. By the end of the century, both England and France had established footholds in North America.

TIMELINE: 1500–1600

1500 Portuguese discovery of Brazil (Cabral)

1509 Spanish settlement of Central America begun; invention of the watch, Germany

1522 First circumnavigation of the globe completed (Magellan and del Cano)

1527 Sack of Rome

1545 Council of Trent called to counter threat of Protestantism

1549 Direct Portuguese rule imposed on Brazil

1500　　　　**1520**　　　　**1540**

1508–12 Michelangelo paints the Sistine Chapel ceiling

1517 Martin Luther's *95 Theses* attacks abuses of the Catholic Church

1519 Habsburg Charles V elected Holy Roman Emperor

1521 Cortés conquers Aztec Empire

1534 Act of Supremacy: Henry VIII of England breaks with Rome

1543 *Of the Revolution of Celestial Bodies* published by Copernicus

1559 Treaty of Cateau-Cambrésis: France forced to concede Habsburg supremacy in Italy

Mannerism

The voyages of discovery showed the world to be much larger than had been imagined and full of curious new lands and creatures. In 1543, Copernicus published his proof that the Sun, not the Earth, was the centre of the planetary system. Long-held scientific beliefs were being challenged as well as religious ones. Against this turbulent background, it is not surprising that the self-confidence of the art of the High Renaissance gave way to the uncertainties of Mannerism, whose principal characteristics were a deliberate flouting of rules as well as wilful eccentricity and distortion.

⊠ **Château de Chambord, Loire Valley**
Francis I's desire to emulate the cultural superiority of Italy found potent expression in the lavish châteaux of the Loire Valley. Chambord, begun in 1519, is the largest. 1,800 workmen were employed in its construction over 30 years.

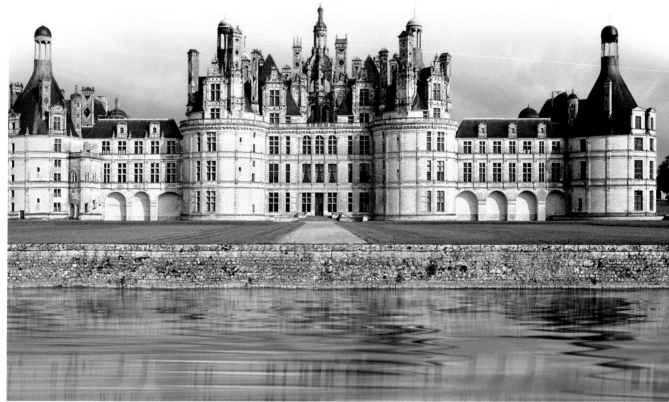

1570 Publication of Palladio's Four Books of Architecture, Italy

1572 St Bartholomew's Day Massacre: slaughter of French Protestants in Paris

1588 Spanish Armada: attempted conquest of Protestant England by Spain

1560   **1580**   **1600**

1565 Dutch Revolt starts: extended attempt to gain independence from Spain; Philippines claimed by Spain

1571 Battle of Lepanto: Ottoman navy defeated by united Christian fleet

1598 Edict of Nantes ends 30-year religious war in France

The High Renaissance

c.1500–27

The years between about 1500 and the Sack of Rome in 1527 saw a prodigious outpouring in Italy in all the visual arts. In Rome, under the energetic patronage of an exceptionally able (and self-promoting) pope, Julius II, Raphael and Michelangelo simultaneously created works of startling novelty. In Venice, the celebrated Titian redefined the possibilities of painting.

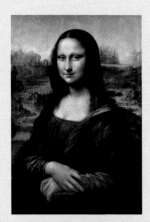

⌃ **Mona Lisa** Leonardo da Vinci, c.1503–05, 77 x 53.5 cm (30 ¼ x 21 in), Paris: Musée du Louvre. Praised by Giorgio Vasari because it "appeared to be living flesh rather than paint".

Idealization is the benchmark of the High Renaissance but it manifests itself in different ways. For Raphael it meant heroic confidence, technical sophistication, and grace. Similar elegance allied to acute psychological insight and astonishingly close observation of the natural world are obvious in Leonardo's works. Both Michelangelo and Titian pioneered more personal if no less heroic styles. The former was astoundingly audacious in his vision of the male form, the latter above all in his mastery of colour.

Subjects

The visionary goal of High Renaissance art was a perfect union of the human and Divine, Christian and pagan antique, nature and imagination. Thus the male nude "made in God's image", the central motif of Michelangelo's painting and sculpture, heroic and often deliberately distorted, has an extraordinary power, which the Church used to convey a spiritual ideal. Yet, although religious subjects generally remained pre-eminent in High Renaissance works, other subjects – whether classical scenes, landscapes, or portraits – became increasingly important, significantly widening the repertoire of Western art. Titian's *poesie*, lyrical and dreamlike "visual poems", began to explore the relationship between the human figure and landscape.

What to look for

The greatest triumph of the High Renaissance was the rebuilding of St Peter's in Rome and its decoration under the leadership of Pope Julius II.

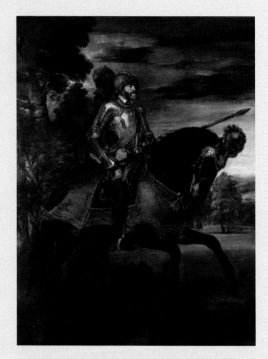

⌃ **The Emperor Charles V on Horseback in Mühlberg** Titian, 1548, 332 x 279 cm (131 x 110 in), oil on canvas, Madrid: Museo del Prado. Drama, idealization, and huge scale are unified by brilliant colouring and daring brushwork.

As a complement to Michelangelo's religious theme in the Sistine Chapel, Raphael decorated the Pope's library with four subjects: Philosophy, Theology, Poetry, and Law. For his interpretation of Philosophy, Raphael drew exclusively on the inspiration and precedents of Greek and Roman Antiquity.

KEY EVENTS

1498	Leonardo completes his huge, psychologically penetrating *Last Supper* in Milan
1504	Michelangelo completes *David* in Florence, the largest statue carved since Antiquity
1506	Foundation stone of Bramante's new (and in the event never finished) St Peter's laid by Julius II
1508–12	Michelangelo's almost single-handed epic labour on the ceiling of the Sistine Chapel, Rome
1528	Renaissance ideals defined by Castiglione in *The Book of the Courtier*

» Raphael was renowned in his own day for his ability to include a huge variety of complex poses and realistic expressions in a single work. Many hundreds of preliminary drawings were made from life.

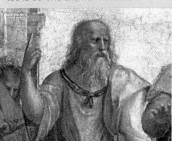

Plato and Aristotle, silhouetted against the sky, are awarded the dominant positions in the picture

» TECHNIQUES

Each figure is a masterful, expressive portrait and each group a model of statuesque harmony and continuous graceful movement. The colour scheme too is serene and harmonious.

The architectural setting was based on designs by Bramante, the leading classical architect in Rome

Euclid, giving a geometry lesson, was a portrait of Bramante

⊼ ***The School of Athens***
Raphael, 1509–11, base 772 cm (304 in), fresco, Vatican: Stanza della Segnatura

Pythagoras, the great Greek mathematician, demonstrates his propositions

Heraclitus was a portrait of Michelangelo, then working on his Sistine ceiling

Raphael included a self-portrait, an indication of the growing status accorded artists

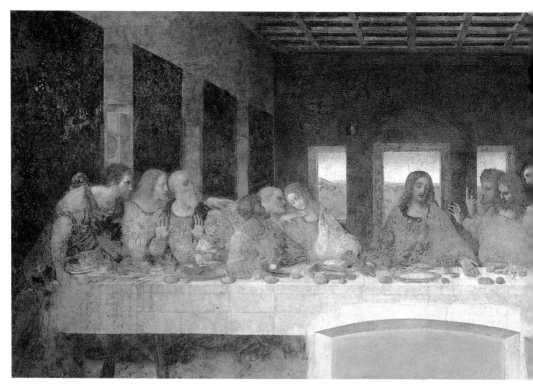

» The Last Supper
1495–97 (post-restoration), 460 x 880 cm (181 x 346 ½ in), mixed media fresco, Milan: Santa Maria delle Grazie. More than a depiction of one event, the fresco refers to other episodes narrated in the Gospels.

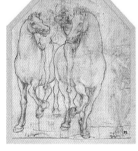

⌃ Two Horsemen *after 1481, 14.3 x 12.8 cm (5 ⅗ x 5 in), metal point drawing, Cambridge: Fitzwilliam Museum.* An example of Leonardo's life-long fascination with animals.

Leonardo **da Vinci**

● 1452–1519 ⚐ ITALIAN ✎ OILS; DRAWINGS; SCULPTURE; FRESCO

A unique, perhaps lonely, genius, Leonardo was the universal Renaissance man – scientist, inventor, philosopher, writer, designer, sculptor, architect, and painter. He had such a fertile mind that he rarely completed anything, and there are relatively few paintings by him. He changed the status of the artist from artisan to gentleman and was pivotal in the creation of the High Renaissance period of Florentine art.

Leonardo was born in Vinci, near Florence. He was the illegitimate son of a notary at a time when illegitimacy was a serious stigma. This may have been a factor that led him to become detached from others.

He trained with Verrochio, but much of his life was spent working at the courts of foreign dukes and princes who, at times, were at war with Florence. The Medici ignored him entirely. After 1483, he worked for Ludovico Sforza, Duke of Milan, but returned to Florence following the French invasion of Milan in 1499. Between 1500 and 1516, he produced many of his most famous paintings.

He spent his last years in the service of Francis I of France and, according to legend, died in the King's arms near Amboise in the Loire Valley. Leonardo's most remarkable legacy is his notebooks filled with writings and sketches, in which he explored his private thoughts about art and science, observations from nature, and diagrams for visionary scientific and mechanical projects.

Style

Leonardo had an insatiable curiosity to find out how everything operated. He then put this into practice (as shown by his keenly observed

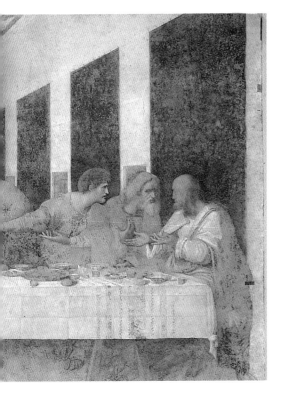

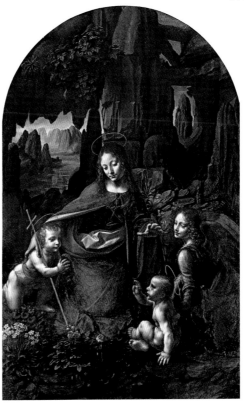

The Virgin of the Rocks c.1508, 189.5 x 120 cm (74 x 47 in), oil on panel, London: National Gallery. Painted for the Milanese Foundation of San Francesco Grande. This is the second version created by Leonardo, showing the infant St John the Baptist adoring the infant Christ accompanied by an angel.

anatomical drawings, his plans for flying machines, and so on). His paintings are multilayered, investigating these subjects; they also explore a wide range of themes – beauty, ugliness, spirituality, man's relationship with nature and God, and "the motions of the mind" (psychology). He was technically inventive, but careless.

What to look for

Why is the *Mona Lisa* (see page 84) so important? The painting created a sensation (c.1510) because it was lifelike in a way that had never been seen before. It comprises a brilliant array of technical and perceptual innovation (the use of oil paint,

a relaxed pose, soft and shadowy figure with no outlines, and *two* landscapes) and demands that the viewer's imagination should supply the inner meaning and missing visual detail. This work of art set a new standard – and it reaffirms that art you have to interact with creatively is always the most memorable.

KEY WORKS: Drawings, c.1452–1510 (London: Royal Collection); *Ginevra de' Benci*, c.1474 (Washington DC: National Gallery of Art); *Cecilia Gallarani / The Lady with an Ermine*, c.1483 Kraków: Czartoryski Museum); *Mona Lisa*, c.1503–06 (Paris: Musée du Louvre)

> The **mind** of the painter should be like a **looking-glass** that is **filled with as many images** as there are **objects placed before him**.
>
> Leonardo da Vinci

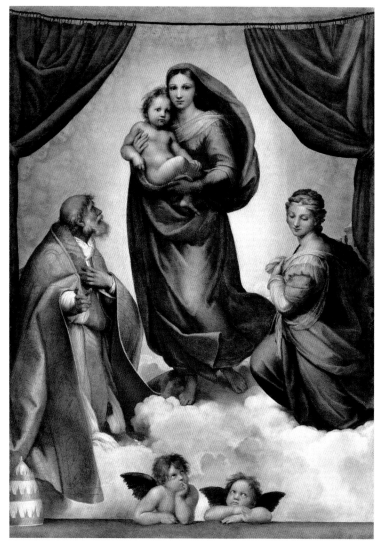

superb draughtsmanship. He projected an ideal at almost every level – which is why he was held up as the model for all ambitious artists until the overthrow of academic art by the Modern movement.

Notice how everything has a purpose, especially how contrast is used to heighten our perception and feeling (one of the oldest and most successful devices): stern men and sweet women; stillness and movement; contemplation and activity; curved line and straight line; tension and relaxation. Observe too the continuity in his works – how a gesture, pose, or movement begun in one part of the body, or in one figure, is carried a stage further in another.

KEY WORKS: *Portrait of Agnolo Doni*, c.1505–06 (Florence: Palazzo Pitti); *The School of Athens*, 1510–11 (see page 85); *Madonna of the Chair*, c.1513 (Florence: Galleria degli Uffizi); *Bindo Altoviti*, c.1515 (Washington DC: National Gallery of Art); *Portrait of Baldassare Castiglione*, pre-1516 (Paris: Musée du Louvre); *The Transfiguration*, 1518–20 (Vatican City: Pinacoteca Vaticana)

⊠ *Pope Leo X with Cardinals Giulio de' Medici and Luigi de' Rossi* Raphael (Raffaello Sanzio), 1518–19, 154 x 119 cm (60 ⅗ x 46 ⅘ in), oil on wood, Florence: Galleria degli Uffizi.

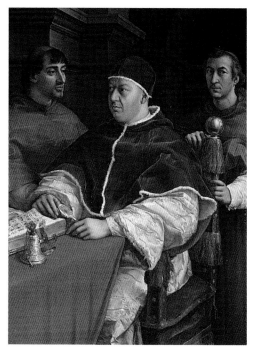

⊼ *The Sistine Madonna*
Raphael (Raffaello Sanzio), 1513, 265 x 196 cm (104 ⅓ x 77 ⅕ in), oil on canvas, Dresden: Gemäldegalerie. This was Raphael's first major work on a theme that was to become a central feature of his art – the Madonna and Child. He reworked the subject with constant variation and invention.

Raphael (Raffaello Sanzio)

◓ 1483–1520 ⚑ ITALIAN ✍ OILS; FRESCO

"Il Divino". A child prodigy who died young, but one of the greatest masters of the High Renaissance and therefore of all time. Profoundly influential, he helped raise the social status of artists from craftsmen to intellectuals.

He had complete mastery of all Renaissance techniques, subjects, and ideas, and used and developed them with apparent ease: deep, emotional, and intellectual expression; total Christian belief; harmony; balance; humanity;

Fra Baccio della Porta
Bartolommeo

c.1474–1517 | ITALIAN | OILS

Fra Bartolommeo was a major Florentine painter who influenced the change in style between the early and High Renaissance.

His large-scale, elaborate altarpieces of throned Madonnas with the Christ child show the main characteristics of the High Renaissance style – monumental, solemn, balanced, with dignified compositions and figures. Fra Bartolommeo replaced the intensely observed detail of the early Renaissance with idealization and generalizations (notice it especially in faces and drapery).

Look for well-fed people with a tendency to chubby cheeks, double chins, and a self-satisfied look. Observe landscapes that look prosperous and well-farmed. Also look for warm colour and light in his works.

KEY WORKS: *Portrait of Savonarola*, c.1495 (Florence: Museo San Marco); *Marriage of St Catherine*, 1511 (Paris: Musée du Louvre); *Mother of Mercy* , 1515 (Lucca, Italy: Museo Nazionale)

Sebastiano del Piombo

c.1485–1547 | ITALIAN | OILS; FRESCO

Sebastiano was a Venetian expatriate and Titian's contemporary, who settled in Rome when Michelangelo and Raphael were there. In 1531, he obtained the sinecure of keeper of the papal seal (made from lead, or "piombo", hence his nickname).

He excelled at painting portraits – which can be magnificent. Otherwise he flirted with relative failure. In his works, he achieved a certain marriage of muscularity and poetry, which makes his figures look like soulful athletes, but the compositions, colour, and figures became overblown as he strove unsuccessfully to keep up with his friend Michelangelo.

Look for rather fierce-looking, muscular people, with good strong hands; dramatic gestures and plenty of foreshortening. There is also an interesting use of perspective. Rich colour and landscape backgrounds maintain his links with

Venice. Is it a misfortune to be talented but not outstanding in an epoch of giants? Do they cause you to live in their shadow and diminish your talent? Or do they inspire you to reach heights you would otherwise not have achieved?

KEY WORKS: *The Daughter of Herodias*, 1510 (London: National Gallery); *Fall of Icarus*, c.1511 (Rome: Villa Farnesina); *Raising of Lazarus*, c.1517–19 (London: National Gallery)

Andrea **del Sarto**

1486–1530 | ITALIAN | FRESCO; OILS

The last significant Florentine High Renaissance painter, Andrea was influenced in subjects, style, and technique by Leonardo, Raphael, and Michelangelo. He synthesized those influences to produce handsome, monumental, religious pictures and portraits, which are harmonious in colour, well balanced, grand in conception and scale, but lack real emotional depth and originality.

KEY WORKS: *Punishment of the Gamblers*, 1510 (Florence: Santissima Annunziata); *Madonna of the Harpies*, 1517 (Florence: Galleria degli Uffizi)

Lamentation over the Dead Christ *Andrea del Sarto, 1524, 238 x 198 cm (93 ¾ x 78 in), oil on wood panel, Florence: Palazzo Pitti.* Forced to flee from the plague, Andrea painted this for the convent where he took refuge.

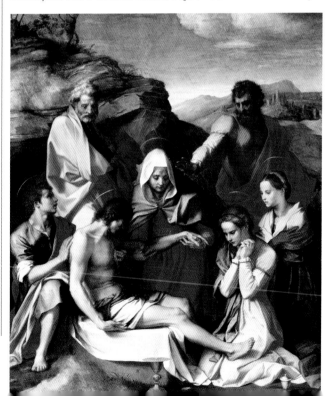

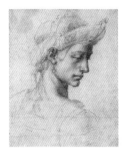

Ideal Head c.1518-20 1504–05, 20.5 x16.5 cm (8 x 6 ½ in), red chalk on paper, Oxford: Ashmolean Museum, University of Oxford, UK.

Michelangelo Buonarroti

● 1475–1564 ⚑ ITALIAN ✍ SCULPTURE; FRESCO; TEMPERA

The outstanding genius (and infant prodigy), Michelangelo cast his influence over all European art until Picasso broke the spell and changed the rules. He was a sculptor first, a painter and architect second. A workaholic, melancholic, temperamental, and lonely soul, he was also argumentative and belligerent and found relationships with others difficult.

Michelangelo was born near Florence, the son of a minor official with noble lineage, and showed his talent at an early age. He had a profound belief in the human form (especially that of the male) as the ultimate expression of human sensibility and beauty. His early work shows the human being as the measure of all things: idealized, muscular, confident and quasi-divine. Gradually that image becomes more expressive, more human, less perfect, fallible, and flawed. More at ease with drawing than painting, he conceived the figure in sculptural terms and used light to model it, so it could be the design for shaping a block of marble.

In paint, he used fiery reds and yellows against grey or blue; employing a wet-in-wet oil paint technique. Look for tempera hatching, reminiscent of a sculptor exploring volume. In his brilliant drawings he explored outline, contour, and volume; twisting poses, full of latent energy; faces, hands, and limbs expressing the full range of human emotions. Endlessly inventive, he never repeated a pose (although he borrowed some from famous Greek and Roman sculptures).

KEY WORKS: *The Entombment*, c.1500–01 (London: National Gallery); *David*, 1501–04 (Florence: Gallerie dell'Accademia); **Sistine Chapel ceiling frescoes**, 1508–12 (Rome: Vatican Museums)

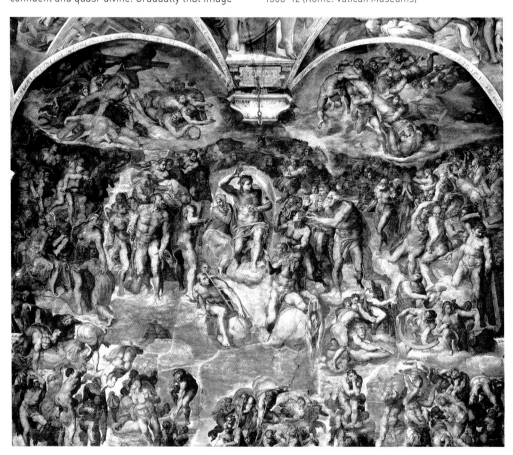

The Last Judgement 1536–41, 1,463 x 1,341 cm (576 x 528 in), fresco, Vatican City: Sistine Chapel.
In the centre of the composition, Christ raises the good with his right hand and dismisses the damned with his left.

Pietà

Michelangelo was only 25 when his *Pietà* was unveiled at St Peter's Basilica in Rome. In this superb work, he removed the subject from its usual sphere. More than a lofty religious symbol, far removed from normal life, it has become a complement to human experience: a sculpture that invites the viewer to share Mary's grief.

Michelangelo took the study of anatomy very seriously. As an adolescent he befriended a priest who allowed him access to dead bodies lying in rest at the church before being buried. Michelangelo did not believe that his Christ should appear superhuman; he wrote that there was no need to conceal the human behind the divine. The work ensured his reputation as one of the Renaissance's finest artists.

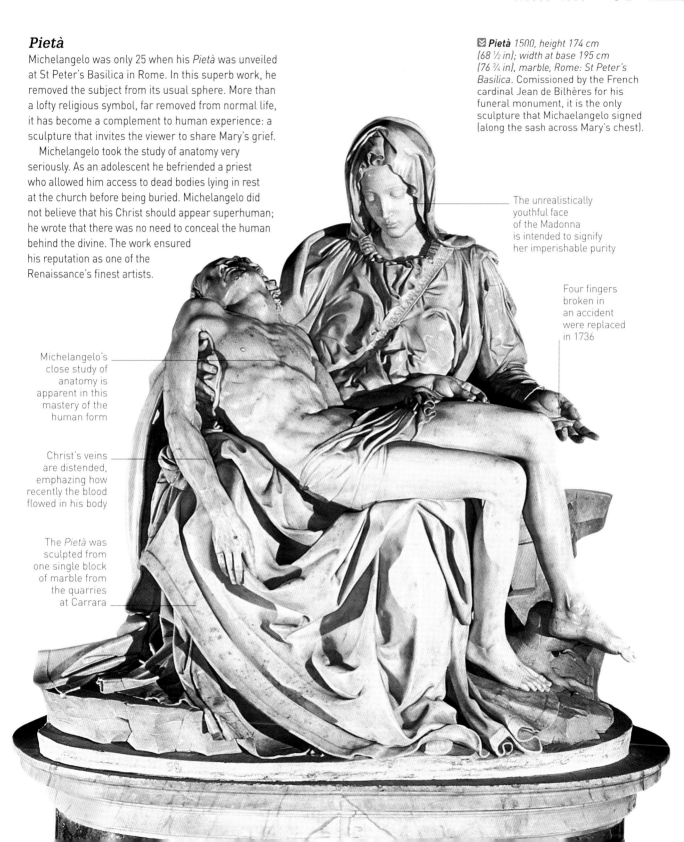

Pietà 1500, height 174 cm (68 ½ in); width at base 195 cm (76 ¾ in), marble, Rome: St Peter's Basilica. Comissioned by the French cardinal Jean de Bilhères for his funeral monument, it is the only sculpture that Michaelangelo signed (along the sash across Mary's chest).

The unrealistically youthful face of the Madonna is intended to signify her imperishable purity

Four fingers broken in an accident were replaced in 1736

Michelangelo's close study of anatomy is apparent in this mastery of the human form

Christ's veins are distended, emphazing how recently the blood flowed in his body

The *Pietà* was sculpted from one single block of marble from the quarries at Carrara

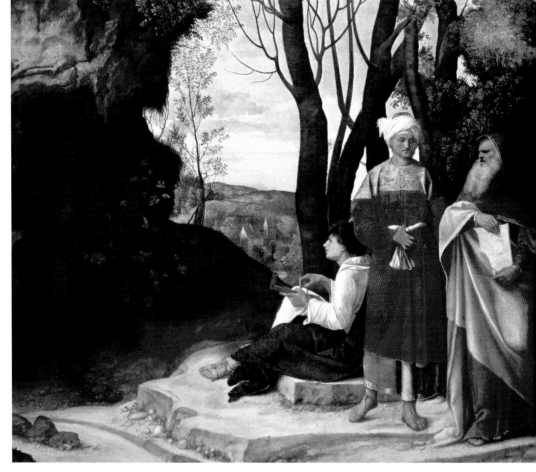

» *The Three Philosophers* *Giorgione, c.1509, 121 x 141 cm (47 ⅗ x 55 ½ in), oil on canvas, Vienna: Kunsthistorisches Museum.* Giorgione was patronized by collectors who enjoyed poetic ambiguity.

Giorgione

● c.1476–1510 ⊞ ITALIAN ✍ OILS

Also known as Giorgio Barbarelli or Giorgio da Castelfranco, Giorgione was the young, short-lived genius of the Venetian School, who ranks in achievement, significance, and importance with the greatest of Renaissance painters. Few works are known to be his for certain.

His small-scale, mostly secular, pictures are consciously poetic, lyrical, and mysterious – carefully observed portraits of youthful and sensitive young men being beautiful. His paintings have dream-like landscape settings. *The Sleeping Venus* and *The Tempest* opened the door for the development of the nude, landscape, and mythological painting on which so much of Western art has depended.

To own an authentic Giorgione has been one of the supreme ambitions of collectors since the Renaissance, so just think how many pictures have falsely or mistakenly had, and still have, the label "Giorgione" attached to them. It is impossible to identify a recognizable technique as so few works are known for certain, and there have been wicked restorations and overcleanings. Look for that indefinable, dreamy Giorgione mood, plus a passion for observing the real world.

KEY WORKS: *Old Woman*, c.1502–03 (Venice: Gallerie dell'Accademia); *The Tempest*, 1505–10 (Venice: Gallerie dell'Accademia); *The Sleeping Venus* 1508–10 (Dresden: Gemäldegalerie)

Jacopo **Palma Vecchio**

● 1480–1528 ITALIAN OILS

Vecchio had a short-lived career for an artist. He was a well-regarded painter of the greatest period of Venetian art and belonged to the same generation as Titian. His less good grandnephew was Palma Giovane (1544–1628). His high-quality pictures are well executed and decorative, but have the misfortune to be emotionally empty (the fate of many artists who just fail to reach the first rank). He had great success with half-lengths of sumptuous blondes masquerading as goddesses and saints in the high-Venetian fashion of the day.

Look for skilful drawing, pleasingly soft and harmonious colouring, and mastery of perspective and the human figure. The most elaborate works seem to be no more than an accumulation of small-scale visions and fine details – lacking the boldness and grandeur they seem to be striving for.

KEY WORKS: *Portrait of a Poet*, c.1516 (London: National Gallery); *A Blonde Woman*, c.1520 (London: National Gallery); *Venus and Cupid* c.1523–24 (Cambridge: Fitzwilliam Museum); *Judith*, 1525–28 (Florence: Galleria degli Uffizi)

Dosso **Dossi**

● c.1479–1542 ITALIAN OILS

Dossi was a somewhat obscure Venetian painter in the mould of Titian and Giorgione – moody, poetic, sensuous, using rich light and colour. He painted myths, allegories, portraits, lush landscapes, and frothy trees. He had a liking for animals. Few works remain, most of which are badly damaged. It is fashionable to say he is wonderful – he ought to be, but he can also be somewhat ungainly and gauche.

KEY WORKS: *Sibyl*, c.1516–20 (St Petersburg: Hermitage Museum); *Melissa*, 1520s (Rome: Galleria Borghese); *Circe and her Lovers in a Landscape*, c.1525 (Washington DC: National Gallery of Art)

Vittore **Carpaccio**

● ACTIVE 1490–1523 ITALIAN TEMPERA

Carpaccio was a notable Venetian storyteller with an eye for homely, factual detail, crowds, and processions. He set his religious and mythological stories within images of his own Venice and thus chronicled his own times. His faithful representation of the visible world is composed of many tiny parts. He was not a pioneer, but a forerunner of later domestic genre painters and recorders of the Venetian scene, such as Canaletto.

KEY WORKS: *The Legend of Saint Ursula*, 1495 (Venice: Gallerie dell'Accademia); *Young Knight in a Landscape*, 1510 (Madrid: Museo Thyssen-Bornemisza)

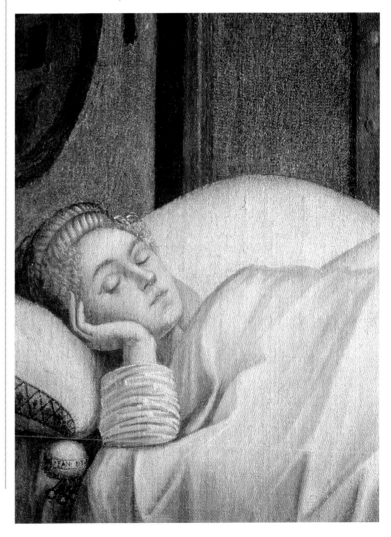

☑ *Dream of St Ursula*
(detail) Vittore Carpaccio, 1495, 23 x 23 cm (9 x 9 in), tempera on canvas, Venice: Galleria dell'Accademia. Carpaccio painted a series of works showing an unusually domesticated interpretation of the martyrdom of St Ursula.

Vincenzo **Catena**

● c.1480–1531 Ⅱ ITALIAN ✍ OILS

Catena was a reputable second-rank Venetian who created good middle-of-the-road paintings. His figures and compositions are uninspired, but light is well-observed and the colours attractive. Everything looks swept meticulously clean in his work – perhaps because cleanliness is next to godliness.

KEY WORKS: *Madonna and Child with the Infant St John the Baptist*, c.1506–1515 (London: National Gallery); *St Jerome in his Study*, c.1510 (London: National Gallery)

Lorenzo **Lotto**

● c.1480–c.1556 Ⅱ ITALIAN ✍ OILS

Lotto was a minor and uneven Venetian painter with a difficult personality. Much travelled, he died a forgotten man.

Lotto's portraits, altarpieces, and allegories have sumptuous colours and a rich, robust style, but are often uncomfortable compositions with overcramped spaces and inexplicable changes of scale. He never quite made all the parts work together. There are influences from many of his contemporaries, but too many borrowings that he never fully absorbs, so that his work can look like a mishmash of everyone else. At times, it even comes close to caricature.

He was at his best in portrait painting, especially conjugal double portraits. He liked searching, soulful expressions and was obsessed with hand gestures and fingers. His works have uncertain anatomy, but good landscape details and bold modelling with light. Look for the stunning oriental carpets in his paintings of interiors. He was much admired by Bernard Berenson, who made a detailed study of his work.

KEY WORKS: *The Virgin and Child with Saints*, 1522, (Boston: Museum of Fine Arts); *St Catherine*, c.1522 (Washington DC: National Gallery of Art); *The Annunciation*, 1527 (Recanati, Italy: Church of Santa Maria sopra Mercanti)

◙ *Christ Carrying the Cross* *Lorenzo Lotto, 1526, 66 x 60 cm (26 x 23 ½ in), oil on canvas, Paris: Musée du Louvre.* Deeply religious, but restless and dissatisfied, Lotto identified with St Jerome, the founder of Western Monasticism.

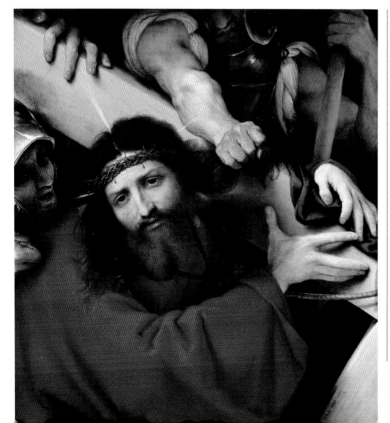

Benvenuto **Cellini**

● 1500–71 Ⅱ ITALIAN ✍ SCULPTURE; ENGRAVING

Cellini was a sculptor and engraver, and a pupil of Michelangelo. He was unpleasant, arrogant, sadistic, and violent. He was exiled from Florence for duelling and committed more than one murder. It was rumoured that Cellini crucified a man and watched him die in order to sculpt a realistic Christ on the cross. He had many influential patrons, including Francis I and Cosimo de' Medici. He was bisexual and was imprisoned twice for sodomy, but also fathered four children. He wrote an entertaining autobiography. Many of his famous works are monumental, but these lack the precision and excellence of his smaller pieces, such as Francis I's golden saltcellar.

KEY WORKS: *Saltcellar, called the "Saliera"*, 1540–43 (Vienna: Kunsthistorisches Museum); *Perseus with the Head of Medusa*, 1545 (Florence: Loggia dei Lanzi)

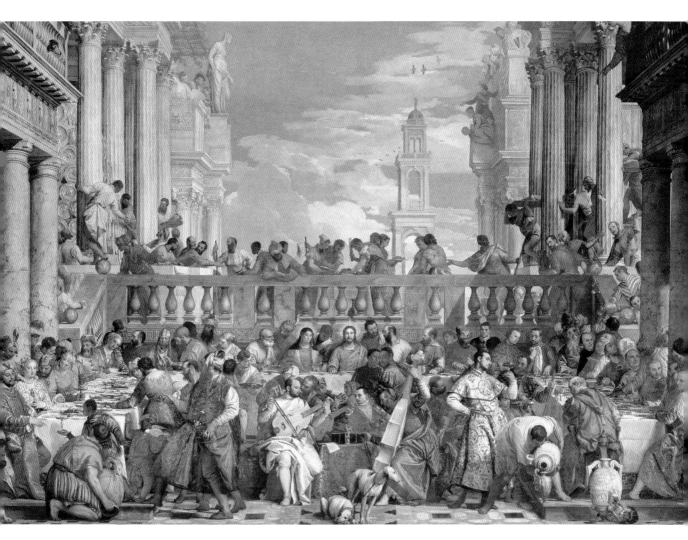

Paolo **Veronese**

🎨 **c.1528–88** 🏳 **ITALIAN** ✍ **OILS**

Paolo Caliari, born in Verona and known as
Veronese, was one of the major Venetians and one
of the greatest-ever creators of decorative schemes.
The son of a stonecutter, his precious talent for
painting was spotted by the Duke of Mantua.

See his work *in situ* – in one of his large-scale
decorative schemes, such as a Venetian church
or a nobleman's villa. Do not look for profound
meaning or a deep experience, but let your
eye have a feast and enjoy the glorious visual
and decorative qualities. Try to spot some of
the illusionistic tricks he used and remember
that these works were intended to go hand in
hand with a particular building – with its space,
architectural detail, and light.

Look for the posh people (his clients), surrounded
by their servants, rich materials, and classy
architecture. And look at the faces. Have they
become bored by too much good living and leisure?
Is that why the dogs and animals often seem more
alive than the people? These are the last days of
the really good times for the Venetian Empire. The
Madonnas and deities who he portrays are really
no more than Venetian nobility in fancy dress.

KEY WORKS: *The Triumph of Mordecai*, 1556
(Venice: San Sebastiano); *Allegory of Love, I
(Unfaithfulness)*, c.1570s (London: National Gallery);
The Finding of Moses, 1570–75 (Washington DC:
National Gallery of Art)

⌃ *Marriage at Cana*
*Paolo Veronese, 1563,
666 x 990 cm (262 ⅕ x
389 ¾ in), oil on canvas,
Paris: Musée du Louvre.*
The scene is a fantasy
interpretation of the
occasion when Christ
turned water into wine.

Titian

● c.1487–1576 ◫ ITALIAN ✍ OILS; FRESCO

Born into a humble family, Tiziano Vecellio, usually known by the shortened version Tiziano, or Titian, was the supreme master of the Venetian School and arguably the greatest painter of the High Renaissance, and of all time. Probably a pupil of Giovanni Bellini, he also worked with Giorgione. He is one of the few painters whose reputation has never been eclipsed or overlooked.

Titian had a miraculous ability with rich colour and luscious paint, and constantly innovated, using new subjects or brilliant reinterpretations. He had a Shakespearean response to the human condition, convincingly showing us tragedy, comedy, realism, vulgarity, poetry, drama, ambition, frailty, and spirituality. He was a genius at creating a psychological relationship between figures so that the space between them crackles with unspoken messages.

Study the faces and the body language – portraits with a thrilling likeness (who was it I met or saw who was just like that?). Also evident is an idealization and understanding of the hidden secrets of his subjects' characters. Was he too wise or discreet to tell quite all that he knew? In his *Bacchus and Ariadne*, Titian chooses to focus on the electrifying moment when Ariadne, daughter of King Menos of Crete, meets Bacchus, the god of wine, and they fall in love at first sight. He later married her, and she was eventually granted immortality. There is an overriding sense of ordered chaos about the painting. Although the scene is crowded, Titian has worked out the composition with great care. Bacchus's right hand is at the centre of the painting where the diagonals intersect. The revellers are all confined to the bottom right. Bacchus and Ariadne occupy the centre and left. Bacchus's feet are still with his companions, but his head and heart have joined Ariadne.

The greatest painter of the Venetian school, Titian was based in Venice for his entire life, inspired by its magical union of light and water. He was one the most successful painters in history, the Renaissance master of colour.

KEY WORKS: *Christ Appearing to the Magdalen (Noli me Tangere)*, c.1514 (London: National Gallery); *The Assumption of the Virgin*, 1515–18 (Venice: Santa Maria Gloriosa dei Frari); *Venus of Urbino*, c.1538 (Italy: Uffizi Gallery); *Portrait of Ranuccio Farnese*, 1542 (Washington DC: National Gallery of Art); *Diana Surprised by Actaeon*, 1556–59 (Edinburgh: National Gallery of Scotland); *The Flaying of Marsyas*, c.1570–75 (Kromeriz, Czech Republic: Château Archiépiscopal)

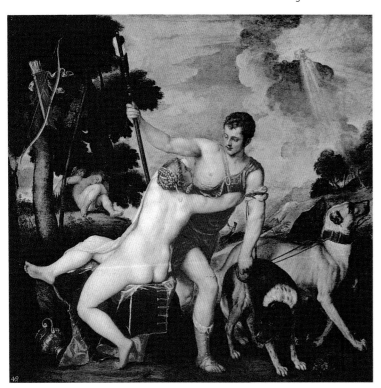

◀◀ *Venus and Adonis* 1553, 186 x 207 cm (73 ¼ x 81 ½ in), oil on canvas, Madrid: Museo del Prado. Titian's sensuous colour tones accentuate the soft and shimmering beauty of the lovers' flesh.

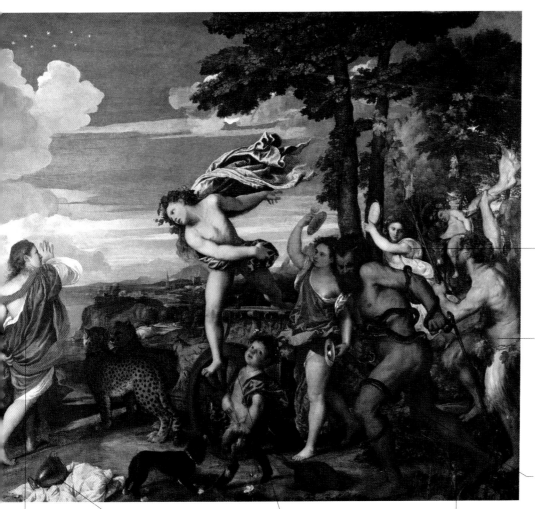

◀◀ *Bacchus and Ariadne*
*175 x 190 cm (69 x 75 in),
oil on canvas, London:
National Gallery.* Titian's
crowning achievements
are his mythological
poesie (poem) paintings.
This work was one of a
series commissioned by
Alfonso d'Este, the duke
of Ferrara in northern
Italy, to decorate his
country house.

The longing glance
that this maenad
exchanges with the
satyr contrasts with the
intense expressions of
the main characters

This drunken satyr,
crowned and girdled
with vine leaves, waves
the leg of a calf above
his head

A maenad crashes
cymbals together in
a riotous procession

Ariadne has been
abandoned by her
lover Theseus,
whom she helped
to escape from
the Minotaur's
labyrinth

Titian's name appears on an
urn in Latin – "TICIANUS
F[ecit]", or "Titian made this
picture". He was one of the
first artists to sign his work

Bacchus's chariot was
traditionally pulled by
leopards. Titian uses artistic
licence by employing
cheetahs for the task

The muscular figure shown
wrestling with the snakes is based
on the antique Roman statue of
Laocoön, which was unearthed in
1506 (see pages 16–17)

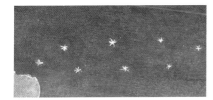

◀◀ **After falling
in love,** Bacchus
took Ariadne's
crown and threw
it into the sky
where it became
the constellation
Corona Borealis.

❯❯ TECHNIQUES

This close-up detail of Ariadne
shows Titian relishing two of
the special qualities of oil
paint: translucent, lustrous
colour, and fine, precise detail.

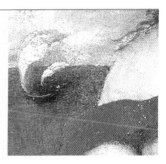

Mannerism

c.1520–1600

Mannerism is the name given to the predominant artistic style of the period bridging the High Renaissance and the Baroque. The term comes from the Italian word *maniere*, meaning "manner" or "style". The cradle of Mannerism was Rome, where the style was developed by artists influenced by the late works of Raphael and Michelangelo. Mannerist tendencies can be noted throughout Europe until after 1700.

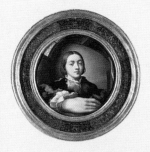

⏶ **Self-Portrait in a Convex Mirror** *Girolamo Parmigianino, c.1523–24, diameter 24.4 cm (9 ⅝ in), oil on wood, Vienna: Kunsthistorisches Museum.*

Mannerism was a reaction to social, political, and religious upheaval. The art of the period became violent, excitable, unnerving, often with a nightmarish, conflicting style; a huge step away from the harmony of High Renaissance. Key figures include Rosso Fiorentino, Jacopo Pontormo, Tintoretto, El Greco, Agnolo Bronzino, and Girolamo Parmigianino.

After the violent Sack of Rome in 1527, Mannerism spread throughout Italy, as terrified artists fled from the city. The subjects of Mannerist works include religious scenes viewed from an unusual aspect; portraits whose sitters wear unexpected expressions; and mythological or allegorical scenes, often characterized by a sinister form of symbolism.

What to look for

Look for distorted or elongated figures, artificial poses, complicated or obscure subject matter, uneasy symbolism, deliberate distortion of space, vivid colour, unreal textures, deliberate lack of harmony and proportion, voyeuristic sexual scenes. Faces in Mannerist works are rich with expression. Figures look deliberately tense or as though suspended halfway through an action. In sculpture, look for sense of movement, realism, exaggerated postures, strongly muscled anatomy. In architecture, look for anti-classicism and distortion of the viewer's expectations.

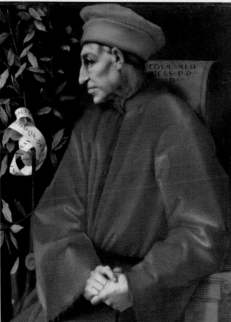

⏵ **Cosimo de' Medici (Il Vecchio)** *Jacopo Pontormo, 1518, 86 x 65 cm (33 ¾ x 25 ⅗ in), tempera on wood, Florence: Galleria degli Uffizi.* A posthumous portrait of Cosimo il Vecchio (1389–1464), founder of the Medici dynasty.

KEY EVENTS	
1520	Death of Raphael. His later works were considered the beginning of Mannerism
1527	Sack of Rome. Mannerism spreads across Italy and into France
c.1528	Jacopo Pontormo finishes his *Deposition*, a Florentine altarpiece in the Mannerist style
1534–40	Girolamo Parmigianino paints *The Madonna of the Long Neck* (see page 102)
1541	Birth of El Greco

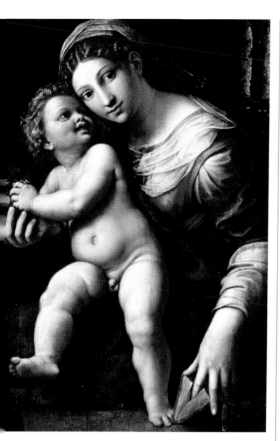

Madonna and Child *Giulio Romano, c.1530–40, 105 x 77 cm (33 ⅓ x 30 ⅓ in), oil on wood, Florence: Galleria degli Uffizi.* The Christ child reaches for grapes – a symbolic reference to the Eucharist, the central Christian sacrament.

Giulio **Romano**

⬤ c.1496-1546 🏛 ITALIAN ✎ CHALKS; FRESCO; OILS

Also known as Giulio Pippi, he was an architect and painter, and a major exponent of Mannerism. Guillo studied under and worked with Raphael and was strongly influenced by his later style, and also by the work of Michelangelo. After Raphael's death, Giulio finished several of his commissions. He was also a pornographer – he designed a series of celebrated and notorious pornographic engravings. Threatened with prison in Rome, Giulio moved to Mantua under the protection of the Gonzaga family. His most famous architectural work is Mantua's Palazzo del Tè.

In paintings, look for a similar style to Raphael, but exaggerated; also look for realism, muscular anatomy, and a strong sexual overtone. In architecture, look for deliberate "mistakes": missing expected features, such as central motifs; optical illusions, for instance, columns that are sturdy but look ready to tumble; or stonework left rough, instead of being smoothly carved and finished.

KEY WORKS: *Crowning of the Virgin (Madonna of Monteluce)*, c.1505–25 (Rome: Vatican Museums); *Mary Magdalene Borne by Angels*, c.1520 (London: National Gallery); *The Holy Family*, c.1520–23 (Los Angeles: J. Paul Getty Museum); *The Fall of the Giants*, 1532–34 (Mantua: Palazzo de Tè)

Giorgio **Vasari**

⬤ 1511-74 🏛 ITALIAN ✎ FRESCO; OILS

Vasari was a Mannerist painter, architect, writer, art historian, and collector. A popular, entertaining man – and an inveterate gossip – whose patrons were said to have enjoyed his storytelling ability as much as his art. Most famous for his volumes of biography, *Lives of the Artists* (1550; reprinted and extended in 1568), which was dedicated to Cosimo de' Medici. Despite inconsistencies, errors, and an overwhelming bias in favour of Michelangelo, it remains an important source for students of Renaissance art.

Vasari's writings have now outshone his other works, but in his time he was a highly successful painter, often decorating the houses of aristocratic families. He was also a respected architect, best known for designing the Galleria degli Uffizi in Florence.

KEY WORKS: *Paul III Directing the Continuence of St Peter's*, 1544 (Rome: Palazzo della Cancelleria); *Uffizi offices in Florence*, 1560-80 (finished by others); *The Prophet Elisha*, c.1566 (Florence: Galleria degli Uffizi); *The Attack on the Porta Camolia at Siena*, 1570 (Florence: Museo Ragazzi)

The Annunciation *Giorgio Vasari, c.1564–67, 216 x 166 cm (85 x 65 ⅓ in), oil on panel, Paris: Musée du Louvre.* This intimate scene formed the centre panel of a triptych for the dominican church of Santa Maria Novella at Arezzo.

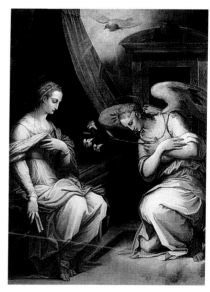

Jacopo **Pontormo**

● 1494–1557 ▥ ITALIAN ✍ OILS; FRESCO

Jacopo Carucci was named after his birthplace, Pontormo, near Empoli in Tuscany. Nervous, hysterical, solitary, melancholic, slow, capricious, and hypochondriacal, he was also a talented painter (good enough, anyway, to have studied with Leonardo). He taught Bronzino.

He painted altarpieces, religious and secular decorative schemes for churches and villas, and portraits. He took Michelangelo's and Dürer's classicism and energy, and contorted them into beguiling works with irrational compositions – figures in complicated but frozen poses – and bright, high-key colours (acid greens, clear blues, and pale pinks). Consciously radical and experimental – in line with his temperament and the political and social moods of his time.

Brilliant drawings. Very good portraits – with elongated and arrogant poses, and sharp observation of character.

Pontormo was one of the originators of the wayward style now known as Mannerism. (Like most good artists he did not care what style he painted in – he just got on with it.) Out of fashion in the 18th and 19th centuries, but has returned to favour in the 20th and 21st. (The word "Mannerism" was not invented or defined until the 20th century.)

KEY WORKS: *The Visitation*, 1514–16 (Florence: Santissima Annunziata); *Deposition*, c.1528 (Florence: Santa Felicità, Cappella Capponi); *Portrait of Duke Cosimo I de' Medici*, c.1537 (Malibu: J. Paul Getty Museum); *Portrait of Maria Salviati*, c.1537 (Florence: Galleria degli Uffizi); *Monsignor della Casa*, c.1541–44 (Washington DC: National Gallery of Art)

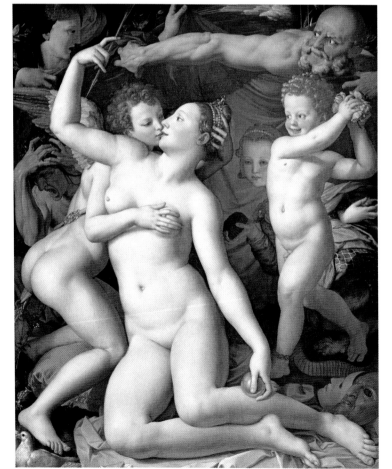

☑ *Venus and Cupid*
Agnolo Bronzino, c.1540–50, 146.5 x 116.8 cm (57 ⅔ x 45 in), oil on panel, London: National Gallery. Designed for King Francis I of France; the meaning of Bronzino's allegory is unclear.

Agnolo **Bronzino**

● 1503–72 ▥ ITALIAN ✍ OILS

Bronzino was best known for his aloof and icy portraits. Court painter to the Grand Duke of Tuscany, he came from a humble background. Bronzino painted with brittle artificiality – he lived in an age when artifice and striking poses reigned supreme. He sums it up in works with rare beauty: note the body language of the poses and faces, which communicate such arrogance, contempt, or insolence; and the equally arrogant ease of his technique, with its superb facility, deliberately complex and artificial compositions, and intense, insolent colours.

Look for flesh that seems to be made of porcelain (as smooth as the people he portrays). Notice the elongated faces and bodies, and eyes that can often seem vacant, like those of a child's doll. Look also for more rarely seen allegories and religious works with intricate designs, involving many figures whose poses are deliberately stolen from Michelangelo.

KEY WORKS: *A Lady with a Dog*, c.1529–30 (Frankfurt: Städelsches Kunstinstitut); *The Panciatichi Holy Family*, 1540 (Florence: Galleria degli Uffizi)

Giovanni Battista **Moroni**

◉ c.1525–78 ꝓ ITALIAN ✍ OILS

The son of an architect. Moroni was an artist
from Bergamo who is best remembered as an
accomplished, if formulaic, painter of low-key,
realist portraits, with good precise detail, in which
the sitters are allowed to speak for themselves
without too much manipulation by the artist. He
had a wide range of sitters, including those from
the middle and lower classes. He possessed a
strong preference for painting figures silhouetted
against a plain background.

KEY WORKS: *Portrait of a Lady*, c.1555–60 (London:
National Gallery); *Portrait of a Man*, mid-1560s
(St Petersburg: Hermitage Museum); *The Tailor*,
1565–70 (London: National Gallery); *Portrait of a
Bearded Man in Black*, 1576 (Boston: Isabella
Stewart Gardner Museum)

Giambologna

◉ 1529–1608 ꝓ FLEMISH ✍ SCULPTURE

Also called Giovanni da Bologna or Jean de
Boulogne, Giambologna was a Mannerist sculptor,
capable of producing both miniatures and
monumental statues with equal ability. Patronized
by the Medici, he established his reputation
with *The Fountain of Neptune* in Bologna and the
equestrian statue of Cosimo de' Medici in Florence.
He studied in Antwerp before arriving in Italy in
around 1550 to study. He lived in Rome before
settling in Florence. His works were hugely
influential on the future of sculpture.

Look for elegant, elongated bodies and limbs,
exaggerated three-dimensional movement, often
in contrary directions ("contraposto"), finely
chiselled facial features, fingers, toes, and nails,
and shimmering, patinated, polished surfaces
that catch the light.

KEY WORKS: *Samson Slaying a Philistine*, c.1561–62
(London: Victoria & Albert Museum); *The Fountain
of Neptune*, c.1563–66 (Bologna: Piazza del Nettuno);
Florence Triumphant over Pisa, c.1575 (Florence:
Museo Nazionale del Bargello); *Edward the
Confessor*, c.1579–89 (Florence: Church of
San Marco); *Hercules and the Centaur*, c.1594–1600
(Florence: Loggia dei Lanzi)

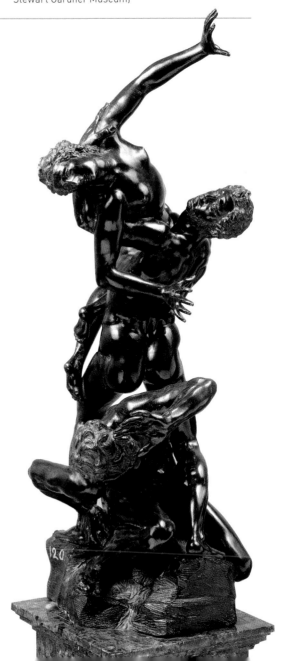

⟫ *The Rape of the Sabines* Giambologna, c.1583,
bronze, Florence: Museo Nazionale de Bargello.
This is a brilliant resolution of the problem of
uniting several figures in a single sculpture.

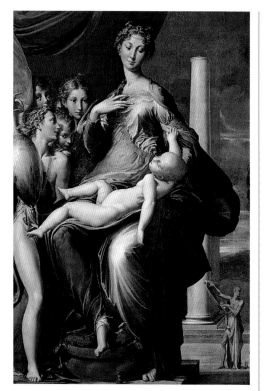

>> *The Madonna of the Long Neck* Girolamo Francesco Maria Mazzola Parmigianino,1534–40, 215 x 132 cm, (84 ¾ x 52 in), oil on canvas, Florence: Galleria degli Uffizi. This work is a union of artificial elegance and spirituality.

Girolamo Francesco Maria Mazzola **Parmigianino**

● 1503–40 Ⓟ ITALIAN ✍ FRESCO; OILS; ENGRAVINGS; DRAWINGS

Parmigianino was a short-lived, precocious, much admired (sometimes referred to as "Raphael reborn"), and very influential artist. He was from Parma, in northern Italy – like his contemporary, Correggio.

Look for beautifully executed, refined, elegant, contrived, and precious works. He was especially great as a portraitist, projecting a cool, reserved, and enigmatic image. His religious and mythological paintings are a paradoxical combination of real and unreal. His art starts with acute observations from life, which he then transforms into fantasies – like a musical composer making variations on a theme. He also produced small-scale panel paintings, large frescoes, and brilliant, prolific drawings. Notice the recurrent bizarre, elongated human figures, their impossibly long necks, and knowing looks (especially in his late work, which was considered very beautiful at the time). Look for the distorted and convoluted perspectives and variety of scales (his style was the epitome of Mannerism). He had a sophisticated line in erotica. His drawings are full of energy, movement, and light; he loved drawing as an activity for its own sake, as well as a tool.

KEY WORKS: *Self-Portrait in a Convex Mirror*, c.1523 (Vienna: Kunsthistorisches Museum); *Vision of St Jerome*, 1527 (London: National Gallery)

Antonio **Correggio**

● c.1494–1534 Ⓟ ITALIAN ✍ OILS; DRAWINGS

Correggio was once hugely revered and popular (especially in 17th and 18th centuries), and was consequently very influential. Now, no longer well known, his virtues are completely out of fashion. His most important works are in Parma, northern Italy.

His works are full of genuine charm, intimacy, and tender emotion, and occasional sentimentality. He chose subjects from mythology and the Bible, and had a lyrical and sensitive style; everything (though immensely accomplished and not unambitious) is gentle – light, colour, and foreshortening. His compositions are complex but satisfying, with easy-to-read subjects displaying pleasing anatomy and relationships, youthful faces, and sweet smiles. He invented the idea of light radiating from the Christ child.

The *in-situ* decorations in Parma are forerunners of the over-the-top illusionistic decorations in Baroque Rome 100 years later (the link from one to the other was Lanfranco). See how he turns the ceiling into an illusionistic sky and then makes exciting things happen in it (Mantegna did this first and Correggio followed him). The charming, sentimental side derives from Leonardo and influenced French Rococo. He liked wistful faces and idealized profiles and produced many fine drawings.

KEY WORKS: *The Mystic Marriage of St Catherine*, c.1526–27 (Paris: Musée du Louvre); *Judith*, 1512–14 (Strasbourg: Musée des Beaux-Arts); *Venus, Satyr, and Cupid*, 1524–27 (Paris: Musée du Louvre); *Venus with Mercury and Cupid*, c.1525 (London: National Gallery)

Paris **Bordone**

● 1500–71 ⚐ ITALIAN ✍ OILS

A painter of portraits, religious works, landscapes, and mythological genre scenes, Bordone was influenced by Giorgione and Titian (despite disliking the latter intensely). He worked for King Francis I of France and was an important member of the first Fontainebleau School. His works, although facially realistic and finely detailed, demonstrate a problem with anatomy and perspective.

KEY WORKS: *Rest on the Flight into Egypt*, 1520–30 (London: Courtauld Institute); *The Presentation of the Ring of St Mark to the Doge*, c.1535 (Venice: Galleria dell'Accademia)

Jacopo **Bassano**

● c.1517–92 ⚐ ITALIAN ✍ OILS

Bassano was the best-known member of the prominent Venetian da Ponte family, who lived at Bassano (where grappa is made).

He was a painter of standard religious subjects, chosen for their power and drama. Note how he interpreted them to make the best of his interest in stocky peasants, animals, stormy mountain landscapes, and spectacular lighting.

Note also how Bassano packs great drama into small spaces – which is why everyone seems to be in such a hurry, and either moving into the picture space or trying to get out of it. Beautifully painted hands and arms; striking light; marvellous, urgent handling of paint, which reflects the drama of the scene as though Bassano were part of it.

KEY WORKS: *The Good Samaritan*, c.1550–70 (London: National Gallery); *Sheep and Lamb*, c.1560 (Rome: Galleria Borghese)

Federico **Barocci**

● 1526–1612 ⚐ ITALIAN ✍ OILS; FRESCO; CHALKS

Barocci was an Urbino-based painter of sentimental religious pictures, who suffered from terrible ill health (at times, evident in his work). Look for sugar-plum colours and soft forms (he was one of the first artists to use chalks), sweetly-faced Madonnas, and well-handled crowds. His work, like cheap, sweet wine, is all sugar and no bite.

KEY WORKS: *Rest on the Flight to Egypt*, 1570–73 (Vatican: Pinacoteca); *Madonna del Popolo*, 1576–79 (Florence: Galleria degli Uffizi)

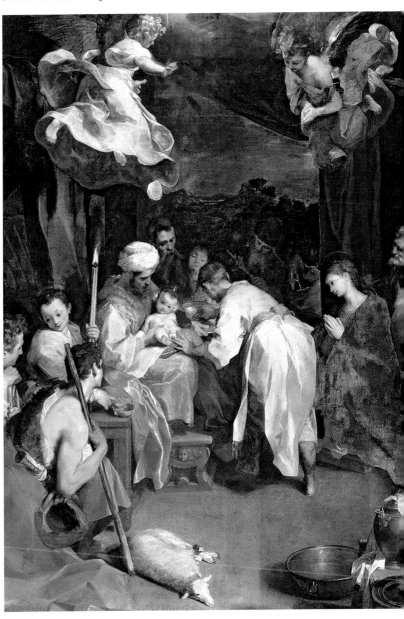

▽ *The Circumcision of Christ* Federico Barocci, 1590, 356 x 251 cm (140 x 98 ⅘ in), oil on canvas, Paris: Musée du Louvre. The significance of the circumcision is that it is the first occasion on which Christ shed his blood.

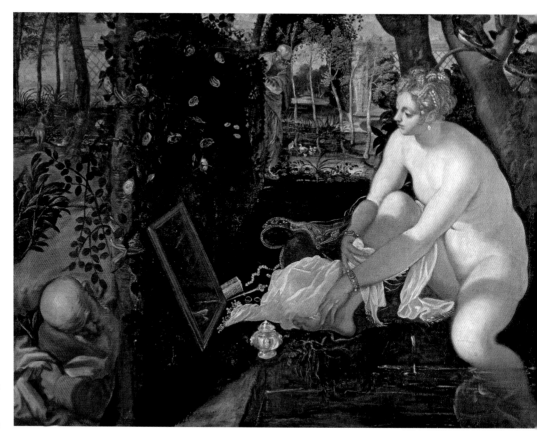

>> *Susanna and the Elders* Jacopo Robusti Tintoretto, 1555–56, 146.5 x 193.6 cm (57 ⅓ x 76 ⅛ in), oil on canvas, Vienna: Kunsthistorisches Museum. A popular subject as it provides an excuse for female nudity.

Jacopo Robusti **Tintoretto**

● 1518–94 ⬛ ITALIAN ⬥ OILS; DRAWINGS

Tintoretto's father was a dyer (*tintore*) – hence his nickname. Very little is known about his life. Although unpopular and unscrupulous, he was one of the major Venetian painters in the generation following Titian; he is said to have trained briefly with the greatest painter of the Venetian School. Very prolific, he was also a formidable draughtsman.

In his monumental and vast religious works and mythologies, everything was treated with the drama, verve, panache, scale – and sometimes the absurdity – of grand opera. Tintoretto used a model stage and wax figures to design his extraordinary and inventive compositions.

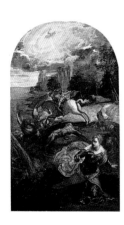

◀ *St George and the Dragon* Jacopo Robusti Tintoretto, c.1570, 158 x 100 cm (62 ⅕ x 39 ⅓ in), oil on canvas, London: National Gallery. Such a small scale is unusual.

His late religious work tended to be gloomy. His thick, hasty brushwork and exciting lighting show his passionate involvement in his creations. He painted portraits of notable Venetians but his busy studio produced many dull efforts.

When you find an extraordinary or off-centre composition, try standing or kneeling to one side so that you view the work from an oblique angle. Tintoretto designed many works to be seen in this way, especially if they were big works for the small or narrow spaces of Venetian churches, where the congregation would be both kneeling and looking up or forward to works hung on the side wall. The anatomy is poor in some of his portraits; the hands don't seem to belong to the bodies.

KEY WORKS: *Summer*, c.1555 (Washington DC: National Gallery of Art); *The Woman who Discovers the Bosom*, c.1570 (Madrid: Museo del Prado); *Christ at the Sea of Galilee*, c.1575–80 (Washington DC: National Gallery of Art)

Rosso **Fiorentino**

● c.1494/5–1540 ▣ ITALIAN ✍ OILS; FRESCO;
TEMPERA; STUCCO

His real name was Giovanni Battista di Jacopo.
Fiorentino was an unconventional, eccentric
painter – a talented early Mannerist and a pupil
of Andrea del Sarto. A member of the first
Fontainebleau School, he was born and worked
in Florence, before moving to Venice, Rome, and
France. His works include a large number of
religious scenes as well as excellent portraits.
He also worked in stucco, decorating the palace
in Fontainebleau with painting and stucco
decorations. He was the official painter of Francis I
from 1532 to 1537; he died in Paris and is credited
with taking Italian Mannerism to France.

Look for lots of movement, bold colours,
prominent muscles, faces filled with expression,
and dreamlike sequences that have a strange
realism to them.

KEY WORKS: *Portrait of a Young Man Holding
a Letter*, 1518 (London: National Gallery); *Musical
Angel*, c.1520 (Florence: Galleria degli Uffizi); *The
Virgin and Child with Angels*, c.1522 (St Petersburg:
Hermitage Museum)

Francesco **Primaticcio**

● c.1504–70 ▣ ITALIAN ✍ OILS;
FRESCO; STUCCO

Primaticcio was born and trained in Bologna and
worked with Giulio Romano in Mantua. In 1532,
he moved to France under the patronage of
Francis I. He became assistant to Rosso Fiorentino
and was appointed official art buyer to the king.
He settled in Fontainebleau (and died in France),
but returned to Italy regularly on art-buying trips.
After the death of Fiorentino, Primaticcio took
over as leader of the Fontainebleau School. After
the death of Francis I, he worked for Henry II as
Surveyor of Works.

Look for paintings and stucco, in high relief,
characterized by sensuality, overcrowded scenes,
tiny heads, and elongated, elegant limbs. He was
influenced by Mannerism, Michelangelo, Cellini,
and Correggio; look for anatomical correctness,
but overly-muscular figures.

KEY WORKS: *The Rape of Helen*, 1530–39
(County Durham, UK: Bowes Museum); *Salle
d'Hercule*, 1530–39, Château de Fontainebleau;
Study of God, 1555 (Los Angeles: J. Paul
Getty Museum)

» **FONTAINEBLEAU** c.1530–1560 & c.1589–1610

The royal palace at Fontainebleau, near Paris, fostered
two brilliant schools of decoration and architecture.
The first – and most influential – was established by
King Francis I in the 1530s. He (1515–47) employed
a variety of artists and artisans: painters, poets,
designers, sculptors, writers, printmakers, architects,
stucco workers, gold- and silversmiths, and textile
workers. Most of the early workers, such as Fiorentino
and Primaticcio, came from Italy, thereby spreading
Italianate art to northern Europe.

The second Fontainebleau School was established
by Henry IV in 1589, after a period of great social
and political unrest in France. The principal painters
included Toussaint Dubreuil, Martin Fréminet,
and Ambroise Dubois.

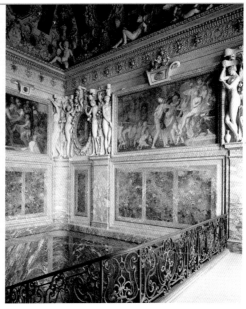

» *Former apartments of Anne de Pisseleu,
Duchesse d'Étampes* Francesco Primaticcio,
1533–44, Château de Fontainebleau. The influence
of the Mannerist style seen here spread quickly
throughout northern Europe.

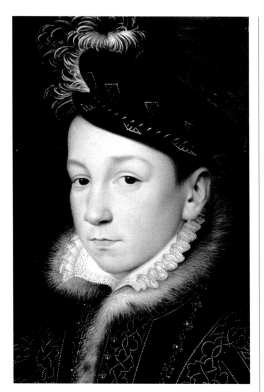

» *Charles IX* François Clouet, 1550–74, 25 x 21 cm (9 ⅘ x 8 ¼ in), *oil on wood, Vienna: Kunsthistorisches Museum.* At the time of painting, the young French king was only aged 11 but had already been reigning for a year. Clouet's portrait invests the young face with firmness and maturity, whilst retaining the bloom of youth.

François **Clouet**

◔ c.1510–72 ⚑ FRENCH ✍ OILS; DRAWINGS

A portrait painter, miniaturist, and draughtsman, Clouet is often confused with his father, Jean Clouet, who trained him; both were favourites of Francis I who nicknamed both "Janet" or "Jehannet". François ran a large, successful studio. He was appointed court painter in 1541 and remained so for Henry II, Francis II, and Charles IX; he retired in 1570. Strongly influenced by the Italianate paintings of first Fontainebleau School, he painted portraits of the nobility and allegorical landscapes. A famous portrait of Francis I – lavish with gold – is attributed to both François and Jean Clouet.

Look for meticulous detail, rich decoration, attention to contemporary fashions, natural-looking facial features, and realistic expression.

KEY WORKS: *François I, King of France*, c.1540 (Florence: Galleria degli Uffizi); *Pierre Quthe*, 1562 (Paris: Musée du Louvre); *Lady in her Bath*, c.1570 (Washington DC: National Gallery of Art)

Niccolò dell'**Abbate**

◔ c.1512–71 ⚑ ITALIAN ✍ OILS; STUCCO

Niccolò was an Italian-born decorator of palaces and portrait painter. He trained in his birthplace, Modena, and later developed a mature style in Bologna. He had a refined, elaborate, mannered, and artificial style playing with fantasy landscapes and themes of love. He settled in France in 1552 to work for the royal court. He was a key link figure between Correggio and Parmigianino (who influenced Niccolò with his elegant figure style) and the French classical landscape painters, such as Claude and Poussin (whom he influenced). He also painted portraits in both Italy and France.

KEY WORKS: *Landscape with the Death of Eurydice*, c.1552 (London: National Gallery); *The Continence of Scipio*, c.1555 (Paris: Musée du Louvre)

Toussaint **Dubreuil**

◔ 1561–1602 ⚑ FRENCH ✍ FRESCO; OILS

Dubreuil was a painter and draughtsman who had a strong association with the second Fontainebleau School. He was apprenticed to Médéric Fréminet, father of Martin Fréminet. He was appointed Premier Painter to Henry IV and worked for him in Fontainebleau and Paris; he is not known to have left France. Little of his work survives, but his reputation as a talented painter remains intact.

He designed large-scale tapestries and painted murals and frescoes, mainly of mythological and classical subjects. He is best known for the frescoes to be found in the Tuileries Palace, Paris. In his lifetime he was famed for painting murals in the Louvre – all destroyed by a fire in 1661. He is credited with forging the link between Mannerism and Classicism.

KEY WORKS: *Angélique and Médor*, 16th century (Paris: Musée du Louvre); *Dicé gives a Banquet for Francus*, c.1594–1602 (Paris: Musée du Louvre); *Hyante and Climène at their Toilette*, c.1594–1602 (Paris: Musée du Louvre); *Hyante and Climène offering a Sacrifice to Venus*, c.1594–1602 (Paris: Musée du Louvre)

El Greco

◉ 1541–1614 ᴾᵁ GREEK/SPANISH
✍ OILS; SCULPTURE

El Greco's real name was Domenikos Theotocopoulos. He was born in Crete and trained in Venice but worked in Spain, hence the name El Greco (the Greek). Arrogant, intellectual, and spiritual, he was a one-off, with a wide range of sources. He was popular with Philip II of Spain until he fell out of favour in 1582.

Art historians can have a good time trying to piece together the sources: directly applied colour (Titian), writhing figures (Michelangelo and Parmigianino), fragmented spaces and jewel-like acid colours (Byzantine mosaics and icons). But to touch the real El Greco, you have to forget this and enter the spiritual world of visionary Christianity. Only then will you appreciate his genius and the significance of his superb technical skills.

The elongated figures, hands, feet, and faces are not intended to describe, but to reveal the inner spirit.

The soaring compositions are about the ascent from the material to the divine. The strange colours are a reflection and revelation of spiritual light. He believed that other-worldly appearances were a better aid to devotion than naturalism. El Greco excelled as a portraitist, painting mainly ecclesiastics or gentlemen; his works reveal the essence and idea of a person rather than a strict likeness. Look for the thrilling draughtsmanship and the tense, probing line that profiles his forms.

KEY WORKS: *St Joseph and the Christ Child*, 1597–99 (Toledo: Museo de Santa Cruz); *Madonna and Child with St Martina and St Agnes*, 1597–99 (Washington DC: National Gallery of Art); *Laocoön*, c.1610 (Washington DC: National Gallery of Art)

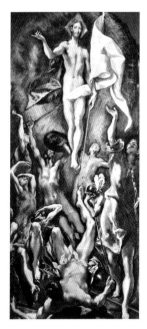

⌃ *The Resurrection*
El Greco, 1584–94, 275 x 127 cm (108 ¼ x 50 in), oil on canvas, Madrid: Museo del Prado. El Greco's late visionary style so displeased the Spanish monarch Philip II, that he lost all royal patronage.

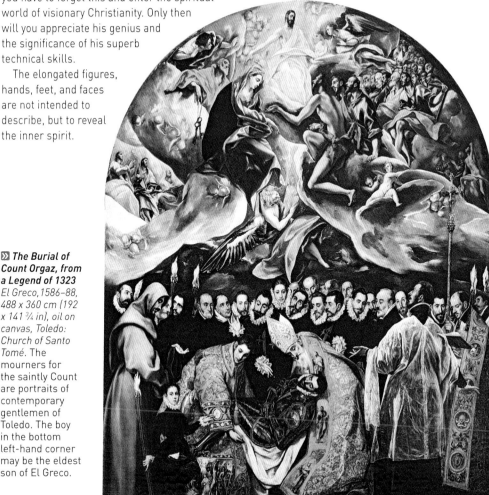

⤤ *The Burial of Count Orgaz, from a Legend of 1323*
El Greco, 1586–88, 488 x 360 cm (192 x 141 ¾ in), oil on canvas, Toledo: Church of Santo Tomé. The mourners for the saintly Count are portraits of contemporary gentlemen of Toledo. The boy in the bottom left-hand corner may be the eldest son of El Greco.

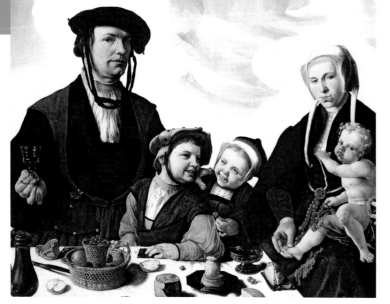

Maerten **van Heemskerck**

⬤ 1498–1574 🏳 DUTCH ✍ OILS; ENGRAVINGS

Van Heemskerck was the leading Haarlem painter of his day. He painted portraits, altarpieces, and mythologies, and was totally transformed by a visit to Rome, 1532–36. Look for classical profiles; Michelangelesque, muscular figures; emotional (unrealistic) faces, gestures, and colours (hot reds, strong pinks, turquoise blue). He adopted Italian idealization rather than northern realism.

KEY WORKS: *The Crucifixion*, c.1530 (Detroit Institute of Arts); *Portrait of a Lady with a Spindle and Distaff*, c.1531 (Madrid: Museo Thyssen-Bornemisza)

⬈ *Family Group* Maerten van Heemskerck, 1530, 118 x 140 cm (45 ½ x 55 in), oil on wood, Kassel (Germany): Staatliche Museen. This portrait is in a vigorous and relatively sober style and dates to before van Heemskerck's visit to Rome. He spent most of his life in Haarlem and became Dean of the Painters' Guild.

Pieter **Aertsen**

⬤ c.1508–75 🏳 DUTCH ✍ OILS

Aertsen was a painter of altarpieces and large-scale peasant subjects as well as monumental genre and still-life scenes (such as a butcher's shop). Many of these have a religious subject hiding in the background. He was good at modelling with light in the Italian manner.

Aertsen also liked movement. He was a Bruegel without the humour and moral observation; a Rubens without the panache and power.

KEY WORKS: *Market Scene*, c.1550 (Munich: Alte Pinakothek); *Butcher's Stall with the Flight into Egypt*, 1551 (Sweden: University of Uppsala); *Cook in front of the Stove*, 1559 (Brussels: Musées Royaux des Beaux-Arts)

⬊ *The Adoration of the Shepherds* Pieter Aertsen (studio of), 16th century, 84.5 x 113.7 cm (33 ¼ x 44 ¾ in), oil on panel, private collection. Many Aertsen altarpieces were destroyed in the Reformation riots.

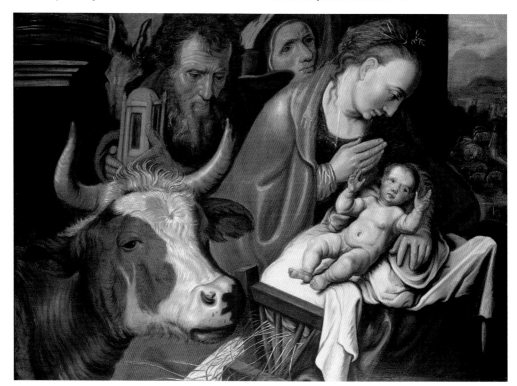

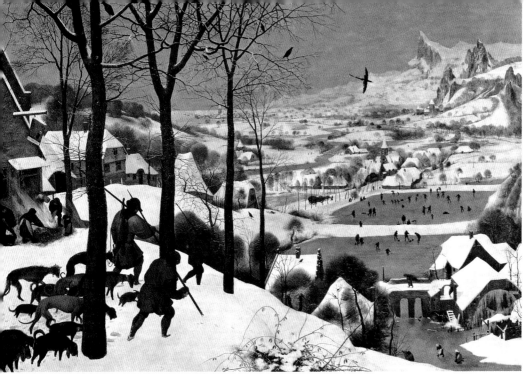

« *Hunters in the Snow – February*
Pieter Bruegel (the elder), 1565, 117 x 162 cm (46 x 63 ¾ in), oil on canvas, Vienna: Kunsthistorisches Museum. This famous series of depictions was commissioned by Niclaes Jonghelinck, a wealthy merchant.

Pieter **Bruegel** (the elder)

● c.1525–69 ▯ FLEMISH ◿ OILS; DRAWINGS

Nicknamed "Peasant" Bruegel because of the subject matter of his paintings, he was the leading Flemish artist of his day whose subjects reflected contemporary religious and social issues. He paved the way for the Dutch masters of the 17th century. His works are brilliant and accurately observed commentaries on the appearance and behaviour of the ordinary people of his day – like a first-rate stage play or TV soap opera. They are powerful because, as well as enjoying the existence and minutiae of his day and age, we can recognize ourselves – especially when he illustrates human follies, greed, and misdemeanours. Like all great artists, Bruegel spoke simultaneously about the personal and the universal.

Bruegel's bird's-eye views place us outside his world (we look down god-like, distanced, and superior); then by the fineness and charm of detail he draws us into it – we are simultaneously in his world and apart from it. Clear outlines and detail lead the eye through each picture. His early work (from Antwerp) is busy and anecdotal; his later work (from Brussels) is simpler and more consciously and artistically composed and organized. He saw the Alps in 1552–53 on his way to Italy.

KEY WORKS: *Netherlandish Proverbs*, 1559 (Berlin: Staatliche Museen); *Children's Games*, 1560 (Vienna: Kunsthistorisches Museum); *The Adoration of the Kings*, 1564 (London: National Gallery), *The Gloomy Day*, 1565 (Vienna: Kunsthistorisches Museum); *The Wedding Feast*, c.1567–68 (Madrid: Museo del Prado)

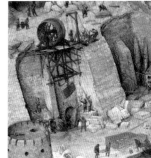

⌃ *The Tower of Babel*
(detail), *Pieter Bruegel (the elder)*, 1563, 114 x 155 cm (45 x 61 in), oil on panel, Vienna: Kunsthistorisches Museum. An attempt to build a tower so tall it would reach up to Heaven.

Marten **de Vos**

● c.1531–1603 ▯ FLEMISH ◿ OILS

A leading painter in Antwerp, Marten de Vos combined Flemish realism and detail with Italianate subjects, grandeur, and idealization (he visited Rome, Florence, and Venice, 1552–58). His works include altarpieces (vertical, with elegant, elongated figures); portraits (Flemish burghers and plain backgrounds); and mythologies (large scale, ambitious, and decorative).

KEY WORKS: *St Paul Stung by a Viper on the Island of Malta*, c.1566 (Paris: Musée du Louvre); *Antoine Anselme and his Family*, 1577 (Bruges: Musées Royaux des Beaux-Arts)

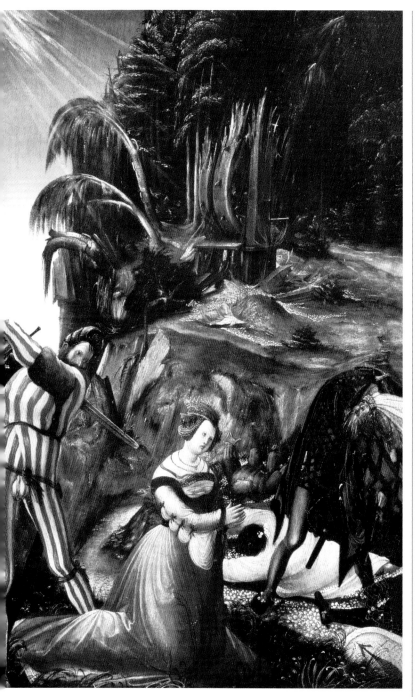

⌃ Beheading of Saint Catherine *Albrecht Altdorfer,*
c.1505–10, 56 x 36 cm (22 x 14 ⅛ in), oil on panel,
Vienna: Kunsthistorisches Museum. Altdorfer
appealed to German humanists wanting to
revive native traditions.

Albrecht **Altdorfer**
◒ c.1480–1538 ⌘ GERMAN ✍ OILS; ENGRAVINGS

Altdorfer mainly painted altarpieces. The
most notable features of his works are strange,
visionary landscapes with eerie light effects, in
which wild nature is in control, with man taking
second place. His output was small and he gave
up painting to go into local government.

KEY WORKS: *Christ Taking Leave of his Mother,*
c.1520 (London: National Gallery); *St Florian*
Altar, c.1520 (Linz, Austria: Monastery of
St Florian; Florence: Galleria degli Uffizi)

Bartholomeus **Spranger**
◒ 1546–1611 ⌘ FLEMISH ✍ FRESCO;
OILS; DRAWINGS

A painter, draughtsman, and etcher, Spranger
was an exponent of late Mannerist style and a
key figure of northern European Mannerism. Born
in Antwerp, he worked in France then moved on to
Rome, where he studied under Taddeo Zuccaro. He
was appointed court painter to the Pope in 1570. In
Vienna he worked for Emperor Maximilian II. Then
he moved on to Prague, where he stayed for the
rest of his life. In 1581, he became court painter
to Emperor Rudolf II. His works were mainly of
mythological or allegorical subjects. He was very
popular in northern Europe and hugely influential
on the Haarlem school.

His works are typical of late Mannerism. Look
for a glut of nudes, improbable poses, a sensual
style, luminosity of skin tone, and exaggerated
features. His paintings have rich colours, finely
executed details, such as jewels and flowers,
and detailed decorations, such as on
background furniture.

KEY WORKS: *Christ, the Saviour of the World,*
16th century (Montauban, France: Musée Ingres);
Diana and Actaeon, c.1590–95 (New York: Metropolitan
Museum of Art); *The Adoration of the Kings,*
c.1595 (London: National Gallery); *Venus and*
Adonis, c.1597 (Vienna: Kunsthistorisches
Museum); *Allegory of Justice and of Prudence,*
c.1599 (Paris: Musée du Louvre)

Adam **Elsheimer**

⬤ 1578-1610 ⚑ GERMAN ✍ OILS;
ENGRAVINGS; DRAWINGS

Elsheimer was a popular, early practitioner of
small-scale, ideal landscapes. He spent his
working life in Italy and had a great influence on
artists such as Rubens, Rembrandt, and Claude.

His paintings are full of the kind of remarkable
precision and detail that you see when looking
down the wrong end of a telescope. All his works
are painted on copper plates, which allows such
fine detail (he must have had brushes with
only one bristle).

Elsheimer often used several sources of light
in one picture, such as a sunset and moon, daylight
and torchlight. He painted charming trees, which
look like parsley.

KEY WORKS: *Nymph Fleeing Satyrs*, c.1605 (Berlin:
Staatliche Museum); *The Flight into Egypt*, 1609
(Munich: Alte Pinakothek)

Giuseppe **Arcimboldo**

⬤ 1527-93 ⚑ ITALIAN ✍ OILS

Arcimboldo was best known
for fantastical faces and bodies
made up of vegetables, trees,
fruit, fish, and the like – he had
the type of artistic curiosity
produced in times of cultural
and political upheaval (as true
in the late 20th century as in
the late 16th century). He
worked mostly in Prague for
Emperor Rudolf II, who was
obsessed with alchemy and
astrology. Arcimboldo returned
to Milan in 1587.

KEY WORKS: *Fire,* 1566 (Vienna:
Kunsthistorisches Museum); *The
Librarian*, 1566 (Balsta, Sweden:
Skoklosters Slott); *Spring, Summer,
Autumn, and Winter (series of four),*
1573 (Paris: Musée du Louvre)

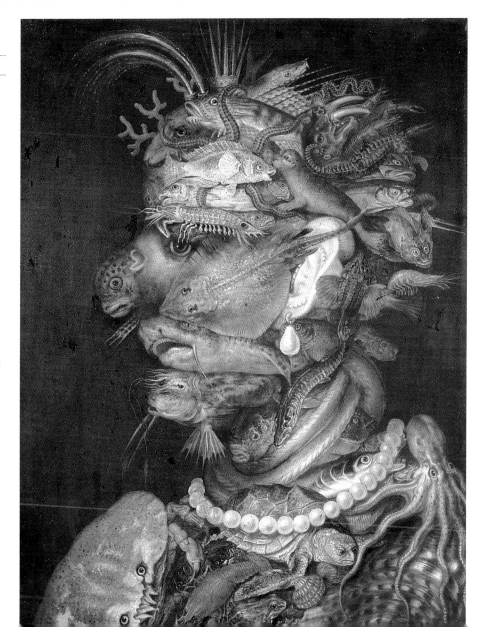

»» ***Water*** *Giuseppe Arcimboldo,
1566, 66.5 x 50.5 cm (26 ⅕ x
20 in), oil on canvas, Vienna:
Kunsthistorisches Museum*. The
four elements – earth, air, water,
and fire – were popular subjects
for series paintings.

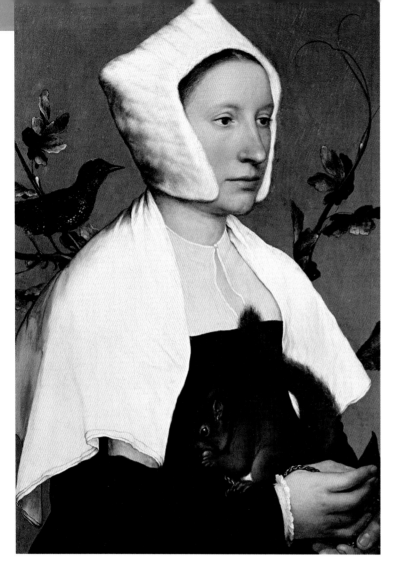

⊼ *Lady with a Squirrel and a Starling* Hans Holbein (the younger), c.1526–28, 56 x 39 cm (22 x 15 1⁄3 in), oil on panel, London: National Gallery. The animals in the painting may allude to the family coat of arms of the sitter, Anne Lovell.

Hans **Holbein** (the younger)

🌐 c.1497/8–1543   🏳 GERMAN/SWISS
🖌 OILS; DRAWINGS

A painter and designer, Holbein is chiefly celebrated as one of the greatest of all portraitists. He was forced to leave Switzerland because of the Reformation. He came to England and established himself successfully as the propaganda portrait painter of the era of Henry VIII. He died of the plague, and very little is known about his life. He was famous above all for his portraits (many of his early religious works were destroyed during the Reformation). There are interesting parallels with official court photographs of the mid-20th century, such as the work of Cecil Beaton: masterly,

memorable, posed, officially commissioned images – in sharp focus – of the monarch and ruling officials, which are self-chosen icons of the political and constitutional system. Holbein also produced more informal and flattering (but never too relaxed) soft-focus images of high society that surrounded the court.

Note the way Holbein draws and models with light (as does a photographer); the remarkable sharp focus detail (stubble on a chin, fur); the intense lighting; the wonderful feel for the structure of a face and the personality inside it. The portraits before the mid-1530s are full of objects (sometimes symbolic); later they are flattened designs on a dark background. The famous album of 80 drawings at Windsor contains lovely, soft-focus, informal portraits.

KEY WORKS: *Portrait of a Woman*, c.1532–35 (Detroit Institute of Arts); *The Ambassadors*, 1533 (London: National Gallery); *Christina of Denmark*, c.1538 (London: National Gallery); *Edward VI as a Child*, c.1538 (Washington DC: National Gallery of Art)

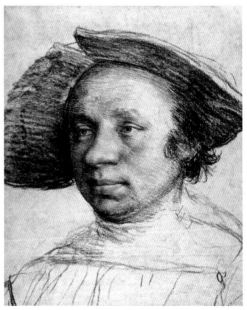

⊼ *Portrait of a Youth in a Broad-brimmed Hat* Hans Holbein (the younger), c.1524–26, 24.5 x 20.2 cm (9 1⁄3 x 8 in) chalk on paper, Derbyshire (UK): Chatsworth House. The artist learned his three-colour pastel technique in France.

Hans **Eworth**

● c.1520–c.1574　🏛 FLEMISH　🖌 OILS

Antwerp-born, Hans Eworth arrived in England in 1549. His works are difficult to identify. Look for very pale faces with tight, hard eyes; carefully observed and outlined figures, encased in lavish costumes and jewellery.

KEY WORKS: *Sir John Luttrell*, 1550 (Private Collection); *Portrait of Elizabeth Roydon, Lady Golding*, 1563 (London: Tate Collection); *Portrait of a Lady*, c.1565–68 (London: Tate Collection)

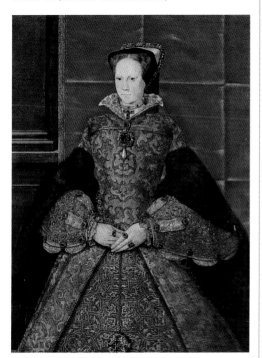

🔼 *Queen Mary I* Hans Eworth, 1554, London: Society of Antiquaries. Painted shortly after her marriage to Philip II of Spain, Mary wears his gift of the famous Peregrina pearl.

Nicholas **Hilliard**

● 1547–1619　🏛 BRITISH　🖌 WATERCOLOURS

The son of an Exeter goldsmith, Hilliard trained as a jeweller. He was the principal portrait painter during the reign of Elizabeth I. Hilliard was especially known for miniatures, which he produced in quantity to pay the bills for a large family. His reputation extended to France, which he visited around 1577–78. Look for innovative oval format, symbolism, French elegance, and fine outline. Life-size portraits of Elizabeth I still exist.

KEY WORKS: *Queen Elizabeth I*, c.1575 (London: National Portrait Gallery); *Robert Dudley, Earl of Leicester*, 1576 (London: National Portrait Gallery); *Young Man Among Roses*, c.1590 (London: Victoria & Albert Museum)

Isaac **Oliver**

● c.1565–1617　🏛 BRITISH
🖌 WATERCOLOURS; DRAWINGS

The son of a Huguenot goldsmith who settled in England in 1568, Oliver painted miniatures (portraits, and mythological and religious images). He was a pupil of Hilliard, but adopted a different style, with strong shadows. His life revolved around the courts of Elizabeth I and James I. A visit to Venice in 1590s led to a softer style and richer colours.

KEY WORKS: *Charity*, c.1596–1617 (London: Tate Collection); *Lodovick Stuart, 1st Duke of Richmond, and 2nd Duke of Lennox*, c.1605 (London: National Portrait Gallery)

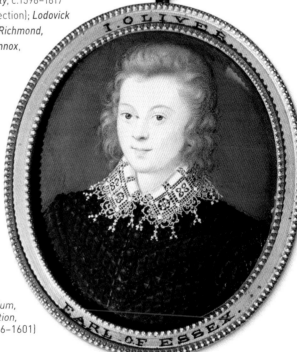

▶▶ *Portrait thought to be of Robert Devereux* Isaac Oliver, c.1590s, miniature, watercolour on vellum, Beauchamp Collection, UK. Devereux (1566–1601) was a favourite of Queen Elizabeth I.

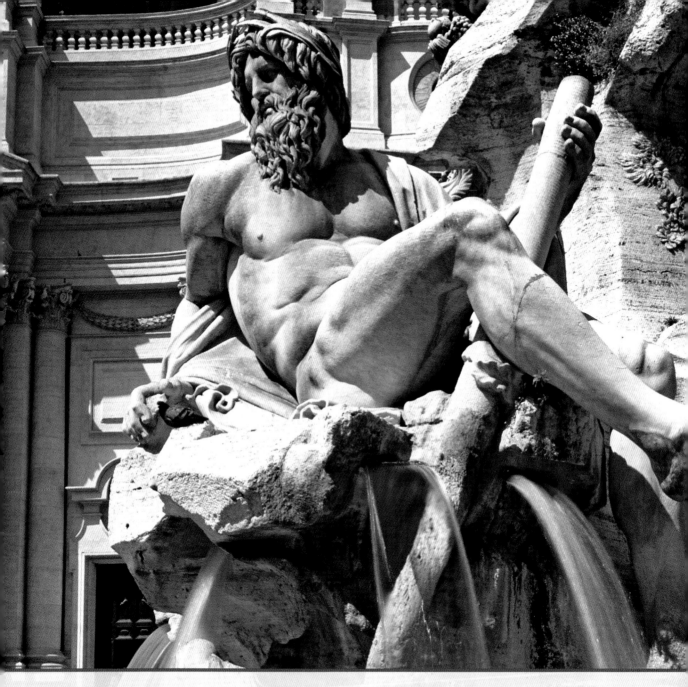

The Baroque Era
c.1600–1700

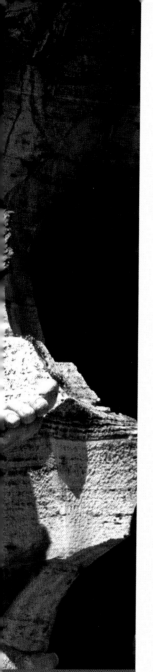

"Baroque" was first used disparagingly to describe something artificially extravagant and complex. Only relatively recently has it been used to denote the art and architecture of the 17th century – an era that saw the creation of some of the most grandiose and spectacular buildings, paintings, and sculpture in the history of art.

The magnificent art and architecture of the period was reminiscent of grand opera, an art form that developed in 17th-century Italy. Artists too assumed a grandeur not known before, sometimes adding to their role of creative practitioner that of impresario, art dealer, courtier, and diplomat.

Ideological division

The reasons for this extravagance lay in societies pulled apart by deep ideological and religious divisions. On one side were those fiercely committed to the absolute authority of the Catholic Church and the "Divine Right of Kings" with their requirements of unquestioning obedience. On the other were those committed to Protestant reform and a belief in self-determination personally and nationally. The former used art without restraint to overwhelm and impress, creating such wonders as the Baroque churches and fountains of Rome and the palace of

◄ Fountain of the Four Rivers *Gianlorenzo Bernini, 1651, marble and travertine, Piazza Navona, Rome.* The magnificence of Bernini's sculptural projects was inspired by a belief that, through art, he was expressing the absolute authority of God and the Catholic Church.

Versailles outside Paris. The latter disapproved of all worldly show, destroying religious art, whitewashing the interiors of churches and dispersing royal and noble collections.

The consequences of this ideological struggle are most clearly seen in three places. In England, Charles I's unyielding insistence on his divine right to rule led to his execution in 1649, the dispersal of his art treasures, and the institution of a Puritan Commonwealth that rejected any form of aesthetic experience. In the Netherlands, the Habsburgs attempted to stem the tide of Protestant revolt, finally conceding and then formally recognizing a compromise which split the Low Countries in two: a Protestant north (Holland) and a Catholic south (Flanders). The new republic of Holland, mercantile and bourgeois, was able to strengthen and expand its trading empire, especially in the East Indies. This new wealth funded a magnificent flowering of art. What the Dutch wanted were landscapes, seascapes, still lifes, and genre scenes of everyday life to hang on the walls of their townhouses, and which they could buy and sell like other commercial goods.

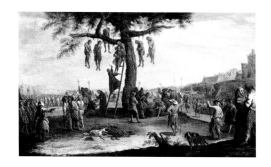

>> *The Hanging, after engraving by Jacques Callot (1592–1635), oil on canvas, Clermont-Ferrand: Musée Bargoin.* Callot's series of engravings "The Miseries of War" illustrated many of the horrors of the Thirty Years' War.

Rise of France

In central Europe the Austrian Habsburgs faced another Protestant revolt, this time in Bohemia. By 1618, this had given rise to general warfare, with other powers sucked in according to their religious affiliations: the Baltic powers, Denmark, and Sweden on the Protestant side against the Habsburgs and their Catholic allies. Religion was the starting point but by the 1630s the war had become a trial of strength between France and the Habsburgs. The Thirty Years' War, as it was afterwards known, was the most brutal yet fought in Europe, carving a swathe of destruction across Germany and leaving perhaps one million dead. In some areas, 40 per cent

of the population was killed. It ended in 1648, with France emerging as the most powerful state in Europe.

This new dominance was brilliantly exploited by Louis XIV, whose direct personal reign lasted 54 years. He asserted his authority by controlling his court from his own vast creation, the largest palace in Europe, Versailles.

Chapelle Royale, Versailles Louis XIV's chapel was begun by royal architect Jules Hardouin-Mansart in 1689. During services the upper balcony was reserved for the royal family, while the nobles stood below.

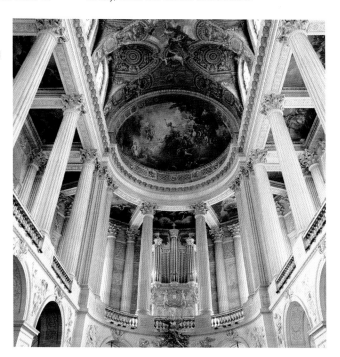

TIMELINE: 1600–1700

1609 Invention of the telescope (Holland); Dutch Revolt ended by treaty between Spain and the Netherlands

1630 Foundation of the English Massachusetts Bay colony

1633 Galileo condemned for heresy by the inquisition

1649 Execution of Charles I in England

1600 **1620** **1640**

1618 Start of the Thirty Years' War

1621 Hostilities renewed between Spain and the Netherlands

1636 French intervene in the Thirty Years' War

1648 Treaty of Westphalia ends the Thirty Years' War

1659 Treaty of Pyrenees confirms French dominance in Western Europe

His brand of absolutist rule – centralizing and martial, visually spectacular and rigidly ceremonial – created a style of kingship that was increasingly imitated at other European courts, notably by Peter the Great in Russia.

A new style of monarchy

In the end the extravagance of Baroque art and architecture and the beliefs that it sought to promote were unsustainable. The future would lie not with unquestioning faith and obedience but with self-reliance. By the end of the century Spain was in decline politically and economically, central Europe was exhausted and devastated, and the Papacy was forced to accept that it would have to live with rival Christian churches. France continued to prosper, but the soon-to-re-emerge power was England, which was evolving a new form of constitutional monarchy and which was destined to supersede Holland as the world's leading trading nation.

》 SCIENCE IN THE 17TH CENTURY

In the course of the 17th century, European monarchs, as well as being generous patrons of the arts, also became sponsors of the sciences, in particular astronomy and physics. State backing was given to science in England in 1662 when the Royal Society was established. A French equivalent, the Académie Royale des Sciences, followed in 1666. The century was characterized by an accelerating scientific revolution. The telescope, the microscope, the slide rule, the thermometer, and the barometer were all invented before 1650. As early as 1609, the Italian scientist Galileo Galilei used a telescope to discover four moons of Jupiter. He made other important observations that confirmed the Copernican theory of the Solar System. By the end of the century, Sir Isaac Newton in England had laid the theoretical foundations of the new science of physics.

《 **Isaac Newton's telescope** As well as discovering the laws of motion and gravity, Newton wrote a comprehensive treatise on optics.

》 **Visit of Louis XIV to the Académie Royale des Sciences in 1667** By the mid-17th century, it was clear that scientific advances would play a key role in the development of states. Official patronage duly followed.

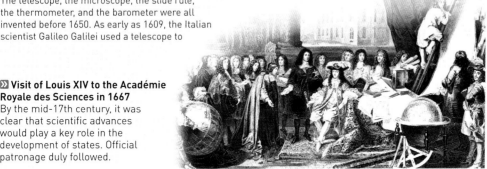

1660 Restoration of the monarchy in England

1667 Completion of Bernini's Piazza, St Peter's, Rome

1683 Ottoman threat contained after siege of Vienna

1688 The Glorious Revolution in England: overthrow of James II

1694 Bank of England founded

1660   **1000**   **1700**

1662 Royal Society established in England

1678 Louis XIV initiates major building works at Versailles

1685 Edict of Nantes revoked: French Protestants face renewed persecution

1689 Accession of Peter the Great, Russia

1699 Habsburgs recover Hungary from Ottomans

The Baroque

c.1590–1700

The dominant style of the 17th century, the Baroque was used by the Catholic Church to proclaim its continuing power. The best examples are found in Italy, Spain, France, Austria, Southern Germany, and Central Europe. It was loved by absolute monarchs who wanted to emphasize their worldly authority and riches.

"The style of absolutism" was used by the Catholic Church as a means of harnessing the magnificence of art to influence the largest possible audience. Exploiting the ideas of Classicism and religious doctrine, work was to be visually stunning and emotionally engaging to reflect the new Counter-Reformation confidence of the Church. The subsequent boldness of the artists' styles translates as huge freestanding sculptures, exaggerated decorations, intensely lit, emotional oil paintings with grand operatic-style themes, and a new architecture, planned around a series of geometrically controlled spaces to create an animated grandeur. Its hallmarks are illusion, movement, drama, rich colour, and pomposity.

Fontana del Moro
Gianlorenzo Bernini, 1653, stone, Rome: Piazza Navona.
Originally designed in 1576 by Giacomo della Porta, the *Fontana del Moro* was then altered by Bernini in 1653. He designed the central statue of a muscular Moor holding a dolphin. The tritons blowing shells, from which water exits, are 19th-century additions.

Subjects

Religious subjects were of paramount importance, especially the lives of saints and martyrs. These included recent saints such as St Ignatius Loyola, founder of the Jesuits, and the Spanish mystic St Teresa of Ávila (both canonized in 1622). Mythological characters, such as the chaste nymph Daphne or Proserpine, raped by Pluto, were used to illustrate religious ideals of purity. Statues of allegorical figures – Peace, Faith, Modesty, Chastity – were also common. Portraits tended to be bombastic and self-consciously dramatic. However, the everyday also found a place with scenes that included taverns, card players, and water sellers.

What to look for

The best examples of secular Baroque decoration are Carracci's rarely seen frescoes for the vault of the sculpture gallery of the Farnese Palace in Rome. To complement the outstanding Farnese collection of Antique sculpture, Carracci created on the vaulted ceiling a picture gallery of mythological scenes illustrating stories from Ovid's *Metamorphoses*. The resulting effect is one of the triumphs of the Baroque ambition – to marry architecture, painting, and sculpture.

KEY EVENTS

1595	Annibale Carracci summoned from Bologna to decorate Farnese Palace, Rome
1601	Caravaggio paints the first of two versions of *The Supper at Emmaus*
1629	Bernini starts work on St Peter's and the Palazzo Barberini
1634	Charles I's Banqueting House, London: ceiling by Rubens completed
1663	Bernini's colonnaded piazza in front of St Peter's
1669	Louis XIV orders massive reconstruction programme at Versailles

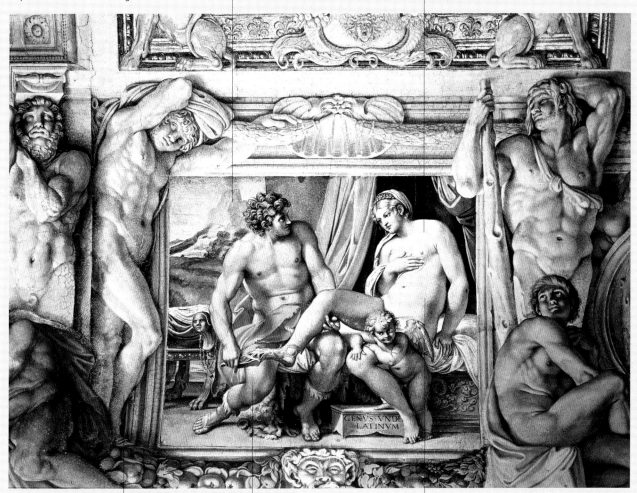

Venus and Anchises *Annibale Carracci, 1597–1604.* Part of Carracci's frescoed cycle depicting *The Loves of the Gods*. Anchises captures the heart of the goddess Venus.

The landscape shows Mount Ida, where Anchises traditionally met Venus

Venus disguised herself as a mortal and seduced Anchises. Their child was Aeneas, the founder of Rome

All the figures are based on studies of live models

Anchises was a Trojan shepherd. He is shown removing Venus's sandal

Venus wore jewels and sweet-smelling perfume. The couch belonged to Anchises

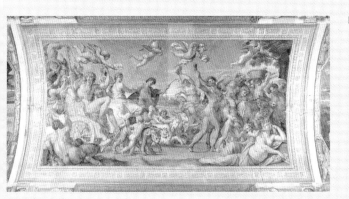

The central panel depicts the triumph of Bacchus and Ariadne, for which the artist made a detailed study of Classical reliefs. So disappointed was Carracci by the small fee he received for the work that he took to drink, and died aged only 49.

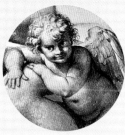

Cupid, the son of Venus, is nearly always shown as a pretty, curly-haired boy who is present whenever love is in the air.

>> **THE SCHOOL OF BOLOGNA** c.1550–1650

Bologna never achieved the artistic pre-eminence of Florence, Venice, or Rome, but nonetheless this ancient university town made a significant contribution to the arts of Italy and Europe. Situated midway between Florence and Venice, the School of Bologna drew inspiration from both, creating its own distinctive style. In particular, Bolognese artists tried to synthesize Florentine classicism with Venetian theatricality, seen most successfully in the works of Carracci, Domenichino, Guercino, and Reni. The Bolognese School style was much imitated in the 18th century, but has been despised for most of the 20th.

Guido **Reni**

● **1575–1642** ⚐ **ITALIAN** ✍ **OILS; FRESCO**

One of the principal Bolognese masters. Greatly inspired by Raphael, he was much admired in the 17th and 18th centuries, and much despised in the 20th. Reni's style was largely influenced by his visits to Rome, the first of which came soon after 1660. His images of intense and idealized (unreal and artificial) emotional experiences are usually religious. His mythological works do not have the same levels of intensity, but are highly polished pieces. He himself was very beautiful but remained celibate – two qualities that are reflected in his paintings, which convey a remote and unapproachable beauty. Are they too self-consciously slick, posed, and theatrical for popular 20th-century taste?

In his work, look for eyeballs rolling up to heaven (as a means of signalling intensity of feeling), and surprisingly subtle and sensitive paint handling.

KEY WORKS: *Deianeira Abducted by the Centaur Nessus*, 1621 (Paris: Musée du Louvre); *Susannah and the Elders*, c.1620 (London: National Gallery); *Lady with a Lapis Lazuli Bowl*, c.1630s (Birmingham: Museums and Art Gallery); *St Mary Magdalene*, c.1634–42 (London: National Gallery)

☑ *Atalanta and Hippomenes* Guido Reni, c.1612, 206 x 297 cm (81 x 117 in), oil on canvas, Madrid: Museo del Prado. Atalanta, the virgin huntress, would challenge her suitors to a race in which losing was punishable by death. Hippomenes distracted her by dropping three golden apples given to him by Venus and thus overtook her.

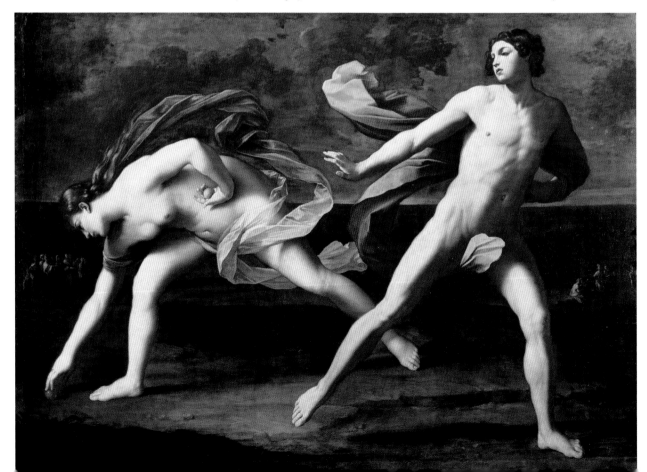

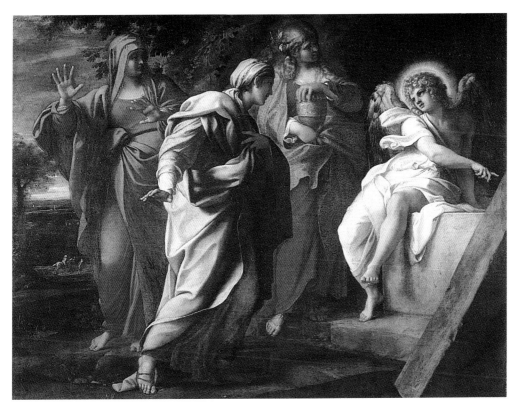

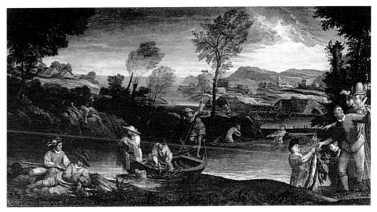

<The Holy Women at
Christ's Tomb* Annibale
Carracci, c.1597–98,
121 x 145.5 cm (47 ⅓ x
57 ⅓ in), oil on canvas,
St Petersburg:
Hermitage Museum.
All the figures are from
studies of live models.

Annibale **Carracci**

● 1560–1609 🏛 ITALIAN 🎨 OILS; FRESCO

Born in Bologna, Carracci lived in Rome from 1595.
He was the most talented member of a brilliant trio
(with brother Agostino and cousin Ludovico). He
revived Italian art from the doldrums that followed
Michelangelo, but was a victim of change of fashion
from around 1850.

The arguments for his greatness are that he is
as good as Raphael (brilliant draughtsmanship,
observation of nude, harmonious compositions);
as good as Michelangelo (anatomical knowledge,
heroic idealization – his frescoes in the Farnese
Palace are at par with Michelangelo's in the
Sistine Chapel); and as good as Titian (richness
of colour). Carracci was original: he invented
caricature and his early genre scenes and
ideal landscapes are full of fresh observation.
He influenced Rubens and Poussin.

The arguments against his greatness are that
he was too eclectic – merely a plagiarist with no
originality, the whole less than the individual
parts. Look who his followers were – the awful
Bolognese School. However, he made a large

number of wonderful drawings, which are full of
humour and personal touches. He had a strong
belief in drawing and observing from life as an
answer to sterile academicism – to the point of
establishing a school to teach it. This belief was
shared in a different way by the Impressionists,
especially Cézanne. Carracci gave up painting
almost entirely in 1606.

KEY WORKS: *The Butcher's Shop*, 1580s (Oxford: Christ
Church Picture Gallery); *Domine Quo Vadis?*, 1601–02
(London: National Gallery)

❯ *Fishing* Annibale
Carracci, 1585–88,
136 x 253 cm (53 ½ x
99 ½ in), oil on canvas,
Paris: Musée du Louvre.
Carracci created the
ideal landscape, in
which a classical vision
of nature becomes the
setting for a narrative.

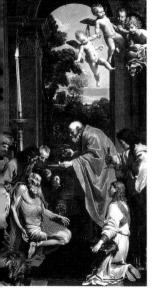

⌃ The Last Sacrament of St Jerome
Domenichino, 1614, oil on canvas, Rome: Vatican Museums.
St Jerome, one of the four fathers of the Christian Church, died near Bethlehem on 30 September 420.

Domenichino

● 1581–1641 ⚲ ITALIAN ✍ FRESCO; OILS; DRAWINGS

Bologna-born, Domenichino worked in Rome and Naples. Look for idealization that is influenced by Raphael and antiquity (unlike his contemporary Caravaggio) and harmonious classical landscapes with mythological themes. His figures have expressive gestures that symbolize emotion but do not embody expression. He was a fine draughtsman (Windsor Castle's Royal Library has a superb collection of his drawings), and an excellent portraitist.

KEY WORKS: *Monsignor Agucchi*, c.1610 (York: City Art Gallery); *Landscape with Tobias Laying Hold of the Fish*, c.1610–13 (London: National Gallery); *St Cecilia with an Angel Holding Music*, 1620 (Paris: Musée du Louvre)

Giovanni **Lanfranco**

● 1582–1647 ⚲ ITALIAN ✍ FRESCO; OILS

Lanfranco was a key figure who established the enthusiasm for the large-scale illusionistic decoration of churches and palaces in Rome and Naples. He painted crowds of figures on clouds floating on ceilings, with extreme foreshortening and brilliant light. Huge scale, excessive, and inspiring – his work needs to be seen *in situ*.

KEY WORKS: *Elijah Receiving Bread from the Widow of Zarephath*, c.1621–24 (Los Angeles: J. Paul Getty Museum); *Moses and the Messengers from Canaan*, 1621–24 (Los Angeles: J. Paul Getty Museum); *Assumption of the Virgin*, 1625–27 (Rome: S. Andrea della Valle); *Ecstacy of St Margaret of Cortona*, c.1630s (Florence: Palazzo Pitti)

⌄ **Christ and the Woman of Samaria** *Giovanni Lanfranco, 1625–28, 66 x 86.5 cm (26 x 34 in), oil on canvas, Oxford: Ashmolean Museum.* Although from an enemy tribe she realized He was a prophet.

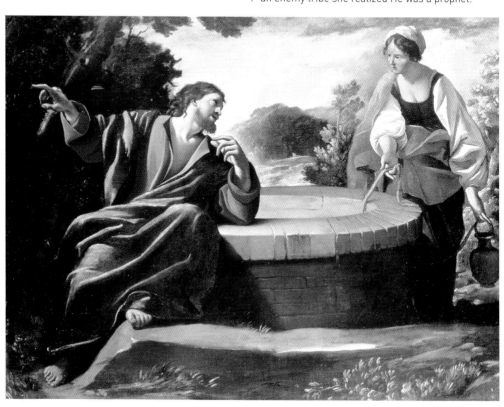

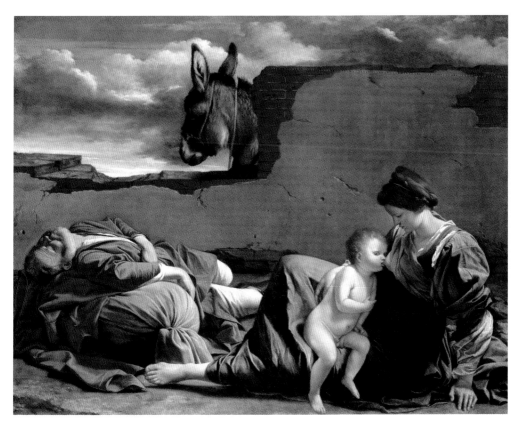

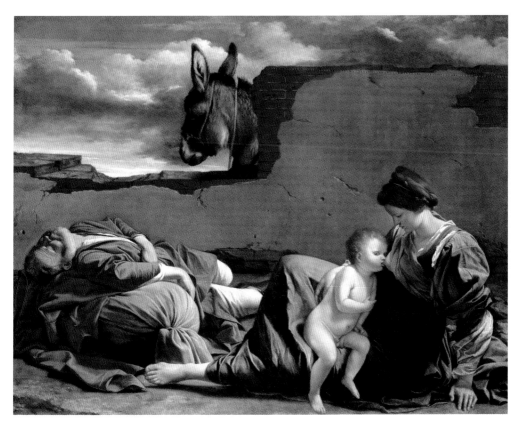 **Rest on the Flight into Egypt** *Orazio Gentileschi, c.1615–20, 175.6 x 218 cm (69 x 85 ⅘ in), oil on canvas, Birmingham (UK): Museums and Art Gallery.* The use of harmonious blues and yellows is typical of Gentileschi.

Orazio **Gentileschi**

● 1563–1639 🏛 ITALIAN 🎨 OILS

Gentileschi was a greatly esteemed Tuscan. He was born in Pisa, but settled in Rome in 1576. He was much influenced by Caravaggio, but without his wild energy and imagination: he domesticated Caravaggio's excesses. Look for large-scale, decorative works, simplified subjects and compositions, cool colours, sharp-edged draperies, and unconvincing realism. In 1626, he became court painter to Charles I of England, a safe choice artistically, if unwise politically.

KEY WORKS: *The Lute Player*, c.1610 (Washington DC: National Gallery of Art); *Annunciation*, 1621–23 (Turin: Galleria Sabauda)

Alessandro **Algardi**

● 1598–1654 🏛 ITALIAN 🎨 SCULPTURE

Algardi was the best sculptor in Baroque Rome after Bernini. The two were great rivals and Algardi's studio seized control when Bernini was briefly out of favour with Pope Innocent X's court for shoddy work on St Peter's. Algardi was more obsessed than Bernini with the classical ideal and the philosophy of the "Antique", so his work is more solid, permanent, and psychologically real than the transitory fluidity of Bernini. His figures are heavily classical in stance, robust, muscular, and powerful. Pieces were often symbolically crafted with careful attention to classical geometry and line. He preferred the statuesque nobility of cool white marble to Bernini's lively movement. Look out for his sensitive terracotta models. His marble reliefs became prototypes for supplanting painted altarpieces with sculptured ones. His intense classicism influenced French Baroque development and he became a great friend of Poussin.

KEY WORKS: *Portrait of Gaspare Mola*, 1630s (St Petersburg: Hermitage Museum); *Tomb of Leo XI*, 1634–44 (Rome: St Peter's); *Decapitation of St Paul*, 1641–47 (Bologna: San Paolo Maggiore); *Pope Liberius Baptizing the Neophytes*, 1645–48 (Paris: Musée du Louvre); *Cardinal Paolo Emilio Zacchia*, 1650s (Florence: Bargello)

Caravaggio

● 1571–1610 📖 ITALIAN ✍ OILS

Michelangelo Merisi da Caravaggio was the only major artist with a serious criminal record (hooliganism and murder). He died of malarial fever at the age of 38. A contemporary of Shakespeare (1564–1616), he was immensely influential.

From his native Milan, Caravaggio moved to Rome in 1592 where two distinct phases in his career occurred: an early period (1592–99), where he learned from the examples of the High Renaissance and the Antique; and a mature period (1599–1606), where he rejected decorum and turned to an exhilarating realism, displaying a complete disregard for proprieties and accepted rules. Nonetheless, he was well-received in Papal circles and executed many important Church commissions. He lived in a state of hyperexcitement, both in life and

≫ **The Supper at Emmaus** *1601, 141 x 196.2 cm (55 ½ x 77 ¼ in), oil and tempera on canvas, London: National Gallery.* Caravaggio painted a second, more subdued version of this work five years later.

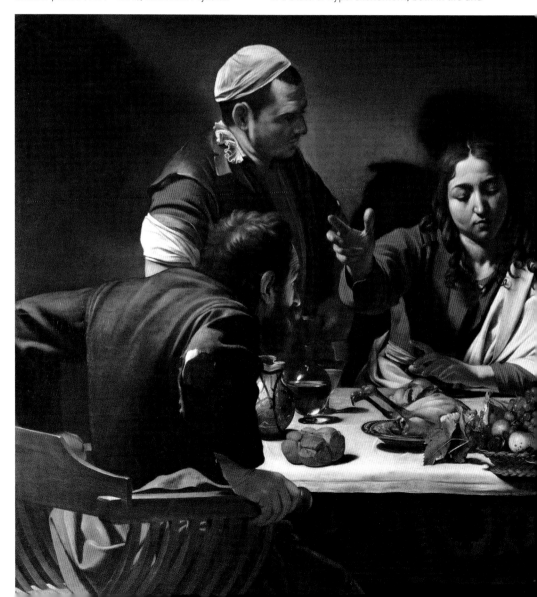

in his art. In 1606, at the height of his success, his tempestuous character led him into a murderous brawl over a wager on a tennis match. He was forced to flee to Malta, where, after another fight, he moved on to Sicily. Wounded in Palermo, Caravaggio died near Naples while waiting for a Papal pardon. It arrived three days after his death. His many followers took up his mantle, ensuring his contribution to the future development of art, notably in Naples, Spain, and the Netherlands. Echoes of Caravaggio's influence are seen in the works of artists as diverse as La Tour, Rembrandt, and Velásquez.

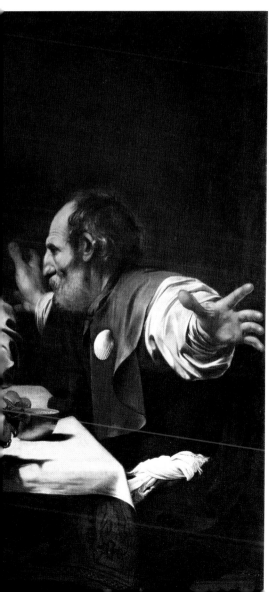

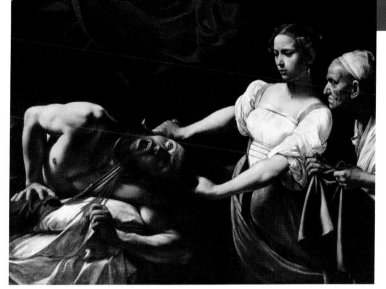

Style

Caravaggio is known for sensational subjects, in which severed heads and martyrdom are shown in gory detail, and young men display charms that suggest decadence and corruption (his tastes were heterosexual, and his girlfriend a prostitute). His biblical subjects show immense moments of dramatic revelation. His use of peasants and street urchins as models for Christ and the saints caused deep offence to many. His technique is equally sensational and theatrical, with tense compositions, masterly foreshortening, and dramatic lighting with vivid contrasts of light and shade (*chiaroscuro*). His later work, after 1606, was hastily executed and is more contemplative and less forceful.

What to look for

Early works by Caravaggio tend to be quite small, with half-length figures and still-life compositions. Later, his figures gained plasticity, and shadows became richer and deeper. Still-life details can contain symbolic meaning; for instance, a fruit that is full of wormholes. Also, look closely at the modelling of flesh to observe the range of subtle rainbow colours used.

KEY WORKS: *Calling of St Matthew*, 1599–1600 (Rome: S. Luigi dei Francesi); *The Conversion of St Paul*, 1601 (Rome: S. Maria del Popolo); *The Incredulity of St Thomas*, 1601–02 (Florence: Galleria degli Uffizi)

🔼 *Judith and Holofernes*
1599, 145 x 195 cm (57 x 76 ¾ in), oil on canvas, Rome: Palazzo Barberini. Caravaggio's interpretation emphasizes real-life drama and shock rather than the symbolism of virtue defeating sin.

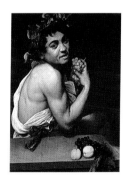

🔼 *The Sick Bacchus*
1591, 67 x 53 cm (26 ⅓ x 20 ⅘ in), oil on canvas, Rome: Galleria Borghese. Most of the early erotic works were commissioned by high-ranking Church dignitaries.

Bartolommeo **Manfredi**

◐ **1593–c.1622** Ⓝ ITALIAN ✍ OILS

A little-known artist who was a successful imitator and follower of Caravaggio, Manfredi painted decadent everyday scenes as well as mythological and religious subjects. He preferred allegorical themes of conflict and discord. His style was more rough and ready than his celebrated master, but he copied Caravaggio's theatrical lighting effects and also foreshortened the action so the viewer feels like an accomplice to the scene. Along with fellow *Caravaggisti* like Valentin, with whom Manfredi was often confused, he influenced northern artists who stayed in Rome (e.g. Honthorst and Terbrugghen).

KEY WORKS: *Cupid Chastized*, 1610 (Art Institute of Chicago); *Allegory of the Four Seasons*, c.1610 (Ohio: Dayton Art Institute); *Cain Murdering Abel*, c.1610 (Vienna: Kunsthistorisches Museum); *The Fortune Teller*, c.1610–15 (Detroit Institute of Arts); *The Triumph of David*, c.1615 (Paris: Musée du Louvre)

Guercino

◐ **1591–1666** Ⓝ ITALIAN ✍ OILS; FRESCO

Guercino's full name was Giovanni Francesco Barbieri Guercino. He came from Bologna and was self-taught and successful in his day. Although now regarded as one of the most important 17th-century Italian artists, he was neglected until recently. He was at his best in his early work, which is lively, natural, and has exciting light and strong colour. He also produced wonderful drawings. The Bolognese pope summoned him to Rome in 1621; thereafter Guercino lost his spontaneity and became boringly classical. "Guercino" means "squint-eyed".

KEY WORKS: *The Dead Christ Mourned by Two Angels*, c.1617–18 (London: National Gallery); *The Woman Taken in Adultery*, c.1621 (London: Dulwich Picture Gallery); *Aurora* (fresco), 1621 (Rome: Ceiling of the Casino, Villa Ludovisi); *The Liberation of St Peter by an Angel*, c.1622–23 (Madrid: Museo del Prado)

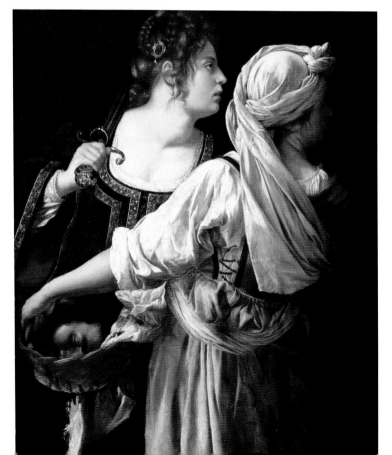

Artemisia **Gentileschi**

◐ **c.1597–c.1652** Ⓝ ITALIAN ✍ OILS

The daughter of Orazio Gentileschi, Artemisia was a better painter. Her tendency towards bloodthirsty themes was probably related to her own dramatic life, including being raped at 19 and tortured during the subsequent court case to see if she was truthful. She chose dramatic subjects, often erotic, bloody, and with a woman as victim or gaining revenge. She was stylistically close to Caravaggio – she made powerful use of foreshortening and *chiaroscuro*. She was the first female member of the Florentine Academy.

KEY WORKS: *Judith Slaying Holofernes*, c.1620 (Florence: Galleria degli Uffizi); *Self-Portrait as the Allegory of Painting*, 1630s (Royal Collection)

◐ *Judith and her Maidservant* Artemisia Gentileschi, 1612–13, 114 x 93.5 cm (44 ⅘ x 36 ⅘ in), oil on canvas, Florence: Palazzo Pitti. These depictions of Old Testament heroines such as Judith appealed greatly to private collectors throughout Europe.

Salvator **Rosa**

● c.1615–73   ITALIAN   OILS; ENGRAVINGS

Rosa was one of the first wild men of art – quarrelsome, anti-authority, self-promoting, and lover of the macabre. He was a poet, actor, musician, and satirist. He is now best remembered for large, dark, stormy, fantastic mountainous landscapes and unpleasant witchcraft scenes (both much collected in the 18th and early 19th centuries). He was said to have fought by day and painted by night.

KEY WORKS: *The Return of Astraea*, 1640–45 (Vienna: Kunsthistorisches Museum); *Human Fragility*, c.1656 (Cambridge: Fitzwilliam Museum); *The Spirit of Samuel Called up before Saul by the Witch of Endor*, 1668 (Paris: Musée du Louvre)

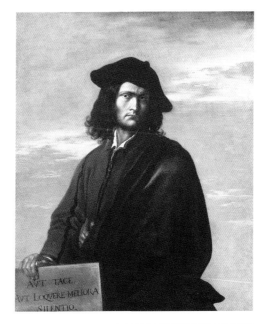

◀ *Self-Portrait Salvator Rosa, c.1641, 116.3 x 94 cm (45 ¾ x 37 in), oil on canvas, London: National Gallery.* The Latin inscription below Rosa's hand means "Be quiet, unless your speech be better than silence." He painted a companion portrait of his mistress Lucrezia whom he portrayed as one of the Muses of Poetry.

Pietro da **Cortona**

● 1596–1669   ITALIAN   FRESCO; OILS; STUCCO

Virtuoso architect, decorator, and painter, Cortona was much sought after by Catholic grandees in Italy and France. He was known as the key creator of Roman High Baroque and for large-scale, extreme, illusionistic paintings, where ceilings open up into a bold, dramatic, rich theatre of space, colour, human activity, architecture, learned allusion, and spiritual uplift.

KEY WORKS: *Allegory of Divine Providence and Barberini Power*, 1633–39 (Rome: Palazzo Barberini); *Glorification of the Reign of Urban VIII*, 1633–39 (Rome: Palazzo Barberini); *Allegories of Virtue and Planets*, 1640–47 (Florence: Palazzo Pitti)

Mattia **Preti**

● c.1613–99   ITALIAN   FRESCO; OILS

Preti was an accomplished painter of large-scale decoration that successfully combines the realism of Caravaggio and the theatricality of grand Venetian painting (it sounds unlikely, but he showed it could be done and thereby had much influence on the development of exuberant Baroque decorations).

KEY WORKS: *Concert*, c.1630 (St Petersburg: Hermitage Museum); *The Marriage at Cana*, c.1655–60 (London: National Gallery); *The Martyrdom of St Paul*, c.1656–59 (Houston: Museum of Fine Arts); *Clorinda Rescuing Sofronia and Olindo*, c.1660 (Los Angeles: J. Paul Getty Museum)

Luca **Giordano**

● c.1634–1705   ITALIAN   OILS; DRAWINGS; FRESCO

Giordano was the most important Italian decorative artist of the late 17th century. Prolific and energetic, he created very theatrical, large-scale work and was a successful decorator of palaces (especially ceilings). He loved mythological subjects, which enabled him to emphasize dramatic action, bold compositions, contrasts of light and dark, silhouettes, violence and lust, and subjects that polarize good and evil. Giordano's last work was the Treasury Chapel ceiling of San Martino, Naples. He was nicknamed "Luca Fa Presto" (Luke works quickly).

KEY WORKS: *The Fall of the Rebel Angels*, 1666 (Vienna: Kunsthistorisches Museum); *Allegory*, 1670 (Los Angeles: J. Paul Getty Museum); *Death of Seneca*, c.1684 (Paris: Musée du Louvre); *Celestial Glory and Triumph of the Habsburgs* (fresco), 1692–94 (Spain: El Escorial)

Gianlorenzo **Bernini**

● 1598–1680 🏴 ITALIAN ✍ SCULPTURE; OILS

Bernini was a devoted Roman Catholic for whom art was the emotional inspiration and glorification of godliness and purity. Although gifted as a painter, he despised the medium, regarding sculpture as the "Truth". He set sculpture free from its previous preoccupation with earthly gravity and intellectual emotion, allowing it to move and soar, giving it a visionary and theatrical quality that it had never had before.

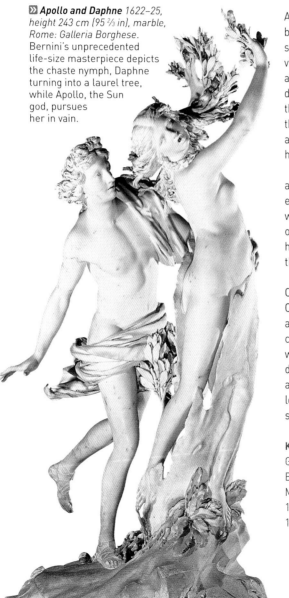

» *Apollo and Daphne* 1622–25, height 243 cm (95 ⅔ in), marble, Rome: Galleria Borghese. Bernini's unprecedented life-size masterpiece depicts the chaste nymph, Daphne turning into a laurel tree, while Apollo, the Sun god, pursues her in vain.

A child prodigy, Bernini had a sparkling personality, brilliant wit, and wrote comedies – qualities that shine through his work in sculpture. He was a virtuoso technically, able to carve marble so it appeared to move and come to life, or had the delicacy of the finest lace. He epitomized the Baroque style with its love of grandeur, theatricality, movement, and passionate emotion, and his finest works are to be found in Rome where he was the favourite artist of the Catholic Church.

At his best, he blended sculpture, architecture, and painting into an extravagant theatrical ensemble, nowhere more so than in his fountains, where the play of water and refractions of light over his sculptured forms of larger-than-life human figures and animals creates a vision that is literally out of this world.

In creating the centrepiece of the Cornaro Chapel – commissioned by Cardinal Federigo Cornaro – Bernini accepted St Teresa's spiritual account of her mystical union with Christ. The central figure is of an angel piercing Teresa's heart with an arrow of divine love. Modern interpretations draw parallels between the appearance of the angel and Cupid, the son of Venus with his love-laden darts. This emphasizes the seemingly sexual quality of the saint's mystical experience.

KEY WORKS: *The Rape of Proserpine*, 1621–22 (Rome: Galleria Borghese); *David*, 1623 (Rome: Galleria Borghese); *Constanza Bonarelli*, 1635 (Florence: Museo Nazionale del Bargello); *Cornaro Chapel*, 1646 (see page 129); *The Blessed Lodovica Albertoni*, 1671–74 (Rome: S. Francesco a Ripa)

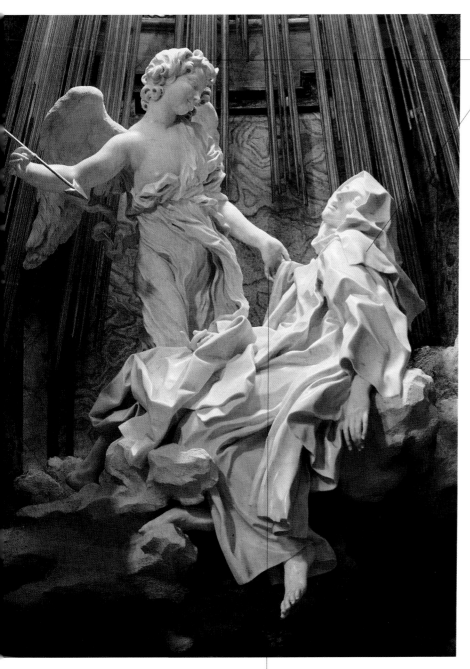

The angel looks adoringly at St Teresa, ready to plunge his arrow into her heart for a second time

Bernini's ability to make marble seem like flowing drapery was one of his most exceptional skills

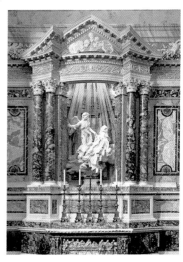

⌃ **The elaborate** and carefully calculated setting brilliantly heightens the full visual impact of the white marble figure group. High above are vaulted painted heavens. The Cornaro family, in privileged front-row loggia boxes, sat below.

》 TECHNIQUES

No sculptor before Bernini used light to accomplish an illusion of life so successfully. Unlike diffused light of the Renaissance, this directed light accentuates the poised moment of action. Warming reds and yellows in the lower human zone balance the religious purity of the white marble group.

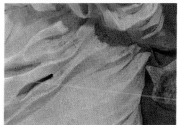

⌃ **Cornaro Chapel** *1645–52, 350 cm (137 ⁴⁄₅ in), marble, gilded wood, bronze, Rome: Santa Maria della Vittoria.* The centrepiece of the lavishly decorated but intimate and candlelit Baroque Church of Santa Maria della Vittoria in Rome is the Cornaro Chapel. It contains one of Bernini's most ambitious works, created to resemble a miniature theatre.

Bernini's attention to detail can be seen in the precise carving of the little finger of the angel's left hand

Nicolas **Poussin**

c.1593–1665 FRENCH OILS

The founder of French classical painting, Poussin was immensely influential on French artists up to (and including) Cézanne. He established the standard to be lived up to.

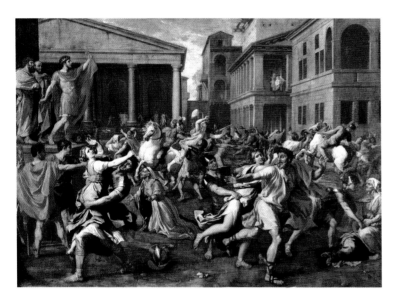

⌃ *The Rape of the Sabines* c.1637–38, 159 cm x 206 cm (62 ½ x 81 in), oil on canvas, Paris: Musée du Louvre. Worried about the declining birth rate, Romulus, Rome's founder, arranged a feast that resulted in young Romans marrying Sabine maidens.

⌄ *Portrait of the Artist* 1650, 97 x 73 cm (38 x 29 in), oil on canvas, Paris: Musée du Louvre. A grave Poussin makes no concession to vanity in his portraiture.

The son of a French farmer, Poussin became inspired when an artist arrived to decorate his village church. He struggled in early years through poverty and ignorance until, during a trip to Paris, engravings of Raphael's works exposed him to the Italian High Renaissance. Poussin then set off for Rome. Except for two years spent as court painter to Louis XIII (1640–42), he worked in the epicentre of Baroque Italy, though he was more at home with the classical style. He did not survive to see his style glorified by the French Academy in the late 17th century.

Poussin's paintings, usually biblical or from Greco-Roman antiquity, are severe, intense, and intellectual in subject matter and style, as well as references. There are complex and allegorical subjects with a moral theme, constant references to classical antiquity, and a hidden geometrical framework of verticals, horizontals, and diagonals into which the figures are placed, and by which they are tied together.

What to look for

Note how the groups of figures are positioned flat on the surface of the picture, like a carved bas-relief (another classical reference). Although notionally in motion, the figures have the stationary quality of statues. Poussin liked well-sculpted nudes, especially muscular backs, arms, and legs, and drapery that could have been carved out of marble. The interweaving arrangements of arms and legs are like an intellectual puzzle (which belong to whom?). The dark-reddish quality of many of Poussin's works is because he painted on a red ground, which is now showing through the oil paint that has become transparent over time.

KEY WORKS: *Cephalus and Aurora*, c.1630 (London: National Gallery); *Landscape with the Ashes of Phocion*, c.1648 (Liverpool: Walker Art Gallery); *The Holy Family*, 1648 (Washington DC: National Gallery of Art)

⌄ *Arcadian Shepherds* c.1648–50, 58 x 121 cm (33 ½ x 47 ½ in), oil on canvas, Paris: Musée du Louvre. The shepherds are examining an inscription that reads, *Et in Arcadia Ego* (Even in Arcadia, I [Death] am ever present).

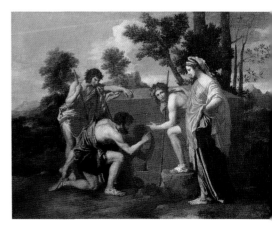

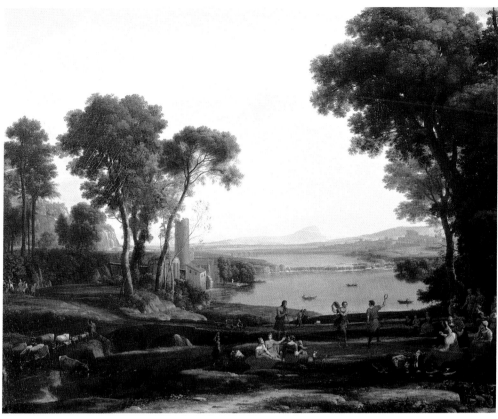

◀◀ *Landscape with the Marriage of Isaac and Rebekah* Claude Lorrain, 1648, 149 x 197 cm (58 x 77 in), oil on canvas, London: National Gallery. The Old Testament story lends artistic respectability to this pastoral landscape.

Moïse **Valentin**

◉ **c.1593–1632** 🏳 **FRENCH** ⚲ **OILS**

The son of an Italian, but from Boulogne in France, Valentin settled in Rome. Most of his known work dates from 1620. A Caravaggisti, he loved the plebeian side of art. More emotional and dramatic than Poussin, he preferred seedy, bawdy scenes.

KEY WORKS: *Christ and the Adulteress*, 1620s (Los Angeles: J. Paul Getty Museum); *The Expulsion of the Money-Changers from the Temple*, c.1620–25 (St Petersburg: Hermitage Museum)

Claude **Lorrain**

◉ **c.1600–82** 🏳 **FRENCH** ⚲ **OILS**

Also called Le Lorrain or Claude Gellée, Claude Lorrain was the originator of the pastoral or picturesque landscape and immensely influential and popular, especially in the 18th and early 19th centuries. Claude worked in and around Rome. His landscapes and seascapes are enjoyable on two levels: as exquisite depictions in their own right; and as a poetic setting for the staging of mythological or religious scenes. Notice how he moves your eye from side to side across the picture in measured steps via well-placed figures, buildings, or paths (*coulisse*), and at the same time takes you from warm foreground to cool, minutely detailed distance (aerial perspective).

A magical painter of light, he was the first artist to paint the sun. He used a formula of well-proven, balanced compositions and colours to produce a serene, luminous, and harmonious atmosphere – although somewhere in the airless heat there is usually a refreshing breeze: a rustle in the tree tops, an unfurling flag, the sails of a boat in the far distance, or birds gliding on a current of air.

KEY WORKS: *The Judgement of Paris*, 1645–46 (Washington DC: National Gallery of Art); *Landscape with Hagar and the Angel*, 1646 (London: National Gallery); *Landscape with Ascanius Shooting the Stag of Silva*, 1682 (Oxford: Ashmolean Museum)

Phillippe de **Champaigne**

◔ c.1602–74 FRENCH ✎ OILS

Born in Brussels, Champaigne arrived in Paris in 1621. He was a brilliant and successful painter of portraits and religious pictures at the court of Louis XIII (and was favoured by Cardinal Richelieu).

His unique, memorable style combined over-the-top Baroque grandeur with severe, crisp, detailed, colourful, and authoritarian austerity – you believe it should not be possible, but he showed that it could be done.

KEY WORKS: *Triple Portrait of Cardinal Richelieu*, 1642 (London: National Gallery); *Moses with the Ten Commandments*, 1648 (St Petersburg: Hermitage Museum); *Ex Voto*, 1662 (Paris: Musée du Louvre)

Gaspard **Dughet**

◔ c.1615–75 FRENCH ✎ OILS; DRAWINGS; ENGRAVINGS

Dughet was the brother-in-law of Poussin. He was very popular in the 18th century, but few works can be confidently attributed to him. He produced decorative landscapes, in which he sometimes tried almost too hard to combine the heroic qualities of Poussin with the pastoral features of Claude. He ought to be very good, but frequently disappoints.

KEY WORKS: *Landscape with Herdsman*, c.1635 (London: National Gallery); *Imaginary Landscape*, c.1645 (New York: The Metropolitan Museum of Art); *A Landscape with Mary Magdalene Worshipping the Cross*, c.1660 (Madrid: Museo del Prado); *Classical Landscape with Figures*, c.1672–75 (Birmingham, UK: Museums and Art Gallery)

Le Nain brothers

◔ c.1588–1677 FRENCH ✎ OILS

Brothers Antoine (c.1588–1648), Louis (c.1593–1648), and Mathieu (c.1607–77) were painters of large-scale mythologies, allegories, and altarpieces, but they are best known for smaller-scale portrayals of peasant groups sitting in an interior, doing nothing much, with dignity.

Note the style; sensitivity when handling light and colour and pleasing and detached powers of observation. It is difficult to assign works as all three brothers signed their work by their surname only. They were admired by Cézanne.

KEY WORKS: *A Landscape with Peasants*, Louis Le Nain, c.1640 (Washington DC: National Gallery of Art); *Peasant Family in an Interior*, Le Nain brothers, c.1640 (Paris: Musée de Louvre); *Four Figures at a Table*, Le Nain brothers, c.1643 (London: National Gallery)

François **Girardon**

◔ 1628–1715 FRENCH ✎ SCULPTURE

Girardon studied antiquities in Rome, then returned to Paris to dominate Sun King Louis XIV's sculptural projects, including decoration of the Louvre, with distinct classical style. His sculptures have unified, muscular bodies, but are lyrical, with careful contrast of gesture and pose. Girardon preferred Poussin's painting as his chief influence rather than his sculptor counterparts. When he died he owned 800 sculptures – the second biggest collection after the king's.

KEY WORKS: *Apollo Tended by the Nymphs*, c.1666 (Château de Versailles); *Monument to Cardinal Richelieu*, 1675–94 (Paris: Sorbonne Church); *Pyramid Fountain*, 1668–70 (Château de Versailles)

Georges de **La Tour**

◔ c.1593–1652 FRENCH ✎ OILS

La Tour was a shadowy figure with few attributed works; many are now in poor condition. He is in fashion with art historians, who are in the process of reconstructing his oeuvre. Was he a major master or an overrated enigma?

His work has two points of focus: peasant scenes (pre-1630s), and nocturnes with spectacular handling of candlelight (post-1630s). He also painted cardsharpers and fortune-tellers.

Note how La Tour paints peasants and saints with unnerving realism: wispy, greasy hair; lined brows and convincing old, dry skin; distinctive horny finger nails and peasant hands; sinister, cunning, piggy eyes. He used strong and beautiful *chiaroscuro* and lighting, and flat, non-existent backgrounds. He was unconvincing when painting young flesh – the faces are wooden and mask-like. He was a master at creating virtuoso candlelight effects (such as the way they make a hand look translucent).

KEY WORKS: *The Payment of Taxes*, c.1620 (Lviv, Ukraine: Lviv National Art Gallery); *Job and his Wife*, 1632–35 (Epinal, France: Musée Départemental des Vosges); *The Repentant Magdalen*, c.1635 (Washington DC: National Gallery of Art)

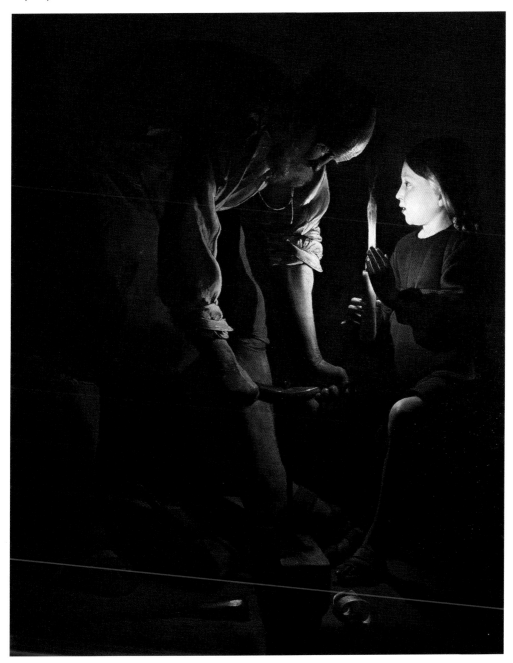

◀◀ *St Joseph the Carpenter* Georges de La Tour, c.1640, 130 x 100 cm (51 ⅛ x 39 ¾ in), oil on canvas, Paris: Musée du Louvre. These humble settings for religious scenes were inspired by a Franciscan-led religious revival.

Velásquez

● 1599–1660 ◫ SPANISH ✎ OILS

Diego Rodríguez de Silva y Velásquez was the great Spanish painter of the 17th century, whose life and work were inextricably linked with the court of King Philip IV. He wasn't a prolific artist but was precocious; while still in his teens he painted pictures that display powerful presence and technical mastery. He was very influential on late-19th-century French avant-garde painting.

Observe the extraordinary and unique interweaving of grandeur, realism, and intimacy, which ought to self-cancel, but result in some of the finest official portraits ever painted. Notice the grand poses, characters, and costumes; eagle-eyed observation (he never flatters or idealizes); and a feeling of sensual intimacy through the use of seductive colours and paint handling. His religious and mythological paintings sometimes fail to convince because he was simply too realistic in his work.

Velásquez had a great sensitivity to light, which is recorded with pin-sharp accuracy in his early work and evoked by loose, flowing paint in later work. See how he makes ambiguous and mysterious use of space, which has the effect of drawing the viewer into the picture and therefore closer to the figures.

He is better with static, solitary poses than with movement or people communicating. There are sensational colour harmonies (especially pink and silver) in his late work.

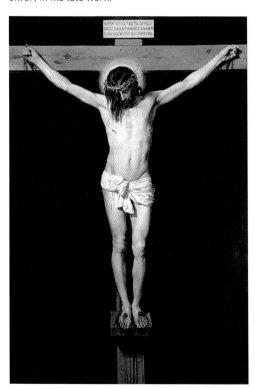

🔼 **Christ on the Cross** *c.1631–32, 248 x 169 cm (96 x 66 ½ in), oil on canvas, Madrid: Museo del Prado.* An early work showing the continuing influence of Spanish polychrome sculpture.

KEY WORKS: *The Forge of Vulcan*, 1630 (Madrid: Museo del Prado); *The Surrender of Breda*, 1634–35 (Madrid: Museo del Prado); *Francisco Lezcano*, 1636–38 (Madrid: Museo del Prado)

🔽 **Waterseller of Seville** *c.1620, 106.7 x 81 cm (42 x 31 ⅘ in), oil on canvas, London: Wellington Museum.* Gifted to the Duke of Wellington by the king of Spain for his victory over Napoleon's army.

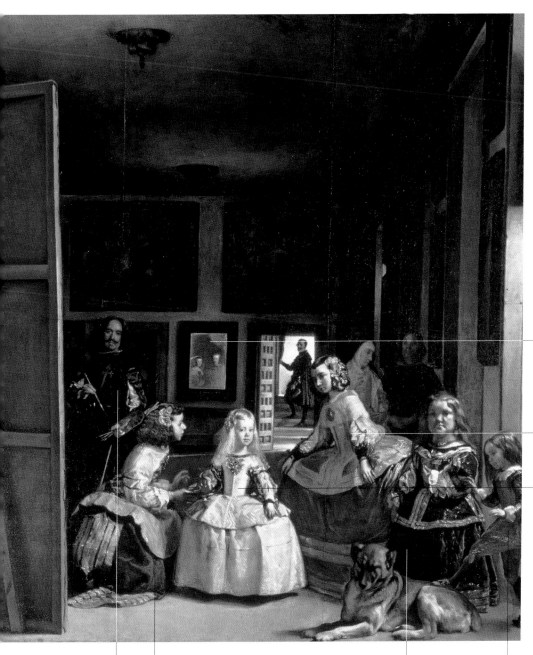

1656, 318 x 276 cm (125 x 108 ½ in), oil on canvas, Madrid: Museo del Prado. In this remarkable group portrait of the Infanta Margarita and her maids of honour, Velásquez – an ambitious courtier – displays cunning as an artist and politician.

The mirror at the end of the room reflects the King and the Queen. The Infanta has come to look at her parents. Velásquez has reversed the rules and expectations of portraiture

A maid of honour awaits the child's orders. Behind her a nun and a priest converse in the shadows

The Infanta Margarita, aged five, is the central figure in the painting

» TECHNIQUES

Velásquez developed a technique whereby details of a painting come into focus only at a certain distance. The maid of honour's lace cuffs are loose brushstrokes that suggest rather than describe.

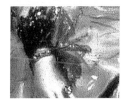

Velásquez portrays himself painting on a large canvas. He wears the cross of the Order of Santiago (St James)

The maid of honour on the left proffers a red terracotta jug on a gold plate to the Infanta

Mari-Bárbola, a court favourite, has grim features and a dark dress, which serve to accentuate the Infanta's delicate beauty

The court jester Nicolasito playfully treads on the huge sleepy mastiff

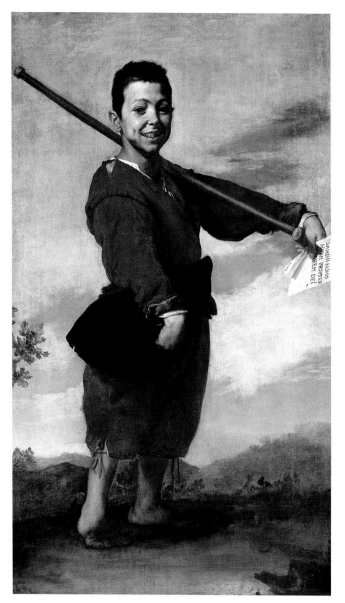

José **Ribera**

⬤ 1591–1652 ⚑ SPANISH ✎ OILS;
ENGRAVINGS; DRAWINGS

Spanish-born Ribera settled in Spanish-owned
Naples in 1616, where he was known as "Lo
Spagnoletto". Naples was one of the main centres
of the Caravaggesque style at the time, and Ribera
was the major Neapolitan painter of the 17th
century. He was particularly good at depicting
martyrdom with powerful images of resigned
suffering. Sometimes the subject matter is
repellant, but the technique is exquisite and this
results in an almost unbearable "can't look but
must" tension. He made brilliant use of *chiaroscuro*
and tenebrism (light coming from a single source
above), and was an early exponent of realism – his
saints and philosophers were real people from the
streets of Naples. Observe his marvellous painting
of textures and surfaces.

He paints old men wonderfully, with leathery
faces, necks, and hands. Notice how the
brush-strokes follow the contours of the flesh,
across a brow, down an arm. He couldn't do
convincing women's or boys' flesh and faces
though. Is his brighter, Venetian-style palette
adopted from the 1630s a step forward or a
step backward? Note that many pictures have
darkened with time.

KEY WORKS: *Martyrdom of St Bartholomew*, c.1630
(Madrid: Museo del Prado); *Apollo Flaying Marsyas*,
1637 (Brussels: Musées Royaux des Beaux-Arts)

◀◀ *The Club Foot José Ribera, 1642, 164 x 92 cm
(64 ⅗ x 36 ⅕ in), oil on canvas, Paris: Musée du
Louvre. In his late work Ribera softens his
dramatic lighting, adopting a looser style with
gentler modelling and airy harmonious tones.*

Francisco de **Zurbarán**

⬤ 1598–1664 ⚑ SPANISH ✎ OILS

"The major painter between Velásquez and
Murillo" (read this as code for good, not great).
Zurbarán's principal patrons were Spanish religious
orders. His most characteristic works are of saints
and monks in prayer or meditation. Like that of
Caravaggio, his work has a hard-edged realism,
employs strong *chiaroscuro* effects, and
demonstrates a smooth technique and care
for precise detail. It has dramatic visual impact,
but generally lacks convincing emotion. Zurbarán
died out of fashion and in financial difficulty.

KEY WORKS: *Beato Serapio*, 1628 (Hartford,
Connecticut: Wadsworth Atheneum); *St Margaret*,
1630–34 (London: National Gallery)

Juan de **Arellano**

● c.1614–76 🏛 SPANISH 🖌 OILS

Arellano was the pre-eminent Spanish flower painter of the 17th century. His detailed, skilful works, often executed and designed as pairs, show bouquets in baskets on rough stone plinths, or in vases of crystal or metal, with a careful balancing of red, white, blue, and yellow. His later work is more loosely painted, with full-blown flowers and curling leaves.

KEY WORKS: *Garland of Flowers with Landscape*, 1652 (Madrid: Museo del Prado); *Irises, Peonies, Convolvuli, and Other Flowers in an Urn on a Pedestal*, 1671 (London: Christie's Images)

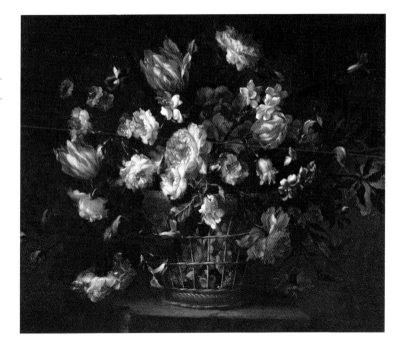

⬆ *Still Life of Flowers in a Basket* Juan de Arellano, c.1671, 84 x 105.5 cm (33 x 41 ½ in), oil on canvas, Bilbao: Museo de Bellas Artes. Spain has a long tradition of still-life painting influenced by Netherlandish art.

Bartolomé **Murillo**

● 1617–82 🏛 SPANISH 🖌 OILS

Regarded until about 1900 as greater than Velásquez and as good as Raphael, Murillo is now the poor man's Velásquez. He was born in Seville to a pious family. As well as good portraits, he produced acres of soft-focus, sentimental religious pictures for the home market and fewer, better, genre scenes for the export market. A Murillo revival campaign is currently under way. It is easy to extol his confident, masterly way with colour, paint handling, and strong composition. His genre scenes are appealing as subjects, and influenced Reynolds and Gainsborough.

KEY WORKS: *The Young Beggar*, c.1645 (Paris: Musée du Louvre); *The Virgin of the Rosary*, c.1649 (Madrid: Museo del Prado); *Two Boys Eating Melons and Grapes*, c.1650 (Munich: Alte Pinakothek)

Juan de **Valdés Leal**

● 1622–90 🏛 SPANISH 🖌 OILS; ENGRAVINGS

Valdés Leal was a Spanish painter and engraver, who founded the Seville Academy of Painting with Murillo. He was a religious painter with a fixation on the macabre. Note the vibrant colouring and dramatic lighting, vivid movements, volatility, verging on the operatic. He loved swirling forms, draperies, grand gestures. His work anticipates the decorative exuberance of the 18th-century Rococo style.

KEY WORKS: *The Assumption of the Virgin*, 1658–60 (Washington DC: National Gallery of Art); *The Immaculate Conception of the Virgin, with Two Donors*, c.1661 (London: National Gallery)

Claudio **Coello**

● 1642–93 🏛 SPANISH 🖌 OILS

Coello was deeply influenced by Rubens, van Dyck, and Titian, whose works were in the Spanish Royal Collection. He studied for seven years in Italy. Painter to Charles II in 1683, his works were often complex and complicated, fussy with exaggerated detail. He pre-empted Rococo and employed loose brushstrokes, a brilliant palette, and moody lighting. His masterpieces are his Titian-style portraits, particularly of Charles II, which capture the degeneracy of the last Hapsburg ruler of Spain.

KEY WORKS: *Self-Portrait*, 1680s (St Petersburg: Hermitage Museum); *The Repentant Mary Magdalene*, 1680s (St Petersburg: Hermitage Museum)

Sir Peter Paul **Rubens**

1577–1640 FLEMISH OILS; DRAWINGS; CHALKS

Rubens was an extraordinary, widely travelled, gifted man of many talents: a painter, diplomat, businessman, and scholar. The greatest and most influential figure in Baroque art in northern Europe, he had a huge output and a busy studio with many assistants, including van Dyck. He was *the* illustrator of the Catholic faith and the divine right of kings.

His large-scale set-piece works, such as ceiling decorations and altarpieces, must be seen *in situ* in order to experience their full impact and glory. However, do not overlook his many sketches and drawings, which are miracles of life and vigour, and the genesis of the major works. Rubens's work is always larger than life, so enjoy the energy and enthusiasm he brought to everything he saw and did. He was never hesitant, never introspective, and was a wonderful storyteller.

There are three possible themes to explore in Rubens's work: 1) Movement – inventive compositions with energetic diagonals and viewpoints; colour contrasts and harmonies that activate the eye; figures at full stretch both physically and emotionally. 2) Muscles – gods built like superman, muscular Christianity in which well-developed martyrs suffer and die with enthusiasm. 3) Mammaries – he never missed a chance to reveal a choice breast and cleavage. Note also the rosy, blushing cheeks, and the business-like eye contact in the portraits.

In his later years Rubens developed a new interest in landscape painting.

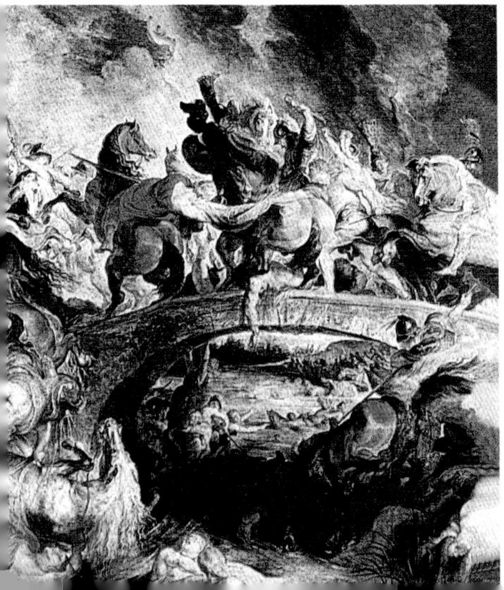

Battle of the Amazons and Greeks *(detail), c.1617, 121 x 166 cm (47 3/5 x 65 1/3 in) oil on panel, Munich: Alte Pinakothek.* Rubens was in Italy from 1600–08 and this work shows the lasting influence of his study of Greco-Roman and Italian Renaissance art.

KEY WORKS: *Samson and Delilah*; *The Life of Maria de Medici series*, c.1621–25 (Paris: Musée du Louvre); *The Garden of Love*, 1632–34 (Madrid: Museo del Prado); *The Judgement of Paris*, 1635–38 (London: National Gallery)

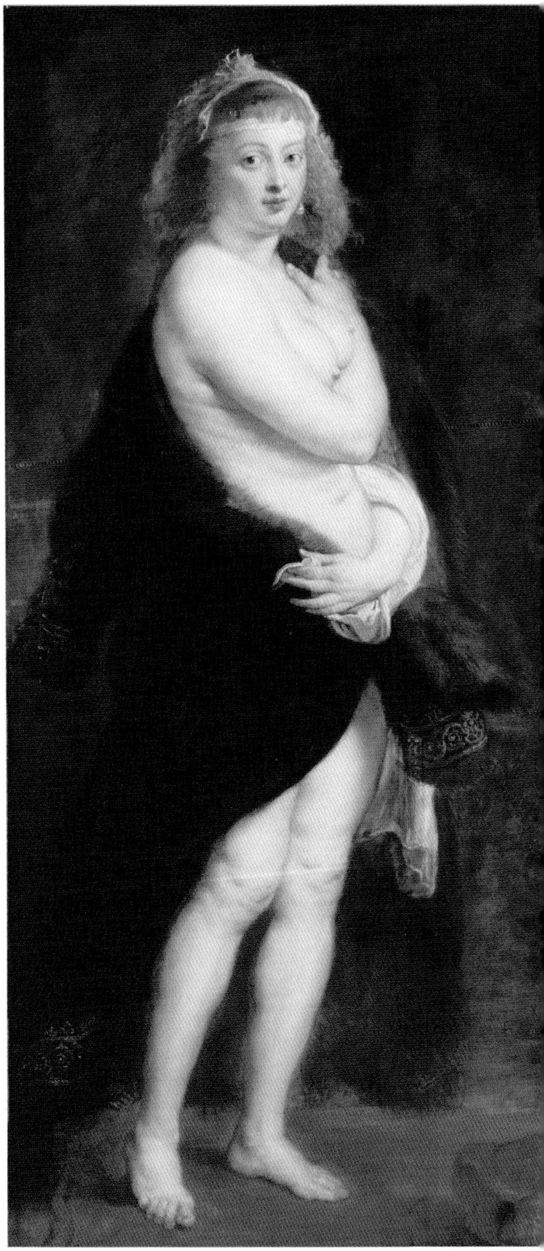

Hélène Fourment in a Fur Wrap *1635–40, 176 x 83 cm (69 1/4 x 32 2/3 in), wood, Vienna: Kunsthistorisches Museum.* Rubens's second wife (who was aged 16 when they married in 1630) was the ideal female model for his art.

The tilt of Delilah's head echoes the statue of Venus above. Note Rubens's expert use of light on Delilah and her flowing clothing

Each of the main characters has specific hand gestures that reveal their mental and physical state

The intertwined hands holding the scissors are a metaphor for the elaborate plot to cause Samson's downfall

Samson's enormous muscular frame was inspired by the work of Michelangelo (see pages 90–91)

Rubens's chiaroscuro treatment of light was strongly influenced by Caravaggio (see pages 124–125)

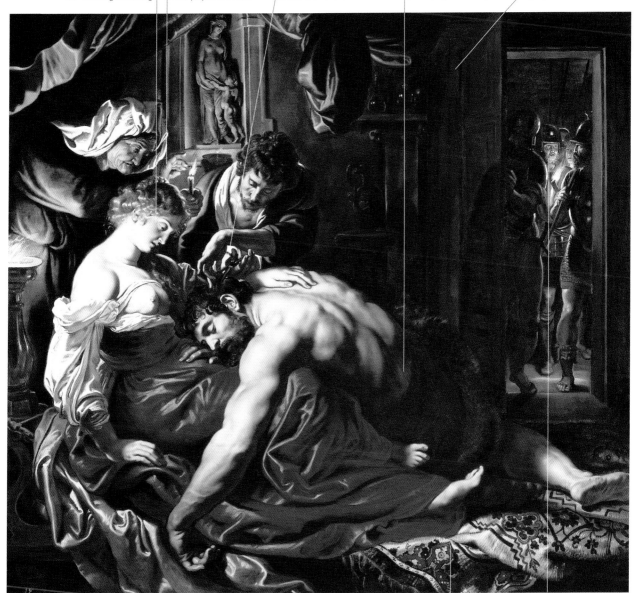

The picture is strewn with rich materials and colours – silks, satins, and embroidery in vibrant reds and golds

The Philistines' faces are lit from below by a flaming torch

⏏ **Samson and Delilah** c.1609, 185 x 205 cm (73 x 80 ½ in), oil on wood, London: National Gallery. Rubens painted Samson and Delilah for close friend and patron Nicolaas Rockox, a rich and influential alderman. Samson's ruin was caused by his lust for the Philistine Delilah, who beguiled him into revealing the secret source of his strength – his uncut hair. Rubens depicts the tense moment when the first lock is cut and the soldiers prepare to gouge out the Israelite's eyes.

Pieter **Brueghel** (the younger)

● 1564–1638 🏴 FLEMISH ✍ OILS; TEMPERA

Pieter was the elder son of "Peasant" Bruegel and made copies and imitations of his father's work. Later, he did fashionable hellfire scenes, which gave him the nickname "Hell" Brueghel (he also retained the 'h' in his name).

KEY WORKS: *Fight between Carnival and Lent*, c.1595 (Bruges: Musées Royaux des Beaux-Arts); *The Adoration of the Magi*, c.1595–1600 (St Petersburg: Hermitage Museum)

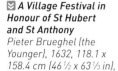

⌄ *A Village Festival in Honour of St Hubert and St Anthony*
Pieter Brueghel (the Younger), 1632, 118.1 x 158.4 cm (46 ½ x 63 ⅓ in), oil on panel, Cambridge: Fitzwilliam Museum.

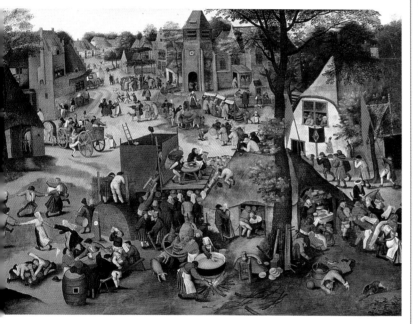

Jan **Brueghel**

● 1568–1625 🏴 FLEMISH ✍ OILS

Jan was the second son of "Peasant" Breugel, and was nicknamed "Velvet" Breughel. He produced flower paintings, landscapes, and allegories with rich, velvety textures; very finely painted. He sometimes worked with Rubens.

KEY WORKS: *The Battle of Issus*, 1602 (Paris: Musée du Louvre); *The Earthly Paradise*, 1607–08 (Paris: Musée du Louvre); *Forest's Edge (Flight into Egypt)*, 1610 (St Petersburg: Hermitage Museum)

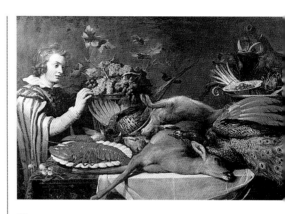

⌃ *Pantry Scene with a Page* Frans Snyders, c.1615–20, 125 cm x 198 cm (49 ⅕ x 78 in), canvas, London: Wallace Collection.

Frans **Snyders**

● 1579–1657 🏴 FLEMISH ✍ OILS

The undisputed master of the Baroque still life, Snyders became as rich as his clients, so was able to consume and enjoy the produce he painted. He was prolific and much imitated – there are many wrong attributions.

Look for market scenes; pantries; large-scale still lifes that groan and overflow with fruit, vegetables, and fish, flesh, and fowl, both alive and dead. Look also for the odd symbol of successful bourgeois capitalism, such as rare imported Wan Li Chinese porcelain. After 1610, he painted hunting scenes, but his best and most freely painted work came after 1630 – geometrically structured compositions, which contain fluidity, rhythm, balance, harmony, and rich colour.

He was much influenced by his visit to Rome in 1608. He collaborated with other artists (for example, he sometimes added the still life or animal component to Rubens's work). There is possible symbolism in the details (grapes as Eucharist, for instance), plus moralizing messages, proverbs, or animal fables. He painted embroidered reality, not far-fetched fantasy.

KEY WORKS: *Still Life with Dead Game, Fruits, and Vegetables in a Market*, 1614 (Art Institute of Chicago); *Hungry Cat with Still Life*, c.1615–20 (Berlin: Staatliche Museen); *Wild Boar Hunt*, 1649 (Florence: Galleria degli Uffizi)

Jacob **Jordaens**

● 1593–1678 🏴 FLEMISH ✍ OILS; WATERCOLOURS; GOUACHE

Jordaens was the leading painter in Amsterdam after the death of Rubens, whose style he emulated. By comparison Jordaens's work seems ill organized, without any clear visual or emotional focus. He is best when not too ambitious, as in genre scenes, and made good portraits. He had a large output from commissions, but quantity trumped quality.

KEY WORKS: *The Artist and his Family in a Garden*, c.1621 (Madrid: Museo del Prado); *The Four Evangelists*, c.1625 (Paris: Musée du Louvre); *The Lamentation*, c.1650 (Hamburg: Kunsthalle)

David **Teniers** (the younger)

● 1610–90 🏴 FLEMISH ✍ OILS

Teniers is best remembered for his lively small-scale paintings of peasant and guardroom scenes (and depicting them misbehaving, as in *Boors Carousing*). After 1651 he was also known for his detailed views of the painting galleries of Archduke Leopold Wilhelm (Regent of the Netherlands). His later work is weak.

KEY WORKS: *The Kitchen*, 1646 (St Petersburg: Hermitage Museum); *An Old Peasant Caresses a Kitchen Maid in the Stable*, c.1650 (London: National Gallery); *Peasants Making Music*, c.1650 (Vienna: Liechtenstein Museum)

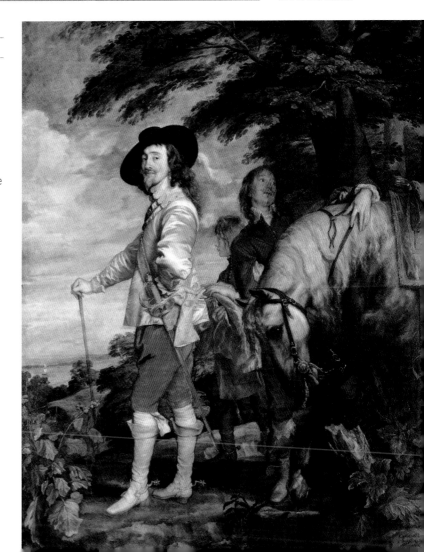

🔽 *King Charles I of England out Hunting*
Sir Anthony van Dyck, c.1635, 226 x 207 cm (104 ½ x 81 ½ in), oil on canvas, Paris: Musée du Louvre. Van Dyck painted 38 portraits of Charles I, of which this is the finest.

Sir Anthony **van Dyck**

● 1599–1641 🏴 FLEMISH ✍ OILS; DRAWINGS

Van Dyck was an Antwerp-born infant prodigy from a family of silk merchants. He is best remembered for his portraits, especially those of the ill-fated court of Charles I of England. He died fairly young.

As well as portraits, look for religious and mythological subjects. He also painted landscape watercolours. His brilliant, restrained technique reflected the elegance, finesse, and impeccable taste and breeding assumed by his sitters – subtly elongated fingers, bodies, noses, and poses, and the rich silks and satins. Even his martyrs suffer with perfect manners. Note that air of aristocratic privilege. He set the ultimate role model, much copied in (notably British) portraiture and life: the aloofness, and reserve adopted by people wishing to appear consciously set apart. These faces never smile; they know their duty and they will fight to retain their privileges to the end. Van Dyck also painted wonderfully sensitive images of children, with realistic details, especially hair.

KEY WORKS: *Portrait of Charles V on Horseback*, 1620 (Florence: Galleria degli Uffizi); *Geronima Brignole Sale and her Daughter Amelia*, c.1621–25 (Genoa: Palazzo Rosso); *James Stewart, Duke of Richmond with Lennox*, 1635–36 (Private Collection); *A Lady as Erminia, Attended by Cupid*, c.1638 (Oxfordshire: Bleinheim Palace)

Dutch Realism

1600s

Seventeenth-century Holland consciously developed a new type of art. Small-scale, well-made, and often full of symbolism and anecdotes, its principal subjects were secular and focused on the present day – landscapes, still lifes, and genre scenes that recorded their daily activities. The Dutch also had a liking for portraits but these too tended to be small-scale and distinctly bourgeois in character.

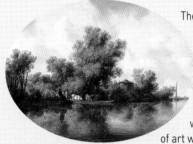

The content of Dutch Realism reflected everyday domestic tastes: sensitive and unpretentious scenes, usually painted with a close attention to detail. This new style of art was made to decorate and please, but it was also created for financial gain. Investing in works of art was a major activity, and trading in works of art was commonplace at all levels of society.

↗ River Landscape with Peasants Ferrying Cattle *Salomon van Ruysdael, 1633, oil on panel, private collection.* These early works are similar in style to Van Goyen.

Subjects

National pride was the main subject. For example, landscapes, although rarely accurate descriptions of exact places, celebrate the particular qualities of the Dutch countryside: flat, neatly cultivated lands with grey skies, heavy with rain. Canals and shipping feature large, including naval battles and storms at sea, both of which threatened their prosperity. Being a nation of market gardeners, they painted

superb flower pieces. Still lifes are full of rich and exotic goods, with glass often in evidence, as it was one of their luxury industries. Domestic scenes are full of themes of love, sexual morality, cleanliness, and household economy and order.

What to look for

Nothing in Dutch art is ever quite what it seems, not even in a still life. The exotic objects, snuffed-out candles, and empty jugs are symbolic of the essential emptiness of earthly possessions, and often there is a skull or other symbol of death – a *momento mori* – a reminder that even for the richest citizen, there is no escape from the inevitability of dying. What is ostensibly an object for visual enjoyment is, in fact, a sober Calvinist discussion.

KEY EVENTS	
1602	Dutch East India Company was founded
1610	Utrecht School established. Group including Terbrugghen also returns from Rome excited by realism
1616	Frans Hals, *alla prima* pioneer, painting directly onto canvas, wins fame with Dutch "Civic Guards" group portrait
1648	Holland becomes an independent republic
1650	Founding of the Delft School with Vermeer as leading exponent
1659	Major late Rembrandt self-portrait. The first artist to practise self-portraiture as a speciality

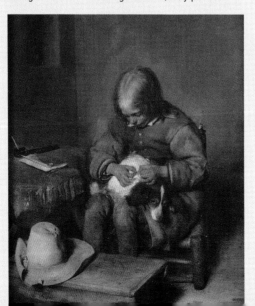

⏩ The Flea-Catcher (Boy with his Dog) *Gerard Terborch, c.1655, 34.4 x 27.1 cm (13 ½ x 10 ⅔ in), oil on canvas, Munich: Alte Pinakothek.*

The shaft of light highlights the central object – the human skull, a principal reminder of mortality; light is a Christian symbol of the eternal

The pitcher may be an allusion to the dangers of drunkeness referred to in Ecclesiastes (Eccl. 10:17)

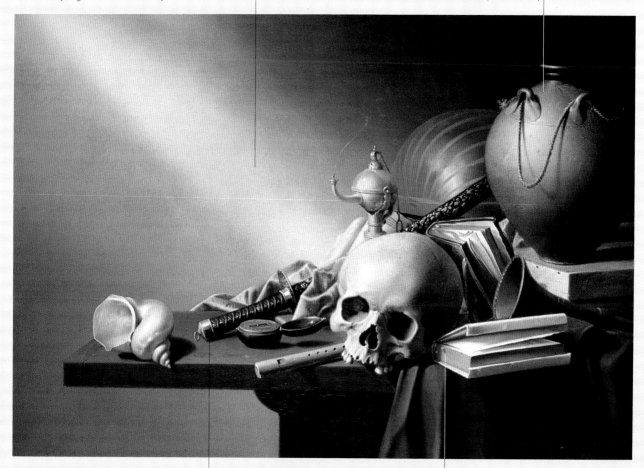

The Japanese sword is a symbol of worldly power, indicating that even the might of arms cannot defeat death

The grief of too much wisdom is represented by a book, symbol of the human quest for knowledge (Eccl. 1:18)

⌃ **The Vanities of Human Life**
Harmen Steenwyck, c.1645, 39 x 51 cm (15 ½ x 20 in), oil on oak, London: National Gallery. A visual sermon based on the Book of Ecclesiastes.

⏩ TECHNIQUES

Dutch painters were the first to establish a tradition of still-life painting: Steenwyck's subject gives him ample scope to show off his technical mastery, attention to detail, and evocation of reflected light on surfaces.

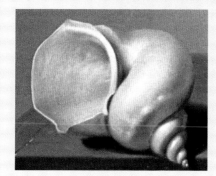

⏩ **The shell is a symbol** of worldly wealth – it would also have been a rare and prized possession in the 17th century. But riches are also a vanity: "As he came forth of his mother's womb, naked shall he return to go... and shall take nothing of his labour" (Eccl. 5:15).

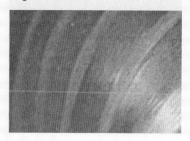

Frans **Hals**

● c.1581–1666 DUTCH OILS

The Laughing Cavalier Frans Hals, 1624, 83 x 67 cm (32 ⅔ x 26 ⅜ in), oil on canvas, London: Wallace Collection. The picture is inscribed "AETA. SVAE 26/Aº 1624" (his age, 26; the year 1624), but the identity of the sitter remains unknown.

Hals was a stay-at-home self-portraitist who never moved from Haarlem in the Netherlands. He was one of the first masters of the Dutch School (preceded Rembrandt). Although successful, he was constantly in debt, perhaps because he had eight children.

Hals painted portraits and group portraits, especially of the "Civic Guards" (all-male social clubs) and members of the newly established Dutch republic, who usually look pink-cheeked, well fed, well dressed, happy, and prosperous. He also painted single genre figures of children and peasantry. He was very influential during the late 19th century when his style, having been totally out of fashion, became much admired by young artists such as Manet.

His exciting, lively, but simple poses are full of animation. He had a unique (for the time) sketchy painting technique, straight onto the canvas, with broad brushstrokes and bright colours, adding to the sense of vivacity. Yet he captured the feel and appearance of different textures – plump flesh, pink cheeks, the shimmer of silk and satin, the intricacy of lace and embroidery. Note the masterly command of beautifully observed, well-formed, expressive eyes.

KEY WORKS: *Young Man with a Skull*, 1626–28 (London: National Gallery); *Mad Babs*, c.1629–30 (Berlin: Staatliche Museum); *Portrait of Willem Coymans*, 1645 (Washington DC: National Gallery of Art); *Portrait of a Man*, early 1650s (New York: Metropolitan Museum of Art)

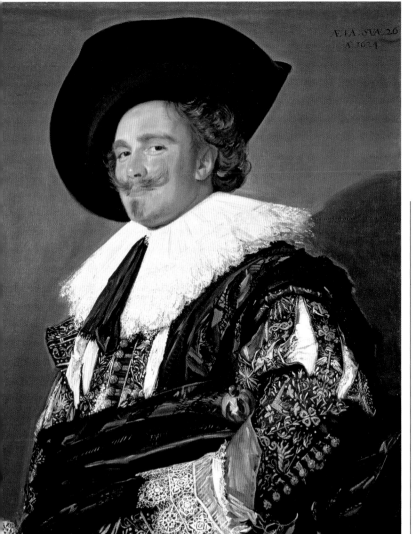

Daniel **Mytens** (the elder)

● c.1590–c.1647 DUTCH/BRITISH OILS

Mytens was the major portrait painter in England before van Dyck. Dutch-born and trained, he arrived in London around 1618 and worked for Charles I. He painted elegant, rather stiff, formally posed portraits (but with insight into personality) which introduced a new level of realism to English art. His best works are his later full-length portraits – powerful, assured, and fluent.

KEY WORKS: *Henry Wriothesley, 3rd Earl of Southampton*, c.1618 (London: National Portrait Gallery); *King James I of England and VI of Scotland*, 1621 (London: National Portrait Gallery); *Endymion Porter*, 1627 (London: National Portrait Gallery)

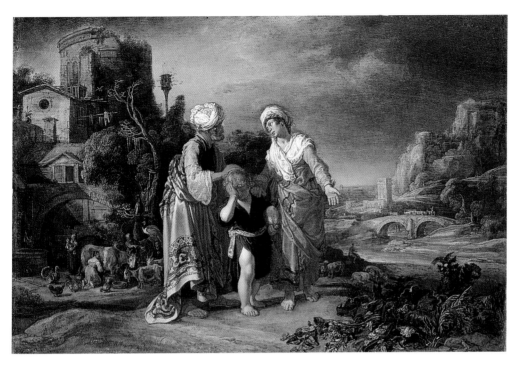

≪ The Expulsion of Hagar *Pieter Lastman, 1612, oil on panel, Hamburg: Kunsthalle.* The drama of the moment when Abraham banished his first son Ishmael and Hagar (Ishmael's mother). It shows an extensive landscape of an equally dark mood.

Pieter **Lastman**

● 1583–1633 DUTCH OILS

Lastman is chiefly remembered as Rembrandt's most influential teacher. He painted lush, narrative pictures, full of gesture and facial expression (see Rembrandt), but spoiled by over-fussy and anecdotal detail.

KEY WORKS: *Abraham on the Way to Canaan*, 1614 (St Petersburg: Hermitage Museum); *Juno Discovering Jupiter with Io*, 1618 (London: National Gallery)

Jan Davidsz **de Heem**

● 1606–84 DUTCH OILS

Born in Utrecht, de Heem lived and worked in Antwerp from 1636. He was famous and successful with his still-life paintings of flowers and groaning, exquisitely laid tables. De Heem had many pupils and imitators.

KEY WORKS: *Still Life with Books*, 1628 (The Hague: Mauritshuis Museum); *Fruit and Rich Tableware on a Table*, 1640 (Paris: Musée du Louvre); *A Table of Desserts*, 1640 (Paris: Musée du Louvre)

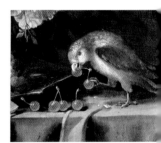

⌂ Still Life of Fruit and Flowers *(detail), Jan Davidsz de Heem, c.1640s, oil on canvas, Burnley, Lancashire: Towneley Hall Art Gallery.* His style became more exotic and opulent after moving to Antwerp.

Hendrick **Terbrugghen**

● 1588–1629 DUTCH OILS

Terbrugghen was the most important painter of the Utrecht School and was deeply influenced by Caravaggio's subjects and style (he spent ten years in Italy). On his return to the Netherlands, he became with Honthorst the leader of the Caravaggism associated with the Utrecht School. His early work has hard, raking light, which throws detail into sharp relief. His later work is softer and quieter, sometimes to the point of stillness and silence. He was fascinated by reflected light. The rediscovery of his sensitive and poetic paintings has been part of the general reappraisal of Caravaggesque art in the 20th century.

KEY WORKS: *Flute Players*, 1621 (Kassel, Germany: Staatliche Kunstsammlungen); *St Sebastian Tended by Irene and her Maid*, 1625 (Oberlin, Ohio: Allen Memorial Art Museum); *The Annunciation*, 1629 (Amsterdam: Stedelijk Museum)

Rembrandt

● 1606–69   ⬛ DUTCH   ✍ OILS; ETCHINGS; DRAWINGS

Rembrandt Harmensz van Rijn is generally considered to be the greatest, but most elusive, Dutch master. He created prolific, stunning masterpieces, treasured in galleries worldwide. However, the Rembrandt Commission currently argues over how many works he painted, which is ultimately a flawed enterprise: you cannot resolve disputed attributions by majority vote in committee. He was also one of the great printmakers, developing the exciting, new, free-flowing surface scratching techniques of etching into copper rather than the heavier deep deliberate cutting of engraving.

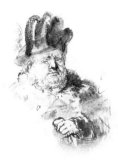

◢ *Studies of Old Men's Heads and Three Women with Children* (detail), c.1635, ink on paper, Birmingham (UK): The Barber Institute of Fine Arts. From a group of rapid sketches using thin pen strokes.

Rembrandt was born in Leiden. He was the son of a miller but, reflecting Dutch social engineering of the period, his modest parents recognized the importance of education, so he was sent to Leiden University. Unlike the Utrecht School founders and Rubens, he never visited Italy to drink at

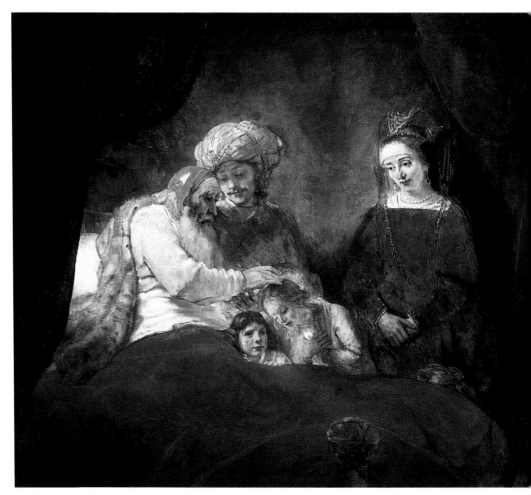

▶ *Jacob Blessing the Children of Joseph* 1656, 175.5 x 210.5 cm (69 x 82 ⅘ in), oil on canvas, Kassel (Germany): Gemäldegalerie. One of Rembrandt's greatest paintings depicting biblical history.

the fountains of Baroque but had access to High Renaissance works and was taught by Dutch "Caravaggio in a tea cup" artist, Pieter Lastman, who had worked in Italy.

Rembrandt's personal life was increasingly touched with tragedy. At first money rolled in, thanks to marrying a successful art dealer's cousin, which resulted in wealthy portrait commissions and quickly-won renown. He inherited his wife's fortune on her early death but later his popularity declined, resulting in debt, bankruptcy, and the loss of his grand house and massive personal art collection. His beloved son, Titus, and housekeeper common-law wife saved him from ruin but when they died (Titus at the age of 27), he was left lonely and poor in his old age, dying 11 months later in Amsterdam.

Subjects and style

Rembrandt's subjects were biblical history (his preference), portraits, and landscapes. He had a unique ability to find all humanity beautiful, in a way that can evoke deep, heart-rending emotions. He never flinched, even in front of the toughest subjects (the Crucifixion, or his own face). In fact he is seen as art's first major self-portraitist as a recognized speciality. His direct honesty and intense personal scrutiny over the years reveal an ageing face of a true human being, not beautiful but with penetrating realism. And this is the secret to his other works. Faces and gestures are the key – he was fascinated by the way faces reveal inner states of mind, and how hand and body language convey emotion. He was also interested in showing emotional crises and moral dilemmas – you sense that he has experienced the intense feelings he portrays.

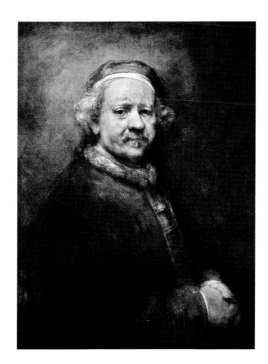

◀ **Self-Portrait at the Age of 63** *1669, 86 x 70.5 cm (33 ⅘ x 27 ¾ in), oil on canvas, London: National Gallery.* This is one of the last of over 75 self-portraits – paintings, drawings, and prints.

What to look for

Observe his emotional manipulation of light and shade – light being warming, purifying, revealing, spiritual; shadow being the domain of the unexplained, the threatening, the evil. He was enthralled by the activity of painting. His early work is detailed and his later work is looser in style. His palette is distinctive: rich, warm, earthy, and comforting. He was intrigued by human skin, especially the fleshy areas around the eye and nose in old faces – no other artist has ever painted them with such care and so convincingly.

KEY WORKS: *The Anatomy Lecture of Dr Nicolaes Tulp*, c.1632 (The Hague: Mauritshuis Museum); *The Storm on the Sea of Galilee*, 1633 (Boston: Isabella Stewart Gardner Museum); *Saskia as Flora*, 1635 (London: National Gallery); *The Blinding of Samson*, 1636 (Frankfurt: Städelsches Kunstinstitut); *Joseph Accused by Potiphar's Wife*, 1655 (Washington DC: National Gallery of Art)

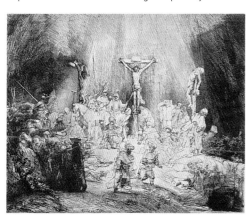

◀ **The Three Crosses** *1653, 38.1 x 43.8 cm (15 x 17 ¼ in), etching, Cambridge: Fitzwilliam Museum.* One of Rembrandt's best etchings: a complex, crowded work, with a stunning exploitation of light and shade.

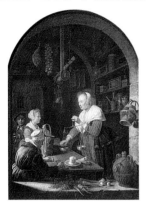

The Village Grocer
Gerrit Dou, 1647, 38.5 x 29 cm (15 x 11 ⅖ in), oil on panel, Paris: Musée du Louvre. Dou often used this composition of figures engaged at a window.

Gerrit **Dou**

1613–75 | **DUTCH** | **OILS**

Also known as Gerard Dou and best remembered as Rembrandt's first pupil (age 15), Dou painted small-scale works in fine detail with a high, glassy finish, using brilliant colours and a focused play of light and shade (he had trained initially as an engraver and glass painter).

He created a conjurer's world, dedicated to self-conscious illusion. He was obsessed with superficial appearance, skilful special effects, and hidden symbolism.

KEY WORKS: *Astronomer by Candlelight*, 1655 (Los Angeles: J. Paul Getty Museum); *Woman at a Window*, 1663 (St Petersburg: Hermitage Museum); *The Hermit*, 1670 (Washington: National Gallery of Art)

Govaert **Flinck**

1615–60 | **DUTCH** | **OILS**

A pupil of Rembrandt in the 1630s, Flinck was strongly influenced by him in style and subject matter, but his works are generally lighter, more elegant, and less serious or gloomy. He was prolific and greatly esteemed in his own day. A recent revival of interest is due to reattributions by the Rembrandt Commission; consequently, several so-called Rembrandts are now said to be by Flinck.

KEY WORKS: *Countryside with Bridge and Ruins*, 1637 (Paris: Musée du Louvre); *Young Shepherdess with Flowers*, c.1637–40 (Paris: Musée du Louvre); *Angels Announcing the Birth of Christ to the Shepherds*, 1639 (Paris: Musée du Louvre)

Ferdinand **Bol**

1616–80 | **DUTCH** | **OILS**

Bol was a pupil of Rembrandt and produced portraits and history paintings very much in the style of his master, to whom his works are often attributed (Rembrandt being more prestigious and his works much more valuable).

Bol liked the formula of posing his sitters by an open window. He also did allegorical and historical paintings for public buildings, such as Amsterdam Town Hall. He possessed a dark early style that became lighter after around 1640. In 1669, Bol married a rich widow and, as a consequence, seems to have given up painting.

KEY WORKS: *Portrait of an Old Lady*, c.1640–45 (Amsterdam: Rijksmuseum); *Jacob's Dream*, 1642 (Dresden: Gemäldegalerie); *David's Dying Charge to Solomon*, 1643 (Dublin: National Gallery of Ireland)

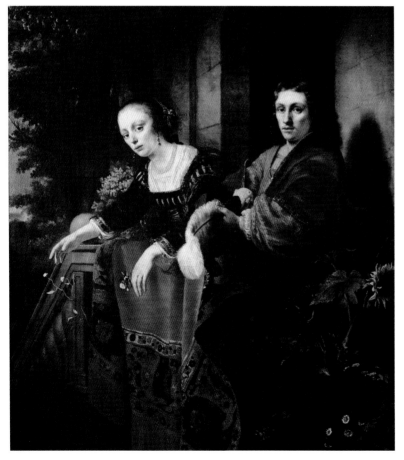

Portrait of a Husband and Wife *Ferdinand Bol, 1654, 171 x 148 cm (67 ⅓ x 58 ¼ in), oil on canvas, Paris: Musée du Louvre.*

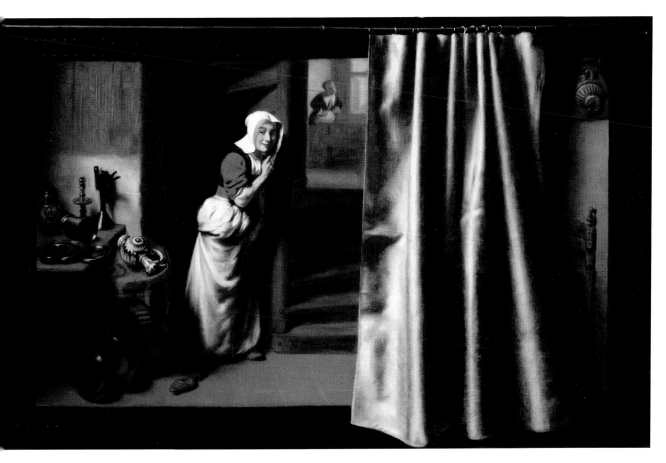

Carel **Fabritius**

● 1622–54 ⊓ DUTCH ⚄ OILS

Fabritius had a tragically short life, and fewer than 10 authenticated works are known, but they show great variety. Immensely talented, he was Rembrandt's best pupil and a highly original and distinctive painter. He made portraits, still lifes, genre, and perspectives. He died in a gunpowder explosion in Delft, near his studio, which destroyed most of his work.

Fabritius used thick, impastoed paint next to thin glazes (like Rembrandt) and preferred cool colours to Rembrandt's dark reds and browns. Sometimes he silhouetted a dark figure against a light background (Rembrandt preferred vice versa).

KEY WORKS: *The Beheading of John the Baptist*, c.1640 (Amsterdam: Rijksmuseum); *The Goldfinch*, 1654 (The Hague: Mauritshuis Museum)

⌃ *An Eavesdropper with a Woman Scolding*
*Nicolaes Maes, 1655, 46.3 x 72.2 cm (18 ¼ x 28 ⅖ in),
oil on panel, London: Harold Samuel Collection.*
Maes succeeded best when combining humour and complicity.

Nicolaes **Maes**

● 1634–93 ⊓ DUTCH ⚄ OILS

Maes is best known for his early genre paintings which often show kitchen life below stairs, or old women asleep (very popular at the time). Later in life he went in for small, elegant, French-style portraits. He used strong *chiaroscuro* (he was a pupil of Rembrandt) and soft focus and liked painting kitchen utensils. Good, but not great.

KEY WORKS: *The Mocking of Christ*, c.1650s (St Petersburg: Hermitage Museum); *A Young Woman Sewing*, 1655 (London: Harold Samuel Collection)

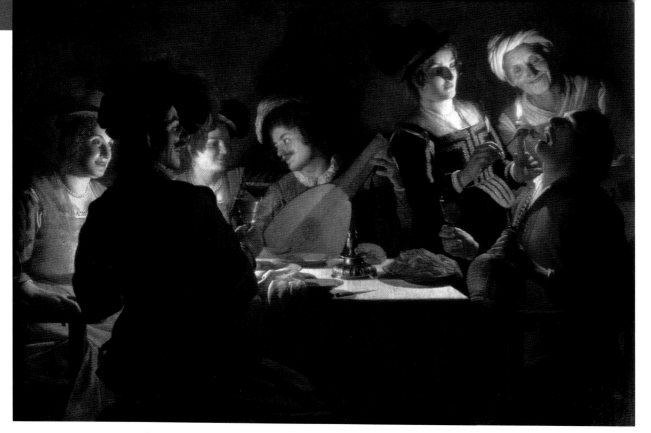

⌃ Supper with the Minstrel and his Lute
Gerrit van Honthorst, c.1619, 144 x 212 cm (56 ⅔ x 83 ½ in), oil on canvas, private collection. This use of artificial light and silhouettes greatly influenced the young Rembrandt.

Gerrit **van Honthorst**

⬤ 1590–1656 🏳 DUTCH ✍ OILS; FRESCO

The only member of the Utrecht School to establish an international reputation, Honthorst studied in Rome from 1610 to 1612. He was much favoured by royal and aristocratic patrons for his history paintings and allegorical decorations. He is best remembered now for his striking illumination by artificial light – he was especially good when he hid the light source and played with silhouette.

KEY WORKS: *Christ Before the High Priest*, c.1671 (London: National Gallery); *Christ in the Garden of Gethsemane (The Agony in the Garden)*, c.1671 (St Petersburg: Hermitage Museum); *Christ Crowned with Thorns*, 1620 (Los Angeles: J. Paul Getty Museum)

Esaias **van de Velde**

⬤ c.1591–1630 🏳 DUTCH ✍ OILS

Van de Velde was one of the founder members of the realist school of Dutch landscapes. His soft, monochromatic scenes (often in winter) are characterized by a feeling of natural, unstagey open space and atmosphere. He showed good detail, especially in the anecdotal figures going about their daily business. He was also a prolific etcher and draughtsman.

KEY WORKS: *Winter Games on the Town Moat*, c.1618 (Munich: Alte Pinakothek); *A Winter Landscape*, 1623 (London: National Gallery); *Villagers Skating on a Frozen Pond*, 1625 (Washington DC: National Gallery of Art)

Willem **van de Velde** (the elder)

⬤ 1611–93 🏳 DUTCH ✍ OILS; PEN AND INK

The elder van de Velde was a talented maritime painter, but eclipsed in popularity by his son Willem. His principal achievements are drawings of ships and small craft, and pen paintings in ink on white canvas or oak panel, with meticulous and accurate detailing. He spent much time at sea with the Dutch fleet, but he emigrated with his family to England (c.1672) to escape political confusion in Holland.

KEY WORKS: *Figures on Board Small Merchant Vessels*, 1650 (Los Angeles: J. Paul Getty Museum); *Dutch Ships Near the Coast*, 1650s (Washington DC: National Gallery of Art); *The Battle of Terheide*, 1657 (Amsterdam: Rijksmuseum)

Willem **van de Velde** (the younger)

● 1633–1707 DUTCH OILS

The precocious son of a hard-working maritime painter, Willem's early work concentrates on accurately drawn and carefully placed fishing vessels on tranquil seas. After 1670, he produced portraits of particular ships, naval battles, and storms at sea. His later work (after 1693) was more freely painted. He worked extensively from his father's drawings.

KEY WORKS: *Ships in a Calm Sea*, 1653 (St Petersburg: Hermitage Museum); *Dutch Vessels at Low Tide*, 1661 (London: National Gallery); *Ships off the Coast*, 1672 (Vienna: Liechtenstein Museum)

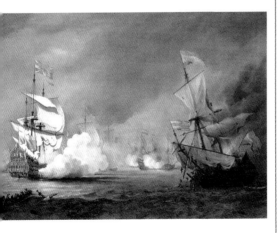

⊼ *Sea Battle of the Anglo-Dutch Wars* Willem van de Velde (the younger), c.1700, oil on canvas, New Haven: Yale Center for British Art. Both the elder and younger van de Veldes were official naval war artists to the English crown. The Anglo-Dutch wars (1652–74) were about control of trade routes.

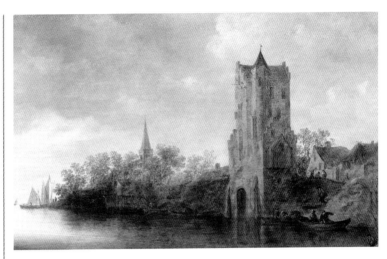

Jan **van Goyen**

● 1596–1656 DUTCH OILS

Van Goyen was one of the most important Dutch landscape painters. Prolific and much imitated, he had many pupils. He repeated the same motifs frequently – Dordrecht, sand dunes, ships, and the Nijmegen River. Van Goyen painted in subdued browns and greys, enlivened by a flash of red or blue. His paintings have attractive light, space, air, and cloud movement. He liked depicting gnarled oaks. He also used high viewpoint and low horizon.

KEY WORKS: *Skaters in Front of a Medieval Castle*, 1637 (Paris: Musée du Louvre); *A Windmill by a River*, 1642 (London: National Gallery); *Fort on a River*, 1644 (Boston: Museum of Fine Arts)

Pieter Jansz **Saenredam**

● 1597–1665 DUTCH OILS; CHALKS; WATERCOLOURS

Saenredam was a supremely gifted painter of architecture – both specific buildings in Dutch towns and the interiors of identifiable churches (the once-decorated Gothic buildings that were whitewashed to satisfy the Protestant belief in plainness). He made meticulous preliminary drawings and measurements. The light-filled church interiors are a metaphor for the universal laws of mathematics and optics.

⊼ *River Landscape with Ferries Docked Before a Tower* Jan van Goyen, 1640s, 64.1 x 94 cm (25 ¼ x 37 in), oil on panel, private collection. The castle is real, the setting imaginary.

KEY WORKS: *Interior of the Marienkirche in Utrecht*, 1638 (Hamburg: Kunsthalle); *Interior of St James's Church in Utrecht*, 1642 (Munich: Alte Pinakothek)

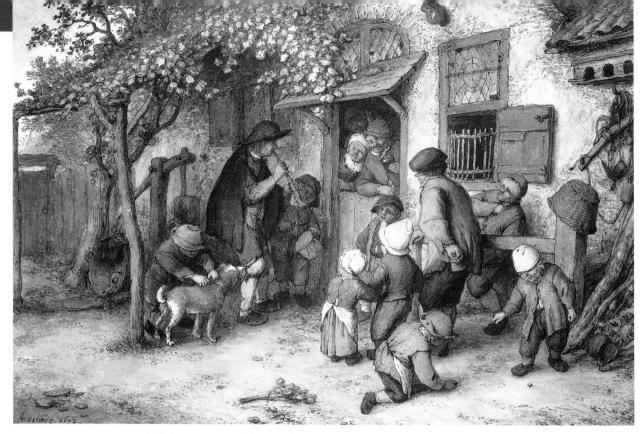

Adriaen **van Ostade**

● **1610–85** 🏳 **DUTCH** ✍ **OILS; DRAWINGS; WATERCOLOURS**

A Haarlem-born specialist in good-natured, uncritical, lowlife scenes of peasants having a good time in their hovels or taverns. Rich, earthy colours suit the mood. Both the peasants' behaviour and Ostade's technique improved as his work developed (perhaps marrying a well-to-do woman toned down his style and subjects). His brother and pupil, Isaak, started with similar subjects. Adriaen later developed silvery-grey landscapes, with good atmosphere and busy human activity.

KEY WORKS: *Rustic Concert*, 1638 (Madrid: Museo del Prado); *A Peasant Courting an Elderly Woman*, 1653 (London: National Gallery)

Salomon **van Ruysdael**

● **c.1600–70** 🏳 **DUTCH** ✍ **OILS**

Van Ruysdael was a prolific and well-known painter of landscapes and riverscapes. He was the uncle of the better known Jacob van Ruisdael.

Van Ruysdael painted scenes that sum up a preconceived idea of Holland (water, flat lands, big skies) – applying a standard formula that was very popular with Dutch collectors. There are also a few late still lifes with hunting themes.

The riverscape formula that he employed inventively juggles the following elements: compositions that always have a diagonal axis; mature trees on a river bank; rowing boats with fishermen; sailing boats with flags; cows; buildings on horizon (town, windmill, church); cloudy skies; evening light on the horizon; and reflections in water. He painted with broad, sweeping brushstrokes, using thin paint on a light ground; the grain of the panel often shows through.

KEY WORKS: *Sailboats on the Wijkermeer*, c.1648 (Berlin: Staatliche Museum); *Landscape with Medieval Castle*, 1652 (Vienna: Liechtenstein Museum); *Dutch Landscape with Highwayman*, 1656 (Berlin: Staatliche Museum); *A View of Deventer seen from the North-West*, 1657 (London: National Gallery)

Aert **van der Neer**

● 1603–77 DUTCH OILS

A specialist in night scenes (gloomily imaginative, with a ghostly full moon or lit by burning candles) and winter landscapes (atmospheric, with pale cold colours and lots of skaters). Van der Neer was also an unsuccessful innkeeper and went bankrupt.

KEY WORKS: *Sports on a Frozen River*, c.1600 (New York: Metropolitan Museum of Art); *River View by Moonlight*, c.1645 (Amsterdam: Rijksmuseum)

Philips **Koninck**

● 1619–88 DUTCH OILS

A pupil of Rembrandt who learned from the master's landscape etchings and went on to produce a formula for large-scale, panoramic landscapes of Holland: high viewpoint; horizon across middle; scudding clouds; small figures to increase sense of vast space; alternating bands of light and dark to give receding space. He was good, but not great.

KEY WORKS: *Wide River Landscape*, 1648 (New York: Metropolitan Museum of Art); *An Extensive Landscape*, 1666 (Edinburgh: National Gallery of Scotland)

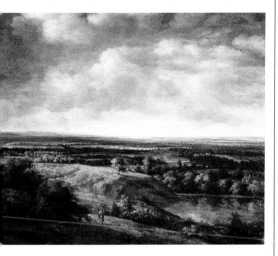

⌃ *An Extensive Landscape* Philips Koninck, 1666, 91 x 111.8 cm (34 ¾ x 44 in), oil on canvas, Edinburgh: National Gallery of Scotland. The equal division of open sky and landscape is typical of Koninck.

Philips **Wouvermans**

● 1619–68 DUTCH OILS

Wouvermans painted small-scale landscapes of horsemen, battle, or hunting scenes (note the trademark white horse). It is unpretentious decorative art at its best, and was highly popular. Simple compositions are characterized by clear, white sky; harmonious, hilly landscape; foreground figures; and elegant colouring.

KEY WORKS: *Horses Being Watered*, 1656–60 (St Petersburg: Hermitage Museum); *Landscape with Bathers*, 1660 (Vienna: Liechtenstein Museum)

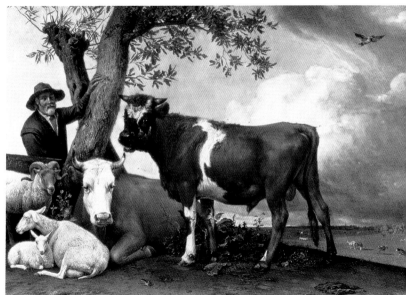

Paulus **Potter**

● 1625–54 DUTCH OILS

Potter was the best painter of cows as well as horses, sheep, and goats. While he is noted for a few life-sized animal pictures, he was more at ease with small-scale representations. He was good at weather, atmospheres, and observation of light. Potter also painted vanitas-type still lifes.

KEY WORKS: *Cattle and Sheep in a Stormy Landscape*, 1647 (London: National Gallery); *The Wolf-Hound*, c.1650 (St Petersburg: Hermitage Museum)

⌃ *The Young Bull* Paulus Potter, 1647, 236 x 339 cm (93 x 133 ½ in), oil on canvas, The Hague: Mauritshuis Museum. This is Potter's most monumental work. His father owned a factory for stamping and gilding leather.

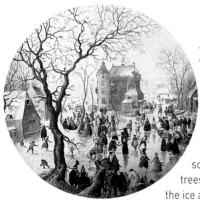

⌂ Winter Scene with Skaters near a Castle
Hendrik Avercamp, c.1608–09, diameter 41 cm (16 ⅕ in), oil on panel, London: National Gallery. These winter scenes were painted in the studio, from sketches for sale in the local art market.

Hendrick **Avercamp**

● 1585–1634 🏳 DUTCH
✍ OILS; WATERCOLOURS

Hendrick Avercamp was a mute painter from Kampen in Holland. He specialized in atmospheric winter scenes, usually in a landscape with bare trees, a pink castle, and a happy throng on the ice and snow. He uses high horizons and warm-coloured buildings that intensify the coldness of sky and snow; the thin painting of his figures gives them vitality and movement.

KEY WORKS: *Winter Scene at Yselmuiden*, c.1613 (Geneva: Musée d'Art et d'Histoire); *Fishermen by Moonlight*, c.1625 (Amsterdam: Rijksmuseum)

Gerard **Terborch**

● 1617–81 🏳 DUTCH ✍ OILS

Precocious and successful, Terborch (or Ter Borch) was one of the finest and most inventive masters of the Dutch School. His small-scale, very beautiful, restrained, and gentle genre scenes show self-absorbed moments of a mundane world being raised to immortality by art. One senses from the acuity of his observation and the minute care with which he applied the paint that he viewed this world, its people, its foibles, its ordinariness, and its objects (not forgetting the dogs) with the greatest of affection and pleasure.

Look for harmonies of brown, gold, and yellow, and silver and grey-blue, exquisitely balanced against dark backgrounds; his love of detail; the rendering of fabrics and the way clothes are made; his ability to draw us quietly into his intimate world and leave a lingering question over the secrets or affections that are being shared; his love of a lady's neck; and the light reflecting off a surface. See how he used gentle symbolism but without overt moralizing.

KEY WORKS: *The Swearing of the Oath of Ratification of the Treaty of Münster*, 1648 (London: National Gallery); *The Message*, c.1658 (Lyon: Musée des Beaux-Arts); *A Lady at her Toilet*, c.1668 (Detroit Institute of Arts)

Aelbert **Cuyp**

● 1620–91 🏳 DUTCH ✍ OILS; WATERCOLOURS

The son of a painter, Cuyp married a wealthy widow in 1658 and neglected his art for local politics.

He produced some of the most beautiful landscapes and riverscapes ever painted. Using Italianate, golden light, he transformed Holland into a dream world, which epitomized the start or end of a perfect day. The patrician classes who commissioned and collected his work appreciated the qualities of order, stillness, security, clarity, everything and everyone in their appointed place, harmony with nature, and a sense of proprietorship and timelessness.

The light floods in from the left, casting long, soft shadows (surprising how few definite shadows there are). Note how the golden light catches just the edges of plants, clouds, or animals, with highlights laid on in thick, impastoed paint. He uses a warm palette of earthy golds and browns contrasted with cool, silvery skies and foliage. Nice ambiguities and easily overlooked

Jacob van **Ruisdael**

● 1628–82 🏳 DUTCH ✍ OILS

Ruisdael was the principal Dutch landscape painter of the second half of the 17th century. His earliest known works date from 1746. He was a prolific painter and about 700 known works are attributed to him. A melancholic person, he was the nephew of Salomon van Ruysdael (c.1600–70; the different spelling occurs regularly in their signatures) and had a second career as a surgeon. His work has a certain amount of stock imagery although he could be quite inventive within the formula: mountains, waterfalls, beaches and dunes, seascapes, and winter scenes. His paintings are descriptive (they have no hidden symbolism) with a yearning for grandeur. Before 1650, he worked on panel but subsequently painted on canvas.

He favoured skies with rain clouds and flying birds (not convincing – looks like a stage backdrop). He was more naturalistic than his predecessors and it is possible to identify species of trees in his paintings (note how he liked rotten trees and broken branches). He was attracted to massive details, such as birds in flight; is it morning or evening? He was much loved and collected in England.

KEY WORKS: *The Sea by Moonlight*, c.1648 (St Petersburg: Hermitage Museum); *Sunset after Rain*, 1648–52 (Cambridge: Fitzwilliam Museum); *A Distant View of Dordrecht with a Milkmaid and Four Cows*, c.1650 (London: National Gallery)

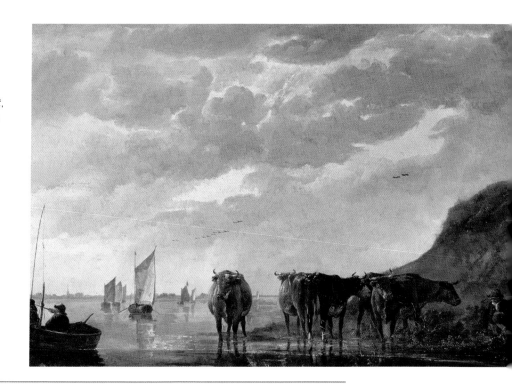

⯈⯈ *A Herdsman with Five Cows by a River* Aelbert Cuyp, c.1650, 45 x 74 cm (17 ¾ x 29 in), oil on wood, London: National Gallery. Works like these were produced on commission for wealthy members of Dordrecht society.

forms and often used a low viewpoint to silhouette features against the sky. His work was painted on dark priming and, as a result, has dark tones.

KEY WORKS: *Panoramic View of Haarlem*, c.1660s (London: Harold Samuel Collection); *Forest Scene*, c.1660–65 (Washington DC: National Gallery of Art); *Oaks by a Lake with Watermills*, c.1665–69 (Berlin: Staatliche Museum)

Jan **van der Heyden**

● 1637–1712 🇳🇱 DUTCH ✍ OILS

Van der Heyden was a prosperous inventor and designer of fire engines and lighting for whom painting was a secondary activity. He is best known for still lifes and meticulous, small-scale topographical and *capriccio* views of towns in the Netherlands and Rhineland.

Famous for dexterous paintings of walls and masonry, he set warm, sharp, detailed bricks against blue skies and fluffy white clouds – satisfying contrasts of warm and cool, hard and

soft. A typical composition is of buildings closing in on one side with an open area leading out of the picture on the other – another good use of contrast.

KEY WORKS: *A View in Cologne*, c.1660–65 (London: National Gallery); *The Inn of the Black Pig at Maarsseveen*, c.1668 (Los Angeles: J. Paul Getty Museum)

Meyndert **Hobbema**

● 1638–1709 🇳🇱 DUTCH ✍ OILS

The last of the major Dutch landscape artists of the 17th-century golden age, Hobbema gave up professional painting when he married in 1668 and became a wine gauger. His range is generally limited to repetitive scenes of finely painted dark landscapes with watermills and cottages round a pool, overgrown trees, and occasional figures.

KEY WORKS: *A Stream by a Wood*, c.1663 (London: National Gallery); *A Watermill*, c.1665–68 (Amsterdam: Rijksmuseum)

Jan **Steen**

◐ c.1626–79 ▥ DUTCH ✍ OILS

Steen, one of the best and most important Dutch genre painters, ran a tavern and owned a brewery. His lively, crowded scenes of taverns, feasts, and households with stock characters and facial expressions (like a TV soap opera – and maybe his works fulfilled a similar need), were prolific and popular. Watch out for his portraits, mythological scenes, religious works, and landscapes.

The lively and easy use of flowing, juicy, fresh colours (rose red, blue-green, pale yellow) adds to the paintings' vitality and reflects their character. Full of symbolism, the genre scenes carry an unambiguous (sometimes heavy-handed) message about drunkenness, idleness, promiscuity, etc.

KEY WORKS: *A Young Woman Playing a Harpsichord*, c.1659 (London: National Gallery); *Skittle Players Outside an Inn*, c.1660–63 (London: National Gallery)

Jan **Both**

◐ c.1618–52 ▥ DUTCH ✍ OILS

A Dutch landscape painter who studied in Rome and introduced the Italianate Arcadian landscape, à la Claude, to Holland. More detailed and literal than Claude (see page 131) , he does not usually make references to classical mythology.

KEY WORKS: *Italian Landscape*, c.1635–41 (Cambridge: Fitzwilliam Museum); *Bandits Leading Prisoners*, c.1646 (Boston: Museum of Fine Arts)

Pieter **de Hooch**

◐ 1629–83 ▥ DUTCH ✍ OILS

De Hooch is a perennially popular Dutch master and one of the best-known and best-loved genre painters. It is known that he died insane, but otherwise, little is known of his life.

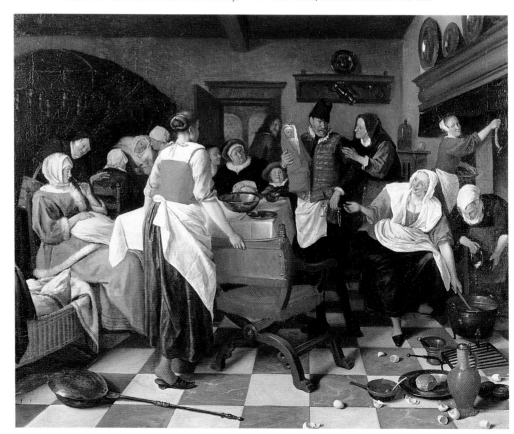

》 The Christening Feast (detail), Jan Steen, 1664, 87.8 x 107 cm (34 ½ x 42 in), oil on canvas, London: Wallace Collection. The complex symbolism indicates that the "father" holding the baby is a cuckold.

His best and most widely recognized works date from his years in Delft (1654–c.1660/61), and generally depict sunny courtyards and sunlit interiors, celebrating well-behaved middle-class life. Before 1655, he painted lowlife peasant and soldier scenes. He moved to Amsterdam and, after 1665, portrayed rich interiors with a bogus view of pseudo-aristocratic life. His very late work (1670s) is feeble, but his best work bears a similarity to that of Vermeer (see pages 158–159), who was his talented contemporary in Delft.

Observe the way he played with, and enjoyed, space and light – he created views from one room to another and used the geometric patterns of the tiled floors and courtyards to construct the illusion of space, flooding them with warm light and leaving the foreground uncluttered. His compositions were carefully designed with well-placed verticals, horizontals, and diagonals, and he used carefully worked-out geometric perspective, usually with a single vanishing point. He also made discreet use of symbols and emblems.

KEY WORKS: *Two Soldiers and a Woman Drinking*, c.1658–60 (Washington DC: National Gallery of Art); *Dutch Courtyard*, c.1660 (Washington DC: National Gallery of Art)

Gabriel **Metsu**

● 1629–1667 🇳🇱 DUTCH ✍ OILS

Metsu was a high-quality painter of intimate, small-scale scenes of well-ordered, polite Dutch households. His carefully organized compositions and meticulous technique and palette reflect the lifestyle of the Dutch bourgeoisie. Many of the objects and still-life details are symbolic; if there is lettering or a document, it is meant to be read as part of the meaning of the picture (a way of drawing you into the intimacy and secrecy of the scene).

Note Metsu's liking for dark interiors – rooms with windows closed or curtains drawn, or a dark corner. His palette is warm and personal, especially his use of reds and browns.

KEY WORKS: *A Soldier Visiting a Young Lady*, 1653 (Paris: Musée du Louvre); *A Dead Cock*, 1653 (Madrid: Museo del Prado)

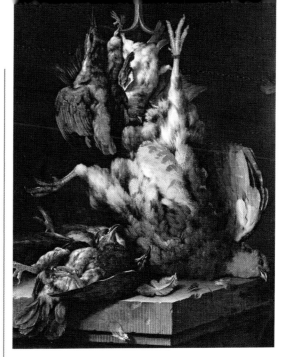

◄ *Still Life* Jan Weenix, c.1690, 49.5 x 38.1 cm (19 ½ x 15 in), oil on canvas, Leeds: City Art Gallery. Weenix's early still lifes caught the eye of the Elector Palatine, who employed him in Düsseldorf from 1702–14.

Jan **Weenix**

● 1640–1719 🇳🇱 DUTCH ✍ OILS

The son of Jan Baptist Weenix (1621–63) who called himself Giovanni Battista, Jan Weenix never visited Italy but continued his father's popular Italianate seaports and courtyard scenes. He also painted hunting trophies and still lifes, and was skilled at textures, such as silk, marble, silver, and glass.

KEY WORKS: *The White Peacock*, 1692 (Vienna: Liechtenstein Museum); *Falconer's Bag*, 1695 (New York: Metropolitan Museum of Art)

Jan **van Huysum**

● 1682–1749 🇳🇱 DUTCH ✍ OILS

One of the most prolific flower painters, van Huysum gained an impressive international reputation. He created ornamental bouquets of asymmetrical flower arrangements, not necessarily of the same season. Look for smooth enamel-like paint; cool tones; vivid blues and greens; a few fruit pieces and landscapes. Whenever possible, he worked directly from life rather than from studies.

KEY WORKS: *Flowers and Fruit*, 1723 (St Petersburg: Hermitage Museum); *Still Life with Flowers*, 1723 (Amsterdam: Rijksmuseum)

Jan **Vermeer**

● **1632–75** ᳀ **DUTCH** ᳀ **OILS**

Vermeer is now regarded as the finest Dutch genre painter. However, he was unrecognized in his own lifetime and remained forgotten until the end of the 19th century.

Only 35 works by Vermeer are known for certain. With a few memorable exceptions, he constantly reworked the same theme: the corner of a room, but with a unique, exquisite, tantalizing observation of the organization of space, light, and enigmatic human relationships.

Look closely: nothing is quite in focus – visually and emotionally he selects that tantalizing fraction of a second just before something that is anticipated, but not yet fully perceived or understood, becomes clear and resolved, and in its full realization, so often disappointing. By stopping short, he requires your

eye and imagination to supply what it most desires to see and feel. This is perceptual and poetic creativity, along with manipulation of breathtaking skill and sensitivity. It makes the eye linger over the seemingly innocent but precisely calculated interplay of cool blues and sensuous yellows and whites.

KEY WORKS: *Kitchen Maid*, c. 1658 (Amsterdam: Rijksmuseum); *Woman Holding a Balance*, c.1664 (Washington DC: National Gallery of Art); *Lady Standing at the Virginal*, c.1670 (London: National Gallery)

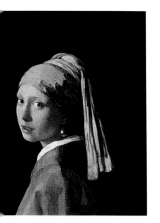

⏶ *Girl with a Pearl Earring* c.1660–61, 46.5 x 40 cm (18 ⅓ x 15 ¾ in), oil on canvas, The Hague: Mauritshuis Museum. In the 1880s, this famous work was sold in Holland for the equivalent of 25 pence (39 cents).

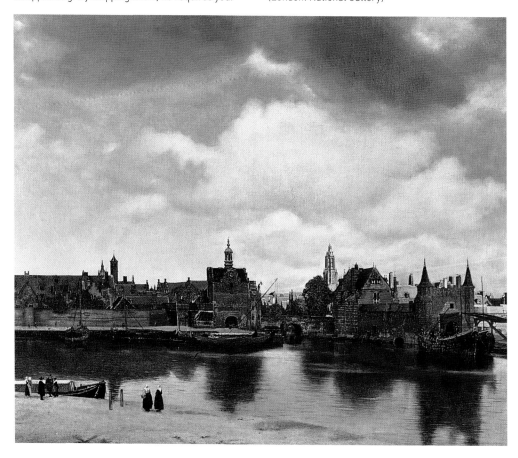

⏷ *View of Delft* c.1660–61, 100 x 117 cm (39 ⅓ x 46 in), oil on canvas, The Hague: Mauritshuis Museum. It is likely that Vermeer used a camera obscura, which projects a slightly fuzzy image. The work was much admired by Marcel Proust.

The source of light is hidden behind a curtain. Note how Vermeer turns highlights into delicate beads of light

The Muse of History carries a trumpet, which symbolizes the fame that can be achieved by an artist

The roof beams create a strong horizontal pattern continued by the map's roller bars. The horizontals and verticals give the picture its mood of stability and calm

The Artist's Studio c.1665, 120 x 100 cm (47 x 39 ½ in), oil on canvas, Vienna: Kunsthistorisches. This is one of Vermeer's later and most ambitious works and it operates on two levels: visually, it is a subtle and intricate arrangement of space and light; intellectually, it is a complex allegory about the art of painting.

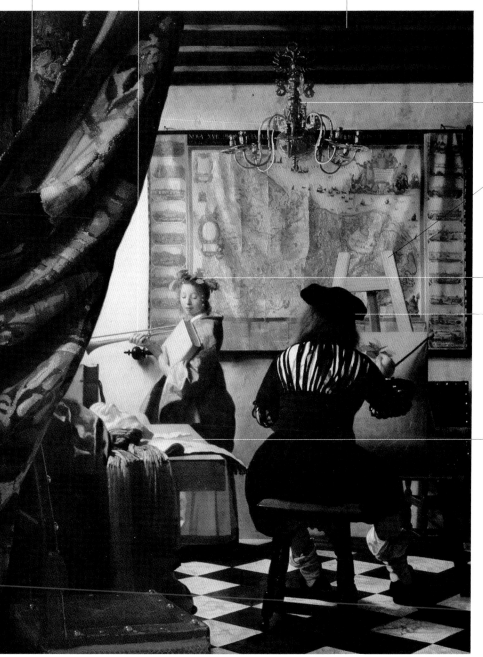

The chandelier is decorated with the two-headed eagle of the Hapsburgs, the Spanish royal family. The lack of candles refers to their waning power: the Northern Dutch provinces gained full independence from Spain in 1648

The artist's easel points with new confidence towards the new republic of Holland

The model represents Clio, the Muse of History, whose attributes are the wreath of laurel and a book

The painter wears a 15th-century costume. It seems that Vermeer is connecting the art of his own era with that of van Eyck and van der Weyden

The line of the tabletop draws the viewer's eye towards a vanishing point just below the bulbous finial of the map's roller bar

❯❯ TECHNIQUES

Vermeer uses the tiles like stepping stones to lead the eye into the composition. The line is reinforced by the angle of the tabletop.

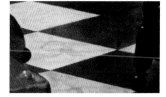

William **Dobson**

⬤ c.1610–46 ▥ BRITISH ✍ OILS

Dobson had a brief career as a painter to the doomed court of Charles I. There are only 50 known paintings; nothing from before 1642. He used a robust, direct style. He painted half-length portraits: red-faced, earthy, male subjects with classical allusions that emphasize the sitter's learning or bravery (or both).

KEY WORKS: *The Executioner with the Baptist's Head*, c.1630s (Liverpool: Walker Art Gallery); *Portrait of the Artist's Wife*, c.1635–40 (London: Tate Collection)

Sir Peter **Lely**

⬤ 1618–80 ▥ DUTCH/BRITISH ✍ OILS

German-born of Dutch parents, Lely settled in England in the early 1640s. He was the principal portrait painter for Charles II and notable for his fashionable, female portraits of richly dressed women with heavy eyes and long fingers. Studio assistants were responsible for much poor-quality work in his name. A few very fine early works show a talent for landscape and observation of unimportant faces. When on form, he had a wonderful feel for light.

KEY WORKS: *Trial by Fire*, 1640s–50s (St Petersburg: Hermitage Museum); *Two Ladies of the Lake Family*, c.1660 (London: Tate Collection); *Barbara Villiers, Duchess of Cleveland*, c.1665 (Private Collection)

✉ *Anne Hyde, Duchess of York* Sir Peter Lely, c.1660s, 182.2 x 143 cm (71 ¾ x 56 ⅓ in), Edinburgh: Scottish National Portrait Gallery. The first wife of James II was reputedly more clever than beautiful.

John Michael **Wright**

⬤ 1617–94 ▥ DUTCH/BRITISH ✍ OILS

Wright was a talented Catholic portrait painter who spent the 1640s and 1650s in Rome and France, and learned the virtues of allegory and elegance. He was a direct contemporary of Sir Peter Lely. Wright established a successful practice during the reigns of Charles II and James II, but his more direct and realistic style never quite suited fashionable taste. He died in poverty.

KEY WORKS: *Elizabeth Claypole (née Cromwell)*, 1658 (London: National Portrait Gallery); *Thomas Hobbes*, c.1669–70 (London: National Portrait Gallery)

Sir Godfrey **Kneller**

⬤ 1646–1723 ▥ GERMAN/BRITISH ✍ OILS

Kneller was German-born, but had settled in England by the age of 30. He was the principal state portrait painter from the reign of Charles II to George I. He established a successful formula – polite, mask-like faces with repetitive mouths and eyes that emphasized status rather than realism or personality. Many sub-standard works were produced by studio assistants.

KEY WORKS: *Portrait of John Banckes*, 1676 (London: Tate Collection); *King Charles II*, 1685 (Liverpool: Walker Art Gallery)

Grinling **Gibbons**

◷ 1648–1721 🏛 BRITISH/
DUTCH ✍ SCULPTURE

Gibbons was England's most famous
woodcarver. Born of English parents
in Rotterdam, he arrived in England
around 1670–71. He had a very
distinct personal style; his sculptures
seem organically alive with cascades
of fruit, leaves, flowers, birds, and fish
tumbling down furniture, panelling,
chimneys, and walls. This famous cravat (right),
à la Venetian needlepoint, was so realistic that an
overseas visitor thought it the standard dress of
an English gent. Writer Sir Horace Walpole often
wore it as a joke. Royal patrons included Charles II,
William III, and George I, as well as major stately
homes, where his work is found today.

KEY WORKS: *Marble font*, c.1680s (London:
St James's Church, Piccadilly); *Ceiling*,
c.1690s (Suffolk: Petworth House)

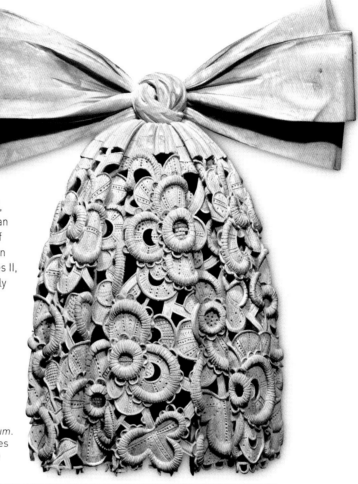

⏩ *Woodcarving of a Cravat* Grinling Gibbons,
c.1690, limewood, London: Victoria & Albert Museum.
This intricately carved piece meticulously imitates
Venetian needlepoint lace, and once belonged to
18th-century collector Sir Horace Walpole.

Sir James **Thornhill**

◷ 1675–1734 🏛 BRITISH ✍ OILS; FRESCO

Ambitious and successful, Thornhill was the only
fashionable and illusionistic English painter of
Baroque wall and ceiling paintings for country
houses and public buildings, such as the Painted
Hall of Wren and Hawksmoor's naval hospital in
Greenwich, London. He retired in 1728 to become
an MP and a country squire. He produced quality
work, but it lacked the necessary histrionic drama
and excess; the British always believed that
foreigners were better at that sort of thing.

KEY WORKS: *Thetis Accepting the Shield of Achilles
from Vulcan*, c.1710 (London: Tate Collection); *Time,
Truth and Justice*, c.1716 (Manchester: City Art Gallery)

Michael **Dahl**

◷ 1659–1743 🏛 SWEDISH/BRITISH ✍ OILS

Dahl was born in Sweden, and settled in
London in 1689. He produced competent
portraits of aristocracy, royalty, and the literati.
He had a languorous, elegant style, but poor
characterization. He was good on draperies;
he used diffused, silvery tones and short
brushstrokes. He was Kneller's principal
competitor. Dahl was prolific and successful.
His earlier works are best.

KEY WORKS: *Self-Portrait*, 1691 (London: National
Portrait Gallery); *Unknown Woman, formerly
known as Sarah Churchill, Duchess of Marlborough*,
1695–1700 (London: National Portrait Gallery)

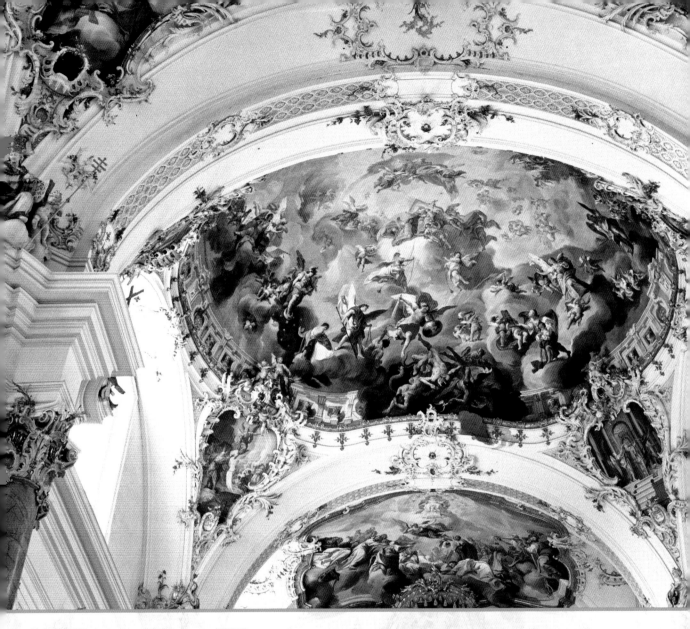

From Rococo to Neoclassicism
c. 1700–1800

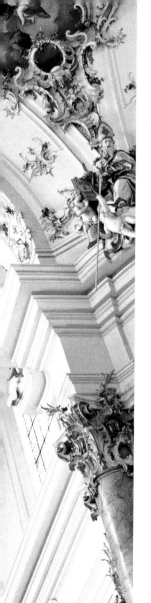

The 17th century had been a period of religious confrontation and warfare. By contrast, the mid-18th century, the Age of Reason, was a period of relative calm in which all the arts developed a refinement and elegance – often small in scale – suited to satisfying simple human needs and longings, rather than supporting ideologies.

At the heart of 18th-century thought and politics was the Enlightenment – a belief that human reason would resolve political and religious dilemmas, explain the workings of the world, the universe, and human nature, and create harmonious relationships in which superstition, tyranny, slavery, and oppression would be eliminated. This emphasis on "a pursuit of happiness" manifested itself in many ways: family life, children, and conjugal love became important; as did education, travel, industriousness, town planning, landscape gardening, parties, music, reading, discussion, food, comfort, and convenience. The Enlightenment also liked intellectual and emotional dualities, not as competing ideologies that would fight each other to the death, but to emphasize that choice was part and parcel of human fulfilment. Thus the art, literature, and philosophy of the 18th century are full of references to the differences between sense and sensibility, frivolity and morality, reason and emotion, indulgence and sobriety, sensuality and self-denial. This duality is equally well represented in the two principal artistic styles of the century: the Rococo with its light-hearted subjects, delicate colours, and asymmetric curves emphasizing frivolity, and sensuality, and Neoclassicism with its serious historical subjects, straight lines, and precise outlines prioritizing morality and self-denial.

France and England

The principles of the Enlightenment were also reflected in the politics of the two major powers, France and England, but expressed in surprisingly different ways, and with very different outcomes. English ideas were

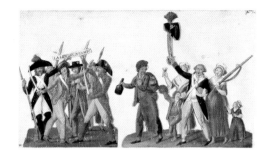

⌃ **Cry of Liberty and the Departure for the Frontier**
Le Sueur brothers, 1792, print, Musée de la Ville de Paris. The French Revolution brought 10 years of political chaos to France, during which the king and his family were executed and Europe was plunged into war.

◖ **Interior of Abbey Church, Ottobeuren, Bavaria**
In the 18th century Germany staged a cultural recovery. Spectacular church interiors were created from a blend of Baroque architecture and Rococo decoration.

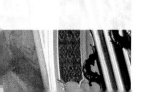

filtered though a prism of robust middle-class pragmatism; French ideas through one of theory, philosophical speculation, and aristocratic otherworldliness.

Both nations benefited from scientific discoveries, population growth, and agricultural revolutions. Both also had substantial colonial territories – chiefly in India and North America – backed by powerful military and naval forces. However Anglo-French rivalry was more than just a question of power politics. Equally importantly, each stood for a fundamentally different approach to government. Catholic France remained committed to the absolutist model of kingship established by Louis XIV. Protestant England, more properly Britain after its formal unification with Scotland in 1707, was rapidly evolving an early form of parliamentary rule. After

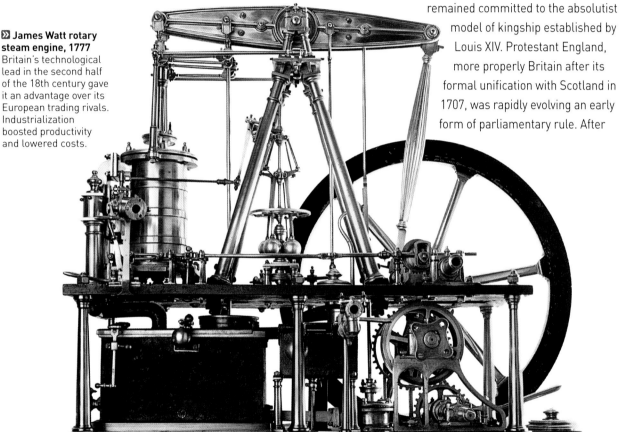

>> **James Watt rotary steam engine, 1777**
Britain's technological lead in the second half of the 18th century gave it an advantage over its European trading rivals. Industrialization boosted productivity and lowered costs.

TIMELINE: 1700–1800

1703 Foundation of St Petersburg by Peter the Great

1714 Hanoverian succession in Britain

1729 Bach's *St Matthew Passion* first performed

1751 Diderot begins publication of *L'Encyclopédie*

1700

1720

1740

1704 Grand Alliance forces under duke of Marlborough defeat French at Blenheim

1715 France ruled by regency of Philippe II, duc d'Orléans, upon death of Louis XIV

1733 War of the Polish Succession becomes Europe-wide conflict

1740 Frederick II the Great of Prussia launches War of Austrian Succession

1763, with the end of the Seven Years' War, Britain's superiority was clear. France had been ejected from India and North America and British naval superiority, the linchpin of its maritime empire, was emphatically confirmed.

Independence and Revolution

British self-confidence received a stinging rebuff with the Declaration of Independence in 1776 by the American colonists. It was the clearest possible statement of the political and philosophical principles of the Enlightenment, modelled on the examples of both France and England, and it succeeded in creating what would eventually grow into a new world power. Britain recovered. Having lost her American colonies, she simply went on to build a second worldwide empire, an Anglo-Scottish enterprise that defined a British national identity, and added enormous wealth to a land already grown rich on modern agriculture, and about to reap the economic benefits of an industrial revolution.

France, on the other hand, was a country that was kept unsteadily afloat by a volatile combination of aristocratic privilege, corruption, and debt, the whole centred on an inept monarchy. In the end, this fatally flawed structure fell apart in the turmoil of the French Revolution of 1789. The

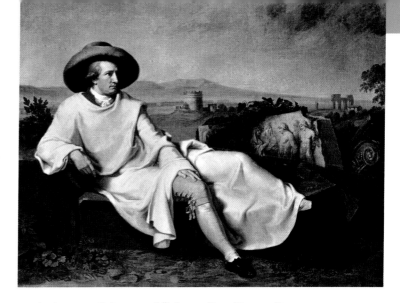

revolutionary rallying cry of "Liberty, Equality, Fraternity" soon became hollow words, as the bloodshed and tyranny of the "Terror" and then the dictatorship of Napoleon usurped the Enlightenment principles that the Revolution had sought to establish.

Elsewhere in Europe the Austrian Habsburgs (Empress Maria Theresa), Prussia (Frederick the Great), and Russia (Catherine the Great) were all growing in influence and power, even if they lacked the global reach of France and England. Poland was on the verge of extinction. Venice and Habsburg Spain were subsiding, the latter despite its still huge Latin American empire. Ottoman Turkey was also shrinking in terms of power and territory, reduced by the end of the century to little more than an impotent bystander.

⬆ *Goethe in the Campagna* Johann Heinrich Wilhelm Tischbein, 1787, 164 x 206 cm (64 ½ x 81 in), oil on canvas, Frankfurt: Städelsches Kunstinstitut. Like many other 18th-century writers and artists, Goethe visited Italy to seek inspiration among the Classical ruins.

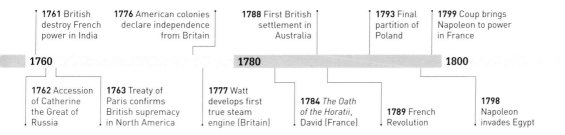

1761 British destroy French power in India

1776 American colonies declare independence from Britain

1788 First British settlement in Australia

1793 Final partition of Poland

1799 Coup brings Napoleon to power in France

1760

1780

1800

1762 Accession of Catherine the Great of Russia

1763 Treaty of Paris confirms British supremacy in North America

1777 Watt develops first true steam engine (Britain)

1784 *The Oath of the Horatii*, David (France)

1789 French Revolution

1798 Napoleon invades Egypt

Jean-Antoine **Watteau**

◉ 1684–1721 🎨 FRENCH ✎ OILS; CHALK

The most important French painter of the first half of the 18th century, Watteau created a fresh, new, unassuming style. He came from a poor family and had indifferent health throughout his short life.

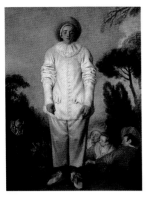

⬆ *Pierrot: Gilles* 1721, 185 x 150 cm (72 ⅘ x 59 in), oil on canvas, Paris: Musée du Louvre. The character Pierrot: Gilles comes from the form of Italian improvised comedy known as *commedia dell'arte*.

Watteau trained as a scene painter at the Paris Opéra from c.1702–07. He then went to work for the curator of the Luxembourg Palace. There he had access to Rubens's *Marie de Medici* series, which was a major influence.

He entered the French Academy with *A Journey to Cythera*, which could not be fitted into any category and for which he received the title of "peintre de fêtes galantes", a variant of the "fête champêtre" or "outdoor feast", which had been applied to the 16th-century outdoor scenes of Giorgione (see page 140).

In 1719, he went to London, possibly to consult a physician, but the English winter aggravated his condition and he died of TB in 1721. His last great work was a shop sign known as *L'Enseigne de Gersaint*, 1721 (Berlin: Staatliche Museen).

Watteau is famous for inventing the *fête galante* or "courtship party"– a stage set and dream world of perfectly mannered human love and harmony with nature, grounded in an acute observation of reality. Never sentimental, there is a melancholy sometimes accredited to his poor health.

His forms are often half-suggested and require completion in the imagination (as in love, where a stolen glance can mean a lot). His statues seem about to become flesh and blood. The very titles of his works – *Rural Pleasures*, *Conversation* – become the spirit of the Rococo: daring, airy, carefree exuberance. When he died, he was developing a more sober blending of his early Flemish realism with his playful *fête galante*.

Curators now find that many of Watteau's paintings are in poor condition, probably due to carelessness with materials. However, he made exquisite red-and-black chalk drawings, gouaches,

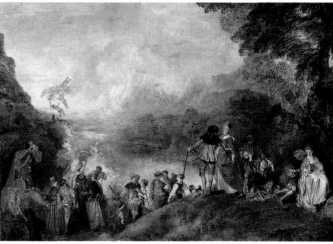

⬆ *A Journey to Cythera* 1717, 129 x 194 cm (51 x 76 ½ in), oil on canvas, Paris: Musée du Louvre. It is not clear from Watteau's composition whether the party is about to go to, or is departing from, the island of Cythera, the birthplace of Venus.

and pastels done from life, which he used as a repertoire for his paintings. These drawings have become important references. During the French Revolution and with Neoclassicism, his reputation suffered, but his colour-flecking techniques influenced Delacroix and the later Post-impressionists.

What to look for

Look for gesture, light, and facial expression to counterpoint frivolity with a melancholy, suggesting the deeper issues of humanity. His delicate brushwork and pastel colours perfectly echo his subject.

KEY WORKS: *The Scale of Love*, c.1715–18 (London: National Gallery); *The Faux Pas*, 1717 (Paris: Musée de Louvre); *Italian Comedians*, c.1720 (Washington DC: National Gallery of Art)

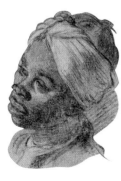

⬆ *Head of a Negro* c.1710–21, chalk on paper, London: British Museum. Watteau was a master of the French technique, *trois crayons*, a combination of red, black, and white chalks set down separately on tinted paper.

Nicolas **Lancret**

● 1690–1743 🏴 FRENCH ✍ OILS

Lancret was a chief follower of Watteau's style, but his own style was more prosaic – he painted only the day-to-day (albeit elegant) reality, whereas Watteau could transform reality and endow it with the magic of poetry and dreams. His works have a cruder colour than Watteau's. Lancret liked theatre subjects. His works were popular with aristocratic collectors.

KEY WORKS: *The Four Ages of Man: Maturity*, 1730–35 (London: National Gallery); *Dance before a Fountain*, c.1730–35 (Los Angeles: J. Paul Getty Museum)

Jean-Baptiste **Pater**

● 1695–1736 🏴 FRENCH ✍ OILS

Pater was Watteau's pupil. Although his subjects and style were similar to Watteau's, his drawing and use of colour lack confidence. Also, his work hasn't got the depth of feeling and the richness of colour that are the hallmarks of Watteau's work.

KEY WORKS: *Les Baigneueses (Women Bathing)*, Early 1700s (St Petersburg: Hermitage Museum); *The Dance*, c.1730 (Los Angeles: J. Paul Getty Museum); *Chinese Hunt*, 1736 (Paris: Musée du Louvre)

Jean **Chardin**

● 1699–1779 🏴 FRENCH ✍ OILS

Chardin was a diligent artist. He exemplified in paint the best qualities of the Age of Reason, producing exquisite small still lifes and genre scenes that demonstrate harmony of order, sober colour, as well as pleasure in simplicity and relationships.

Note his loving observation of light and handling of paint. His choice of subjects and his style reflect his modest, open personality with love of craftsmanship. The surfaces and textures of the still lifes are so believable that you want to touch them – you know exactly what everything is and where it is in space. The genre scenes crystallize moments of simple, restful intimacy, such as childish pleasures, Experience teaching Youth, and the dignity of domestic labour. The symbolism is simple and easy to understand.

KEY WORKS: *The House of Cards*, c.1735 (Washington DC: National Gallery of Art); *The Young Schoolmistress*, c.1735–36 (London: National Gallery)

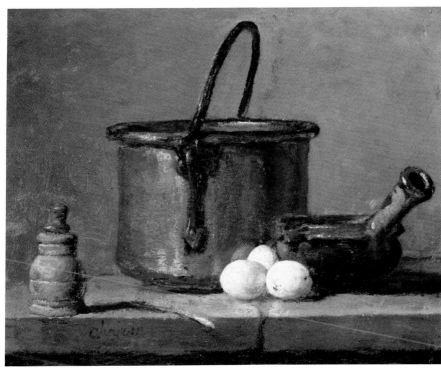

》 *Still Life* Jean Chardin, c.1732, 16.8 x 21 cm (6 ⅔ x 8 ¼ in), oil on panel, Detroit Institute of Arts. Although a member of the prestigious Royal Academy in Paris, Chardin was criticized for not attempting more ambitious subjects. The son of a master carpenter, and a man of simple tastes, he preferred to perfect what he knew he could do best.

The Rococo

1921 | FRENCH | OILS

By the early 18th century, the heroic certainties of the Baroque were giving way to the elegant intricacies of the Rococo (from the French "rocaille", meaning "shellwork", a recurring motif in Rococo interior decoration). A conspicuously courtly painting style, it appealed to sophisticated, aristocratic patrons. As a reflection of a supremely cultivated society, it was briefly supreme.

In Rococo, light colours and deft brushwork predominate, with a premium on highly finished, shimmering surfaces in which the depiction of gorgeous fabrics, melting skin tones, and luxuriant landscape backgrounds – often overgrown, never threatening – is relished for its own sake. In the hands of its most outstanding exponents – the French painters Boucher and Fragonard, and the Italian Tiepolo – the result is a captivating, idealized world, elegant and seemingly effortless. Draperies flow, limbs intertwine, smiles entice and eyelids flutter. Allure is everything.

Sophisticated 18th-century society placed a premium on intimacy. It was a shift in taste precisely reflected by Rococo art, above all in France. In place of the large scale of the Baroque, whether antique or religious, Rococo painting concentrated on aristocratic dalliance, small scale and highly wrought.

Antiquity became a matter of scantily clad shepherdesses,

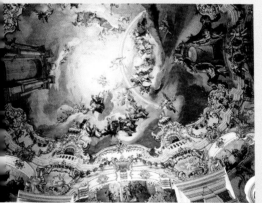

▲ **The Last Judgement** (ceiling fresco) Johann Baptist Zimmermann, c.1746–54, fresco and stucco, Wies (Germany): Wieskirche. German artists fused architecture and painting to create light-filled interiors, which soar into visions of heaven.

◄◄ **"Education de l'Amour"** (modelled by Etienne Falconet after Boucher), c.1763, 30.5 cm (12 in), porcelain. The subject matter, self-evidently sexual, is as typical as the handling: eroticism meets highly finished treatment.

bosoms daintily exposed, ravished by muscular young giants. The Rococo rarely lent itself to religious subjects, but Tiepolo successfully linked the two.

What to look for

Boucher's works epitomized the gorgeous colours, highly finished surfaces, and technical sophistication of the Rococo. It was an art that was self-consciously pleasing, reflecting the privileged aristocratic world that brought it into being. As early as the mid-18th century, however, Rococo was being criticized for these apparent frivolities: by the French Revolution in 1789, what was left of Rococo sentiment had been obliterated. Yet at its best, Rococo encapsulated much more than aristocratic frippery.

KEY EVENTS	
1702	Flemish-born Watteau arrives in Paris
1714	Death of Louis XIV
1717	Watteau paints his elegiac *A Journey to Cythera* (see page 166)
1750	Tiepolo spends three years at Würzburg. Completes the decorative cycle in 1752–53 with fresco of the *Continents*, the world's largest painting, over the main staircase
1775	Boucher appointed director of the French Academy
1767	Fragonard paints his airy masterpiece, *The Swing* (see page 228)

Putti underline the classical origins of this scene as well as its essential unreality

Soft background lighting focuses attention on the principal figures in this tableau

To seduce Frigone, Bacchus transformed himself into a bunch of grapes. She swoons as her arm touches the fruit

Precise painting of an apparently naturalistic setting highlights a new interest in landscape

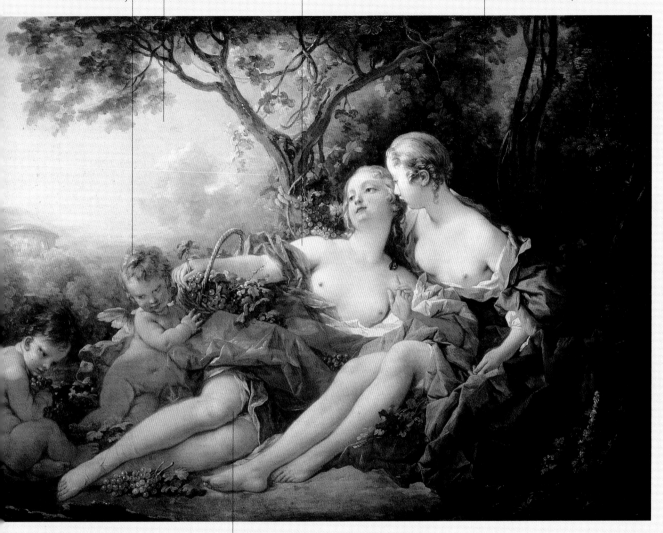

⌃ *Bacchus and Erigone* François Boucher, 1745, 99 x 134.5 cm (39 x 53 in), oil on canvas, London: Wallace Collection. For Boucher, classical myths made most sense when transformed into scenes of ravished innocents. Seduction, here aided by the (fatal) promise of wine, is a recurring theme.

Flesh tones are precisely and lovingly rendered, exemplified in Erigone's delicate, elegant legs, sensually curved and exposed.

⟫ TECHNIQUES

Darkened leaves are lit so that they appear iridescent at the edges from the light of the shaded sun. Similar light plays seductively on the girls' exposed breasts.

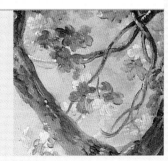

François **Boucher**

⬤ **1703–70** 🏛 **FRENCH** ✍ **OILS**

Boucher was a key artist of the sumptuous, overindulgent *ancien régime* of Louis XV, and a favourite of Madame de Pompadour. He epitomizes the full-blown Rococo style.

He created lavish images of, and for, a world of self-indulgent luxury – the mid-18th century French royal court (wonderful paintings all the same). He was most magnificent with his depictions of classical gods, who (according to him) enjoyed a similar lifestyle; as well as his heavily sentimental pastoral and genre scenes. He designed for royal tapestry works and porcelain factories and became King's Painter in 1765.

Notice the acres of soft, pink flesh set among frothy and false vegetation; lavish silks, satins, and lace in the portraits – all painted with great technical skill and caressing sensuality; a brilliant marriage between his patrons' needs (the subject matter) and style and technique – one of the hallmarks of great painting.

KEY WORKS: *The Breakfast*, 1739 (Paris: Musée du Louvre); *Diana Bathing*, 1742 (Paris: Musée du Louvre)

Jean-Baptiste **Greuze**

⬤ **1725–1805** 🏛 **FRENCH** ✍ **OILS**

Greuze was best known for his sentimental storytelling genre pictures and images of young children, which were part of his later work. Early on he had aspirations as a history painter and played to a pre-French Revolution audience that turned luxury and idleness into an art form. Greuze became very successful but fell into obscurity with the revolution and died in poverty. He had an unpleasant personality.

His overriding feature is excess of emotion – overexpressive faces and overdramatic gestures. You know what feeling he was trying to convey (or do you, in fact?) but, like bad acting, it can seem so false you may well be moved to laughter rather than tears.

Greuze had many weaknesses: false emotion, bad composition, poor drawing, unattractive colour. In fairness, he did make some striking portraits, which are good and worth looking for.

KEY WORKS: *Boy with Lesson Book*, c.1757 (Edinburgh: National Gallery of Scotland); *Spoilt Child*, 1765 (St Petersburg: Hermitage Museum)

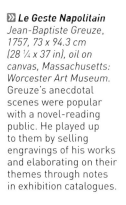

》 *Le Geste Napolitain*
Jean-Baptiste Greuze, 1757, 73 x 94.3 cm (28 ¼ x 37 in), oil on canvas, Massachusetts: Worcester Art Museum.
Greuze's anecdotal scenes were popular with a novel-reading public. He played up to them by selling engravings of his works and elaborating on their themes through notes in exhibition catalogues.

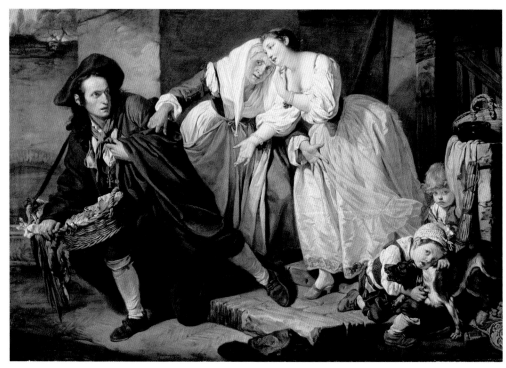

Jean-Honoré **Fragonard**

◉ 1732–1806 ⁌ FRENCH ✍ OILS; CHALKS

Fragonard was precocious and successful – he was much favoured by the *ancien régime* for his easy-to-enjoy, virtuoso, and titillating private paintings. He rejected the trappings of official art and died in poverty after the French Revolution.

He liked pink cheeks and heaving bosoms, sidelong glances, passionate embraces, and futile resistance. Even his drapery, landscape backgrounds, foliage, and clouds froth with equal erotic intensity.

His exciting, nervous, but confident style suits his subjects; his seductive pink-and-green palette and soft, dappled light prefigure Renoir. He painted hands with long, sensuous fingers. Note the lap dogs and fleshy statues ready to join the fun. Look for occasional early works in a "correct" official style – which he soon rejected.

KEY WORKS: *Bathers*, c.1765 (Paris: Musée du Louvre); *Young Girl Reading*, c.1776 (Washington DC: National Gallery of Art); *The Stolen Kiss*, c.1788 (St Petersburg: Hermitage Museum)

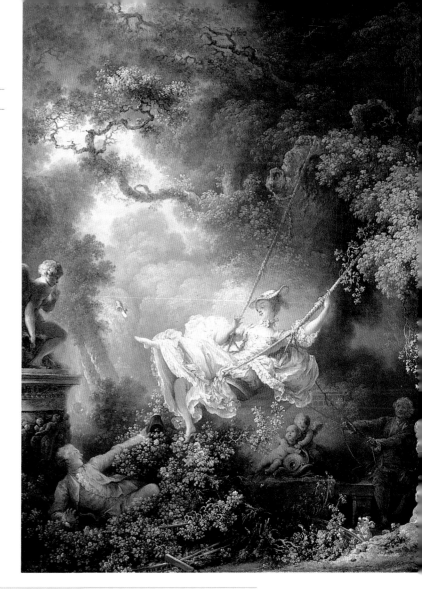

⏩ *The Swing (Les hasards heureux de l'escarpolette)* *Jean-Honoré Fragonard, 1767, 81 x 65 cm (32 x 25 ½ in), oil on canvas, London: Wallace Collection.* The trees were inspired by the Tivoli Gardens in Rome.

Sebastiano **Ricci**

◉ 1659–1734 ⁌ ITALIAN ✍ OILS

Ricci is known for decorative painting at its best. He created standard mythological and religious paintings, which were an engaging eyeful of easy compositions, fresh colour, and attractive people. There is no pretentious intellectualizing or moralizing in his work. Ricci worked in the Venetian tradition.

KEY WORKS: *The Rape of the Sabine Women*, c.1700 (Vienna: Liechtenstein Museum); *Esther before Ahasuerus*, c.1730 (London: National Gallery)

Marco **Ricci**

◉ 1676–1729 ⁌ ITALIAN ✍ OILS; DRAWING

Marco Ricci, the nephew of Sebastiano Ricci, worked in England from 1708 to 1716. He collaborated with his uncle on several religious and mythological pieces. Ricci also developed his own line of fresh, frothy, and light-filled fantasy or semi-topographical landscapes.

KEY WORKS: *Fishing Boats*, 1715 (Los Angeles: J. Paul Getty Museum); *Landscape with Ruins*, 1725 (Los Angeles: J. Paul Getty Museum)

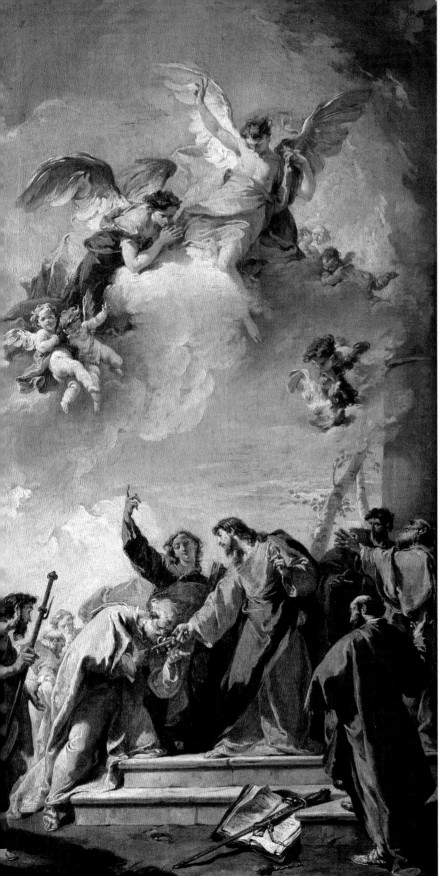

Giovanni Antonio **Pellegrini**

🌐 1675–1741 🏛 ITALIAN 🎨 OILS

Pellegrini was a well-travelled Venetian painter (he went to Germany, Vienna, Paris, Netherlands, and England). His works are bright, appealing, airy, illusionistic, and decorative compositions on a large scale (very much the Venetian tradition, but brought up to date), which were influential in creating a fashion and demand for this type of work, especially in England.

KEY WORKS: *Rebecca at the Well*, 1708–13 (London: National Gallery); *The Marriage of the Elector Palatine*, 1713–14 (London: National Gallery); *Bacchus and Ariadne*, c.1720–21 (Paris: Musée du Louvre)

Giovanni Battista **Pittoni**

🌐 1687–1767 🏛 ITALIAN 🎨 OILS

Pittoni is known as the poor man's Tiepolo. He had a flashy, richly coloured, loosely painted style, which is more of a mishmash of earlier Venetian artists and borrowings from Tiepolo than truly original. His work – religious, historical, and mythological subjects – was much sought after in his lifetime, both at home and abroad, which shows that commercial and critical success is sometimes (often?) achieved by showing off, rather than through genuine talent.

KEY WORKS: *St Prosdocimus Baptizing Daniel*, 1725 (York: City Art Gallery); *An Allegorical Monument to Sir Isaac Newton*, 1727–29 (Cambridge: Fitzwilliam Museum)

◀ ***The Delivery of the Keys to St Peter*** *Giovanni Battista Pittoni, c.1710–67, 82 x 42 cm,(32 ⅓ x 16 ½ in), oil on canvas, Paris: Musée du Louvre.* Christ entrusts the keys of heaven to the disciple, Peter, watched by cherubs.

Rosalba Giovanna **Carriera**

● 1675–1758 🏛 ITALIAN ✍ PASTELS

Rosalba Giovanna Carriera is known for her highly successful portraits in pastels, which cleverly combine delicacy and graciousness with spontaneity, plus a judicious realism that neatly negotiates the fine divide between honesty and flattery. She was much sought after by the rich and fashion-conscious as she took her artistic skills round the capital cities of Europe. It was she who inspired Maurice-Quentin de La Tour to use pastel.

KEY WORKS: *Self-Portrait with a Portrait of her Sister*, 1709 (Florence: Galleria degli Uffizi); *Young Lady with a Parrot*, c.1730 (Art Institute of Chicago)

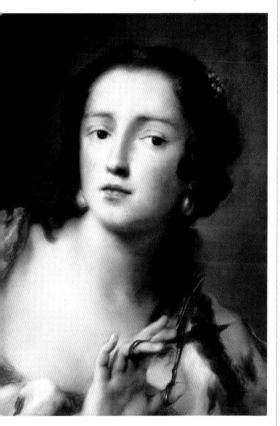

⬆ *Caterina Sagredo Barbarigo as "Bernice"*
Rosalba Giovanna Carriera, c.1741, 44.5 x 31.8 cm (17 ½ x 12 ½ in), pastel on paper mounted on canvas, Detroit Institute of Arts. One of the last works that the artist produced – in 1745, she went blind.

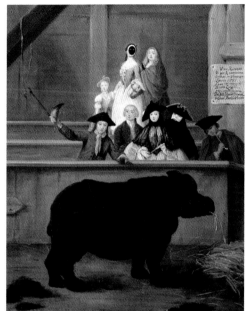

◀ *Exhibition of a Rhinoceros at Venice*
Pietro Longhi, 1751, 60 x 47 cm (23 ⅔ x 18 ½ in), oil on canvas, London: National Gallery. The rhino is exhibited for the amusement of revellers, one of whom brandishes its horn.

Pietro **Longhi**

● 1702–85 🏛 ITALIAN ✍ OILS; CHALKS

Longhi was the Italian counterpart to Lancret and Hogarth (see pages 167 and 180), in successfully catching the 18th-century taste for scenes of everyday life – in his case, Venetian goings-on from aristocracy to lowlife. They still sparkle with spontaneity and sharp, dispassionate observation.

KEY WORKS: *Theatrical Scene*, c.1752 (St Petersburg: Hermitage Museum); *The Display of the Elephant*, 1774 (Houston: Museum of Fine Arts)

Giandomenico **Tiepolo**

● 1727–1804 🏛 ITALIAN ✍ OILS; FRESCOES

The son of Giambattista, with whom he worked on major projects and whose style he successfully imitated. He flourished in his own right (without his father's celestial inspiration and vision), preferring scenes of everyday life and witty anecdote. He was a skilled draughtsman and printmaker.

KEY WORKS: *The Marriage of Frederick Barbarossa*, c.1752–53 (London: National Gallery); *The Building of the Trojan Horse*, (London: National Gallery)

Giambattista **Tiepolo**

● 1696–1770 🏳 ITALIAN ⚄ OILS; FRESCOES

Giovanni Battista Tiepolo was the last great Venetian decorator in the Renaissance tradition. The most celebrated fresco painter of the 18th century, he was famed for his ceaseless invention, astonishing fluency, and ability to tackle huge decorative schemes in record time.

His great works *in situ* (Venice, the Veneto, Madrid, Würzburg) are a miraculous combination of fresco and architecture on a vast scale, where walls and ceilings seem to disappear, revealing a celestial, luminous, shimmering vision of happily radiant gods, saints, and historical and allegorical figures in an epic fantasy world. They constitute one of the greatest artistic experiences of all time.

Observe his brilliant storytelling and illusionistic perspective. The settings of Tiepolo's frescoes were always crucial – they allowed him to create works that extended the real space into his imaginary painted world. He had a confident technique and used luminous colours. His large-scale schemes were the result of teamwork (when painting architectural settings, this was especially crucial). His preliminary sketches show a deft, delicate technique with flickering dark outlines that weave under and over colour, giving life and crispness. He loved rich textures and theatrical gestures, but always avoided cliché and frivolity.

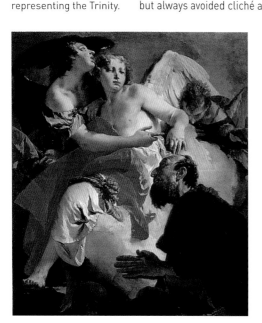

🔽 *Abraham and the Three Angels*
c.1720–70, oil on canvas, Venice: Scuola Grande di San Rocco. The Bible tells how the prophet Abraham offered a meal to three angels, representing the Trinity.

KEY WORKS: *Queen Zenobia Addressing her Soldier*, c.1730 (Washington DC: National Gallery of Art); *The Olympus*, c.1750s (Madrid: Museo del Prado); *Allegory of the Marriage of Rezzonico to Savorgnan*, 1758 (Venice: Ca' Rezzonico: Museo del Settecento)

🔼 *Apollo Bringing the Bride* 1750–51, 6.97 × 14.07 m (22⅚ × 46⅙ ft), ceiling fresco, Würzburg Palace: Imperial Hall. In this fresco, Germany, where Apollo is bringing the medieval Princess Beatrice to her marriage, is transmuted into a vision of 16th-century Venice.

Tiepolo revelled in his mastery of extreme foreshortening. These magnificent horses testify to his virtuosity and his unique brand of epically elegant heroism

Though only a fragment of a building is shown, and from a steeply angled perspective, it implies a strongly imagined architectural setting

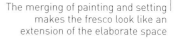

The merging of painting and setting makes the fresco look like an extension of the elaborate space

Pale, limpid colours add
luminosity to the airy
magnificence of the sky. Large,
cloud-flecked areas are daringly
left blank, increasing the sense
of heroic expansiveness

The Sun God Apollo escorts
Beatrice to her wedding. She is
dressed as though in a painting
by Veronese, the 16th-century
Venetian painter, who had a
profound influence on Tiepolo

Allegorical figures
usher the chariot
bearing Apollo and
Beatrice towards
the princess's
future husband

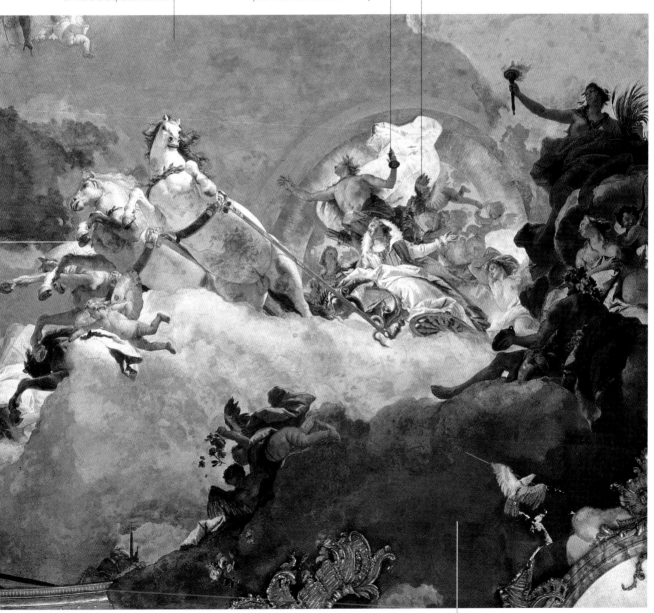

Clouds and figures spill
over the frame of the
fresco into the room

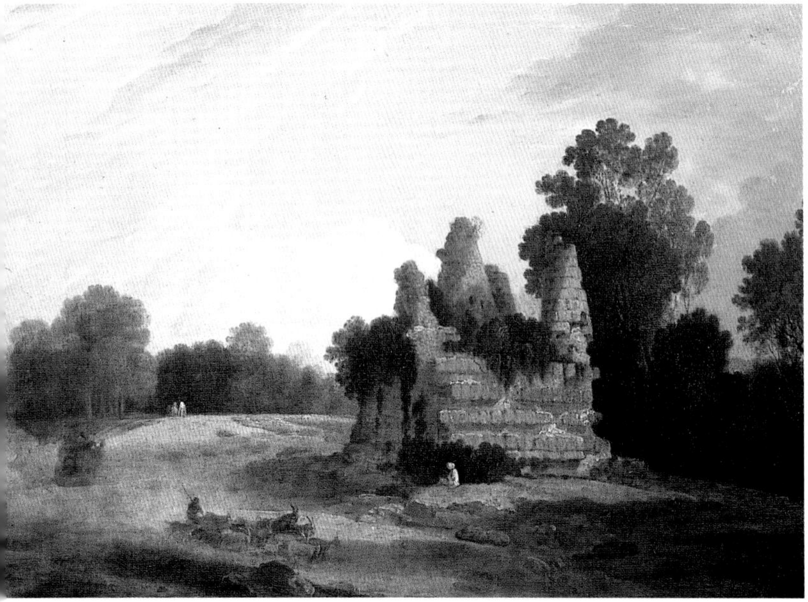

Ruins with Figures *Giovanni Paolo Panini, 1738, 38.1 x 27.9 cm (96 ¾ x 70 ⅘ in), oil on canvas, Wilton (UK): Wilton House.* Panini trained in architectural drawing.

Giovanni Paolo **Panini**

c.1691–1765 ITALIAN OILS

Also known as Pannini, he was a highly successful view painter, contemporary of Canaletto, who anticipated Neoclassical taste. Panini was born in Piacenza and trained in the school of stage designers in Bologna. He worked in Rome, and was much admired by the French. He had a good line in picturesque, ancient ruins, and views and events in modern Rome. His drawings were much sought after in his day.

KEY WORKS: ***Roman Ruins with Figures***, c.1730 (London: National Gallery); ***The Sermon of St Paul Amid the Ruins***, 1744 (St Petersburg: Hermitage Museum); ***Roman Ruins with a Prophet***, 1751 (Vienna: Liechtenstein Museum)

THE GRAND TOUR 18TH CENTURY

Once-in-a-lifetime tour around Europe to see the major sights and works of art, and to experience life and broaden horizons. It was very much the done thing in the early 18th and 19th centuries, especially for young English gentlemen, who would return home with quantities of works of art with which they filled their country homes. An elegant portrait painted in Rome by the Italian artist Batoni was the typical Grand Tour souvenir-cum-status symbol.

Giovanni Antonio **Canaletto**

1697–1768 ITALIAN OILS; DRAWINGS; ENGRAVINGS

Canaletto was the most famous Venetian view painter of the 18th century, much loved and collected by English Grand Tourists. He also painted views of England.

His early views of Venice (1720s to 1730s) are his best, being surprisingly subtle and poetic (his later works tend to become mechanical and dull). He made stunning use of perspective and composition

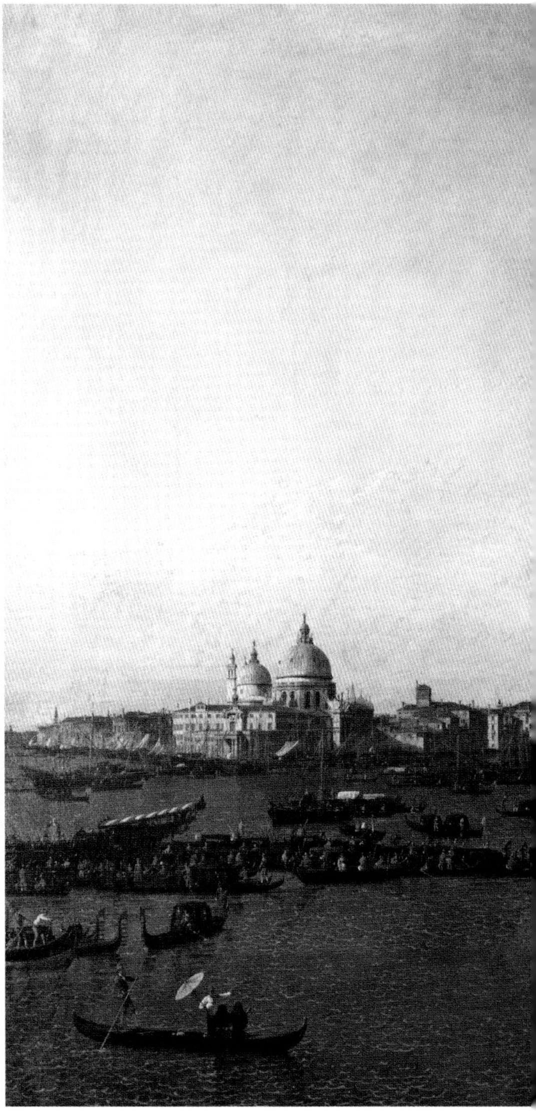

(he may have used a camera obscura). The views are not of reality, but cunning fictions. He was one of the few painters able to capture not just the light and feel of Venice, but also the pageantry and history of a once-great empire in its dying years.

See the way he enlivens perspective with crisp, accurate, architectural details and opens up a scene by using several different viewpoints in one work. He shows clever use of light and shade with a judicious balance of both: razor-sharp shadows and an exciting, unexpected fall of light on a wall. There are many delightful, original, anecdotal details (particularly figures), first-hand observation, and a sense of something (unseen) happening around the corner. He also produced exciting, fluent drawings and sketches.

KEY WORKS: *The Stonemason's Yard*, 1726–30 (London: National Gallery); *Rome: The Arch of Constantine*, 1742 (Windsor Castle, England: Royal Collection); *London, St Paul's Cathedral*, 1754 (New Haven: Yale Center for British Art); *A View of the Ducal Palace in Venice*, pre-1755 (Florence: Galleria degli Uffizi)

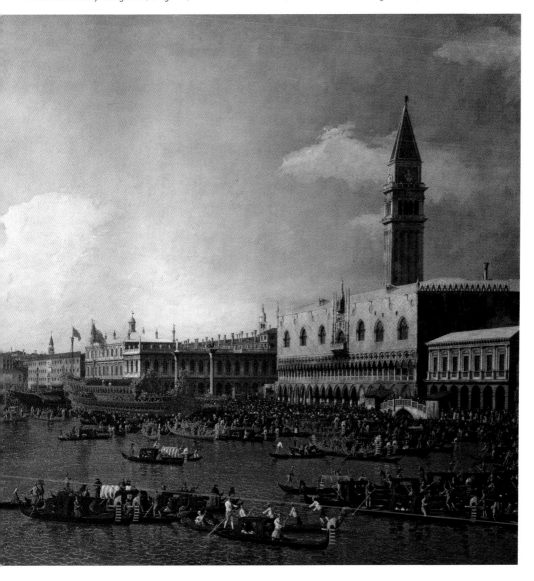

◀ *The Basin of San Marco on Ascension Day* Giovanni Antonio Canaletto, c.1740, 122 x 183 cm (48 x 72 in), oil on canvas, London: National Gallery. Every year on Ascension Day, the Doge of Venice went to the Lido to perform a ceremony whereby Venice was "married" to the Adriatic Sea. The Doge's golden barge is moored ready.

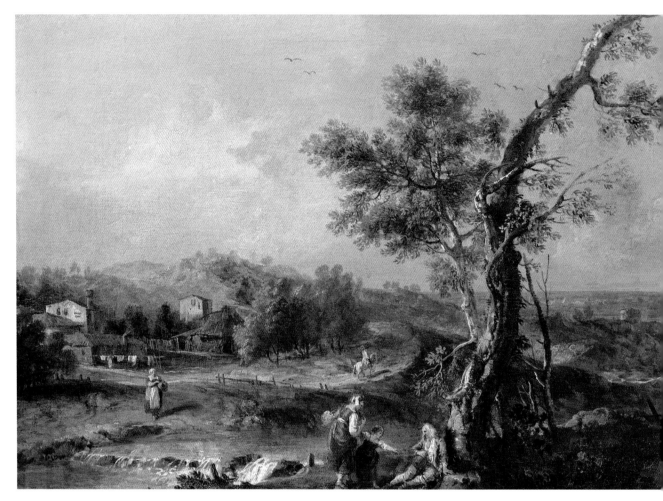

⌂ *An Italianate River Landscape* Francesco Zuccarelli, 105.3 x 89.8 cm (41 ½ x 35 ⅓ in), oil on canvas, London: Christie's Images. Zuccarelli's work was usually made to become part of a decorative room setting.

Francesco **Zuccarelli**

◐ 1702–88 ▥ ITALIAN ✍ OILS

A Florentine painter of Venetian-style high quality, Zuccarelli produced sugary, softly coloured, easily painted pastoral landscapes and cityscapes. He was much admired by collectors of his day (especially the English, who favoured his soft, Rococo style and made him a founder member of the Royal Academy). Once spoken about in the same breath as Canaletto, he is now virtually forgotten.

KEY WORKS: *Landscape with a Woman Leading a Cow*, 1740s (St Petersburg: Hermitage Museum); *Landscape with the Education of Bacchus*, 1744 (Los Angeles: J. Paul Getty Museum); *Landscape with Shepherds*, 1750 (Los Angeles: J. Paul Getty Museum)

Pompeo Girolamo **Batoni**

◐ 1708–87 ▥ ITALIAN ✍ OILS

Batoni was a highly successful portrait painter, especially of English visitors to Italy on the Grand Tour. His works are polished and finely painted. He paid careful attention to detail (lace, stitches in clothing), with beautiful results. He established a formula that favoured stock poses with smart clothes, ruins in the background, and dogs at the feet – or both. He knew exactly what his snobbish clientele wanted and provided them with it.

KEY WORKS: *Christ in Glory with Four Saints*, 1736–38 (Los Angeles: J. Paul Getty Museum); *Time Orders Old Age to Destroy Beauty*, 1746 (London: National Gallery)

Francesco **Guardi**

● 1712–93 ITALIAN OILS; DRAWINGS

A prolific Venetian view painter and the best-known member of a family of painters, Guardi was widely collected in the 18th century, but his paintings sold for half the price of Canaletto's.

His charming Venetian scenes capture the spirit of the city more by atmosphere and mood than by topographical accuracy. The cool, misty, relaxed, small-scale style is in complete contrast with the intense, busy, sharp, and bigger-scale style of Canaletto (their works are usually hung together).

Note the inaccurate perspective and seeming indifference when people or buildings get out of scale; suppression of detail; the loose style of painting; and hazy, cool colours and sombre palette.

KEY WORKS: *A Seaport and Classical Ruins in Italy*, 1730s (Washington DC: National Gallery of Art); *St Mark's Square*, c.1760–65 (London: National Gallery); *Venice: The Grand Canal with the Riva del Vin and Rialto Bridge*, c.1765 (London: Wallace Collection); *An Architectural Caprice*, 1770s (London: National Gallery)

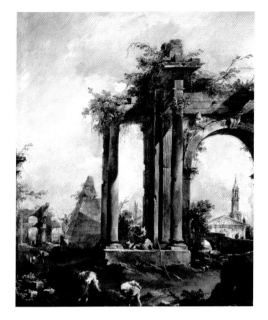

⬘ **Landscape with Ruins** *Francesco Guardi, c.1775, 72 x 52 cm (28 ⅓ x 20 ½ in), oil on canvas, London: Victoria & Albert Museum.* Guardi had a liking for *capricci* – fantasy townscapes with real and imaginary buildings.

Bernardo **Bellotto**

● 1720–80 ITALIAN OILS

Bellotto was a nephew of Canaletto, from whom he learned his trade. Bellotto left Italy in 1747 because of family problems, never to return. His colouring is generally more sombre than his uncle's.

Bellotto painted views of northern European towns, commissioned by the old-fashioned, aristocratic patrons who ruled them and who employed him on a salary as court painter (Dresden, Vienna, and Warsaw).

His impressive, large-scale works are distinguishable from Canaletto's by their different subject matter and cooler, blue-green, silvery palette (he painted on darkly primed canvases). There is less imaginative use of space (used only a standard single-viewpoint perspective), but a better response to trees and vegetation. His anecdotal detail is good, but the figure-painting is more crude than Canaletto's.

KEY WORKS: *Dresden, the Frauenkirche and the Rampische Gasse*, 1749–53 (Dresden: Gemäldegalerie); *The Neustädter Market in Dresden*, 1750 (Dresden: Gemäldegalerie); *Architectural Capriccio*, c.1765 (San Diego Museum of Art); *Entrance to the Grand Canal, Venice*, c.1745 (Cambridge: Fitzwilliam Museum)

⬙ **View of Warsaw from the Royal Castle** *Bernardo Bellotto, 1772, oil on canvas, Warsaw: National Museum.* Bellotto's views of Warsaw were used in the reconstruction of the city after 1945.

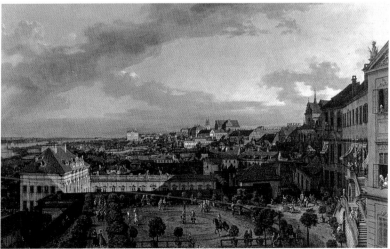

William **Hogarth**

● 1697–1764 ▥ BRITISH ✍ OILS; ENGRAVINGS

Considered the "father of English painting", Hogarth was a quirky, argumentative anti-foreigner, who'd had a tough childhood. Talented both as a painter and printmaker, he laid the foundations that led to Reynolds and the Royal Academy.

Hogarth is best known for his portraits (individual and group), and modern, moral subjects – slices of contemporary life, which were often developed as a series (for instance, *The Rake's Progress* and *Marriage à la Mode*). In neither does he idealize or criticize. He simply shows people and their behaviour for what they are.

He was brilliant as a storyteller, and also a very fine handler of paint, producing confident drawing and colour-rich textures. He painted attractive, open faces in portraits and was especially good at representing children. His work shows engaging anecdotal details coupled with a "warts and all" realism, but we are left to draw our own moral conclusions.

KEY WORKS: *The Strode Family*, 1738 (London: Tate Collection); *The Graham Children*, 1742 (London: National Gallery); *The Shrimp Girl*, c.1745 (London: National Gallery)

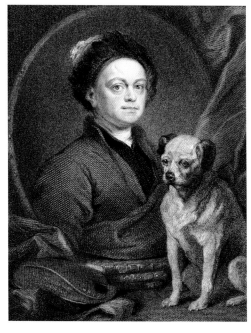

⌃ *Self-Portrait William Hogarth, engraving, private collection*. Hogarth helped to establish the first permanent public display of English art at the Foundling Hospital in central London.

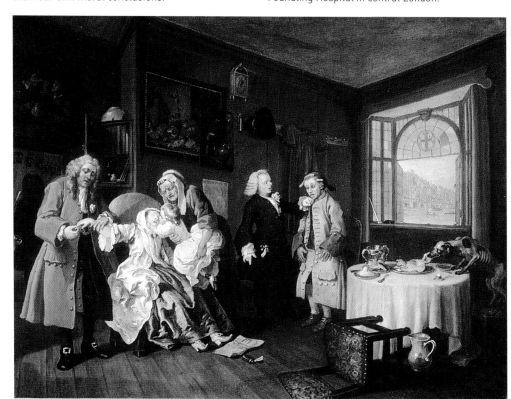

≫ *Marriage à la Mode: VI, The Lady's Death* William Hogarth, c.1743, 70 x 91 cm (27 ½ x 35 ⅗ in), oil on canvas, London: National Gallery. The final grimly comic scene in a story of a disastrous fashionable marriage.

Allan **Ramsay**

● 1713-84 ▢ BRITISH ✎ OILS; DRAWINGS

Ramsay was an interesting and successful Scottish portrait painter who worked mainly in London, from 1739. His early work is often laboured and derivative, his later work, from the 1760s onwards, is better. He was at his best with small and intimate three-quarter-length portraits, especially of women; these have a lovely softness, charm, and delicacy.

The turn of the head on the body gives life to the figures, in spite of repetitive and unimaginative poses. His intensity of observation is worthy of the best still-life painters: note the detail on costumes; the eyes, where even the colour of the iris is noted exactly; and the beautiful use of light.

KEY WORKS: *Richard Mead*, 1740 (London: National Portrait Gallery); *Miss Janet Shairp*, 1750 (Aberdeen: Art Gallery and Museums)

Sir Joshua **Reynolds**

● 1723-92 ▢ BRITISH ✎ OILS

Reynolds is best known for his portraits. He raised the status of portraiture, the arts generally, and the social standing of artists in Britain. He was a discriminating collector of old-master prints and drawings, well connected, and first President of the Royal Academy.

His principal achievement is the brilliant way in which he used allusion and cross-references to enhance the dignity of his sitters and turn portraiture into a type of history painting, with lots of references to classical mythology, antique statues, and architecture. His sitters are often in the poses of well-known examples of Greek and Roman sculpture or the Madonna and Child. He was especially good with children, but terrible as a "history" painter.

Reynolds made inventive use of hands and gesture to bring life and character to his figures. In 1781, he went to Flanders and Holland, and afterwards one can see the influence of Rubens and Rembrandt on his work. He had poor technique – his pictures are often in bad condition because of his use of inferior materials such as bitumen and carmine.

KEY WORKS: *Self-Portrait Shading the Eyes*, 1747 (London: National Portrait Gallery); *Commodore Keppel*, 1753-54 (Greenwich, London: National Maritime Museum); *Lady Caroline Howard*, 1778 (Washington DC: National Gallery of Art)

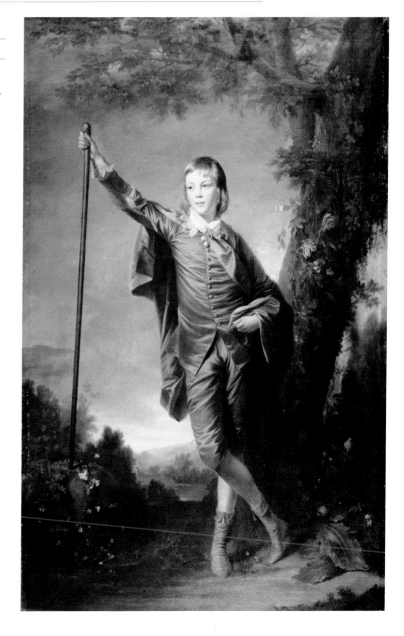

》 *Master Thomas Lister (The Brown Boy)* Sir Joshua Reynolds, 1764, 231 x 139 cm (91 x 55 in), oil on canvas, Bradford, UK: Art Galleries and Museums. The pose mimics an antique statue of Mercury.

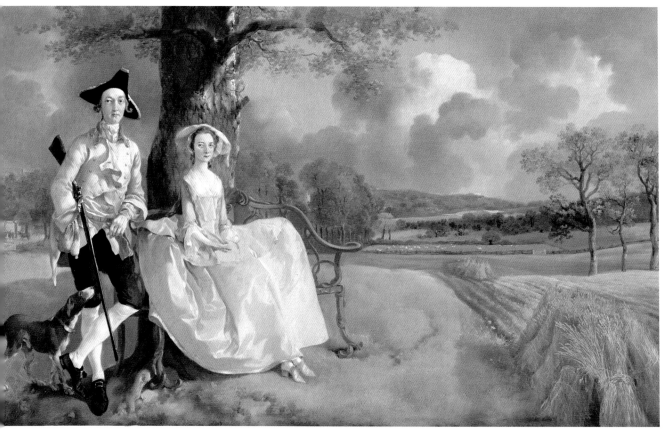

☆ **Mr and Mrs Andrews**
Thomas Gainsborough, c.1749, 71 x 120 cm (28 x 47 in), oil on canvas, London: National Gallery. The newly married couple sit in their estate, the topography of which is precisely recorded.

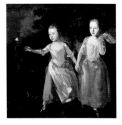

Thomas **Gainsborough**

⬤ 1727–88 🏴 BRITISH ✍ OILS

Gainsborough was best known for his portraits (which he could sell), although his heart was more in landscapes (which were difficult to sell). An amorous man, he was fashionable and successful.

Born in Sudbury, Suffolk, he went to London in 1740 and studied engraving before setting up as a portrait painter in 1752. His sensibility and instinct, as well as his imaginative, experimental craftsmanship were the antithesis to Reynolds's intellectualism and bad technique. His portraits after 1760 are of natural, untheatrical poses – gorgeous best clothes and hats and sympathetic observation and response to character in a face (especially that of a pretty woman). His landscapes

《 **The Painter's Daughters Chasing a Butterfly**
Thomas Gainsborough, c.1759, 113.5 x 105 cm (44 ⅔ x 41 in), oil on canvas, London: National Gallery. Observed with love, aged 7 and 11.

are imaginary, lyrical, poetic – a conscious escape from a hard day's labour. Gainsborough made lovely, free chalk drawings as well as prints. His paint handling was wonderful; used very thinly, freely, and sketchily, enabling him to capture the shimmer of silks and satins, the rustle of breeze-touched foliage, the natural blush on a girl's cheek, or rouge on a matron's face. There are parallels with early Mozart (1756–91): the interweaving of structure and texture, light-hearted seriousness, and physical pleasure of being alive. His early works lack the easy relaxation of the later works; they are charming, but the portrait figures look like dolls and the landscapes concentrate on detail rather than atmosphere.

KEY WORKS: *The Blue Boy*, c.1770 (San Marino: Huntingdon Art Collections); *Portrait of Anne, Countess of Chesterfield*, c.1777 (Los Angeles: J. Paul Getty Museum); *Mrs Richard Brinsley Sheridan*, c.1785 (Washington DC: National Gallery of Art)

Gavin **Hamilton**

● 1723-98 ◨ BRITISH ✍ OILS

Hamilton, a Scottish-born resident of Rome, was an archaeologist, painter, and picture dealer. He was also a pioneer of the international, archaeological, and severely intellectual branch of Neoclassicism, but was outpaced by other, better, painters. He also painted portraits and conversation pieces endowed with an austere charm.

KEY WORKS: *Dawkins and Wood Discovering the Ruins of Palmyra*, 1758 (Edinburgh: National Gallery of Scotland); *Achilles Lamenting the Death of Patroclus*, 1763 (Edinburgh: National Gallery of Scotland)

James **Barry**

● 1741-1806 ◨ BRITISH ✍ OILS

Barry was a highly gifted Irish-born history painter. He became a professor at the Royal Academy, only to be expelled in 1799. After writing a critical open letter in the press, he was the only artist to be expelled from the Royal Academy until the 21st century. He aimed for the top, creating large-scale history paintings on the scale of Raphael's Vatican frescoes. He was such a difficult person that he ruined his own opportunities and died lonely.

KEY WORKS: *The Progress of Human Knowledge and Culture*, 1777–83 (London: Royal Society of Arts); *Portrait of Samuel Johnson*, c.1778–80 (London: National Portrait Gallery)

Johann **Zoffany**

● C.1734-1810 ◨ GERMAN/BRITISH ✍ OILS

Zoffany was a German-born painter who made his career in Rome and London from 1760. He lived in India from 1783 to 1789. He made a fortune by painting native princes and British colonialists. His delightful informal group portraits are his best works and they capture the ease and confident prosperity of Georgian upper-class society. Look for good anecdotal details: sporting, artistic, and literary activities.

KEY WORKS: *The Academicians of the Royal Academy*, 1772 (Royal Collection); *Charles Townley's Library at 7, Park Street, Westminster*, 1781–83 (Burnley, UK: Towneley Hall Art Gallery)

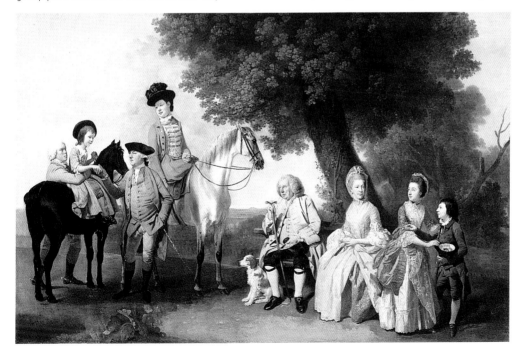

◀ *The Drummond Family* Johann Zoffany, c.1769, oil on canvas, New Haven: Yale Center for British Art. Zoffany's portraits were popular with George III and Queen Charlotte, who became his patrons.

Angelica **Kauffmann**

● 1741–1807　◉ SWISS　✍ OILS

Kauffman is best known for her work done in England (1765–80). She was very successful with elegant, delicate portraits, history paintings, and decorations in the style of Reynolds for houses by Robert Adam. She was partial to sentimental figures with pink faces and cheeks.

KEY WORKS: *Rinaldo and Armida*, 1771 (New Haven: Yale Center for British Art); *Ariadne Abandoned by Theseus*, 1774 (Houston: Museum of Fine Arts); *Self-Portrait Hesitating Between the Arts of Music and Painting*, 1775 (Yorkshire, UK: Nostell Priory)

Richard **Cosway**

● 1742–1821　◉ BRITISH　✍ WATERCOLOURS; OILS

Cosway was best known as the most fashionable and outstanding miniaturist of the 18th century. Look for long, aquiline noses with very noticeable nostrils and shadows under the nose. He painted a few unsuccessful large-scale oils. He married Maria Hadfield (1759–1838), a successful Irish/Italian painter, miniaturist, and illustrator. He was a friend of the Prince of Wales (later Prince Regent).

KEY WORKS: *Self-Portrait*, c.1770–75 (New York: Metropolitan Museum of Art); *Group of Connoisseurs*, 1771–75 (Burnley, UK: Towneley Hall Art Gallery); *Portrait of Mrs Marley*, c.1780 (Washington DC: Hillwood Museum and Gardens); *Unknown Lady of the Sotheby or Isted Families*, c.1795 (Cambridge: Fitzwilliam Museum)

Sir Henry **Raeburn**

● 1756–1823　◉ BRITISH　✍ OILS

Raeburn was the best-ever Scottish portrait painter. A no-nonsense character, he was just as happy playing golf or speculating in property (he went bankrupt). He was the first Scots painter to be knighted. Note the matinée-idol style of portraiture – heroic stances and soft focus with "alone but self-assured" poses, often against

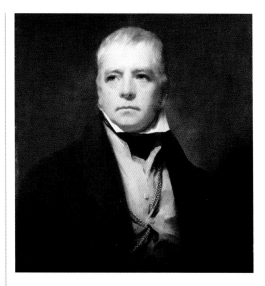

⬒ *Portrait of Sir Walter Scott* Sir Henry Raeburn, 1822, 75.5 x 59 cm (30 x 23 in), oil on canvas, Scottish National Portrait Gallery. Scott's "Waverley" novels made him the most important and influential Scottish novelist of the time.

dramatic skies and landscape backgrounds. His work is at its best with handsome, strong-jawed male figures, looking vaguely dishevelled and adopting the stern, faraway look. He was never at home with female sitters, who often look dull and plain, but was very good with children. His figures are bathed in light and animated by the brilliant, inventive, theatrical play of light over face and costume. Look for pink faces and rich colours. He had a strong, confident, broadly brushed technique using square brushes straight onto coarse canvas, without underdrawing – he painted directly from life, with carefully observed tones and shadows. His best works have no alterations or reworkings – he became messy and clumsy when forced to make changes. Raeburn's down-to-earth, confident method is in harmony with the temperament he saw in (or imposed on?) his sitters. Note the single dab of bright highlight on noses.

KEY WORKS: *Miss Eleanor Urquhart*, c.1793 (Washington DC: National Gallery of Art); *William Glendonwyn*, c.1795 (Cambridge: Fitzwilliam Museum); *Isabella McLeod, Mrs James Gregory*, c.1798 (Aberdeenshire: Fyvie Castle); *Mrs Scott Moncrieff*, c.1814 (Edinburgh: National Gallery of Scotland)

The English Landscape Tradition

18TH CENTURY

From as early as 1750, a distinctive tradition of landscape painting was emerging in England, partly a reflection of 18th-century English landscape gardening – the subtle re-ordering of nature for aristocratic patrons in imitation of the classical landscapes of 17th-century painters like Claude Lorrain. In the hands of a series of exceptional painters, it developed into a rich celebration of a distinctively English approach to nature.

Reaching a peak of achievement in the hands of Turner and Constable, English artists drew on several sources for inspiration. An inherent interest in the pastoral qualities of the English countryside and the subtle nuances of its seasons was bolstered by theoretical discussions on the different qualities of picturesque and sublime scenery, by studies of the Dutch and Italian masters, and by first-hand experience of the contrasting virtues of the landscape of the Roman Campagna.

The art of watercolour painting, small-scale, delicate, understated, was a particular English accomplishment practised by both amateurs and professionals. Starting as essentially topographical, and as an embellishment for drawings, it blossomed into an art form in its own right, its transparent washes ideally suited to capturing the most subtle qualities of light filtered through clouds, and reflections on water or snow.

⬙ *The White House* Chelsea Thomas Girtin, 1800, *watercolour on paper, private collection.* Turner greatly admired Girtin's brilliant watercolour technique and later said "Had Tom Girtin lived, I would have starved."

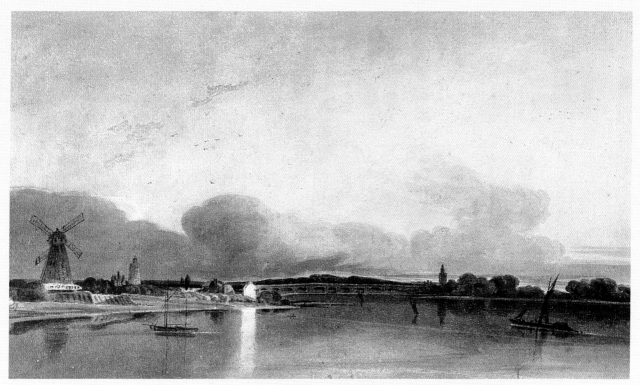

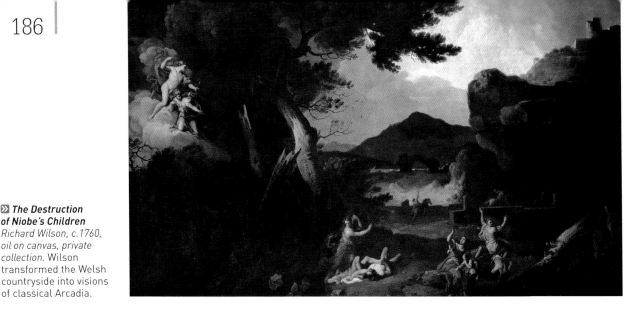

▶▶ *The Destruction of Niobe's Children*
Richard Wilson, c.1760, oil on canvas, private collection. Wilson transformed the Welsh countryside into visions of classical Arcadia.

Richard **Wilson**

● c.1713–82 🏳 BRITISH ✍ OILS

The first major British landscape painter, Wilson produced lovely, direct topographical views and sketches, which were influenced by Dutch masters. He is especially known for successful set-piece works that are a synthesis of idealized classical formulae and actual places. His work shows great sensitivity to light, notably during and after his visit to Italy 1750–57, but it can become overfamiliar and repetitious.

KEY WORKS: *Caernarvon Castle*, c.1760 (Cardiff: National Museum of Wales); *The Valley of the Dee*, c.1761 (London: National Gallery); *Lake Albano*, 1762 (Washington DC: National Gallery of Art)

Alexander **Cozens**

● 1717–86 🏳 RUSSIAN/BRITISH ✍ DRAWINGS

Born in Russia, but educated in Rome, Cozens was an English landscape draughtsman known for his watercolour landscapes and etchings. He was fascinated by systems and famous for his method of using accidental blots on a piece of paper as visual inspiration out of which an idea, such as a landscape, might develop.

KEY WORKS: *The Valley of the Rhone*, 1746 (London: Tate Collection); *A Blot: Landscape Composition*, 1770–80 (London: Tate Collection)

John Robert **Cozens**

● 1752–97 🏳 BRITISH
✍ WATERCOLOURS; DRAWINGS

John Robert Cozens, the melancholic son of Alexander Cozens, was a landscape painter. He was well travelled (the Alps and Italy). His early watercolours, prefiguring those of Turner, are wonderful. In them, he shows how a landscape can be a vehicle for emotion and mood when made with imagination and inventive techniques. Cozens created luminous skies full of atmosphere, space, and light. In 1793, he went insane.

KEY WORKS: *Satan Summoning his Legions*, c.1776 (London: Tate Collection); *Sepulchral Remains in the Campagna*, c.1783 (Oxford: Ashmolean Museum)

Thomas **Girtin**

● 1775–1802 🏳 BRITISH
✍ WATERCOLOURS; OILS

Girtin was potentially a rival to Turner, but he died of consumption at the age of 27. He painted brilliant watercolours that pushed the interpretation of landscape and watercolour technique through to new frontiers. He had a wonderful sense of colour and of the noble grandeur of nature.

KEY WORKS: *Village Along a River Estuary in Devon*, 1797–98 (Washington DC: National Gallery of Art); *Lindisfarne*, c.1798 (Cambridge: Fitzwilliam Museum)

William **Marlow**

🌐 1740–1813 🏛 BRITISH ✍ WATERCOLOURS; OILS; DRAWINGS

Marlow was a successful, topographical painter in watercolour and oils. He travelled widely in the UK, France, and Italy and painted successful Grand Tour souvenir views, seascapes, river scenes, and portraits of country houses. He created satisfying, balanced compositions and was able to capture the cool light and well-ordered topography of England, as well as the intense light and more dramatic topography of Italy.

KEY WORKS: *The Pont Royal*, c.1765–68 (Cambridge: Fitzwilliam Museum); *View of the Tiber and the Ripetta with St Peter's in the Distance*, c.1768 (Northamptonshire, UK: Boughton House); *A Post-House near Florence*, c.1770 (London: Tate Collection)

🔽 *The Pont du Gard, Nîmes* William Marlow, *c.1767, 38 x 56 cm (15 x 22 in), oil on canvas, London: Charles Young Fine Paintings.* Marlow travelled in France and Italy in 1765–66, painting Grand Tour souvenir views.

Jacques Philippe de **Loutherbourg**

🌐 1740–1812 🏛 FRENCH/BRITISH ✍ OILS; DRAWINGS

Loutherbourg was a painter and stage designer from Strasbourg, who settled in England in 1771. He produced stagey landscapes and seascapes. He was important as a link between the old Arcadian classical landscape traditions and the new realism and Romanticism of Turner and Constable. He also painted battle scenes and biblical subjects in an energetic style. He was one of the first to celebrate the delights of English scenery.

KEY WORKS: *Landscape with Cattle*, c.1767 (London: Dulwich Picture Gallery); *The Falls of the Rhine at Schaffhausen*, 1788 (London: Victoria & Albert Museum)

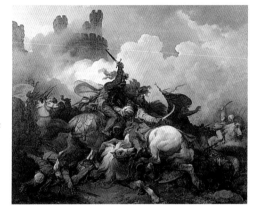

🔽 *Battle Between Richard I Lionheart (1157–99) and Saladin (1137–93) in Palestine* Jacques Philippe de Loutherbourg, c.1790, oil on canvas, Leicester: New Walk Museum.

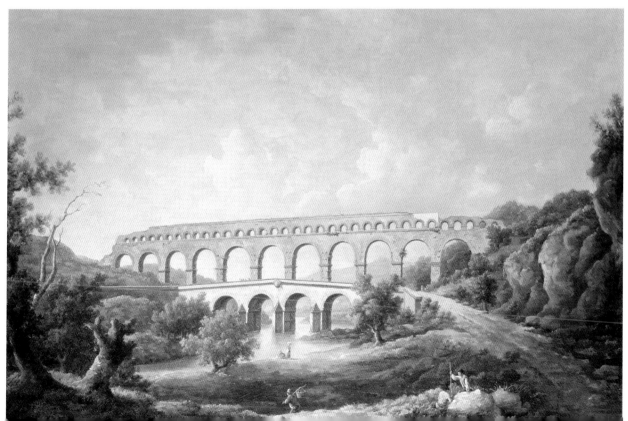

Joseph **Wright**

● **1734–97** | BRITISH | OILS

Known as "Wright of Derby", he was a talented and versatile painter, but out of the mainstream. He developed new and original subjects: night scenes, scientific experiments, and early industrial forges. His paintings often have unusual light effects and offer fascinating insights into the Age of Reason and the nascent Industrial Revolution. He painted goodish, occasionally great, portraits.

KEY WORKS: *A Philosopher Lecturing on the Orrery*, 1766 (Derby, UK: Derby Museum and Art Gallery); *An Experiment on a Bird in the Air Pump*, 1768 (London: National Gallery); *Mrs John Ashton*, c.1769 (Cambridge: Fitzwilliam Museum)

David **Allan**

● **1744–96** | BRITISH | OILS; DRAWINGS

The Scottish Hogarth, Allan was deeply influenced by a visit to Rome. He wanted to be remembered as a history painter (*de rigueur* at the time, but it was not his forte). However, Allan was a successful portrait painter and established the tradition of Scottish genre paintings with anecdotal illustrations of Scottish life and history.

KEY WORKS: *John, the 4th Duke of Atholl and His Family*, c.1773 (Private Collection); *The Connoisseurs*, 1783 (Edinburgh: National Gallery of Scotland); *A Neapolitan Music Party*, c.1775 (Private Collection)

George **Stubbs**

● **1724–1806** | BRITISH | OILS

Stubbs was the greatest-ever painter of the horse, hunting, racing, and horsebreeding, and also painted scenes of rural life. He was successful, with powerful patrons, but always a loner.

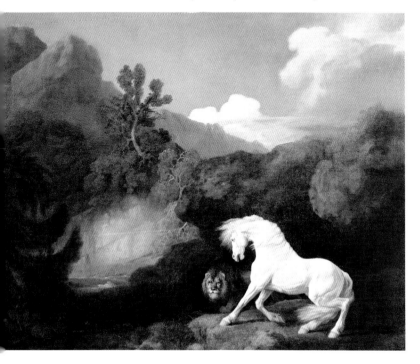

His book, *Anatomy of the Horse* (1766), is one of the most remarkable publications on art and science. Stubbs's deep, personal fascination with the anatomy and character of the horse touched something more widespread and profound: man's relationship with nature (wholly dependent on the horse until the invention of mechanical power) – plus the mid-18th-century belief in rational investigation as a means of understanding the natural world and comprehending the qualities of beauty. He produced wonderful, measured, modest pictures that exemplify the saying "beauty is truth, truth beauty".

His paintings are models of rational beauty: subtle, careful, half-concealed geometry of horizontal and vertical structures around which play curving cadences (like Mozart); a loving observation of space, anatomy, and the unspoken relationship between animal and man. He was a stunning draughtsman. His exquisite, harmonious, gentle colour has too often been tragically destroyed by insensitive cleaning and restoration.

KEY WORKS: *Mares and Foals beneath Large Oak Trees*, c.1764–68 (Private Collection); *Cheetah and Stag with Two Indians*, c.1765 (Manchester: City Art Gallery)

« *A Horse Frightened by a Lion* George Stubbs, 1770, 94 x 125 cm (37 x 49 in), oil on canvas, Liverpool: Walker Art Gallery. Stubbs's inspiration was not real life but an Antique sculpture he saw in Rome in 1754.

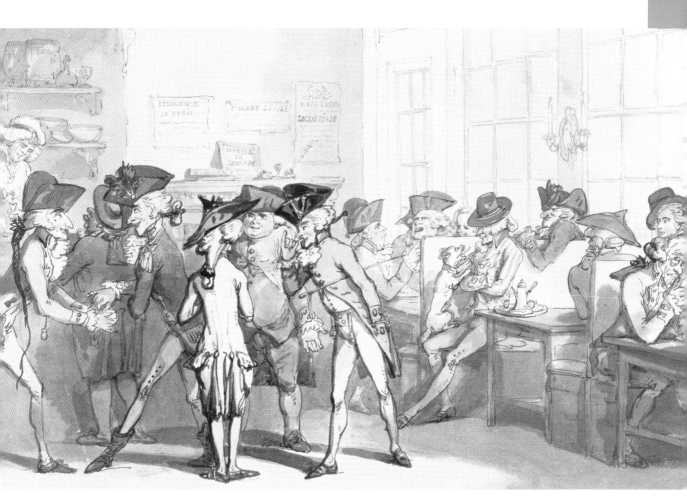

⌃ *A French Coffee House* Thomas Rowlandson, 1790s, 23 x 33 cm (9 x 12 ⅘ in), pen and ink with watercolour on paper, Cambridge: Fitzwilliam Museum. Revolutionary France was a popular subject for British caricaturists.

Thomas **Rowlandson**

◉ 1756–1827 🏳 BRITISH ✍ DRAWINGS; PRINTS

A prolific draughtsman and printmaker, Rowlandson was a chronicler of 18th-century life and morals. He had huge technical facility, enthusiasm for life, and an eye for detail and character, which he expressed with an admirable economy of line. Rowlandson walked the tightrope between observation and caricature with skill.

KEY WORKS: *Box-Lobby Loungers*, 1785 (Los Angeles: J. Paul Getty Museum); *The Dinner*, 1787 (St Petersburg: Hermitage Museum)

Jacques-Laurent **Agasse**

◉ 1767–1849 🏳 SWISS ✍ OILS

Swiss-born and Paris-trained (by J. L. David, and as a vet), Agasse worked in England. He was known for his faithfully observed, meticulously executed paintings of animals and their owners or keepers. Although a truly great painter, he had a small output and died poor and unknown; in those days, animals were not considered a serious art subject (they still aren't today).

KEY WORKS: *Sleeping Fox*, 1794 (Private Collection); *The Nubian Giraffe*, 1827 (Windsor Castle, England: Royal Collection)

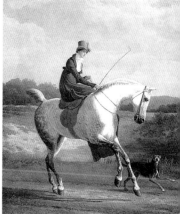

⊠ *Miss Casenove on a Grey Hunter* Jacques-Laurent Agasse, c.1800, 30.5 x 25.5 cm (12 x 10 in), oil on canvas, private collection. The artist was much influenced by Stubbs in both subject matter and technique.

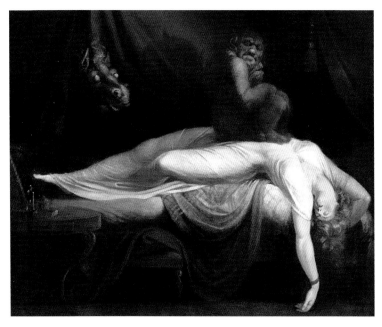

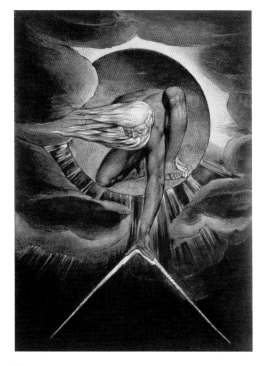

⚑ **The Nightmare**
Henry Fuseli, 1781, 101 x 127 cm (39 ¾ x 50 in), oil on canvas, Michigan: Detroit Institute of Arts. The woman represents Fuseli's lost love, Anna Landolt.

Henry **Fuseli**

● **1741–1825** ◫ SWISS/BRITISH
✍ OILS; DRAWINGS

A Swiss-born eccentric, Fuseli was also known as Johann Heinrich Füssli. Inspired by Michelangelo, Shakespeare, and Milton, he made highly dramatic interpretations of literature with intense facial expressions and overdeveloped body language. His defective technique ruined many of his oil paintings.

Fuseli's drawings are wonderful; he also had a special line in female cruelty and bondaged males. He was obsessed with women's hair.

KEY WORKS: *Lady Macbeth Sleepwalking*, c.1784 (Paris: Musée du Louvre); *Oedipus Cursing His Son Polynices*, 1786 (Washington DC: National Gallery of Art)

William **Blake**

● **1757–1827** ◫ BRITISH ✍ ENGRAVINGS; WATERCOLOURS; DRAWINGS

Blake was a true visionary, inspired and driven by inner voices and sights, but neglected in his lifetime. His early work was within the current Neoclassical style. In time, his work transformed the graceful, symbolic fauna of Neoclassicism and became more visionary. He had originality in imagery, technique, and symbolism and created mostly small(ish) works on paper – watercolours and drawings – and a combination of these with print techniques. Blake's imagery and symbolism are highly personal but at heart is the wish to express his dislike of all forms of oppression. He championed creativity over reason; love over repression; individuality over state conformity. He believed in the liberating power of the human spirit.

Look for idealized human figures with spiritual expressions, and a fascination with fire and hair, which are stylized. His works often have Biblical sources, especially from the Old Testament.

KEY WORKS: *Newton*, 1795 (London: Tate Collection); *Job and his Daughters*, 1799–1800 (Washington DC: National Gallery of Art)

⚑ **The Ancient of Days** *William Blake, 1824, 23 x 17 cm (9 x 6 ⅔ in), etching with watercolour, pen, and ink on paper, Manchester: Whitworth Art Gallery.* Blake's God is an oppressive lawmaker imprisoning the imagination.

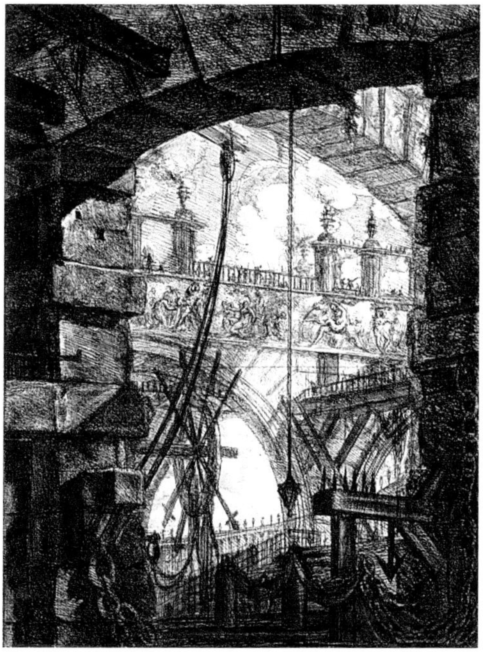

Carceri d'Invenzione (Prisons) Plate IV
Giovanni Battista Piranesi, 1760, 54.5 x 41.5 cm (21 ½ x 16 ⅓ in), etching, Hamburg: Kunsthalle.
Piranesi was also a successful restorer and dealer in Roman art and artefacts.

Giovanni Battista **Piranesi**

1720–78 | ITALIAN | ENGRAVINGS

Piranesi was an architect, archaeologist, and printmaker (etchings). Venetian-born, he settled in Rome in 1740 and made a reputation from popular prints of ancient and modern Rome. He used inventive imagery, which moved from archaeological exactitude to dramatic, overwhelming Romantic grandeur, made all the more powerful by a brilliant technique and a mastery of perspective, light, and shade. His most original works are images of fantastic prisons, which are Surrealist before their time. His etching work was continued by his son, Francesco.

KEY WORKS: *Round Tower*, c.1749 (St Petersburg: Hermitage Museum); *The Gothic Arch*, c.1749 (Washington DC: National Gallery of Art); *The Well*, 1750–58 (Washington DC: National Gallery of Art)

Anton Raphael **Mengs**

1728–79 | GERMAN | OILS; FRESCO

"The German Raphael", Mengs was a founder of Neoclassicism, and one of the foremost artists of his day. He worked in Germany, Italy, and Spain. He was a committed teacher with an active studio and wrote an influential theoretical treatise.

Mengs is proof that having the right credentials – being well taught, and obeying all the currently correct aesthetic principles – does not lead to lasting fame. His religious paintings, mythologies, and portraits consciously aimed to contain the best of Raphael (expression), Correggio (grace), and Titian (colour). In a way they do, but in spite of their competence they look lifeless and contrived.

Note his paint surface that looks like polished lacquer. His compositions and poses are so carefully calculated as to be merely stagey: notice how in the portraits the head often turns in one direction while the hands and body turn in the other. He painted flesh and faces that look impossibly healthy. His works have rich textures and colours (especially a velvety royal blue, rich bottle-green, and dusky pinks). Mengs's portraits are now considered better than his history paintings.

KEY WORKS: *Noli me Tangere*, 1771 (London: National Gallery); *The Immaculate Conception*, 1770–79 (Paris: Musée du Louvre)

Franz Xaver **Messerschmidt**

1736–83 | AUSTRIAN | SCULPTURE

Messerschmidt was a sculptor, trained by his uncles, whose Baroque busts won early approval with the Austrian Court. Later, he was influenced by famous Roman Republican heads after a visit to Rome and his style became more Neoclassical. He is famous for his "Character Heads", a series of busts, many self-portraits, in which he explored facial distortions and grimaces after he started to suffer from delusions and paranoia. He thought the work would help heal and protect him from evil spirits.

KEY WORKS: *Character Heads: The Gentle, Quiet Sleep; The Hanged; The Lecher; The Arched Evil*, 1770–83 (Vienna: Österreichische Galerie)

Neoclassicism

1770–1830

Neoclassicism was a deliberate reaction against the decorative priorities of the Rococo. It was a self-conscious return to what were thought of as the absolute, severe standards of the ancient world. On the whole, it generated huge, dull paintings of "improving" history subjects, but its most brilliant exponent, the painter David, radically fused contemporary political concerns with a new artistic language.

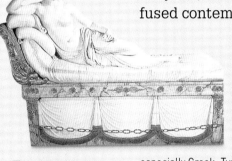

⌃ **Paolina Bonaparte Borghese as Venus**
Antonio Canova, 1808, marble, Rome: Galleria Borghese. Canova, who settled in Rome after 1779, was the most influential Neoclassical sculptor. He brought an exceptionally finished technique to the ideals of Greek purity.

The German theorist and art historian, Johann Winckelmann, decisively influenced Neoclassicism, by persuasively advocating the "noble simplicity and calm grandeur" of ancient art, especially Greek. Typically, Neoclassical works are measured, grave, and self-consciously noble. Colour schemes are often sombre, though with brilliant highlights, and paint is applied with smoothly precise consistency. Light falls evenly, draperies are simple and chaste, poses invariably sternly heroic.

Overwhelmingly, subjects from Classical literature and history were favoured. Religious subjects always co-existed uneasily with Neoclassicism, not surprisingly since the vast majority of Classical art was pagan. Greece and Republican (not Imperial) Rome furnished most subjects. Self-sacrifice and self-denying heroism were recurring themes, underlining the supposed moral worth and superiority, and thus truth, of ancient art.

What to look for

The Oath of the Horatii is a landmark painting of Neoclassical art, a deliberate celebration of the art, life, and stern moral values of Republican Rome. Authoritative, heroic, and impeccably composed, it is a statement of moral and political ideals. Three brothers (the Horatii) swear allegiance to the Roman Republic, but are also bound by ties of love to an enemy family, the Curatii. They choose loyalty to the state over personal emotion.

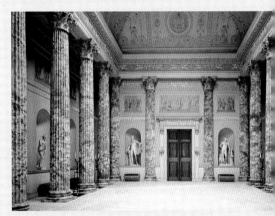

⌃ **Kedleston Hall, Derbyshire** *c.1760.* Interior of the marble hall designed by Robert Adam, with columns and plasterwork by Joseph Rose. Following a visit to Rome in 1754, Adam sought to emulate the grandeur of ancient buildings in a series of opulent and imposing English houses, such as Kenwood House, Hampstead, and Stone House, Buckingham.

KEY EVENTS

1738	Excavations begin at Herculaneum, and at Pompeii in 1748
1755	Publication of Winckelmann's *Thoughts on the Imitation of Greek Works of Art*
1775	French Revolution begins. The Bastille, symbol of the *ancien régime*, is stormed
1806	Work begins on the Arc de Triomphe by sculptor Claude Michel Clodion
1815	Restoration of the French monarchy and final overthrow of Napoleon at Waterloo

Each of the three Doric arches frames a group of figures, suggesting both their isolation and their ties to each other

The dominant colour of the male grouping is a vivid red, the colour of passion and revolution

>> **Sabina (right) is one of the Curatii**, but married to one of the Horatii. Camilla (left), a Horatii, is betrothed to a Curatii. She will be killed by her brother for lamenting her lover's death.

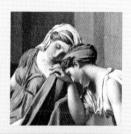

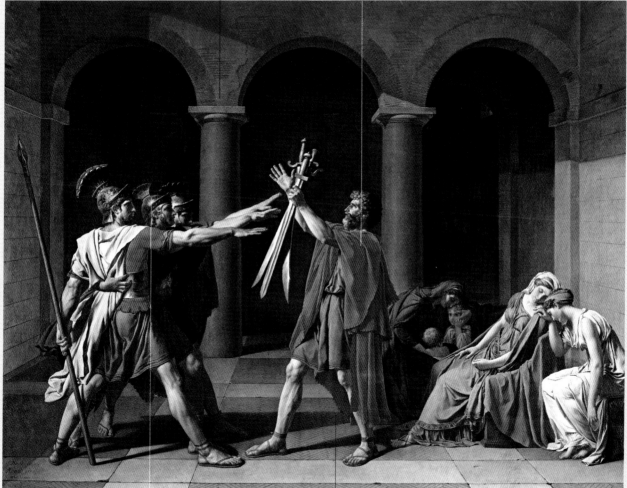

⌃ **The Oath of the Horatii**
Jacques-Louis David, 1784, 330 x 425 cm (130 x 167 in) oil on canvas, Paris: Musée du Louvre. The picture became a rallying cry for the French Revolution. Ironically, it had been commissioned by Louis XVI.

The helmets, swords, and togas are copied from known Roman examples

The shadow of death is cast by the men over the children and their grandmother

>> **TECHNIQUES**

Despite its massive size, *The Oath of the Horatii* is painted with the fine, polished technique usually found in a small Dutch still life.

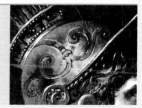

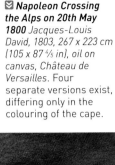

Napoleon Crossing the Alps on 20th May 1800 *Jacques-Louis David, 1803, 267 x 223 cm (105 x 87 ⅘ in), oil on canvas, Château de Versailles. Four separate versions exist, differing only in the colouring of the cape.*

Jean-Antoine **Houdon**

● 1741–1828 ⚑ FRENCH ✍ SCULPTURE

Houdon was one of the most important French sculptors of the 18th century. He was born in France and died there; he studied in Rome after receiving the *Prix de Rome* in 1761 and was famed in his lifetime throughout Europe and America. He survived the French Revolution. The majority of his works are portrait busts. Houdon was famously commissioned to sculpt George Washington, for which he visited North America. He was influenced by the Baroque before becoming a Neoclassicist; his works emulate the busts of ancient Greece and Rome.

KEY WORKS: *St Bruno*, 1767 (Rome: S. Maria degli Angeli); *George Washington as the Modern Cincinnatus*, 1788 (Richmond: Virginia State Capitol)

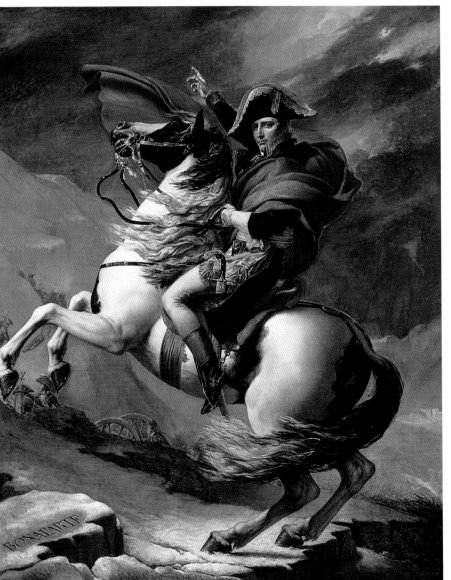

Jacques-Louis **David**

● 1748–1825 ⚑ FRENCH ✍ OILS; DRAWINGS; CHALKS

David was deeply involved in the politics of the French Revolution and the Napoleonic Empire, and died in exile in Brussels. He was the founder of French Neoclassical painting, but was an arts administrator and a creative genius. He applied the precision of a painter of miniatures on a massive scale. He had stern moral and artistic rules: behind the theatre and storytelling is the ideological commitment to art as a public and political statement in the service of the state. The body language and facial expressions of his characters were used as drama. There was no place for ambiguity.

Observe his attention to detail, especially in hands, feet, tassels, armour, and stones. His flesh is as smooth as porcelain, with never a hair in sight. His portraits of victors of the French Revolution have direct, busy-body eyes. Even shadows and light seem to have been disciplined and regimented. His love of antiquity and archaeological accuracy (Roman noses everywhere) are obvious. You have to experience the sheer physical size of the big set pieces at first hand.

KEY WORKS: *The Oath of the Horatii*, 1784–85 (Paris: Musée du Louvre); *The Death of Socrates*, 1787 (New York: Metropolitan Museum of Art); *Death of Marat*, 1793 (Brussels: Musée d'Art Moderne); *Madame Récamier*, c.1800 (Paris: Musée du Louvre)

Claude-Joseph **Vernet**

● 1714–89 🏛 FRENCH 🖌 OILS

Vernet established a successful formula for rather stagey, evocative views of Italianate landscapes, coastlines, and especially shipwrecks, much admired by 18th-century collectors. His major project (commissioned by Louis XV) was 16 views of major French seaports (1753–65).

KEY WORKS: *View of Naples*, 1748 (Paris: Musée du Louvre); *The Town and Harbour of Toulon*, 1756 (Paris: Musée du Louvre)

Elisabeth **Vigée-Lebrun**

● 1755–1842 🏛 FRENCH 🖌 OILS

Vigée-Lebrun was a successful portraitist in the last years of the *ancien régime*; she was also a member of the French Academy. Vigée-Lebrun was best at sentimental, lushly coloured portraits of fashionable women (she allegedly painted Marie Antoinette 25 times). She left France in 1789 to tour Europe, and later wrote a good autobiography.

KEY WORKS: *Hubert Robert, Artist*, 1788 (Paris: Musée du Louvre); *Madame Perregaux*, 1789 (London: Wallace Collection)

📩 *Portrait of a Young Woman* Elisabeth Vigée-Lebrun, *c.1797, 82.2 x 70.5 cm (32 ⅓ x 27 ¾ in), oil on canvas, Boston: Museum of Fine Arts.* The artist organized famous parties at which guests wore Greek costume.

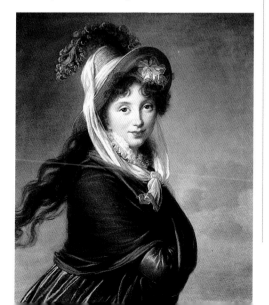

Antonio **Canova**

● 1757–1822 🏛 ITALIAN 🖌 SCULPTURE

Canova was the leading Neoclassical sculptor and certainly the most celebrated artist. He enjoyed huge fame across Europe and was widely credited with reviving the "lost art" of sculpture and was frequently compared with the best of the ancients. He combined astonishingly accomplished technique – his best works are highly finished – with a rare talent for the human figure, females especially, in a variety of winningly graceful poses. Many group sculptures can only be appreciated in the round, i.e. from different viewpoints, so they are no longer dependent on architectural settings. It is significant that many of his later works were created for museums rather than patrons, underlining the changing status of the artist.

Born in Treviso, Canova moved to Venice where he opened a studio in 1774. He visited Rome and Naples as his interest in Neoclassicism developed. In 1781, he settled permanently in Rome. He enjoyed early success with monuments to popes Clement XIV (1782–87) and Clement XIII (1787–92). In 1797, the French invasion forced him into exile in Vienna, but in 1802 he accepvted commissions from Napoleon after visiting Paris. Canova's most famous work was of Napoleon's sister, Pauline Borghese, in 1808. After 1815, he visited Paris again overseeing the return of looted Italian art, with a side trip to London. In 1817, a grateful pope granted him the title of Marchese (Marquis) of Ischia.

KEY WORKS: *Daedalus and Icarus*, 1779 (Venice: Museo Correr); *Theseus Slaying a Centaur*, 1780s (Vienna: Kunsthistorisches Museum); *The Penitent Magdalene*, 1796 (Genoa: Palazzo Bianca); *Pauline Borghese as Venus*, 1808 (see page 192)

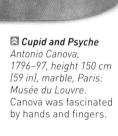

🔺 *Cupid and Psyche*
Antonio Canova, 1796–97, height 150 cm (59 in), marble, Paris: Musée du Louvre. Canova was fascinated by hands and fingers.

Bertel **Thorvaldsen**

● c.1770–1844 🏳 DANISH ✍ SCULPTURE; OILS

Denmark's most important Neoclassicist, he is ranked alongside Canova, although his works lack the Italian's sensitive surfaces. His career took off with the statue *Jason with the Golden Fleece*.

Stationed mainly in Rome, he preferred to work from copies instead of employing live models. A museum was built in his honour in Copenhagen (1839–48).

KEY WORKS: *Hebe*, 1806 (Copenhagen: Thorvaldsens Museum); *The Triumph of Alexander the Great*, 1810s (Preston, UK: Harris Museum and Art Gallery)

Benjamin **West**

● 1738–1820 🏳 AMERICAN ✍ OILS

Born in Pennsylvania, West was the first American artist to achieve international recognition. Trained and based in Europe after 1760, he became the second President of the Royal Academy, London after Joshua Reynolds, and was employed by George III (who lost the American colonies).
His work is an acquired taste for modern eyes.

West's style is second-hand, that is, derived, if not exactly copied, from others. He had the enviable ability of anticipating the next fashion and was thus always successful and in the public eye. His early large works often portray obscure literary subjects and have a stiff, rather flat, wooden style

that caught the taste for the Neoclassical. From 1770 onwards, West cleverly adapted Neoclassicism by delivering the same heroic message using modern rather than ancient history – this was popular with the public and collectors, and shook up less progressive artists. He later anticipated Romanticism by introducing melodramatic subjects of death and destruction with powerful contrast of light and shade. He was also a popular portraitist.

KEY WORKS: *Venus Lamenting the Death of Adonis*, 1768 (Pittsburgh: Carnegie Museum of Art); *Colonel Guy Johnson*, c.1775 (Washington DC: National Gallery of Art); *The Burghers of Calais*, 1789 (Windsor Castle, UK: Royal Collection)

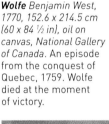

🔽 *The Death of General Wolfe* Benjamin West, 1770, 152.6 x 214.5 cm (60 x 84 ½ in), oil on canvas, National Gallery of Canada. An episode from the conquest of Quebec, 1759. Wolfe died at the moment of victory.

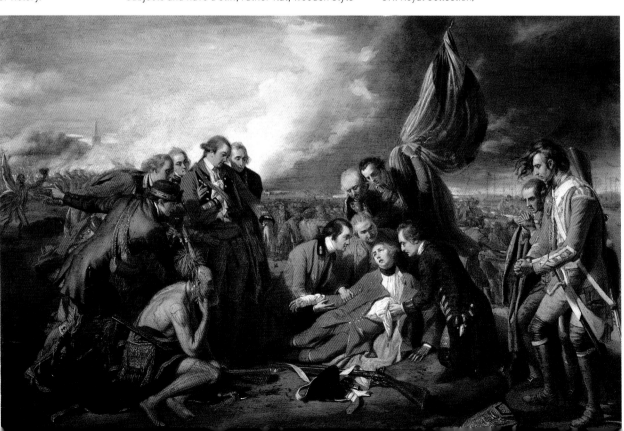

John Singleton **Copley**

1738-1815 AMERICAN OILS

Copley was the greatest American painter of the colonial period. He was self-taught. Slow, earnest, and indecisive as a person, he was assured, talented, and pioneering as a painter. The son of poor Irish immigrants, he married well.

He had two careers and styles. Pre-1774, in Boston, he established himself as the leading portrait painter. His decisive and sober works show his, and his sitters', liking for empirical realism. Note the precise line, clear detail and enumeration of material objects, and severe contrasts of light and dark. In 1774, he left Boston, fearful that he would be dubbed a pacifist and Tory hanger-on.

Note how he adapted to the grand-manner style of portrait painting (more decorative, pompous, and frothy) after his visit to Italy. It did his portraiture no good, but he achieved great success in London with huge-scale modern-history paintings (heroic actual events presented as though they were moral tales from Ancient History). He faced a late, melancholic decline as he went out of fashion and felt exiled (he never returned to the US).

KEY WORKS: *Paul Revere*, c.1768–70 (Boston: Museum of Fine Arts); *The Copley Family*, 1776–77 (Washington DC: National Gallery of Art); *Watson and the Shark*, 1778 (Washington DC: National Gallery of Art); *The Three Youngest Daughters of George III*, 1785 (Windsor Castle, England: Royal Collection)

Ralph **Earl**

1751-1801 AMERICAN OILS

The prominent member of a family of craftsmen and artists; a loyalist who left for England in 1778, returning in 1785. Noted for portraits of Connecticut patrons – typically, a plain likeness in their own familiar setting. His sketches of sites of the battles of Lexington and Concord were turned into popular prints. He was a bigamist, carouser, and a failed businessman.

KEY WORKS: *The Striker Sisters*, 1787 (Ohio: Butler Institute of American Art); *Dr. David Rogers*, 1788 (Washington DC: National Gallery of Art); *Mrs Noah Smith and her Children*, 1798 (New York: Metropolitan Museum of Art)

» THE RISE OF AN AMERICAN SCHOOL

From the mid-18th century, a number of painters appeared in Colonial America. This may have been a measure of growing American prosperity but the colony's cultural insecurity was underlined by the fact that they all trained in Europe, falling under the influence of Neoclassicism. The best known, Benjamin West, settled permanently in England. As late as 1784, when the State of Virginia commissioned a statue of George Washington, it turned to a Frenchman, Jean-Antoine Houdon. A distinctively American school did not emerge until the 19th century.

Gilbert **Stuart**

1755-1828 AMERICAN OILS

The penniless, uneducated son of a Rhode Island tobacconist, Stuart was a heavy drinker, often in debt, bad-tempered, and addicted to snuff. He was also a highly successful portrait painter and America's first virtuoso exponent of the grand manner.

Trained in Edinburgh (1772) and London (1775) as an assistant to Benjamin West, he produced Romantic, dignified portrait images of independence and self-assurance, softly modelled and silhouetted against a plain background. Stuart painted almost every contemporary of note, especially Washington. Of his 114 portraits of Washington, only three were from life; the rest are replicas

His characteristic features and touches are a pinkish-green palette; a white dot on the end of a shiny nose; light shining on a forehead; and rapid execution without preliminary drawing.

KEY WORKS: *The Skater*, 1782 (Washington DC: National Gallery of Art); *The Athenaeum Portraits*, 1796 (Washington DC: National Portrait Gallery); *George Washington and Martha Washington*, 1796 (Boston: Museum of Fine Arts)

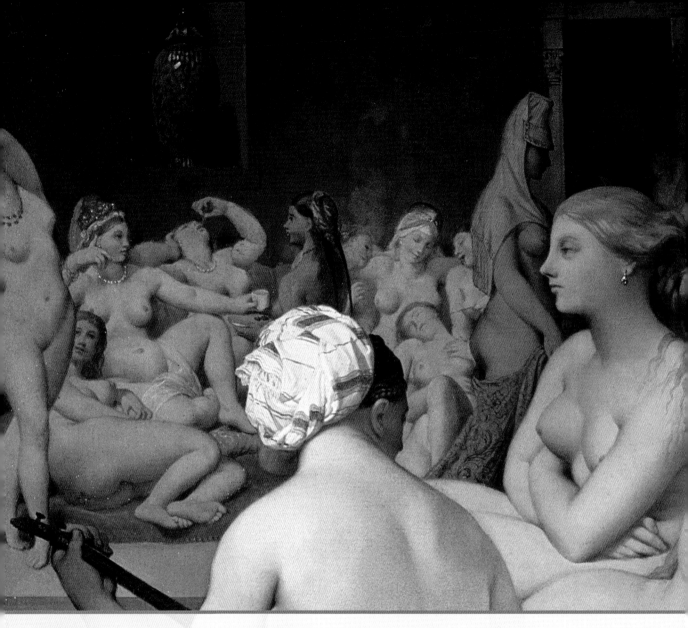

Romantic and
Academic Art
c.1800–1900

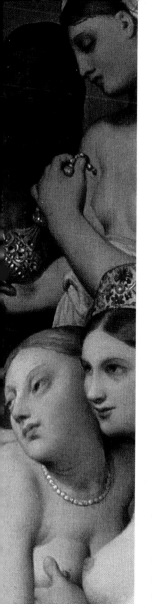

The art of the 19th century was complex and multifaceted. Radical new styles were invented that delighted some and caused deep offence to others. Old styles were revived or combined in unexpected ways. Some artists followed the market, motivated by money; others were willing to starve for the purity of their art.

Romanticism was embraced by those who wanted to redefine the place of art and humankind in a rapidly changing world. Academicism was supported by those who resisted change and wanted art to maintain the cultural and social status quo. These attitudes to the art of the era reflect the complex politics of the 19th century.

The Napoleonic era

In Europe, the decisive event of the early part of the century was the resurgence of France under the galvanizing influence of Napoleon. What had begun in 1789 as a struggle for liberty evolved into a war of conquest. In 1812, at the height of Napoleon's success, French rule extended across almost the whole of western Europe. Only Britain, Portugal, and Scandinavia remained free of French control.

Nationalism and revolution

Napoleon's defeat in 1815 restored Europe's pre-revolutionary status quo, but ideas of liberty, once planted, proved tenacious.

◪ *The Turkish Bath* (detail), Jean-Auguste-Dominique Ingres, 1863, diameter 198 cm (78 in), oil on canvas, Paris, Musée du Louvre. Ingres embodies the 19th-century taste for Classical academic style, combining it with exotic Orientalism.

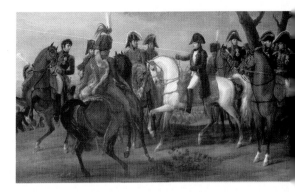

⌃ *Napoleon Giving Orders before Austerlitz* Antoine-Charles Horace Vernet, 1808, oil on canvas, 380 x 645 cm (150 x 254 in), Château de Versailles. The memory of Napoleon influenced French politics throughout the 19th century.

Growing demands for self-rule by oppressed minorities saw Belgium, Greece, Serbia, and Romania emerge as independent nations by the end of the century. Popular nationalism also drove the unification of Italy (after 1859) and of Germany (after 1866).

There was fierce reaction against self-rule by conservative regimes, above all the multi-national Austrian Empire. These conflicting ideologies clashed in 1848 when Poles, Czechs, and Hungarians rose against their Austrian rulers, engulfing central and eastern Europe in revolution. France, which had already seen the abdication of one king in 1830, was also swept by popular uprisings, forcing a second king to abdicate and the inauguration of a new republic. In 1852, this was replaced by the Second Empire under Napoleon III, Napoleon's nephew.

The crushing defeat of France in the Franco-Prussian War of 1870–71 provided the final impetus for the unification of Germany. In its wake, Germany's southern states committed themselves to the powerful new Prussian-dominated German Empire and, following the downfall of Napoleon III, France established the Third Republic.

Industrialization

Britain became increasingly aloof from European affairs, preoccupied with its vast empire and the consequences of industrialization. First Britain, and then Europe after 1850, were changing rapidly from rural to urban societies amid great social upheaval. Britain had set the pace but France, and, significantly, Germany proved ever more effective rivals. Huge new industrial cities appeared, with railways, steam ships, and the electric telegraph causing a revolution in communications.

≫ PHOTOGRAPHY

Photography was first demonstrated to the wider world by Louis-Jacques-Mandé Daguerre in 1839. In its early years it was used principally for studio portraits, mimicking those painted for the wealthy at a fraction of the cost. Gradually, however, it replaced drawing as the most immediate method of making a record of visual appearance. In the 1870s, US-based English photographer Eadweard Muybridge, using a battery of cameras with fast shutter-speed, began to make studies of horses and humans in motion. This allowed people to see for the first time the action of a galloping horse.

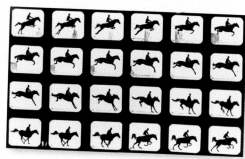

⌃ **Muybridge photographs** of a jumping horse

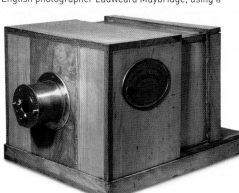

《 **Early Daguerre camera** from the 1840s

TIMELINE: 1800–1900

1804 Napoleon declares himself emperor of France

1812 Napoleon defeated in Russia

1825 First passenger steam train (Britain)

1837 Accession of Queen Victoria (Britain)

1839 Photographs by Louis Daguerre exhibited in Paris

1852 Accession of Napoleon III

1859 Publication of Darwin's *Origin of Species*

1800   1820   1840

1805 Spanish–French fleet defeated at Trafalgar

1815 Napoleon defeated at Waterloo; Congress of Vienna restores pre-revolutionary order

1830 Abdication of Charles X in France and accession of more liberal regime under Louis-Philippe

1838 Invention of first electric telegraph (Britain)

1848 Nationalist uprisings in central Europe repressed; last French king deposed

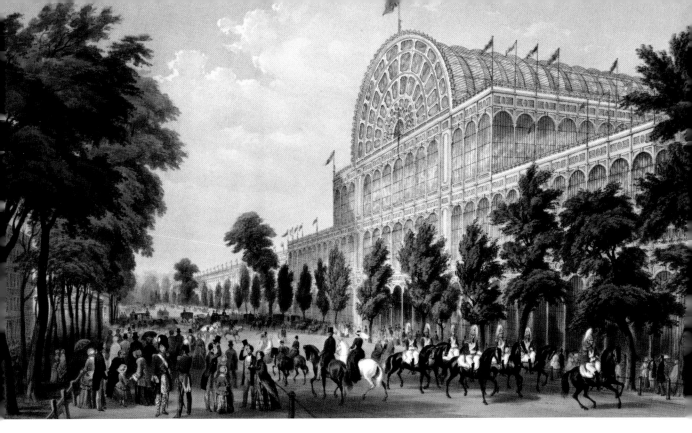

After the trauma of the Civil War of 1861–65, America established a new, confident identity and continued to expand westwards adding new states to the Union. It too became a major industrial power.

Europe and the world

At the same time an important shift in attitude towards Europe's overseas colonies took place. Originally the goal had been trade rather than territory. After about 1870 empire in itself came to be seen as desirable. Europe's states engaged in a frenzied race to take over as much of the globe as they could.

The impact of these enormous changes was highly significant for continental European art especially in France, though less so for Britain and America. From 1870 onwards, the principles that had governed the western tradition for over 400 years began to dissolve. The Modern was being born.

The Crystal Palace in Hyde Park, London
Built for the Great Exhibition of 1851, the iron-and-glass structure was 563 m (1,848 ft) long. Industrial processes and goods were displayed from all round the world.

1863 Paris Salon rejects Manet's *Déjeuner sur l'Herbe*; first Salon des Refusés held

1876 Bell patents telephone (Britain)

1885 Development of first automobile (Germany)

1860

1880

1900

1861 Unification of Italy; abolition of serfdom in Russia

1867 Dual monarchy of Austria-Hungary established

1870–71 Franco-Prussian War and unification of Germany

1884 Berlin Conference initiates "scramble" for Africa

1894 Invention of wireless telegraphy (Marconi)

Francisco **Goya**

● 1746–1828 ⚲ SPANISH ✑ OILS; ENGRAVINGS; DRAWINGS

A solitary and lonely figure, Goya was one of the most accomplished artists of a truly talented age. He produced an extraordinary range of powerful work, and was one of the greatest portrait painters of all time.

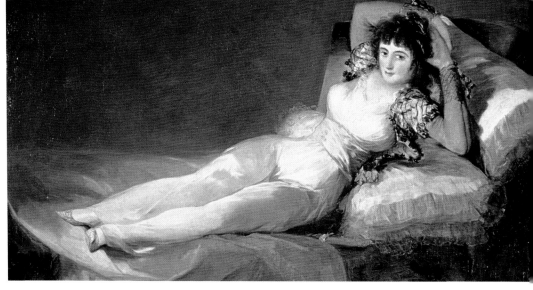

» The Clothed Maja
c.1800, 95 x 190 cm
(37 ⅓ x 78 ⅘ in), oil on canvas, Madrid: Museo del Prado. Goya painted a nude and a clothed Maja, both were commissioned by the licentious prime minister, Godoy.

**▾ Here Neither,
Plate 36, The Disasters of War** 1810–14,
published 1863, 15.8 x 20.8 cm (6 ⅕ x 8 ⅕ in),
etching, private collection. Goya created a series of 82 prints showing the brutality of war.

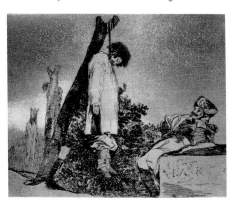

Born near Saragossa, the son of a master gilder, Goya was apprenticed as a church decorator before attending the Madrid Academy. He was an undistinguished student but was helped in his early years by Francisco Bayeu (1734–95) whose sister he married. He was deeply influenced by the paintings of Titian, Rubens, and Velásquez which he saw in the Spanish Royal collection. By astuteness and diligence he became First Painter to the King, but, liberal minded and independent, he welcomed the ideas leading to the French Revolution. He suffered many hardships, in particular total deafness, and died in exile in Bordeaux.

What to look for

Goya's overriding interest was appearances and human behaviour.

He understood youth and age, hope and despair, sense and sensibility, sweet innocence and the most savage aspect of man's inhumanity to man. His art is about Spain and the obsessions of his own day, but also about all time. Hauntingly memorable, he is never judgmental (he simply shows human behaviour as it is), and his brilliant technique with paint, colour, drawings, prints, is always ravishingly beautiful to look at, even when his subject matter is horrific.

Portraits

Usually it is the viewer who asks questions about the subject of a portrait, but with Goya it is his sitters who seem to be looking at you and scrutinizing your view of the human condition.

KEY WORKS: *Therese Louise de Sureda*, c.1803–04 (Madrid: Museo del Prado); *The Duke of Wellington*, 1812–14 (London: National Gallery); *The Third of May 1808*, 1814 (Madrid: Museo del Prado)

Antoine-Jean **Gros**

● 1771–1835 ⚲ FRENCH ✍ OILS

David's most famous pupil and the most successful painter of the early Napoleonic period. Despite a Neoclassical background, Gros was a crucial precursor of Romanticism. He had David's ability to manage huge-scale compositions with many figures, yet drew his subject matter from modern life, not the Antique. His best-known work is *Napoleon in the Plague House at Jaffa* (1804), which portrays Napoleon as a Christ-like figure surrounded by dying French troops. Note the loose, brilliant handling of paint, strong contrasts of light and shade, and an interest in Eastern exoticism. His later works became increasingly sterile and he was eventually driven to suicide.

KEY WORKS: *Sappho at Leucate*, 1801 (Bayeux: Musée Baron Gérard); *Napoleon on the Battlefield at Eylau*, 1808 (Paris: Musée du Louvre)

Anne-Louis **Girodet-Trioson**

● 1767–1824 ⚲ FRENCH ✍ OILS; PEN AND INK

Also known as Anne-Louis Girodet de Roucy or Roussy, he was a male painter of aristocratic portraits, associated with the court of Napoleon I. He was renowned for refusing to paint faces he did not find psychologically interesting. A talented, capable, and in-demand painter, Girodet-Trioson gave up art in his mid-40s after inheriting a large sum of money and became a writer.

KEY WORKS: *The Sleep of Endymion*, 1792 (Paris: Musée du Louvre); *Napoleon Bonaparte Receiving the Keys of Vienna at the Schloss Schönbrunn, 13th November 1805*, 1808 (Château de Versailles)

Jean-Auguste-Dominique **Ingres**

● 1780–1867 ⚲ FRENCH ✍ OILS; DRAWINGS

One of the major heroes of French art and the master of high-flown academic illusionism, Ingres was a great admirer of the Italian Renaissance and Raphael. He had a tortured, uptight personality.

His work conveys total certainty – his subjects were well established and officially approved: portraits, nudes, and mythologies, all painted with the high "finish" required by the Academy. He created the most manicured paintings in the history of art – everything was carefully arranged (hair, hands, poses, clothes, settings, faces, smiles, attitudes, even light) – and some of the most exquisite drawings ever made, with a total mastery of line and precise observation.

Notice the way he (usually but not always) manipulated this artificial idealism and fused realism with distortion, so that the end result is alive and thrilling, and never dead academicism: chubby hands with tapering fingers (can look like flippers), strange necks, and sloping shoulders. He had an interest in mirrors, painting figures that are reflected in them. Maybe his (and his society's) whole world had that glassy reality/unreality of the looking glass?

KEY WORKS: *La Grande Odalisque*, 1814 (Paris: Musée du Louvre); *The Apotheosis of Homer*, 1827 (Paris: Musée du Louvre)

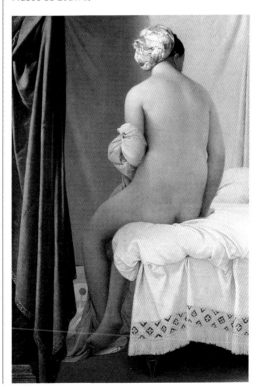

⟪ The Valpinçon Bather
Jean-Auguste-Dominique Ingres, 1808, 146 x 98 cm (57 ½ x 38 ½ in), oil on canvas, Paris: Musée du Louvre. To produce artistic harmony, the body is distorted: for example, the back is anatomically too long.

Romanticism

18TH AND 19TH CENTURIES

As the rationalism promised by the Enlightenment dissolved in the bloodshed of the French Revolution, artists struggled to come to terms with a world that had plunged from apparent certainty into chaos. Perhaps predictably, the results were mixed. Heroic individualism defined Romanticism. It also marked a decisive break with the conformities of the past.

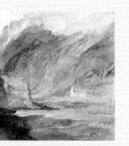

⌃ *Couvent du Bonhomme, Chamonix* J. M. W. Turner, c.1836–42, 24.2 x 30.2 cm (9 ½ in x 12 in), watercolours, Cambridge: Fitzwilliam Museum. Turner transformed the calm certainties of late 18th-century landscape painting by giving a new expressive freedom to colours and brushwork.

It is no surprise that Romanticism resists neat categorization; a single definition is impossible. Self-expression in the modern sense – that the artist is not just uniquely well equipped to see into the human soul but has a duty to do so – inevitably led to a huge variety of artistic styles. The desire to see everything as larger than life frequently expressed itself in bold colour, vigorous brushwork, themes of love, death, heroism, and the wonders of nature. It appealed particularly to northern European temperaments and flourished most creatively in Germany, Britain, and France.

Heightened emotions dominated. Artists turned away from the logical and rational, allowing themselves freedom to express raw, usually suppressed feelings. Movement, colour, and drama were actively championed, and exoticism was favoured. This was a world of vast, elemental forces, which were frequently destructive, and almost always beyond the reach of man to control. Landscapes became larger, brooding, and more threatening. For the first time, the subconscious was recognized as a mainspring of human activity.

In stark contrast to the optimism of the 18th century, humanity was seen as small, vulnerable, and subservient to nature.

What to look for

The Romantics believed in the freedom of the individual. They were not interested in compromise – it was better to be a heroic success or a total failure. Géricault's masterpiece, *The Raft of the Medusa*, encapsulated these virtues and took art into the realm of political protest. It theatrically recreated a real-life incident when the captain of a shipwrecked French frigate saved himself and abandoned the passengers and crew. Here, the survivors see the vessel that will save them. The story and the painting scandalized the French nation. Whereas David's art (see page 194) encouraged service to the state, Géricault castigates the state for abandoning those who serve.

KEY EVENTS

1789	French Revolution
1793	Execution of Louis XVI: apparent triumph of new liberal French political order followed by the Terror
1798	Wordsworth and Coleridge publish *Lyrical Ballads*, a key document of Romantic feeling; Schlegel coins term "romantic poetry"
1799	Napoleonic coup: Bonaparte becomes First Consul and in 1804, he is made Emperor
1814	Constable's *Stour Valley and Dedham Church* appears as does Goya's great anti-war polemic *The Third of May*

⌄ *Monk by the Sea* Caspar David Friedrich, 1809, 110 x 172 cm (43 ⅓ x 67 ¾ in), oil on canvas: Berlin Staatliche Museen. Friedrich excelled in images of an implacable nature under whose vast skies man inevitably shrank.

The storm clouds are pierced by light, a symbol of hope

Rescue offers no consolation to a distraught father grieving over his dead son

An individual silhouetted against a dramatic sky features in many of Géricault's works

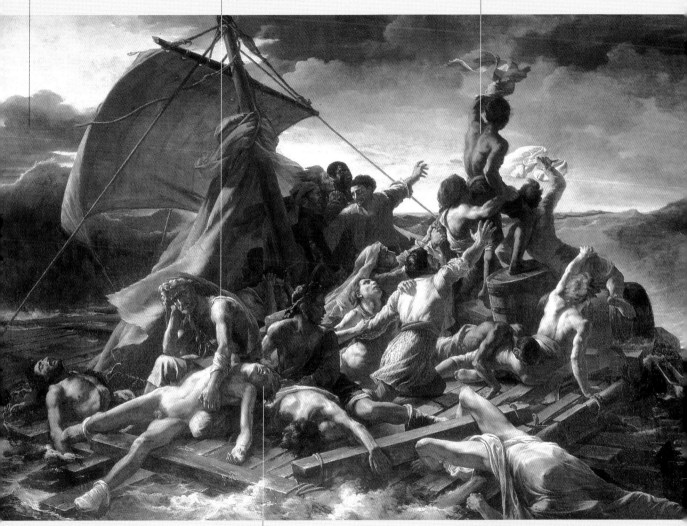

⌃ The Raft of the Medusa
Théodore Géricault, 1819, 491 x 716 cm (193 x 282 in), oil on canvas, Paris: Musée du Louvre. Géricault's huge painting was intended to challenge the newly restored monarchy and a smug bourgeoisie.

Géricault visited the local hospital to study the sick and dying, in pursuit of authenticity

❯❯ TECHNIQUES

The dark, sombre mood of the painting is not entirely deliberate. Géricault used bitumen, a tar-based pigment, to add lustre to his colour scheme. Once dry, it deteriorates. The picture is not just blackening, it is at risk of disintegrating before our eyes.

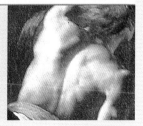

Eugène **Delacroix**

● 1798-1863 ▣ FRENCH ✍ OILS; DRAWINGS; PASTELS

Delacroix was the leading French Romantic painter. Naturally aloof, he had an intensely passionate nature and was popular in society. It is suspected that his natural father was the statesman Talleyrand, who stole his mother's affection and his father's government appointment.

In spite of a classical education Delacroix's interest was with moments of supreme emotion, such as sexuality, struggle, and death. A close friend of Baudelaire and Victor Hugo, he was inspired by Dante and Byron, as well as by politics, historical events, wild animals, and North Africa. After the 1830s he withdrew from society to work on official commissions, but these sapped his frail health and he died alone in Paris.

Delacroix used colour as his main means of expression and he had a sound grasp of colour theory. His art keeps the eye constantly on the move. He loved thick paint, rich textures, lush reds and intense coppery greens. He had complex working methods which produced much preliminary work, often sketches.

In *Liberty Leading the People* the palate is deliberately sombre in order to heighten the brilliance of the flag. He had high hopes for its critical reception, and he signed it prominently in red to the right of the young patriot. However the proletarian emphasis was considered so dangerous that the painting was removed from public view until 1855.

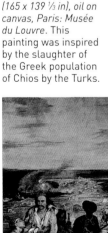

▽ *Scenes from the Massacre of Chios* 1824, 419 x 354 cm (165 x 139 ⅓ in), oil on canvas, Paris: Musée du Louvre. This painting was inspired by the slaughter of the Greek population of Chios by the Turks.

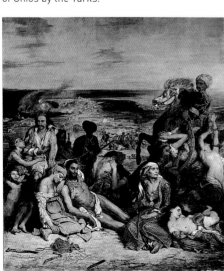

KEY WORKS: *Orphan Girl at the Cemetery*, 1824 (Paris: Musée du Louvre); *The Death of Sardanapalus*, 1827 (Paris: Musée du Louvre); *Odalisque*, 1825 (Cambridge: Fitzwilliam Museum); *The Barque of Dante*, 1822 (Paris: Musée du Louvre)

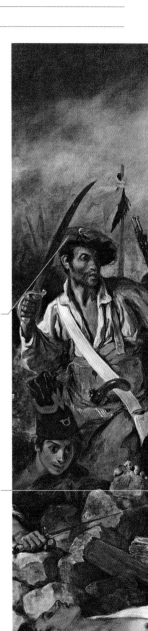

≫ *Liberty Leading the People* 1830, 260 x 325 cm (102 x 128 in), Paris: Musee du Louvre. This work commemorates the political uprising in Paris in July 1830, when Parisians took to the streets in revolt against the regime of Charles X.

The range of social classes supporting the revolution is conveyed by the variety of hats worn by the street fighters – top hats, berets, and cloth caps

A mortally wounded citizen strains to take a last look at Liberty. The artist echoes the colours of the flag in the dying patriots clothing

The bodies of the dead and dying are illuminated dramatically. One of Delacroix's brothers fought alongside Napoleon and died at the Battle of Friedland.

Liberty wears a Phrygian cap, a symbol of freedom, and bears the tricolour flag, the symbol of the 1789 revolution

The young patriot to the right of Liberty represents a popular hero named Arcole, who was killed in the fighting

Emerging from the gunsmoke are the towers of Notre Dame. Delacroix was present at the uprising

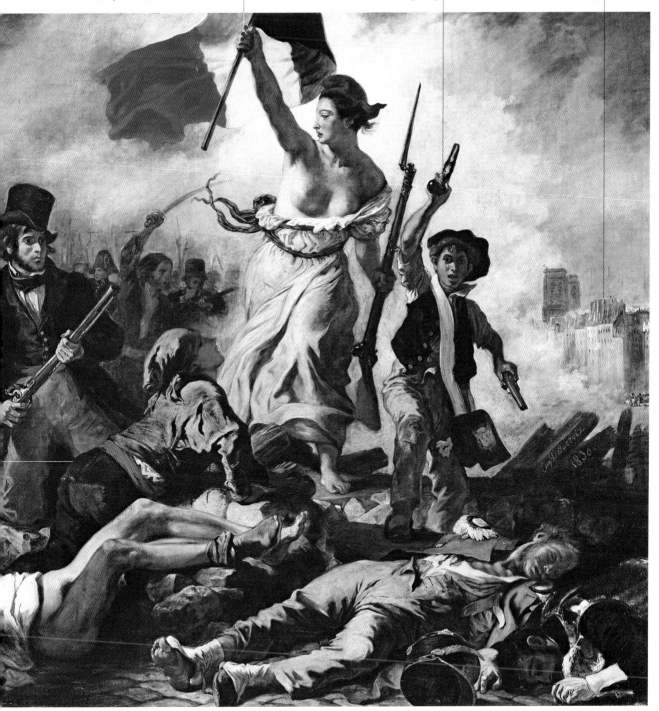

Théodore **Géricault**

● 1791–1824   ⁂ FRENCH   ✍ OILS; DRAWINGS

A true Romantic, Géricault was unorthodox, passionate (about horses, women, and art), temperamental, depressive, virile, and inspiring. He had an early death after falling from a horse. He was wealthy and only painted when he felt like it. His work was hugely influential on Delacroix.

Géricault had two main subjects: horses and moments of danger or uncertainty (and he often combined both). His early work was much influenced by Rubens (rich colour and movement) and Michelangelo (muscles and monumentality). He scandalized the French art and political establishments, and changed the rules of art with *The Raft of the Medusa* – the first rendering of a contemporary political subject in a manner truly comparable with the grandest history painting (see page 205). His talents extended further: he also produced stunning, innovative lithographs.

Géricault's compositions are memorably simple: he often used a silhouette against a dramatic sky, lifting the eye up to a single point of climax near the top of the picture. He depicted soulful human beings and horses (the expression in the horse's eye is the same as in the human's). Note his trick of turning the human face one way and the horse the other. His strong sense of colour and lively paint handling were sometimes ruined by the use of bitumen and poor-quality technique (he was a lazy student and should have studied harder).

KEY WORKS: *A Horse Frightened by Lightning*, 1813–14 (London: National Gallery); *Officer of the Hussars*, 1814 (Paris: Musée du Louvre)

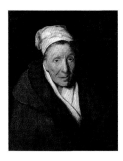

⌃ *Portrait of a Woman Addicted to Gambling*
Théodore Géricault, c.1822, 77 x 65 cm (30 ⅓ x 25 ½ in), oil on canvas, Paris: Musée du Louvre. A psychiatrist encouraged Géricault to paint portraits of the insane.

Richard Parkes **Bonington**

● 1802–28   ⁂ BRITISH   ✍ OILS; WATERCOLOURS

Bonington – known as the English Delacroix, with whom he worked closely – painted lovely, small-scale, fresh, and luminous oils and watercolours of picturesque places (Normandy, Venice, and Paris), and costume history pieces, all done with consummate skill and ease. A genius, he died of consumption, aged 26 – a sad and early loss.

KEY WORKS: *Venetian Campanili*, c.1826 (Maidstone Museum and Art Gallery); *The Corsa Saint' Anastasia, Verona, with the Palace of Prince Maffet*, 1826 (London: Victoria & Albert Museum)

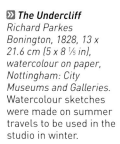

⧉ *The Undercliff*
Richard Parkes Bonington, 1828, 13 x 21.6 cm (5 x 8 ⅛ in), watercolour on paper, Nottingham: City Museums and Galleries. Watercolour sketches were made on summer travels to be used in the studio in winter.

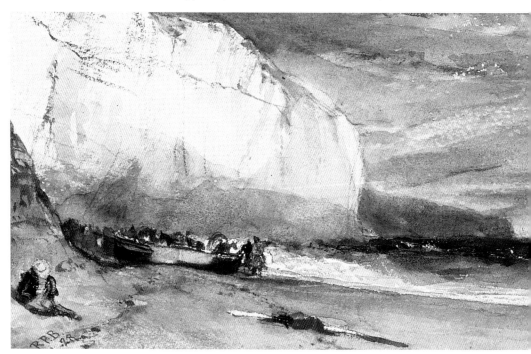

Caspar David **Friedrich**

● 1774–1840 ⚑ GERMAN ✍ OILS; DRAWINGS;
WATERCOLOURS

Although he is now the best-known German
Romantic landscape painter, Friedrich was
neglected in his day. He came into his own
later, influencing late-19th-century Symbolists.

He was born at Greifswald, near the Baltic coast,
but later settled permanently in Dresden. Although
a meticulous and careful painter of small pictures,
Friedrich was full of big ideas. His Romantic
relationship with nature was intensely spiritual and
Christian, and loaded with symbolism. His work is
also full of yearning: for the spiritual life beyond
the grave; for greatness; for intense experience.
He studied nature's details closely, but all his
landscapes are imaginary or composite – painted
out of his head, not sitting in front of nature.

Look for his symbolism; for instance, oak
trees and Gothic churches that represent
Christianity; dead trees as death and despair;
ships as the transition from the here and now to
other-worldliness; figures looking out of windows
or at the horizon. Also, times of day and the
seasons, when one state is about to become

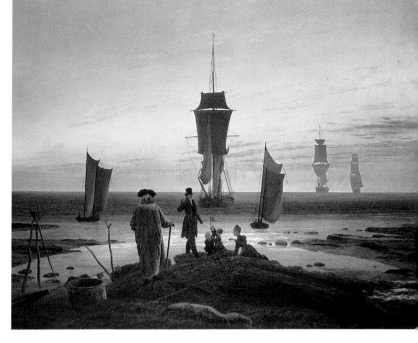

another – sunrise turning to sunset, or winter
turning to spring. These stand for spiritual
transition and the hope of resurrection.

KEY WORKS: *The Cross in the Mountains*, 1808 (Berlin:
Staatliche Museum); *Wanderer above the Sea of Fog*,
1817–18 (Hamburg: Kunsthalle); *The Polar Sea*, 1824
(Hamburg: Kunsthalle)

◢ *The Stages of Life*
Caspar David Friedrich,
c.1835, 72.5 x 94 cm
(28 ½ x 37 in), oil on
canvas, Leipzig: Museum
der bildenden Künste.
The five ships
correspond to the
figures on the shore,
each at a different
stage of life's journey.

Philipp Otto **Runge**

● 1777–1810 ⚑ GERMAN ✍ WATERCOLOURS;
CHALKS; PEN AND INK

Runge was born in Germany, where he spent most
of his short life: he died aged 33. He studied at the
Copenhagen Art Academy for two years, and was
also a musician and lyricist. Runge knew Friedrich
and met Goethe. His art brought him little fame in
his lifetime, but he was recognized posthumously
for his sharp – often naïve – style and vivid use
of colour. Greatly interested in the properties of
colour, Runge wrote a hugely influential treatise
about it, *Die Farbenkugel* (The Colour Sphere),
which has remained pivotal to the study and
teachings of colour.

He tried to express the harmony of the universe,
painting pantheistic, mythical subjects as well
as portraits. Look for intense (often symbolic)
colour and the use of local German landscapes
as the background to religious and genre paintings.

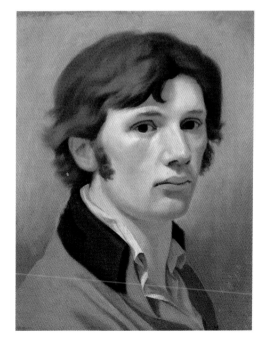

◁ *Self-Portrait* Philipp
Otto Runge, 1802, 37 x
31.5 cm (14 ½ x 12 ⅓ in),
oil on canvas, Hamburg:
Kunsthalle. Runge
hoped to create a
new art that would
fill the voids created
by Revolution and
the collapse of the
old certainties.

KEY WORKS: *The
Hülsenbeck Children*,
1805–06 (Hamburg:
Kunsthalle); *The Child
in the Meadow*, 1809
(Hamburg: Kunsthalle);
The Great Morning,
1809–10 (Hamburg:
Kunsthalle)

>> **THE NAZARENES** 1809–c.1830

A group of Roman Catholic German and Austrian painters who were brought together in Vienna as the Lukasbrüder (Brotherhood of St Luke) in 1809 by art students Friedrich Overbeck and Franz Pforr. They wished to revive German religious art in the manner of Perugino, Dürer, and the young Raphael. From 1810, they lived and worked in a monastery in Rome, where they welcomed others who shared their ideals of intensely spiritual subject matter and the religious properties of light. They were nicknamed the Nazarenes and they dressed like monks. They were a major influence throughout Europe, including on the early Pre-Raphaelites.

Peter von **Cornelius**

● 1783–1867 ▥ GERMAN ✍ OILS; FRESCO

Cornelius was responsible for bringing frescoes back into prominence in the 19th century. His early works are Neoclassical, but later works evince the influence of German Gothic. He spent several years in Rome (from 1811), where he joined the Nazarenes (see box). He was commissioned by Louis I of Bavaria to paint the frescoes in Munich's Glyptothek (1819–30), the museum of ancient art designed by Leo von Klenze. He visited England in 1841 to advise on frescoes for the new Houses of Parliament. He also worked on frescoes for Frederick William IV of Prussia in Berlin but the project was cancelled after the revolution in 1848. Cornelius was also an accomplished book illustrator, most notably of Goethe's *Faust*.

KEY WORKS: *The Vision of the Rabenstein*, 1811 (Frankfurt: Städelsches Kunstinstitut); Joseph *Interpreting Pharaoh's Dream*, 1816–17 (Berlin: Nationalgalerie); *The Recognition of Joseph by his Brothers*, 1816–17 (Berlin: Nationalgalerie)

John **Trumbull**

● 1756–1843 ▥ AMERICAN ✍ OILS

Trumbull was ambitious, pretentious, unfortunate (with an uncanny sense of bad timing), and finally embittered. He was the first college graduate (Harvard) in the US to become a professional painter (although his parents thought art a frivolous and unworthy activity).

His main aim was to excel in history painting, but this was going out of fashion. He took as his subjects the recent history of the triumphs of revolutionary American colonies. He completed eight of a projected series of thirteen works, and was commissioned by a somewhat unenthusiastic Congress to do four for the rotunda of the Capitol in Washington. He struggled to achieve success and had to earn his way as a portrait painter, which he disliked.

Look for stagey compositions, theatrical lighting, and good, convincing faces done from life. He served with Washington, but then went to London and was arrested and very nearly executed in reprisal for the hanging of a British agent in America; he was imprisoned instead. He went back to the US, and then returned to London in 1808 – but any hope of success was dashed by the war of 1812. His last work was his autobiography, which was published in 1841.

KEY WORKS: *The Sortie Made by the Garrison of Gibraltar*, 1789 (New York: Metropolitan Museum of Art); *Mrs William Pinkney (Ann Maria Rodgers)*, c.1800 (San Francisco: Fine Arts Museums); *Declaration of Independence*, 1817 (Washington DC: United States Capitol Rotunda)

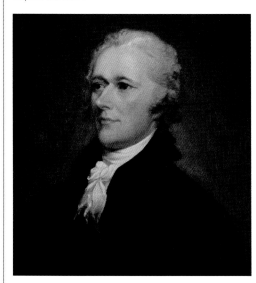

⌃ *Portrait of Alexander Hamilton* John Trumbull, *c.1806, 77 x 61 cm (30 ¼ x 24 ¼ in), oil on canvas, Washington DC: White House.* The man who founded the First Bank of the United States.

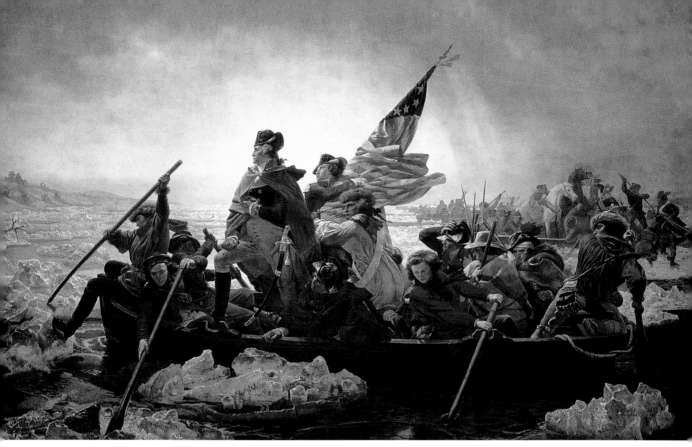

Emanuel Gottlieb **Leutze**

🌐 1816–68 🏛 AMERICAN/GERMAN ✍ OILS;
DRAWINGS

German-born, Leutze was raised in Philadelphia.
He returned to Düsseldorf in 1841 to study history
painting and stayed there (making it a Mecca for
US artists). He was noted for creating large,

memorable, easy-to-understand, patriotic scenes
of American history, including *Westward Ho* for the
capitol, Washington DC.

KEY WORKS: *Columbus before the Queen*, 1843
(New York: Brooklyn Museum of Art); *Westward
the Course of Empire Takes its Way*, 1861–62
(Washington DC: Capitol Collection)

⬆ *Washington Crossing
the Delaware River,
25th December 1776*
*Emanuel Gottlieb Leutze,
1851 (Copy of an original
painted in 1848), 378.5 x
647 cm (149 x 254 ¾ in),
oil on canvas, New York:
Metropolitan Museum
of Art. Exhibited in
New York in 1851,
it sold for $10,000.*

Edward **Hicks**

🌐 1780–1849 🏛 AMERICAN ✍ OILS

Hicks had a Quaker upbringing. Initially, he
learned the trade of decorative coach painting.
An otherwise untrained artist with a primitive
style, he is best known for his *Peaceable Kingdom*
paintings illustrating Isaiah 11:6–9 (words are
sometimes inscribed round the picture) – the belief
in a peaceful coexistence. Quakers disapproved
of art but illustrating Isaiah was acceptable.

He painted at least 60 different versions
of *Peaceable Kingdom* between 1816 and 1849.
The animals' expressions change from tense

and fearful to sad and resigned, reflecting the
current political divisions among the Quakers;
in the background William Penn concludes a
treaty with the Indians. Late in his life, Hicks
also painted depictions of the Declaration of
Independence and Washington crossing the
Delaware River.

KEY WORKS: *The Falls of Niagara*, c.1825 (New York:
Metropolitan Museum of Art); *Noah's Ark*, 1846
(Philadelphia: Museum of Art); *The Cornell Farm*,
1848 (Washington DC: National Gallery of Art)

John **Constable**

1776–1837 BRITISH OILS

One of the great landscape painters, Constable pioneered a new type of plein-air painting based on the direct observation of nature. He believed that nature, with its freshness, sunlight, trees, shadows, streams, and so forth, was full of moral and spiritual goodness. He was a devoted family man.

KEY WORKS: ***Dedham from Langham***, c.1813 (London: Victoria & Albert Museum); ***Weymouth Bay***, 1816 (London: National Gallery); ***Hampstead Heath***, 1821 (Manchester: City Art Gallery); ***The Hay Wain***, 1821 (London: National Gallery); ***Salisbury Cathedral from the Meadows***, 1831 (London: National Gallery)

Constable's subject matter was limited – he only painted the places he knew best. He seemed to know every square inch of ground and all the local day-to-day activity. Note how the light in the sky and the fall of light on the landscape are directly connected (not so in Dutch landscapes). His sketches (not on public display) have a direct spontaneity absent from the more laboured, finished paintings (especially the "six-footers") with which he hoped to make his reputation.

How did he get that sense of dewy freshness? Look at the way he juxtaposed different greens and introduced small accents of red to enliven them. Note too the layering of clouds to create perspective recession; the figures are sometimes almost hidden in the landscape. Constable's late works are much more emotional, darker, and more thickly painted.

To many people, *The Hay Wain* represents a nostalgic image of the English countryside, with mankind working in perfect harmony with nature. Constable was in fact trying to create a new subject matter for painting. At the time it was painted, there was an economic depression in agriculture, with riots and farms burned down. Constable put all his efforts into this picture, but when first exhibited, it failed to sell and he was hurt by the constant rejection of his work.

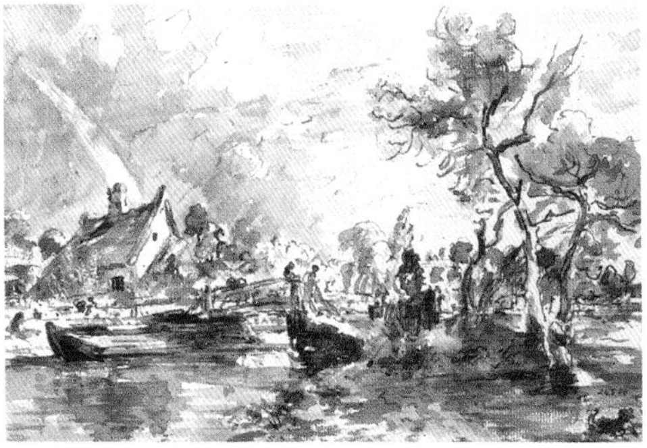

Flatford Old Mill Cottage on the Stour *c.1811, pen and wash, London: Victoria & Albert Museum.* Constable combined a detailed objective study of nature with a deeply personal vision of his childhood scenery.

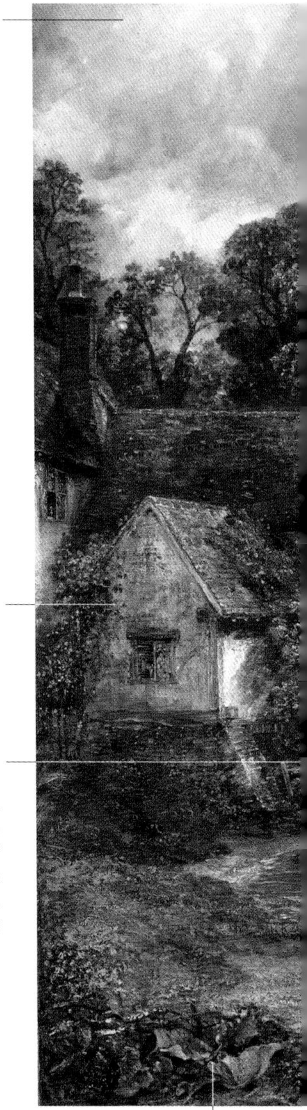

The carefully observed high, billowing clouds are a special feature of this part of eastern England, caused by water vapour drawn up from the nearby Stour Estuary

The cottage on the left is still known as Willy Lot's cottage. He was a deaf and eccentric farmer who lived there for over 80 years; he would have been the inhabitant at the date of this picture

Outside the cottage, a woman is washing clothes. This detail shows Constable's traditional palette of earth colours, and his highlights of thick white paint

Behind this work lie many small sketches made in the open air over several years. The final painting was made at Constable'studio in London

☑ **The Hay Wain** *1821,*
130 x 185 cm (51 x 73 in),
oil on canvas, London:
National Gallery.
This scene of harmonious
nature was derived from
Constable's boyhood
memories. The son of
a wealthy miller, he
was familiar with
country life.

The play of
light and shadow
over the land is
consistent with the
pattern of light and
clouds in the sky

》 TECHNIQUES

If you look carefully you can see that all the areas of
green are an interweaving of many different shades,
and there are touches of red, such as in the figure of the
man fishing. Red is the complementary colour to green,
and so intensifies its impact. Similarly, Constable
infuses the water with brown and orange hues.

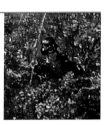

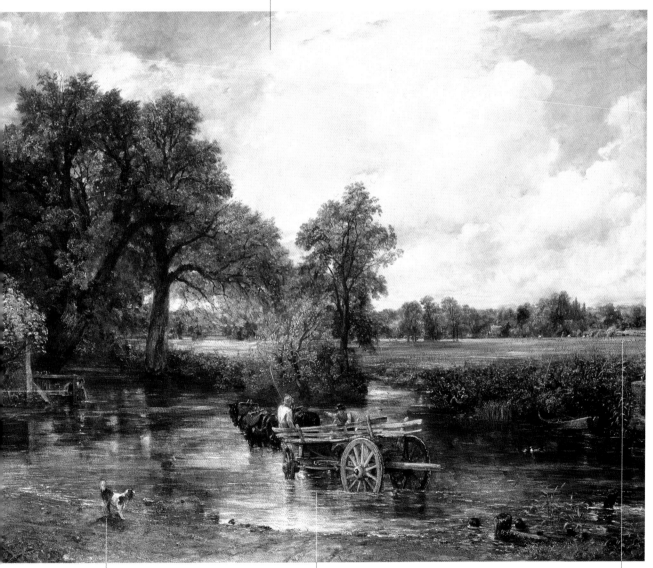

The dog is an essential part
of the composition, leading
the eye towards the focus
of interest – the hay wain

The hay wain is being
directed to the ford that leads
to the reapers. The water
cools the legs of the horses

In the far distance, it is
possible to see haymakers in
the fields carrying scythes,
and loading hay onto a cart

» THE NORWICH SCHOOL 1803–1880s

An important English school of artists founded by John Crome that grew from the Norwich Society of Artists (founded 1803). The group produced landscapes, coasts, and marine scenes from around Norwich and Norfolk, and favoured outdoor painting, as opposed to studio work. They used both oils – as favoured by Crome – and watercolours – favoured by

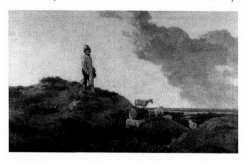

⌂ View of Mousehold Heath, near Norwich
John Crome, c.1812, 54.5 x 81.2 cm (21 ½ x 32 in), oil on canvas, London: Victoria & Albert Museum. "Old Crome" was self-taught and worked only part-time as a painter.

John Sell Cotman, who took over as president after Crome's death. From 1805 until 1833, an annual exhibition was held in Norwich (the only exceptions being the years 1826 and 1827). This school was 19th-century England's only successful attempt at establishing a regional artistic scene, in emulation of the many Italian examples. It was a provincial school in every aspect as the artists were actively patronized by local wealthy families, who bought their works and hired them as drawing tutors. Artists of the Norwich School continued working through the 1830s.

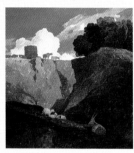

» The Marl Pit
John Sell Cotman, c.1809–10, 30 x 26 cm (11 ¾ x 10 ¼ in), watercolour on paper, Norwich: Castle Museum & Art Gallery. Cotman's early watercolours are noted for their simplicity and translucency.

John **Varley**

● 1778–1842 ⚐ BRITISH ✍ WATERCOLOURS

Varley was a sublime Romantic watercolour painter, whose landscapes are contemporaneous with Turner's and who similarly began the development from topographical drawings to fully developed watercolour painting. He was most influential as a teacher (of Linnel, Cox, Holman Hunt *et al*).

KEY WORKS: *View of Bodenham and the Malvern Hills, Herefordshire*, 1801 (London: Tate Collection); *A Half-Timbered House*, c.1820 (Boston: Museum of Fine Arts)

David **Cox**

● 1783–1859 ⚐ BRITISH
✍ WATERCOLOURS; OILS

Cox was well travelled (France, Flanders, and Wales). He lived in Hereford, London, Birmingham and produced talented, small-scale, freely executed oils and watercolours that capture the spontaneity

of rapidly shifting light and breezes, experienced in the open air. Cox was one of the few painters to make one feel wind and rain (the French Impressionists rarely, if ever, attempted it).

KEY WORKS: *Moorland Road*, 1851 (London: Tate Collection); *Rhyl Sands*, c.1854 (London: Tate Collection)

James **Ward**

● 1769–1859 ⚐ BRITISH ✍ OILS; ENGRAVINGS

Ward was memorable mostly for his large-scale pictures of animals, and landscapes bursting with Romantic drama and emotion. A notable work is the vast *Gordale Scar* (Tate Collection) with its bulging-eyed heroic cattle, exaggerated cliffs, and stormy skies. However, Ward was not appreciated in his time – he died in poverty – although he was an inspiration to Géricault.

KEY WORKS: *Bulls Fighting*, c.1804 (London: Victoria & Albert Museum); *Gordale Scar*, 1811–15 (London: Tate Collection)

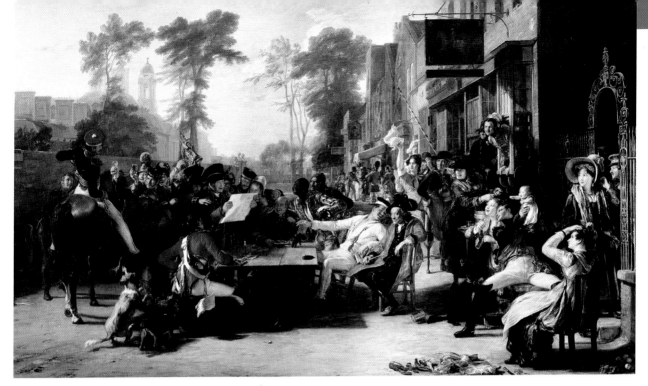

Sir David **Wilkie**

● 1785–1841 🏛 BRITISH 🎨 OILS

Wilkie was Scottish, direct, down-to-earth, and ambitious. His individual style, which embraced the narrative subjects of everyday life and loaded them with authentic detail, was very influential throughout Europe. His manner became more contrived and Romantic after a visit to the Continent in 1825–28. He was much admired by the Prince Regent (George IV) who bought Wilkie's paintings and ignored Turner and Constable.

KEY WORKS: *The Letter of Introduction*, 1813 (Edinburgh: National Gallery of Scotland); *Self-Portrait*, 1813 (Pau: Musée des Beaux-Arts)

John **Linnell**

● 1792–1882 🏛 BRITISH
🎨 WATERCOLOURS; OILS

Linnell was a romantic landscape painter who was successful commercially. He provided artistic and financial support to Blake and Palmer. Linnell was an eccentric, argumentative, radical non-conformist, best known for his rural landscapes, often showing labourers at work or rest. He believed that landscape paintings could carry a religious message – hence their intense visionary quality and style.

KEY WORKS: *Leading a Barge*, c.1806 (London: Tate Collection); *Kensington Gravel Pits*, 1811–12 (London: Tate Collection); *Mid-day Rest*, 1863 (Manchester: City Art Gallery)

Samuel **Palmer**

● 1805–81 🏛 BRITISH 🎨 WATERCOLOURS; ENGRAVINGS

A child prodigy from Kent (the "Garden of England"), Palmer had a very intense pastoral and Christian vision – nature as the gateway to a revelation of paradise. He made exquisite, magical, small drawings in the 1820s, with microscopic details. After his marriage in 1837, he turned to a less intense, classical, pastoral vision.

KEY WORKS: *Self-Portrait*, c.1825 (Oxford: Ashmolean Museum); *Early Morning*, 1825 (Oxford: Ashmolean Museum); *In a Shoreham Garden*, c.1829 (London: Victoria and Albert Museum)

🔼 *The Chelsea Pensioners Reading the Waterloo Dispatch* Sir David Wilkie, 1822, 97 x 158 cm (38 ¼ x 62 ¼ in), oil on wood, London: Wellington Museum. This painting was commissioned by the Duke of Wellington.

In 1877, correspondents to The Times attacked Turner's lack of accuracy, such as incorrect rigging, the sun setting in the east, and the mast of the steamer incorrectly shown behind the smokestack

Turner combined his early training in watercolours with the scope for variation in the texture of oils to form a style involving washes of great fluidity with impasto details to evoke different surfaces

>> *The Fighting Téméraire* 1839, 90.7 x 121.6 cm (35 ³/₄ x 48 in), oil on canvas, London: National Gallery. Turner lived in revolutionary times – he witnessed the dawn of the steam age and observed the French Revolution and the rise and fall of the Napoleonic Empire. In this late work, he explores these themes, together with his Romantic response to the beauty of nature. Turner chose never to sell his picture and The National Gallery acquired it in 1856 as part of the Turner Bequest.

Turner exploits the appearance and symbolism of the setting sun by contrasting it with a delicate new moon, and repeating the fiery glow in the burning gases from the smokestack

The *Téméraire* was a ship of the line with 98 guns. She took her name from a French ship captured at Lagos Bay in 1759

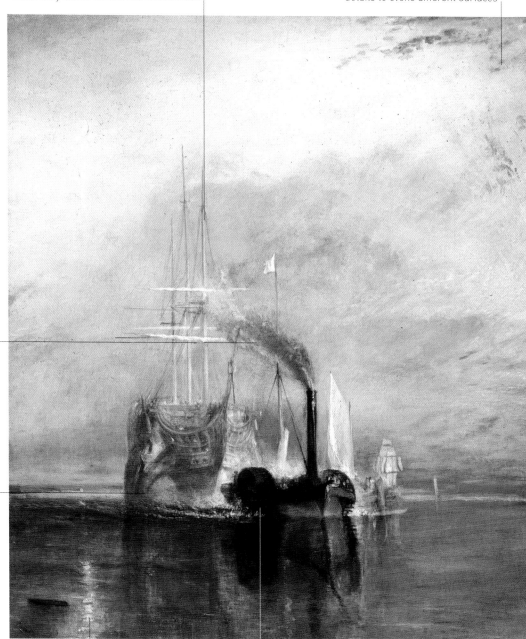

The silver light of a crescent moon, reflected in the water, illuminates the ship and gives it a ghost-like quality

The first paddle-wheel steamboat was launched in 1783 and the first steam warship in 1815

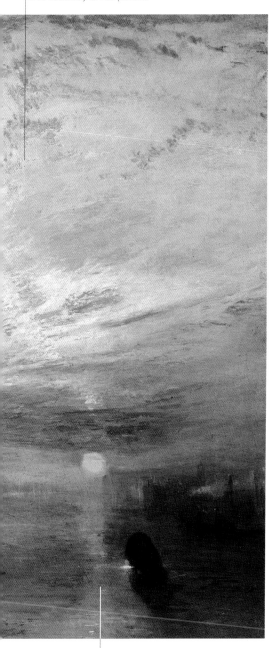

Turner was able to use recently discovered synthetic pigments such as chrome yellow to bring brightness and intensity to his palette

Turner's treatment of light and handling of paint influenced Monet, who studied his works in London in 1870

J. M. W. **Turner**

● 1775–1851 ⚑ BRITISH ✍ OILS; WATERCOLOURS; ENGRAVINGS

The champion of Romantic landscape and seascape, Turner is the greatest British painter yet. His art was at its best when inspired by a subject that resonated with history and with a sense of time, fate, and nature.

Turner was able to portray nature in all her moods, from the most lyrical to the stormiest and most destructive. He had a deep, personal response to nature, using wide-ranging sources of inspiration. He applied a remarkable range of working methods, with fascinating technical and stylistic innovation, especially in his watercolours and later work. Turner had an enduring interest in light, and a deep reverence for the old masters.

Look for the sun – where it is; what it is doing; its physical qualities, but also its symbolism (rising, setting, hiding, warming, frightening, and so on). Turner's early "old master" style changed dramatically after his visit to Italy in 1819, and he introduced a brighter palette and freer style and imagery. Note the detail in his watercolours and the complex personal symbolism. He left sketchbooks that show how he worked.

On September 6th, 1838, Turner was a passenger on a steamboat when he witnessed the *Téméraire* being towed up the Thames to be broken up. Turner always carried a notebook in his pocket and made sketches of this historic event, which he later transformed into his masterpiece.

KEY WORKS: *Mortlake Terrace*, c.1826 (Washington DC: National Gallery of Art); *Norham Castle, Sunrise*, c.1835–40 (London: Tate Collection); 1842 *Snowstorm: Steam-Boat off a Harbour's Mouth*, c.1835–40 (London: Tate Collection); *Approach to Venice*, c.1843 (Washington DC: National Gallery of Art)

» *Rain, Steam, and Speed – The Great Western Railway* c.1840, 90.8 x 121.9 cm (35 ¾ x 48 in), oil on canvas, *London: National Gallery*. Turner was inspired by his own journey on a steam train.

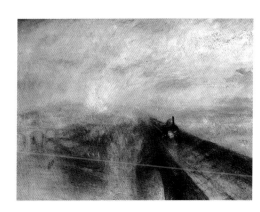

The Academies

1562–LATE 19TH CENTURY

Academies were the official institutions, funded by a princely ruler or a state, that arranged and promoted exhibitions, organized art education, and dictated rules and standards. Enormously influential between the mid-17th and late 19th centuries, the first academy was founded in Florence in 1562.

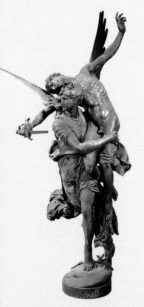

▲ *Gloria Victis Marius Jean Antonin Mercie, 1874, height 140 cm (55 ⅛ in), bronze, Paris: Musée de la Ville*. Archetypal academic sculpture.

The academy par excellence was the French Royal Academy, founded in 1648 under Louis XIV and directed by Charles Le Brun. It had a monopoly of exhibitions and hiring models for life classes, awarded scholarships, and established branches in provincial cities and in Rome. A remarkable example of the imposition of centralized bureaucracy on the arts, its example was widely followed, e.g. in Berlin in 1696, Vienna 1692, St Petersburg 1757, Stockholm 1735, and Madrid 1752, as well as in many principalities and municipalities in Germany, Switzerland, Italy, and Holland. The exception was London where the Royal Academy was, and remains, private and independent.

The 19th century

Academies were at their most stultifying and conservative in the mid- to late 19th century, especially in France with its annual salon that was much patronized by Napoleon III and his Empress Eugénie. In many ways, their most important achievement was to provoke young artists to react against them, e.g. Courbet and Manet in France, and the various Secession movements in Central Europe (see page 268).

▽ *Empress Eugénie (1826–1920) Surrounded by her Ladies-in-Waiting Franz Xavier Winterhalter, 1855, 300 x 402 cm (118 ¼ x 158 ¼ in), oil on canvas, Compiègne: Musée National du Château.*

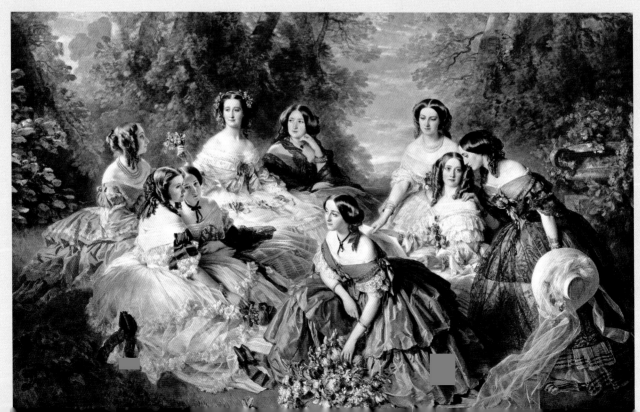

Alexandre **Cabanel**

⬤ 1823–89 🏳 FRENCH ✍ OILS

One of the pillars of the establishment of late 19th-century Paris, Cabanel was conventional and much sought after. He painted nudes, allegories, and portraits. Now it looks like academic painting at its worst – weak technique, garish colours, and banal subjects. A warning that much-praised contemporary art can be dire.

KEY WORKS: *The Birth of Venus*, 1862 (Paris: Musée d'Orsay); *Death of Francesca da Rimini and Paolo Malatesta*, 1870 (Paris: Musée d'Orsay); *The Life of St Louis*, 1870s (Paris: Pantheon)

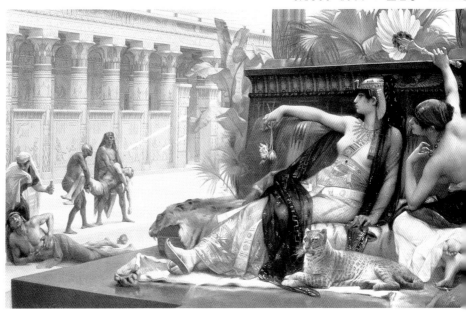

⌃ *Cleopatra Testing Poisons on those Condemned to Death* Alexandre Cabanel, 1887, 87.6 x 148 cm (34 ½ x 58 in) oil on canvas, private collection.

William-Adolphe **Bouguereau**

⬤ 1825–1905 🏳 FRENCH ✍ OILS

Bouguereau was the archetypal conservative pillar of the French academic system in its final years. He refused to abandon the language and manners of a debased Classical tradition.

He delighted his public with large-scale theme paintings and a dazzlingly accomplished technique. However, his work now looks curiously stilted and unconvincing – a dinosaur of art history. His lofty rhetorical subject matter (for example, nude Venuses) invites us to suspend disbelief in reality, but his style, which apes the reality of photography, contradicts or denies the invitation. Characteristic features are smooth, hairless, firm flesh and rosy nipples, which anticipate (inspire?) the airbrushed girlie pin-ups of World War II or *Playboy* magazine. His paintings of everyday peasant life are more convincing than his grander works because they do not aim so high and do not demand suspension of disbelief to the same degree. Art which aspires to be so great must have a seamless unity between subject and style.

KEY WORKS: *Young girl Defending Herself against Eros*, c.1880 (Los Angeles: J. Paul Getty Museum), *A Little Shepherdess*, 1891 (London: Christie's Images); *Cupidon*, 1891 (London: Roy Miles Fine Painting)

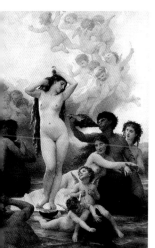
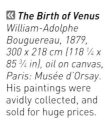

◧ *The Birth of Venus* William-Adolphe Bouguereau, 1879, 300 x 218 cm (118 ¼ x 85 ¾ in), oil on canvas, Paris: Musée d'Orsay. His paintings were avidly collected, and sold for huge prices.

Franz Xaver **Winterhalter**

⬤ 1805–73 🏳 GERMAN ✍ OILS

Winterhalter was a smooth-mannered, popular portrait painter, notably of the European monarchy in their 19th-century golden age as he captured their preferred self-image – royalty as bourgeoisie. His works combine formality, intimacy, and anecdote. He worked rapidly, straight onto canvas, with an impersonal style. He also made lithographs.

KEY WORKS: *Princess Leonilla*, 1844 (Los Angeles: J. Paul Getty Museum); *The First of May*, 1851 (Windsor Castle, UK: Royal Collection)

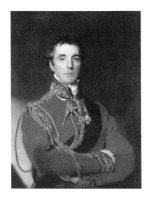

⌃ Portrait of Arthur Wellesley (1769–1852) 1st Duke of Wellington
Sir Thomas Lawrence, 1814, oil on canvas, London: The Wellington Museum. Lawrence painted portraits of all the European victors over Napoleon.

Sir Thomas **Lawrence**

● 1769–1830 ▥ BRITISH ✍ OILS

The precociously talented son of an innkeeper, Lawrence went on to become the leading portrait painter of the day, but over-production led to uneven quality in his work.

His paintings have style, elegance, and haughty confidence. Lawrence was the chosen portrait painter of the ruling class of the richest and most powerful nation on Earth – they believed it and he confirmed it. They were also hungry for an aesthetic experience; his portraits revealed this side of their personalities and gave a strong aesthetic thrill.

Observe the inventive, dramatic, self-conscious poses; flowing dresses, flowing hair; heads confidently turned on overlong necks, to show off; long arms; finely formed, sloping shoulders; rich colours; luscious, free-flowing paint applied with total confidence and sensual pleasure; and above all, dark eyes, with crisp, white highlights that are deep pools of romantic experience and feeling.

KEY WORKS: *Elizabeth Farren*, 1790 (New York: Metropolitan Museum of Art); *Mrs Isaac Cuthbert*, c.1817 (Paris: Musée du Louvre); *Samuel Woodburn*, c.1820 (Cambridge: Fitzwilliam Museum); *Sir John Julius Angerstein*, c.1823–28 (London: National Gallery)

Sir Edwin **Landseer**

● 1802–73 ▥ BRITISH ✍ OILS; SCULPTURE; ENGRAVINGS

Hugely successful and much admired by Queen Victoria, Landseer had a prolific output of sentimental portraits and animal and sporting pictures (he had a particular affinity with Highland cattle, stags, lions, and polar bears). He was in tune with his times – his animals express the key Victorian virtues: nobility, courage, pride, success, conquest, male dominance, and female subservience.

Landseer's small plein-air sketches are as good as anything done by Constable or his French contemporaries.

KEY WORKS: *The Old Shepherd's Mourner*, 1837 (London: Victoria & Albert Museum); *Dignity and Impudence*, 1839 (London: Tate Collection)

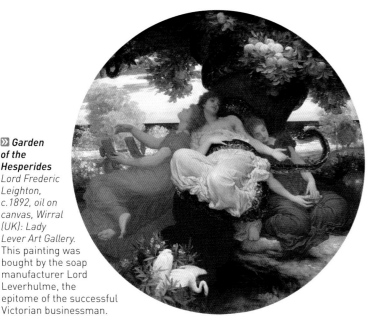

⊠ Garden of the Hesperides
Lord Frederic Leighton, c.1892, oil on canvas, Wirral (UK): Lady Lever Art Gallery. This painting was bought by the soap manufacturer Lord Leverhulme, the epitome of the successful Victorian businessman.

Lord Frederic **Leighton**

● 1830–96 ▥ BRITISH ✍ OILS; SCULPTURE

The first British painter to be made a Lord, Leighton was educated in Europe. He aimed to be, and was called, the Michelangelo of his day. Adept at art politics and diplomacy, he was very successful and counted Queen Victoria among his buyers.

Leighton's works are immaculate and faultless in every way: they display a wonderful technique and draughtsmanship; there is superb, sophisticated, and inventive handling of light, colour, composition; and correct academic subject matter (portraits, biblical and mythological themes). So why are his works so often cold, aloof, and soulless? Because overt support for the status quo always wins support from those with most to lose – but lasting fame requires real innovation.

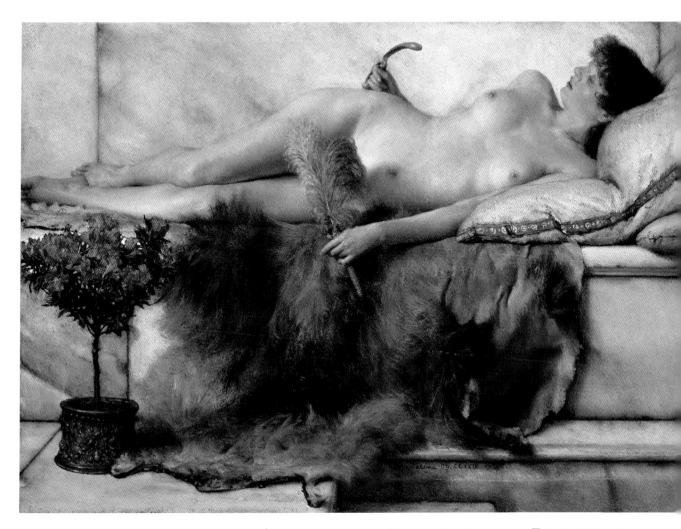

Look for borrowings from (and homages to) Michelangelo and other great Italian and French masters (Titian, Ingres). Also, note the places where he lets go and, instead of playing the pompous, god-like, so-called great artist, is himself: sketches from nature, occasional quirky oil painting, joy at painting white textures. Then the warmth and freshness absent from his "official" works begin to come across.

KEY WORKS: *Cimabue's Madonna Carried in Procession through the Streets of Florence*, 1853–55 (London: National Gallery); *On the Nile*, 1868 (Cambridge: Fitzwilliam Museum); *Athlete Struggling with a Python*, 1874–77 (London: Tate Collection); *Study of a Nubian Young Man*, 1880s (London: Bonhams)

Sir Lawrence **Alma-Tadema**

● 1836–1912 📖 BRITISH ✍ OILS

Alma-Tadema was Dutch-born, but naturalized British. He was highly successful with the Victorian business classes for whom he produced fashionable, meticulously painted, erotic but safe fantasy images of the leisured classes of Greece and Rome – usually the women in private with their clothes off. He was a dedicated archaeologist and used photographs and his own site drawings.

KEY WORKS: *Phidias and the Parthenon*, 1868 (Birmingham, UK: Museums and Art Gallery); *The Sculptor's Model*, 1877 (Private Collection)

⌃ *The Tepidarium* Sir Lawrence Alma-Tadema, 1881, 24 x 33 cm (9 ½ x 13 in), oil on panel, Wirral, UK: Lady Lever Art Gallery. In the 1880s, Alma-Tadema's paintings often fetched higher prices than quality old masters.

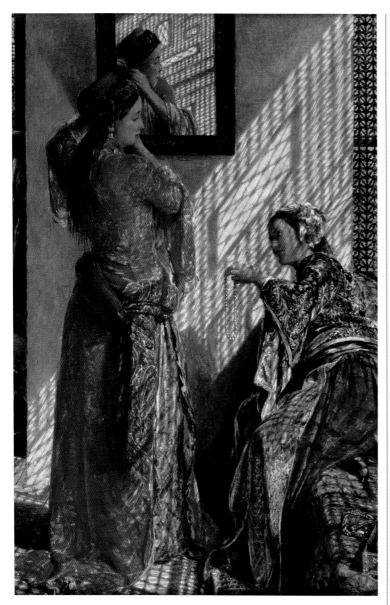

⌃ *Indoor Gossip, Cairo*
John Frederick Lewis, 1873, 30.4 x 20.2 cm (12 x 8 in), oil on panel, Manchester: Whitworth Art Gallery. Personally, Lewis preferred the solitude of Egypt's deserts to the bustling social life of Cairo.

John Frederick **Lewis**

◔ 1805–76 ⚑ BRITISH ✍ WATERCOLOURS; OILS; ENGRAVINGS

The best-known member of a prolific artistic dynasty, Lewis is famous for his impressive scenes of Egyptian markets, bazaars, and harems, using intricate watercolour technique (clever use of gouache) and obsessive detail. He also produced oil paintings, which were not as good. His early work had sporting, wildlife, and topographical subjects. He visited Spain and Morocco (1832–34) and lived in Egypt from 1841 to 1851.

KEY WORKS: *A Syrian Sheik, Egypt*, 1856 (Cambridge: Fitzwilliam Museum); *The Coffee Bearer*, 1857 (Manchester: City Art Gallery); **The Door of a Café in Cairo**, 1865 (London: Royal Academy of Arts)

Christen **Købke**

◔ 1810–48 ⚑ DANISH ✍ OILS

Købke was a short-lived, gifted painter (he died of pneumonia) who caught the prevailing Biedermeier middle-class desire for reassuring portraits of themselves and their dwelling places. The liveliest works are his sketches from nature (from which he made finished exhibition paintings). He travelled in Italy in 1838–40. He was rejected by the Academy.

The luminous calm evident in his works hides a quiet national pride and strong sense of moral virtues. Both sentiments are essential Biedermeier qualities and are revealed in his attention to detail, emphasis on cleanliness and orderliness (which is probably unreal and overexaggerated), and understated symbolic details.

KEY WORKS: *Portrait of Frederik Sødring*, 1832 (Copenhagen: Hirschsprungske Samling); *A View of a Street in Copenhagen*, 1836 (Copenhagen: Statens Museum for Kunst); *The Northern Drawbridge to the Citadel in Copenhagen*, 1837 (London: National Gallery)

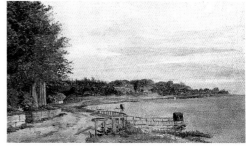

⌃ *River Bank at Emilliekilde* *Christen Købke, c.1836, 19 x 31 cm (7 ½ x 12 ¼ in), oil on canvas, Paris: Musée du Louvre.* Købke's famous lake scenes were painted in the studio from numerous outdoor drawings and sketches.

Richard **Dadd**

● **1817–86** 🏛 **BRITISH** ✍ **OILS**

Known as "Mad Dadd", he murdered his father in 1843 and was locked up, but his doctors encouraged him to continue with his painting. Dadd has become famous for the meticulous and obsessively detailed paintings of fairy subjects that he made in the 1850s.

KEY WORKS: *The Flight out of Egypt*, 1849–50 (London: Tate Collection); *Mercy: David Spareth Saul's Life*, 1854 (Los Angeles: J. Paul Getty Museum); *The Fairy Feller's Master-Stroke*, 1855–64 (London: Tate Collection)

Thomas **Cole**

● **1801–48** 🏛 **AMERICAN** ✍ **OILS**

Cole was British-born (Bolton, Lancashire), but his family emigrated to the US in 1818. He was a major figure in American art – the founder of the Hudson River School and the US tradition of the grand landscape. He was romantic, conservative, melancholic, and his outlook was often at odds with a world given to fast-changing materialism. His early picturesque Hudson River landscapes (done in the 1820s) interpret the American rural scene through the European conventions of the picturesque and sublime. His later work gets larger in scale and is overlaid with literary and moralizing ideas, which he also expresses in verse and diaries. Cole combines landscape with biblical and historical themes, which to modern eyes can go completely over the top in the manner of bad operas or Hollywood spectaculars.

The motivation for the earlier works is a genuine response to the beauties of relatively virgin US nature – unsullied by too much tourism, development, or artistic interpretation (unlike Europe). The motivation for the later work is his anxiety regarding the clash between this nature and an aggressive material culture, which he feared would gobble it up. Cole's five-painting series "The Course of Empire" and his four-part series "The Voyage of Life" predict the rise and fall of American culture.

KEY WORKS: *Distant View of Niagara Falls* (Art Institute of Chicago), 1830; *The Course of Empire: The Savage State*, 1836 (New York Historical Society); *View on the Catskill – Early Autumn*, 1837 (New York: Metropolitan Museum of Art); *Schroon Mountain, Adirondacks,* 1838 (Ohio: Cleveland Museum of Art); *The Notch of the White Mountains*, 1839 (Washington DC: National Gallery of Art)

》 THE HUDSON RIVER SCHOOL

The Hudson River School was a loosely organized group of American painters whose founding father, Thomas Cole, painted picturesque views of the beautiful Hudson River Valley in Upper New York State in the 1820s, thereby establishing a new tradition for landscape painting in the US. Most of the artists associated with the school travelled widely throughout the US and worked in New York. They often painted the Hudson River landscape interspersed with other scenes taken from all over the country. The group's vigour waned after the Civil War (1861–65), but it had a great influence on the Luminist School that followed.

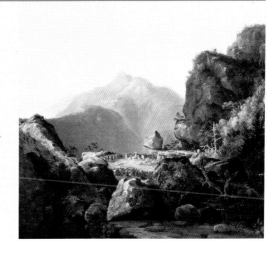

》 Scene from "The Last of the Mohicans" *Thomas Cole, 1827, oil on canvas, New York: Fenimore Art Museum.* This is one of four works inspired by James Fenimore Cooper's novel.

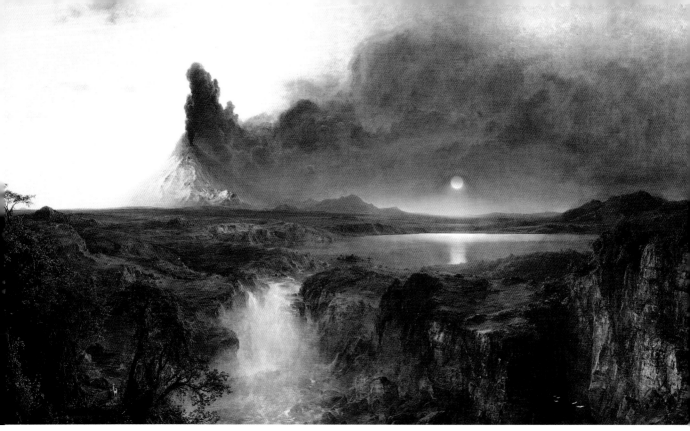

⌃ *Cotopaxi* *Frederic Edwin Church, 1862, 122 x 216 cm (48 x 85 in), oil on canvas, Michigan: Detroit Institute of Arts.* Church made two visits to South America, following in the footsteps of German explorer Alexander von Humboldt. He sketched Ecuador's Cotopaxi volcano in 1857.

Frederic Edwin **Church**

● 1826–1900 ⊓ AMERICAN ✍ OILS

The greatest American landscape painter, Church combined detailed observation of nature with the heroic, sublime vision of Romantics such as Turner. He was God-fearing and patriotic (and it shows).

His large-scale, stunning vistas or panoramas of North and South America have natural phenomena (Niagara Falls), mountains, and dramatic light (blood-red sunsets) at the fore. He used high viewpoints, which give a birdlike feeling of being free to go anywhere, and combined this with the quasi-scientific observation of microscopic

details – indicating his deep spiritual belief in the morality of Nature and presence of God in both its largest and smallest features.

Note the thrilling shafts of light falling on the landscape; exquisite painting of distant mountains and waterfalls; and sharp, bright colours (he used new, heavy metal pigments). At his peak, in the 1860s, he had a long, slow decline (he suffered from bad rheumatism in his hands).

KEY WORKS: *Heart of the Andes*, 1859 (New York: Metropolitan Museum of Art); *Aurora Borealis*, 1865 (Washington DC: National Gallery of Art); *Niagara Falls*, 1867 (Edinburgh: National Gallery of Scotland)

Martin Johnson **Heade**

● 1819–1904 ⊓ AMERICAN ✍ OILS

Heade was an important Luminist and long-lived hack portraitist who "came good" after meeting Frederic Church in 1859. He is best known for his haunting landscapes of flat lands with low horizons. He produced simple, clear compositions – wide, open spaces where each element is placed with

the utmost precision. He had a special ability to show that mysterious, ominous light that precedes a storm. He is also remembered for his travels to Brazil, where he did notable paintings of hummingbirds and orchids.

KEY WORKS: *Approaching Thunderstorm*, 1859 (New York: Metropolitan Museum of Art); *Seascape: Sunset*, 1861 (Detroit Institute of Arts)

Fitz Hugh **Lane**

1804–65 AMERICAN OILS

Lane was a leading member of the Luminist School and a master of the frozen moment, creating scenes of eerie unpopulated stillness with a golden light that suffuses all. He also made paintings of ships and coastlines. His work is the visual equivalent of transcendentalism in literature – the search for the essence of a reality beyond appearance.

KEY WORKS: *The Golden State Entering New York Harbour,* 1854 (New York: Metropolitan Museum of Art); *Off Mount Desert Island,* 1856 (New York: Brooklyn Museum of Art)

Thomas **Moran**

1837–1926 AMERICAN OILS

Moran was a self-taught, Irish-English émigré raised in Philadelphia. He made his reputation after a pioneering visit to Yellowstone (1871), depicting its natural grandeur in the style of Turner's Romanticism. His watercolours are built up from pencil underdrawing and were influenced by Turner. He also painted scenes of Venice, Long Island, and California.

KEY WORKS: *Nearing Camp, Evening on the Upper Colorado River,* 1882 (Bolton, UK: Museums, Art Gallery, and Aquarium); *The Much Resounding Sea,* 1884 (Washington DC: National Gallery of Art); *The River Schuylkill,* 1890s (Private Collection)

Albert **Bierstadt**

1830–1902 GERMAN/AMERICAN OILS

Bierstadt was German-born, but raised in Massachusetts. He painted large-scale landscapes of the American West during the era of early railroads, with low viewpoints, convincing but fanciful compositions, good anecdotal detail, and crisp use of light and shade. Bierstadt did for the American West what Canaletto did for Venice. He also worked in Switzerland and Bermuda. He made brilliant oil sketches.

KEY WORKS: *A Storm in the Rocky Mountains,* 1866 (New York: Brooklyn Museum of Art); *Among the Sierra Nevada Mountains, California,* 1868 (Washington DC: National Museum of American Art)

George Caleb **Bingham**

1811–79 AMERICAN OILS

Born in Virginia and brought up in Missouri, he was the first significant painter from the Midwest. He had a decade of brilliance (1845–55) painting scenes of the American frontier, and "jolly flatboatmen". Contrived simple compositions bathed in golden light. Bingham was as formal as Poussin and as proudly documentary of his new Republic as any 17th-century Dutch master.

KEY WORKS: *Ferrymen Playing Cards,* 1847 (Missouri: St Louis Art Museum); *Country Politician,* 1849 (San Francisco: Fine Arts Museum)

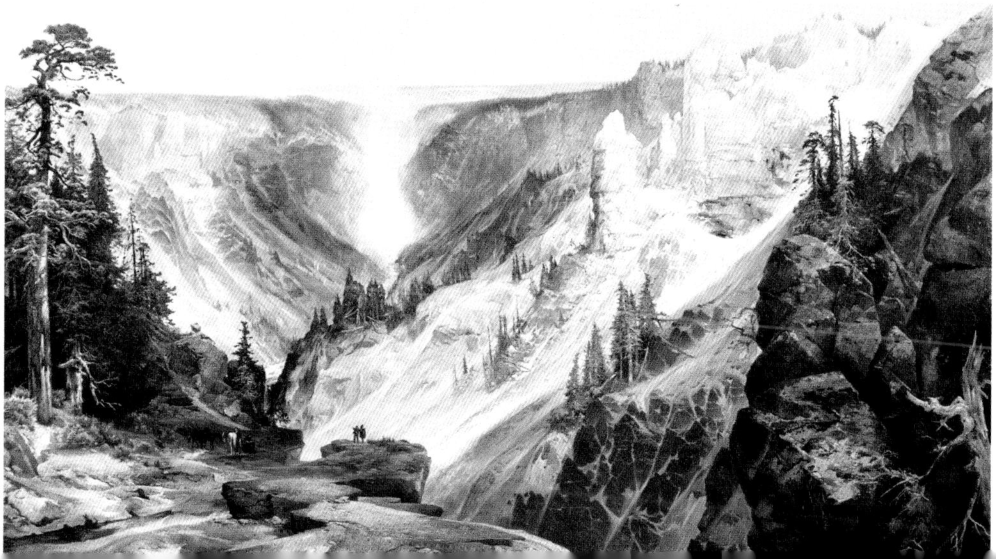

The Grand Canyon of the Yellowstone *Thomas Moran, 1872, 245.1 x 427.8 cm (96 ½ x 168 ½ in), oil on canvas, Washington: Smithsonian Art Museum.* This painting was inspired by joining a government expedition to Yellowstone.

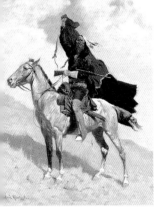

⏫ **The Blanket Signal**
*Frederic Remington
c.1896, oil on canvas,
Houston: Museum of
Fine Arts.* One of the
Native Americans
employed by the United
States Army as
irregulars, a military
trend Remington
strongly supported
in the 1890s.

✉ *Eight Bells* Winslow
*Homer, 1886, 64.5 x
77.2 cm (25 ⅔ x 30 ⅔ in),
oil on canvas, Andover
(USA): Addison Gallery
of American Art.* Homer
lived for many years
on the Atlantic
seaboard in Maine.

Frederic **Remington**

⏺ 1861–1909 ⅋ AMERICAN ✍ OILS; SCULPTURE

The most famous painter of the cowboy West,
Remington also made sculptures. He was haunted
by the notion that he was a mere illustrator
(he was), rather than a "proper" artist – in his
late works he experimented unsuccessfully with
Impressionism and arty ideas. Pro the US cavalry
and unsympathetic to Indians, he was a friend of
Theodore Roosevelt's.

Remington was a great myth-maker, who
liked to promote the idea that he was a former
cowboy and a US cavalry officer. In fact, he was
Yale-educated and lived mostly in New York.

His images of the "good" whites protecting "their"
territory against the savage "foreign" Indians were
consciously adopted by Hollywood cowboy movie
directors. Reproductions of his illustrations in
Harper's Weekly and other popular publications
made Remington a household name throughout
the US. He also spent time as a journalist,
covering the Indian Wars between 1890–91
and the Spanish-American War (in Cuba) of
1898. A keen writer, he published eight books.

KEY WORKS: *The Mexican Major,* 1889 (Art Institute of
Chicago); *Aiding a Comrade,* c.1890 (Houston: Museum
of Fine Arts); *The Advance-Guard, or the Military
Sacrifice,* 1890 (Art Institute of Chicago)

Winslow **Homer**

⏺ 1836–1910 ⅋ AMERICAN ✍ OILS;
WATERCOLOURS

One of the great 19th-century painters, Homer
could interpret nature to reflect the American
pioneering spirit. He was well travelled in the US,
England, and the Bahamas and was self-taught.

He created highly satisfying, virile images:
sea paintings of the Atlantic coast, images of
down-to-earth, practical people, especially when
coping with adversity; modern women; and robust
children. He made a pragmatic exploration of light
and colour, and produced strong, well-designed,
boldly painted pictures. He also painted exquisite,
fresh, fluid watercolours. His work has a strong
narrative content (he started out as a magazine
illustrator), but he lifted his art beyond the ordinary
by infusing it with a sincerely felt, underlying moral
message, and a subtle ambiguity of meaning.

His no-nonsense painting is in tune with its
subject matter, time, and place. He had the ability
to simplify and used strong
contrasts of light and shade.
Note the solid unhesitating
draughtsmanship and frequent
use of a silhouetted figure, often
in heroic attitude. He employed
the imagery of children as a
metaphor for the future of
America. Note also the
progression of his style and
subjects as they grow larger,
stronger, more confident, and
freer with age and experience.

KEY WORKS: *Snap the Whip,* 1872
(Ohio: Butler Institute of American
Art); *Tending Sheep,* Houghton
Farm; c.1878 (Private Collection);
The Herring Net, 1885 (Art Institute
of Chicago); *The Sharpshooters,*
c.1900 (London: Christie's Images)

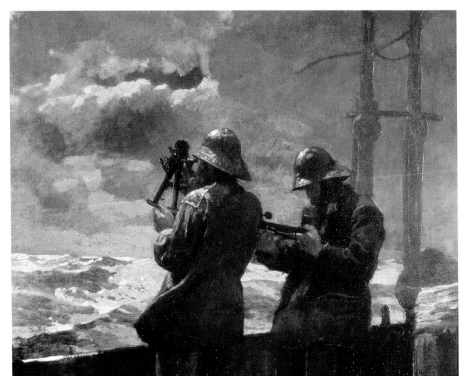

Thomas **Eakins**

● 1844–1916 〔ᴾ〕 AMERICAN ✑ OILS

Philadelphia-born, Eakins studied in Paris and
Spain, and taught at the Pennsylvania Academy.
Said by some to be the greatest American artist,
he was little honoured in his lifetime. He had a
pragmatic but difficult, unyielding personality.
He was a keen boatman.

His frank, candid portraits are of people from
a fairly narrow social circle. Eakins had more
interest in status, achievement, and position
in society than in personality – and responded
best to achievers. From 1869 onwards, his work
featured successful professionals. His later
works were more dreamy. He had a deep interest
in science, medicine, and how things work, and
used human anatomy, motion, and perspective
to make his pictures work.

Look for imaginative poses and movement;
workman-like hands; rich, dark colour harmonies;
atmospheric 19th-century interiors. He used
extra objects or incidents to tell the story behind
a portrait, and light to animate compositions.
He liked colour and emotion, but was even more
interested in shadows – notice how he used them
to create space. Has any other painter observed
shadows so accurately?

KEY WORKS: *The Biglin Brothers Racing*, 1872
(Washington DC: National Gallery of Art); *The Gross
Clinic*, 1875 (Philadelphia: Thomas Jefferson
University); *William Rush carving his Allegorical Figure
of the Schuylkill River*, 1877 (Philadelphia Museum of
Art); *The Swimming Hole*, 1884–85 (Texas: Modern Art
Museum of Fort Worth)

⬙ **Max Schmidtt in a Single Scull** *Thomas Eakins,
1871, 83 x 118 cm (32 ¹/₄ x 46 ¹/₄ in), oil on canvas,
New York: Metropolitan Museum of Art.*

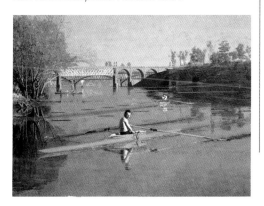

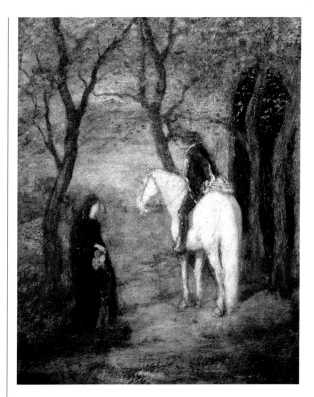

⬙ **Roadside Meeting** *Albert Pinkham Ryder, 1901,
38.1 x 30.5 cm (15 x 12 in), oil on canvas, Ohio:
Butler Institute of American Art.* Like many
symbolist painters, Ryder was an admirer
of the poet Edgar Allen Poe.

Albert Pinkham **Ryder**

● 1847–1917 〔ᴾ〕 AMERICAN ✑ OILS

Ryder was an erratic, bohemian character who
painted brooding, romantic scenes such as *Jonah
and the Whale*, *Siegfried and the Rhinemaidens*, and
boats on stormy moonlit seas. He used jewel-like
colours and thick, cumbersome paint, but his
technique was poor and the use of bitumen meant
most of his paintings have been damaged beyond
repair. He was considered to represent the height
of poetic sensibility and was somewhat of a guru
figure for the likes of Hartley and Pollock.

KEY WORKS: *Siegfried and the Rhinemaidens*, 1888–91
(Washington DC: National Gallery of Art); *The Forest
of Arden*, c.1888–97 (New York: Metropolitan Museum
of Art); *The Race Track (Death on a Pale Horse)*,
c.1896–1908 (Ohio: Cleveland Museum of Art)

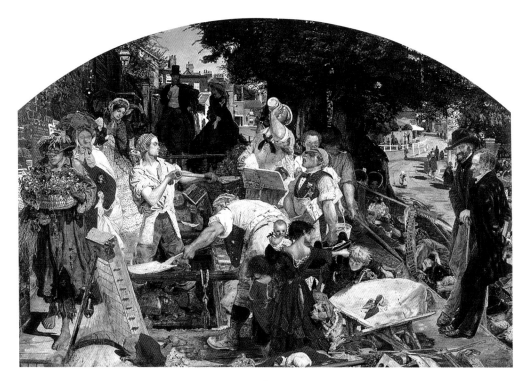

» *Work* Ford Madox Brown, 1852–65, 137 x 197.3 cm (54 x 77 ⅔ in), oil on canvas, Manchester: City Art Gallery. Brown's picture is intended to show that manual workers are as fit a subject for art as intellectuals and aristocrats.

John **Ruskin**

● **1819–1900** ▥ **BRITISH** ✎ **WATERCOLOURS**

Ruskin was most important as a critic and writer. As a painter, he had a central belief in the supremacy of truth to nature (not the same as a slavish imitation of nature), but abandoned this belief after 1858. His intensely observed and detailed watercolours reflect his passion and knowledge of nature, geology, and architecture.

KEY WORKS: *J. M. W. Turner*, c.1840 (London: Royal Academy of Arts); *View of Bologna*, c.1845–46 (London: Tate Collection)

Ford Madox **Brown**

● **1821–93** ▥ **BRITISH** ✎ **OILS; WATERCOLOURS; DRAWINGS**

Brown trained in France and was a follower of the Pre-Raphaelites. He created highly detailed works – landscapes painted in the open air and figurative works containing social commentaries on contemporary life. He was too idiosyncratic to be successful in his own day.

KEY WORKS: *The Seeds and Fruits of English Poetry*, 1845–51 (Oxford: Ashmolean Museum); *The Last of England*, 1855 (Cambridge: Fitzwilliam Museum)

Dante Gabriel **Rossetti**

● **1828–82** ▥ **BRITISH** ✎ **OILS; WATERCOLOURS; DRAWINGS**

Rossetti was a painter, poet, and the leading Pre-Raphaelite. He had a complicated love life and died of alcohol and drug abuse.

His early Pre-Raphaelite work is awkward and stiff at times. He went in for romantic medieval themes, but is best known for images of erotic *femmes fatales*, painted from the 1860s onwards. They are characterized by luscious lips, sinuous hands, and thick, glistening hair. He was a brilliant draughtsman but his painting technique is suspect. Look for works of much intensity (a desirable state of existence for artistic folk at the time) and fine, heavily worked watercolours.

KEY WORKS: *Beata Beatrix*, 1864 (London: Tate Collection); *Proserpina*, 1874 (London: Tate Collection)

The Pre-Raphaelites

19TH CENTURY

The Pre-Raphaelite Brotherhood (PRB) was formed in London in 1848 by seven ambitious young students and artists. They were in rebellion against what they regarded as the unimaginative attitude of the Royal Academy. They sought to establish a new style, endowed with moral sincerity and inspired by Italian art of the 14th and 15th centuries, that is, prior to Raphael. The PRB held together for only five years, but its continuing influence was wide reaching.

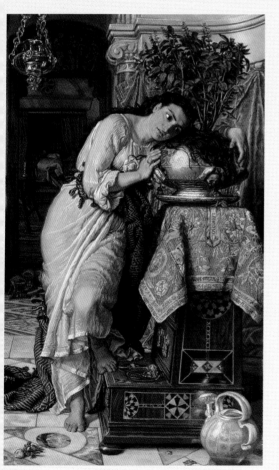

Isabella and the Pot of Basil William Holman Hunt, 1867, 60.7 x 38.7 cm (23 x 15 in), oil on canvas, Wilmington: Delaware Art Museum. Based on Keats's poem; the model was Holman Hunt's pregnant wife.

The Pre-Raphaelites drew their inspiration from literature, especially the Bible, Shakespeare, the Romantics, and contemporary poets, such as Browning and Tennyson. They were also inspired by medievalism, especially Malory's *Morte d'Arthur*. They developed their own paint colours and came up with a new technique of painting on a "wet white" background, so the colours shone with luminosity. Women feature heavily in their works, especially those of Dante Gabriel Rossetti and Edward Burne-Jones.

What to look for

A vivid use of colour – sometimes exquisite, at other times gaudy. Note the scenes of chivalry and deep emotion; sentimentalism; strong literary references, with the same scene often painted by several artists; rich and quite obvious symbolism. They often used one another as models, so look for recognizable portraits and self-portraits among genre paintings. In their early paintings, seek out the stylized "PRB" monogram.

KEY EVENTS

1848	The Pre-Raphaelite Brotherhood holds its first meeting at 7 Gower Street, London
1850	The meaning of "PRB" revealed by mistake to a journalist
1855	Pre-Raphaelite paintings are shown at the Paris Exhibition
1857	Rossetti meets William Morris and Burne-Jones, a new generation of Pre-Raphaelites

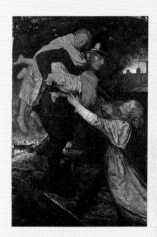

The Rescue Sir John Everett Millais, 1855, 121.5 x 83.6 cm (48 x 33 in), oil on canvas, Melbourne: National Gallery of Victoria. Millais had witnessed the death of a fireman during a rescue.

William Holman **Hunt**

● 1827–1910 🄿 BRITISH ✍ OILS; WATERCOLOURS

A founder member of the Pre-Raphaelite Brotherhood, Hunt was its most consistent exponent. He was religious, obsessive, and stubborn, producing work with insistent moralizing and didactic themes. He was a true Victorian, who verged on greatness but whose obsession with detail and colouring can be intense to the point of unpleasantness.

KEY WORKS: *Our English Coasts*, 1852 (London: Tate Collection); *The Scapegoat*, 1854 (Wirral, UK: Lady Lever Art Gallery)

Sir John Everett **Millais**

● 1829–96 🄿 BRITISH ✍ OILS; DRAWINGS

Millais was an infant prodigy who became extremely fashionable, rich, and famous. He was a founder member of the Pre-Raphaelite Brotherhood and a pillar of the Royal Academy (becoming its president in 1896).

His early work (up to the 1850s) was genuinely Pre-Raphaelite, with a meticulous, tight style, strict observation of nature, and choice of moral themes. The later work is more freely painted, with subjects overtly designed to catch the fashion of the times and sell well – sentimental scenes, historical romances, portraits (he needed the money with eight children and a lavish lifestyle to support).

His virtuoso craftsmanship and attention to detail (natural and historical) make it all look so easy. Look out for delightful, often humorous, sketches; note also the commercial prints made from his paintings, which sold as well as current-day rock group recordings.

KEY WORKS: *Ophelia*, 1851–52 (London: Tate Collection); *The Blind Girl*, c.1856 (Birmingham, UK: Museums and Art Gallery); *The Ransom*, 1860–62 (Los Angeles: J. Paul Getty Museum)

John **Brett**

● 1831–1902 🄿 BRITISH ✍ OILS

He was a devotee of Ruskin and emulator of Holman Hunt, creating early, intensely detailed, high-coloured landscapes that are a *tour de force* of precise observation and technique. He went on painting trips to Italy and the Alps (as approved by Ruskin). Although commercially more successful, his later works (especially panoramic views of the ocean) were flabbier than his earlier works.

KEY WORKS: *Glacier of Rosenlaui*, 1856 (London: Tate Collection); *Florence from Bellosguardo*, 1863 (London: Tate Collection)

George Frederick **Watts**

● 1817–1904 🄿 BRITISH ✍ OILS; SCULPTURE

Watts aimed to emulate the grandeur and achievements of Titian and Michelangelo and was known in his day as "England's Michelangelo". He produced portraits, allegories, and landscapes that reflect the influence of his two exemplars but can now seem pompous and overambitious. His portraits are his best work.

KEY WORKS: *Choosing*, 1864 (Private Collection); *Sir Galahad*, 1880s (Liverpool: Walker Art Gallery)

Sir Edward Coley **Burne-Jones**

● 1833–98 🄿 BRITISH ✍ OILS; WATERCOLOURS

A quiet, retiring, otherworldly painter, with a streak of shrewdness, Burne-Jones became famous and successful after 1877. His paintings reflect his character and one aspect of the age he lived in. His early medieval and mythological subjects are heavily laden with mysticism and symbolism that look back to a "golden" age, chosen to fulfil a wish to escape from modern urban and industrial reality. Yet the large-scale,

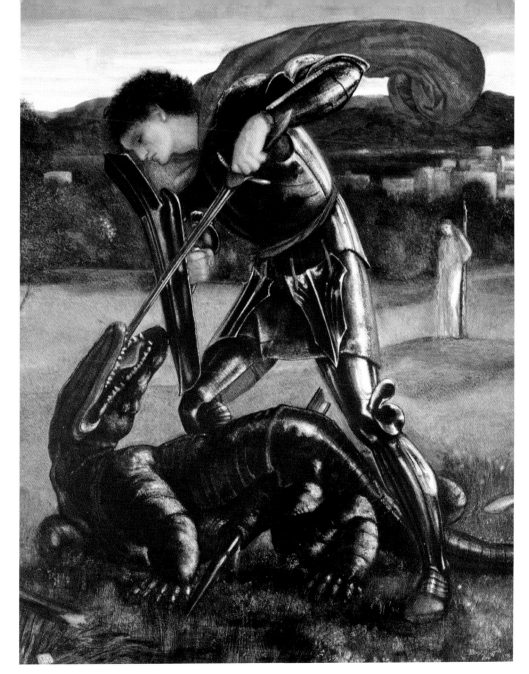

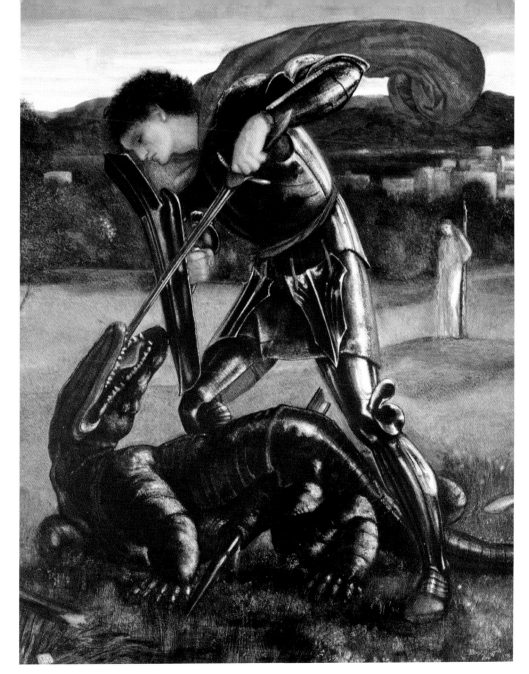 **St George and the Dragon** *Sir Edward Coley Burne-Jones, 1868, gouache on paper, London: William Morris Gallery.* Burne-Jones worked closely with William Morris from 1855–59. This painting post-dates his visit to Italy with Ruskin in 1862.

precise style, fascination with materials and realistic details are very worldly, showing a personal (and typical Victorian) duality.

He had a highly developed sense of design (due to his closeness to William Morris, who encouraged him to become an artist instead of following a career in the Church) and a technique that shows a love of meticulous craftsmanship (due to his closeness to Ruskin).

He was also influenced by early Renaissance art (such as that of Botticelli). He produced successful designs for tapestry and stained glass; and illustrations for texts of medieval and classical legends.

KEY WORKS: *The Beguiling of Merlin*, 1872–77 (Liverpool: Lady Lever Art Gallery); *King Cophetua and the Beggar Maid*, 1880 (London: Tate Collection)

Realism

c.1855–1900

Realism was the progressive movement in art and literature in the mid-19th century (especially in France). It began in earnest in 1855, with an exhibition of works by Gustave Courbet. Its centrepiece, *The Painter's Studio*, had been refused by the Universal Exhibition, so Courbet set up his own in a nearby tent. The artist produced a manifesto to go with his exhibition, which he entitled *Le Réalisme*.

Realism was concerned with social realities, and wanted to show fact rather than ideals or aesthetics. It rejected Academic art as being too artificial, and Romanticism as being too concerned with the imagination. Realists wanted to cut through the hypocrisy manifest in society and art. As such, the movement became a mechanism for social change, with a committed political agenda. It was associated with new, democratic ways of thinking, with anti-establishment causes, and with championing individuals' rights. The movement was highly influential, spreading into Germany, Russia, the Netherlands, and the US. Realism also influenced literary giants such as Tolstoy, Balzac, Zola, Dickens, and Flaubert.

The subject matter is diverse: portraits, groups, landscapes, and genre scenes. Refusing to hark back to historic or pastoral idylls, Realism dealt with the harshness of life, such as human degradation and poverty, as well as with natural landscapes and human emotions. Whereas artists had traditionally romanticized the poor and their harsh existence, Realists wanted to depict the truth. Above all, they painted what they saw in everyday life, rejoicing in the contrariness of the natural world. The movement had a strong following, with artists from other traditions often borrowing the ideas and language of Realism.

What to look for

Courbet's masterpiece, *The Painter's Studio*, although painted early in his career, is a manifesto of Realism in which he sets out his central beliefs and opinions. It shows his studio in Paris with three groups of figures. The artist is in the centre. To his right are his friends – "those who thrive on life". To his left are those who "thrive on death", not just his enemies (notably the head of state, Napoleon III), but also the evils he fought against, as well as the exploited and oppressed, among whom he includes the poor, the destitute, and the losers in the struggle for life.

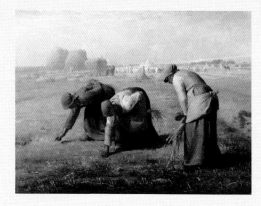

▶ **The Gleaners**
Jean-François Millet, 1857, 83 x 111 cm (33 x 44 in), oil on canvas, Paris: Musée d'Orsay. In 1857, Millet was described by one critic as "a great painter who walks in clogs the road of Michelangelo".

KEY EVENTS

1848	Revolution in France; rise to power of Napoleon III
1850	Courbet's *Stonebreakers*, remarkable for its social realism, shown at Salon
1855	Universal Exhibition. Courbet mounts rival show, including *The Painter's Studio*
1863	Manet's *Le déjeuner sur l'herbe* at Salon des Refusés
1867	Publication of Émile Zola's first major realist novel, *Thérèse Raquin*

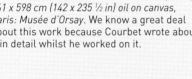

⬇ **The Painter's Studio** Gustave Courbet, 1855, 361 x 598 cm (142 x 235 ½ in) oil on canvas, Paris: Musée d'Orsay. We know a great deal about this work because Courbet wrote about it in detail whilst he worked on it.

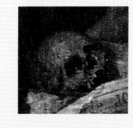

◄ The skull is the archetypal symbol of death. It is resting on top of a newspaper. This is Courbet's unambivalent comment on the critics who shaped 19th-century opinion.

The oppressed include a Chinese man, a Jew, an Irishwoman, a poacher, a war veteran, and a labourer

A figure in the pose of Christ crucified symbolizes Academic art, which Courbet rejected

The central figure here is the writer Champfleury, the founder of Realism in literature

Light enters through a window on the right side – the side of life. A skylight also lit the studio

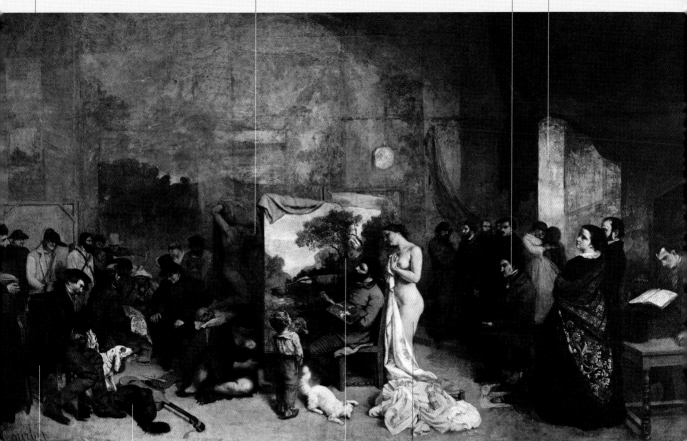

Wearing huntsman's dress is Napoleon III, Emperor of the French Second Empire

A large floppy hat with a feather, a cloak and dagger, and a guitar – the typical accessories of the Romantic artist

On the easel is a large landscape, depicting the artist's own homeland. Well lit, it puts the figures behind in shadow

The naked woman represents unadorned truth guiding Courbet's brush

Gustave **Courbet**

⬤ **1819–77** 🏴 **FRENCH** ✍ **OILS**

Courbet was the radical scourge of corrupt Second Empire France and the tedious old-fashioned traditions of the French Academy. He was the major exponent of 19th-century Realism.

He chose large-scale subjects (such as life, death, destiny, the ocean, the forest) and often produced physically large paintings. He had a brilliant, gutsy technique with thick paint. His works portray toughness and realism – real people carrying out unglamorous, everyday activities. Courbet had an intimate knowledge of all the activities, people, and places he painted, and valued down-to-earth, provincial life more highly than fashionable Parisian glamour.

His work can range from the most brilliantly inspired and executed artworks to sloppy, uninspired, and bad painting. Note the very unusual rich green, especially in his landscapes – it is not artistic licence: in his beloved homeland (Ornans, near Besançon) the copper in the soil turns the vegetation that colour. The area is worth visiting not only for its stunning beauty, but also to see what it was that inspired him and how real his "realism" is. Note also his prominent red signature – what a big ego!

KEY WORKS: *A Burial at Ornans*, 1849–50 (Paris: Musée d'Orsay); *The Source of the Loue*, 1864 (Washington DC: National Gallery of Art); *The Cliff at Etretat after the Storm*, 1869 (Paris: Musée d' Orsay)

Henri **Fantin-Latour**

⬤ **1836–1904** 🏴 **FRENCH** ✍ **OILS; PRINTS**

A painter of allegories inspired by music (especially Wagner), still lifes, and stodgy, wooden portraits with sitters who look distinctly uncomfortable or bored. Flowers and fruit are highly worked and end up looking artificial. Fantin-Latour benefitted from close connections with his more gifted artistic contemporaries.

KEY WORKS: *Flowers and Fruit*, 1865 (Paris: Musée d'Orsay); *Portrait of Edouard Manet*, 1867 (Art Institute of Chicago)

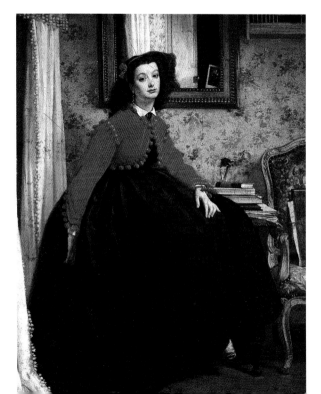

James **Tissot**

⬤ **1836–1902** 🏴 **FRENCH** ✍ **OILS; PRINTS; DRAWINGS**

Tissot was French, but lived in London between 1871 and 1882, where he became a highly successful, fashionable painter of small-scale polished depictions of society (especially slim-waisted women) at play. He had a brilliant technique, which compensated for lack of depth and insight. His late religious conversion following the death of his much-painted mistress led to Bible illustrations.

KEY WORKS: *London Visitors*, 1874 (Ohio: Toledo Museum of Art); *The Gallery of HMS Calcutta*, c.1876 (London: Tate Collection)

◈ *Portrait of Mlle. L. L.* James Tissot, 1864, 124 x 100 cm (48 ¾ x 39 ½ in), oil on canvas, Paris: Musée d'Orsay. His art was attacked by critics Oscar Wilde, Henry James, and John Ruskin for its appeal to the *nouveaux riches*.

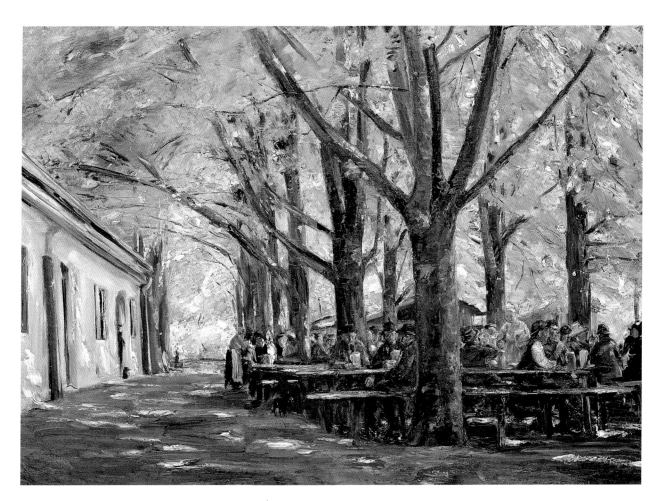

Max **Liebermann**

● 1847–1935 🏳 GERMAN ✍ OILS; PRINTS

Liebermann was a successful painter of middle-class daily life and places – an updated replay of Dutch 17th-century and Biedermeier art. He produced freely painted, not very difficult paintings, which reassured his clients and appealed to modern-day nostalgia. He used the earth-colour palette of the old masters, not the modern rainbow palette of the French Impressionists.

KEY WORKS: *An Old Woman with Cat*, 1878 (Los Angeles: J. Paul Getty Museum); *The Flax Spinners*, 1887 (Berlin: National Gallery); *Memorial Service for Kaiser Friedrich at Kösen*, 1888–89 (London: National Gallery); *The Ropewalk in Edam*, 1904 (New York: Metropolitan Museum of Art)

Carl **Larsson**

● 1853–1919 🏳 SWEDISH ✍ WATERCOLOURS; OILS; PRINTS

Larsson was a key Swedish artist whose idealized illustrations of his own country cottage (rustic furniture, scrubbed floors, simplicity) were internationally influential and established the idea of the Scandinavian style. He also painted large-scale decorative, allegorical murals, portraits, and self-portraits. He became a manic-depressive after 1906.

KEY WORKS: *Breakfast under the Big Birch*, 1896 (Stockholm: National Museum); *Watering the Plants, Sitting Room - View Two*, 1899 (Private Collection); *The Midwinter Sacrifice*, 1914–15 (Stockholm: National Museum); *Indian Summer*, c.1915 (Private Collection)

⌃ *A Country Brasserie, Brannenburg, Bavaria*
Max Liebermann, 1894, 70 x 100 cm (27 ½ x 39 ⅓ in), oil on canvas, Paris: Musée d'Orsay. Liebermann was regarded as a cultural enemy by the Kaiser because he admired modern foreign art (like French Barbizon and Impressionism), and rejected German nationalist and academic traditions.

Jean-Baptiste-Camille **Corot**

● **1796–1875** 🇫🇷 **FRENCH** ✍ **OILS**

A major landscape painter of the 19th century, Corot was a bridge between the English landscape tradition and French Impressionism. He was kind, gentle, and unusually unegocentric for an artist.

His late, best-known paintings (post-1860) – silvery green, soft focus, lyrical landscapes – are based on remembered emotions ("souvenirs") and sketches from nature. But, notice, too, the earlier artificial, more conventional (academic and sometimes ludicrous) landscapes; he also made enchanting figure paintings. He was much copied and faked – there are said to be more fake Corots in the US than all his genuine pictures put together.

His best works are the small plein-air, on-the-spot sketches called *pochades*. They show wonderful observation of light and clouds in the sky and empirical exploration of space; note how he tightens the soft focus with sharp, dark accents.

KEY WORKS: *The Forum Seen from the Farnese Gardens*, 1826 (Paris: Musée du Louvre); *Ville d'Avray*, c.1867–70 (New York: Brooklyn Museum of Art)

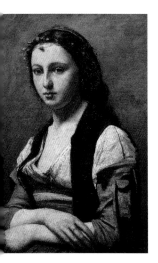

⊼ **Woman with a Pearl**
Jean-Baptiste-Camille Corot, 1868-70, 70 x 55 cm (27 ½ x 21 ⅔ in), oil on canvas, Paris: Musée du Louvre. Corot has based the woman's pose – hands crossed over one another, head turned towards us – on Leonardo da Vinci's masterpiece the *Mona Lisa*.

⊠ **The Third-Class Carriage** *Honoré Daumier, 1864, 20.3 x 29.5 cm (8 x 11 ¾ in), watercolour, ink wash, and charcoal on paper, Baltimore: Walters Art Museum.* Railways brought the rural poor to Paris seeking employment and a new life.

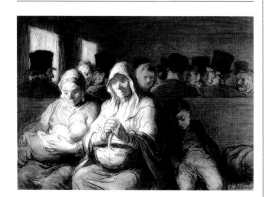

Honoré **Daumier**

● **1808–79** 🇫🇷 **FRENCH** ✍ **PRINTS; DRAWINGS; OILS; SCULPTURE**

Daumier is called the "greatest 19th-century caricaturist", but is much more because he reveals universal truths about the human condition. His subjects are French men and women living in a corrupt, greedy, bourgeois regime (the French Second Empire), but the message is timeless.

His compelling images observe the absurdities and obsessions of husbands, wives, lawyers, politicians, artists, actors, etc. He was never judgmental or unkind, even though his work was censored. He had a prolific output: prints especially (he was a pioneer of lithography), watercolours, sketches; some oil paintings after 1860. But he was never comfortable with the scale and technique. He was at his best with a smaller and more spontaneous scale and medium.

Notice his captivating facial expressions, body language, hands – all speaking volumes. His use of light, shade, and atmosphere is as good as Rembrandt's. His works have a probing, lively line. He produced miraculous, small clay-model caricatures of politicians. He ignored the rich and famous, and was never successful commercially. He made the everyday sublime and moving.

KEY WORKS: *The Laundress*, c.1860s (Paris: Musée d'Orsay); *The Print Collector*, c.1860 (Glasgow Museums); *Advice to a Young Artist*, after 1860 (Washington DC: National Gallery of Art); *The Studio*, c.1870 (Los Angeles: J. Paul Getty Museum)

Théodore **Rousseau**

● **1812–67** 🇫🇷 **FRENCH** ✍ **OILS**

Rousseau was an important pioneer of plein-air painting and a principal figure of the Barbizon School, thereby linking Constable to Monet. He allowed nature to speak for itself, abolishing the convention of inserting human figures in order to animate or interpret the landscape. Rousseau trod a difficult and not always successful path between Romanticism and Realism.

He was excited by woods and trees and sought to convey both the spirit (Romanticism) and appearance (Realism) of nature. Look at the differences between the small-scale sketches painted on the spot and the larger detailed works he made in the studio. His paintings have dramatic skies, such as one finds on autumn evenings. Some of his works have darkened with time.

KEY WORKS: *Sunset in the Auvergne*, 1830 (London: National Gallery); *Paysage panoramique*, 1830–40 (Cambridge: Fitzwilliam Museum)

Jean-François **Millet**

1814–75 FRENCH OILS; ENGRAVINGS

Millet was the son of a Normandy farmer. He painted the final scenes of a rural world and lifestyle at the moment when it was beginning to disappear because of the industrialization of France.

His small-scale works describe a self-contained world of humble people working on and with the land. He portrays, depending on your point of view, either the dignity, or the cruelty, of manual peasant labour. His works show a magical stillness, silence, and peace which is not overloaded with drama or symbolism.

Notice the low viewpoint, so you feel you are standing on the same level as the people you see. There is freshly observed light; a sense of direct contact with the land, the light, and the atmosphere. He works directly onto the canvas – so you can often see *pentimenti* (alterations), the way he worked the paint, and his carefully considered line. It is as if his style and working methods were a sort of parallel with the way in which his peasants work the land.

KEY WORKS: *The Winnower*, 1847–48 (London: National Gallery); *The Sower*, 1850 (Boston: Museum of Fine Arts); *Peasant Girls with Brush-wood*, 1852 (St Petersburg: Hermitage Museum)

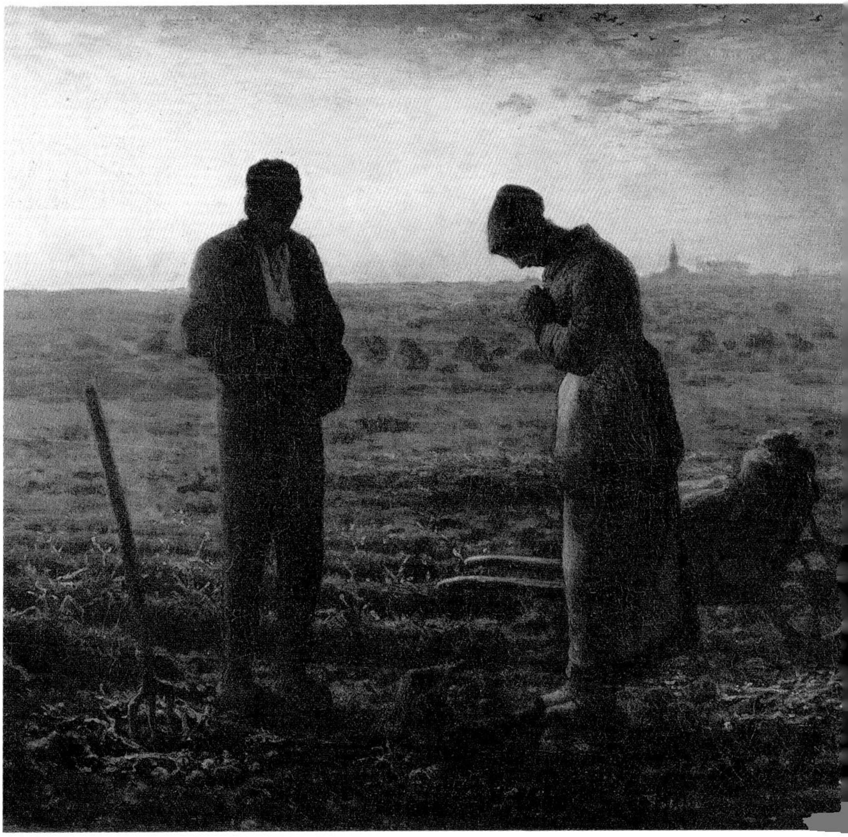

The Angelus *Jean-François Millet, 1857–59, 55.5 x 66 cm (26 x 29 in), oil on canvas, Paris: Musée d'Orsay.* This picture was a star exhibit at the Paris World Fair of 1867; vast numbers of reproductions were sold.

Eugène **Boudin**

1824–98 FRENCH OILS; WATERCOLOUR

Boudin is best known for charming small-scale beach scenes of holidaymakers on the Normandy coast (Trouville), dressed up in their crinolines and bonnets on cloudy, breezy days. He had a sketchy style and was an exponent of plein-air spontaneity, a forerunner of the Impressionists (he had a great influence on the young Monet). He also painted scenes of Venice, Holland, and France. If you can't sense the breeze, it's probably not a Boudin.

KEY WORKS: *Approaching Storm*, 1864 (Art Institute of Chicago); *Ville d'Avray*, c.1867–70 (New York: Brooklyn Museum of Art)

» PLEIN-AIR PAINTING AND THE BARBIZON SCHOOL c.1840–1870

The Barbizon school was a group of progressive mid-19th century painters who worked in and around the French village of Barbizon near Paris, in the forest of Fontainebleau. The leader of the school was Theodore Rousseau. The group made landscape as important as portraiture and genre painting, and paved the way for Impressionism.

The Barbizon painters promoted the concept of "plein-air" painting – paintings were begun and completed in the open air instead of inside the studio, or studio paintings that consciously set out to capture on canvas the qualities and sensations of being outside in the open air.

Edouard **Manet**

● 1832–83 ᴾᵁ FRENCH ✍ OILS; PRINTS; ENGRAVINGS

Manet's ambition was to be officially honoured as the true modern successor of the old Masters. From a good Parisian family, good-looking, charming, strong, worldly-wise, and very gifted, he was born for such a role.

Manet was fascinated by modern city and commercial life, cafe society and travel, and had close friendships with avant-garde artists and writers. The critics and academic artists could see his talent but thought that his fascinating and ambiguous subject matter of modern urban and suburban life, and his "playing card" style, were unacceptable parodies of their revered traditions. Constant rejection of his art caused a nervous breakdown in 1871; he died from syphilis, aged 51.

Manet's personal, very visual, sketchy painting technique with large areas of flat colour was unique at the time, although much influenced by Velasquez and Goya. His work is often a paradoxical combination of intimacy and aloofness, and in his renderings of private relationships there is often a key figure who is a detached and uninvolved observer. *Olympia* was first shown at the official Paris Salon of 1865. It caused a storm of outraged protest. Manet considered it to be his greatest work and he never sold it.

KEY WORKS: *Déjeuner sur l'Herbe*, 1862–63 (Paris: Musée d'Orsay); *The Balcony*, 1868–69 (Paris: Musée d'Orsay); *Gare Saint-Lazare*, 1873 (Washington DC: National Gallery of Art)

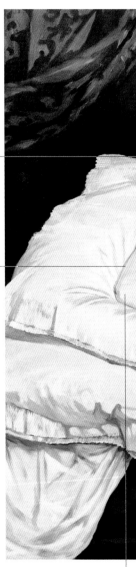

▶ *Olympia* 1863, 130 x 190 cm (51 x 75 in), oil on canvas, Paris: Musée d'Orsay. Manet's painting pays tribute to Giorgione's *Sleeping Venus* (see page 92), but it caused a storm of outraged protest.

Olympia makes direct eye contact with the viewer, as does the cat (bottom right), which is disturbed from sleep by our arrival

Manet's creation is not the goddess Venus but a young woman in a recognizable role. She is explicitly naked with pearls at her neck and ears, and an orchid in her hair

Olympia was seen not as a modern interpretation of a respected theme, but as a crude parody of an artistic tradition. It was obvious to everyone that the reclining woman was a prostitute.

☑ *The Bar at the Folies-Bergère*
1881–82, 97 x 130 cm (38 x 51 in), oil on canvas, London: Courtauld Institute of Art. Upper-class dandies like Manet rubbed shoulders with workers and prostitutes at the Folies-Bergère. The bottles (from beer to champagne) symbolize this interaction.

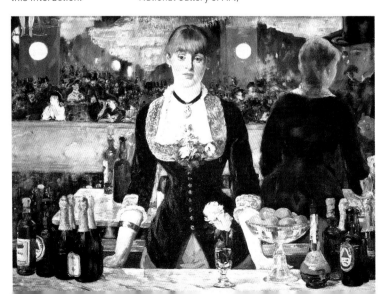

》TECHNIQUES

The candid style shows Manet at his best. He uses a bold composition with strong outlines to the forms. There is virtually no shadow or modelling with soft light. There is no fine detail, but the colour harmonies are very subtle. Some critics saw this style as merely incompetent when compared with that of Ingres (see page 203), and it was described as crude.

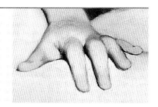

The servant brings in flowers – a gift from a previous admirer – but Olympia does not acknowledge her presence. She is ready and waiting for her next client: the spectator of the painting

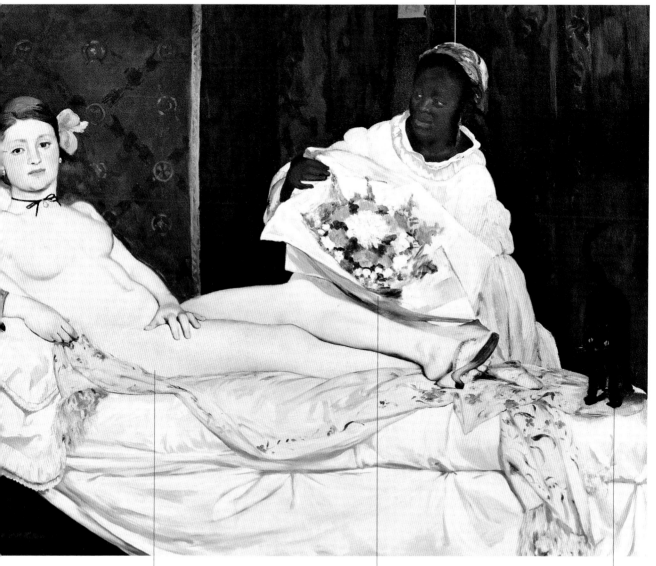

The model is 30-year-old Victorine Meurent – a professional model, who became a painter herself, but died an alcoholic.

The bouquet symbolically suggests the pleasures offered by Olympia. Manet was a master of still life, which he often painted for his own pleasure

Manet used black to bring a rich tonality and elegance to his work. Black is one of the most difficult of pigments for an artist to exploit as it can easily overwhelm and kill all other colours and qualities

Impressionism

1860s–1880s

Impressionism marked the birth of modern painting. Never consciously revolutionary, its aim was simply to depict the immediacy of the world with complete fidelity. Yet, in seeing this as accidental, the product of transitory light conditions and chance moments, it prompted a strikingly different pictorial language that began the overthrow of the naturalistic tradition of the Renaissance.

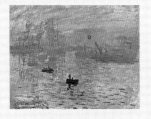

⌃ *Impression: Sunrise* Claude Monet, 1872, 48 x 63 cm (19 x 24 ¾ in), oil on canvas, Paris: Musée Marmottan. Nominally a view of the harbour of Le Havre, this "impression" gave birth to the name of the art movement.

Delicate, mosaic-like brushstrokes in light, brilliant colours intended to capture an instant briefly glimpsed, define Impressionism. The artists aimed at more than just spontaneity. By replacing tonal gradations – the gradual lightening or darkening of a colour to suggest shadows and depth – with tiny dabs of pure colour, the Impressionists pointed to a new way of seeing. But, although almost every major avant-garde French painter of the period was influenced by Impressionism, only Pissarro, Sisley, and Monet, the giant of the movement, remained consistently true to its goals.

Subjects

The here and now dominated Impressionism. Whether it was picnics, boating parties, still lifes, railway stations, city views, or sun-flooded landscapes vibrantly alive with colour, the emphasis was on the world immediately surrounding the painter. The modern world became paramount. Just as importantly, the studio was abandoned for painting on the spot directly onto the canvas. Plein-air (literally, "open-air") painting (see page 237) not only demanded immediacy on the part of the painter – the speed of work required was a key reason for the fragmented, shimmering visual language

《 *Little Dancer, Aged 14* Edgar Degas, 1880–81, height 97.8 cm (38 ½ in), polychrome bronze with muslin, satin ribbon and wood base, private collection. Three-quarters life size, the bronze figure is dressed in real fabrics of silk and gauze.

of Impressionism naturally placing a premium on landscapes and outdoor scenes. It was a decisive rejection of the Academy's ponderous "official" history-painting.

What to look for

Impressionism was almost universally derided as "unfinished". Critics complained that its subjects were trivial and its execution crude, an apparently deliberate flaunting of the accepted canons of Academic painting. Renoir's *Boating Party* encapsulates Impressionism's unshackled *joie de vivre*. It unapologetically celebrates the pleasures of youth and summer. Yet Renoir's most enduring achievement was to combine the visual imperatives of Impressionism, above all in his quivering, feathery brushwork, with the traditions of European figure painting. However, his seeming spontaneity was the product of painstaking labour.

KEY EVENTS

1869	Monet and Renoir establish key characteristics of Impressionism, painting at Bougival on the Seine
1870	Monet and Pissarro in London, escaping Franco-Prussian war; joined by Sisley (1871)
1874	Critic derisively coins name "Impressionism" at first exhibition
1881	Renoir increasingly abandons Impressionism after visiting Rome
1886	Last Impressionist exhibition held
1890	Monet begins epic cycles, repainting same subjects in different conditions

M. Fournaise was the proprietor of the restaurant

Baron Raoul Barbier, a close friend of Renoir, is chatting to the proprietor's daughter

Paul Lhote, wearing pince-nez glasses, flirts with the actress Jeanne Samary. He had a reputation as a ladies' man

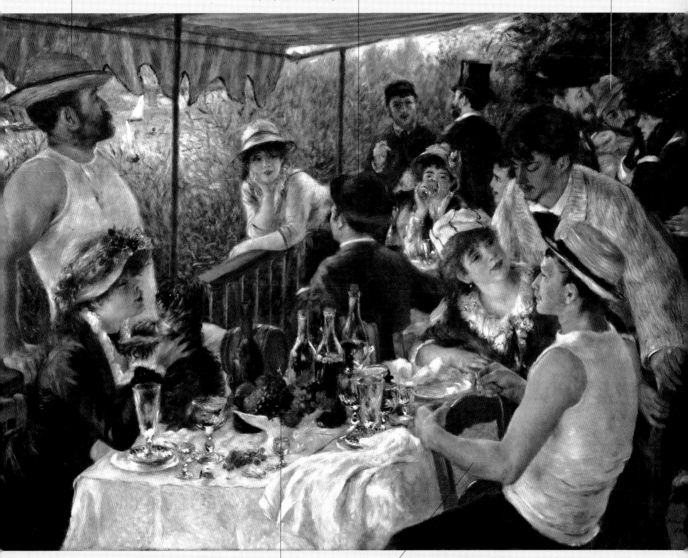

The debris of this meal is a sparkling achievement – its spontaneity is deceptive, since Renoir constantly reworked the painting

Deep in conversation, the man in the straw hat is Gustave Caillebotte, a fellow artist (see page 243)

The Boating Party
Pierre-Auguste Renoir, 1881, 129.5 x 173 cm (51 x 68 in), oil on canvas, Washington DC: Phillips Collection. The figures are portraits of Renoir's friends, carefully arranged into rhythmic groups.

⟩⟩ TECHNIQUES

Renoir paints with a palette of rainbow colours on a white background using short broken brushstrokes. The shadows are blue rather than black.

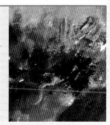

Claude **Monet**

● 1840-1926 ⚑ FRENCH ✍ OILS

The true leader of the Impressionists, Monet was constantly exploring "What do I see and how do I record it in painting?".

He had an interest in observing and painting that most elusive quality, light – notably in the "Series" paintings, where he painted the same subject dozens of times, under different light conditions (Rouen Cathedral, haystacks, scenes in London). He spent 40 years (the second half of his life) creating his garden, at Giverny, from scratch – a subject that he could control in every detail (except the light). He would sit in the middle of it and paint it.

Stand back and enjoy the imagery – familiar and nostalgic for us now, but challenging and modern in its day. Or stand close up to his compositions and enjoy the complexity, texture, and inter-weaving of paint and colour. Note the thick, crusty paint, which gets thicker as the light gets more interesting – particularly when it catches the edges of objects.

KEY WORKS: *The Petit Bras of the Seine at Argenteuil*, 1872 (London: National Gallery); *Impression: Sunrise*, 1872 (see page 240); *The Haystacks, or The End of Summer, at Giverny*, 1891 (Paris: Musée d'Orsay); *The Houses of Parliament, London*, 1904 (Paris: Musée d'Orsay); *Waterlilies*, 1920–26 (Paris: Musée de l'Orangerie)

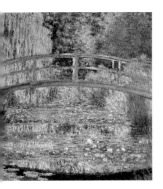

⬆ **Waterlily Pond**
Claude Monet, 1899, 88.3 x 93.1 cm (34 ¾ x 36 ⅔ in), oil on canvas, London: National Gallery. One of a series of 18 paintings depicting the Japanese bridge in Monet's water garden.

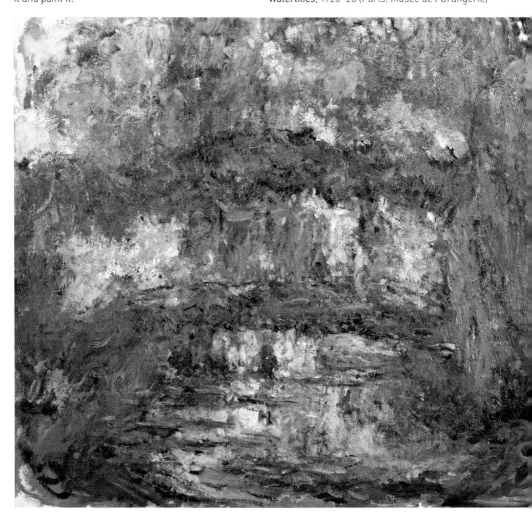

⏩ **The Japanese Bridge at Giverny** *Claude Monet, 1918–24, 89 x 100 cm (35 x 39 ⅓ in), oil on canvas, Paris: Musée Marmottan.* In old age, Monet's eyesight deteriorated because of cataracts and he depended on instinct and memory to paint his later works.

Pierre-Auguste **Renoir**

● 1841-1919 〚U〛 FRENCH ✍ OILS

Renoir was one of the first Impressionists, but soon developed an individual and un-Impressionist style. He is best remembered for his lyrical paintings of pink, buxom young girls. He was very prolific.

He is the greatest ever master of dappled light, which pervades all his work, giving it a seductive, sensual, and soft-focus quality. While the early works have bite and observation, the late works become rather repetitive at times. Did he never become bored by all that comfortable, pink, female flesh, which makes one think of soft feather cushions and Turkish Delight?

See how the sensuality of his technique marries with the subject matter: long, free brushstrokes of warm colour, which caress the canvas. Note the blushes on the cheeks and the obsession with small, firm breasts. The early works have cooler colours, more black, and less mush.

KEY WORKS: *The Gust of Wind*, c.1872 (Cambridge: Fitzwilliam Museum); *The Parisienne*, 1874 (Cardiff: National Museum of Wales); *The Boating Party*, 1881 (see page 241); *Girl Combing her Hair*, 1907–08 (Paris: Musée d'Orsay)

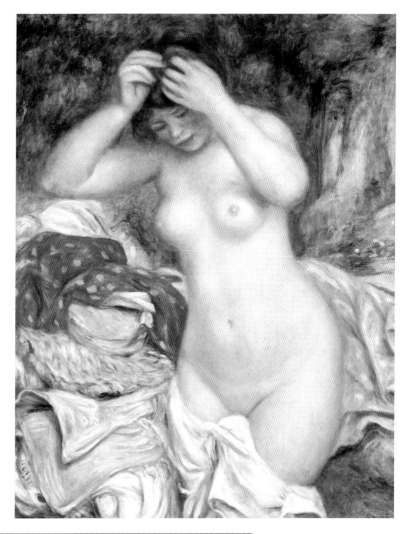

» *Bather Arranging her Hair* Pierre-Auguste Renoir, 1893, 92 x 74 cm (36 ½ x 29 in), oil on canvas, Washington DC: National Gallery of Art. Renoir was much influenced by Delacroix and Ingres. Socially conservative, he destroyed many works he deemed inadequate.

Gustave **Caillebotte**

● 1848-94 〚U〛 FRENCH ✍ OILS

Caillebotte was a second-rate painter who knew what talent was (he was one of the first collectors of great Impressionist paintings), and who occasionally showed some in his own work.

He had typical Impressionist subject matter and technique (very similar to Monet and Manet). He painted scenes of everyday contemporary Paris, especially street scenes with exaggerated, plunging perspectives. While his work was interesting, it was also essentially derivative, and hampered by being too anecdotal – it could often be one of those illustrations for a 19th-century novel that visualize a specific phrase or sentence in the text.

Caillebotte has a recognizable pink-green-blue-purple palette – often too strident and he overdoes the purple. He has cropped compositions, which are influenced by photography.

KEY WORKS: *Woman at a Dressing Table*, c.1873 (Private Collection); *The Floor Strippers*, 1875 (Paris: Musée d'Orsay); *Rue de Paris, Wet Weather*, 1877 (Art Institute of Chicago); *View of Rooftops (Snow)*, 1878 (Paris: Musée d'Orsay); *At the Café, Rouen*, 1880 (Rouen: Musée des Beaux-Arts)

Berthe **Morisot**

● 1841–95 ⚑ FRENCH ✍ OILS; WATERCOLOURS

Morisot was a member of the Impressionists and a convivial hostess, the go-between for the writers, poets, and painters in that circle. She had an attractive, free, delicate style derived from Manet (she married his brother, Eugène). Her works are, in effect, an autobiographical diary.

KEY WORKS: *The Harbour at Lorient,* 1869 (Washington DC: National Gallery of Art); *Portrait of the Artist's Mother and Sister,* 1869–70 (London: National Gallery)

Camille **Pissarro**

● 1830–1903 ⚑ FRENCH ✍ OILS; WATERCOLOURS; DRAWINGS

A reclusive, curmudgeonly, and unsettled artist, Pissarro nonetheless takes his place as one of the major Impressionists and Post-Impressionists. He was always an anarchist and always poor.

Pissarro chose a wide range of subjects: landscapes (the Seine valley), modern cityscapes (Paris, Rouen – note the factory chimneys), still lifes, portraits, and peasant scenes (especially laundresses). He was most confident in his later work, but never really settled into a style with which he was completely at ease or that was completely his own. He progressed from dark, early landscapes to Impressionism and experiments with Divisionism, then back to Impressionism.

He often chose high viewpoints (such as cityscapes painted from windows). His developed palette is quite chalky and pale, with predominant greens and blues. Surfaces are thickly painted (sometimes patchily) with a sketchy look, as if they could be worked further if he could decide what to do with them (a sign of his uncertainty?). Note the play of contrasts in content: rural against industrial; transient against permanent; natural against artificial; old against new; warm against cool.

KEY WORKS: *View from Louveciennes*, 1869–70 (London: National Gallery); *Autumn*, 1870 (Los Angeles: J. Paul Getty Museum); *The Climbing Path, L'Hermitage Pontoise*, 1875 (New York: Brooklyn Museum of Art)

☑ *The Bridge at Moret*
Alfred Sisley, 1893, 73.5 x 92.5 cm (29 x 36 ⅔ in), oil on canvas, Paris: Musée d'Orsay. Sisley had to earn a living as a painter when the family silk business collapsed in 1870.

Alfred **Sisley**

● 1839–99 ⚑ BRITISH/FRENCH ✍ OILS

Often called "The forgotten Impressionist", Sisley was the most underrated of the group, then and now. He was born in Paris to British parents. Like Constable, Sisley only painted places he knew well and he particularly responded to the Seine and Thames valleys. He also liked well-structured compositions (notice the verticals, horizontals, and diagonals). He cleverly used structural details, such as roads and bridges to take the eye through the landscape and link all the parts together.

Note the interesting use of colour combinations (especially pinks and greens, blues and purples) to produce the sensation of light.

KEY WORKS: *Women Going to the Woods*, 1866 (Tokyo: Bridgestone Museum of Art); *The Walk*, 1890 (Nice: Musée d'Art et d'Histoire)

Edgar **Degas**

● 1834–1917 ⚑ FRENCH ✍ OILS; PASTELS; PRINTS; SCULPTURE

Degas was one of the greatest draughtsmen of all time. He successfully bridged the gap between the old master tradition and modernity. Degas was shy, haughty, conservative, and single.

Each picture shows a self-contained and self-absorbed world. Even when the subjects of his portraits make eye contact, they give nothing away. Ballet and racing scenes are a means of exploring complex space and movement. His technique, his extraordinary capacity for drawing, and his attention to detail are equally self-absorbed – one of those rare, perfect unions between subject matter and means of expression.

Degas was fascinated by meticulous, innovative craftsmanship. He experimented in many media: pastel, prints, and sculpture. He was also interested in photography – he borrowed and used the cropped effect brilliantly. He worked and reworked the same subject or theme to achieve ever greater understanding and perfection. Notice how often he used the receding diagonal as the main armature for his compositions. He had astonishing colour sensitivity, even when he was old and nearly blind.

KEY WORKS: *The Dancing Class*, 1873–76 (Paris: Musée d'Orsay); *The Absinthe Drinker*, 1876 (Paris: Musée d'Orsay); *Madame René de Gas*, 1872–73 (Washington DC: National Gallery of Art)

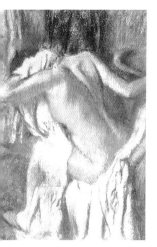

◩ *Woman Drying Herself* Edgar Degas, c.1888–92, 103.8 x 98.4 cm (49 x 38 ¾ in), pastel, London: National Gallery. Degas increasingly worked with soft waxy pastels as his eyesight deteriorated, reliant on touch and feel.

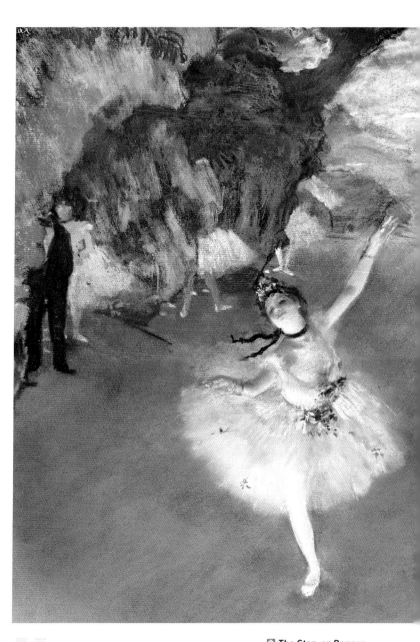

> ❝ **Anyone** can have a **talent** at **25.** The difficulty is to have **talent at 50!** ❞
>
> **Edgar Degas**

⬢ *The Star, or Dancer on the Stage* Edgar Degas, c.1876–77, 60 x 44 cm (23 ¾ x 17 ⅓ in), pastel on paper, Paris: Musée d'Orsay. Degas's technique shows the same qualities of precision and balance as classical ballet.

Childe **Hassam**

● 1859–1935 🏛 AMERICAN ✍ OILS; PRINTS

America's foremost Impressionist artist, Hassam painted more than 4,000 oils and watercolours and is best known for his post-1917 "flag paintings", where brightly coloured, flags at wartime parades act as a symbol of patriotism. In his earlier work, the emphasis was on *contre-jour*.

Next to the French, it was the Americans who were the best and largest group of Impressionists. However, they were late in the day by 20 years – post-1890s, as they did not often visit Paris until the 1880s. Before that, they had tended to learn their art in Germany.

KEY WORKS: *Grand Prix Day*, 1887 (Boston: Museum of Fine Arts); *Evening in New York*, c.1890 (Houston: Museum of Fine Arts); *Avenue of the Allies, Great Britain*, 1918 (New York: Metropolitan Museum of Art)

Mary **Cassatt**

● 1844–1926 🏛 AMERICAN ✍ OILS; PRINTS

The daughter of a wealthy family, Cassatt settled in Paris. She mixed with the avant-garde and helped American collectors spend their loot. A friend of Degas, she also helped the Impressionists. She produced attractive works with a strong sense of design, courageous colour, and cropped, angled viewpoints that captured personal, meaningful moments of the well-to-do. She was influenced by Degas, Japanese prints, and Ingres.

KEY WORKS: *Musical Party*, 1874 (Paris: Musée du Petit Palais); *Mother about to Wash her Sleepy Child*, 1880 (Los Angeles County Museum of Art); *Young Woman Sewing in the Garden*, 1880–82 (Paris: Musée d'Orsay); *Girl Arranging her Hair*, 1886 (Washington DC: National Gallery of Art)

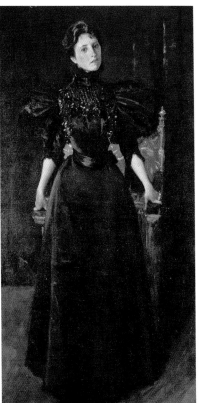

William Merritt **Chase**

● 1849–1916 🏛 AMERICAN ✍ OILS

A prolific and versatile artist from a prosperous background, Chase was successful, gregarious, witty, and a flashy dresser, cultivated in the European manner (a friend of Whistler). He developed two distinct styles, both direct and spontaneous. His early works are dark, heavy, elegant portraits (style learned in Munich). They become light-filled French-Impressionist-style scenes of Long Island (Shinnecock) after the 1890s.

KEY WORKS: *Portrait of Moses Swaim*, 1867 (Indianapolis: Museum of Art); *At the Seaside*, c.1892 (New York: Metropolitan Museum of Art); *The Brass Bowl*, 1899 (Indianapolis: Museum of Art)

◀ *Portrait of a Lady in Black* William Merritt Chase, c.1895, 182.9 x 91.4 cm (72 x 36 in), oil on canvas, Detroit Institute of Arts. Chase is best known for his spirited portraits and still lifes in oil.

Julian Alden **Weir**

● 1852–1919 🏛 AMERICAN ✍ OILS; WATERCOLOURS; DRAWINGS

Weir was the most academically successful American Impressionist. He studied in Paris and was conservative in technique and temperament. While Weir's early work was much influenced by Manet, his later work is closer to Monet. He was most successful in his smaller works, particularly in watercolour and silverpoint. He became president of the National Academy of Design.

KEY WORKS: *Union Square*, c.1879 (New York: Brooklyn Museum of Art); *Willimantic Thread Factory*, 1893 (New York: Brooklyn Museum of Art); *The Red Bridge*, 1895 (New York: Metropolitan Museum of Art)

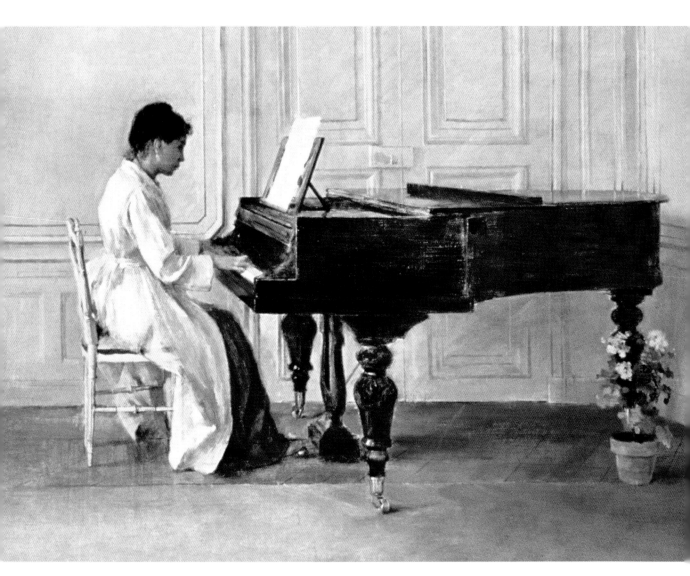

Theodore **Robinson**

⬤ 1852–96 🏴 AMERICAN ✍ OILS

Robinson was the leading American Impressionist painter. He made several visits to France between 1876 and 1892, and was a close friend of Monet, whom he had met at Giverny in 1887. He painted landscapes and vignettes of village and farm life. He found East Coast American light too bright compared with the light in France, and had difficulty painting it. Robinson died relatively young, his later years marred by ill health and poverty.

In the US, Robinson was a pioneer, but his Impressionist style is cautious by French standards – his compositions are rather static and the brushstrokes too carefully considered. Sometimes, he worked from photographs, which he used by squaring up – traces of the grid can occasionally be seen on the canvas.

KEY WORKS: *Self-Portrait*, c.1884–87 (Washington DC: National Gallery of Art); *Watching the Cows*, 1892 (Youngstown, Ohio: Butler Institute of American Art); *Low Tide, Riverside Yacht Club*, 1894 (Washington DC: National Gallery of Art)

⬘ *At the Piano*
Theodore Robinson, 1887, 41.8 x 64.2 cm (16 ½ x 25 ¼ in), oil on canvas, Washington DC: Smithsonian Institute. Known only as Marie, the true identity of Robinson's mysterious model remains unknown, despite her appearance in numerous works.

Auguste **Rodin**

● 1840–1917 ⩎ FRENCH ✍ SCULPTURE

Rodin is the glorious triumphant finale to the sculptural tradition that starts with Donatello. He is rightly spoken of in the same breath as Michelangelo, although they were quite different – Michelangelo carved, while Rodin moulded.

☑ *The Burghers of Calais* 1884–89, height 201.7 cm (79 ½ in), bronze, Washington DC: Hirshhorn Museum. One of a number of casts of Rodin's original plaster model. It was commissioned by the city of Calais to commemorate six 14th-century civic heroes.

Rodin was a shy workaholic who rose from impoverished beginnings. He was also untidy, a friend of poets, and physically enormous. He became an international celebrity and was deeply charismatic and attractive.

He carried out an extraordinary and enriching hide-and-seek exploration with the processes of his art, and the relationship between intellectual and artistic creativity. His famous set-piece projects (such as *The Gates of Hell*) evolved over many years. He also sculpted portraits, nudes, and small models, which show ideas in evolution. Observe the ways in which he used the fluidity of clay and plaster (even when cast in bronze) to release his figures, human feelings, and the unknown forces in nature. He was fascinated with biological procreativity.

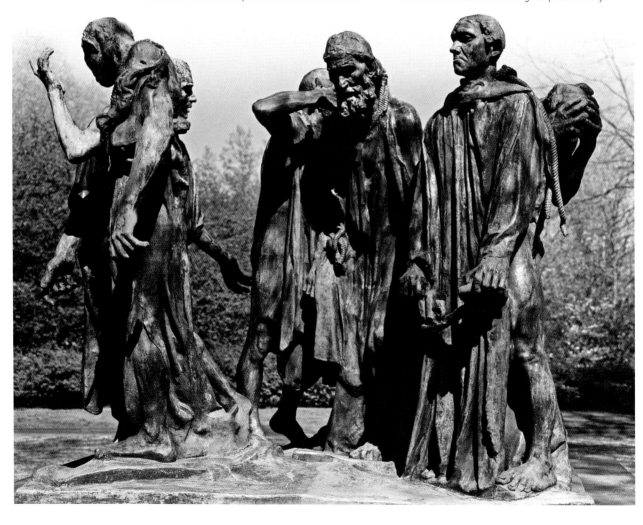

Note his stunningly beautiful recreation of (often large) hands, embraces, kisses, and whole body poses as an expression of human libido and anima (Rodin always worked from life, even when borrowing from antiquity or classics). Bases are important because he made his figures grow out of them. He washed his figures in light (try and see them in natural light). He used studio assistants or commercial firms to make large-scale versions of his original models – what you see may never have been touched by Rodin (he wanted to disseminate his work widely).

He married his lifetime companion Rose Beuret in 1917 in Meudon, Paris, at the age of 77. Rose died two weeks later and Rodin nine months after. A cast of *The Thinker* overlooks his grave in Meudon.

The Kiss, one of Rodin's masterpieces, was originally part of his huge *The Gates of Hell*. The statue eventually became an independent work because the blend of eroticism and pure happiness did not fit the damnation theme of *The Gates of Hell*. The sculpture depicts the illicit lovers, Francesca da Rimini and Paolo Malatesta, whose story is told in Dante's masterwork *The Divine Comedy* (1321). Francesca was stabbed to death by her husband Giovanni as she exchanged her first kiss with his brother Paolo after falling madly in love with him.

KEY WORKS: *The Thinker*, 1880–81 (Private Collection); *The Gates of Hell*, 1880–1917 (Paris: Musée d'Orsay); *Andromeda*, c.1885 (Private Collection); *Sinner*, c.1885 (St Petersburg: Hermitage Museum)

The figures appear to emerge preformed from the stone. Rodin believed man and woman were one entity united through erotic love

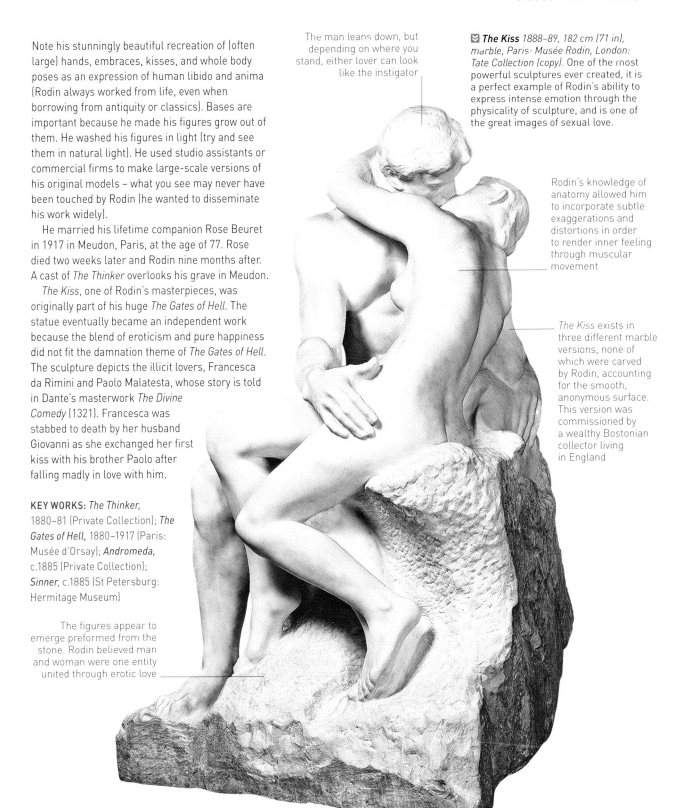

The man leans down, but depending on where you stand, either lover can look like the instigator

The Kiss 1888–89, 182 cm (71 in), marble, Paris· Musée Rodin, London: Tate Collection (copy). One of the most powerful sculptures ever created, it is a perfect example of Rodin's ability to express intense emotion through the physicality of sculpture, and is one of the great images of sexual love.

Rodin's knowledge of anatomy allowed him to incorporate subtle exaggerations and distortions in order to render inner feeling through muscular movement

The Kiss exists in three different marble versions, none of which were carved by Rodin, accounting for the smooth, anonymous surface. This version was commissioned by a wealthy Bostonian collector living in England

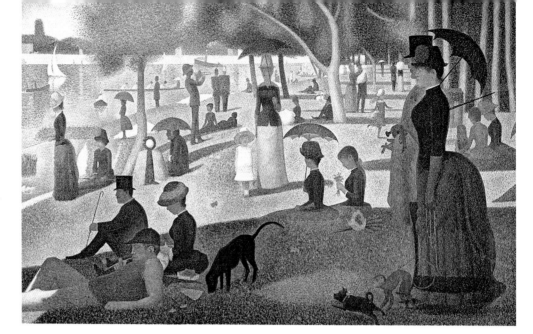

>> *A Sunday Afternoon on the Island of La Grande Jatte* Georges Seurat, 1884–86, 207.5 x 308 cm (81⅔ x 121 ¼ in), oil on canvas, Art Institute of Chicago. Seurat laboured extensively over this piece, reworking the original as well as numerous preliminary drawings and oil sketches.

Georges **Seurat**

● 1859–91 |Ⅱ FRENCH ✍ OILS; DRAWINGS

A shy, reclusive man, Seurat died from meningitis at the age of 31, having produced very great work. He was the originator of Pointillism and Divisionism.

His subjects are modern life and places. His work can seem austere and rigid because he painted according to worked-out theories, not what he saw or felt. He applied the latest ideas of colour and optical mixing – painting separate dots of pure colour on the canvas (Pointillism), which mix and vibrate in the eye and are intended to give the same sensation as light itself. He used a formula of lines to express emotion: upward diagonal = happiness; downward diagonal = sadness; horizontal = calmness.

Colour theories don't work in practice because pigments lose their brightness and the mixing in the eye tends to end up as a grey mush. Why did he ignore the significance of vertical lines? He made wonderful drawings using soft black crayon on textured paper, and tiny, free, preliminary sketches for his big works. He used colour borders that complement the areas of colour in the picture. There is hidden symbolism and references to old masters in the set-piece figure paintings.

KEY WORKS: *Bathers at Asnières*,1884 (London: National Gallery); *The Circus*, 1891 (Paris: Musée d'Orsay)

Paul **Signac**

● 1863–1935 |Ⅱ FRENCH ✍ OILS

Frenchman Signac was a follower and disciple of Seurat. Through his work and writings he was the chief promulgator of the theory and practice of Divisionism. He moved from observed outdoor scenes to studio-based subjects, and from small dots to larger brushstrokes. He produced good plein-air watercolours. His own work was overly theoretical and tidy, but despite this he influenced others (Matisse, for instance).

A keen yachtman, Signac spent a lot of time on the Mediterranean and Atlantic coasts; harbour scenes became his favourite subjects.

KEY WORKS: *Gas Tanks at Clichy*, 1886 (Melbourne: National Gallery of Victoria); *Lighthouse at Groix*, 1925 (New York: Metropolitan Museum of Art)

>> DIVISIONISM

In Divisionism, colour effects are obtained optically rather than by mixing colours on the palette: i.e. small areas of pure colour are put side-by-side on the canvas so that at a distance the eye cannot differentiate between them, but mixes them together and so experiences another colour (optical mixing). This was more convincing as a theory than in practice. Seurat was its originator, but he died young, and so Signac became its chief promulgator. Pointillism is Divisionism as practised by Seurat, using small dots of colour.

James Abbott McNeill
Whistler

1834–1903 **AMERICAN**
OILS; ENGRAVINGS

Whistler was small, egocentric, quarrelsome, witty, and a dandy. Born in Massachusetts, he later lived in Europe (France and England). A leading figure of the Aesthetic movement, he developed a new style of painting and role for the artist. He was a contemporary of Oscar Wilde.

Look for painting as an aesthetic object and experience – the subject matter taking second place to the visual pleasure of colour and form. Note the subtle harmonies of soft colour, carefully placed shapes, and suppression of detail. The artist chose simple subjects, expressive of mood. His portraits say little about the sitter's personality. Why was he so tentative? Was he never at ease with painting? Arguably his best works are his prints, in which he never lacked self-confidence.

The thin paint surface belies the fact that he worked and reworked his pictures, wiping away his efforts until he had reached his notion of perfection (which must have been agonizing for his portrait sitters). Some works are still in their original frames, designed by Whistler to harmonize with the painting. Look for his famous "butterfly" signature, which he used after 1870. Much influenced by Japanese art, he became interested in Oriental art and decoration in general. Velásquez and Manet (he had to be up to date and in the forefront of fashion) were also influences. He played a major role in introducing modern ideas to British art.

KEY WORKS: *The White Girl*, 1862 (London: Tate Collection); *Nocturne: Blue and Gold*. 1872–77 (London: Tate Collection); *Arrangement in Grey and Black: Portrait of the Painter's Mother*, 1871 (Paris: Musée d'Orsay); *Nocturne in Black and Gold: The Falling Rocket* (see page 253); *Upright Venice*, 1879–80 (Private Collection)

⊠ *Mother and Child on a Couch* James Abbott McNeill Whistler, c.1870s, watercolour, London: Victoria & Albert Museum. Whistler wished his art to look effortless. The hidden reality was very different.

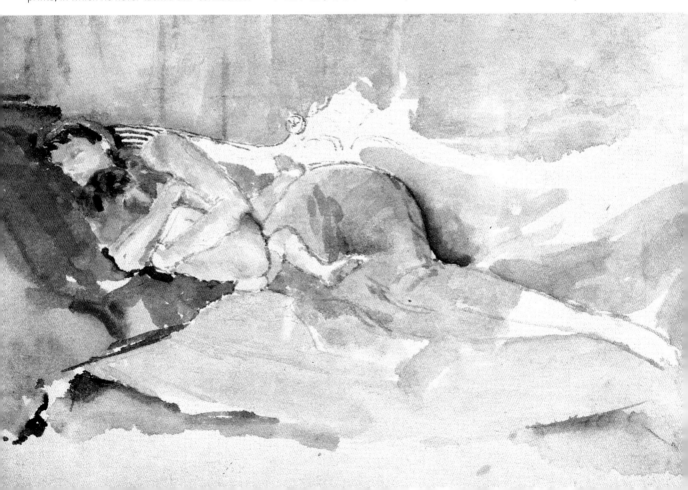

Symbolism and Aestheticism

LATE 19TH CENTURY

From the mid-19th century, a literary cult developed in France that explored the mystical, the spiritual, and the morbid. It found an outlet in the visual arts in Symbolism, "the ambiguous world of the indeterminate", in the words of the painter Odilon Redon. Across the Channel in England, it was echoed by Aestheticism.

Prompted by the poet Théophile Gautier, who had argued for the rejection of conventional morality and the primacy of "pure sensation", a series of poets and painters in France increasingly elaborated a world in which imagination was allowed free rein. For Gustave Moreau, and to some extent the more classically minded Puvis de Chavannes, it was a means of infusing Academic figure painting with an allusive and richly imaginative new pictorial language. Odilon Redon, whose later painting was based directly on his dreams, went further still. Semi-human figures inhabit fantastic landscapes made more mysterious by brushwork that eventually approached the abstract.

The idea that art could be an end in itself with no higher purpose – whether moral, spiritual, or political – than the pursuit of pure "artistic sensation", reached a peak towards the end of

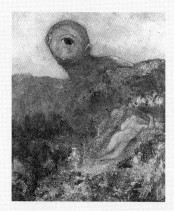

◁ **The Cyclops**
Odilon Redon, c.1914, oil on canvas, Otterlo, Netherlands: Kröller-Müller Museum. Redon's highly personal vision later made him a hero of the Surrealists.

the 19th century. In England, it was exemplified by the Aesthetic movement. Oscar Wilde was its best-known literary exponent, the American-born Whistler its chief (and most notorious) champion in the visual arts, going so far as litigation in court to defend the integrity of the movement. This was "a crusade on behalf of beauty", a "poetic passion", which utterly rejected utilitarianism in favour of the exquisite.

What to look for

Seeing colour and form, irrespective of their subject matter, as expressive in themselves had been a commonplace idea since the days of Delacroix. But Whistler went much further – his nominal subject matter is dissolved until it becomes nothing but a complex interplay of colour and form infinitely delicately rendered. The result is a beguiling, haunting surface pattern.

» JAPANESE ART

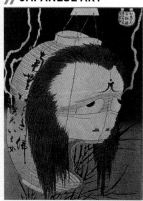

The impact of Japanese prints on the transformation of the visual arts in Europe in the second half of the 19th century was crucial. Their use of everyday subjects, unusual viewpoints, tilted perspectives, bold, flat colours, and strong outlines amounted to a pictorial language entirely different to anything then known in the West.

◁ **Japanese Ghost** Katsushika Hokusai, 1830s, woodblock, London: Victoria & Albert Museum. From series of One Hundred Stories, this features a woman turned into a lantern on her death, a theme that resonated with the Symbolists' obsession with spiritual transformation.

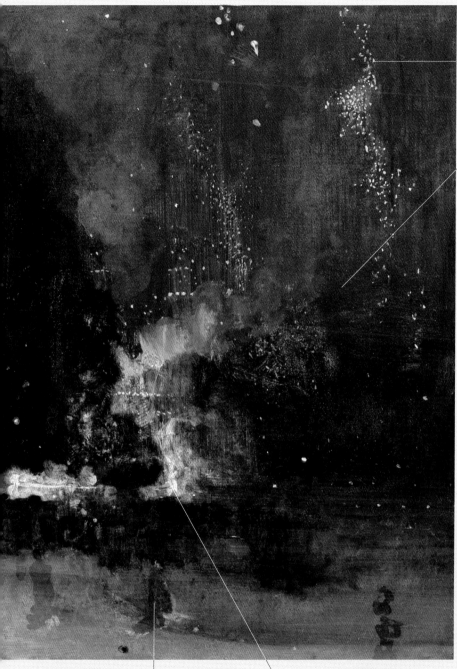

The painting captures the drama and beauty of the fleeting instant in which a rocket explodes, scattering a shower of sparks into the night

Whistler was deeply influenced by Japanese prints, in particular their non-naturalistic handling of space and concentration on expressive surface patterns

》 TECHNIQUES

Rather than build up thick layers of paint, Whistler would wipe away his mistakes to leave only a thin film of transparent paint. The loose, light brushwork and subtle colour harmonies were influenced by Velásquez.

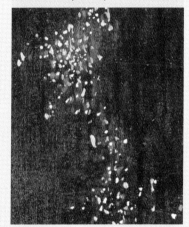

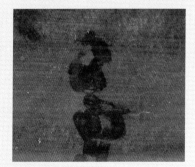

⌂ **Whistler's unusual signature** is similar to the collector's seals found on Chinese art. He was an enthusiastic and early collector of Oriental blue and white porcelain.

⌂ **Nocturne in Black and Gold: The Falling Rocket**
James Abbott McNeill Whistler, c.1875, 60 x 47 cm (23 ¾ x 18 ½ in), oil on panel, Detroit Institute of Arts.

In the foreground, Whistler has given the suggestion of spectators to lend scale and focus to the scene

Like the Impressionists, Whistler continually sought ways to represent immediacy and the constantly changing nature of light

Gustave **Moreau**

⬤ 1826–98 FRENCH ✍ OILS; WATERCOLOURS; DRAWINGS

An intense, talented, prolific, workaholic, and successful artist, Moreau was determined to revive the tradition of history painting (actually in terminal decline) and to rival the greatest old masters.

He was noted for erudite, imaginative, literary, and mythological subjects. His idiosyncratic style is halfway between the strange, fantasy world of Bosch and the surreal dreamworld of Max Ernst. His work is sometimes dark and mysterious, sometimes bright and shimmering, but always sinister, oozing romantic decadence and symbolism. He used deeply worked surfaces and textures with inventive impasto, glazes, and colours that unlocked his imagination.

He produced a huge quantity of sketches and watercolours; these preceded his finished oil paintings, either as experiments or to work out their final design and details. His late watercolours (and some unfinished oils) are as free and sketchy as modern abstraction. He was active at the same period as the Impressionists, who were everything

he was not. A gifted teacher, he influenced many who seem impossibly far removed from his style (such as Matisse). Moreau was much influenced by a tour of Italy (1857–59).

KEY WORKS: *Diomedes Devoured by Horses*, 1851 (Los Angeles: J. Paul Getty Museum); *Orpheus*, 1865 (Paris: Musée d'Orsay); *Salomé*, 1876 (Paris: Musée Gustave Moreau); *The Apparition*, 1876 (Cambridge: Fogg Art Museum)

Pierre **Puvis de Chavannes**

⬤ 1824–98 FRENCH ✍ OILS

Puvis de Chavannes was internationally sought after in his day as the leading painter of large-scale murals to decorate public buildings. He worked on canvas, which was then affixed to walls. His smaller works were also admired by avant-garde painters such as Seurat, Gauguin, and Munch.

His statuesque figures in landscapes are the direct descendants of the great Classical tradition. He had a very recognizable dry technique, using a chalky white colouring with a stiff style that made his work look like a fresco. His was a valiant but ultimately unsuccessful attempt to make the Classical and Academic tradition relevant to the modern world. He tried to touch big emotions such as hope and despair, but missed the target: his work now looks at best decorative, at worst, lifeless.

His archaic, flat style searched for a "modern" simplification of form and colour, and a timeless monumentality for the figure, detached from literary connections; it was only in the next generation (Matisse) that this would be fully unlocked. To do his work full justice, it needs to be seen *in situ* in the elaborate Beaux-Arts Renaissance-revival buildings that he decorated (and which were themselves to be overtaken by the simplified architecture of Modernism).

KEY WORKS: *The Beheading of St John the Baptist*, c.1869 (London: National Gallery); *The Prodigal Son*, c.1879 (Washington DC: National Gallery of Art); *Young Girls by the Edge of the Sea*, 1879 (Paris: Musée d'Orsay); *The Poor Fisherman*, 1881 (Paris: Musée d'Orsay); *Woman on the Beach*, 1887 (St Petersburg: Hermitage Museum)

» Hesiod and the Muse
Gustave Moreau, 1891, 59 x 34.5 cm (23 x 14 in), oil on canvas, Paris: Musée d'Orsay.

Arnold **Böcklin**

● 1827–1901 〔Ⅱ〕 SWISS ✍ OILS

A leading German Symbolist painter, Böcklin was Swiss-born and Düsseldorf-trained, but most influenced by Italian art (especially Raphael). He was a meticulous craftsman of Classical, mythological figures in intense moody landscapes that are intended to trigger dream-like reveries. Very much in the languid *fin de siècle* fashion, his work can now seem cloying and artificial.

KEY WORKS: *Self-Portrait with Death as a Fiddler,* c.1871–74 (Berlin: Staatliche Museen); *The Isle of the Dead*, 1883 (Berlin: Staatliche Museen)

Odilon **Redon**

● 1840–1916 〔Ⅱ〕 FRENCH ✍ OILS; PASTELS; PRINTS; DRAWINGS

Redon became one of the principal *fin de siècle* Symbolist artists, and was a Surrealist before his time. His *oeuvre* divides in two: pre- and post-1894. His early small-scale black-and-white drawings and prints had neurotic, introspective subject matter (he had a classic Freudian, unhappy childhood). After 1894, he overcame his neuroses and his art blossomed into radiant colour and joyful subject matter. His inspiration came from the inner mind, not the outer eye. Today, he is better known for his later work.

His poetic, contemplative works have no specific meaning. His fascinating early subject matter anticipated Surrealism – floating heads, curious creatures, strange juxtapositions, all drawn from the depths of the imagination (and from Symbolist writers such as Poe and Baudelaire). Observe his very fine drawing and print techniques, with beautiful tonal treatments. Later, he developed an exquisite pastel technique and the ability to produce saturated, unreal colours of astonishing richness and intensity.

KEY WORKS: *The Trees*, 1890s (Houston: Museum of Fine Arts); *Ophelia Among the Flowers*, c.1905–08 (London: National Gallery); *The Shell*, 1912 (Paris: Musée d'Orsay); *Anemones and Lilacs in a Blue Vase*, 1914 (Paris: Petit Palais)

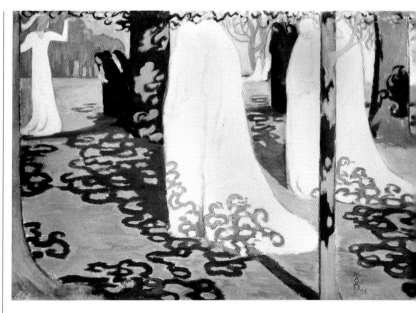

⬆ **Procession under Trees** Maurice Denis, 1892, 56 x 81 cm (22 x 32 in), oil on canvas, private collection.

Maurice **Denis**

● 1870–1943 〔Ⅱ〕 FRENCH ✍ OILS; FRESCO

Denis was a leading Symbolist who led the reaction against Impressionism. He was a founder member of the Nabis.

There is no realistic representation and insignificant subject matter: the small-scale easel painting is king. The result is paintings with a deliberately flat, decorative, stylized or Art Nouveau appearance; strange colours; and trivial, everyday subjects. He was effective with his stage and costume design and book illustrations. A committed Catholic who applied his art to the service of church decoration.

KEY WORKS: *Gaulish Goddess of Herds and Flocks*, 1906 (Munich: Neue Pinakothek); *Orpheus and Eurydice*, 1910 (Minnesota: Minneapolis Institute of Arts)

Aubrey **Beardsley**

● 1872–1998 〔Ⅱ〕 BRITISH ✍ DRAWINGS; PRINTS

Beardsley was self-taught, a workaholic, and a master of sinuous, sensual, erotic (sometimes pornographic), black-and-white drawings and prints. He was brilliant but controversial, a member of the circle around Oscar Wilde. Highly original and gifted, he was capable of capturing the essence of *fin de siècle* decadence. Beardsley had a boring private life – his eroticism was all in his mind. He died in France aged only 25.

KEY WORKS: *Salome*, 1892 (New Jersey: Princeton University Library); *How King Arthur Saw the Questing Beast*, 1893 (London: Victoria & Albert Museum); *A Nightpiece*, 1894 (Cambridge: Fitzwilliam Museum)

Thomas Wilmer **Dewing**

● 1851–1938 ⅏ **AMERICAN** ✍ **OILS**

Dewing painted accomplished works depicting elegant, stately, distant women in tastefully furnished interiors or wandering in lush, dreamy landscapes. His paintings were often large in scale and turned into Japanese-style screens. He also produced studies for the above, pastels, and silverpoints. His work is a good example of Aestheticism – a potpourri of Pre-Raphaelites, Whistler, and Japan. Note also the elaborate, custom frames he used.

KEY WORKS: *The Letter*, 1895–1900 (New York: Metropolitan Museum of Art); *Lady with a Lute*, 1886 (Washington DC: National Gallery of Art); *The Gossip*, c.1907 (Minnesota: Minneapolis Institute of Arts)

John Singer **Sargent**

● 1856–1925 ⅏ **AMERICAN** ✍ **OILS; DRAWINGS**

Sargent was the last successful portrait painter in the grand manner. Born in Florence, he lived mostly in Europe. He was very talented, successful, and rich. He captured the spirit of the golden age that perished in World War I.

In the 1880s and 1890s, he succeeded with large-scale portraits of the *nouveaux riches* of the UK, the US, and France, showing them at their glittering best, in flattering and relaxed poses. After 1900, he painted the English aristocracy but made them more formal and aloof. However, he grew bored with faces and spoilt clientele: look for his preferred small-scale, plein-air landscape sketches, intimate glimpses of family and friends, and rapid charcoal sketches. He also produced uninspired, time-consuming murals for public buildings in Boston (1890–1921).

He had a brilliant oil technique – his assured fluid paint and bold compositions matched the confident faces and expensive, well-cut clothes of his sitters. His real interest was in light (he was friendly with the Impressionists, especially Monet) and precise matching of tones. He trained in Paris to use *au premier coup* technique – one exact brushstroke and no reworking. His watercolour technique was less assured. He was influenced by Velásquez and his work successfully bridges the divide between the Old Masters and Impressionism.

KEY WORKS: *Daughters of Edward Darley Boit*, 1882 (Boston: Museum of Fine Arts); *Madame X (Madame Pierre Gautreau)*, 1883–84 (New York: Metropolitan Museum of Art); *Mrs. Adrian Iselin*, 1888 (Washington DC: National Gallery of Art); *The Bridge of Sighs*, c.1905 (New York: Brooklyn Museum of Art)

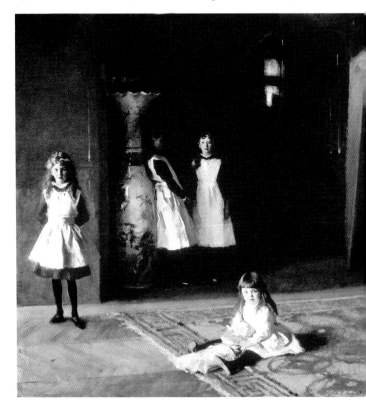

⟫ *The Daughters of Edward Darley Boit* John Singer Sargent, 1882, 221 x 221 cm (87 x 87 in), oil on canvas, Boston: Museum of Fine Arts. The painting was enthusiastically reviewed by Henry James in 1883.

Walter Richard **Sickert**

⬤ 1860–1942 ⊓ BRITISH ✍ OILS; PRINTS

The leading British painter of the Impressionist and Post-Impressionist period, Sickert had personal links with French artists such as Degas. His style is perhaps best described as a French idiom spoken with a very strong English accent.

He painted down-to-earth subjects – street scenes, music halls, and prostitutes – with a disregard for fashion, in a palette of muddy colours, and thick, heavily worked paint. He was fond of and used the sense of intimacy and unobtrusive observation – a quality of photography. Images for many of his late works were taken from newspapers, which destroyed any sense of intimacy. He was a fine craftsman – his pictures are carefully composed, sometimes with striking or unusual viewpoints, behind which lay much work and preliminary drawing. Note the careful and diligent application of paint in his work, his unusual colour combinations, and interesting light effects. In his late work, look for the lines of the underlying grid he used for enlarging the photographs. He also made good etchings.

KEY WORKS: *Interior of St Mark's, Venice*, 1896 (London: Tate Collection); *La Hollandaise*, 1906 (London: Tate Collection); *Jack the Ripper's Bedroom*, c.1906 (Manchester: City Art Gallery)

Joaquin **Sorolla y Bastida**

⬤ 1863–1923 ⊓ SPANISH ✍ OILS; PRINTS

Born and raised in Valencia, Sorolla y Bastida was a prolific and internationally acclaimed painter with an easy, fluent style. He bridged the divide between old masters and Moderns (like Sargent and Zorn). He painted beach scenes, landscapes, society portraits, and genre scenes; he had an enviable facility with light effects. His works show a nice balance between (social) realism and idealism. He painted directly onto canvas – fast.

KEY WORKS: *The Relic*, c.1893 (Bilbao: Museo de Bellas Artes); *Wounded Foot*, 1909 (Los Angeles: J. Paul Getty Museum); *Court of Dances*, 1910 (Los Angeles: J. Paul Getty Museum)

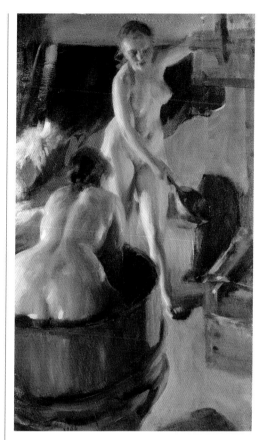

« *Girls from Dalarna Having a Bath* Anders Zorn, 1908, 86 x 53 cm (33 ⅘ x 20 ⅘ in), oil on canvas, Stockholm: Nationalmuseum.

Anders **Zorn**

⬤ 1860–1920 ⊓ SWEDISH ✍ WATERCOLOURS; OILS; PRINTS

Zorn was a prolific, talented, and very successful painter with a popular line in worldly-looking, fleshy nudes in plein-air settings. He also painted elegant portraits of the rich and famous. He had a virtuoso, free paint technique, which cleverly – like Manet – suggests an equality with the Old Masters (Titian) and the modern (the Impressionists); and also (falsely) spontaneity. He made brilliant watercolours, etchings, and the odd sculpture.

KEY WORKS: *Mrs Walter Rathbone Bacon*, 1897 (New York: Metropolitan Museum of Art); *Mrs John Crosby Brown*, c.1900 (New York: Metropolitan Museum of Art); *Hugo Reisinger*, 1907 (Washington DC: National Gallery of Art); *Dagmar*, 1911 (Private Collection)

Post-Impressionism

LATE 19TH/EARLY 20TH CENTURY

However liberating Impressionism was, its concentration on surface appearance and the moment inevitably limited its emotional range. From about 1880, a number of painters sought to fuse the new visual freedom generated by Impressionism with greater emphasis on form and content. The four giants of the Post-Impressionist era were Cézanne, Gauguin, Seurat, and Van Gogh.

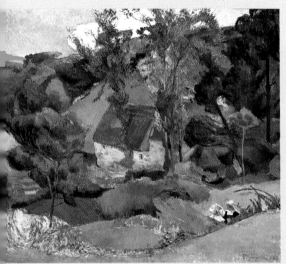

Modern life provides the dominant subject matter in Post-Impressionist works. Seurat pioneered a new monumentality, producing large-scale groups of figures painted using precise dots of paint, a technique known as divisionism. Cézanne achieved a similar sense of grave serenity by very different means, painstakingly reworking his paintings to reveal the underlying visual structures. Gauguin and Van Gogh both sought ways to express troubled, often dream-like emotions. Gauguin used flat colour and distorted perspective, Van Gogh favoured harsh colours and strong outlines.

△ **Landscape at Pont Aven** *Paul Gauguin, 1888, oil on canvas, Private Collection.* Gauguin developed his non-naturalistic style during a stay in Pont Aven, Brittany.

What to look for

The sheer variety of styles covered by the term Post-Impressionism highlights a crucial feature of the period: that the absolute standards governing Western art established in the Renaissance no longer applied. This belief, which has remained unchallenged ever since, was the first claim that art was what the artist asserted it to be. Furthermore, "truth" in art did not have to mean naturalism, the attempt to show the world as it actually is. This inevitably led to a wide diversity of styles with the result that the term Post-Impressionism can only really be applied to the period rather than a particular style. Whereas Cézanne's work was intensely contemplative and minutely observed, Van Gogh's was tortured and highly expressive.

▽ **Van Gogh's Bedroom at Arles** *Vincent van Gogh, 1889, oil on canvas, Art Institute of Chicago.* This is the third version of the painting that Van Gogh produced. It was painted for his mother whilst he was recovering from a mental breakdown.

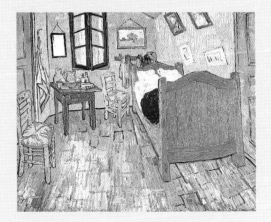

KEY EVENTS

1886	Van Gogh joins brother in Paris. Cézanne moves to Provence. Term "Neo-Impressionism" coined
1888	Van Gogh moves to Arles; after bouts of madness, shoots himself in 1890
1889	Norwegian Edvard Munch comes to Paris; *The Scream*, (1893) combines northern brooding with Symbolist imagery
1891	Gauguin goes to Tahiti; returns to Paris 1893, then back to the Pacific 1895
1895	Cézanne's first major show

Paul **Gauguin**

● 1848–1903 〓 FRENCH ✍ OILS; SCULPTURE; PRINTS

Gauguin was a successful stockbroker who, at the age of 35, abandoned his career and family to become an artist. Yearning for the simple life, he died, unknown, from syphilis, in the South Seas. He had a decisive influence on the next generation (including Matisse and Picasso).

⌵ *Nevermore* 1897, 60.5 x 116 cm (23 ⅘ x 45 ⅔ in), oil on canvas, London: Courtauld Institute of Art. Gauguin had a poetic ability to evoke moods that were haunting, ambiguous, and suffused with melancholy.

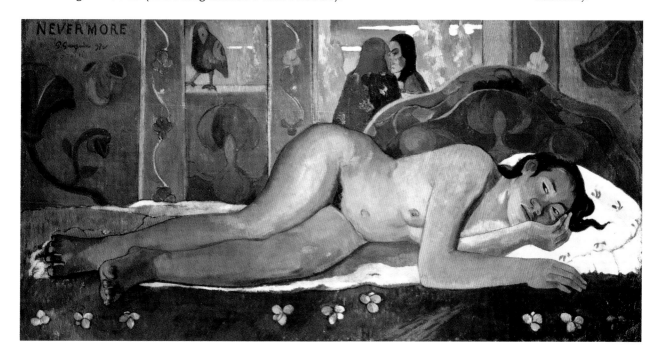

Gauguin's best work is from his visits to Pont Aven in Brittany (especially in 1888), and from Tahiti (1890s). He expressed powerful subjects with a strong sense of design: bold, flattened, simplified forms and intense, saturated colours. He was constantly searching for personal and spiritual fulfilment and was attracted to Tahitian women, so many of his works are full of sexual and spiritual yearning. He produced woodcarvings, pottery, and sculpture.

Although an acute observer of nature, he believed that the source of inspiration had to be internal, not external (which sparked a major quarrel with Van Gogh). Hence, look for symbolic, not natural, colours; and complex, sometimes biblical, symbolism. There is plenty of scope for detective work on his visual sources. They include South American art, Egyptian art, medieval art, Cambodian sculpture, Japanese prints, and Manet.

KEY WORKS: *The Vision After the Sermon*, 1888 (Edinburgh: National Gallery of Scotland); *The Yellow Christ*, 1889 (Buffalo, NY: Albright-Knox Art Gallery); *Where Do We Come From?*, 1897 (Boston: Museum of Fine Arts); *Primitive Tales*, 1902 (Essen: Museum Folkwang); *Riders on the Beach*, 1902 (Essen: Museum Folkwang)

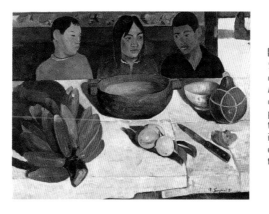

◀ *The Meal* 1891, 73 x 92 cm (28 ¾ x 36 ¼ in), oil on canvas, Paris: Musée d'Orsay. Rich colouring and distorted perspective combine to produce a work that is part still life, part enigmatic portrait of three Tahitian children.

Vincent **van Gogh**

● 1853–90 DUTCH OILS; DRAWINGS; ENGRAVINGS

Van Gogh was a happy child who became grim, impoverished, melancholic, difficult to love, and suicidal – but he painted works that are now among the best known, best loved, and most expensive in the world.

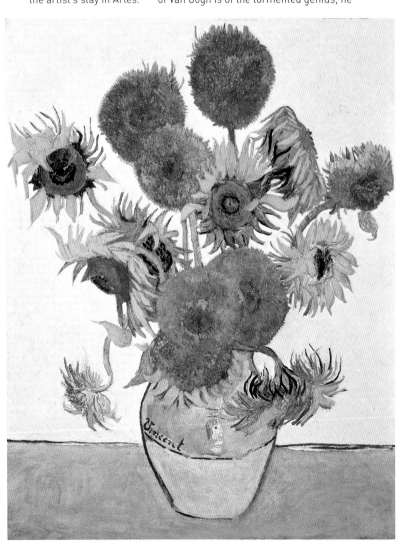

Sunflowers *1888, 92.1 × 73 cm (36 ½ × 28 ¾ in), oil on canvas, London: National Gallery.* This is one of twelve sunflower paintings by Van Gogh, most of which were done during the artist's stay in Arles.

Van Gogh took up painting at the age of 27 and wanted his art to be a consolation for the stresses and strains of modern life. His subjects are wholly autobiographical, tracing every moment and emotion in his life. Whilst the popular image of Van Gogh is of the tormented genius, he was also an educated, cultured man, who, despite the rapid pace of his output, put deep thought and planning into his art.

Life and works

Van Gogh came late to his artistic vocation, after years of unfulfilling careers, failed love affairs, poverty, and spiritual crises. Dismissed from his post as lay preacher for his too literal interpretation of Christ's command to give away worldly goods to the poor, he found a new mission in art. His early subjects were Dutch peasants and workers, whose honest struggle he sought to portray. This moralistic tone disappeared from his later art, which, under the influence of Impressionism and Japanese woodcuts that he encountered on his move to Paris, developed into an expressive, swirling style. An unsuccessful attempt to found an artists' co-operative at Arles with Gauguin led to a breakdown (he cut off part of his left ear during a quarrel), and he briefly entered an asylum in 1889. Although this was an enormously productive period, his depression finally overcame him, and he died at his own hand, virtually unknown to the art world, leaving 800 paintings and 850 drawings, completing 200 paintings in his last 15 months alone. His obsessive letters to his devoted brother, Theo, which often explain work in detail, formed the source material for the cult that continues to grow around him.

Style

Van Gogh had an instinctive, self-taught, hurried style that is instantly recognizable. He used paint straight from the tube, applied as thick as furrows; strange perspectives; firm outlines, like a child's drawing; and a thrilling use of colour, which takes on a life of its own. He distorted form and colour in order to express inner feelings, moving away from the reproduction of literal visual appearances towards a symbolic and expressive synthesis.

His swirling brushwork bristles with energy and emotional power. He was able to endow inanimate objects with human personality (as did his favourite author, Charles Dickens), so that his yellow chair becomes a symbol or image of Van Gogh himself. He had a passionate belief in the importance of first-hand observation, which can be electrifying; but he also used colour symbolism, with yellow being especially significant in his works. He ranks with Cézanne and Gauguin as the greatest of the Post-Impressionist artists.

KEY WORKS: *Portrait of Theo van Gogh*, 1887 (Amsterdam: Van Gogh Museum); *Van Gogh's Chair*, 1888 (London: National Gallery); *The Cafe Terrace on the Place du Forum, Arles, at Night*, 1888 (Otterlo: Kröller-Müller Museum); *The Bedroom at Arles*, 1889 (Paris: Musée d'Orsay); *Irises*, 1889 (Los Angeles; Getty Center); *The Church at Auvers-sur-Oise*, 1890 (Paris: Musée d'Orsay)

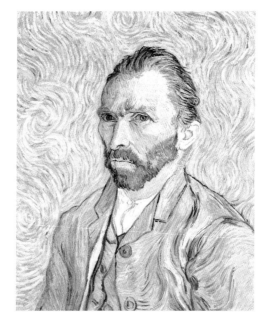

◄ *Self-Portrait* 1889, 65 × 54.5 cm (25 × 21½ in), oil on canvas, Paris: Musée d'Orsay. Four months after his breakdown in Arles in 1889, Van Gogh made this painting in the asylum at St Remy.

▼ *Starry Night* 1889, 73 × 92 cm (29 × 36 in), oil on canvas, New York: Museum of Modern Art. At the time he was planning *Starry Night*, Van Gogh was reading a collection of poems by the American writer Walt Whitman, one of which uses similar imagery to this work.

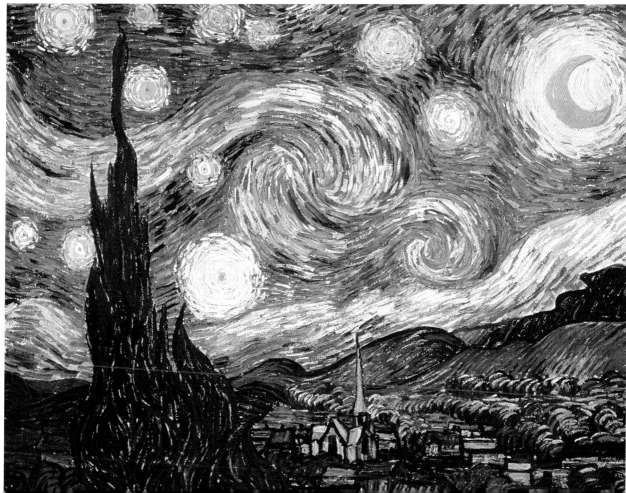

KEY WORKS: *Buckwheat Harvest*, 1888 (New York: Josefowitz Collection); *Study of Breton Women*, c.1888–90 (Quimper, France: Musée des Beaux-Arts)

Emile **Bernard**

● 1868–1941 🇫🇷 FRENCH ✍ OILS

A close friend of Gauguin, Van Gogh, and Cézanne, Bernard painted his own competent versions of Gauguin's style (clear outline; solid, flat colour).

He was good, but not as good as he thought (although he did influence the Nabis). Bernard is most important now for his writings – especially his interviews with Cézanne – and as the editor of Van Gogh's letters. In the 1920s, he gave up painting and retired to Venice to write.

Paul **Sérusier**

● 1864–1927 🇫🇷 FRENCH ✍ OILS

Sérusier's stiff, decorative style (firm outline, bright, flat colours, and simplification) is largely indebted to Gauguin, with lesser borrowings from Egyptian and medieval art. His favoured subject was Breton women at work. A disciple of Gauguin, he spread his ideas and was a founder member of the Nabis. He was well-heeled and popular with fellow artists, but was too hung up on theory; he needed to loosen up his art.

KEY WORKS: *Farmhouse at Le Pouldu*, 1890 (Washington DC: National Gallery of Art); *Breton Landscape*, 1895 (Boston: Museum of Fine Arts)

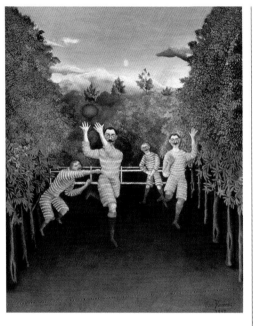

⏩ The Rugby Players
Henri Rousseau, 1908, 100.5 x 80.3 cm (39 ²⁄₃ x 31 ²⁄₃ in), oil on canvas, New York: Guggenheim Museum.

Henri **Rousseau**

● 1844–1910 🇫🇷 FRENCH ✍ OILS; WOODCUTS; SCULPTURE

Rousseau was a minor customs official who took up painting on retirement to supplement his pension. He was lionized by the young avant-garde because of the childlike vitality of his work.

His work has an unconscious (genuine) naïvety. He painted like a child, but on a bigger scale. He had all the qualities of a child, including the "art is my favourite subject" enthusiasm; wobbly perspective; smiley faces; big signature; obsession with arbitrary detail (every leaf on a tree, or every blade of grass), and a desire to please. He usually worked around a simple idea with a central single object. He did what most children grow out of, or are taught not to do; he is a reminder that we may flourish best and achieve unexpected recognition if we are what we are and do not constantly strive to be what we are not.

KEY WORKS: *Self-Portrait of Rousseau, from L'Ile Saint-Louis*, 1890 (Prague: National Gallery); *Tiger in a Tropical Storm*, 1891 (London: National Gallery); *The Sleeping Gypsy*, 1897 (New York: Museum of Modern Art)

☑ The Talisman *Paul Sérusier, 1888, 27 x 21 cm (10 ½ x 8 ¼ in), oil on panel, Paris: Musée d'Orsay. Sérusier's landscape was named The Talisman because it had such a great influence on the development of Symbolism.*

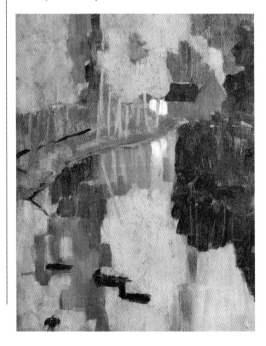

Félix **Vallotton**

⬤ 1865–1925 🏴 SWISS ✍ OILS;
WOODCUTS; SCULPTURE

There was a short period when Félix Vallotton was
at the forefront of new ideas (1890–1901), painting
scenes of everyday life in original, simplified form
(he disliked straight lines and preferred curves,
round tabletops, etc.)

Vallotton was influenced by Japanese prints and
the French Symbolists. He produced good, often
satirical, prints amongst otherwise forgettable,
traditional, realistic works.

KEY WORKS: *Seated Female Nude*, 1897 (Musée
de Grenoble); *Interior*, 1903–04 (St Petersburg:
Hermitage Museum); *Woman in a Black Hat*,
1908 (St Petersburg: Hermitage Museum)

Henri de **Toulouse-Lautrec**

⬤ 1864–1901 🏴 FRENCH
✍ OILS; PRINTS

Toulouse-Lautrec was the epitome
of the bohemian artist: he was a
crippled aristocrat who haunted
the Parisian cafés and brothels, and
commemorated their inhabitants
in art of supreme quality.

There is extraordinary immediacy
and tension in his work, resulting
from his mastery of his subject matter
and technique. The prostitutes and
drunks, although sometimes close
to caricature, are shown without
sentiment or criticism – he loved
them and understood them. The
brilliant, wiry draughtsmanship and
thin, nervous paint seem to reflect
their uncertain, shadowy world; you
sense that he was part of that world,
not just an observer.

The economy of the brushstrokes
and the simplicity of the materials
are as direct and basic as his subjects.
He used paint thinned with turpentine
that allowed fine, rapid marks, and
unprimed cardboard, which he did not
try to disguise – exploiting its rawness
and colour and the way it absorbs
diluted oil paint.

KEY WORKS: *La Toilette*, 1889 (Paris:
Musée d'Orsay); *At the Moulin Rouge*,
1892 (Art Institute of Chicago); *Jane Avril
Dancing*, 1892 (Paris: Musée d'Orsay)

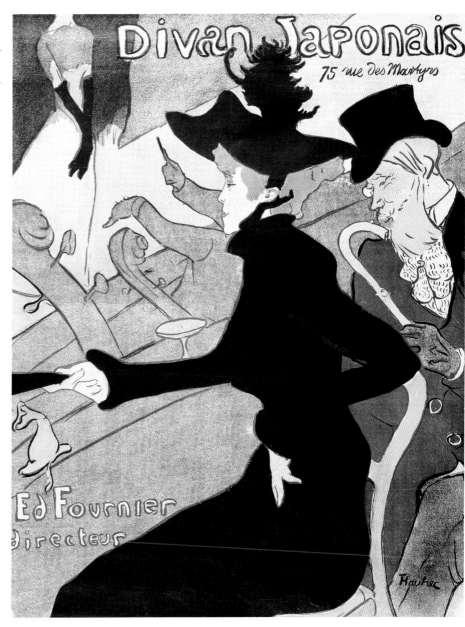

☑ *Le Divan
Japonais* Henri
de Toulouse-Lautrec,
1892, 76.2 x 59.7 cm
(30 x 23 ½ in),
lithograph, Paris:
Bibliothèque
Nationale. Passionate
about lithography,
Toulouse-Lautrec
created many
posters advertising
Montmartre nightlife.

Paul **Cézanne**

● 1839–1906 ⓟ FRENCH ☝ OILS; WATERCOLOURS; DRAWINGS

Cézanne is considered both the mother and father of modern art. He was a solitary, pioneering, and difficult workaholic. He thought that his life and work were failures.

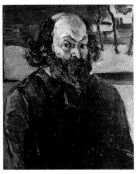

⌃ *Self-Portrait*
*c.1873–76, 64 x 53 cm
(25 ⅕ x 20 ⅘ in), oil on
canvas, Paris Musée
d'Orsay.* Cézanne was
hailed by Picasso as
"My one and only
master... father
of us all."

Cézanne's ambitious businessman father from Aix-en-Provence terrified his son, who was saved by his own determined artistic sensibility. His father eventually allowed him to go to Paris to study art, giving him a small allowance, and later left him a fortune. Cézanne never had to sell his work to live – a rare privilege. In 1870, he married Hortense Fiquet and they had one son, Paul.

Cézanne's early efforts were as inept as his social behaviour, and he was rejected as "incompetent" by the École des Beaux Arts. His subsequent lifelong struggle to find a coherent way of painting resulted miraculously in work that became a key influence on modern art. His first one-man show in 1895 caused huge excitement for young artists such as Matisse and Picasso.

His last years were marked by loneliness and ill health. Already suffering with diabetes, he died from pneumonia after being soaked in a downpour whilst painting outdoors.

Style

At the heart of Cézanne's painting was a determination to continue the highly disciplined French Classical tradition epitomized by Poussin,

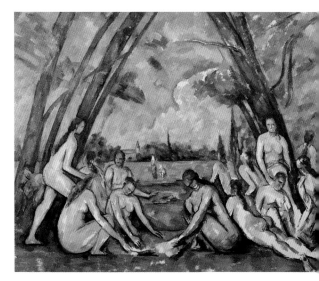

⌃ *The Large Bathers c.1900–05, 208 x 249 cm
(81 ¾ x 98 in), oil on canvas, Philadelphia: Museum
of Art.* Cézanne never painted from naked
models, but assembled his nude compositions
from photographs.

but to do so outdoors and "from nature". In all his works, he combines a remarkable faithfulness to what he observes with a deep awareness of his emotional response. His palette is usually restricted to earthy greens, ochres, and blues, and there may be an instinctive underlying grid-like structure, as if to hold the composition together and define the different areas.

Cézanne did not originate new subjects; his originality was in his way of seeing and painting. For example, his landscapes often took him weeks or months to achieve. The difficulty was that the detail was always changing as the light changed – and even as he moved position. In other words, there never came a moment when he deemed any work to be finished – one of the reasons for his sense of failure, and why he rarely signed his work.

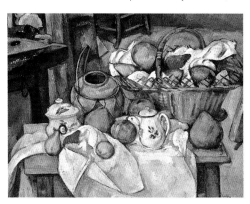

⏩ *Still Life with Basket*
*1888–90, 65 x 81 cm
(25 ¾ x 31 ½ in), oil on
canvas, Paris: Musée
d'Orsay.* Cézanne
worked so slowly that
the fruit often rotted
and he had to substitute
plaster replicas.

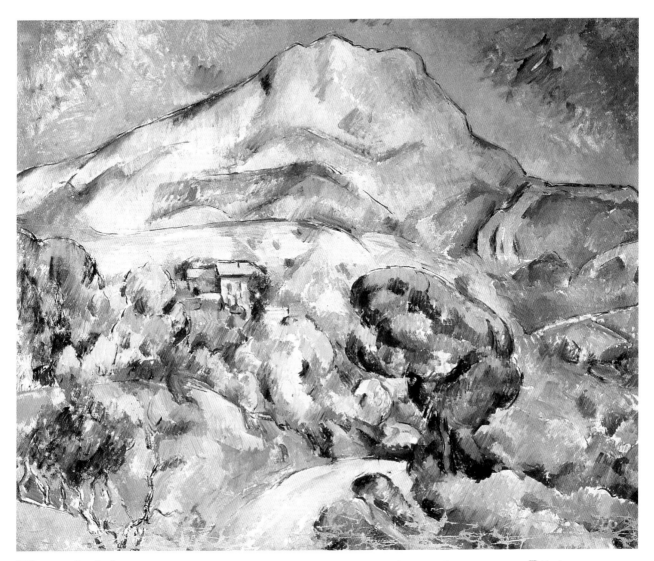

What to look for

His works have multilayered significance – central to Cézanne are the same (traditional) subjects painted over and over again. He did this in a constant attempt to record accurately what he saw, to express what he felt, and to produce an aesthetically satisfying picture. While it was not easy – as these goals are constantly changing and are often in conflict – he achieved it in the works of 1885–1901. Cézanne's paintings have an extraordinary power, as though you were seeing through his eyes.

Examine the marks that he made – small, precise, beautiful, and each in place for a reason. He only made marks when he had seen and felt something. He also wove them together to produce a harmony of colour and design. Every picture surface trembles with the thrill and anxiety of his intense seeing, feeling, and making.

KEY WORKS: *The Artist's Father*, 1866 (Washington DC: National Gallery of Art); *The Abduction*, c.1867 (Cambridge: Fitzwilliam Museum); *The Temptation of St Anthony*, 1869–70 (Zurich: Bührle Collection); *The Card Players*, 1892–95 (London: Courtauld Institute of Art); *Still Life with Apples and Oranges*, c.1895–1900 (Paris: Musée d'Orsay); *Le château noir*, 1900–04 (Washington DC: National Gallery of Art)

⌃ *Montagne Sainte-Victoire with Trees and a House*
1896–98, 78 x 99 cm, (31 x 39 in), oil on canvas, Moscow: Museum of Modern Art of the West. Mont Sainte-Victoire is a well-known landmark near Aix-en-Provence, painted frequently by Cézanne.

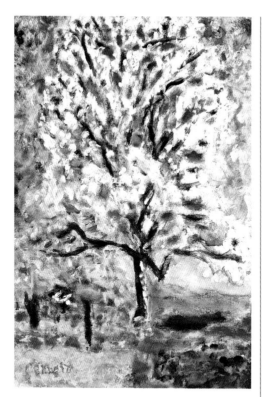

⟫ The Almond Tree in Blossom *Pierre Bonnard, 1947, 55 x 37.5 cm (21 ⅔ x 14 ¾ in), oil on canvas, Paris: Musée National d'Art Moderne.* This is Bonnard's last painting, which he was still perfecting whilst on his deathbed.

Pierre **Bonnard**

◗ 1867–1947 〽 FRENCH ✍ OILS; DRAWINGS

Bonnard was one of the great masters of colour. Though less intellectual than Matisse, he shared his view that art should be a celebration of life and a source of visual joy.

He painted the places, rooms, and people that he knew most intimately, notably his neurotic, bath-obsessed wife, Marthe. His early work is progressive. His later work is deeply personal and stands outside the mainstream. He created lovely, free drawings that are masterpieces of observation. The paintings were done in his studio from memory and from black and white notes and sketches.

Stand well back and see how he created thrilling spaces (rich, textured foregrounds and hazy distances). Walk forwards and see how glorious colour harmonies take over and the detail of flickering brushwork and subtle colour weavings fill your eye. His work became brighter with age.

KEY WORKS: *The Letter*, c.1906 (Washington DC: National Gallery of Art); *Table Set in a Garden*, c.1908 (Washington DC: National Gallery of Art); *Bathing Woman, Seen from the Back*, c.1919 (London: Tate Collection)

Edouard **Vuillard**

◗ 1868–1940 〽 FRENCH ✍ OILS; PRINTS

Vuillard was a shy, highly talented painter and printmaker who was at the forefront of new artistic ideas up to 1900, after which he retreated into his own comfortable, intimate world.

He is best known for his glimpses of middle-class life – mostly cluttered domestic interiors. He had a nervous style, with busy surfaces that flicker with light or allow the image to build up like a mosaic. He was fascinated by repeating patterns, such as woven material or wallpaper. He used a rich, earthy palette and had a warm sense of colour.

He pioneered simple design, strong colour, and energetic brushwork. An enthusiastic photographer, his works have a snapshot-like quality.

KEY WORKS: *Landscape: Window Overlooking the Woods*, 1899 (Art Institute of Chicago); *Portrait of Théodore Duret*, 1912 (Washington DC: National Gallery of Art)

◩ Mother and Child *Edouard Vuillard, 1900, 51.4 x 50.2 cm (20 ¼ x 19 ¾ in), oil on board, private collection.* Vuillard never married, but remained deeply devoted to his widowed mother, who was a dressmaker.

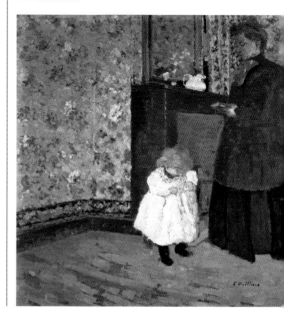

Sir William **Nicholson**

● 1872-1949 ▣ BRITISH ✑ OILS; PRINTS

Nicholson was a highly accomplished painter of landscapes, portraits, and still lifes, with an easy, fluid, intimate style and a wonderful eye for observation, composition, colour, and light – and an ability to edit out the superfluous. He was successful, and knighted for his achievements. He also made poster and theatre designs, and woodblock prints. He was Ben Nicholson's father.

KEY WORKS: *Beerbohm*, 1905 (London: National Portrait Gallery); *The Lowestoft Bowl*, 1911 (London: Tate Collection)

Ferdinand **Hodler**

● 1853-1918 ▣ SWISS ✑ OILS

Creator of monumental figure paintings, portraits, and landscapes, Hodler painted modern narratives and allegories with a confident drawing style and strong outlines. He used powerful, intensified colour; his hatched brushstrokes and broken colour give optical vibrancy. He sometimes falls into the trap of the pompously overserious statement. Hodler liked silhouetted figures or mountains against a sky.

KEY WORKS: *Tired of Life*, 1892 (Munich: Neue Pinakothek); *Silence of the Evening*, c.1904 (Winterthur, Switzerland: Kunstmuseum)

Lovis **Corinth**

● 1858-1925 ▣ GERMAN ✑ OILS; WATERCOLOURS; PRINTS

Corinth's work is rarely seen outside Germany. An ambitious, gifted Prussian, he tried to reinvent the tradition of the Old Masters in a modern idiom.

In his traditional style, he painted established subjects (portraits, still lifes, mythologies), using an earthy palette and was influenced by Old Masters, especially Rembrandt and Hals. In his modern style, he painted frank, direct interpretations. Note his free and expressive paint-handling – he used painting as a personal and emotional release. After a stroke in 1911, his work became increasingly loose, reflecting his physical handicap, awareness of death, isolation (he disliked Modernism), and melancholy at the German Empire's defeat in 1918.

Impressively versatile, he produced stunning, small, late watercolours and prints, which he found easier to handle after his stroke and which show thrilling emotional and technical invention. His plein-air landscapes (especially those around his house at Walchensee, Bavaria) hover between Impressionism and Expressionism and were a great commercial success in Berlin. The compositions in late works often lean curiously to the left. He painted a series of self-portraits every year on his birthday (after 1887).

KEY WORKS: *Nude Girl*, 1886 (Minnesota: Minneapolis Institute of Arts); *Centaurs Embracing*, 1911 (London: Courtauld Institute of Art); *Samson Blinded*, 1912 (Berlin: Staatliche Museum); *Magdalen with Pearls in her Hair*, 1919 (London: Tate Collection); *Self-Portrait with Straw Hat*, 1923 (Basel, Switzerland: Kunstmuseum)

Carl **Milles**

● 1875-1955 ▣ SWEDISH ✑ SCULPTURE

The greatest Swedish sculptor, and one of the most famous sculptors since Rodin (who was a big early influence), Milles is best known for his large-scale fountains, which show his grasp of architecture. He travelled widely in Europe and later taught in the US, where he did most of his best work.

He combined eclectic influences from his travels into a highly individual style. He fused classical and Nordic cultures to create vigorous, unusual groupings. His figures are full of vitality, while his fountains are conceived as an architectural whole: the figures must be viewed against the background of sky and water.

KEY WORKS: *Folke Filbyter (Le cavalier de la légende)*, 1920s (Lidingö, Sweden: Millesgården); *Pegasus and Bellerophon*, 1940s (Iowa: Des Moines Art Center)

Secession and Art Nouveau

LATE 19TH/EARLY 20TH CENTURY

In the 1890s, several groups of painters in Vienna, Munich, and Berlin sought to break away from the official academies and promote new ideas and styles. They labelled their new groupings *Sezession*, and their avant-garde exhibitions created considerable outrage and scandal. In the end, these groups were splintered by internal politics, leading to further breakaway associations.

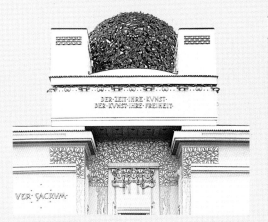

» Façade of Secession Building, Vienna
The new home for art, designed and built in just six months in 1898, was a rejection of the traditional architectural styles of the Austro-Hungarian empire.

KEY EVENTS

1892	Rejection of Munch's early work by Berlin Artists' Association. German artists start Munich Secession
1897	Klimt breaks away from the main Austrian academy and patron, Künstlerhaus, and establishes hugely successful exhibition (57,000 visitors) and magazine *Ver Sacrum*
1898	Leading German Impressionist Max Liebermann starts Berlin Secession movement
1900	First of Hector Germain Guimard's Art Nouveau designs for the Paris Metro

Vienna Secession

This movement was founded by Gustav Klimt, who aimed to put Vienna on the international stage artistically by pursuing new avant-garde ideas, with links to other progressive artists all over Europe. In particular, Klimt wanted to create a union between the fine arts of painting and sculpture and architecture, and the applied arts of design and decoration.

Art Nouveau

French for "new art"; also known as *Jugendstil* or *Sezessionstil* in Austria, and *Stile Liberty* in Italy. Art Nouveau describes a highly decorative style, most often seen in architecture and the applied arts, which was at the forefront of fashion in the 1890s. It aimed to reject historical influences and create one encapsulating style for all the arts. The French-speaking version is organic and free-flowing; the German/Scottish version is geometric.

☑ *Sarah Bernhardt Alphonse Mucha, 1896, colour lithograph, Prague: Mucha Trust.* Mucha was a Czech painter and designer who settled in Paris. His work was important in the development of French Art Nouveau.

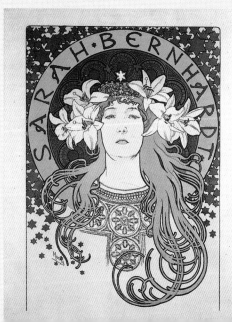

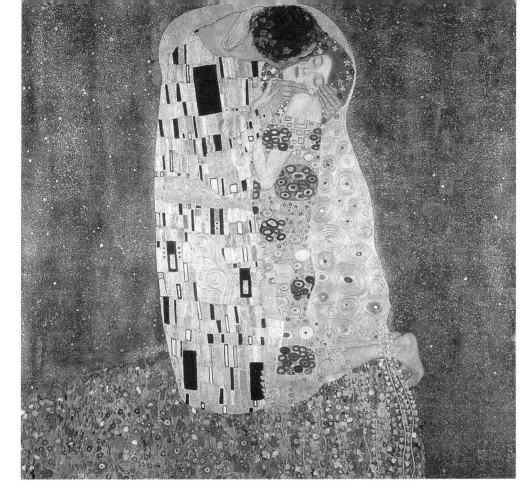

 The Kiss *Gustav Klimt, 1907–08, 180 x 180 cm (71 x 71 in), oil on canvas, Vienna: Österreichische Galerie.* The couple are surrounded by a cloud of gold, intended as a symbolic expression of the power of love.

Gustav **Klimt**

🌐 1862–1918 🏳 AUSTRIAN ✍ OILS; MIXED MEDIA; DRAWINGS

Klimt was an enormous bear of a man with a voracious and tireless sexual and visual appetite. He never married but he had many lovers and fathered four children.

The intense, introverted subject matter reflects Klimt's own personality (he was an oversexed workaholic), and *fin de siècle* Vienna (neurotic, idle, adulterous, gossipy, deeply conservative, but also packed with original talent and fresh ideas from Freud, Richard Strauss, Mahler, and so on). It also expresses his wish to explore modern sensibility and break free from old, stifling taboos and restrictions, and his wish to demolish the snobby distinction between the fine artist and the craftsman.

Klimt's brilliant, inventive technique reflects his training (at the School for Decorative Arts, where he learned craft techniques), and his fascination with Egyptian art (flat and decorative) and Byzantine art (gold and mosaic). Notice the sensitive hands, hidden faces, and private symbolism – he worked through suggestion rather than description in order to touch the inner feeling rather than the outward show.

KEY WORKS: *Judith*, 1901 (Vienna: Österreichische Galerie); *Emilie Floege,* 1902 (Vienna: Historisches Museum der Stadt Wien); *Danae*, 1907–08 (Private Collection); *Hope II*, 1907–08 (New York: Museum of Modern Art); *Baby*, 1917–18 (Cradle) (Washington DC: National Gallery of Art)

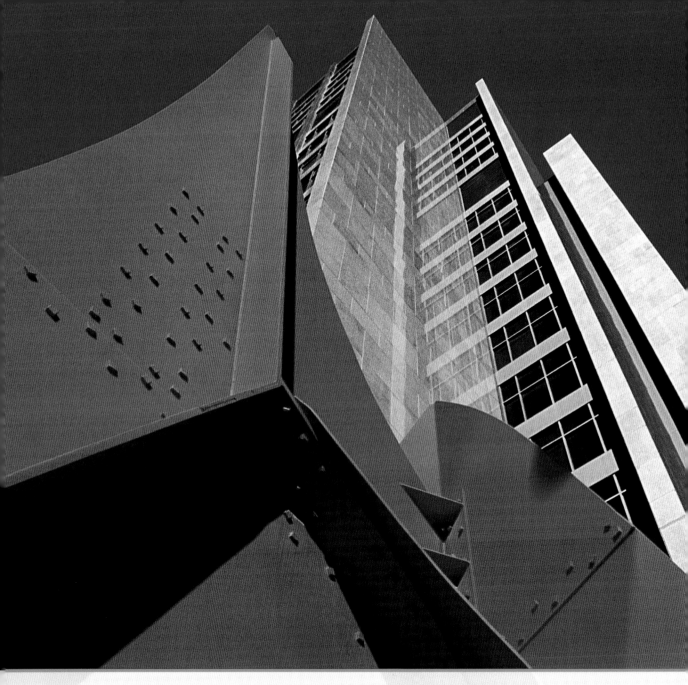

Modernism
c.1900–1970

Young artists and writers in Western Europe welcomed the dawn of the 20th century with excitement and great expectation. They hoped and believed it would usher in a new era fuelled by technological advances and democratic ideals that would result in economic and social improvements for the great majority of humankind.

Artists, architects, and engineers were to be at the heart of creating this brave new modern world that was to look different from anything seen before. In many ways their dreams were realized. The plethora of new styles and technical innovations that followed in rapid succession radically changed art and the environment, and testified to a freedom of thought and expression that was at times bewildering in its range and diversity.

Confrontation

What the idealists failed to predict, however, was the effectiveness of the forces that would seek to destroy, and very nearly extinguish, these new freedoms. They could not foresee the fierceness of the political confrontations or the terrifying destruction of human life and material environment that would ensue.

The World Wars

The principal manifestations of the political struggles were the two World Wars (1914–18 and 1939–45). By 1919, after more than four

*** Young Lady and Her Suite** Alexander Calder, 1970, painted steel, height 10 m (33 ft), Detroit, Michigan. One of the dreams of the first generation of Modern artists and architects was the creation of an ideal city.

years of debilitating warfare on the Western Front, Britain and France emerged victorious. As the world's leading colonial powers, they could still assert their dominant position, despite the growing realities of American financial and political aspirations and power. Germany, by contrast, was prostrate, politically and economically in turmoil, Austria–Hungary was destroyed as a single entity, and Russia embarked on a communist experiment that would bring misery and death to millions. After 1929, the Western economies, including that of the US, suffered a debilitating depression. Germany and the Soviet Union established totalitarian regimes that were irreconcilably opposed in their political ideologies, but had many features in common.

Soon after the onset of war in 1939, France was forced into ignominious surrender, and Britain into lonely defiance. In the end it was the unlikely alliance between American manufacturing might and Soviet manpower that secured a victory over Nazi Germany.

After 1945, Europe had to acknowledge the reality of American dominance of the Western world. Neither Britain nor France

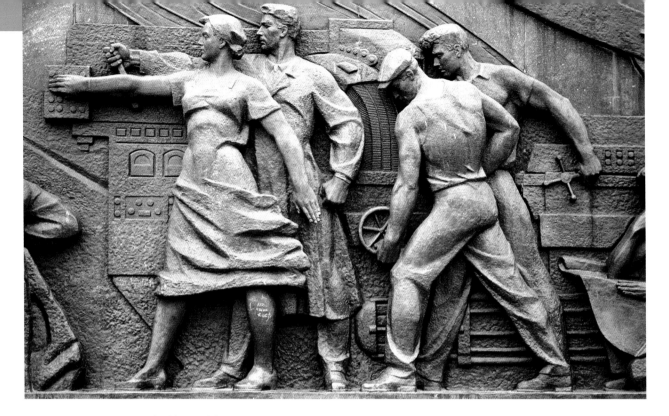

Frieze showing heroic Soviet workers, Moscow Soviet art, like Nazi art, was monumental and deeply conservative. Both regimes ruthlessly crushed any form of individual expression.

had been able to contain the growth of pre-war fascism in Europe, or offer a creditable alternative to communism.

Recovery

The efforts of France and Britain after the war to hold on to their empires were doomed. Europe entered a period of austerity and introspection. From the late 1940s it was the threat of conflict between the US and the Soviet Union that defined international relations. Further, after 1949, a new factor was added to the balance of world power: the threat of nuclear war and the prospect of humankind's complete self-destruction.

By 1970, the picture was very different. Whereas Germany in 1945 was a country reduced to rubble and occupied by its former enemies, its Western entity now boasted the largest economy in Europe. Over the same period, almost every Western country enjoyed an unprecedented period of economic growth. The roots of this lay in the spectacular buoyancy of the US economy in the 1950s

TIMELINE: 1900–1970

1900 Freud's *The Interpretation of Dreams* published, Vienna

1914–18 First World War

1929 Wall Street Crash precipitates global slump

1938 Hitler annexes Austria and border regions of Czechoslovakia

1939 German invasion of Poland sparks World War II

1900   **1910**   **1920**   **1930**

1907 Picasso's *Les Demoiselles d'Avignon*

1917 Russian Revolution

1919 Versailles peace settlement shrinks Germany and dissolves Austria–Hungary

1933 Hitler elected German chancellor

1936 Stalinist purges in the USSR; Spanish Civil War begins (to 1939)

and 1960s. American financial aid to Western Europe, through the Marshall Plan, launched in 1947, kick-started Europe's war-ravaged economies, and thereafter America's dynamism and its tempting vision of a consumer society, drove developments around the world. Even the economies of Soviet-dominated Eastern Europe grew. The European Economic Community which started idealistically in 1957, soon slipped into strategies for securing comfortable prosperity rather than achieving any great ideal.

The Avant-Garde

Avant-Garde art, with its strong ideological and moral agenda, flourished most fruitfully where there was an urgent desire for a change of the existing tyrannical or unstable status quo, or a tradition of radical political action. France, Russia,

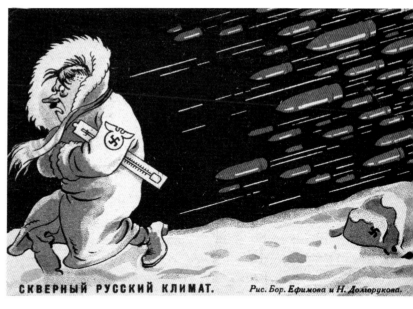

СКВЕРНЫЙ РУССКИЙ КЛИМАТ.　Рис. Бор. Ефимова и Н. Долгорукова.

◰ Soviet postcard from World War II Hitler suffers in the Russian winter as he runs from a hail of shells. All countries in the war used art to project their propaganda messages.

◁◁ Chrysler Building, New York This landmark Art Deco skyscraper, was conceived in prosperity, but opened six months after the Wall Street Crash.

Germany, and Holland were at the forefront, followed by Italy and Spain. In Britain and the US, where freedom of speech and political stability was taken for granted, early Modern Art was initially of less interest. However, in the 1930s and 1940s, refugees from Europe took their avant-garde ideas to the US in particular, where they received a warm welcome. But then, as memories of the hardships of the Great Depression and war began to recede, and the free and easy lifestyle offered by consumer society seduced the creative imagination, their innovative art soon fell prey to commercial exploitation.

1945 German surrender ends war in Europe; atomic bomb dropped on Hiroshima; Japanese surrender

1955 Warsaw Pact established

1956 Anti-Soviet uprising in Hungary suppressed

1962 Andy Warhol's *Twenty-five Colored Marilyns*, New York

1969 US succeeds in landing men on the moon

1940　**1950**　**1960**　**1970**

1941 German invasion of the Soviet Union

1947 New York takes over from Paris as the capital of the artistic avant-garde

1957 Treaty of Rome: EEC created

1962 Cuban missile crisis

1967 Year of "Flower Power" and growing protests against war in Vietnam

Henri **Matisse**

● 1869–1954   FRENCH   OILS; SCULPTURE; COLLAGE; DRAWINGS

Matisse celebrated the joy of living through colour. He was a major hero of the Modern movement and one of its founders. A slow worker and methodical, he was professorial and social, but never convivial.

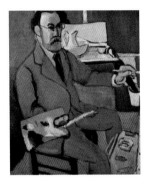

⊿ *Self-Portrait* 1918, 65 x 54 cm (25 ¾ x 21 ¼ in), oil on canvas, Le Cateau-Cambrésis: Musée Matisse. Matisse at the age of 49. He was 12 years older than his great rival Picasso.

Matisse first studied law in Paris and worked as a legal clerk before taking up art studies at the influential Académie Julian and under Gustave Moreau at the École des Beaux-Arts, where he met several of the future Fauves. He came to art late and almost by chance, when, aged 21, he was given a box of paints while recovering from an appendicitis operation.

In the late 1890s, he experimented with Divisionism and absorbed a deep knowledge of colour theory. In 1899, he turned to Cézanne. Although penniless, he bought from art dealer Ambroise Vollard a small Cézanne, *Bathers*, which he kept all his life and used as inspiration at low or critical moments of his career. Coming from the grey cold light of northern Europe, the discovery of the brightness and warmth of Mediterranean light, which he first experienced in Collioure, on the French-Spanish border in the summer of 1904, was a revelation.

From 1905–07, as the foremost Fauve painter, he was champion of the young avante-garde, and opened a school for young artists. His *Notes of a Painter* (published 1908) is one of the most important statements of the principles of modern art. At this period he also visited Morocco and came under the influence of Islamic and Persian art, both of which emphasize pattern and bold but subtle colour. In the 1920s, Matisse settled semi-permanently in Nice, and his art continued to flourish with ever-increasing richness, and fascination with light and colour, even

when he was a bedridden invalid, with very few false turnings. In many ways his later years are among his most fertile and inventive, as he experimented with paper cut-outs and collages, the illustrations for *Jazz* and *La Cirque*, plus the stained glass windows and vestments for the Chapel of the Rosary at Vence, near Nice.

Subjects and style

Look for his life-enhancing, joyous combination of subject matter (notably the open window, still life, and female nude), and his glorious colour, which takes on a life of its own and is free to do its own thing, without necessarily imitating nature. He explored colour independently from subject matter and turned it into something you want to touch and feel. As a result he loved exploring the exotic, especially oriental fabrics and ceramics with their strong decorative feel and heightened colours. This is brilliantly explored in his superb *Odalisque* nudes of 1920–25. His late gouaches on paper cut-outs enabled him to carve into colour. He was also a brilliant and innovative

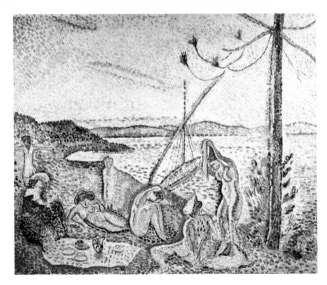

≫ *Luxe, calme, et volupté (Luxury, Serenity, and Pleasure)* 1904, 98 x 118 cm (38 ¾ x 46 ½ in), oil on canvas, Paris: Musée d'Orsay. One of Matisse's most emblematic paintings, much influenced by Cézanne's *Bathers*.

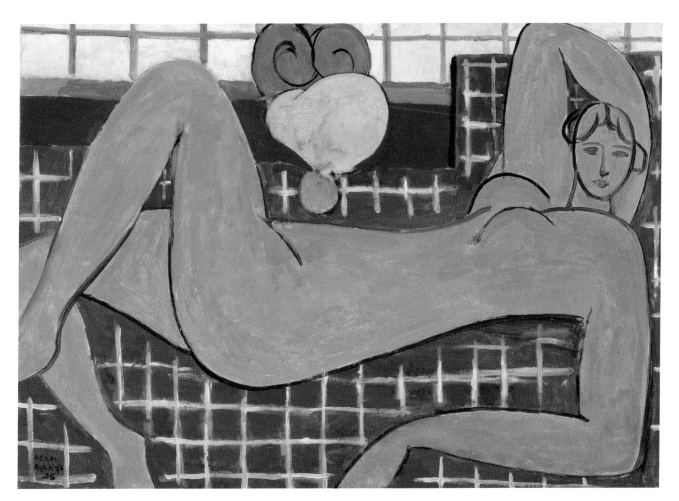

printmaker – the apparent simplifications in his work are deceptive: they were only reached after much thought and alteration.

What to look for

Matisse's work explores the full range of what colour can do, by crowding, juxtaposing, intensifying, relaxing, purifying, heating, and cooling. Look for white spaces around bright colours, allowing them to "breathe" and reach their full visual potential. The open brushwork is deliberate, to give movement and life to the colour and to register Matisse's own presence and activity. Matisse said he dreamt of an "art of balance and purity and serenity, devoid of troubling or depressing subject matter... a soothing, calming influence... like a good armchair". It was this apparent lack of or

need for controversy that puzzled Picasso. If in their earlier years they had competed for leadership of the avant-garde, in later life they kept a respectful distance, each aware of the other's innovations, even influenced by them, yet never in competition. Matisse's principal concern was always with colour, and the way it could be used to create form, emotion, and sensation. In his own words, "I am unable to distinguish between the feeling I have for life and my way of expressing it."

KEY WORKS: *The Joy of Living*, 1905–06 (Pennsylvania: Barnes Foundation); *Statuette and Vases on an Oriental Carpet*, 1908 (Moscow: Pushkin Museum); *The Black I–IV*, 1909–c.1929 (London: Tate Collection); *Reclining Nude Back*, 1927 (Private Collection); *The Snail*, 1953 (London: Tate Collection)

⌃ *Large Reclining Nude*
1935, 66 x 92.7 cm (26 x 36 ½ in), oil on canvas, Maryland: Baltimore Museum of Art. Matisse reworked this picture 22 times, altering the background and model's proportions until he was satisfied.

»» LES FAUVES 1900–07

The name was given to the movement at the 1905 Salon d'Automne exhibition held in Paris. Art critic of the review *Gil Blas* Louis Vauxcelles insultingly labelled the brightly coloured style of the paintings as the work of wild beasts (*fauves*). But the group, loosely formed around liaisons between the artists about the turn of the century, loved the term.

Matisse and Derain studied together in 1898 and Vlaminck, a friend of Derain, was introduced two years later. They were heavily influenced by van Gogh and Cézanne, as well as the Pointillism of Seurat. Colour harmony was a central theme, although the dotted style eventually gave way, in the main, to wide choppy brushstrokes of stunning pure colour, freely applied in flat patterns. It embodied Derain's ideal of "colour for colour's sake". Now an object could generate its own brightness. The chief group members were Matisse, Dufy, Derain, Vlaminck, and Braque. One of the principal places of inspiration was Collioure in the South of France. By 1907, most of the artists had moved on to explore new personal ideals.

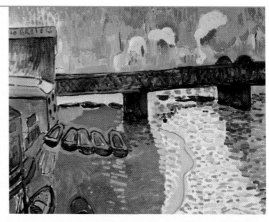

⌃ **Charing Cross Bridge** *André Derain, 1906, 81.2 x 100.3 cm (32 x 39 ½ in), oil on canvas, Washington DC: National Gallery of Art*. Derain was influenced by Monet's paintings of the River Thames.

⌄ **Tugboat at Chatou**
Maurice de Vlaminck, 1906, 50 x 65 cm (19 x 25 in), oil on canvas, private collection. Vlaminck and Derain were named the "Chatou Couple" after the Paris suburb where they painted together.

Maurice de **Vlaminck**

⬤ **1876–1958** 🏳 **FRENCH** ✎ **OILS; DRAWINGS**

Vlaminck was both a volatile and boastful character who made a brief splash as one of the avant-garde Fauve artists in France c.1905–06. As a youth, he earned an income from his winnings as a racing cyclist, and from performing as an orchestral violinist. The turning point in his life was meeting Derain, by chance, on a train in 1899.

His early landscapes are full of colour, thickly and freely painted, and with strong simplified designs. They express the mood of adventure and experimentation that captured the imagination of progressive young French artists at the time. Vlaminck's later landscapes degenerated into a boring formula; superficially they look modern, but they are not.

Separate the subject matter of his work (which is actually not very innovative) from the way it is painted (which is), and maybe question the reason for this balancing of old and new. Vlaminck used a not very subtle palette of four colours – red, blue, yellow, and green – but wove them together to create a strong visual "fizz".

KEY WORKS: *The Blue House*, 1906 (Minnesota: Minneapolis Institute of Arts); *Tugboat on the Seine, Chatou*, 1906 (Washington DC: National Gallery of Art); *View of the Seine*, c.1906 (St Petersburg: Hermitage Museum); *Still Life*, c.1910 (Paris: Musée d'Orsay); *The River*, c.1910 (Washington DC: National Gallery of Art)

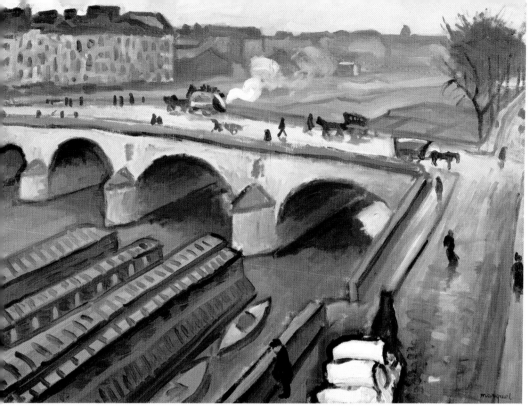

◄◄ *The Seine at Paris*
*Albert Marquet, c.1907,
65 x 81 cm (25 ¾ x
31 ⅔ in), oil on canvas,
private collection.*
Fauvist Marquet is
well known for his
panoramic views of
the Seine and of various
French ports, which
feature docks, cranes,
tugs, and ships
at anchors.

Albert **Marquet**

● 1875–1947 ◫ FRENCH ✍ OILS;
WATERCOLOURS; DRAWINGS

Marquet, who studied under Moreau with Matisse,
developed an appealing and poetic style: strong,
simple design; clear, harmonious colour; the
elimination of unnecessary detail (Matisse
compared him favourably with the Japanese
artist Hokusai). He produced small-scale works
in oil and watercolour. The scenes of Paris,
around the Seine, and French ports are the
most effective and popular.

KEY WORKS: *André Rouveyre*, 1904 (Paris: Musée
d'Orsay); *Le Pont-Neuf*, 1906 (Washington DC: National
Gallery of Art); *Winter on the Seine*, c.1910 (Oslo:
National Gallery)

André **Derain**

● 1880–1954 ◫ FRENCH ✍ OILS;
SCULPTURE; DRAWINGS

Derain is best remembered as Matisse's main
partner in creating Fauvist paintings in the South of
France, in the early 20th century. He was one of the
first artists to take an interest in African sculpture.

His early works were extremely influential in the
development of the use of colour in Modern art. He
stayed (mostly) with traditional landscape themes,
with an important series of views of London (the
River Thames) painted in 1906. Then, he unwisely
abandoned colour and concentrated on form. His
later work is mediocre and currently overrated.

His early work is notable for attractive paint
handling, open brushwork, and strong, confident
compositions. He made subtle use of colour,
exploiting harmonies as well as contrasts,
and placing half-tones and full tones together.
He intensified local colours, but unlike Matisse
never abandoned them: thus skies are
always blue, leaves green (Matisse's skies
can be yellow, green... anything).

KEY WORKS: *Portrait of Matisse*, 1905 (London:
Tate Collection); *Charing Cross Bridge* (see
opposite); *The Pool of London*, 1906 (London:
Tate Collection); *Southern France*, 1927
(Private Collection)

Expressionism and Abstraction

EARLY 20TH CENTURY

Expressionism and Abstraction were key early trends in the development of Modern Art, and their influence continues in full force to the present day with many different individual styles. Early practitioners wanted art to become more like music, conveying emotion and meaning by suggestion, heightened sensation, and free association, rather than by description of forms and appearances.

» Storm Tide in Hamburg *Oskar Kokoschka, 1962, 90 x 118 cm (35 ¾ x 46 ½ in), oil on canvas, Hamburg: Kunsthalle.* Painted in the year of his first retrospective at the Tate Gallery, London.

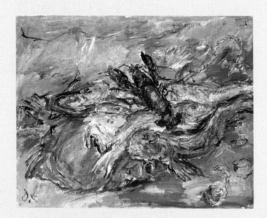

☑ Fabeltier *Franz Marc, 1912, 14.3 x 21.4 cm (5 ⅔ x 8 ⅔ in), woodcut, Hamburg: Kunsthalle.* In 1911, Marc embarked on a series of paintings of animals; these have since become the cornerstone of his reputation.

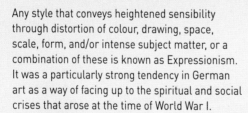

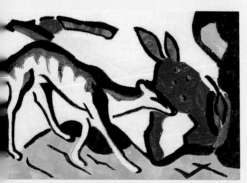

Any style that conveys heightened sensibility through distortion of colour, drawing, space, scale, form, and/or intense subject matter, or a combination of these is known as Expressionism. It was a particularly strong tendency in German art as a way of facing up to the spiritual and social crises that arose at the time of World War I.

A true example of abstract art has intellectual or emotional meaning (or both), but does not represent or imitate any visible object or figure. Good abstract art is not easy to get to grips with, but it will reward the effort involved. You may need to see a large number of works together as well (for example, in an exhibition devoted to one artist) to begin to see fully and understand what the artist is trying to convey. One piece in a mixed show is often – frankly – meaningless, because all that you can hope to notice are the eye-catching or superficial qualities.

What to look for

Starting out as a figurative painter, Wassily Kandinsky was among the first to create a truly abstract art in which colour and form take on an expressive life of their own. He believed that abstract art could be as profound as the greatest figurative painting of the Renaissance. Painted at the height of his creative powers, *Black Frame* encapsulates his theories about the emotional properties of shape, line, and colour. It was painted after Kandinsky settled in Germany for the second time in 1921. He had left his academic posts in Russia disillusioned with the outcome of the Revolution.

KEY EVENTS	
1910	Kandinsky paints his first abstracts
1911	Kandinsky writes the abstract artists' chief treatise *On the Spiritual in Art* and establishes Der Blaue Reiter group
1914	Outbreak of World War I. Several artists are killed in action, including Franz Marc and August Macke
1919	Weimar Republic takes control in Germany. Period of cultural and artistic diversity. Egon Schiele dies in influenza pandemic
1934	Expressionism condemned as "degenerate art" by Nazi party

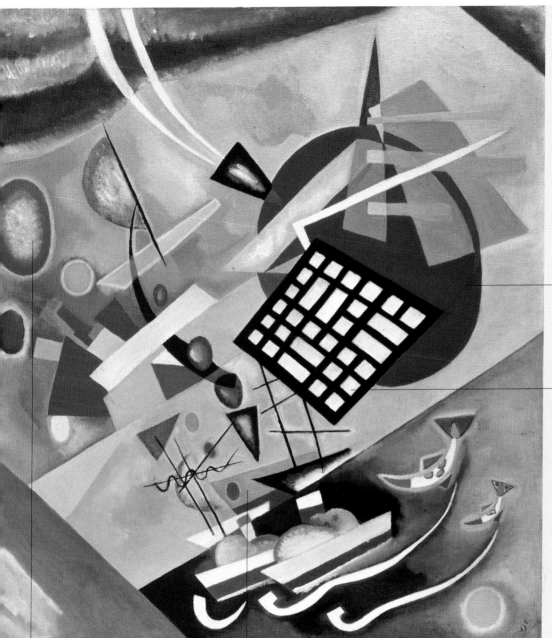

◀ ***Black Frame***
Wassily Kandinsky, 1922, oil on canvas, Paris: Musée National d'Art Moderne. Painted just after Kandinsky began teaching at the Bauhaus. This painting should not be analysed intellectually but allowed to reach those parts of the brain that respond to music.

The artist contrasts curved lines, which are "mature", with angular lines, which are "youthful"

For Kandinsky, horizontal lines were "cold and flat" and verticals were "warm and high"; acute angles were "warm, sharp, and active" and right angles were "cold and controlled"

Red was described as giving "the impression of a strong drum beat", whereas green was "the attenuated sounds of a violin"

According to Kandinsky's theories, yellow possesses a capacity to "attain heights unbearable to the eye and the spirit"

❯❯ TECHNIQUES

Works such as this were planned and executed with the utmost care and precision by Kandinsky. Colours, angles, and the places where lines touched and planes overlapped had to be absolutely exact.

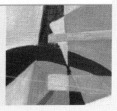

Edvard **Munch**

● 1863–1944 NORWEGIAN ✍ OILS; PRINTS; WOODCUTS

Munch is the best-known Scandinavian painter, and a forerunner of Expressionism. His early life was tortured by sickness, death, insanity, rejection, unhappy love affairs, and guilt – a textbook case for Freud.

Observe the way Munch worked through his neuroses in his paintings. The best, most intense, works were made before his nervous breakdown in 1908. They are full of recognizable (almost clichéd) images of isolation, rejection, sexuality, and death, but he had a rare ability to portray such intimate emotions in a universal way, so that we can recognize and even come to terms with our own inner fears, as well as being able to touch his. He made anxiety beautiful.

The sketchy, unfinished style, using scrubby paint (with scratch marks from the handle of the brush), alongside simple and balanced compositions reveals much of his inner uncertainty and search for peace and stability. Look for intense colour combinations, strange flesh colours, an obsessive interest in eyes and eye sockets, and phallic symbols. His woodcuts, which exploit the grain of the wood, are some of the most accomplished things he did.

Much like van Gogh, by whom he was deeply influenced, Munch devised a startling visual language to give expression to the neuroses that dogged his life: despair, rejection, and loneliness. The primal quality of *The Scream* – Munch painted two versions – conveys this profound sense of alienation and nightmare with shocking directness.

KEY WORKS: *The Sick Child*, 1885–86 (Oslo: National Gallery); *Starry Night*, 1893 (Los Angeles: J. Paul Getty Museum)

Lurid reds, greens, and yellows fill the sky, their unnaturalness a striking metaphor for the central figure's despair

The strong, unsettling diagonal of the bridge and rail contrast with the opposing diagonal of the water. The horizon is relatively high and strongly emphasized. The principal figure is placed firmly in the centre of the picture

Staring, hollow eyes on a skull-like face are a recurring feature of Munch's deeply disturbed figures

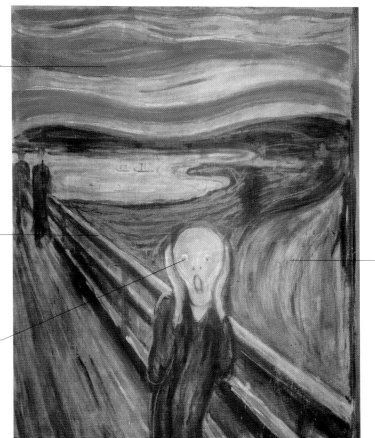

The Scream *1893, 91 x 73 cm (35 x 29 in), oil, tempera, and pastel on cardboard, Oslo: National Gallery.* One of the world's most recognizable paintings, it was a part of Munch's *The Frieze of Life*, "a poem about life, love, and death". The project occupied him for much of his life: an attempt to find pictorial means to represent inner turmoil and angst.

A near formless landscape suggests a world dissolving into chaos. Like the vivid sky, these patterns prefigure fully abstract painting

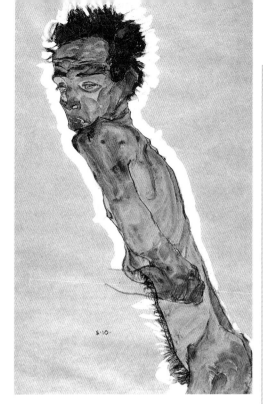

⌃ **Self-Portrait Nude** *Egon Schiele, 1910, 110 x 35.5 cm (43 x 14 ½ in), oil on canvas, Vienna: Graphische Sammlung Albertina.* Schiele often isolated his figures against a plain background – like specimens on a dissecting table.

Egon **Schiele**

⬤ 1890–1918 🏛 AUSTRIAN ✍ OILS;
WATERCOLOURS; DRAWINGS

Schiele was an intense, tragic, short-lived genius whose art expressed his own self-destructive personality and the claustrophobic introspection of Sigmund Freud's Vienna. He died, together with his pregnant young wife, in the great flu epidemic of 1918.

His art concentrates on sexually intense subjects, including portraits, self-portraits, and (at end of his life) religious works. Look for isolated, single figures, often shown in silhouette; couples or groups of figures in highly charged relationships; bodies in contorted positions; gaunt faces lost in inner thoughts; cityscapes in Art-Nouveau style. A precocious, gifted draughtsman, Schiele also made many drawings and watercolours. His paintings have a tense, nervous, probing outline, rapidly filled with colour, which gives them a strong sense of immediacy and urgency.

His work can still extract a genuine gasp, if not the shock or horror of 100 years ago. It attracted fierce opposition from conservative society, and he was arrested and imprisoned on the charge of immorality. He was, however, recognized and successful in advanced circles. He saw the human figure or spirit as an animal rather than a moral being. Schiele insisted on absolute freedom for creative individuality and self-determination.

KEY WORKS: *Mourning Woman*, 1912 (New York: Museum of Modern Art); *Houses on the River*, 1914 (The Old Town) (Madrid: Museo Thyssen-Bornemisza)

Emil **Nolde**

⬤ 1867–1956 🏛 GERMAN ✍ OILS;
WATERCOLOURS; PRINTS; ENGRAVINGS

A pioneering Expressionist and member of Die Brücke, Nolde's art hides a unique radical-regressive complexity. He was very interested in non-European "primitive" art, but believed in racial purity and the concept of a master race.

This was Expressionism done with flair, manifesting its strengths (spontaneity, passion, visual challenge) and its weaknesses (too strident, soon ran out of steam). A creator of landscapes, seascapes (his best work), and figure painting, he used bright, clashing colours and thick paint, resulting in simplification and a conscious crudeness. He had an instinct for colour; this is most apparent when his work is seen from a distance. He was a prolific watercolourist (1941–45).

His early work was on the cutting edge of the avant-garde, but he never developed – he was painting the same work in 1940 as in 1910 (but only Beckmann was able to sustain such original levels of Expressionist creativity and freshness after the age of 40). He was a fully paid-up Nazi and never understood why the regime rejected his art – perhaps he was a curious case of arrested development, artistically and politically?

KEY WORKS: *Young Black Horses*, 1916 (Dortmund: Museum am Ostwall); *Orchids*, 1925 (Private Collection)

⬇ **The Dancers** *Emil Nolde, 1920, oil on canvas, Stuttgart: Staatsgalerie.* Nolde had been much influenced by a visit to New Guinea in 1913, saying "Everything which is primeval and elementary captures my imagination."

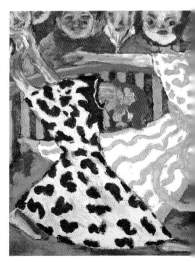

>> **DIE BRÜCKE** 1910–13

Die Brücke was an important avant-garde group of German Expressionists based in Dresden, founded by Kirchner, Schmidt-Rottluff, Heckel, and Fritz Bleyl. They expressed radical political and social views through modern, urban subject matter or landscapes and figures. Later associated artists included Nolde, Pechstein, and Van Dongen. They were influenced by the latest Parisian ideas and primitive non-European art. Look for bright colours, bold outlines, and deliberately unsophisticated techniques (most of the group were without proper training). They were influential in the revival of the woodcut as an expressive medium.

☑ *Berlin Street Scene*
Ernst Ludwig Kirchner, 1913, 121 x 95 cm (47 ⅓ x 37 ½ in), oil on canvas, Berlin: Brücke Museum. Kirchner moved to Berlin in 1911 and became fascinated by the edginess of street life.

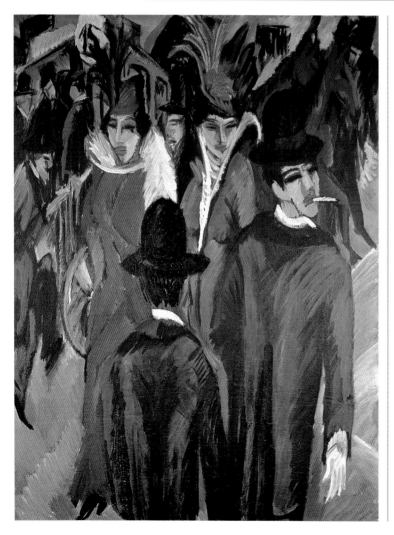

Otto **Müller**

● 1874–1930 🏳 GERMAN ✍ PRINTS; OILS

Müller was an important but short-lived contributor to the German avant-garde, from 1910 to 1913 (Die Brücke) . He produced powerful images of nudes in landscape with "primitive", rough texture, bold outline and colour, deriving from Matisse and the Cubists. He painted gypsy subjects after 1920.

KEY WORKS: *Two Bathers*, c.1920 (Washington DC: National Gallery of Art); *Adam and Eve*, 1920–22 (San Francisco: Fine Arts Museums)

Ernst Ludwig **Kirchner**

● 1880–1938 🏳 GERMAN ✍ PRINTS; OILS; SCULPTURE

Kirchner was a key member of Die Brücke. Sensitive, prone to mental and physical breakdown after terrible war experiences, he expressed the schizophrenic mood of his times in a highly charged, tense, Expressionist style. Kirchner had a sketchy, wiry technique, making use of heightened, intensified colour. He committed suicide.

KEY WORKS: *Artillerymen*, 1915 (New York: Guggenheim Museum); *Self-Portrait as a Soldier*, 1915 (Oberlin, Ohio: Allen Memorial Art Museum)

Max **Pechstein**

● 1881–1955 🏳 GERMAN ✍ PRINTS; OILS; ENGRAVINGS

A leading member of Die Brücke, Pechstein was a painter and engraver who also designed decorative projects and stained glass. Called "the Giotto of our time", he had a characteristic flat style, using pure, unmixed colours and lyrical subjects of figures, nudes, and animals in landscape. He was influenced by Matisse and Oceanic art. His commercial success alienated his fellow avant-garde artists.

KEY WORKS: *Nelly*, 1910 (San Francisco: Museum of Modern Art); *Seated Nude*, 1910 (Berlin: Staatliche Museum)

Erich **Heckel**

◗ 1883-1970 🏳 GERMAN ✍ PRINTS; ENGRAVINGS

Heckel was a leading German Expressionist (a Die Brücke member). He was untrained, but painted powerful, pessimistic images of nudes, portraits, sickness, and anguish with a corresponding fierce and angular style, using strident colours. His landscapes are more decorative.

KEY WORKS: *The Village Pond*, 1910 (Hannover: Sprengel Museum); *Two Men at Table*, 1912 (Hamburg: Hamburger Kunsthalle)

Karl **Schmidt-Rottluff**

◗ 1884-1976 🏳 GERMAN ✍ OILS; PRINTS; WOODCUTS; SCULPTURES

A leading German Expressionist and member of Die Brücke, Schmidt-Rottluff was noted for his instinctive, forceful, angular, monumental style, which used consciously harsh colour and aggressive simplification. His later style (after 1945) was softer and more fluid, but still involved intense colour. He made powerful woodcuts and lithographs. He was reviled by the Nazis.

KEY WORKS: *Gap in the Dyke*, 1910 (Berlin: Brücke Museum); *Red Tower in the Park*, 1910 (Frankfurt: Städel Museum)

Wassily **Kandinsky**

◗ 1866-1944 🏳 RUSSIAN ✍ OILS; PRINTS

Kandinsky was one of the pioneers of the Modern Movement and reputedly the painter of the first abstract picture. He lived in Germany from 1896 to 1914 and from 1921 to 1933, and taught at the Bauhaus in the 1920s.

He worked slowly from increasingly simplified figurative work through to sketchy abstracts and then hard-edged abstract. He had a complex, multifaceted personality. Kandinsky cultivated an intellectual rather than instinctive approach to art, backed up by much theoretical writing, but at the same time he had a strong physical

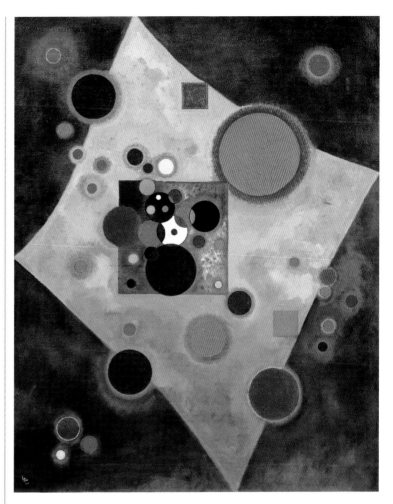

sensitivity to colour, which he could hear as well as see (a phenomenon known as synaesthesia, or union of the senses).

Stand close to the paintings, let them fill your field of vision, then try to relax the eye and the mind so the colour and shapes reach that part of the brain that responds to music – don't analyse them, but float into them and let yourself go. If you have never looked at a picture this way before, it can be a strange, exhilarating, spiritual experience, but it will need time and patience.

KEY WORKS: *St George I*, 1911 (St Petersburg: Hermitage Museum); *Improvisation 31 (Sea Battle)*, 1913 (Washington DC: National Gallery of Art); *Several Circles*, 1926 (New York: Guggenheim Museum)

⌃ *Accent in Pink* Wassily Kandinsky, 1926, 100 x 80 cm (39 ¼ x 31 ½ in), oil on canvas, Paris: Musée National d'Art Moderne. Painted in the same year that the Bauhaus published his major treatise *Point and Line to Plane*.

›› DER BLAUE REITER 1911–14

An important, loosely grouped association of avant-garde German Expressionists, Der Blaue Reiter was based in Munich. Kandinsky and Marc were the key members, but the group included Klee, Macke, and Münter. Their name, meaning "The Blue Rider", came from the Kandinsky painting used on the cover of their *Almanac*. They wanted to put spiritual values into art and used abstraction, simplification, and the power of colour as a means of doing this.

›› **The *Almanac* of 1912** included articles and illustrations by Der Blaue Reiter artists and the composer Arnold Schoenberg, and even a play by Kandinsky.

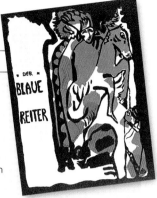

Gabriele **Münter**

● 1877–1962 ⚑ GERMAN ✍ OILS

Strongly influenced by Fauvism, Münter was a leader of Der Blaue Reiter, and Kandinsky's partner and mistress from 1903 until 1914. During this time she painted bold, expressive, original, and colourful still lifes and landscapes. She broke for good from Kandinsky in 1917 and ceased to paint.

KEY WORKS: *Interior*, 1908 (New York: Museum of Modern Art); *Future (Woman in Stockholm)*, 1917 (Ohio: Cleveland Museum of Art)

Franz **Marc**

● 1880–1916 ⚑ GERMAN ✍ OILS

Son of a Munich painter, Marc was a key member of Der Blaue Reiter group. He was the author of richly sourced, very personal art, which explores a vision of a unified world in which animals and the rest of nature exist in perfect harmony. He combined progressive French Cubist structure; Matisse-like expressive colour; Kandinsky's spiritualism; and old-fashioned, German Romantic notions of nature. By 1914, his work had become more abstract. He was killed at Verdun.

KEY WORKS: *The Tiger*, 1912 (Munich: Städtische Galerie im lenbachhaus); *Animals*, 1913 (Moscow: Pushkin Museum); *The Mandrill*, 1913 (Munich: Sammlung Moderne Kunst)

August **Macke**

● 1887–1914 ⚑ GERMAN ✍ OILS; WATERCOLOURS

A leading German Expressionist of Der Blaue Reiter group, Macke was the most French in outlook and expression with a joyful, rather than anguished, agenda. He made lyrical use of clear, vibrant colour, and figurative subject matter. A possibly great talent, he died, aged 27, in the first German offensive in World War I.

KEY WORKS: *Garden on Lake Thun*, 1913 (Munich: Städtische Galerie im Lenbachhaus); *Woman in a Green Jacket*, 1913 (Cologne: Museum Ludwig)

James **Ensor**

● 1860–1949 ⚑ BELGIAN ✍ OILS; ENGRAVINGS

A talented loner, Ensor is remembered for his eccentric, brightly coloured, nervously painted, and macabre imagery (skulls, skeletons, self-portraits, suffering Christ), much of it derived from childhood memories of objects in his parents' souvenir shop. His best work was made between 1885 and 1891 (he tended to repeat himself after that). He received belated recognition for his high-quality drawings and engravings, as well as his paintings.

KEY WORKS: *Still Life with Ray*, 1892 (Bruges: Musées Royaux des Beaux-Arts); *Still Life with Sea Shells*, 1923 (Boston: Museum of Fine Arts)

›› *Christ's Triumphant Entry into Brussels* James Ensor, 1888, 258 x 431 cm (101 ¾ x 169 ⅔ in), oil on canvas, Los Angeles: J. Paul Getty Museum. An early masterpiece motivated more by a belief in the future triumph of socialism than in Christian religion.

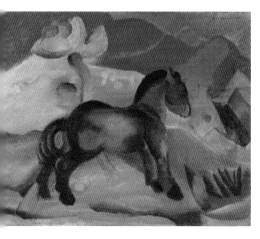

⬙ *Little Blue Horse* Franz Marc, 1912, 58 x 73 cm (22 ¾ x 28 ¾ in), oil on canvas, Saarbrücken (Germany): Saarland Museum. Marc thought that animals had an inherent innocence that gave them access to greater truths than humans, and that their fate paralleled the apocalyptic future to be visited on mankind.

Käthe **Kollwitz**

◔ 1867–1945 🏴 GERMAN ✑ PRINTS; SCULPTURE; WOODCUTS; WATERCOLOURS; ENGRAVINGS

Kollwitz became one of the great printmakers (especially of black-and-white woodcuts), and was also a sculptor. She placed great emphasis on strength of emotion, and of the human body (she saw it as monumental), and gave importance to expressive hands and faces.

   She chose personal themes – mother and child, her son's death in World War I, self-portraits. Politically committed and a social reformer (but never revolutionary), she was much honoured (except by the Nazis).

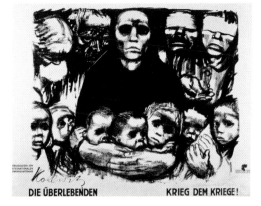

⬢ **The Survivors; War against War; Anti-War Day 21 September 1924** *Käthe Kollwitz, 1924, print, Florida: Holocaust Museum. The poster was published by the International Federation of Trade Unions, Amsterdam.*

KEY WORKS: *Weavers' Revolt Series*, 1895–98 (Berlin: Käthe-Kollwitz-Museum); *Peasants' War Series*, 1902–08 (Berlin: Käthe-Kollwitz-Museum); *The Widow I, the Mothers, and the Volunteers*, 1922–24 (New York: Museum of Modern Art)

Oskar **Kokoschka**

◔ 1867–1945 🏴 GERMAN ✑ OILS; PRINTS; WATERCOLOURS

Kokoschka was from the same generation as Sigmund Freud, and was also from Vienna. He was best known for his powerful Expressionist portraits and self-portraits, very freely painted and rich in colour. He also painted landscapes and townscapes. He responded best to strong, famous faces and views. Kokoschka was a deep-thinking and deep-feeling humanist.

KEY WORKS: *Bride of the Wind*, 1914 (Basel, Switzerland: Kunstmuseum); *Jerusalem*, 1929–30 (Detroit Institute of Arts)

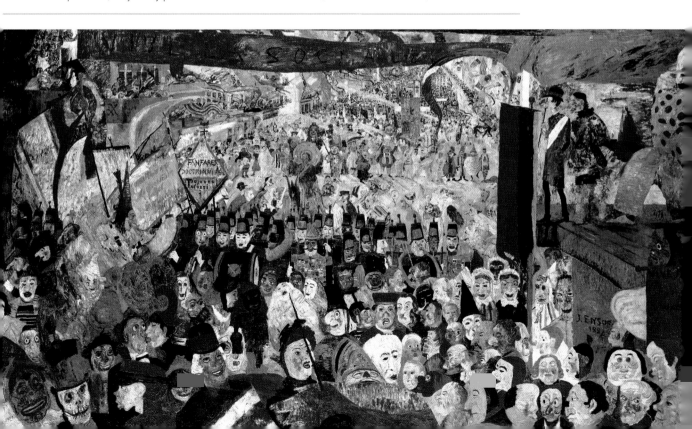

Pablo **Picasso**

● 1881–1973 📖 SPANISH ✍ OILS; SCULPTURE

Picasso was the undisputed master and chief innovator of the Modern movement. You have to go back to Michelangelo to find anyone of equal genius or stature. He was convivial and energetic, and led a turbulent, intense, and often unhappy personal life (his many love affairs are legendary). His output was vast; he was equally inventive as painter, sculptor, printmaker, ceramicist, and theatre designer.

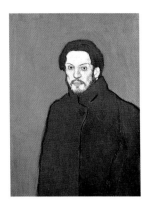

⬆ *Self-Portrait*, 1901, 81 x 60 cm (40 x 23¾ in), oil on canvas, Paris: Musée National Picasso. The starving artist aged 20, painted in Paris during his "Blue Period".

Born into an artistic family in Barcelona, Picasso's prodigious talent showed itself early. He visited Paris for the first time in 1909, and he divided his early years between France and Spain, developing his "Blue Period", with its themes of death and deprivation. Then, in 1904, he settled permanently in France, evolving his "Rose Period", with images of the circus and harlequins. By 1907 he was the champion of the avant-garde and the pioneer of Cubism (see page 288). Although deeply committed to Spain, its art, and its people, Picasso effectively lived in voluntary exile, based in Paris, where he became the focus for the emerging School of Paris, and latterly in the south of France. Passionately opposed to Franco's nationalist political regime, which he attacked in his art, he vowed never to set foot in his land of birth while Franco lived. The dictator outlived him by 32 months.

Paintings

His paintings display a bewildering range of technical and stylistic originality: he was the master of Classicism, Symbolism, and Expressionism; the inventor of Cubism, and an anticipator of Surrealism. However, pure abstraction never interested him. Central to his art was a wide-ranging post-Freudian response to the human figure and the human condition – with frequent intimate references to sex and death, sometimes blissful, sometimes anguished. All his work was highly egocentric in some way, but he had the rare ability to turn self-comment into universal truths.

Out of many themes, two invite immediate exploration: the almost daily autobiography from ambitious half-starved young hopeful, to husband and womanizer, to sexually frustrated old man; and the ease with which he switched styles, images, and techniques, always conscious of which was the most appropriate for his subject matter and mood.

Sculpture

There is a tendency to judge Picasso by his paintings whereas his true forte was for works in 3-D. These became more numerous and interesting as he grew older (while the quality of his paintings declined after 1939). Here, too, he was the master of traditional techniques and a dazzling innovator through welding, constructions, and ceramics. In fact, many two-dimensional works are simply ideas that itch to be realized in 3-D.

KEY WORKS: *Child with a Dove*, 1901 (London: National Gallery); *Family of Saltimbanques*, 1905 (Washington DC: National Gallery of Art); *The Lovers*, 1923 (Washington DC: National Gallery of Art); *Guernica*, 1937 (Madrid: Museo Nacional Centro de Arte Reina Sofía)

⮞ *Weeping Woman* 1937, 55 x 46 cm (21 ⅔ x 18 in), oil on canvas, Melbourne: National Gallery of Victoria. Showing typical Cubist distortion, the model for this depiction of grief is said to be Picasso's mistress, Dora Maar. The picture was used as a study for *Guernica* (1937), painted in response to the German bombing of that Spanish city in 1937.

⊠ *Les Demoiselles d'Avignon*, *1907,*
244 x 233 cm (96 x 92 in), oil on canvas,
*New York: Museum of Modern Art.*This
celebrated painting is now hailed as
one of the most momentous paintings
in the history of art. Yet, for 30 years,
it was known only to a handful of
Picasso's friends and was hardly
ever seen in public until purchased
by MoMA, New York in 1938.

Archaic Spanish
(Iberian) sculpture
influenced these
faces. In March
1907, Picasso
acquired two
such pieces

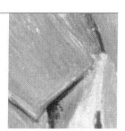
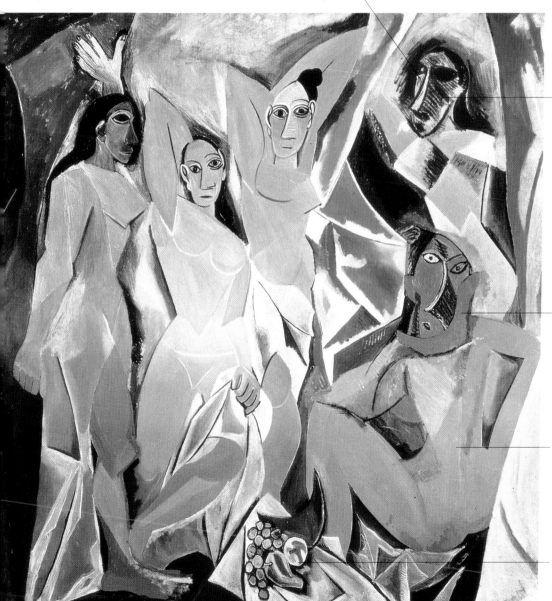

These faces were
repainted after
Picasso had a
"revelation" about
African sculpture
at the Ethnographic
Museum, Paris
in 1907

This figure begins
to explore what
became a hallmark
of Cubism: different
viewpoints and
profiles in a
single figure

Picasso believed
that art could have
a redemptive power.
Here the target is
prostitution and
sexual disease

Picasso would later
turn this type of
still-life imagery
into small, brightly
painted sculptures

Cubism

1907–1918

Cubism was the most significant art and design innovation of the 20th century, similar in effect and consequence to the invention of the internal combustion engine, manned flight, and wireless communications – all of them developed at about the same time. The principles of Cubism were worked out from 1907 to 1914.

The movement's inventors were Picasso and Braque. Their early Cubist works were all small-scale, with conventional subjects such as still life, landscape, and the human figure. The great innovation was the use of fragmented and chopped-up forms, creating an effect like a jigsaw that has been put together with the pieces wrongly joined. The works of 1910–11 are given the label "Analytical Cubism", and used monochromatic paint on canvas. In the works after 1912, the artists also stuck on the contents of wastepaper baskets – this development is known as "Synthetic Cubism".

Principles

Cubism rewrote the rules and expectations as to how paintings and sculpture could be made. Paintings were no longer like a window, but a forum where almost anything might happen. Sculpture was to be open and transparent rather than a solid object. Any sort of material, however humble or everyday, could be used to make art. In the eyes of the Cubists, art was to be about cumulative experience rather than mere observation.

KEY EVENTS	
1907	Picasso's *Les Desmoiselles d'Avignon* (see p.287) introduces the principle of collapsing form and figure distortion
1909	Braque and Picasso work closely as a team to create the first "Analytical Cubist" works
1911	Picasso's *The Guitar* is first sculpture made by constructing parts rather than reducing
1913	Birth of collage and *papiers collés* as "Synthetic Cubism" evolves
1918	Cubism's effects influence Italian and Russian Futurist/Orphic movements

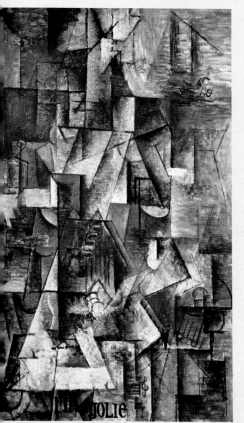

⌃ *Woman with a Guitar (Ma Jolie)* Pablo Picasso, 1911, 100 x 65 cm (39 ⅓ x 25 ¾ in), oil on canvas, New York: Museum of Modern Art. The woman in the title is Picasso's mistress Eva Gouel, who died in 1915 at the age of 30.

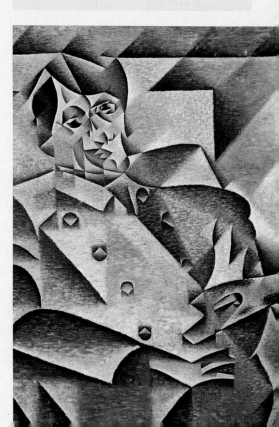

⏵ *Portrait of Pablo Picasso* Juan Gris, 1912, 93 x 74 cm (36 ¾ x 29 ¼ in), oil on canvas, Art Institute of Chicago. Gris wished to acknowledge Picasso as the father of the new artistic era.

Georges **Braque**

⬤ 1882–1963 ᴾᵁ FRENCH ✍ OILS;
MIXED MEDIA

Braque was one of the most innovative and majestic painters of the 20th century. He built on the example of Paul Cézanne and the 18th century to lift decorative painting (especially still life) to new heights.

One of the key early leaders of the avant-garde, he produced important Fauve paintings, and then invented Cubism with Picasso. His later work concentrates on still life, the human figure, and studio interiors. Enjoy the way he develops the visual language of Cubism, and his unerring instinct for colour, texture, and paint. This is work that delights the eye, in the way romantic music delights the ear, and touches the heart rather than the intellect.

Cubist innovations included the use of letters, *papiers collés*, sand mixed with paint, and trompe-l'oeil wood graining. Braque used rich, earthy colours and images built up layer by layer. His works show a wonderful sense of controlled freedom as he moves images and details around to create lyrical harmonies of colour, line, and shape (he loved music and you can sense it going through his head as he paints). His late work is famous for the bird image as a simple symbol of human spiritual aspiration.

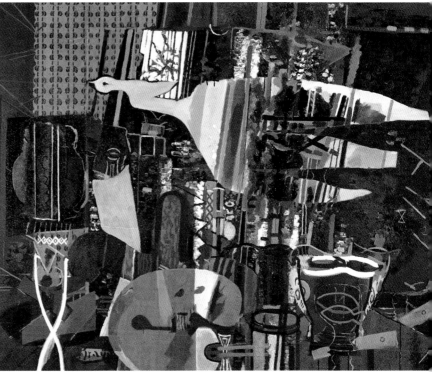

KEY WORKS: *Landscape near Antwerp*, 1906 (New York: Guggenheim Museum); *Café-Bar*, 1919 (Basel, Switzerland: Kunstmuseum); *Le Guéridon*, 1921–22 (New York: Metropolitan Museum of Art); *Still Life: Le Jour*, 1929 (Washington DC: National Gallery of Art)

⬆ *Studio V* Georges Braque, 1949, 145 x 175 cm (57 x 68 ¾ in), oil on canvas, private collection. In later life, he rarely left the intimacy of his studio for subject matter, transforming everyday objects, such as guitars, table tops, and fruit bowls into masterpieces of colour and form.

Juan **Gris**

⬤ 1887–1927 ᴾᵁ SPANISH ✍ OILS; SCULPTURE;
COLLAGE

Gris was third in the hierarchy of the inventors of Cubism (after Picasso and Braque), concentrating mainly on still life.

He moved to Paris from Spain in 1906, and in his formative years was a satirical cartoonist. In 1911, he turned to avant-garde painting as a serious pursuit.

He achieved a masterly reinterpretation of traditional still life. Stand back and see how his meticulously crafted, stylish, highly decorative pictures look like expensive jewellery; they are often (and very effectively) shown in elaborate frames like mounts for brooches. Stand close to them and play the Cubist game of piecing together the final image from the fragmented images and clues.

He often used a dark palette to great effect, especially blacks and blues. His works have complex geometric designs and grids, with the images slipping in and out of the different planes, and playful use of lettering and speckled patterns. His brilliant and inventive *papiers collés* get better as they get older, browner, and more antique. Are they somehow reminiscent of French 18th-century marquetry furniture and its fine craftsmanship?

KEY WORKS: *Bottle of Rum and Newspaper*, 1914 (New York: Guggenheim Museum); *Still Life*, 1917 (Minnesota: Minneapolis Institute of Arts)

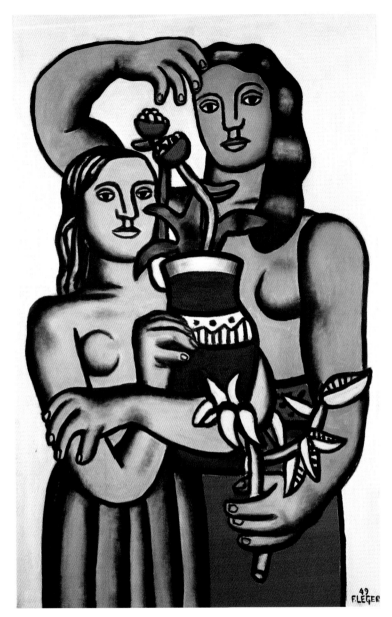

⏫ *Two Women holding a Pot of Flowers* Fernand Léger, c.1920s, oil on canvas, private collection. Léger often painted two women together, exploring their forms and using flowers as symbols of fertility.

Fernand **Léger**

⬭ **1881–1955** 📖 **FRENCH** ✎ **OILS**

Léger was one of the giants of the Modern Movement and an ardent believer in the moral and social function of art and architecture. He was refreshingly cheerful and an extrovert.

His ambition was to create a new democratic art for and about ordinary people. He achieved it through strong, straightforward imagery, style, and technique: the modern, blue-collar worker and his family at work and play, plus the machine-made objects of their world. He shows muscular happiness and spiritual joy in an ideal world where work and play become one (if it can be so for children, why can it not be so for adults?).

Léger was simple but not simplistic. He had a modern, moral message, which was romantic and idealistic but also challenging (a fresh reaffirmation of "man the measure of all things"). He produced simple images and designs that contain sophisticated spatial and colour relationships. He also made beautiful and strong drawings, stage sets, tapestries, murals, films, books, and posters – he believed art should touch and transform all corners of everyday life. He portrayed hands as pieces of machinery. His early Cubist work was pioneering.

KEY WORKS: *The Smokers*, 1911–12 (New York: Guggenheim Museum); *The Wedding*, 1912 (Paris: Musée National d'Art Moderne); *The Mechanic*, 1920 (Ottawa: National Gallery of Canada); *The Two Sisters*, 1935 (Berlin: Staatliche Museum); *The Grand Parade*, 1954 (New York: Guggenheim Museum)

Julio **González**

⬭ **1876–1942** 📖 **SPANISH** ✎ **SCULPTURE; DRAWINGS; OILS**

González was one of the first artists to use iron as a sculptural medium. He was taught by his goldsmith/sculptor father how to use metals, but he spent his early years mainly as a painter.

After meeting Picasso in Barcelona, González moved to Paris where he was reacquainted with his fellow countryman and they struck up a lifelong friendship. Making jewellery and metalwork occupied González up until the 1920s, but at the age of 50 he made a total commitment to sculpture, concentrating specifically on welded metal as a material. Look for semi-abstract works on a grand scale, incorporating Picasso's brutal humour.

KEY WORKS: *Woman with Hair in a Bun*, 1929–34 (Art Institute of Chicago); *Head Called "The Rabbit"*, 1930 (Madrid: Reina Sofía National Museum); *Daphné*, 1937 (Madrid: Reina Sofía National Museum)

Jacques **Lipchitz**

⊖ 1891–1973 〔〕 LITHUANIAN ✑ SCULPTURE

A talented sculptor of Lithuanian origin, Lipchitz settled in Paris in 1909 and emigrated to the US in 1941. He was an early, sensitive, and personal interpreter of Cubism in traditional materials (plaster, stone, terracotta, and bronze) in the 1920s. This led to a more figurative, arabesque style, then to a flirtation with Surrealism and, finally, complex Symbolism. He was always original, if sober and monumental.

KEY WORKS: *Seated Figure*, 1917 (Ottawa: National Gallery of Canada); *Mother and Child*, 1949 (Alabama: Birmingham Museum of Art)

Frank **Kupka**

⊖ 1871–1957 〔〕 FRENCH/CZECH ✑ OILS; DRAWINGS

Kupka was a natural anarchist who settled in Paris at the age of 24 and stayed forever. He was one of the first to create a true abstract art, characterized by solid, geometric blocks of colour. He had the potential to develop as a great pioneer of abstraction, but lacked an underlying philosophical drive and the single-minded dedication to fulfil it – he was distracted by too many ideas.

KEY WORKS: *Vertical and Diagonal Planes*, c.1913–14 (New York: Metropolitan Museum of Art); *The Coloured One*, c.1919–20 (New York: Guggenheim Museum)

Raoul **Dufy**

⊖ 1877–1953 〔〕 FRENCH ✑ OILS; WATERCOLOURS; DRAWINGS

Dufy was a talented painter who in the early days might have made the big time with Braque and Matisse – but he lacked their grit. He is best known for accomplished, colourful, decorative works, much admired by the fashionable beau monde of the 1920s and 30s. Look for free, linear drawing; clear, floating colours; and easy subjects such as horse racing and yachting.

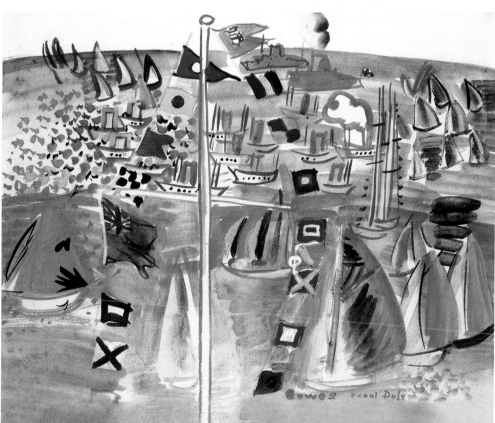

◀ *The Regatta at Cowes*
Raoul Dufy, 1934, 82 x 100 cm (32 ¼ x 39 in), watercolour on paper, private collection.
Dufy was not interested in art theories or questioning the meaning of life. His vivacious art, which included book and stage design, was much praised in the 1930s–1950s.

KEY WORKS: *The Baou de Saint-Jeannet*, 1923 (London: Tate Collection); *Mother and Child*, 1949 (Alabama: Birmingham Museum of Art)

Maurice **Utrillo**

⬤ **1883–1955** 🏴 **FRENCH** ✍ **OILS**

Utrillo was a popular painter known for his unchallenging, crustily painted views of Montmartre, characterized by sharp perspectives and deserted streets. His best work was from c.1908 to 1916. His later work is less gloomy and contains small figures. He had a history of mental instability.

KEY WORKS: *Saint-Denis Canal*, 1906–08 (Tokyo: Bridgestone Museum of Art); *Marizy-Sainte-Geneviève*, c.1910 (Washington DC: National Gallery of Art)

Georges **Rouault**

⬤ **1871–1958** 🏴 **FRENCH** ✍ **OILS; DRAWINGS**

Rouault was an important French painter with a highly individual style. An unhappy loner, he deliberately stood outside the mainstream of Modern art.

He chose losers and the exploited as his subjects, expressing through them his bleak view of life and the activities and rituals used by human beings as they prey on each other in a struggle for survival. He was one of the very few committed Christian artists of the 20th century.

Rouault used faces to convey expression and his dark palette reflected his gloomy subjects. The black outlines and his choice of colours give his paintings the appearance of stained glass and there is an icon-like quality in his figures.

KEY WORKS: *Nude with Raised Arm*, 1906 (St Petersburg: Hermitage Museum); *Christ in the Outskirts*, 1920 (Tokyo: Bridgestone Museum of Art)

Kees van **Dongen**

⬤ **1877–1968** 🏴 **FRENCH** ✍ **OILS**

Van Dongen was Dutch-born but was considered an honorary Frenchman (he settled in Paris in 1897). He is best remembered for the work he produced from 1905 to 1913: they are genuinely original, boldly painted works, in saturated vibrant colours, which made him one of the leading Fauve painters and placed him almost on a par with Matisse. While van Dongen's later work is lively, it is also somewhat repetitive and unimaginative.

KEY WORKS: *The Red Dancer*, 1907 (St Petersburg: Hermitage Museum); *Woman in a Black Hat*, 1908 (St Petersburg: Hermitage Museum)

Robert **Delaunay**

⬤ **1885–1941** 🏴 **FRENCH** ✍ **OILS**

Delaunay was one of the pioneers of modern art. He sought new types of subject matter and made an early breakthrough to abstract painting. He was much supported by his Russian-born wife, Sonia, who produced equally talented art in a similar style, and was also a theatre and textiles designer.

Delaunay's early work takes modern themes such as cities, the Eiffel Tower, manned flight, and football. He used colour in a free and highly inventive way, most famously in his discs, which are abstract, lyrical, full of light and pleasure, and intended to celebrate the emotional and joyful impact of pure colour.

KEY WORKS: *Simultaneous Open Windows*, 1912 (London: Tate Collection); *Homage to Blériot*, 1914 (Basel, Switzerland: Kunstmuseum)

Marc **Chagall**

⬤ **1887–1985** 🏴 **RUSSIAN/FRENCH** ✍ **OILS**

Chagall was a Russian-born Hasidic Jew whose inspiration was his early cultural roots. His unique and personal marriage of subjects, themes, and quirky, personal style perpetuate an enduring air of childlike innocence and wonder. He was very prolific – producing paintings, prints, ceramics, stained glass, murals – which inevitably led to uneven quality. His best paintings were his early works; his worst late work is sugary, sentimental, and slight (but has never lost its popularity). Chagall concentrated on major stained-glass projects after 1950. Do the odd floating heads and bodies and his combination of simultaneous events in one picture reflect his own strange, peripatetic life and consequent cultural eclecticism?

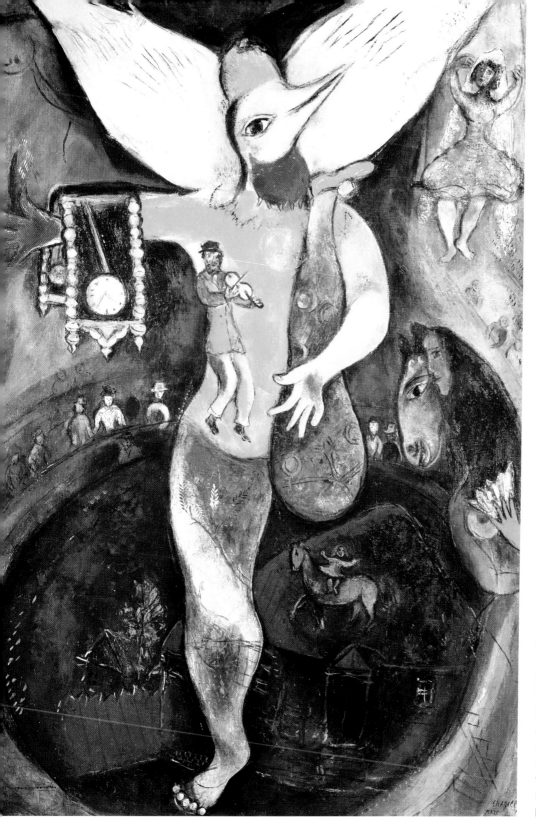

◀◀ *The Juggler* Marc Chagall, 1943, 132 x 100 cm (52 x 39 ⅓ in), oil on canvas, private collection. Chagall settled in France in 1914. His art combines Russian folk art, Cubist fragmentation, and Expressionist colour.

KEY WORKS:
The Fiddler, 1912–13 (Washington DC: National Gallery of Art); *Paris through the Window*, 1913 (New York: Guggenheim Museum); *The Rooster*, 1929 (Madrid: Museo Thyssen-Bornemisza); *War, 1917*, 1964–66 (Zürich: Kunsthaus)

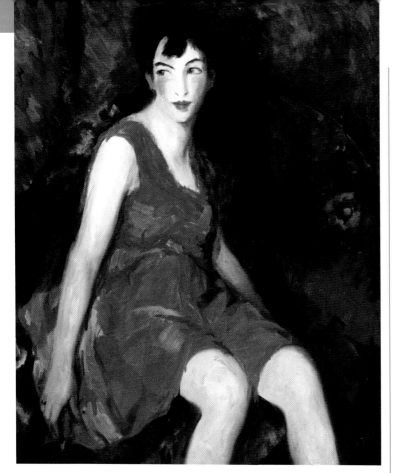

⬆ The Little Dancer
Robert Henri, c.1916–18, 102.8 x 82.5 cm (40 ½ x 32 ½ in), oil on canvas, Youngstown, Ohio: Butler Institute of American Art. Henri produced a number of paintings of dancers – some of unknowns like the model for this portrait, others of stars such as Isadora Duncan.

Robert **Henri**

⬤ 1865–1929 AMERICAN ✎ OILS; DRAWINGS

Henri was a charismatic, hard-drinking, rebellious, and anarchic man, but a great teacher and believer in young people. He chose down-to-earth, urban subjects (note his portraits of "my people" – Irish peasants, Chinese coolies, American Indians) and had a direct, "real" style using dark tonal contrast, limited colour, and liquid brushstrokes.

The leader of the Ashcan School, in 1908 he founded The Eight, who put together the first art exhibition independently curated by artists in the US. Henri links Eakins (he studied at Pennsylvania Academy) and Manet (he was in Paris from 1888 to 1890) – and his students: George Bellows, Stuart Davies, Edward Hopper, Rockwell Kent, Man Ray, and Trotsky (yes, Trotsky), who was in New York in 1917.

KEY WORKS: *The Irish Girl*, c.1910 (Phoenix, Arizona: ASU Art Museum); *Himself*, 1913 (Art Institute of Chicago)

George **Luks**

⬤ 1867–1933 AMERICAN ✎ OILS; WATERCOLOURS; DRAWINGS

A vaudeville comedian, Luks was also pugnacious, a braggart, and hard-drinking. He painted Ashcan School scenes of New York lower-class life, but ignored the reality of poverty and overcrowding, favouring the romance of teeming humanity, male supremacy, and adventure. Note his bravura brushwork. He painted notable watercolours of his native Penn mining country.

KEY WORKS: *Allen Street*, c.1905 (Chattanooga, Tennessee: Hunter Museum of American Art); *The Café Francis*, c.1906 (Youngstown, Ohio: Butler Institute of American Art); *The Bersaglieri*, 1918 (Washington DC: National Gallery of Art)

William James **Glackens**

⬤ 1870–1938 AMERICAN ✎ DRAWINGS; OILS

Philadelphia-born, Glackens studied in Paris and was a protégé of Robert Henri. Initially a newspaper illustrator, he produced attractive and competent images of everyday New York life (interiors and exteriors), overtly derived from Manet and the Ashcan School. His work is popular imagery/illustration aspiring to the level of art.

KEY WORKS: *East River Park*, c.1902 (New York: Brooklyn Museum); *May Day, Central Park*, c.1905 (San Francisco: Fine Arts Museum); *Italo-American Celebration, Washington Square*, c.1912 (Boston: Museum of Fine Arts)

》 **ASHCAN SCHOOL** c.1891–1919

A progressive group of American painters and illustrators, comprising Sloan, Bellows, Glackens, Luks, and Henri. They believed that art should portray the everyday, sometimes harsh, realities of life – especially New York city life – and rejected officially sanctioned art (which they said was "fenced in with tasselled ropes and weighed down with bronze plates"). They generally painted gritty, poor, urban scenes in a spontaneous, unpolished style.

John **Sloan**

● 1871–1951 ⊞ AMERICAN ✍ OILS; DRAWINGS

Sloan was a member of the Ashcan School. He started as an illustrator/cartoonist with socialist sympathies but was opposed to the idea of art as propaganda. He produced New York scenes of the working classes, but modified harsh reality with an ideal of honest, cosy, vaguely erotic, urban happiness. Sloan caught fleeting moments well. After 1914, he worked in Santa Fe, but lost the plot after 1928. He made superb etchings.

KEY WORKS: *Wake of the Ferry*, 1907 (Washington DC: Phillips College); *Austrian-Irish Girl*, c.1920 (Washington DC: Hirshhorn Museum)

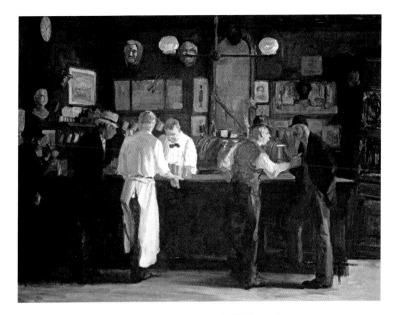

⊠ *McSorley's Bar* John Sloan, 1912, 66 x 81.2 (26 x 32 in), oil on canvas, Detroit Institute of Arts. Sloan was a regular at this then men-only, working-class, Irish tavern in New York. Some of his sketches still decorate the walls today.

George Wesley **Bellows**

● 1882–1925 ⊞ AMERICAN ✍ OILS; PRINTS; DRAWINGS

Bellows was a leading member of the Ashcan School. His best period was pre-1913, when he tackled tough, gritty subjects, such as construction sites (Penn Station), slum dwellers, and boxing matches – depictions of raw energy. His later work is too self-conscious and affected by theories of symmetry and the Golden Section.

KEY WORKS: *Cliff Dwellers*, 1913 (Los Angeles: County Museum of Art); *Mrs T in Cream Silk, No.2*, 1920 (Minnesota: Minneapolis Institute of Arts)

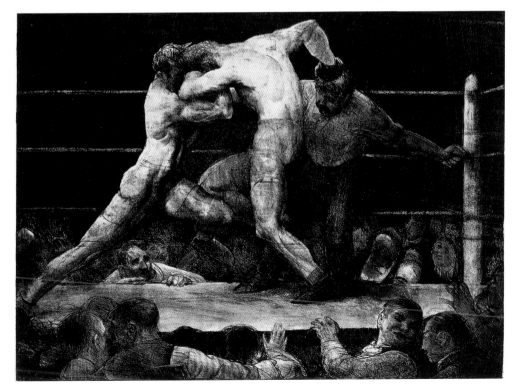

◁ *A Stag at Sharkey's* George Wesley Bellows, painted 1909, 47 x 60.4 cm (18 ½ x 23 ¾ in), lithograph by George Miller (1917), Houston, Texas: Museum of Fine Arts. Bellows's evocation of an illegal boxing match was acclaimed at the time as a landmark of realism.

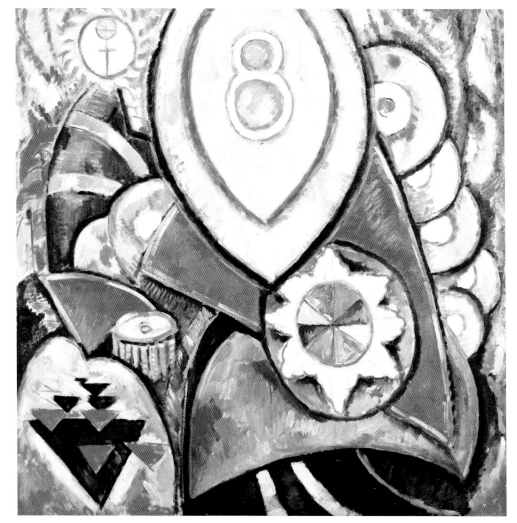

Painting, No.48
*Marsden Hartley,
1913, 119.8 x 119.8 cm
(47 ¼ x 47 ¼ in), oil on
canvas, Brooklyn
Museum of Art, New
York.* This key work
shows the influence of
Delaunay and Kandinsky
in its geometric
arrangements and
colour relationships.

Marsden **Hartley**

● 1877–1943 AMERICAN OILS;
PRINTS; DRAWINGS

Marsden Hartley was the greatest American
artist of the first half of the 20th century:
original and mystical.

His early Impressionist work was followed
by paintings influenced by the German
Expressionists, whom he knew (he met
Kandinsky and Jawlensky in Berlin and Munich
c.1913). He experimented with abstraction. His
"Portrait of a German Officer" series (which
commemorates his male lover) is the major
monument of early American Modernism.
He later produced several important series of
paintings in Provence (France), New Mexico, and
Maine. Hartley used vigorous brushstrokes
and jarring colour contrasts, such as rust and
acid green.

KEY WORKS: *The Aero*, 1914 (Washington DC: National
Gallery of Art); *Mount Katahdin, Maine*, 1942
(Washington DC: National Gallery of Art)

Max **Weber**

● 1881–1961 RUSSIAN/AMERICAN
 WOODCUTS; OILS; CHALKS

Russian-born, Weber was a gifted artist. He studied
with Matisse in Paris in 1905–08 and produced
important Cubist paintings. He was one of the
first Americans to use the modern idiom. Later,

he produced Expressionist work (à la Soutine), drawing on Jewish subjects based on Russian memories. Weber moved easily between established styles, with pleasing results but compromised originality.

KEY WORKS: *Interior of the Fourth Dimension*, 1913 (Washington DC: National Gallery of Art); *Rush Hour,* 1915 (Washington DC: National Gallery of Art)

Patrick Henry **Bruce**

● 1881–1937 American ✎ OILS; DRAWINGS

Bruce was a member of an old Virginia family. An early American Modernist, he visited Paris in 1904 and was influenced by Matisse, Stein, and Delaunay. He produced good semi-abstract still lifes with spare, geometric shapes, primary colours, hot pinks, and thick paint like cake icing. He was unrecognized and his work did not sell. He gave up painting, destroyed his work, and sold antiques; he later committed suicide.

KEY WORKS: *Painting*, 1922–23 (New York: Whitney Museum of American Art); *Still Life: Transverse Beams*, 1928–32 (Washington DC: Hirshhorn Museum)

Stanton **Macdonald-Wright**

● 1890–1973 American ✎ OILS

Macdonald-Wright was an avant-garde American painter. He studied in Los Angeles and went to live in Paris in 1913. He developed Synchronism – an abstract, kaleidoscopic symphony of swirling, fragmented rainbow colours derived from French artists such as Delaunay. He lost the plot on his return to the US.

KEY WORKS: *Dragon Trail*, 1930 (Washington DC: Hirshhorn Museum); *Mural for the Santa Monica Library*, 1934–35 (Washington DC: Smithsonian American Art Museum)

Arthur Garfield **Dove**

● 1880–1946 American ✎ DRAWINGS; OILS; MIXED MEDIA

Dove was a shy, reclusive farmer *manqué*, and a keen sailor. He was the first American artist to paint an abstract picture (1907–09). He produced small-scale lyrical work, derived from a love of land and seascape, full of natural shapes, rhythms, and essences of nature; he also made witty collages and assemblages. He was unappreciated in his lifetime.

KEY WORKS: *Foghorns*, 1929 (Colorado Springs: Fine Arts Center); *Reflections*, 1935 (Indianapolis: Museum of Art)

Burgoyne **Diller**

● 1906–65 American ✎ OILS; SCULPTURE

Diller was one of the most important American abstract artists. He produced 3-D abstract painted reliefs and geometric paintings. He used simple shapes, primary colours on white or black, and understated brushwork. He was much influenced by Mondrian and Dutch De Stijl (see page 316), both as to style and his aspiration for social and spiritual reformation.

KEY WORKS: *Untitled*, 1932 (*Three Men with Hats in City Street*) (Ohio: Cleveland Museum of Art); *Second Theme*, 1949 (New York: Metropolitan Museum of Art)

Stuart **Davis**

● 1894–1964 American ✎ OILS

A leading American Cubist, Davis initially trained in advertising (it shows to his advantage), and studied with Robert Henri (see page 294). From 1924, he developed striking and individual abstract paintings and collages, notable for bright colours and jazzy rhythms. He borrowed motifs from popular culture and is considered a progenitor of Pop Art. He was fascinated by urban scenes and advertising posters.

KEY WORKS: *House and Street*, 1931 (New York: Whitney Museum of American Art); *The Mellow Pad*, 1945–51 (Private Collection)

Constantin **Brancusi**

● 1876–1957 🏴 ROMANIAN/FRENCH ✍ SCULPTURE

Brancusi was a seminal figure in 20th-century art, with a profound influence on sculpture and design. Born into a Romanian peasant family, he settled in Paris in 1904. A student of Rodin, Brancusi remained indifferent to honour and fame.

Brancusi's work shows a tireless refinement and search for purity. He constantly reworked selected themes – children, human heads, birds, and modular columns. He was interested in abstract ideals such as the purity of primordial (simple) forms, but was never an abstract artist – a reference to a recognizable nature is always present. He placed great emphasis on the inherent qualities of materials. He touches something very basic in the human psyche – as soothing as the sound of the waves of the sea.

Endless pleasure can be derived from the contemplation of pure line, simplicity of form (such as an egg shape), light reflecting off surfaces, materials unadorned and unadulterated. Notice the bases that are an integral part of the whole work. His studio became a work of art in its own right because of the way he grouped his work in it to bring out comparisons and reflections of light.

KEY WORKS: *The Kiss*, 1909 (Paris: Montparnasse Cemetery); *Mademoiselle Pogani*, 1920 (Paris: Musée National d'Art Moderne); *Princess X*, 1916 (Paris: Musée National d'Art Moderne); *Maquettes for the Endless Column*, 1937 (Paris: Musée National d'Art Moderne)

When seen in the round, the graceful elongated curve, which is neither symmetrical nor geometrical, suggests soaring movement

Light radiates from the gently undulating surface of the polished bronze like a beam of sunlight

❝ Simplicity is not an end in art but we **arrive at simplicity** in spite of ourselves. ❞

Constantin Brancusi

⧆ *Bird in Space* 1923, bronze, 144 cm (56 ¾ in), Paris: Musée National d'Art Moderne. In 1926, the New York customs officials refused to believe that Brancusi's sculpture was art and imposed the duty appropriate to manufactured metal objects (40 per cent).

From 1900 to 1950, Paris was the centre of artistic innovation, attracting artists, collectors, dealers, and connoisseurs from all over the world. All the major innovations from Cubism to Surrealism originated in Parisian studios, and could be first seen there in avant-garde exhibitions. This diversity of styles, artists, and activity has been labelled loosely as the "Ecole de Paris" (School of Paris).

Chaïm **Soutine**

⬤ 1893–1943 〽 FRENCH ✎ OILS

Soutine was a Lithuanian-born Jew who worked in Paris. Inspired by Rembrandt, he was undisciplined, tragic, and depressive. He was unknown in his own lifetime although he was recognized and supported by a few dedicated collectors.

Look for portraits, landscapes, and flayed carcasses. He had a wide emotional range – from angelic choirboys to dead meat. At a distance, the paintings look controlled and neat, but close up, the churning distortions and paint handling become dominant.

KEY WORKS: *Self-Portrait*, 1916 (St Petersburg: Hermitage Museum); *Landscape at Ceret*, c.1920 (London: Tate Collection); *Side of Beef*, 1925 (Buffalo: Albright-Knox Art Gallery)

Amedeo **Modigliani**

⬤ 1884–1920 〽 ITALIAN ✎ OILS; SCULPTURE

Modigliani was a neurotic, spoilt, tubercular, drug-addicted, woman-beating, poverty-stricken but talented pioneer who achieved a genuine and satisfactory synthesis between the priorities of the Old Masters and those of modern art.

Modigliani created very recognizable portraits, mostly of his artistic friends and mistresses, and splashy nudes, both highly stylized, simplified, painterly, poetic, decorative, and moody. Note the inclined heads with long faces on long necks; elongated noses; almond-shaped eyes with a glazed and faraway stare, which show the influence of his original, gifted, carved stone sculptures and his own study of African and Oceanic art.

He cleverly combined many influences: African art; Art Nouveau; Matisse-like simplification; Cézanne- and Cubist-like fragmentation of space; Picasso-like intensity; and caricature. Would he have gone on to greater things or was he finally burned out? His early death probably saved his reputation.

KEY WORKS: *Head*, c.1911–12 (London: Tate Collection); *Paul Guillaume*, 1916 (Milan: Galleria d'Arte Moderna); *Chaïm Soutine*, 1917 (Washington DC: National Gallery of Art); *Nude on a Blue Cushion*, 1917 (Washington DC: National Gallery of Art)

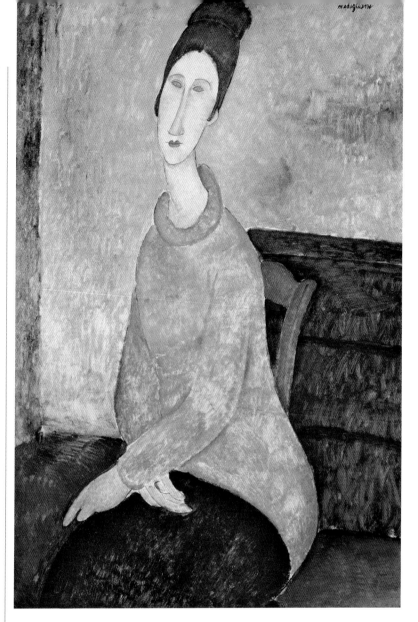

⬙ *Jeanne Hébuterne in a Yellow Jumper*
Amedeo Modigliani, 1918–19, 100 x 65 cm (39 ⅓ x 25 ¾ in), oil on canvas, New York: Guggenheim Museum. Jeanne was the artist's common-law wife and frequent subject.

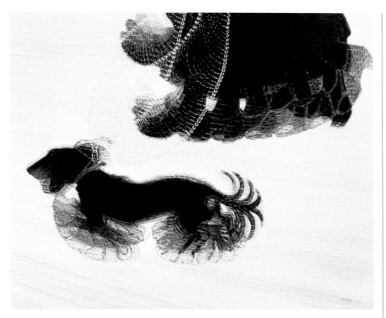

⌃ Dynamism of a Dog on a Lead *Giacomo Balla, 1912, 89 x 109 cm (38 ¾ x 43 ¼ in), oil on canvas, New York: Albright-Knox Art Gallery.* Balla created the illusion of speed in this painting by superimposing several images in layers.

Giacomo **Balla**

⬤ 1871–1958 ⚑ ITALIAN ✍ OILS; SCULPTURE; MIXED MEDIA

Balla was a leading Italian Futurist who had a brief, important, innovative, key period from 1912 to 1916. He was interested in sensations: speed, flight, movement, and light, which he represented by using fragmentation and colour – progressing from Divisionism via Cubism to clean-cut Abstraction. His work declined after 1916 into decorative figuration. He also produced theatre design and poems.

KEY WORKS: *Girl Running on a Balcony*, 1912 (Milan: Civica Galleria d'Arte Moderna); *Mercury Passing in Front of the Sun*, 1914 (Private Collection)

》 FUTURISM 1909–15

Originating in Italy (although it had adherents elsewhere), Futurism was one of the most important early avant-garde art movements, and the only one not to be centred on Paris. Its main figures included Boccioni, Balla, Carrà, Severini, Wyndham Lewis, and Joseph Stella. It was widely influential, with aims set out in a series of manifestoes urging a break with the past. Futurism noisily promoted a worship of machinery, speed, modernity, and revolutionary change, using the latest avant-garde styles such as Cubism.

Umberto **Boccioni**

⬤ 1882–1916 ⚑ ITALIAN ✍ OILS; SCULPTURE

Boccioni was a leading Futurist painter and sculptor who embraced the verve of modern life and enjoyed conflict. He joined a World War I bicycle brigade, but died falling from a horse at the age of 34.

His work was pioneering in subject and style. He was interested in highly charged modern subjects, such as dynamic, collective experience (crowds and riots); movement and speed; memories and states of mind shown as continuous time; emotions and experiences beyond the incidental trivia of time and place. He was innovative in adopting French Cubist interlocking planes and fragmentation, then adding colour as a means of representing his ambitious subjects.

His work is always on a small scale and not always successful – Boccioni's ambitions often outran his technical abilities and the means at his disposal. Ditto for his sculptures, of which only four remain. He is to later artists what Blériot's flying machine is to jet aircraft.

KEY WORKS: *Street Noises Invade the House*, 1911 (Hanover: Niedersächsische Landesmuseum); *Dynamism of a Cyclist*, 1913 (Milan: Collection Gianni Mattioli); *Dynamism of a Man's Head*, 1914 (Milan: Civico Museo d'Arte Contemporanea); *The Charge of the Lancers*, 1915 (Milan: Ricardo Jucker Collection)

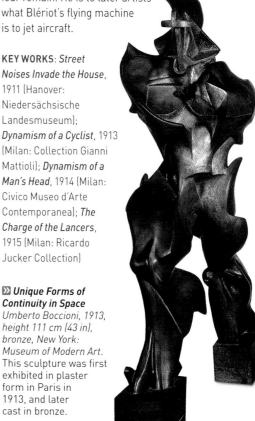

》 Unique Forms of Continuity in Space *Umberto Boccioni, 1913, height 111 cm (43 in), bronze, New York: Museum of Modern Art.* This sculpture was first exhibited in plaster form in Paris in 1913, and later cast in bronze.

Carlo **Carrà**

● 1881–1966 ⚑ ITALIAN ✎ OILS

Carrà was a prominent Futurist painter and later a leading figure in the Metaphysical movement. His early works combined Futurism's dynamism with a Cubist feel for structure. Under Chirico's influence he turned to Metaphysical painting, but later rejected the avant-garde and advocated a return to a more naturalistic type of art. Carrà was also an influential critic and a writer on art.

KEY WORKS: *Horsemen of the Apocalypse*, 1908 (Art Institute of Chicago); *The Funeral of the Anarchist Galli*, 1911 (New York: Museum of Modern Art)

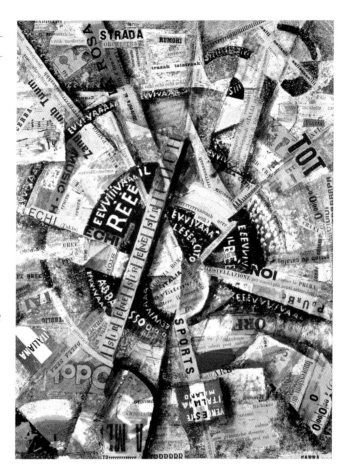

» *Interventionist Demonstration*
Carlo Carrà, 1914, 38.5 x 30 cm (15 ¼ x 11 ½ in), collage, Venice: Peggy Guggenheim Collection. The spiralling collage was inspired by a plane dropping leaflets onto the Piazza del Duomo, Milan.

Gino **Severini**

● 1883–1966 ⚑ ITALIAN ✎ OILS; GOUACHE; DRAWINGS

Severini was one of the creators of Futurism. He was a painter, stage designer, writer, and intellectual. He lived long and was adaptable.

His early work was dull, until he discovered Impressionism (in Paris, 1906). His most significant works are his Futurist paintings, 1911–16, which have dynamic subjects, such as trains, buses, city streets, dancers, and war machinery – all of them animated by Cubist fragmentation and strong colours. After 1916 his paintings become less dynamic and more formally pure, with precise adherence to geometric rules. In the 1920s he made mural decorations (especially mosaics in churches); and in the 1930s, grand Fascist monuments.

Severini's work is of uneven quality – the Futurist paintings can be very good, or else very formulaic and trite. His later work is hardly known outside Italy. Like other bright sparks of the early avant-garde (such as Derain), he had only a brief period of real significance. Does a lasting reputation require longevity and large output more than talent? Fascist Italy (unlike its equivalent in Germany or Russia) produced some very fine architecture and public art. Why? And does evil political patronage irrevocably taint the art?

KEY WORKS: *Dynamic Rhythm of a Head in a Bus*, 1912 (Washington DC: Hirshhorn Museum); *Red Cross Train Passing a Village*, 1915 (New York: Guggenheim Museum); *Suburban Train Arriving in Paris*, 1915 (London: Tate Collection); *Still Life with Fish*, 1958 (San Francisco: Fine Arts Museums)

(Percy) Wyndham **Lewis**

⬤ 1882–1957 ◫ **BRITISH** ✎ **OILS; DRAWINGS; MIXED MEDIA**

Lewis was a painter, writer, and journalist. He was an angry young man who, along with his fellow Vorticists, brought Modern art to Britain. He later became a right-wing misfit and an admirer of Fascism.

His work is always angular and awkward, rather like the artist himself. His powerful and original early work was among the first abstract art in Europe. He was also the author of very strong drawings and paintings of World War I battlefields (he was an official war artist). His later portraits were interesting.

Note his skilled, spikey draughtsmanship and his personal and innovative use of Cubist and Futurist styles and ideas. He makes inventive, creative use of faceted space and figures to explore the concept of the man-cum-machine. He was happier with words than images.

KEY WORKS: *Praxitella*, c.1921 (Leeds: City Art Gallery); *The Mud Clinic*, 1937 (New Brunswick, Canada: Beaverbrook Art Gallery)

⬙ A Battery Shelled
(Percy) Wyndham Lewis, 1919, 182.8 x 317.8 cm (72 x 125 in), oil on canvas, London: Imperial War Museum. Lewis was one of several young professional artists employed by the government to record their experience of the battlefront.

❯❯ VORTICISM 1913–15

An avant-garde British art movement, Vorticism was short-lived but significant as the first organized movement towards abstraction in English art. It took Cubist and Futurist ideas, aiming to shake up the stuffy British art world. Its lynchpin was Percy Wyndham Lewis, editor of *Blast*, the Vorticist review. Another prominent figure was Christopher Richard Wynne Nevinson, who had a brief flowering as a leading member of the English avant-garde, producing his best work as an official war artist in World War I. The movement foundered after its sole exhibition in 1915, but left a legacy on the development of British modernism.

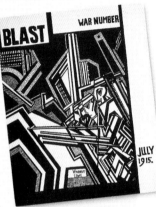

❯ Front cover of the Blast War Number, featuring a Wyndham Lewis woodcut. The issue included articles by Ezra Pound (who coined the movement's name) and T. S. Eliot.

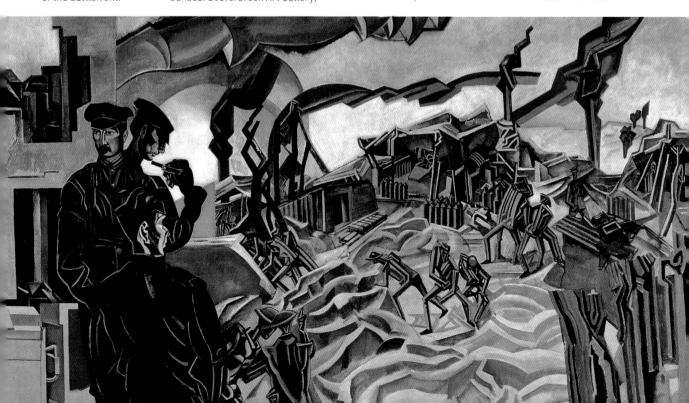

Edward **Wadsworth**

● 1889-1949 🏴 BRITISH ✑ TEMPERA

Wadsworth was a successful member of the avant-garde who ran through the voguish styles of his time: geometric and Cubist pre-1914; representational in the 1920s; a figurative Surrealist in the 1930s; abstract in the 1940s. He produced rather good work, in a derivative way. His skill at Cubist fragmentation led him to design and paint ship camouflage in World War I.

KEY WORKS: *Abstract Composition*, 1915 (London: Tate Collection); *Satellitium*, 1932 (Nottingham: Castle Museum); *The Perspective of Idleness*, 1940 (Bolton, UK: Museums, Art Gallery, and Aquarium)

David **Bomberg**

● 1890-1957 🏴 BRITISH ✑ OILS;
DRAWINGS; PRINTS

Bomberg was the son of Polish Jewish immigrants. He was briefly on the cutting edge of the avant-garde (c.1914) when he pioneered Cubism and Vorticism in Britain. He then changed style and produced gloomy, minor Expressionist paintings.

KEY WORKS: *In the Hold*, 1913-14 (London: Tate Collection); *The Mud Bath*, 1914 (London: Tate Collection)

William **Roberts**

● 1895-1980 🏴 BRITISH ✑ OILS; DRAWINGS;
WATERCOLOURS

Roberts was an individual Modernist who developed an interesting and curiously homely version of the working man/urban life/machine-age imagery and style pioneered by Léger. His early experience as an advertising-poster designer is (perhaps too) evident, and his weakness is that he established a formula that became overrepetitive. He was a member of the pioneering Vorticists, c.1914.

KEY WORKS: *The Return of Ulysses*, 1913 (London: Tate Collection); *People at Play*, c.1920 (London: Christie's Images)

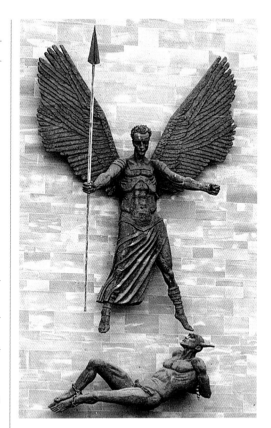

◀◀ *St Michael Vanquishing the Devil*
Jacob Epstein, 1958, height 600 cm (236 ¼ in), bronze, Coventry Cathedral (UK). Epstein created a number of large-scale biblical subjects, hoping to encourage a "new hope for the future".

Sir Jacob **Epstein**

● 1880-1959 🏴 AMERICAN/
BRITISH ✑ SCULPTURE; OILS; DRAWINGS

An audacious and original sculptor, Epstein was frequently attacked by conservative critics for indecency. He studied in Paris (1902–05), where he developed a lasting interest in ancient and primitive sculpture, which inspired much of his later work. He settled in England in 1905, and carried out a series of controversial commissions, labelled as obscene by his critics. He was influenced by Picasso, Modigliani, and Brancusi in Paris whilst working on Oscar Wilde's tomb, and associated with Wyndham Lewis and the Vorticists in London. In later years he concentrated on bronze portrait busts of luminaries, which were widely admired.

KEY WORKS: *The Rock Drill*, 1913–14 (London: Tate Collection); *Rima*, 1922 (London: Hyde Park); *The Tomb of Oscar Wilde*, 1912 (Paris: Père Lachaise Cemetery)

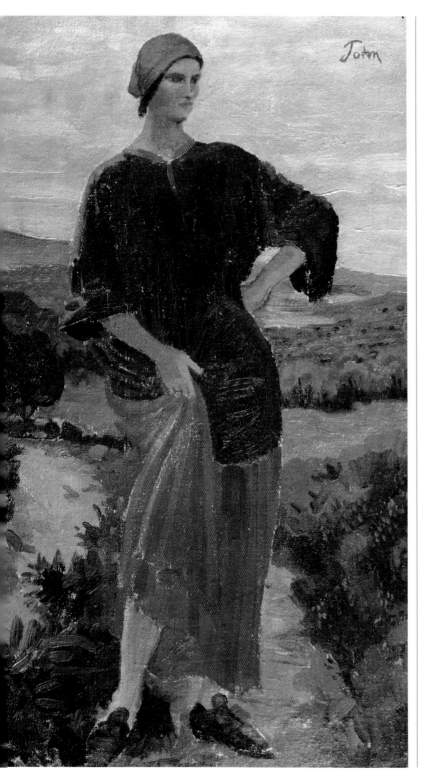

Augustus **John**

● 1878–1961 ⚑ BRITISH ✍ OILS;
DRAWINGS; CHALKS

John was truly gifted and one of the best draughtsmen of any period. His romantic, bohemian temperament made him an increasing misfit – he should have lived in the first half of the 19th century, not the 20th. His wonderful early pieces show his great originality and talent; after 1918, it went to seed and he ended up doing competent, unexceptional work – although it was always recognizably John.

His best works were his early drawings and his sensitive, simplified, intensely coloured landscapes – a personal interpretation of Post-Impressionism. He painted society portraits with style and panache. He is unjustly underrated and deserves reinstatement.

KEY WORKS: *William Butler Yeats*, 1907 (Manchester: City Art Gallery); *The Smiling Woman*, c.1908 (London: Tate Collection)

« *Dorelia in a Landscape* Augustus John, c.1916, 62 x 41 cm (24 ⅔ x 16 in), oil on canvas, private collection. Gypsy life fascinated John. Dorelia (Dorothy McNeil) was his mistress, and, after his wife's death, his lifelong companion.

Gwen **John**

● 1876–1939 ⚑ BRITISH ✍ OILS

The sister of Augustus John and the mistress of Rodin, Gwen John was the author of tight, overintense (neurotic?), minutely worked, rather monochromatic portraits and interiors. She had a sensitive talent, but was limited in range and is currently overrated compared with her brother.

KEY WORKS: *Girl Holding a Rose*, c.1910–20 (New Haven: Yale Center for British Art); *Interior (Rue Terre Neuve)*, c.1920s (Manchester: City Art Gallery)

Robert Polhill **Bevan**

● 1865–1925 🏳 BRITISH ✍ OILS; DRAWINGS

Bevan was an interesting, underrated painter who studied in Paris in the 1890s and met Gauguin at Pont-Aven, in Brittany. He painted traditional subjects, with a successful, if limited, individual Modernist style – stiff, angular, simplified, with luminous colours. Bevan was rather better than the contemporaneous Bloomsbury set (Bell, Fry, and Grant).

KEY WORKS: *Hawkridge*, 1900 (Private Collection); *The Cab Horse*, c.1910 (London: Tate Collection); *Parade at Aldridge's*, 1914 (Boston: Museum of Fine Arts)

Sir Alfred **Munnings**

● 1878–1959 🏳 BRITISH ✍ OILS; DRAWINGS

The brilliant and successful Munnings was an artist who believed (like his clientele) that anything "modern" was a horrible mistake. Though blind in one eye, he had acute vision. Socially he saw only what he wanted to see. He was president of the Royal Academy.

Munnings is remembered primarily for his hunting and racing portraits of humans and horses. He had rare flashes of inspiration, but too often his work lapses into a stock formula: half-way horizon, human upper torsos and heads plus horses' heads and ears silhouetted against a sky piled high with clouds. Though fascinating as social documents, such paintings are his least interesting artistically. He always painted a good "picture", just as some writers always write a good "story".

He was at his best when at his most informal and inventive – in his pictures of horse fairs, local races, landscapes, or gypsies. Within them (and tucked away in portraits), note his genius for capturing a specific light effect, the play of light on a landscape or on horses' flanks, movement, unexpected viewpoints, and spontaneous slices of life. Munnings never doubted his own talent or the values that he celebrated (and it shows).

KEY WORKS: *Shrimp on a White Welsh Pony*, 1911 (Dedham, England: Castle House); *The Friesian Bull*, 1920 (Wirral, UK: Lady Lever Art Gallery)

Mark **Gertler**

● 1891–1939 🏳 BRITISH ✍ OILS

A talented artist from a poor, Jewish immigrant family, Gertler came to inhabit the fringes of the elitist Bloomsbury set. He shared their interest in modern French art and painted better than they did. His work includes figure studies (back views of nudes) and still lifes. He had a talent for design and paint handling. Depression finally led to suicide.

KEY WORKS: *Head of the Artist's Mother*, 1910 (London: Victoria & Albert Museum); *Merry-Go-Round*, 1916 (London: Tate Collection)

》 THE BLOOMSBURY GROUP 1920s–1930s

A loosely-knit group of writers, artists, poets, and designers, taking their name from the London district where they were based. An intellectual élite in rebellion against Victorian restrictions, priding themselves on their sexual freedom but frequently accused of snobbery. On the artistic side, they practised and promoted modern French art. Vanessa Bell, Duncan Grant, and Roger Fry were the artistic leading lights: their output was variable, but their self-confidence unshakeable.

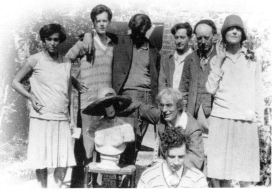

》 **A Group of "Bloomsberries"** in Vanessa Bell's Sussex garden. Grant is third from the right; Fry has his arm around the bust.

»» DADA 1915–22

The first of the modern anti-art movements, with strands in Europe and New York, Dada's prominent figures (Arp, Duchamp, Ernst, Man Ray, and Picabia) deliberately used the absurd, banal, offensive, and tatty to shock and to challenge all existing ideas about art, life, and society. The name (French for "hobby-horse") was probably chosen by randomly inserting a penknife into a dictionary.

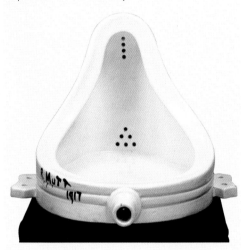

☒ **Fountain (Urinal)** *(replica, original lost), Marcel Duchamp, 1917 (remade 1964), height 61 cm (24 in), porcelain, London: Tate Collection.* This was intended for display at a US exhibition; the artist had decamped to America in 1915.

Francis **Picabia**

● 1879–1953 ⚐ FRENCH ✍ OILS; MIXED MEDIA

Picabia was a quixotic, anarchic character, best remembered for his involvement with Dada. He flirted with Cubism, Expressionism, and Surrealism. His most effective work was in his "machine style" phase (1913–1920s), when he used the inspiration of technical drawings to produce telling images that comment ironically on man's relationship with machines (often with erotic overtones).

KEY WORKS: *I See Again in Memory My Dear Udnie*, 1914 (New York: Museum of Modern Art); *Very Rare Picture on Earth*, 1915 (New York: Guggenheim Museum)

Marcel **Duchamp**

● 1887–1968 ⚐ FRENCH ✍ OILS; SCULPTURE; MIXED MEDIA

The father of Conceptual art, Duchamp is applauded as one of the great gurus and heroes of the Modern Movement, but his work is possibly one of its greatest bores (it is possible to achieve both at the same time).

The ragbag of his few works are now icons of the Modern Movement (notably the urinal; see left). None are very interesting to look at per se, but Duchamp was the first to propose that the interest and stimulus of a work of art can lie solely in its concept or intellectual content – it doesn't matter what it looks like, as long as you can pick up the message.

To speak ill of Duchamp is to invite the wrath and derision of the modern art establishment. However, although he was significant in his day, his work is quite limited and now looks distinctly tired. Not quite a case of the Emperor's clothes, but time to say that the suit is now threadbare and old-fashioned. A brilliant, charming but arrogant, intellectual thug who continues to mesmerize and intimidate the art world from beyond the grave.

KEY WORKS: *Nude Descending Staircase, No.2*, 1912 (Philadelphia: Museum of Art); *The Bride Stripped Bare by her Bachelors, Even*, 1915–23 (Philadelphia Museum of Art)

Kurt **Schwitters**

● 1887–1948 ⚐ GERMAN ✍ COLLAGE; MIXED MEDIA; OILS; SCULPTURE

Schwitters was a pioneering, poetic, romantic loner who used the fragments no one bothered with to make sense of a world that he found politically, culturally, and socially mad – Germany from 1914 to 1945. He ran a successful, pioneering advertising agency from 1924 to 1930. He died in England as a refugee. Schwitters was influential, especially in the 1960s and 1970s.

His small-scale "Merzbilder" collages were created in great number and with extraordinary care, in composition, content, and arrangement. He used material that he literally picked up in the streets of his native Hanover. His work of 1922–30 is more consciously constructed (and influenced by Russian Constructivism and Dutch De Stijl). He produced a few high-quality, traditional paintings and sculptures as a deliberate contrast to his avant-garde activities.

His early roots were in Dada, but he was never political, polemical, or satirical. His work is always personal or autobiographical – the artist as sacrificial victim or spiritual leader. His major (manic) project was "Merzbau" – a whole building filled with personal *objets trouvés* – a collage gone mad. (It was destroyed by Allied bombs in 1943; a successor near Oslo was destroyed by fire in 1951.) He made a poignant attempt to create a new beauty on the ruins of German culture.

KEY WORKS: *Merzbild 5B (Picture-Red-Heart-Church)*, 1919 (New York: Guggenheim Museum); *Merz 163, with Woman Sweating*, 1920 (New York: Guggenheim Museum); *Merz Picture 32A (The Cherry Picture)*, 1921 (New York: Museum of Modern Art)

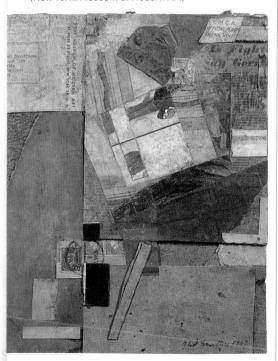

⊼ *YMCA Flag, Thank You, Ambleside* Kurt Schwitters, 1947, mixed media, Kendal, Cumbria (UK): Abbot Hall Art Gallery. *The title refers to the Lake District, in England, where the artist settled in 1945.*

Jean (Hans) **Arp**

● 1886–1966 ⚲ FRENCH ✍ COLLAGE; SCULPTURE; OILS

A poet, painter, and sculptor as well as an experimenter, best remembered for wood reliefs, cardboard cut-outs, torn paper collages, and (after 1931) stone sculptures. His early work is modest in scale and appearance. Arp liked simplicity, biomorphic shapes, and chance. He took natural forms and sought to perfect their shape and inner spirit. A founder of Dada and Surrealism.

KEY WORKS: *Collage with Squares Arranged According to the Laws of Chance*, 1916–17 (New York: Museum of Modern Art); *Birds in an Aquarium*, c.1920 (New York: Museum of Modern Art)

⏩ *Head* Jean (Hans) Arp, 1929, 67 x 56.5 cm (26 ⅓ x 22 ¼ in), relief, private collection. *Arp regarded his simplified shapes as emblems of natural growth and forms, using light-hearted inspiration from plants, animals, and man.*

John **Heartfield** (Helmut Herzfelde)

● 1891–1968 ⚲ GERMAN ✍ PHOTOMONTAGE

An artist and journalist, and a founder of Dada in Berlin in 1910, Heartfield is perhaps best known for developing political photo-montage in Berlin in the 1920s and 1930s. He took refuge in England from 1938 to 1950, and then settled in East Germany.

Heartfield had an intense social and political commitment (left wing, anti-Nazi), and anglicized his name as a protest against German nationalism. He was the original manipulator of media imagery and lettering, producing biting and memorable satire, highly expressive of its age.

Notice the economy of means: Heartfield knew exactly what he wanted to say and went for the jugular with one simple, unforgettable image – less is more.

KEY WORKS: *Adolf the Superman: Swallows Gold and Spouts Junk*, 1920 (Berlin: Akademie der Künste); *Five Fingers has the Hand*, 1928 (New York: Smithsonian Cooper-Hewitt National Design Museum)

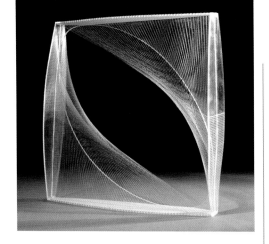

>> *Linear Construction in Space No. 1* Naum Gabo, 1944–45, height 30 cm (11 ¾ in), plastic and nylon thread, University of Cambridge: Kettle's Yard. Gabo created form through the description of space rather than mass.

Naum **Gabo**

● 1890–1977 ⚑ RUSSIAN ✍ SCULPTURE

Also known as Naum Neemia Pevsner, Gabo was a peripatetic, self-taught pioneer of Russian Constructivism. He lived in Russia, Germany, Paris, London, and the US. He worked closely with his elder brother, Antoine Pevsner. His 3-D work emphasizes modern materials (such as Plexiglas), space, light, and kinetic movement. Gabo expressed sophisticated aesthetic values plus social ideals – a vision of a transcendental order.

KEY WORKS: *Head No. 2*, 1916 (London: Tate Collection); *Construction in Space with a Crystalline Centre*, 1938–40 (Museum of London)

⊻ *Birth of the Universe* Antoine Pevsner, 1933, 75 x 105 cm (29 ½ x 41 ⅓ in), oil on canvas, Paris: Musée National d'Art Moderne. Pevsner's later work was characterized by spiralling three-dimensional forms.

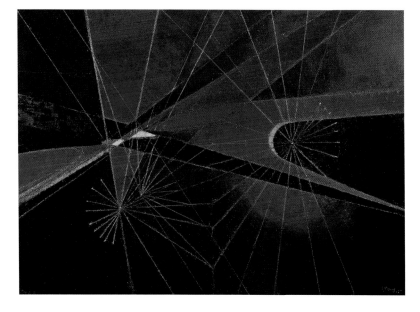

>> CONSTRUCTIVISM 1917–21

Constructivism was an important Russian avant-garde movement. Vladimir Tatlin, later joined by Rodchenko and brothers Antoine Pevsner and Naum Gabo, developed "constructed" architectural art to reflect the modern world. They were concerned with abstraction, space, new materials, 3-D form, and social reform. Soviet disapproval meant the group members dispersed across Europe, influencing the fields of architecture and decoration, and the Bauhaus and De Stijl movements.

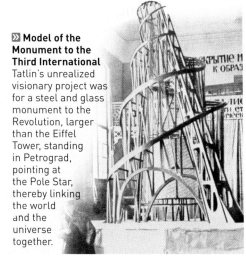

>> **Model of the Monument to the Third International** Tatlin's unrealized visionary project was for a steel and glass monument to the Revolution, larger than the Eiffel Tower, standing in Petrograd, pointing at the Pole Star, thereby linking the world and the universe together.

Antoine **Pevsner**

● 1886–1962 ⚑ RUSSIAN/FRENCH ✍ OILS; MIXED MEDIA; SCULPTURE

Pevsner was the leading exponent of Russian avant-garde, non-objective art, and a creator of 2-D and 3-D pieces. He was fascinated by modern technology and engineering. He made conscious use of modern materials such as Perspex, glass, and iron. Note his mastery of the dynamics of spherical surfaces, the way he loves to use projections in space and expresses the poetry of technology, especially flight. Pevsner left Russia (together with his brother Naum Gabo) in 1921 and settled in Paris in 1923. He died a much-respected figure.

KEY WORKS: *Construction in Space*, 1929 (Basel, Switzerland: Kunstmuseum); *Anchored Cross*, 1933 (New York: Guggenheim Museum)

El **Lissitsky**

1890–1941 RUSSIAN PRINTS; SCULPTURE; MIXED MEDIA

Lissitsky was a pioneering Modernist architect and artist. He was a creator of Constructivist abstractions, which developed the links between art, design, and architecture, and art as a material and spiritual experience.

KEY WORKS: *Untitled*, c.1919–20 (New York: Guggenheim Museum); *Proun*, c.1923 (New York: Guggenheim Museum)

Aleksandr **Rodchenko**

1891–1956 RUSSIAN PHOTOGRAPHY; OILS; PRINTS; SCULPTURE

An active Bolshevik with strong ideals, Rodchenko believed that art must be in the service of the Revolution to create an ordered, technological society. He always demanded active participation from viewers. Rodchenko was rejected by Stalin.

KEY WORKS: *Line and Compass Drawing*, 1915 (New York: Museum of Modern Art); *Composition*, 1916 (Private Collection)

Vladimir **Tatlin**

1885–1953 RUSSIAN MIXED MEDIA; SCULPTURE; OILS

Tatlin was the heroic, legendary founder of Russian Constructivism. He lived in Paris in 1913 and was much influenced by Picasso and Futurism. Tatlin was famous for his relief constructions, especially corner reliefs, and his never-built tower (*Monument to the Third International*). He made stage and industrial designs in the 1920s and believed in art at the service of Revolution. He was a deadly rival of Malevich. Tatlin died in obscurity.

KEY WORKS: *The Fishmonger*, 1911 (Moscow: Tretyakov Gallery); *Mother and Child*, c.1912–13 (Private Collection)

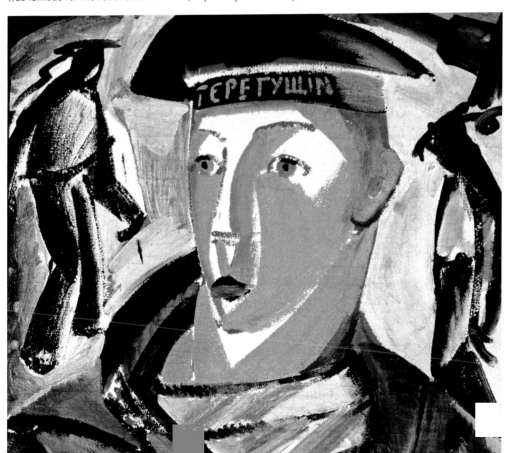

The Sailor (Self-Portrait) *Vladimir Tatlin, 1911–12, 71.5 x 71.5 cm (28 ¼ x 28 ¼ in), tempera on canvas, St Petersburg: State Russian Museum.*

Max **Beckmann**

⬤ 1884–1950 🏳 GERMAN ✍ OILS;
WOODCUTS; DRAWINGS

Beckmann was one of the great painters of the
20th century. He was generally overlooked because
he was never one of the Modernist "gang", and is
difficult, even now, for officialdom to pigeonhole.
To sustain such Expressionist intensity and
quality is a rare (unique?) achievement.

He produced beautiful, expressive, sombre
paintings; rich colours, strong drawing. He made
many portraits, self-portraits, and allegories full of
symbolism. His works are very much of their time,
but do not belong to any "school" or "ism". Their
underlying theme is the human condition and
concern for the triumph of the human spirit.

Beckmann's use of black (one of the most
difficult pigments) is stunning and worthy of Manet;
his understanding of the human condition is worthy
of Rembrandt. His work charts a central vein of the
spiritual anguish of 20th-century Europe. Born
into the gifted, optimistic generation of the 1880s,
he experienced the horrors of World War I and
the collapse of civilized values in Germany
in the 1920s and 1930s. In 1937, classed as a
"degenerate" by the Nazis, he chose voluntary
self-exile in Amsterdam. In 1947, he emigrated
to the US, where he taught and painted.

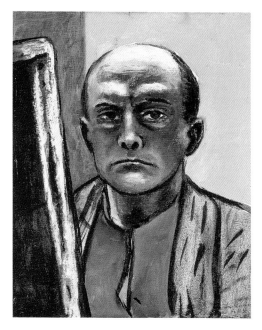

⬆ *Self-Portrait in Olive and Brown* Max Beckmann,
1945, 60.3 x 49.8 cm (23 ¾ x 19 ¾ in), oil on canvas,
Detroit Institute of Arts. Beckmann painted this
while he was writing his autobiography.

KEY WORKS: *The Dream*, 1921 (Missouri: St Louis Art
Museum); *Departure*, 1932–33 (New York: Museum
of Modern Art); *Journey on the Fish*, 1934
(Stuttgart: Staatsgalerie)

⟫ THE NAZIS AND DEGENERATE ART 1930s

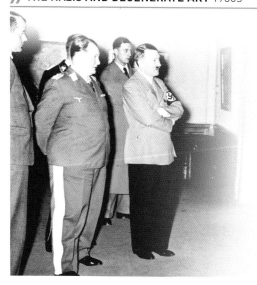

Nazi ideologues believed that any art that did not
conform to a bourgeois ideal of well-crafted,
figurative images portraying ideal heroism or
comfortable day-to-day living was the product of
degenerate human beings and perverted minds. The
German term, *entartete Kunst*, was coined by Hitler
and the party's chief theoretical spokesperson, Alfred
Rosenberg. "Degenerate" modern artists could not
exhibit or work, and many confiscated works were
burnt. A Nazi-backed touring exhibition of modern
and abstract art (with works by Beckmann, Dix,
Grosz, Kandinsky, Mondrian, and Picasso) opened in
1937 to show how foul Degenerate art was. The plan
backfired and introduced modern art to huge crowds.

◀ *Adolf Hitler and Hermann Goering, probably at
the 1937 exhibition.* Before he rose to power, Hitler
supported himself through painting and continued
to paint throughout his life.

Otto **Dix**

◗ 1891–1969 🏛 GERMAN ✎ PRINTS;
DRAWINGS; MIXED MEDIA

Dix was a mocking, bitter observer and recorder
of German society during World War I and the
1920s and 1930s as its moral and social values
collapsed. He was anti-Nazi. Ugliness
fascinated him – note his powerful distortion of
realistic observation with intense line, detail, and
acid colour; his expressive portraits of friends;
and powerful engravings. He was recognized
only after 1955.

KEY WORKS: *Card-Playing War Cripples*, 1920
(Private Collection); *The Artist's Parents*, 1921
(Basel, Switzerland: Kunstmuseum)

George **Grosz**

◗ 1893–1959 🏛 GERMAN ✎ PRINTS;
DRAWINGS; OILS

Grosz is best remembered as the biting and
original chronicler of the sad and corrosive
period of Germany's history between 1918
and the rise of Hitler.

   His small-scale works (especially prints and
drawings) are of a consciously artless, angular,
modern style (in the sense of uncomfortable,
provocative, and anarchic). They chronicle the
uncomfortable truth behind the respectable
bourgeois façade. Grosz was fascinated by street
life yet, for all his apparent criticism of it, he seems
to end up loving the ugly corruptness he records.

   Note the repetition of certain stock types and
faces; poisonous colours and artless style to create
a feeling of instability and menace. He was an early
user of photomontage. His terrifying personal
World War I experiences made him a pessimist,
misanthrope, and political activist (Communist).
His style softened c.1924 after marriage and
fatherhood. He emigrated to the US in 1933
and reverted to being a graphic artist.

KEY WORKS: *Suicide*, 1916 (London: Tate Collection);
Grey Day, 1921 (Berlin: Nationalgalerie); *Pillars of
Society*, 1926 (Berlin: Staatliche Museum)

Christian **Schad**

◗ 1894–1982 🏛 GERMAN ✎ OILS;
PRINTS; COLLAGE

Schad was a painter who also made collages and
prints (woodcuts), and took photos in the manner of
Man Ray (see page 322). He was best known for his
Neue Sachlichkeit work – a cool, uncompromising,
critical depiction of the German bourgeois society
of the 1920s, including cold, steely portraits. The
exaggerated, emphasized detail serves to highlight
its emptiness. The alienating spaces show how
things and people become disconnected.

KEY WORKS: *Agosta, the Pigeon-Chested Man, and
Rasha, the Black Dove*, 1929 (London: Tate Collection);
Operation, 1929 (Munich: Städtische Galerie)

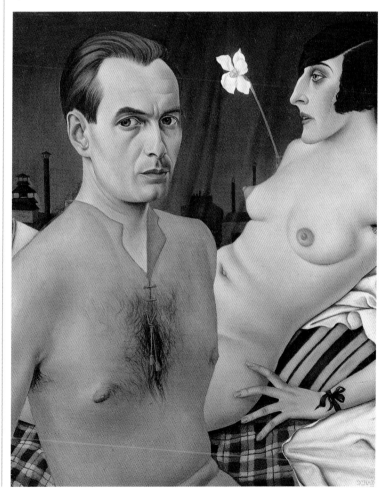

🔲 *Self-Portrait with
Model* Christian Schad,
1927, 76 x 62 cm (30 x
24 ¼ in), oil on canvas,
London: Tate Collection.
Neue Sachlichkeit
(New Objectivity)
describes a tendency
for German art, after
1925, to turn away from
Expressionism. Schad
abandoned painting
in the Nazi era.

Paul **Klee**

⊖ 1879–1940 SWISS MIXED MEDIA;
DRAWINGS

Klee was a prolific author of drawings, watercolours, and etchings. He was a dedicated teacher at the Bauhaus, and a talented poet and musician. He had a fey, spiritual character and was one of the most original pioneers of the Modern movement.

He was the creator of the chamber music of modern art – finely wrought, small-scale works in many media, which are reminiscent in some ways of medieval manuscript illumination (perhaps he drew on this tradition?). Note his quirky, personal imagery and the delicate, unpretentious abstracts. His work is always very sensual, visually and mentally, and delightfully and poetically odd. He had an exquisite colour sense and produced neat, precisely worked surfaces.

Don't try to understand or intellectualize Klee – just enjoy his work and follow him wherever he chooses to take your eye and imagination (one of his well-known writings is called "Taking a line for a walk"). Above all, let him take you back to the realm of childhood curiosity, imagination, and humour. You will return to adulthood immensely refreshed, enriched, and stimulated.

KEY WORKS: *Ancient Sound*, 1925 (Basel, Switzerland: Kunstmuseum); *Ad Parnassum*, 1932 (Hamburg: Kunsthalle); *Diana in the Autumn Wind*, 1934 (Bern, Switzerland: Kunstmuseum); *Death and Fire*, 1940 (Bern, Switzerland: Kunstmuseum)

◙ *The Golden Fish* Paul Klee, 1925–26, 50 x 69 cm (19 ¾ x 27 ¼ in), oil and watercolour on paper and board, Hamburg: Kunsthalle. In 1925 Klee joined the staff of the Bauhaus, published his *Pedagogical Sketchbook*, and displayed his work at a Surrealist exhibition in Paris.

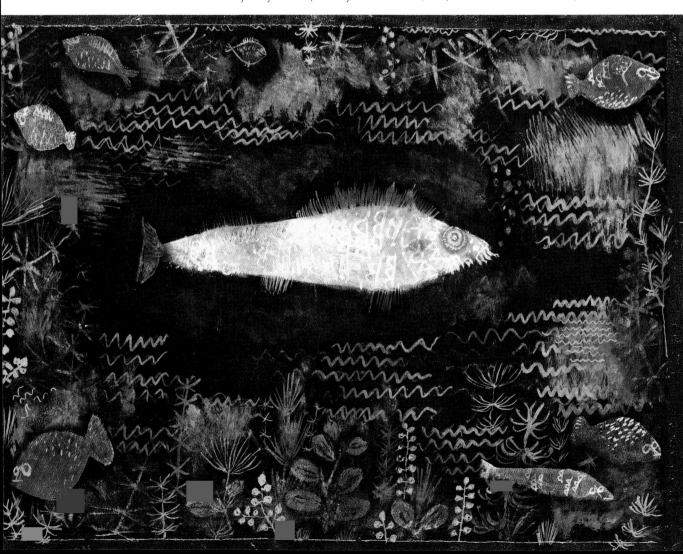

THE BAUHAUS 1919–33

The Bauhaus was the most famous modern art school, on which so many others have been modelled, and was highly influential in the fields of architecture and design. Its teachers included Albers, Feininger, Klee, Kandinsky, Moholy-Nagy, and Schlemmer. It opened in Germany in 1919 and was closed by the Nazis in 1933. The New Bauhaus was set up in Chicago by Moholy-Nagy in 1937. The Bauhaus tried to teach the virtues of simple, clean design; abstraction; mass production; the moral and economic benefits of a well-designed environment; democracy and worker participation.

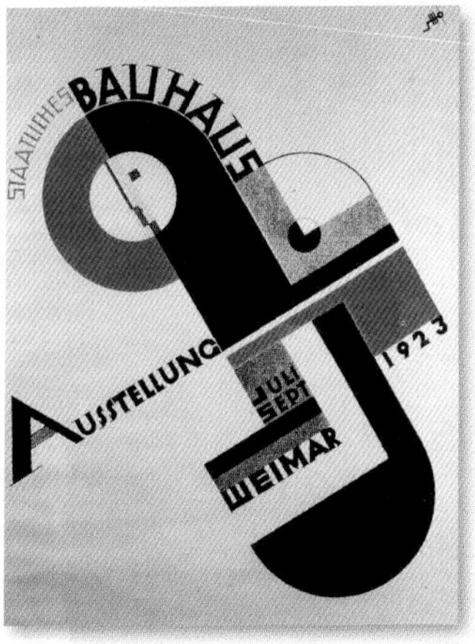

Poster by Joost Schmidt for the Bauhaus Exhibition in Weimar, July–September 1923. Bauhaus artists recognized early the importance of graphic design and used it as a medium to express a corporate identity for the school.

Lyonel **Feininger**

1871–1956 AMERICAN/GERMAN
WOODCUTS; DRAWINGS; WATERCOLOURS

Son of a concert violinist, Feininger was born and based in New York, but spent most of his life in Germany (1887–1937). He had a quiet, personal style, akin to a pane of broken glass in which buildings and seascape are the central subject. He blended Cubist fragmentation of form (he studied in Paris) and the misty light and dreaminess of Romanticism (his German heritage). A founder of the Bauhaus, he remained there until it was closed in 1933. He was a talented printmaker (etchings). He influenced set designs for early films such as Max Reinhardt's *The Cabinet of Doctor Caligari*.

KEY WORKS: *The Bicycle Race*, 1912 (Washington DC: National Gallery of Art); *Sailing Boats*, 1929 (Detroit Institute of Arts); *Market Church at Evening*, 1930 (Munich: Alte Pinakothek)

László **Moholy-Nagy**

1895–1946 HUNGARIAN/GERMAN
COLLAGE; PHOTOMONTAGE; DRAWINGS; PRINTS

Moholy-Nagy was a lawyer-turned-artist and theoretical writer. He was a Geometric Abstract artist and leading member of, and teacher at, the Bauhaus. He provided the basis for the New Photographer's movement. Moholy-Nagy sought to create order and clarity using design, abstraction, architecture, typography, constructions, and photography. He settled in Chicago in 1937.

KEY WORKS: *Photogram*, 1923 (Los Angeles: J. Paul Getty Museum); *A II*, 1924 (New York: Guggenheim Museum); *Dual Form with Chromium Rods*, 1946 (New York: Guggenheim Museum)

At Coffee *László Moholy-Nagy, c.1926, 28.3 x 20.6 cm (11 ¼ x 8 ¼ in), vintage gelatin silver photograph, Houston: Museum of Fine Arts.* Moholy-Nagy tried to expand the scope of photography with experimental techniques and innovative compositions. An inspirational teacher, his influence on art and design training has been profound.

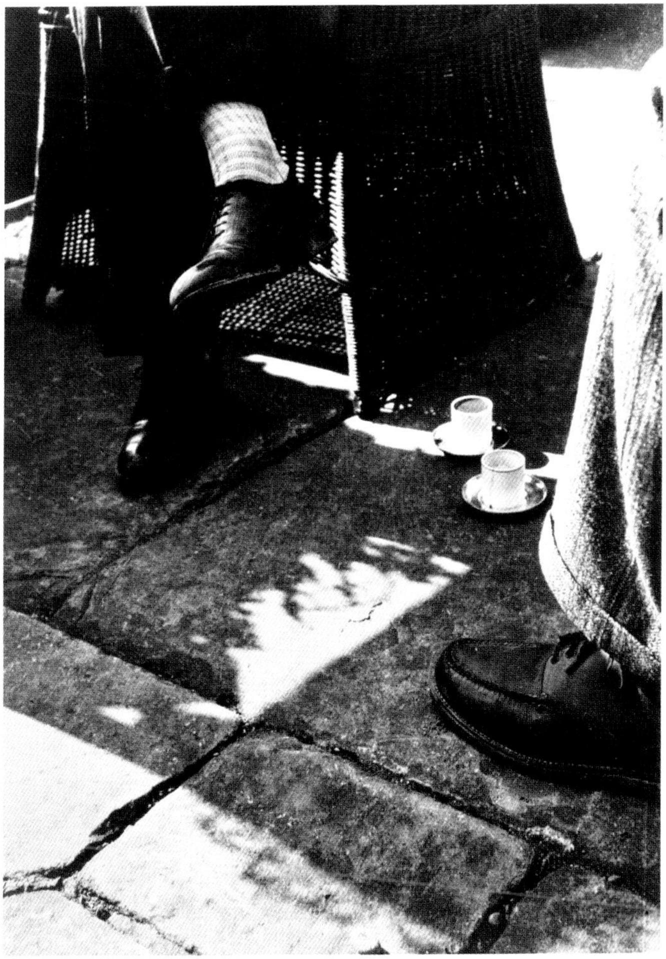

Josef **Albers**

● 1888–1976 GERMAN/AMERICAN
✍ PRINTS; WOODCUTS; OILS

Albers was one of the great artist-educators of the Modern movement. A pillar of the Bauhaus (1923–1933), he emigrated to the US in 1933.

His highly original work combines investigations into perception with a simple beauty. He is best known for his "Homage to the Square" series (1949–70), in which he experiments with nests of squares that explore values of light and degrees of temperature in contrasting colours and hues. Albers uses the square because it is the most static geometric form, and so able to accentuate colour relationships. He was also an accomplished photographer and designer in stained glass.

"Homage to the Square" sounds boring, but is visually fascinating because Albers understood that you can never predict scientifically what colour is going to do, and how it constantly catches you unaware and delights you. "Homage to the Square" is the ultimate proof of this, but you need to get involved and experiment (by half closing your eyes, for instance) to really enjoy and appreciate what is going on.

KEY WORKS: *Glass, Color, and Light*, 1921 (New York: Metropolitan Museum of Art); *Study for Homage to the Square Mild Scent*, 1965 (Hamburg: Kunsthalle)

Oskar **Schlemmer**

● 1888–1943 GERMAN ✍ OILS; PRINTS; SCULPTURE

A leading member of the Bauhaus, Schlemmer was a painter and sculptor. He was most effective and at ease designing mural decorations for the ballet and theatre. He preferred simplification, the interplay of shape and form, and reflective inner states of mind to expression and dramatic impact. Schlemmer liked quiet exploration and experiment.

KEY WORKS: *Head in Profile, with Black Contour*, 1920–21 (San Francisco: Fine Arts Museums); *Group of Fourteen Figures in Imaginary Architecture*, 1930 (Cologne: Wallraf-Richartz-Museum); *Bauhaus Stairway*, 1934 (New York: Museum of Modern Art)

» DE STIJL 1917–31

De Stijl (from the Dutch for "the style", was the name of a group of Dutch artists, and the journal they published – the 1920s' most influential avant-garde art magazine. Members and contributors included Piet Mondrian, Theo van Doesburg, and the architect and designer Gerrit Rietveld. The collective advocated a geometrical type of abstract art, simplification, social and spiritual form, seeking laws of harmony that would be equally applicable to life and art.

» *Red Blue Chair* designed by Gerrit Rietveld, 1918. The hard surfaces and strong colours are a rejection of familiarity and sentimentality in favour of dynamic rationality.

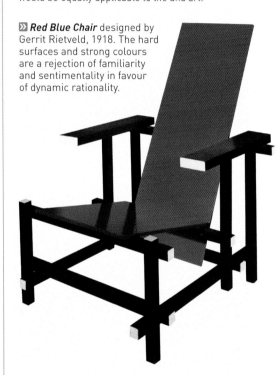

Piet **Mondrian**

● 1872–1944 DUTCH ✍ OILS; MIXED MEDIA

One of the pioneers of pure abstract art, Mondrian was an austere, reclusive character who hated the green untidiness of nature. He was theoretically and intellectually influential in his lifetime, but had no commercial success.

The most familiar works are the abstracts of the 1920s and 1930s. They have simple elements: black, white, and primary colours only, horizontal and vertical lines. His aim was to find and express a universal spiritual perfection, but his imagery has become a commonplace of 20th-century commercial design. Look out, also, for his late, jazzily colourful work, completed in New York. His slow and painstaking progress through Symbolism and Cubism to abstraction repays patient study.

You have to see Mondrian's work in the flesh to understand it. Reproductions make his abstracts look bland, mechanical, and easy, with immaculate, anonymous surfaces. In fact, you can (and are supposed to see) the brush marks, the alterations, the hesitations – the struggle to achieve that

balance and purity that he desperately wanted, but found so hard to attain. Note also the deliberate small scale and intimacy of most of his work.

KEY WORKS: *The Grey Tree*, 1912 (The Hague: Gemeentemuseum); *Pier and Ocean*, 1915 (Otterlo, Netherlands: Kröller-Müller Museum); *Tableau No. IV with Red, Blue, Yellow, and Black*, 1924–25 (Washington DC: National Gallery of Art); *Composition in Red and Blue*, 1939–41 (Private Collection)

Broadway Boogie Woogie Piet Mondrian, 1942–43, 127 x 127 cm (50 x 50 in), oil on canvas, New York: Museum of Modern Art. © 2005 Mondrian/Holtzman Trust, c/o HCR International, Warrenton, Virginia, USA

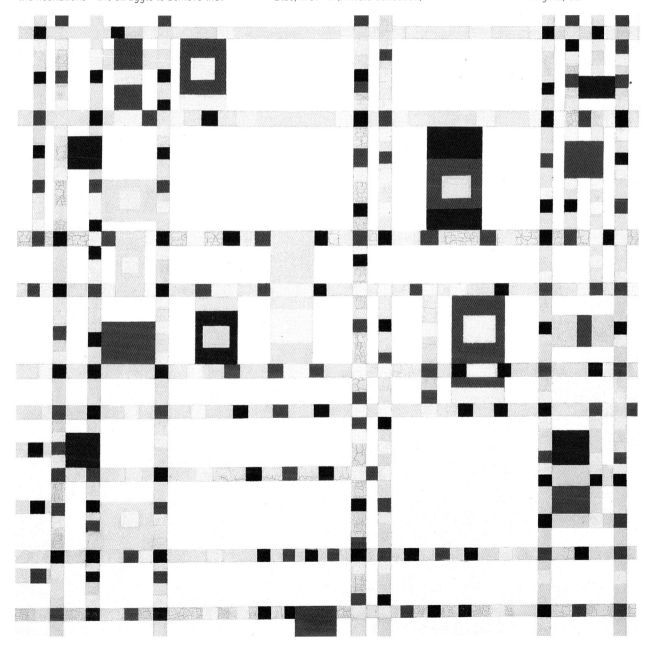

Surrealism

1920s–1930s

Surrealism was the most influential avant-garde movement of the inter-war years. Its chief goal, asserted by its founder and leader, André Breton, was to meld the unconscious with the conscious to create a new "super reality" – a *surréalisme*. Cubism, Dada, and Freud were its starting points. Its enduring influence can be found notably in present-day advertising and avant-garde humour.

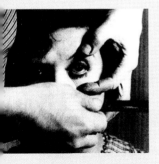

⏏ **Still from the 1929 Surrealist film** *Un Chien Andalou* **by Salvador Dalí and Luis Buñuel**. Film was an ideal medium for Surrealism. Buñuel, working closely with Dalí, created a disconcerting and deliberately unfathomable masterpiece.

Perhaps not surprisingly for a movement whose origins were largely literary and which actively championed anarchy, Surrealism in the visual arts almost immediately developed a bewildering variety of styles. It could be highly finished, aiming at a kind of heightened realism (Dalí), or, at the other end of the spectrum, entirely abstract (Miró). In whatever style it was executed, it generally aimed to surprise, often to shock, frequently to disturb, and always to create a dream-like atmosphere, sometimes specific, and at other times vague and suggestive.

Subjects

The personal nature of the subconscious necessarily resists categorization; Surrealist subject matter literally knew no limits. Ernst experimented with a visual equivalent of stream of consciousness writing: *frottage* – rubbings taken from worn surfaces to create chance patterns. Magritte's deadpan paintings exploit enigmatic juxtapositions,

often sexual. Arp, a painter and sculptor, favoured simple, vaguely biomorphic shapes, seemingly randomly assembled, in bold, flat colours.

What to look for

Ernst was the most complete Surrealist artist in that he experimented with all techniques: figuration, abstraction, and collage. In the pioneering work *Oedipus Rex*, he explores methods of creating imagery that were to become a common-place of Surrealist painting. In particular, he synthesizes his study and understanding of Freud's ideas, notably about the juxtaposition of polarities such as the rational/irrational, constructive/destructive, dead/alive, with his own experiences and desires. Oedipus means "swollen foot"; in Greek mythology he was the hero who unwittingly killed his father, married his own mother, and gouged out his eyes on realizing what he had done. Freud's Oedipus Complex is an inability to break the infantile dependence on parents, and become fully mature.

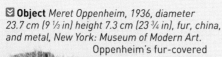

✉ **Object** *Meret Oppenheim, 1936, diameter 23.7 cm (9 ⅓ in) height 7.3 cm (23 ¾ in), fur, china, and metal, New York: Museum of Modern Art.* Oppenheim's fur-covered cup, saucer, and spoon encapsulate Surrealism's determination to subvert the everyday world.

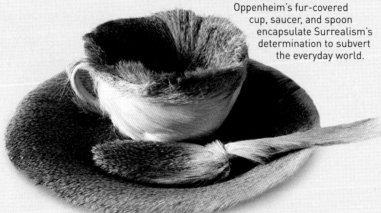

KEY EVENTS	
1919	André Breton and Philippe Soupault write *Les Champs Magnétiques*
1924	First *Surrealist Manifesto* issued, largely written by Breton, in Paris
1930	Breton formally allies Surrealism with the Proletarian Revolution
1936	London International Surrealist Exhibition held
1938	Leon Trotsky and Breton write *Manifesto for an Independent Revolutionary Art*
1939	Outbreak of World War II sees exodus of Surrealist artists to New York

The hand that cracks the nut is a metaphor for sexual intercourse. The spike and the arrow stand for pain, and the distorted scale suggests the struggle in gender relationships

The mechanical device that pierces the finger was used to punch holes in the feet of chickens to mark their age. It suggests pain, penetration, and intercourse

In Freudian analysis, the balloon and the birds represent a longing for escape and freedom

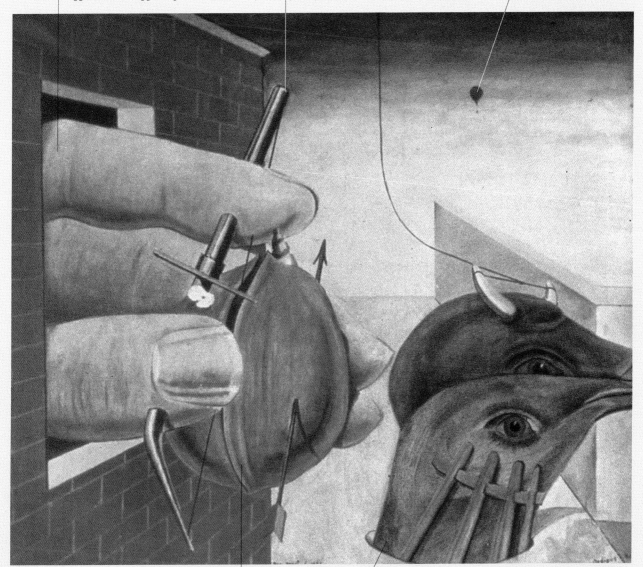

⌃ *Oedipus Rex* Max Ernst, 1922, 93 x 102 cm (36 ⅔ x 40 in), oil on canvas, private collection. Ernst knew he had to escape the dominance of his father, who was an academic painter and devout Catholic.

The psychosexual interpretation is that the nut represents the female (the crack suggesting the vulva)

Ernst was obsessed by birds, death, and gender ever since his pet cockatoo died on the day his sister was born. The birds have human, upside-down eyes

≫ TECHNIQUES

Paint is applied in a precise but anonymous manner. Imagery has been copied from magazines and prints. Ernst was a self-taught painter and a pioneer of collage.

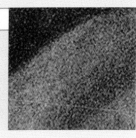

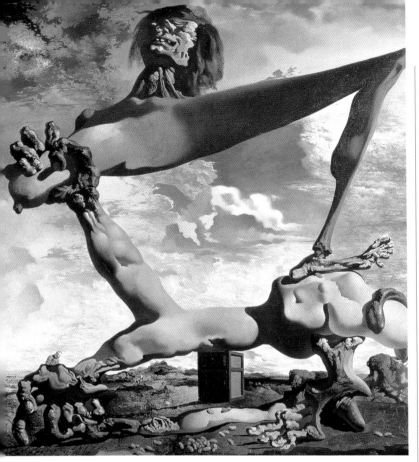

⌃ **Soft Construction with Boiled Beans: Premonition of Civil War** *Salvador Dalí, 1936, 110 x 83 cm (43 ⅓ x 32 ⅔ in), oil on canvas, Philadelphia: Museum of Art.* The second half of the painting's title was added on the outbreak of the Spanish Civil War.

Salvador **Dalí**

⏀ 1904–89   ⚑ SPANISH   ✍ MIXED MEDIA; OILS; SCULPTURE

Dalí was a flamboyant self-publicist, and one of the most popular painters of the 20th century. He made a brief but major contribution to Surrealism.

He was an artist of astonishing technical precosity and virtuosity. He mastered almost any style (see his early work), finally choosing one based on the detailed, "realistic", 17th-century Dutch masters – instantly popular and recognizable as "very skilful" (the optical illusions are breathtaking). Ultimately he was just a flashy showman with a big ego and a long moustache – like a singer who churns out popular arias in a spectacular way, but is devoid of any real expression, meaning, or freshness.

There is one exception to the above. Look for the works of 1928–33, which are great and profound. Briefly, as a true pioneer of the Surrealist movement, Dalí created works to explore his "paranoia-critical method". Using Freudian ideas about dreams and madness, he produced obsessional images in which detailed reality is suddenly transformed into different, intricate, and disturbing images – technically and imaginatively brilliant. He ought to have persisted with it.

KEY WORKS: *Seated Girl Seen from the Rear*, 1925 (Madrid: Museo Nacional Centro de Arte Reina Sofia); *Surrealist Composition with Invisible Figures*, c.1936 (Private Collection); *Christ of St John of the Cross*, 1951 (Kelvingrove, Glasgow: Art Gallery and Museum)

Max **Ernst**

⏀ 1891–1976   ⚑ GERMAN   ✍ PRINTS; COLLAGE; SCULPTURE; OILS

One of the leading Surrealists, Ernst lived in France after 1921 (and in the US from 1941 to 1953). After serving in World War I, he became, with Jean Arp, his lifelong friend, the leader of the Dada movement in Cologne.

His witty and inventive experimentation unites subject and technique to great effect. He was a pioneer of the Surrealist desire to explore the subconscious and create a sense of disturbing out-of-this-world reality. His experimental techniques were a means of activating or liberating his own imagination and, by extension, ours. Don't be tempted into an overly serious, analytical, or historical approach to his work. Relax, and enter into the imaginative play he sets up.

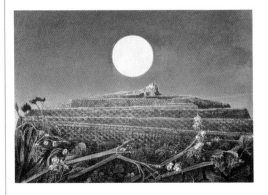

⌃ **The Entire City** *Max Ernst, 1935, 60 x 81 cm (23 ¾ x 31 ¾ in), oil on canvas, Zürich: Kunsthaus.* The artist created a whole series of works portraying cityscapes, using different media, including oils and frottage.

Look for his own childhood memories, such as forests and little bird "Loplop". Enjoy his unusual techniques: witty play with collaged images (one of the first to use them); frottage (rubbed patterns); and décalcomania (liquid paint patterns), where accident is used to liberate images in the subconscious. His early strange, figurative images seem to be painted dreams. Although his work is always imaginative, his later work is more abstract and lyrical, and loses bite. His work is best when on a small scale.

KEY WORKS: *Massacre of the Innocents*, 1921 (Private Collection); *The Elephant Celebes*, 1921 (London: Tate Collection); *La Toilette de la Mariée*, 1940 (Venice: Peggy Guggenheim Gallery)

André **Masson**

● 1896–1987 ᴾᵁ FRENCH ✍ MIXED MEDIA; DRAWINGS; ENGRAVINGS; SCULPTURE

Masson was an artist whose reputation and influence is better known than his work. Deeply affected by World War I injuries, he was a leading Surrealist who explored the irrational and subconscious in intense, finely wrought paintings and drawings. He disliked order, preferring experimentation and spontaneous action. He lived in the US after 1940 and had a big impact on the Abstract Expressionists.

KEY WORKS: *Pedestal Table in the Studio*, 1922 (London: Tate Collection); *Card Trick*, 1923 (New York: Museum of Modern Art)

Yves **Tanguy**

● 1900–55 ᴾᵁ FRENCH ✍ OILS

Tanguy was a self-taught Surrealist who, from c.1927, evolved (but never developed further) a style of imaginary landscapes (or sea beds?) full of weird and curiously compelling half-vegetable, half-animal forms.

KEY WORKS: *The Look of Amber*, 1929 (Washington DC: National Gallery of Art); *Promontory Palace*, 1931 (New York: Guggenheim Museum)

Joan **Miró**

● 1893–1983 ᴾᵁ SPANISH ✍ MIXED MEDIA; CERAMICS; SCULPTURE; PRINTS

Miró was a leading Surrealist painter and sculptor: experimental, unconventional, and influential. He searched for a new visual language, purged of stale meanings and appealing to the senses.

Miró is best known for his abstract and semi-abstract works – highly structured, poetic, and dreamy; simple forms floating on fields of colour. Let them suggest anything (especially something biological, sexual, primitive). Enjoy the naughty thoughts, silliness, colour, beauty, light, warmth.

He used a limited number of forms, but repeated and made rhymes of them. He drew on an (unconscious) memory bank of natural and landscape forms, which suggest generative power in nature. He experimented with "magic realism" before breaking into a new style c.1924.

KEY WORKS: *Le Port*, 1945 (Private Collection); *The Red Sun Gnaws at the Spider*, 1948 (Private Collection); *Woman and Bird in the Moonlight*, 1949 (London: Tate Collection)

✉ *Harlequin's Carnival* Joan Miró, 1924, 66 x 93 cm (26 x 36 ¾ in), oil on canvas, Buffalo: Albright-Knox Gallery. Miró claimed that his imagery was sometimes the result of hallucinations caused by extreme hunger.

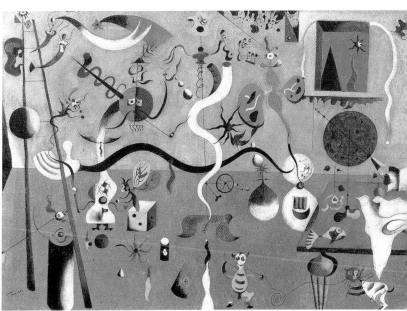

▽ *The Aged Emak Bakia*
Man Ray, 1970, after the original of 1924, height 46 cm (18 ¼ in), silver, private collection. The sculpture is named after an earlier Man Ray Surrealist film of 1927, *Emak Bakia*, which means "leave me alone" in Basque.

Man Ray

● **1890–1976** ⚐ **AMERICAN**
✍ **PHOTOGRAPHY; PRINTS; MIXED MEDIA**

Man Ray was the creator of memorable avant-garde Surrealist images, usually photographic. He was inventive (imaginatively and technically), witty, and anarchic. He cultivated a carefree persona with a maxim that the least possible effort would give the greatest possible result. He painted documentary portraits of the Dada and Surrealist heroes.

KEY WORKS: *Silhouette*, 1916 (New York: Guggenheim Museum); *Duchamp with Mill*, 1917 (Los Angeles: J. Paul Getty Museum)

Meret **Oppenheim**

● **1913–85** ⚐ **GERMAN**
✍ **SCULPTURE; MIXED MEDIA**

Oppenheim will always be remembered for her Surrealist fur teacup *Object* (see page 318). She produced engaging, delicate, whimsical work on many themes, and in many media and styles, individually slight but collectively expressing her refusal to be categorized and pinned down. She had a free spirit and disliked prescribed roles, especially for women. Witches and snakes are recurring images.

KEY WORKS: *Object (Le Déjeuner en Fourrure)*, 1931 (Houston: Museum of Fine Arts); *Sitzende Figur mit verschränkten Fingern*, 1933 (Bern, Switzerland: Kunstmuseum); *Red Head, Blue Body*, 1936 (New York: Museum of Modern Art)

Sir Roland **Penrose**

● **1900–84** ⚐ **BELGIAN** ✍ **OILS**

Penrose was a rich and eccentric painter, writer, dilettante, connoisseur, and collector – another shining example of the uniquely British "gifted amateur". A friend of Picasso and Ernst, he was a champion of Surrealism. He made and painted good (if derivative) Surrealist works.

KEY WORKS: *Night and Day*, 1937 (Private Collection); *The Last Voyage of Captain Cook*, 1936–67 (London: Tate Collection)

Paul **Delvaux**

● **1897–1994** ⚐ **BELGIAN** ✍ **OILS**

Delvaux was a loner who created a limited and repetitive *oeuvre* of finely detailed, vaguely erotic, and symbolic, night-time, dreamland images based on themes of naked women, semi-deserted railway stations or landscapes, and classic buildings. He was admired by, but not allied with, the true Surrealists. Delvaux was influenced by Magritte and the De Chirico exhibition of 1926.

KEY WORKS: *A Siren in Full Moonlight*, 1940 (New Haven: Yale Center for British Art); *The Red City*, 1941 (Private Collection)

René **Magritte**

● **1898–1967** ⚐ **BELGIAN** ✍ **OILS; GOUACHE; PRINTS**

Magritte was a leading Surrealist painter who made a virtue of his bowler-hatted, cheap-suited provincialism. He was famous for his use of everyday objects plus a deadpan style, creating mildly disturbing images that suggest the dislocated world of dreams.

He painted small(ish) oil paintings and used a deliberately banal technique, without aesthetic virtue – imagery is everything. He transformed the familiar into the unfamiliar with weird juxtapositions, changes of scale and texture, and by defying expectation. The titles of his works (sometimes chosen by friends) are deliberately designed to confuse and obscure. His best work dates from the 1920s and 1930s. He changed style after 1943. He worked as a freelance advertising artist from 1924 to 1967.

Magritte used classic Freudian symbols and references – death and decay (coffins, night); sex (naked women, pubic parts); phallic symbols (guns, sausages, candles). His themes were claustrophobia (closed rooms, confined spaces = sexual repression?) and yearning for liberty (blue sky, fresh landscapes). He witnessed his mother's suicide at age 13. His work risked becoming a tired formula (his very late work is), but was saved by an active imagination and a sense of the absurd.

KEY WORKS: *The Menaced Assassin*, 1926 (New York: Museum of Modern Art); *Reproduction Prohibited*, 1937 (Rotterdam: Museum Boijmans Van Beuningen); *The Song of Love*, 1948 (Private Collection); *Golconde*, 1953 (Houston: Menil Collection)

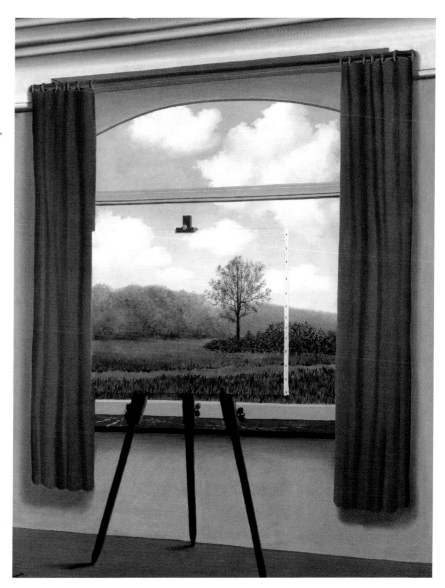

» **The Human Condition** *René Magritte, 1933, 100 x 81 cm (39 ⅔ x 32 in), oil on canvas, Washington DC: National Gallery of Art.* Magritte was influenced by the German philosopher, Kant, who argued that humans can rationalize but not understand "things-in-themselves".

Matta

● 1911–2002 ⚑ CHILEAN ✍ OILS; PRINTS; DRAWINGS

Roberto Sebastián Echaurren, or Matta, was a revolutionary spirit who was born in Santiago but settled in France in 1933 and became an early Surrealist. Like many other artists, he left for the US when World War II broke out but resettled in Paris in 1954. The author of strange, dream-like paintings with complex spaces and totem-like figures, he had a poetic agenda: searching for links between the cosmos, the eroticism of the human body, and the human psychic space. He intended his work to exalt freedom and aid mankind's struggle against oppression.

KEY WORKS: *Psychological Morphology*, 1939 (Toronto: Art Gallery of Ontario); *La Rosa*, 1943 (Ohio: Cleveland Museum of Art)

Sir Stanley **Spencer**

● **1891–1959** 📖 **BRITISH** ✍ **OILS; DRAWING**

Spencer was a difficult, argumentative but inspired personality with a unique and personal vision and great talent. He preached, practised, and illustrated sexual liberation at a time when such things were "not done".

His work shows English eccentricity at its best and most convincing. He disregarded prevailing conventions (social and moral, as well as artistic), and had an utterly personal agenda and unshakeable belief in his own vision and ability. The focus of his life and major work was around his home village of Cookham, which he saw as an earthly paradise. It also provided the setting for his profound belief in the return of Christ for and among ordinary people.

Observe his humanity, humour, and acerbic wit. He had a dry, careful, deliberately outdated technique inspired by early Italians, Pre-Raphaelites, and Dutch and Flemish painters. A masterly and inspired draughtsman his best works are his religious and World War I subjects. His potboiler landscapes earned him money. Like all true visionary eccentrics, he managed to be separate from his own time and era yet totally of it.

KEY WORKS: *The Centurion's Servant*, 1914 (London: Tate Collection); *The Resurrection: Cookham*, 1924–26 (London: Tate Collection); *Self-Portrait with Patricia Preece*, 1936 (Cambridge: Fitzwilliam Museum); *A Village in Heaven*, 1937 (Manchester: City Art Gallery)

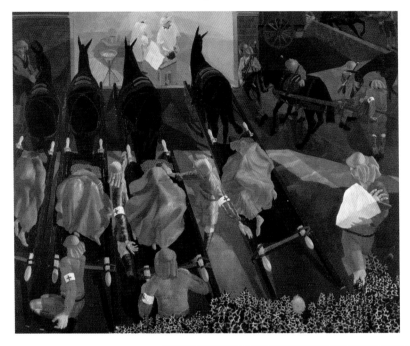

◀◀ *Travoys Arriving with the Wounded at a Dressing Station, Smol, Macedonia* Sir Stanley Spencer, 1916, 183 x 218.5 cm (72 x 86 in), oil on canvas, London: Imperial War Museum. Spencer served in the army as a medical orderly and infantryman.

Paul **Nash**

● **1889–1946** 📖 **BRITISH** ✍ **OILS; MIXED MEDIA; PHOTOGRAPHY**

One of the best British artists before 1950, Nash successfully blended an English pastoral vision with an awareness of European modern art. The voice of "I am English first and foremost, of Europe but not in Europe."

His small-scale works in oil, pastel, or watercolour show a deeply personal first-hand response to landscape, coastline, the sun, moon, and objects in nature. He was careful in every sense and very English, of a certain type: self-contained, serious, gentle, parochial, romantic, polite, self-assured, independent, but not too progressive. He used spare, well-focused imagery and style and an earthy English palette. He worked as a war artist in both world wars. He focused on the trench landscape and its destruction in World War I and flight and aircraft in World War II. His capacity for juxtaposing the unexpected and transposing one object into another by association links him with the Surrealists. Note how he abstracted from nature and organized his perceptions, feelings, and paintings to capture the essential feel of a place – the so-called "genius loci".

KEY WORKS: *Mineral Objects*, 1935 (New Haven: Yale Center for British Art); *Circle of Monoliths*, 1937–38 (Leeds: City Art Gallery); *Monster Field*, 1939 (South Africa: Durban Art Gallery); *Totes Meer (Dead Sea)*, 1940–41 (London: Tate Collection)

Ivon **Hitchens**

⬤ 1893–1979 📖 BRITISH ✍ OILS; DRAWINGS

Hitchens was a sensitive painter who made a slow, patient progress from figuration to abstraction. His main theme was landscape, often in long horizontal format, in which colour and form are increasingly abstracted to simple elements. Among the first in England to sustain a development of post-Cubist painting, he also painted still lifes and nudes.

KEY WORKS: *Balcony at Cambridge*, 1929 (London: Tate Collection); *Winter Stage*, 1936 (London: Tate Collection)

Henry **Moore**

⬤ 1898–1986 📖 BRITISH ✍ SCULPTURE; DRAWINGS

Moore was a gritty, ambitious Yorkshireman, one of the best-known British modern masters. His work was a popular choice for international sculptural monuments but looks best in a landscape setting rather than a gallery or city square.

His romantic response to nature and the human figure is often expressed as a synthesis of the two, so that his forms can be read simultaneously as organic nature (rocks, cliffs, trees), and as human figures. He consciously rejected Renaissance notions of ideal beauty, but was much influenced by Mexican, Egyptian, and English medieval sculpture. Direct carving and truth to materials were an imperative of his early work; this was gradually replaced by a desire for monumentality.

Walk around his sculptures to investigate the constantly changing relationships between the different parts. Moore was fascinated by the reclining nude, and mother-and-child images. He investigated ideas in his drawings and was a superb sculptural draughtsman. He flirted with Surrealism in the 1930s and made important war drawings in the 1940s. His work declined when he used assistants for late public monuments.

KEY WORKS: *Mother and Child*, 1936–37 (Leeds: City Art Gallery); *UNESCO Reclining Figure*, 1957 (forecourt of UNESCO headquarters, Paris); *Mirror Knife Edge*, 1976–77 (Washington DC: National Gallery of Art)

⬇ *Reclining Figure*
(LH 175) Henry Moore, 1936, height 64 cm (25 ¼ in), elmwood, West Yorkshire: Wakefield Art Gallery. Created when Moore believed in the idea of "truth to materials".

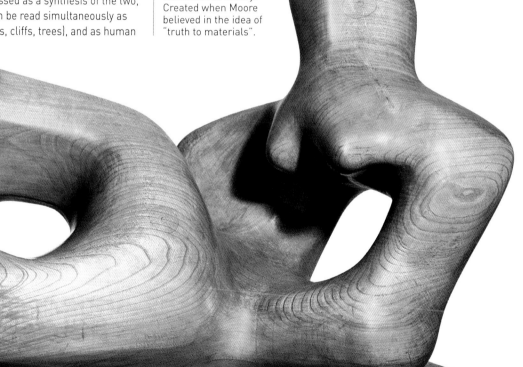

Ben **Nicholson**

● 1894–1982 ◗ BRITISH ✍ OILS; SCULPTURE

Doyen of the St Ives School, Nicholson was a pioneer of abstract art in Britain, and one of the UK's first modern artists. Son of Sir William Nicholson, he married Barbara Hepworth in 1934.

Nicholson moved easily between a pared-down figuration and pure abstraction, making interesting use of materials and scratched textures. The lean, athletic look and sense of calculation rather than spontaneity was central to his competitive persona, which enjoyed playing games (ball and psychological). His work shows his debt to modern European art – Cubism, Mondrian, and Braque. He chose traditional subject matter (landscapes and still lifes) for his paintings, reliefs, and drawings.

Notice the way in which he imposed English virtues of politeness or understatement on the unruly appearance of the European avant-garde, making it as well-tailored as a Savile Row suit and as well-mannered as a game of gentlemen's cricket (both express deep passions as well as reserve). Does the fact that his work looks equally at home in modern or traditional, country or urban, British or European settings suggest that it is bland – or does it mean it is the essence of international savoir-faire?

KEY WORKS: *St Ives Bay: Sea with Boats*, 1931 (Manchester: City Art Gallery); *White Relief*, 1935 (London: Tate Collection); *February 1956 (menhir)*, 1956 (New York: Guggenheim Museum)

≫ ST IVES GROUP 1940s–1960s

St Ives in Cornwall became a creative colony for British artists after the arrival in 1939 of sculptor Barbara Hepworth and her then husband Ben Nicholson, who had discovered retired fisherman painter Alfred Wallis on an earlier visit to the town. Wallis's naïve paintings later inspired many of the group, which included artists Terry Frost, Patrick Heron, and sculptor Henry Moore.

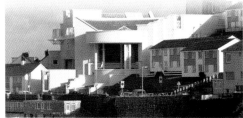

◪ *September 1963 Ben Nicholson, 1963, oil and collage on fibrocement, private collection*. In the 1930s, Nicholson explored abstraction through carved relief sculptures. In the 1950s, he returned to the theme, making constructions out of boards that he cut, assembled, and painted.

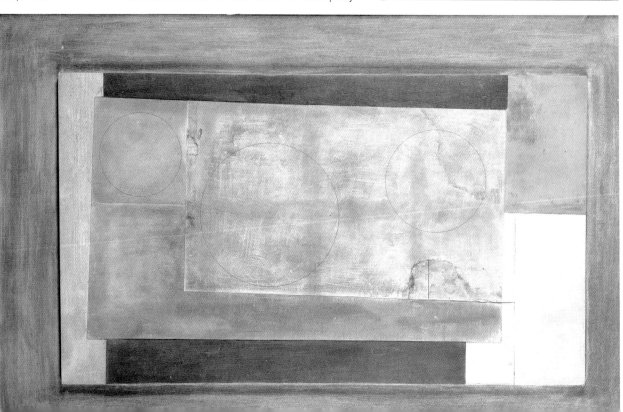

Dame Barbara **Hepworth**

● 1903-75 ◫ BRITISH ✍ SCULPTURE

Hepworth was a leading member of the first generation of British modern masters. She expressed in sculpture, for the first time, the tradition of English Romantic landscape. She was much honoured and revered both in her lifetime and subsequently.

Look for a deeply emotional response to, and identification with, nature and landscape. Her inspiration came from light, the seasons, natural materials, and the mysteries of nature. She searched for (and found) fundamental essences and elements. These were distilled and abstracted, for instance, into simplified forms and pure colour as in the work of Matisse (she had contact with the French avant-garde in 1932), although Hepworth's starting point was nature, not the human figure. She made some geometric carvings in the 1930s. She also made beautiful drawings.

She had a lifelong belief in truth to materials – taking stone, wood, bronze (after 1950) and revealing the unique quality of each individual piece, adapting the final form to its own peculiarities. She initiated and developed pierced form to explore materials and evoke nature's mystery and organic growth. She used strings to express emotional response and tension. Greek titles, after her visit to Greece in 1953, indicate her respect for the Classical tradition.

KEY WORKS: *Doves*, 1928 (Manchester: City Art Gallery); *Minoan Head*, 1972 (Cambridge: Fitzwilliam Museum)

⬆ *Involute 1* Dame Barbara Hepworth, 1946, height 45.7 cm (18 in), white stone, private collection. Pierced abstract form became a distinctive feature, allowing Hepworth to explore the physical essence and inherent poetry of her materials. Her first such piece dates from 1931–32.

John **Piper**

● 1903-92 ◫ BRITISH ✍ OILS; PRINTS

Piper was a serious, well-regarded painter and printmaker notable for a very personal, stylized, romantic imagery of landscape and architecture, especially churches and stately homes. He was also a book illustrator and a designer for the theatre and of stained glass windows. Once the epitome of acceptable modernity, his work can look dated, but is coming back into fashion.

KEY WORKS: *Beach with Starfish*, 1933–34 (London: Tate Collection); *Autumn at Stourhead*, 1939 (Manchester: City Art Gallery)

Graham **Sutherland**

● 1903-80 ◫ BRITISH ✍ ENGRAVINGS; OILS

Sutherland's work is a fascinating example of English tradition and modern idiom cohabiting. His landscapes reveal a fascination with organic forms and metamorphosis. His portraits (his best work?) show a fascination for facial forms that contain the inner personality (like a fossil in a rock). He is still underrated.

KEY WORKS: *Somerset Maugham*, 1949 (London: Tate Collection); *Christ in Glory*, 1962 (Coventry Cathedral)

José Clemente **Orozco**

● 1883–1949 🇲🇽 MEXICAN ✍ OILS;
WATERCOLOURS

Orozco was one of the three great Mexican muralists (with Diego Rivera and David Alfaro Siqueiros). His public-building murals, in a cold and austere style, are based on his experiences of the Mexican Revolution and Civil War, showing the struggles and sacrifices of the people and the pain of needless suffering.

KEY WORKS: *Fresco series*, 1926 (Mexico City: Casa de los Azulejos); *The Coming and the Return of Quetzalcoatl*, 1932–34 (New Hampshire: Dartmouth College)

Diego **Rivera**

● 1886–1957 🇲🇽 MEXICAN ✍ OILS; FRESCO

Rivera was a giant – 6 ft, 21 stone, with a charismatic personality (political revolutionary and turbulent love life); and in the quantity and scale of his work. A Marxist, loved and financed by US mega-capitalists, he represents social realism at its most convincing. The large-scale murals he created in the 1920s and 1930s were designed for public spaces and express a utopian view of society – they are political statements of art in the service of society. His vision was a union between Mexico's indigenous history and a machine-age future in which past, present, the hereafter, nature, science, humanity, male and female, and all races and cultures coexist in harmony. He revived the art of monumental, true fresco, physically and conceptually.

The way he turned his vision into vast, crowded images is truly miraculous. He synthesized first-hand knowledge of pre-Columbian art, Modernism (Cubist space), realism, and early Renaissance frescoes (the monumental, simplified forms of Giotto, Masaccio, and Piero) into brilliantly organized and controlled decorative pageants, with a storyteller's instinct for memorable detail. Rivera also produced seductive, smaller-scale easel paintings and sketches: portraits, figures, narrative scenes, and still lifes.

KEY WORKS: *Still Life*, 1913 (St Petersburg: Hermitage Museum); *Table on a Café Terrace*, 1915 (New York: Metropolitan Museum of Art); *The Aztec World*, 1929 (Mexico City: Palacio Nacional)

David Alfaro **Siqueiros**

● 1896–1974 🇲🇽 MEXICAN ✍ OILS; ACRYLICS

A prolific painter and writer who was deeply involved in progressive, political causes in Mexico in the 1920s and 1930s, Siqueiros is revered as Mexico's greatest painter.

He produced solemn (gloomy?) works with strong political commitment – art in the service of the people's revolution. Look for monumental, sculptural peasants and faces; direct, earthy subjects. He was technically accomplished and quietly experimental (he made very early use of industrial paints and drip techniques), and was unshakeably consistent in his style and belief.

His crowning achievements are the vast *in situ* murals in Mexico, which are revolutionary manifestos in their own right and exploit daring, cinema-inspired angles and perspectives.

KEY WORKS: *Zapata*, 1931 (New York: Metropolitan Museum of Art); *Seated Nude*, 1931 (San Francisco: Fine Arts Museums)

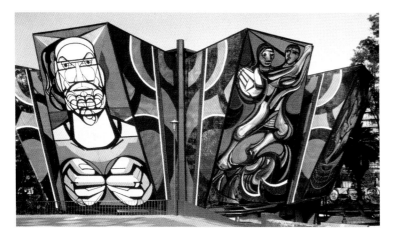

◀ *The March of Humanity in Latin America* David Alfaro Siqueiros, 1964, area 4,645 sq. metres (50,000 sq. ft), mural painting, Mexico City: Polyforum Siqueiros. Siqueiros considered this his greatest achievement and the union of all his discoveries.

Frida **Kahlo**

● 1907–54 🏛 MEXICAN ✍ OILS

Kahlo was one of the best-known Mexican painters. She created powerful, figurative images that synthesized her sufferings, both physical (she was crippled in a car accident aged 18) and emotional (her stormy marriage to Diego Rivera), along with an exploration of themes of Mexican politics and identity. Is her art essentially parochial, or does it touch deeper levels of emotion?

KEY WORKS: *Self-Portrait with Monkey*, 1938 (Buffalo: Albright-Knox Art Gallery); *The Two Fridas*, 1939 (Mexico City: Museo de Arte Moderno); *Self-Portrait with Cropped Hair*, 1940 (New York: Museum of Modern Art)

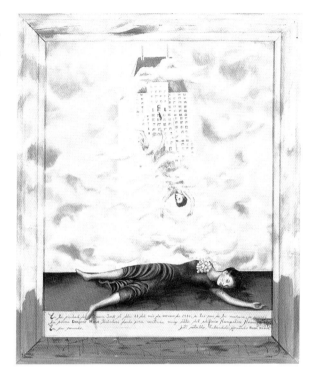

» **Suicide of Dorothy Hale** *Frida Kahlo, 1939, 59.7 x 49.5 cm (23 ½ x 19 ½ in), oil on masonite with painted frame, Arizona: Phoenix Art Museum.* Dorothy Hale was a beautiful socialite who, after losing her husband and her financial security, threw herself to her death from the window of her New York apartment.

Giorgio **Morandi**

● 1890–1964 🏛 ITALIAN ✍ OILS; ENGRAVINGS

Morandi was reclusive, isolated, and gifted, best known for his post-1920 still lifes of simple objects (such as bottles) of great delicacy and seductive, poetic simplicity. His works are small scale, low key and almost monochrome, almost abstract, to be enjoyed in silence. His pre-1920 metaphysical paintings are good and he made beautiful etchings.

KEY WORKS: *Still Life*, 1948 (Parma: Fondazione Magnani-Rocca); *Still Life*, 1957 (Hamburg: Kunsthalle)

Giorgio **de Chirico**

● 1888–1978 🏛 ITALIAN ✍ OILS; SCULPTURE

De Chirico was the originator of metaphysical painting. A melancholic curmudgeon with a brief period of true greatness around 1910–20, he made haunting paintings of deserted Italianate squares with exaggerated perspectives, irrational shadows, trains, clocks, oversized objects, and a sense of latent menace and ungraspable meaning. He was much influenced by Nietzsche. Late work is weak.

KEY WORKS: *The Uncertainty of the Poet*, 1913 (London: Tate Collection); *The Painter's Family*, 1926 (London: Tate Collection)

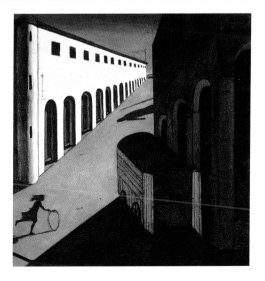

« *The Mystery and Melancholy of a Street* Giorgio de Chirico, 1914, 88 x 72 cm (34 ⅔ x 28 ⅓ in), oil on canvas, private collection. De Chirico's poetic suggestions of the unpredictable were an inspiration for the Surrealists.

Hans **Hofmann**

● 1880–1966 ◫ GERMAN/AMERICAN ✎ OILS; DRAWINGS

Hofmann was a pioneering, but only moderately successful, abstract painter (his style was never fully resolved – principally large squares modified by thick pigment and bright colour). Hugely gifted and influential as a teacher, he was the key figure in bringing news of the European giants (like Picasso) to the younger generation of soon-to-be American Abstract Expressionists.

KEY WORKS: *Autumn Gold*, 1957 (Washington DC: National Gallery of Art); *City Horizon*, 1959 (San Francisco: Museum of Modern Art)

✉ *Tango Elie Nadelman, c.1918–24, height approx. 88 cm (34 ⅓ in), cherry wood and gesso, Houston: Museum of Fine Arts.* Impressed by American popular culture, the artist also borrowed from folk art to make observations about high society.

Elie **Nadelman**

● 1882–1946 ◫ POLISH/AMERICAN ✎ SCULPTURE

A gifted Polish sculptor of great charm, Nadelman moved to Paris in 1904. His Parisian style was eclectic in the Classical Greek tradition. He moved to London around 1914 before emigrating to New York at the onset of World War I. There he counted cosmetics queen Helena Rubinstein among his patrons and she commissioned Nadelman to create a set of marble heads for her beauty salons. In 1919, he married an heiress and became a pioneer collector of folk art. He himself created charming folk art – inspired wood sculptures (with a hint of the Hellenistic). After a decade of living the high life he lost everything financially in the economic depression that followed the Wall Street Crash of 1929.

His sculptures often have the silhouettes of figures in Seurat's paintings. His work is an interesting and

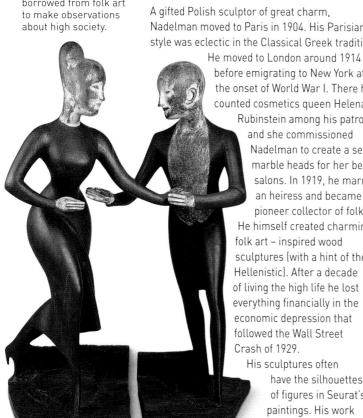

successful synthesis of ancient and modern, the common denominator being a search for purity in form and materials.

KEY WORKS: *Classical Head with Headdress*, 1908–09 (Wisconsin: Milwaukee Art Museum); *Standing Female Nude*, c.1909 (Washington DC: Hirshhorn Museum)

Balthus

● 1908–2001 ◫ FRENCH ✎ OILS

His full name was Balthasar Klossowski de Rola Balthus. Self-taught and precocious, with Polish antecedents, he was well-connected intellectually (Bonnard and Rilke were family friends). A recluse, he worked against the modern grain and was ideologically opposed to abstract art and determined to establish the importance of craftsmanship.

He painted landscapes and portraits and his work probes the area between innocence and perversity, reality and dream. Note the slow and careful workmanship. His work is an affirmation of time-honoured virtues such as precise draughtsmanship, oil paint, observation from life, conscious creation of beauty, muted tones, delicate colour, light, and the primacy of the human figure.

KEY WORKS: *The Living Room*, 1941–43 (Minnesota: Minneapolis Institute of Arts); *Sleeping Girl*, 1943 (London: Tate Collection)

Louise **Nevelson**

● 1899–1988 ◫ RUSSIAN/AMERICAN ✎ SCULPTURE; MIXED MEDIA; OILS

Born Louise Berliawsky in Kiev (the family emigrated to the US in 1905), Nevelson was brought up with wood (the family business was timber) and was always dedicated to being a sculptor (to the point of abandoning her husband and child). She only discovered her signature style in the 1950s – open-sided boxes made into reliefs, each box containing an assortment of forms created from wood scraps, painted in monochrome, usually black.

Her sculpture is most impressive when on a large scale. It is distinguished work that carries within it the sort of accumulated experience and mysterious gravitas that comes with old age. It must be absorbed slowly just like the company or wisdom of the ancients. This is a welcome reminder that no one is ever too old to be creative: Nevelson's best work was done in her 70s and 80s.

KEY WORKS: *White Vertical Water*, 1941–43 (Minnesota: Minneapolis Institute of Arts); *Sky Cathedral*, 1958 (Buffalo: Albright-Knox Art Gallery)

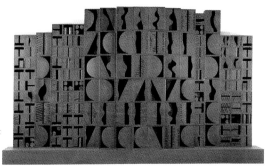

◀ *Mirror Image 1*
Louise Nevelson, 1969, height 534 cm (210 ¼ in), painted wood, Houston: Museum of Fine Arts. Nevelson took the boxes that she had previously used as pedestals for her work and turned them into art, filling them with carved wooden forms. This inspiration led her to create wall-sized assemblages.

Joseph **Cornell**

● 1903–72 [PU] **AMERICAN** ✍ **SCULPTURE; MIXED MEDIA; OILS**

Cornell created strange, small-scale imaginative boxes. Though often pigeonholed as Surrealist, they are poetic reveries rather than Freudian dream worlds. He lived a lonely, reclusive life in Flushing, New York, with his mother and crippled brother, scouring junk shops for bits and pieces which he filed away meticulously.

Many of the reveries are about travel that he never undertook (maps and images of Paris, for instance) or film stars he never met. He often tinkered for years with the images and contents of individual boxes. The glass fronts of the boxes symbolically separate the real world from the dream. There is no sexual imagery – he disapproved of Surrealism's "unhealthy" aspects.

KEY WORKS: *Tilly Losch*, 1935 (Private Collection); *Untitled (The Hotel Eden)*, 1945 (Ottawa: National Gallery of Canada)

Grant **Wood**

● 1892–1942 [PU] **FRENCH** ✍ **OILS; TEMPERA**

Wood painted fantastical, childlike landscapes, and portraits, murals, and stained glass. His quirky work reflects old-fashioned virtues: sobriety, strict parents, and sexual morality. He had a painstaking, stiff, old-fashioned style, and often worked in tempera. Iowa-raised, Wood was the (closet gay) altar boy of American regionalism.

American Gothic is as famous in American art as the *Mona Lisa* is in Italian art, and just as enigmatic. Does it parody the chaste and sober

virtues it proclaims or is it admiring of them? The work never reveals the answer, and he never confessed to anyone.

KEY WORKS: *American Gothic*, 1930 (Art Institute of Chicago); *The Midnight Ride of Paul Revere*, 1931 (New York: Metropolitan Museum of Art); *Daughters of the Revolution*, 1932 (Ohio: Cincinnati Art Museum)

Charles **Sheeler**

● 1883–1965 [PU] **AMERICAN** ✍ **OILS; PHOTOGRAPHY**

Sheeler was a dour, romantic painter and photographer who turned the industrial landscape into works of art as carefully calculated, precise, and free of human presence as any mass-produced objects. He worked for Henry Ford and shared his belief that factories are temples of worship. He replaced the sublimity of wild nature with the sublimity of the urban landscape. In 1959, he suffered a stroke and had to give up painting and photography.

KEY WORKS: *Fugue*, 1940 (Boston: Museum of Fine Arts); *Aerial Gyrations*, 1953 (San Francisco: Museum of Modern Art); *Stacks in Celebration*, 1954 (New York: Berry-Hill Galleries)

▶ *Steam Turbine* Charles Sheeler, *1939, 56 x 45.7 cm (22 x 18 in), oil on canvas, Ohio: Butler Institute of American Art.* The fifth in the series of six "Power" paintings commissioned by *Fortune* magazine.

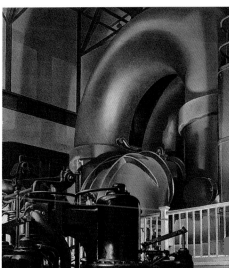

Charles **Demuth**

● 1883–1935 🇺🇸 AMERICAN 🖌 OILS;
WATERCOLOURS

Demuth was the leading Precisionist of the 1920s
and 1930s. He produced small-scale views of
industrial architecture (factories, water towers, and
silos), carefully painted with a front-on view and an
emphasis on simplified geometry. Note his subtle
colours and acute observation of light and shade,
and the total absence of any human presence.

KEY WORKS: *My Egypt*, 1927 (New York: Whitney
Museum of American Art); *I Saw the Figure
Five in Gold*, 1928 (New York: Metropolitan
Museum of Art)

Edward **Hopper**

● 1882–1967 🇺🇸 AMERICAN 🖌 OILS;
ENGRAVINGS; WATERCOLOURS

Hopper was a taciturn, monosyllabic, New York
inhabitant with a small-town puritan upbringing,
who became a successful and quintessentially
American painter.

His imagery is the American urban landscape
and its inhabitants; also Cape Cod and Maine.
His observation and ability to record light
(notably harsh, electric light) were marvellous.
His technique was spare, lean, and tough (like
many of his subjects). He had a strong sense
of colour and the ability to create tense,
confined spaces. He was influenced by
photography and the movies (he was an
avid moviegoer) and Impressionism (he
visited Paris in 1906–07 and 1909–10).

How was Hopper able to make the commonplace
and banal so uneasy, significant, and memorable?
Was it his magic way with light or his ability to
simplify and generalize – to express a universal
mood, not just an anecdotal story? His subtle space
distortions create a sense that something is wrong
or about to happen. Similar talents were shown by
the great black-and-white movie producers (like
Hitchcock) – many of Hopper's pictures could be
stills from a movie.

KEY WORKS: *Early Sunday Morning*, 1930 (New York:
Whitney Museum of American Art); *Cape Cod Evening*,
1939 (Washington DC: National Gallery of Art);
Nighthawks, 1942 (Art Institute of Chicago)

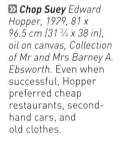

⟫ *Chop Suey* *Edward
Hopper, 1929, 81 x
96.5 cm (31 ¾ x 38 in),
oil on canvas, Collection
of Mr and Mrs Barney A.
Ebsworth*. Even when
successful, Hopper
preferred cheap
restaurants, second-
hand cars, and
old clothes.

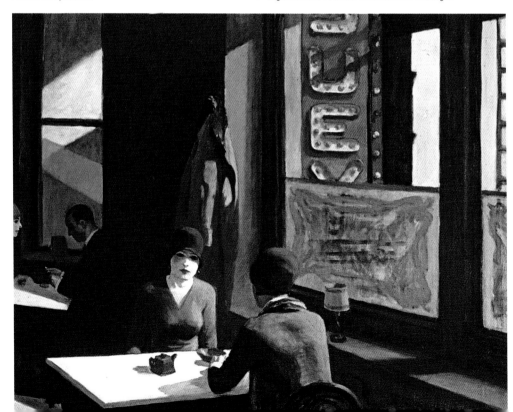

Grandma **Moses**

● 1860–1961 📖 AMERICAN ✍ OILS

Née Anna Mary Robertson, Moses was a self-taught farmer's wife from Virginia in Vermont who, in the 1930s, aged over 70, became a celebrity. Her paintings are in a naïve style with nostalgic images of idyllic rural life, full of women and children. She copied details from popular prints; her work was in turn endlessly reproduced as greeting cards, wallpaper, and fabrics.

KEY WORKS: *My Hills of Home*, 1941 (New York: University of Rochester); *Black Horses*, 1942 (Private Collection); *Making Apple Butter*, 1958 (Art Institute of Chicago)

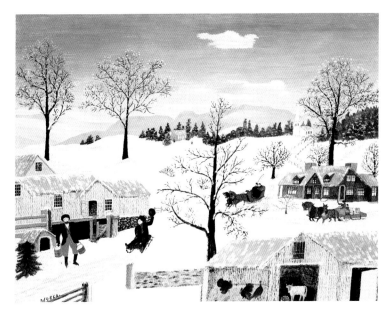

⊠ *Down on the Farm in Winter* Grandma Moses, 1945, 49.5 x 60 cm (19 ½ x 23 ⅜ in), oil on masonite, Tokyo: Fuji Museum. Grandma Moses spent most of her life on a farm, first as hired help, and then as the wife of a farmer. Many of her paintings depict her memories of that time.

Georgia **O'Keeffe**

● 1887–1986 📖 AMERICAN ✍ OILS

O'Keeffe was an influential but one-off artist, outside the mainstream of modern art. Her work will probably be remembered and valued far longer than many other 20th-century names that are currently in fashion or overpraised.

Her intense and exotic imagery lay in that intriguing area between figuration and abstraction. She made very powerful images of nature and architecture, which have a strong period feel of the 1920s, 1930s, and 1940s. Her ability to simplify and intensify colour, movement, and pattern has something in common with the best of the classic Disney cartoons, notably *Fantasia*, with which her work was contemporary (Walt Disney: 1901–66).

Many of her paintings have the shifting and fantastic qualities seen in cloud patterns in the sky. Look for plants and flowers (often in close-up), mountains, and animal bones. Note how she transformed all of them into something that has a strong unreal, even surreal, poetic life: mountains become flesh; plants become organisms like sea anemones; skulls live and see. She used unusual and intense colour combinations and bold simple patterns.

KEY WORKS: *Black Iris*, 1926 (New York: Metropolitan Museum of Art); *Ranchos Church*, 1929 (Washington DC: Phillips College); *Jack-in-the-Pulpit No. IV*, 1930 (Washington DC: National Gallery of Art); *Red Hills with White Shell*, 1938 (Houston: Museum of Fine Arts); *White Iris No.7*, 1957 (Madrid: Museo Thyssen-Bornemisza)

Thomas Hart **Benton**

● 1889–1975 📖 AMERICAN ✍ OILS

Considered the High Priest of American Regionalism, Benton came from a national, political family and was a cantankerous, homophobic, anti-Modern, energetic self-publicist. He was a determined painter of subjects that proclaim the authentic virtues of the Midwest, non-urban American life – bulging, restless figures

in heaving swirling spaces. Benton was a keen user of deliberately coarse and vulgar colours. He was very popular, and his works influenced Jackson Pollock.

KEY WORKS: *Martha's Vineyard*, c.1925 (Washington DC: Corcoran Gallery of Art); *Cattle Loading, West Texas*, 1930 (Andover, Massachusetts: Addison Gallery of American Art); *Roasting Ears*, 1930 (New York: Metropolitan Museum of Art)

Jacob **Lawrence**

1917–2000 AMERICAN OILS

Lawrence's was the first voice of an authentic art by and for African-Americans. Born in Atlanta, he resided in Harlem. He researched and understood the Great Migration and Ku Klux Klan persecution. He is most famous for the "Migration" series – 60 small powerful paintings in a spare, lean, modern style with intense colours, which are strengthened by their understatement and the lack of any expression of hatred.

KEY WORKS: *The Migrants Arrived in Great Numbers*, 1940-41 (New York: Museum of Modern Art); *The Wedding*, 1948 (Art Institute of Chicago); *Street to Mbari*, 1964 (Washington DC: National Gallery of Art)

Mark **Tobey**

1890–1976 AMERICAN OILS

Tobey was a sensitive artist who developed a very personal abstract style, serene and luminous, from small calligraphic marks and gestures. This did not happen until the mid-1940s when he was aged over 50 (he was a contemporary of Picasso, rather than Pollock). He was influenced by spiritual faith (a convert to Bahai), Far East calligraphy, Amerindian art, and Japanese woodcuts.

KEY WORKS: *Fragments in Time and Space*, 1956 (Washington DC: Hirshhorn Museum); *Advance of History*, 1964 (New York: Guggenheim Museum); *Composition*, 1967 (San Francisco: Fine Arts Museums)

David **Smith**

1906–65 AMERICAN SCULPTURE

Smith created beautiful, inventive, poetic works made from iron, steel, and found objects, which he welded, manipulated, and coaxed into constructions of great originality. His quiet modesty, honest beliefs, and deep feeling touched his work with a profound sense of the presence of fundamental and universal forces, and of human worth. One of the most influential and original modern sculptors of his generation.

KEY WORKS: *Hudson River Landscape*, 1951 (New York: Whitney Museum of American Art); *Books and Apple*, 1957 (Harvard University: Fogg Art Museum); *Cubi XXVII*, 1965 (New York: Guggenheim Museum)

Jackson **Pollock**

1912–56 AMERICAN OILS; ENAMELS; MIXED MEDIA

A pioneering abstract painter of the New York School, nicknamed "Jack the Dripper", Pollock was a tortured alcoholic who swung between sensitivity and machismo, elation and despair.

His work is at its best when on a large scale, such as 4 x 7 m (12 x 24 ft), as it is only then that the passionate, heroic, monumental nature of his

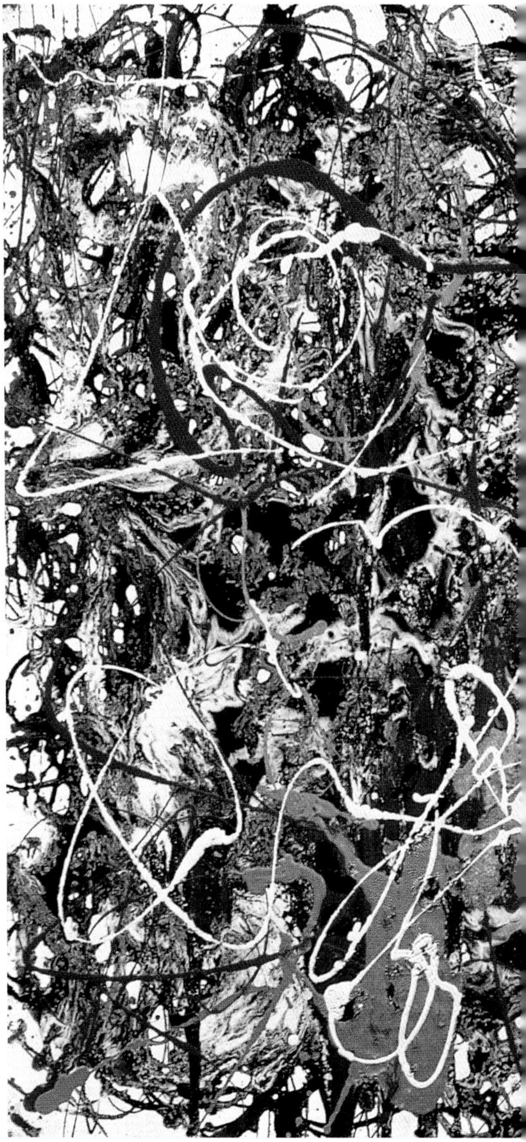

achievement becomes fully apparent. (A child of five cannot conceive or create on this scale.) He put the canvas on the floor and stood in the middle with a can of paint – he consciously wanted to be "in" the painting and to become physically part of it.

Look for the rhythms and flow in the threads of paint (they may be instinctive, but they are never arbitrary or careless). How many separate layers of paint can you see? It is just about possible to reconstruct his movements, and so be "in" the painting at second hand. But why no footprints?

KEY WORKS: *Blue Poles (Number 11, 1952)*, 1952 (Canberra: National Gallery of Australia); *Number 1, 1950 (Lavender Mist)*, 1950 (Washington DC: National Gallery of Art); *The Deep*, 1953 (Paris: Musée National d'Art Moderne)

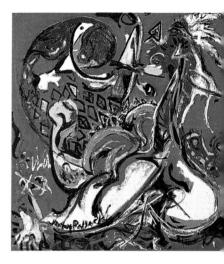

⌃ *The Moon-Woman Cuts the Circle* *Jackson Pollock, 1943, 109.5 x 104 cm (43 x 41 in), oil on canvas, Paris: Musée National d'Art Moderne*. Inspired by a North American Indian myth about the moon and the feminine.

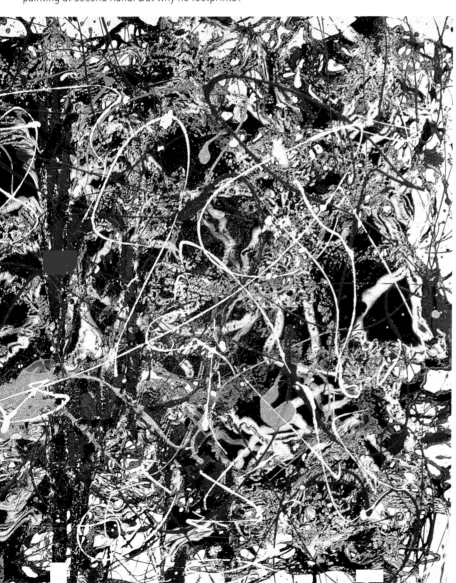

≪ *Number 6 Jackson Pollock, 1948, 57 x 78 cm (22 ⅔ x 30 ¾ in), oil on paper laid down on canvas, private collection*. Pollock first showed his drip paintings in 1948 at the Betty Parsons Gallery, New York.

Abstract Expressionism

LATE 1940s–1950s

Abstract Expressionism was the first original American art movement growing out of the human tragedies of the Great Depression and World War II, reaching maturity in the early years of the Cold War. Faced with the possibility of the denial of freedom of expression and the extinction of the human race, artists felt compelled to assert their individuality.

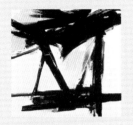

⏏ *Ballantine* Franz Kline, 1958–60, oil on canvas, Los Angeles: County Museum of Art. Kline's early work was black-and-white; later he used colour. The spontaneity is illusory: each "gesture" was painted slowly and deliberately.

It grew out of Surrealism but was never a coherent movement and it had no programme. Styles were wholly personal. New York now replaced Paris as the capital of artistic creativity. Among its leaders, Jackson Pollock dripped and flung paint onto his giant canvases, torn between the desire to allow chance to determine how it fell and to control the final result. Mark Rothko's immense areas of subtly modulated colour had precise, meditative ends in mind.

Sometimes energized forms (such as Pollock's) were intended to be a near documentary account of the artist's struggle to create in his or her direct encounter with the canvas. Other artists aimed to express the deepest and most universal of human emotions and anxieties in distorted figurative images, or fields of pure, deliberately modulated or contrasting colour. Yet as with music, ultimately all Abstract Expressionist works can only be felt intuitively rather than understood.

What to look for

Heroic imperatives dominate Abstract Expressionism. It is alternately bold and assertive, contemplative and questioning. Its impact derives in large measure from scale, large canvases – "portable murals" – that overwhelm and dazzle, seeming to draw the spectator into what can feel like a parallel universe. Texture is important, too, whether Pollock's rivulets and rivers of paint, Clyfford Still's thick, almost relief-like blocks of colour, or Rothko's layers of thinly applied colour. Rothko, however, spoke for them all when he said "... if you are moved only by the colour relationships, you miss the point ... I'm interested only in exploring basic human motions."

⏷ *Man on the Dunes* Willem de Kooning, 1971, oils, private collection. Part of the artist's passionate outpourings during the 1970s when his painting became an extreme frenzy of bold colours and paint layering smeared by newspapers.

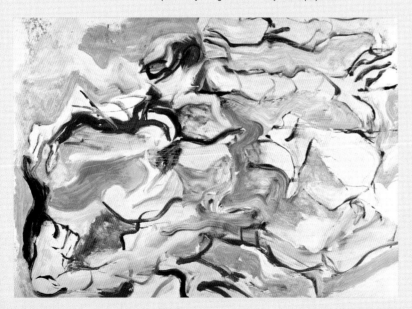

KEY EVENTS

1943	Rothko, Still, and Adolph Gottlieb assert the basic goals of their art in a letter to *The New York Times*
1946	*New Yorker* art critic Robert Coates coins the term "Abstract Expressionism"
1947	Pollock develops new style of Surrealist-influenced "automatic" painting, dripping paint onto huge canvases laid on the ground
1956	Pollock killed in car crash
1970	Rothko, suffering from deep depression, commits suicide in his studio

⟨⟨ *The Black and the White*
*Mark Rothko, 1956, 238 x 136 cm
(93 ¾ x 53 ½ in), oil on canvas,
Harvard: Fogg Art Museum.*
Abstract Expressionist works
were displayed unframed so
that they would be perceived
as a "presence" rather
than a tangible object.

Within a limited
range, Rothko's
colours have an
exceptional richness,
a seemingly infinite
series of subtle
gradations

Black in Rothko's
hands achieves a
gentle luminosity:
the sense of an
"infinite void"
is palpable

》 TECHNIQUES

In a typical motif, Rothko paints two
hazy, soft-edged blocks of colour,
the upper stacked weightlessly
over the lower, with both appearing
to hover over a delicate red base.
The effect of the work is deliberately
sublime, inducing a kind of
quasi-religious experience.

Mark **Rothko**

● 1903–70 �📧 AMERICAN ✍ OILS

A melancholic Russian émigré who settled in the US at the age of 10, Rothko became a leading member of the New York School and a pioneer of Colour Field abstract painting. He committed suicide.

His deceptively simple abstract paintings have deliberately plain, soft-edged shapes and luminous, glowing colours. His work is at its best seen on a large scale, completely filling a space such as the Rothko room at Tate Modern or the chapel at St Thomas University. Look for his early work to see how slowly and carefully he reached this final, very personal, expression.

Treat the works with the respect and care with which they were created and give them time to reach you. Move around them to get to know them; stand close to the works, relax, wait, so that the colour completely fills your field of vision and seeps through your eyes into your mood and feelings. Rothko said his paintings were about "tragedy, ecstasy, and doom" – about fundamental (and romantic) emotions and passions.

KEY WORKS: *Multiform*, 1948 (Canberra: National Gallery of Australia); *Untitled (Violet, Black, Orange, Yellow on White and Red)*, 1949 (New York: Guggenheim Museum); *Green and Maroon*, 1953 (Washington DC: Phillips College)

Willem **de Kooning**

● 1904–97 �📧 DUTCH/AMERICAN
✍ OILS; SCULPTURE

De Kooning was a Rotterdam-born painter and decorator who went to New York in 1926. He became one of the most consistent and longest-lived Abstract Expressionists.

He produced his best work between 1950 and 1963. One of the few artists to achieve a genuine synthesis between figuration and abstraction – the image (most famously, the woman) and the abstract expressive gesture coexist and interact as equal partners. After 1963 he lost control and direction, turning out work with arbitrary gestures, flabby colours, and splodgy decoration. His last paintings were, sadly, feeble (he had Alzheimer's disease).

He had a wonderful colour sense, using thrilling and unusual colour juxtapositions, and complex textures and interweaving of paint, which are a pleasure to look at. He created a truly exciting balance and tension between uncontrolled freedom and conscious control; between aggression and beauty; between abstraction and figuration (as skilled, daring, and breathtaking as a high-wire act). In the complexity of paint and imagery lurk subtle layers of meaning. Who can or will explain the tortured female?

KEY WORKS: *Woman and Bicycle*, 1952–53 (New York: Whitney Museum of American Art); *Marilyn Monroe*, 1954 (Private Collection)

Franz **Kline**

● 1910–62 �📧 AMERICAN ✍ OILS

Kline was a leading Abstract Expressionist who grew up in the industrial coal-mining region of Pennsylvania. He studied in Boston and London, lived a lonely life in New York, and died young.

At first, his big black-and-white abstract paintings from the 1950s and 1960s look like enlarged Chinese calligraphy. They are typical for their time: gestural, personal, spontaneous, moody, and full of existential angst. But, further acquaintance shows that this is the opposite of what they are.

Kline was not spontaneous. He worked out the compositions and placing of the brush marks very carefully. He painted well-balanced, serene pictures with astonishing cerebral and sensual harmony. Visitors to a Kline exhibition become noticeably deeply engaged with the works and each other.

KEY WORKS: *Ballantine*, 1948–60 (Los Angeles: County Museum of Art); *Chief*, 1950 (New York: Museum of Modern Art)

Robert **Motherwell**

● 1915-91 ▣ AMERICAN ✍ OILS; COLLAGE

Motherwell was an urbane, erudite, fluent, and influential painter, writer, and philosopher who was a leading Abstract Expressionist. He was married to Helen Frankenthaler.

His abstract paintings, drawings, and collages are always elegant. His work ranges from small-scale, intimate collages to grand, large-scale paintings. He enjoyed paint, accident, the unexpected, and calculated simplicity. Note the restrained use of colour.

His major achievement, the "Elegies to the Spanish Republic" series of paintings (more than 150 canvases done over his lifetime), form a deeply emotional response to the Spanish Civil War and Motherwell's realization that civilization can regress. The collages he built around wine labels, cigarette wrappers, and music are a diary of association, not an autobiography.

KEY WORKS: *Personage (Autoportrait)*, 1943 (New York: Guggenheim Museum); *Black on White*, 1961 (Houston: Museum of Fine Arts)

Barnett **Newman**

● 1905-70 ▣ AMERICAN ✍ OILS; SCULPTURE

Newman was a leading Abstract Expressionist, who developed a personal style of large-scale Colour Field painting that attempted to touch emotions and aspirations beyond the power of words to express.

Look for everything or nothing. If you see the intense colour fields with the simple vertical stripes as nothing more than that, you will not see much. But if you see, for example, the red background drawing aside to reveal an expanding opening into an infinite blue space (the blue stripe), or the yellow stripe as a flash of cosmic light, then you will see everything.

KEY WORKS: *Moment*, 1946 (London: Tate Collection); *Dionysius*, 1949 (Washington DC: National Gallery of Art)

☑ ***Vir Heroicus Sublimis*** *Barnett Newman, 1950–51, 242.2 x 513.6 cm (95 ⅜ x 213 ¼ in), oil on canvas, New York: Museum of Modern Art.* The title means "sublime heroic man" and is an exploration of transcendent experience.

Adolph **Gottlieb**

◐ 1903–74 ᴾᵁ AMERICAN ✍ OILS

Gottlieb was a well-known Abstract Expressionist, but was too sch ematic to be one of the great artists. He had two styles: pictographs and loose compartments filled with schematic and symbolic shapes (he was into Freud and Surrealism), which he produced from 1941 to 1951; and imaginary semi-abstract landscapes, typically with a simple, round, celestial body floating above loosely painted earthly chaos, which he created from the 1950s onwards.

KEY WORKS: *Romanesque Façade*, 1949 (Champaign, Illinois: Krannert Art Museum); *Ascent*, 1958 (New York: Adolph and Esther Gottlieb Foundation)

Clyfford **Still**

◐ 1904–80 ᴾᵁ AMERICAN ✍ OILS

One of the leading Abstract Expressionists, Still was intense, serious, painterly, heroic, romantic, and difficult to live with. A sensitive intellect in a rugged exterior, he was brought up in the big open spaces of Alberta, Canada, and Washington.

His early figurative work explored the relationship between humans and landscape. His later large-scale (for their time) abstract paintings are heavily worked, having rough surfaces with thick paint. He used intense colours and simple "imagery" consisting of flames or flashes of colour on a field of single colour, with a vertical format for paintings and "images". His works manifest a deliberate cragginess, intransigence, and awkwardness that reflect both the character of the artist and the agenda shared by his fellow Abstract Expressionists.

You have to spend time with the paintings and be prepared to meet the artist halfway. Still saw art as a moral power in an age of conformity; life as a force pitted against nature – especially earth and sky. Thus the vertical "necessity of life" arises from the horizontal. He continued the 19th-century tradition of Romantic landscape.

KEY WORKS: *Jamais*, 1944 (New York: Guggenheim Museum); *1953*, (London: Tate Collection)

Sam **Francis**

◐ 1923–94 ᴾᵁ AMERICAN ✍ ACRYLICS; WATERCOLOURS; PRINTS; SCULPTURE

Francis took up art as therapy while recovering from spinal injuries as a World War II fighter pilot. He made large-scale abstracts in which splattered and dribbled pure, translucent colour floats with weightless ease over a white background, conjuring up a magical, open, light-filled space.

KEY WORKS: *Red and Pink*, 1951 (San Francisco: Museum of Modern Art); *Around the Blues*, 1956–57 (London: Tate Collection)

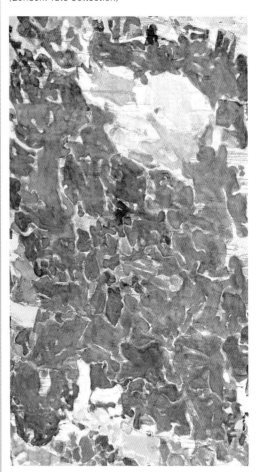

⊠ **In Lovely Blueness** *Sam Francis, 1955–57, 300 x 700 cm (118 x 275 ¾ in), acrylic on canvas, Paris: Musée National d'Art Moderne.* Francis was inspired by memories of light patterns on his hospital ceiling and the Pacific sky.

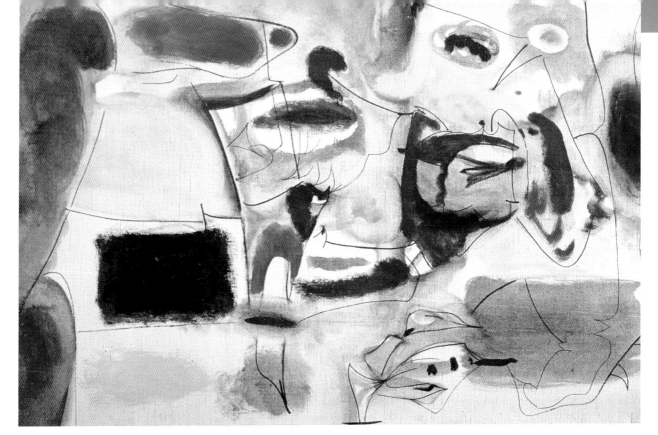

Arshile **Gorky**

◉ 1904–48 ◫ ARMENIAN/AMERICAN ✍ OILS

Gorky emigrated from Turkey to the US in 1920. He had an original lyrical, gentle, and poetic abstract painterly style, deriving inspiration from landscape and nature. He used natural colours and biomorphic forms influenced by Miró and Surrealism. As with many fellow Abstract Expressionists, his early death was tragic. He committed suicide after cancer, a car accident, and a disastrous studio fire.

KEY WORKS: *The Artist and his Mother*, 1926–29 (New York: Whitney Museum of American Art); *Hugging/Good Hope Road II*, 1945 (Madrid: Museo Thyssen-Bornemisza)

Richard **Diebenkorn**

◉ 1922–93 ◫ AMERICAN ✍ OILS

Considered an American-West Coast Matisse (whom he was much taken with), Diebenkorn was talented, influential, and very visual, but lacked a true master's range and tough-minded certainty.

His early abstracts (abstraction from nature) of 1948–56 were reactions to specific places (colour, topography, and light). Note the vigorous figurative work from 1956, with bold, simple designs, glowing colour, and juicy paint. He returned to abstraction with the Ocean Park series (from 1966); these works are large-scale, translucent, investigative, and statuesque. It is important to see his pieces by natural light – hard, artificial light kills subtleties. Don't rush: let the eye bask and play.

His most confident work is figurative. His abstracts are always oddly tentative – justified as sensitive, responsive, and so on, but somehow he could never reach that final distillation of sensation that so distinguishes Matisse. His early abstract work can be repetitive and unstructured, and can kill colour. Yet he demonstrated a stunning response to light (as good as Hopper's) and produced lovely small-scale work (cigar-box lids 1976–79). His late work was also small, as a heart disease prevented him from working large scale.

KEY WORKS: *Seated Nude, Black Background*, 1966 (Private Collection); *Seated Figure with Hat*, 1967 (Washington DC: National Gallery of Art)

⬈ *Untitled* Arshile *Gorky, 1946, 53.3 x 73.6 cm (21 x 29 in), mixed media, private collection.* In the 1940s, Gorky spent part of each year in Virginia, where his wife's family had a farm, making drawings in the countryside, then exploring multiple versions of the shapes and colours he had observed.

Jean **Tinguely**

◐ 1925–91 🏴 SWISS ✍ SCULPTURE; MIXED MEDIA

Tinguely was the creator of bizarre, unpredictable, clanking machines – made from junk – which move and whizz, sometimes to the point of self-destruction. His work is highly original and very humorous. He thought that change was the only constant in life. Tinguely delighted in expressing an anarchic freedom (against neat, orderly Switzerland?). He married Niki de Saint-Phalle and worked with her on his most famous work, *Beaubourg Fountain*.

KEY WORKS: *The Sorceress*, 1961 (Washington DC: Hirshhorn Museum); *Débricollage*, 1970 (London: Tate Collection); *Beaubourg Fountain*, 1980 (Paris: Centre Pompidou)

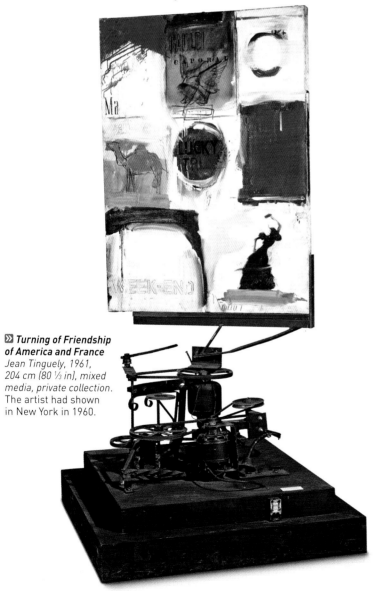

≫ *Turning of Friendship of America and France*
Jean Tinguely, 1961, 204 cm (80 ⅓ in), mixed media, private collection. The artist had shown in New York in 1960.

≫ **CoBrA** 1948–51

First founded in Paris by Belgian poet and essayist Christian Dotrement, the group were mainly inspired by their Marxist beliefs. Its members included Karel Appel, Asger Jorn, and Pierre Alechinsky; their art was experimental and sympathetic to Expressionism and Surrealism but showed its greatest affinity to folk art and children's art, and to the works of Paul Klee and Joan Miró. CoBrA's name was adopted from the names of the three capital cities of the countries of its principal members: Co from Copenhagen, Br from Brussels, and A from Amsterdam.

Asger **Jorn**

◐ 1914–73 🏴 DANISH ✍ OILS; DRAWINGS

A founder member of CoBrA, Jorn painted bold and free, intensely coloured, gestural works, sometimes abstract, sometimes with figurative imagery. He was at the forefront of European art until the mid-1960s, when Pop Art became the fashion.

KEY WORKS: *My Spanish Castle*, 1953 (Boston: Museum of Fine Arts); *The Three Sages*, 1955 (Brussels: Musées Royaux des Beaux-Arts); *Letter to My Son*, 1956–57 (London: Tate Collection)

Karel **Appel**

◐ 1921–2006 🏴 DUTCH ✍ OILS; SCULPTURES; DRAWINGS; PRINTS; CERAMICS

An important postwar artist and founder member of CoBrA, Appel was recognizable for thickly painted, brightly coloured Expressionist paintings that attempted to capture the spontaneity of children's painting, but also benefited from adult sophistication/organization and aesthetic sensibility, together with an ability to create on a large scale. Appel also produced scenery for a ballet.

KEY WORKS: *Burned Face*, 1961 (Private Collection); *Hip Hip Hooray*, 1949 (London: Tate Collection); *People, Birds, and Sun*, 1954 (London: Tate Collection)

Pierre **Alechinsky**

◉ 1927– 🏳 FRENCH ✍ OILS;
ACRYLICS; PRINTS

A painter and printmaker, Alechinsky
creates decorative, joyful, abstract
paintings, notable for their spontaneity,
lightness of touch, and glowing
translucent colour. He often uses the
formula of a central panel surrounded
by complementary border of small
calligraphic images. He makes
pleasure-giving work that is mercifully
free from introspection.

KEY WORKS: *Hors de Jeu*, 1962 (Rome:
L'Archimede – Galleria d'Arte); *To Day
Red Hot, Too Hot*, 1964 (San Francisco:
De Young Museum)

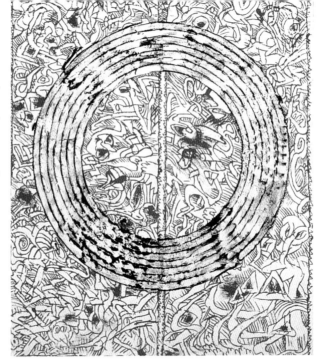

◀◀ *Octave* Pierre
Alechinsky, 1983,
print, private collection.
A one-time member
of the CoBrA group,
Alechinsky settled
in Paris in 1951, gaining
an interest in Japanese
calligraphy and visiting
the Far East.

Nicolas **de Staël**

◉ 1914–55 🏳 FRENCH ✍ OILS

An orphaned Russian aristocrat émigré who took
French citizenship in 1948, De Staël started with
an admiration for Old Masters, not Modernism. He
evolved a successful style that bridged the divide
between figuration and abstraction, using thick,
tactile paint, rich colours, and simple forms
suggestive of landscape or still life. De Staël
committed suicide at Antibes in the south of
France. His work is neglected.

KEY WORKS: *Composition*, 1950 (London: Tate
Collection); *Le Parc des Sceaux*, 1952 (Washington DC:
Phillips College); *Mediterranean Landscape*, 1953
(Madrid: Museo Thyssen-Bornemisza)

Jean **Dubuffet**

◉ 1901–85 🏳 FRENCH ✍ OILS;
SCULPTURE; PRINTS

Dubuffet was a painter, sculptor, printmaker,
collector, and writer who was also the son of
a wine merchant. He turned full-time artist in
1942 after an early life of the wine trade, military
service, divorce, and dilettantism. He developed a
challenging and consciously anti-aesthetic, anti-art
establishment style – but ended up as the art
establishment's favourite example of radical chic.

His art went through a succession of cycles.
In each case he had a thought-out agenda and
different experiments with materials, which he
then promoted via exhibitions: 1942–50 portraits
and graffiti; early 1950s obese nudes in smeary oil
paint; late 1950s "Earth" themes and sand-gravel
textures; 1960s black outlined "jigsaw" style and
polystyrene sculpture. He sought intensity, not
beauty. He promoted Art Brut and tapped into the
unschooled creativity of children and psychotics.

Dubuffet raised naïvety to the highest level of
sophistication. He knew exactly what he was doing –
one of the few occasions where this "game" works.
The trouble with most *faux naïf* work is that you
have no idea (unless told) whether the work is to be
admired because it is by an untrained and innocent
eye, or by an overeducated sophisticate trying to
amaze us by how "simple" he or she can be.

KEY WORKS: *Spinning Round*, 1961 (London: Tate
Collection); *The Triumpher*, 1973 (Périgny-sur-Yerres,
Paris: Dubuffet Foundation)

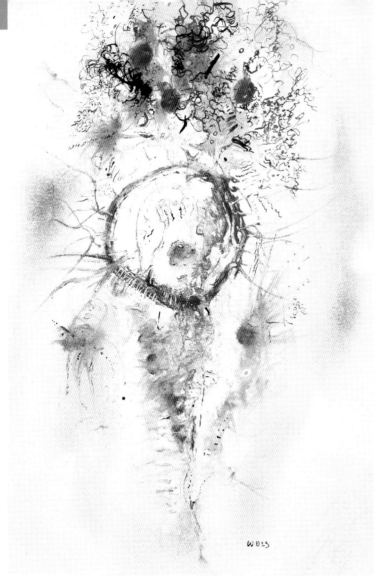

Alfred Otto Wolfgang Schulze **Wols**

⊖ 1913–51 ᴾᵁ GERMAN/FRENCH ✍ OILS; WATERCOLOURS; DRAWINGS

Wols was a lost soul, typical of many dispossessed, destitute, and unhappy people who were victims of political and social upheavals in central Europe during this era. He found solace in artistic activity and drink. Born in Germany, he lived in France.

He made small-scale works in oils and watercolours. The oils are often composed of compulsive pouring, smearing, spraying, and scratching. The watercolours frequently have an obsessive concern with detail. What distinguishes Wols from many lesser jotters and scribblers is the quantity, consistency, and integrity of his work. Unrecognized in his lifetime, he persisted with, and pioneered, a new style of expressive abstraction.

He was remarkable for his attention to detail. Every mark is there for a reason (the sign of real integrity.) Try to see a group of works together: the end result, individually and collectively, is a remarkable record of someone using art to rise above hardships that killed many others – literally or spiritually. Together they are strangely beautiful and moving to look at and be with.

KEY WORKS: *Painting*, 1944–45 (New York: Museum of Modern Art); *Bateau*, 1951 (Boston: Museum of Fine Arts)

Pierre **Soulages**

⊖ 1919– ᴾᵁ FRENCH ✍ OILS; PRINTS

Soulages produced large-scale, heavily textured, gestural, painterly abstracts in which black is predominant. This was intended to be more visual than emotional in impact; for him, black was the means of making light and colour visible and alive.

KEY WORKS: *Painting, 23 May 1953*, 1953 (London: Tate Collection); *Painting, 195 x 130 cm, 6 August 1956*, 1956 (Canberra: National Gallery of Australia)

César (César Baldaccini)

⊖ 1921–1998 ᴾᵁ FRENCH ✍ SCULPTURE; MIXED MEDIA

César is celebrated for constructions and compressions in metal, often with unusual material, such as car parts. He created very visual, human, witty, and active work. He liked animal skeletons, bones, and surfaces like bats' wings. His work with paper and plastic lacks strength and tension (as if the material bored him?) and can be kitsch. He made disturbing self-portraits.

KEY WORKS: *Italian Flags*, 1960s (Private Collection); *Thumb*, 1965 (Martigny, Switzerland: Fondation Pierre Gianadda)

Yves **Klein**

◉ 1928–62 🏳 FRENCH ✍ MIXED MEDIA; SCULPTURE

Klein was untrained (except at judo), uneducated, and a megalomaniac dreamer, who had a brief, high-profile, and influential presence.

His paintings, objects, and records of "happenings" (notably those saturated with his trademark IKB "International Klein Blue") give a unique, intense glow. The rhetoric he and his supporters used is huge: blue is the infinite immateriality of the heavens; blue fills the space between object and viewer with spiritual energy; blue leads to a Zen-like transcendental experience, and so on. With a leap of imagination similar to his own, this is possible. Klein was also infamous for his scandalous behaviour throughout his short-lived career.

Is the attraction of his objects in the aesthetic and spiritual experience they seek to convey? Or is it that they were and remain as instantly recognizable and as chic as the Gucci loafer or Chanel No. 5 – all of them proclaiming the possessor to be a (self-elected) member of the international club of connoisseurship and savoir-faire? Is this the first example of art as a high-class fashion accessory? And, if so, is it any the worse for that?

KEY WORKS: *IKB 79*, 1959 (London: Tate Collection); *Untitled Blue Monochrome (IKB 82)*, 1959 (New York: Guggenheim Museum); *Requiem Blue*, 1960 (Houston: Menil Collection)

Armand Fernandez **Arman**

◉ 1928–2005 🏳 FRENCH ✍ SCULPTURE; CONCEPTUAL ART

Arman was a stimulating and witty manipulator of objects whose work was more visual than conceptual. An avid collector since childhood, his father was a furniture and knick-knack dealer and his grandmother, an obsessive accumulator of junk.

He had an obsessive interest in manufactured objects (such as keys, car parts, machines, dolls, or paint tubes), which he transformed through accumulations, combustions, and cut-ups. Out of

context, their repetitive agglomeration and luxurious or bizarre presentation (for instance Perspex boxes, resin beds, and wall mounts), endow them with a kind of poetry. Cut-up musical instruments or charred furniture simultaneously shock and make you reappraise the true function of objects.

KEY WORKS: *Accumulation of Sliced Teapots*, 1964 (Minneapolis: Walker Art Center); *Diana (Noli me tangere)*, 1986 (Toronto: Miriam Shiell Gallery); *Self-Portrait-Robot*, 1992 (Florence: Galleria degli Uffizi)

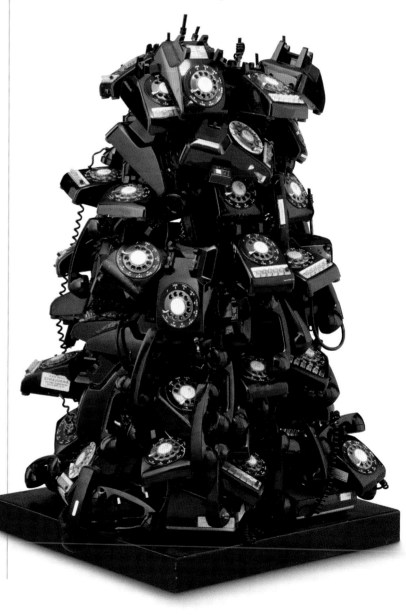

☑ *Office Fetish* Armand Fernandez Arman, 1984, 76.2 x 76.2 cm (30 x 30 in), rotary telephones and metal poles, Detroit Institute of Arts. Along with Yves Klein and Jean Tinguely, Arman was a member of the Nouveaux Réalistes, who rejected painting and used real materials in their works.

Henri **Michaux**

● 1899–1984 🏴 BELGIAN ✍ OILS; DRAWINGS; ENGRAVINGS; SCULPTURE

Michaux was the author of highly original, experimental, introverted paintings. He sought to use art as an escape from the material world and worked very rapidly, without preconceptions. He used wash and diluted inks for his watercolours, as they do not allow for revision and second thoughts. After 1956, he sometimes worked under the influence of the hallucinogenic drug mescalin.

KEY WORKS: *Meidosems*, 1948 (Boston: Museum of Fine Arts); *La bataille des éperons d'or*, 1960 (Brussels: Musées Royaux des Beaux Arts)

◩ *The Andes Cordillera* *Henri Michaux, 1958, 40 x 30 cm (15 ¾ x 11 ¾ in), gouache on paper, private collection.* Even before he used drugs, Michaux regarded painting as an art of psychic improvisation.

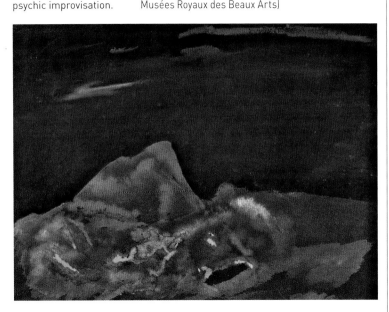

Hans **Hartung**

● 1904–89 🏴 GERMAN/FRENCH ✍ OILS; ACRYLICS; PRINTS

Hartung is recognized as one of the first painters of gestural abstraction. His style is spontaneous, neat, wiry, free, with pencil lines crawling over the paper and brushstrokes that have some of the characteristics of Chinese calligraphy but are never uncontrolled or arbitrary. His strong sense of (complex) composition and colour identifies him as European rather than American. His aim was to create images expressing his innermost being. His paintings are not always as spontaneous as they look: they may be enlarged versions of small, free sketches, in which he replicates the gestures or accidental marks (but does that make the end result any less valid?).

KEY WORKS: *T-1954-20*, 1954 (Canberra: National Gallery of Australia); *Lines and Curves*, 1956 (San Francisco: Fine Arts Museums)

Marcel **Broodthaers**

● 1924–1976 🏴 BELGIAN ✍ SCULPTURE; PHOTOGRAPHY; INSTALLATIONS; VIDEO

Broodthaers was an unsuccessful poet turned untrained artist (in 1964), who created bizarre objects and installations or exhibitions of objects and real works of art. His aim? To investigate issues such as the meaning of art; the definition of art; art institutions and power structures; the art market and aesthetics – and in doing so to challenge received opinion. His work is subtle, humorous, influential, and successful.

KEY WORKS: *Armoire charbonnée (Armoire à charbon)*, 1966 (Brussels: Musées Royaux des Beaux Arts); *Le drapeau noir. Tirage illimité*, 1968 (Brussels: Musées Royaux des Beaux Arts)

Panamarenko (Henri van Herwegen)

● 1940– 🏴 BELGIAN ✍ SCULPTURE; INSTALLATIONS

Panamarenko is an eccentric visionary who designs weird Leonardo-like machines. They do not work in reality but they do wonders for the imagination. The theme of his works is liberating humanity from physical constraints by suggesting ways to jump further, to fly, to defy gravity, to reinvent time and space, and so on. They are beautiful machines.

KEY WORKS: *Feltra*, 1966 (Ghent: Stedelijk Museum voor Actuele Kunst); *Aeroplane*, 1967 (Wolfsburg: Kunstmuseum); *The Aeromodeller*, 1969–71 (New York: Dia:Chelsea)

Friedensreich **Hundertwasser**

● 1928–2000 ⚲ AUSTRIAN ✎ OILS; MIXED MEDIA

Hundertwasser produced small, detailed, richly coloured, ornamental and jewel-like abstract works, often with a spiral motif, which is organic and labyrinthine in character (a deliberate metaphor for the self-regenerative processes of life). He used mixed media, gold and silver, wrapping paper, and jute. His work is refreshingly romantic and lyrical.

KEY WORKS: *460 Hommage au Tachisme*, 1961 (Vienna: KunstHausWien); *224 The Big Way*, 1955 (Vienna: Österreichische Galerie)

Günther **Uecker**

● 1930– ⚲ GERMAN ✎ SCULPTURE

Uecker's typical work (after 1955) consists of nails hammered into a board that are arranged in patterns that are reminiscent of electromagnetic fields. Monotony and repetition are deliberate and integral to his work. Motivated by Zen and visions of purity and silence, he believes that he should establish harmony between people and nature.

KEY WORKS: *Tactile Rotating Structure*, 1961 (Venice: Peggy Guggenheim Collection); *TV 1963*, 1963 (Marl: Skulpturenmuseum Glaskasten)

》 **FLUXUS** 1962–1970s

Originating in Germany and literally meaning "flow", the Fluxus movement advocated a shift from aesthetics to ethics in artistic values. It held a similar attitude to that of Dadaism, promoting artistic exploration and socio-political activism. Ignoring art theories, members often created mixed-media works from found materials and developed the performance art movement, called "Aktions" or "Happenings". Fluxus artists shifted the importance from what an artist creates to the artist's actions, opinions, and emotions.

》 *Literature Sausage* Dieter Roth, 1967, 63 cm (25 in), mixed media, Hamburg: Kunsthalle. The work consists of a novel by Alfred Andersch, ground up and stuffed into sausage skins.

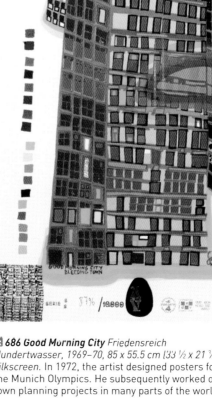

△ *686 Good Morning City* Friedensreich Hundertwasser, 1969–70, 85 x 55.5 cm (33 ½ x 21 ¼ in), silkscreen. In 1972, the artist designed posters for the Munich Olympics. He subsequently worked on town planning projects in many parts of the world.

Renato **Guttuso**

● 1912–87 🏴 ITALIAN ✎ OILS; WATERCOLOURS

Guttuso was much praised in the 1950s, when considered by many left-wing critics to be on the cutting edge of the avant-garde; his social realist works were seen as an antidote to American gestural abstraction; thus, he did capture something specific about postwar European art and politics. He was a founder-member of the anti-Fascist association Corrente. His originality declined rapidly after the late 1950s when his work became derivative (too many borrowings from Picasso and Goya).

KEY WORKS: *Crucifixion*, 1941 (Rome: Galleria Nazionale d'Arte Moderna); *Sulphur Miners*, 1949 (London: Tate Collection)

☑ ***Death of a Hero*** Renato Guttuso, 1953, 88 x 103 cm (34 ⅔ x 40 ½ in), oil on canvas, London: Estorick Collection. The artist was staunchly anti-Fascist and a resistance fighter. After the war he became a Communist politician.

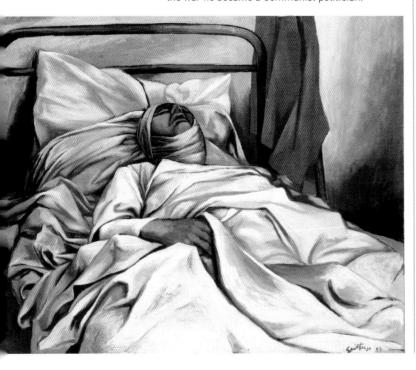

Alberto **Burri**

● 1915–95 🏴 ITALIAN ✎ COLLAGE

Burri was a doctor-turned-artist who had some success in the 1950s with work that was original for the time, using sacking and other non-arty materials, to produce serious looking collages. There must be a connection to doctors bandaging patients and using splints – he simulated blood with splashes of red paint. A commentary on the state of postwar Europe?

KEY WORKS: *Abstraction with Brown Burlap (Sack)*, 1953 (Turin: Galleria Civica d'Arte Moderna e Contemporanea); *Composition*, 1953 (New York: Guggenheim Museum)

Lucio **Fontana**

● 1899–1968 🏴 ARGENTINIAN/ITALIAN ✎ OILS; SCULPTURE; CERAMICS; INSTALLATIONS

Fontana was an unknown who in middle age became a significant figure in postwar European art, finding a successful, if limited, "formula" that was in tune with the mood of the times.

He is most famous for monochrome canvases with single or multiple precision cuts, and for canvases and supports that have been pierced or lacerated. He can be very good indeed – but can be oh so dull! It is better to see several works together – a single work can look merely superficial or silly.

The cuttings and piercings had a meaning in the 1960s, as part of a (then new, but now worn out) exploration of the meaning of existence and the role of art. They are perhaps now best seen as engaging period pieces with an innocent 1950s or 1960s view of the creative act, and gesture to a bid for freedom (he was over 50 when he started them). His earlier ceramic work searched for freedom of expression, but he needed a different medium to find full utterance.

KEY WORKS: *Spatial Concept*, 1958 (London: Tate Collection); *Spatial Concept: Expectations*, 1959 (New York: Guggenheim Museum); *Nature*, 1959–60 (London: Tate Collection)

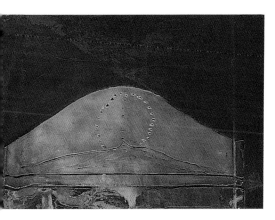

⬈ **Composition LXIV** *Antoni Tàpies, 1957, 97 x 162 cm (38 ¼ x 63 ¾ in), mixed media on canvas, Hamburg: Kunsthalle.* Tàpies was a key member of the Spanish Dau al Set ("the seventh side of the dice" in Catalan), an artistic alliance inspired by Dada and Surrealism, which reacted against the intellectual stagnation of postwar Spain. Tàpies in particular concentrated on the materiality of paint.

Antoni **Tàpies**

⬤ 1923–2012 ⚑ SPANISH ✎ MIXED MEDIA; OILS; PRINTS

Tàpies was a talented, self-taught artist whose best work dates from the 1950s and early 1960s, when he used coarse materials to produce sombre heavily textured canvases expressing the uncertain, stressed mood of Cold War Europe. His later work is less convincing because it is less in tune with the times. The highly praised, so-called avant-garde art of the 1970s and 1980s was anticipated by Tàpies's work.

KEY WORKS: *Great Oval or Painting*, c.1955 (Bilbao: Fine Arts Museum); *Le Chapeau Renversé*, 1967 (Paris: Musée National d'Art Moderne)

Juan **Muñoz**

⬤ 1953–2001 ⚑ SPANISH ✎ SCULPTURE; INSTALLATIONS

Born in Madrid, Muñoz studied in London and New York. He created large-scale installations that fill a whole gallery, such as marquetry floors with extreme false perspective, constructions with architectural elements (such as iron balconies) that have distorted scale, and groups of figure sculptures in unexplained silent relationships. He created feelings of disequilibrium, danger, and absurdity.

If the new museums of modern and contemporary art are no longer places for individual, spiritual, and aesthetic refreshment, nor for genuinely eye-opening artistic and political challenge, but are effectively adult adventure playgrounds driven by management targets for admissions, budgets, shop sales, fund raising, and commercial sponsorship (and why not? – everyone and everything must move with the times), then these (and other similar works) are good-quality content for them.

KEY WORKS: *Last Conversation Piece*, 1984–85 (Washington DC: Hirshhorn Museum); *Dwarf with a Box*, 1988 (London: Tate Collection); *Double Bind*, 2001 (London: Tate Collection)

Eduardo **Chillida**

⬤ 1924–2002 ⚑ SPANISH ✎ SCULPTURE

Chillida was a Basque artist, notable for abstract constructions, mainly in forged or welded iron, that combined several Spanish influences: modern, such as Picasso, and traditional, such as old farm implements. These sculptures are sometimes monumental, but are always graceful – often without a base, so they touch the ground with a dancer's lightness. Many of them have interlocking and embracing themes.

KEY WORKS: *Tximista (Lightning)*, 1957 (Washington DC: Hirshhorn Museum); *Modulation of Space*, 1963 (London: Tate Collection); *Silent Music II*, 1983 (New York: Metropolitan Museum of Art)

⬇ **Berlin** *Eduardo Chillida, 2000, iron sculpture, Berlin-Tiergarten: Bundeskanzleramt.* The installation of Chillida's sculpture in the Court of Honour of the Berlin Federal Chancellery coincided with the opening of his own dedicated museum, the Museo Chillida-Leku, in his home town of Hernani.

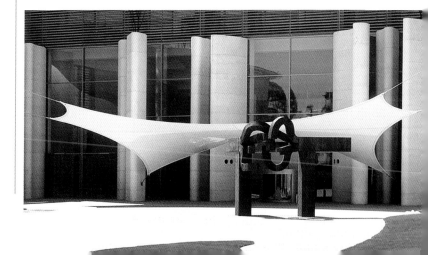

Laurence Stephen **Lowry**

● 1887–1976 British OILS

Lowry was a quirky painter who became critically and commercially successful with his instantly recognizable scenes of the bleak north of England – industrial landscapes inhabited by busy "stick" people. His "spontaneous naïvety" appeals to critics and intellectuals, his everyday directness to popular taste. At his best he is very good indeed, at all levels.

KEY WORKS: *An Organ Grinder*, 1934 (Manchester: City Art Gallery); *The Fever Van*, 1935 (Liverpool: Walker Art Gallery)

Victor **Pasmore**

● 1908–98 BRITISH OILS; SCULPTURE

Pasmore was an interesting pioneer of British abstraction. He started as a spare-time painter (1927–37), then became a full-time figurative painter who went abstract in 1948 (it was a difficult decision for him). His line and form were very sensitive (over sensitive and contrived?) His spare, cool, calculated, consciously artificial works can now look dated.

KEY WORKS: *Parisian Café*, 1936–37 (Manchester: City Art Gallery); *Chiswick Reach*, 1943 (Ottawa: National Gallery of Canada)

Sir Terry **Frost**

● 1915–2003 BRITISH OILS

Frost was a leading St Ives Group painter, who produced sensitive early works with gentle, fundamental shapes and colours abstracted from nature, often invoking sensations of movement, flight, or waves. His later work is more purely abstract. He drew inspiration from the natural world, wanting to convey the ecstatic and poetic experiences he found in nature.

You could go round a Sir Terry Frost exhibition looking for modern art influences and colour theories (they are there to be found and that is all some people do), but what a waste of an opportunity that would be. If you go round looking for sunlight, water, leaves, and woods, and your memory or evocation of them and their interaction with you, your sight, or your emotions, you will be as uplifted as if you had spent an ideal day in the country.

KEY WORKS: *Brown and Yellow*, c.1951–52 (London: Tate Collection); *Green, Black, and White Movement*, 1951 (London: Tate Collection); *Blue Moon*, 1952 (London: Tate Collection)

» **Red and Blue** *Sir Terry Frost, 1959, 127 x 76 cm (50 x 30 in), oil on canvas, Leicester: New Walk Museum.* Frost began to paint after being taken prisoner during the German invasion of Crete in 1943.

Roger **Hilton**

◗ 1911–75 ⚑ BRITISH ✎ OILS; GOUACHE

Hilton produced gutsy paintings, sometimes abstract, and sometimes with rudimentary female or abstract forms. He delighted in colour, paint, and the female form, causing offence and maintaining a rough humour in the face of considerable personal problems.

KEY WORKS: *January*, 1957 (London: Tate Collection); *Oi Yoi Yoi*, 1963 (London: Tate Collection)

Sir Sidney **Nolan**

◗ 1917–92 ⚑ AUSTRALIAN ✎ OILS

Widely travelled and acclaimed, Nolan was one of the few contemporary artists to have established a place for narrative, mythological painting, notably the "Ned Kelly" (romantic Australian outlaw) series. His distinctive style combines abstraction and figuration, and conveys a strong sense of the heat and emptiness of the vast Australian landscape. Nolan was an exponent of expressive brushwork and colour.

KEY WORKS: *The Trial*, 1947 (Canberra: National Gallery of Australia); *Kelly in Spring*, 1956 (London: Hayward Gallery); *Carcass*, 1953 (Private Collection)

Patrick **Heron**

◗ 1920–99 ⚑ BRITISH ✎ OILS; PRINTS

Heron is greatly revered and respected as one of the pioneers of large-scale, post-war abstract art in the UK. He had a difficult, combative personality and his last years were marked by illness and personal tragedy.

He was the creator of a prolific and impressive body of work that is intensely visual, colourful, and inspired by personal emotion and things seen. He was one of the few artists who sought to bridge the gap between the European aesthetic sensibility and American direct rawness. If possible, see his work in daylight – preferably sunlight – so the individual colours and colour contrasts and interactions reach their full potential of Mediterranean intensity.

His most powerful work dates from the late 1960s and early 1970s – big works with intense, simple, hard-edged colour forms that generate intense colour sensations and pulsating spaces. Stand close to them for the full power to develop in your eye. His earlier work shows the inspiration of landscape, seascape, and the light of Cornwall. His later works were looser in style. Nevertheless, everything he created was done with very great, but not always obvious, technical exactitude.

KEY WORKS: *Boats at Night*, 1947 (London: Tate Collection); *Vertical: January*, 1956 (London: Tate Collection); *Red and Yellow Image*, 1958 (London: Tate Collection)

Alan **Davie**

◗ 1920–2014 ⚑ BRITISH ✎ OILS; PRINTS

Davie was an unusual but well-regarded painter, who worked in a totally individual manner. He was a talented athlete and jazz musician, as well as a prolific artist. His work is all about trying to express the inexpressible and how to reach the primal and mystical forces of humankind (the sort of experience that the hippy generation sought). If you cannot accept the possibility of the occult, or are unwilling to travel with him, his work will remain meaningless and appear no more than a design for a cover to a handbook on Indian mysticism.

He needs a large scale to express fully the magnitude of his endeavours. His early work is thickly painted in an Abstract Expressionist style. From the 1960s, he worked in a figurative style, full of signs and symbols that were highly reminiscent of Indian art and decoration.

KEY WORKS: *Thoughts for a Giant Bird*, 1940s (London: Bonhams); *Entrance to Paradise*, 1949 (London: Tate Collection); *Peggy's Guessing Box*, 1950 (Venice: Peggy Guggenheim Gallery)

Leon **Kossoff**

● 1926– ⚑ BRITISH ✍ OILS

Kossoff is a somewhat shadowy and neglected figure, influenced by his Jewish cultural heritage. The human figure is always central to his work, which is of high quality, very thickly and crudely painted, in a strongly Expressionist style. He is inclined to gloominess, although his swimming-bath series is full of life.

KEY WORKS: *Portrait of Father*, 1978 (Edinburgh: National Gallery of Modern Art); *Two Seated Figures No. 2*, 1980 (London: Tate Collection)

Frank **Auerbach**

● 1931– ⚑ BRITISH ✍ OILS

German-born, but British by adoption, Auerbach chiefly produces small-scale paintings with paint that can be as thick as the crust of a loaf, the result of constant revisions piled on one another. His images are mostly of central, urban London, but he also does nudes. His work is an almost defiant declaration that although the art of painting may be considered out of fashion, it will certainly never die.

KEY WORKS: *The Sitting Room*, 1964 (London: Tate Collection); *Jym I*, 1981 (Southampton: City Art Gallery)

R. B. **Kitaj**

● 1932–2007 ⚑ AMERICAN/BRITISH ✍ OILS; PASTELS

Kitaj was born in the US, but settled in the UK in the 1960s. He maintained and advanced a definition of art that is central to European painting in the "grand manner" – life drawing, literary subjects, the exposition of human, intellectual, and moral issues.

Kitaj had a very personal style and made large-scale, "exhibition" pieces, with many personal and biographical references, sometimes hidden. There were cross-references to literature and philosophy, sometimes to specific passages. He was concerned with the Jewish diaspora, and was a fine draughtsman and an instinctive colourist. Kitaj was independent of eye and mind, and (to his credit) is difficult to pigeonhole. His refusal to compromise was seen as arrogant which is why he was savaged by art critics in Britain in 1994 (but not in the US). As a consequence, he withdrew into himself, and to Los Angeles.

KEY WORKS: *The Murder of Rosa Luxembourg*, 1960 (London: Tate Collection); *The Ohio Gang*, 1964 (New York: Museum of Modern Art); *The Hispanist (Nissa Torrents)*, 1977–78 (Bilbao: Fine Arts Museum)

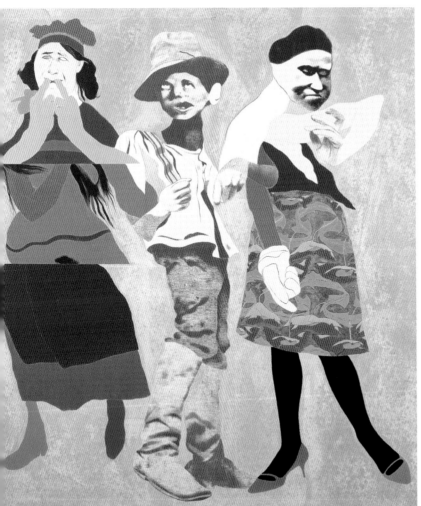

◀ *Value, Price, and Profit, or Production of Waste* R. B. Kitaj, 1963, 152.4 x 152.4 cm (60 x 60 in), oil on canvas, private collection. Kitaj's self-image was that of a pilgrim existing in a cold, ugly, and exploitative world, whose saving grace was the warmth generated by human creativity and intellect.

Francis **Bacon**

⬤ 1909–92 🏳 BRITISH ✍ WATERCOLOURS; OILS; DRAWINGS

Bacon was one of the most significant figurative painters of the postwar period. Largely self-taught, he was a loner, personally and artistically. His long-term significance has yet to be assessed and will depend on whether he is followed. He was a late developer – and produced nothing of sustained significance until his late 30s, then there were 20 years of very powerful work. After about 1971 (aged 61 and following the death of his lover, George Dyer), his work declined into a repetitive formula.

Bacon showed genuine originality in his imagery, in the way he constructed, and in his handling of paint. His central image is of an isolated figure, usually male, often naked, under stress, in bare, brightly lit, or coloured space: this was said by Bacon (and others) to indicate the condition of postwar Europe and modern human isolation. His work is beautifully crafted, with controlled drawing and line, and tense, emotional colour. There is creative interplay between what he intended and what happened accidentally.

Like many contemporary artists, he suffered from unhelpful excess of praise, but in truth, he had only one image and one emotion, which he repeated with variation.

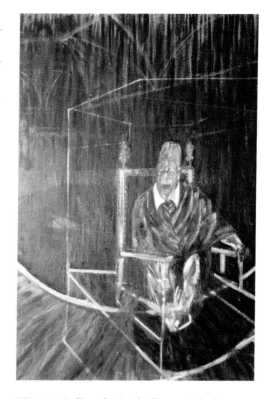

KEY WORKS: *Three Studies for Figures at the Base of a Crucifixion*, 1964 (London: Tate Collection); *Study after Velasquez I*, 1950 (New York: Tony Shafrazi Gallery); *Three Figures in a Room*, 1965 (Paris: Musée National d'Art Moderne); *Study for Head of Lucian Freud*, 1967 (Private Collection)

◧ *Pope I – Study after Pope Innocent X by Velásquez* Francis Bacon, 1951, 197.8 x 137.4 cm (78 x 54 in), oil on canvas, Aberdeen: Art Gallery and Museums. An existential protest against authoritarian political power.

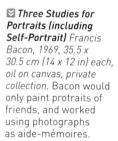

◩ *Three Studies for Portraits (including Self-Portrait)* Francis Bacon, 1969, 35.5 x 30.5 cm (14 x 12 in) each, oil on canvas, private collection. Bacon would only paint protraits of friends, and worked using photographs as aide-mémoires.

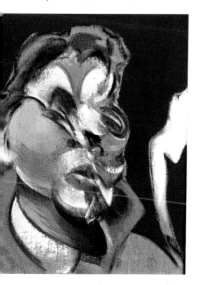

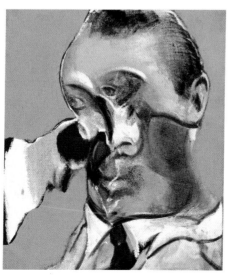

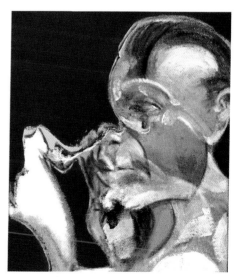

Lucian **Freud**

● 1922–2011 ⚐ BRITISH ⬕ OILS

A German-born grandson of Sigmund Freud (the founder of psychoanalysis), Lucian Freud became a British subject in 1939.

His main subject was the human figure, often naked, posed artificially as models in a studio. Sometimes, he painted views from windows, but anything other than the human figure he considered "frivolous". All his models were known to him, so there is an intimate sense of deep knowledge (perhaps even love), not detachment. His work reveals extraordinary powers of concentration (which is not the same as intensity). His portraits are powerful.

Look how carefully the eyes are painted and how much of the inner person they reveal, even when closed. How well he knew all those blemishes, bulges, lumps, private parts of the flesh that we study and examine intimately in our own bodies, but rarely see or care to look at in others. He knew every corner of his studio and the space that the models occupied. He knew exactly what he could do with his paint – and what he couldn't.

KEY WORKS: *In the Silo Tower*, 1940–41 (Private Collection); *Girl with Roses*, 1947–48 (London: British Council); *Naked Woman*, 1988 (Missouri: St Louis Art Museum)

Sir Anthony **Caro**

● 1924–2013 ⚐ BRITISH ⬕ SCULPTURE

Caro was often proclaimed as the leading contemporary British sculptor. He studied engineering at Cambridge (which shows) and worked with Henry Moore (which doesn't).

He created sculpture constructed out of heavy metal, which was usually welded together, recycling the elements of the engineering and construction industries (plates, beams, propellers). There is emphasis on structure, space, horizontals, verticals, and constructions hugging the ground or tabletop, like well-organized scrap. He displays truth to industrial materials. His early work (1960s) is brightly painted; his later work is undecorated other than with carefully controlled rust.

Beneath the modern outer garment is a deeply traditional soul – solid, honest, plain speaking, down-to-earth, making no-frills work that emphasizes the basic values (space, construction, materials); but he can be didactic and schoolmasterish, suggesting deep-seated, sometimes stubborn, suburban values (and none the worse for that). It isn't an art of fantasy or poetic imagination.

KEY WORKS: *Sculpture 3*, 1961 (Venice: Peggy Guggenheim Gallery); *Early One Morning*, 1962 (London: Tate Collection)

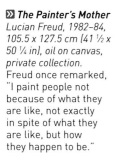

⏵ The Painter's Mother
Lucian Freud, 1982–84, 105.5 x 127.5 cm (41 ½ x 50 ¼ in), oil on canvas, private collection.
Freud once remarked, "I paint people not because of what they are like, not exactly in spite of what they are like, but how they happen to be."

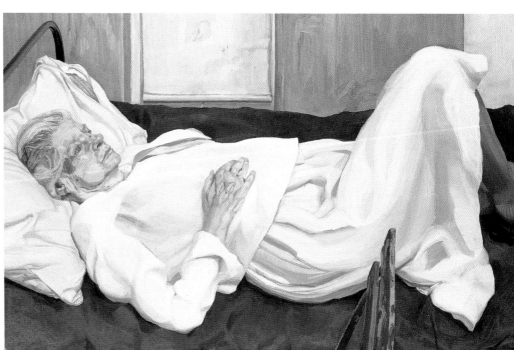

Michael **Andrews**

● 1928–95 🄟 BRITISH ✍ ACRYLICS; OILS

Andrews produced sensitive work that reflected his inner personality. He made large-scale paintings of places and people he knew well and felt deeply about. He possessed a delicate, unassertive technique (mainly working with spray-painted acrylic). Andrews was a shy, reclusive personality. A painstakingly slow worker (hence few works), he was totally absorbed by his subjects and activity. He possessed an English sensibility to light and nature.

KEY WORKS: *The Colony Room*, 1962 (London: Tate Collection); *The Deer Park*, 1962 (London: Tate Collection)

Bridget **Riley**

● 1931– 🄟 BRITISH ✍ OILS; WATERCOLOURS; PRINTS

An eminent major abstract painter, Riley has a strong international reputation and a lifelong dedication to exploring both the visual and emotional properties of colour. She has travelled widely.

She creates intensely visual, abstract paintings whose appearance and form (large scale, stripes, blocks of colour) do not result from any theory or formula but are a means of using colour and form to create sensations of light and space.

The colours interact at the edges and generate the illusion of other colours or jumps of colour. Some colours leap forwards and others back. Dark (often black) stripes create a rhythmic pulse across the surface. There is deep emotional as well as visual involvement.

KEY WORKS: *Winter Palace*, 1981 (Leeds: Museums and Art Gallery); *Fall*, 1963 (London: Tate Collection); *Orphan Elegy I*, 1978 (London: British Council)

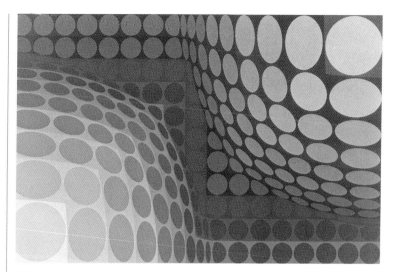

Victor **Vasarely**

● 1908–97 🄟 HUNGARIAN/FRENCH ✍ OILS; PRINTS

Vasarely was one of the key figures in the creation of Op art in the 1950s. Hungarian-born, he was awarded French citizenship in 1959. He produced hard-edge abstract paintings designed to create powerful optical effects and illusions that can often be explored and activated by moving around the paintings. His work was satisfying, but limited.

KEY WORKS: *Neves II*, 1949–58 (London: Tate Collection); *Quasar*, 1966 (San Francisco: Fine Arts Museums)

Morris **Louis**

● 1912–62 🄟 AMERICAN ✍ OILS; ACRYLICS

Louis created large-scale lyrical works. The subject matter is colour, which is trickled and floated onto bare canvas in such an inventive way that, if you suspend disbelief, the pigment can seem to be rivers, waterfalls, and liquid mists of fresh pure colour (if you can enjoy a landscape, why not this?). His work is easy-going but satisfying.

KEY WORKS: *Tet*, 1958 (New York: Whitney Museum of American Art); *Gamma Epsilon*, 1960 (Private Collection)

⬆ *Bi-Vega* Victor Vasarely, 1974, 114 x 79 cm (45 x 31 in), screenprint, London: Hayward Gallery. Vasarely regarded the artist as a workman who produces prototypes for reproduction by others.

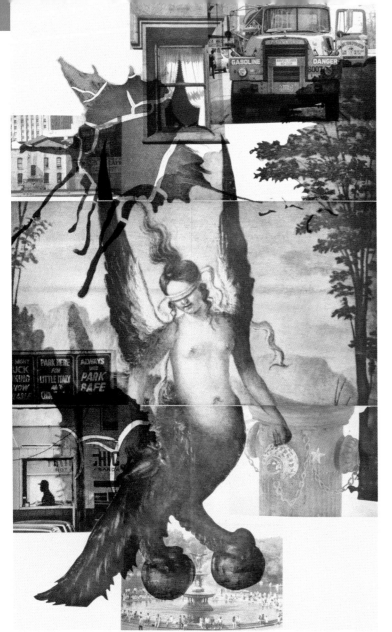

Robert **Rauschenberg**

⬬ 1925–2008 🎨 AMERICAN ✍ PRINTS; MIXED MEDIA

Rauschenberg was a major pioneering postwar artist. Prolific, creative, and influential; very New York, he was deeply committed to international co-operation for social change and human rights.

He produced a very consistent, personal, and visual work that explored how to make materials (screen printing, paint, found objects, papers, fabrics, or metals) and images (from contemporary media, words, abandoned urban detritus) work together. The whole constitutes a chronicle of his own activities and of his culture and times. Like Canaletto, he produced works that mirror a particular society, reflecting, distorting, or glamorizing it, and sought after by its members as souvenirs.

He had a passionate involvement, with an underlying innocence (not naïvety) and took evident delight in collecting material and putting it together, without self-consciousness or rules. His best work is beautiful to look at, technically intriguing, layered, memorable, and puzzling. Rauschenberg's work declined from the 1980s, becoming impersonal and overblown.

KEY WORKS: *Bed*, 1955 (New York: Leo Castelli Gallery); *Odalisk*, 1955–58 (Cologne: Museum Ludwig); *Soviet/American Array II*, 1988 (Detroit Institute of Arts)

◀◀ *Bellini Robert Rauschenberg, 1986, 143.5 x 88.9 cm (56 ½ x 35 in), intaglio printed in colour on woven paper, Detroit Institute of Arts.* A late work that combines high and low art imagery.

Larry **Rivers**

⬬ 1923–2002 🎨 AMERICAN ✍ OILS; SCULPTURE; MIXED MEDIA; COLLAGE

Rivers was a multifaceted bohemian: painter, poet, and jazz musician from a Russian-Jewish émigré family. He was an influential guru and created versatile and many-sided works, which are difficult to summarize – they can switch, within the same work, between figuration and abstraction, sharp detail and lush brushstrokes. One of the parents of Pop Art, Rivers' was also one of the first to use mass-media imagery. He also reworked famous hackneyed paintings.

KEY WORKS: *Washington Crossing the Delaware*, 1953 (New York: Museum of Modern Art); *Camels*, c.1962 (Cambridge: Fitzwilliam Museum); *French Money*, 1962 (Private Collection); *Living at the Movies*, 1974 (Ohio: Canton Museum of Art)

Alexander **Calder**

● 1898–1976 ⦿ AMERICAN ✍ SCULPTURE; GOUACHE

The man who gave the world the mobile, thus transforming the history of sculpture, Calder was the child of a sculptor father and painter mother. He trained as an engineer, draughtsman, and painter.

Enjoy the movement and *joie de vivre* in his mobiles (from the 1930s) – famous, delicately balanced constructions of wire and discs painted in primary colours or black. Tiny or large scale, they are marvels of endless variety. The stabiles are steel constructions firmly planted on the ground and immobile but their swooping shapes suggest movement. His early work includes wire figures and a circus of tiny figures, which he could animate.

Let the child in you come alive and forget worldly cares. Animate the mobiles into life (a breath of wind is usually enough); walk around and through the large stabiles to explore their life. Deceptive simplicity and soothing unpredictability are among the life-enhancing qualities of Calder's works. If you must speak art jargon, talk about drawing in space, negative space, spatial relationships, form, and colour. He also created wonderful, energy-filled gouaches.

KEY WORKS: *Lobster Trap and Fish Tail*, 1939 (New York: Museum of Modern Art); *The Spider*, 1940 (Private Collection)

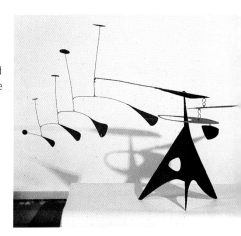

⌃ *Blue Feather*
Alexander Calder,
c.1948, 106.6 x 139.7 x 45.7 cm (42 x 55 x 18 in),
painted sheet metal and wire, private collection. This piece combines Calder's two inventions: the "stabile" (the static base) and "mobile" parts.

Ellsworth **Kelly**

● 1923– ⦿ AMERICAN ✍ OILS; PRINTS; DRAWING

Kelly is one of the contemporary masters, who has continued Matisse's exploration of colour. In his work, the traditional values of painting – technical perfection, visual pleasure, spiritual uplift – are still alive and well.

His very simple, large canvases are saturated with pure colour. Let the eye and the mind relax fully and absorb the colours, shapes, and the razor-sharp edges. Enjoy them for what they are and let them play on the imagination, stretch the eye and unfold in the mind's eye. Look at the meticulously painted surfaces (he always uses oil paint for richness of colour).

His works are sometimes to be enjoyed as objects seeming to float on the wall; sometimes to be seen as spaces through the wall giving onto fields of blue (sky or sea?), or red (earth or fire?). He mixes his own colours, and what he creates is a final distillation of something once seen in the world (especially architecture). He can uplift the eye and the spirit as refreshingly as chilled champagne. The canvases must be in pristine condition (damage and dirt ruin the purity and experience).

KEY WORKS: *Rebound*, 1959 (London: Anthony d'Offay Gallery); *Red Curve*, 1960s (Private Collection); *Blue, Green, Yellow, Orange, Red*, 1966 (New York: Guggenheim Museum)

Philip **Pearlstein**

● 1924– ⦿ AMERICAN ✍ OILS; PRINTS; DRAWING

Pearlstein is a leading figurative painter with a raw, objective style depicting the human body as it appears, with the minimum of interpretation.

Notice the artificiality within the reality: highly finished surfaces (rather than imitation of perceived textures), hidden or cut-off faces, and odd viewpoints. The artificiality forces the question "why?", which in turn demands an answer or

interpretation. Pearlstein claims to have given dignity back to the figure by rescuing it from both Expressionist and Cubist distortion, and from pornographic exploitation. His early, pre-1960s work is Abstract Expressionist.

KEY WORKS: *Nude Torso*, 1963 (New York: National Academy of Design); *Male and Female Nudes with Red and Purple Drape*, 1968 (Washington DC: Hirshhorn Museum); *Model in Green Kimono*, 1974 (San Francisco: Fine Arts Museums)

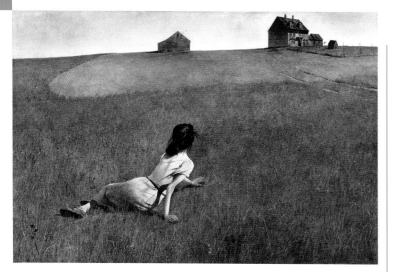

⤒ **Christina's World**
Andrew Wyeth, 1948,
82 x 121 cm (32 x 47 in),
tempera on gessoed
panel, New York: MoMA.
The inspiration for this
painting was the sight
of a neighbour, part
paralysed by polio,
crawling across a field.

Andrew **Wyeth**

⬤ c.1917–2009 🏳 AMERICAN ✍ TEMPERA;
WATERCOLOURS

Wyeth was the son of a famous book illustrator.
He first achieved fame with the watercolours
he painted in Maine in the late 1930s. He had
a brilliant realist technique, was popular and
much collected, but was unjustly derided by
many contemporary critics and curators.

His subjects were carefully chosen and all
had deep personal meaning. At first sight they
may look ordinary, but part of Wyeth's magic was
his ability to make the commonplace hauntingly
memorable. He was unconcerned by fashion
or being up to date. His large-scale paintings
were done in tempera (not oil), which was
painstakingly slow to work with and enabled
him to exploit his love of fine detail and focus
on the quality of draughtsmanship rather
than painterliness.

Observe the way he heightened realism
by using strong design and unusual, artificial
compositions; note also the way he contrasted
fine detail with large areas of abstraction. His
watercolours and dry-brush paintings were
painted in a frenzy (they were often tossed onto
the ground, which is why they may have smudges,
tears, or attached pieces of vegetation).

KEY WORKS: *Winter*, 1946 (North Carolina Museum
of Art); *Wind from the Sea*, 1947 (Washington DC:
National Gallery of Art); *Snow Flurries*, 1953
(Washington DC: National Gallery of Art)

Claes **Oldenburg**

⬤ 1929– 🏳 SWEDISH/AMERICAN
✍ SCULPTURE; MIXED MEDIA

Oldenburg was born in Europe, but brought
up in the US (his father was appointed Swedish
Consul in Chicago, 1936). He is one of Pop Art's
most original and inventive talents.

His highly inventive creations work on several
levels by constantly reversing normal expectations.
He starts with commonplace consumer-society
objects (such as a hamburger or a typewriter)
and metamorphoses them into something
strange and comical by altering their scale,
texture, or context. He also asks questions about
what constitutes a painting, sculpture, work of
art, or a consumer object.

He enjoys experimenting with paradox and
contradiction. He mocks the self-absorbed
seriousness of consumer society but is always
teasing and humorous, never threatening. He
has always been a compulsive drawer, even as
a child, forever imagining transpositions that
carry witty and significance resonances – such
as a woman's lipstick, which becomes a rocket
with a warhead and doubles as a sculptural
monument in a public place.

KEY WORKS: *Two Cheeseburgers with Everything
(Dual Hamburgers)*, 1962 (New York: Museum of
Modern Art); *Lipsticks in Piccadilly Circus, London*,
1966 (London: Tate Collection)

Jim **Dine**

⬤ 1935– 🏳 AMERICAN ✍ OILS; ACRYLICS;
MIXED MEDIA; PRINTS; INSTALLATIONS

Dine is one of the pioneers of Pop Art. His work
has a strong biographical element in which tools
(childhood memories of grandfather's hardware
store), paint, palettes (artist's studio), and domestic
objects, are prominent. His work is full of wit and
simple poetry, released by sensitive juxtaposition
of objects, colour, and stencilled labels.

KEY WORKS: *Bedspring*, 1960 (New York:
Guggenheim Museum); *Pearls*, 1961 (New
York: Guggenheim Museum)

Pop Art

1950s–1960s

Pop Art emerged independently in New York and London in the mid-1950s, and remained the dominant avant-garde movement until the late 1960s. In America, its initial motivation was a reaction against the self-absorption of Abstract Expressionism and a determination that art should re-engage with the real world. In the US, Pop Art celebrated the new consumer society; in Britain, there was always an undertow of nostalgia.

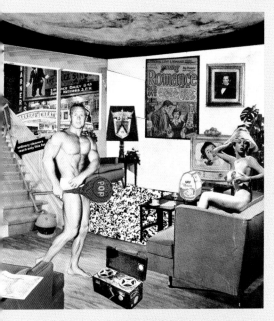

⬆ *Just what is it that Makes Today's Homes so Different, so Appealing?* Richard Hamilton, 1956, 26 x 24.8 cm (10 ¼ x 9 ¾ in), collage, Tübingen: Kunsthalle. Witty, mocking, challenging: Pop Art is born.

In Pop Art, the commonplace and the ordinary dominate: famously, Coca-Cola bottles, hamburgers, comic strips, household products, images from newspapers, advertisements – in short, almost anything produced by Western consumer society. In part, this was because Pop Art held that it was the duty of art to take the modern world as its subject. By extension, in an age of mass production, styles aimed at anonymity.

KEY EVENTS	
1952	Independent Group (IG) formed in London: actively seeks to celebrate "pulp imagery"
1955	Robert Rauschenberg's *The Bed*, key proto-Pop Art work
1958	English critic Lawrence Alloway coins term "Pop Art"; Jasper Johns has first one-man show in New York
1962	Pop Art announces itself with its first major exhibition, held at the Sidney Janis Gallery in New York. Lichtenstein, Warhol, Oldenburg, and other artists are present

What to look for

As with pop music, look for a world of youthful energy, more excited by mass advertising than the obscurities of high and abstract art. Pop Art was designed to be consciously different, irreverent, easy to look at and remember. Fun and economic freedom, however banal and cheap, were considered more interesting than contemplating life's deepest mysteries.

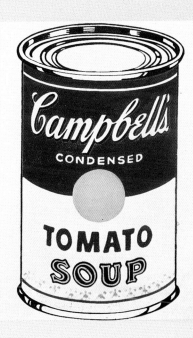

⏩ *Campbell's Soup Can* Andy Warhol, 1962, 90.8 x 60.9 cm (35 ¾ x 24 in), screen print, New York: Leo Castelli Gallery. Bold, simple, and unadorned: in short, Pop Art epitomized, the everyday made epic.

Wayne **Thiebaud**

◔ 1920– ⚐ AMERICAN ✐ OILS

Thiebaud paints portraits, landscapes, and still lifes, which are lavishly executed in thick, buttery paint and clear, bright colours. He takes a loving but unromantic interest in the anonymous faces and products seen in the supermarket, cafeteria, or deli. His simplified style comes from his early experience as an advertising artist and cartoonist. He paints clear light, and thick blue shadows you feel you can touch.

KEY WORKS: *Display Cakes*, 1963 (San Francisco: Museum of Modern Art); *Freeway Curve*, 1979 (San Francisco: Museum of Modern Art)

Roy **Lichtenstein**

◔ 1923–97 ⚐ AMERICAN ✐ ACRYLICS; OILS; SCULPTURE

Lichtenstein was a leading American Pop artist with an instantly recognizable style. At first sight, his work appears to be just large-scale blow-ups of comic-book images.

He had a great ability to defy expectations with wit and elegance – nothing is what it seems. He transformed comic-book images, traditionally dismissed as mere trash, into elegant large-scale paintings, which are in the tradition of a serious art gallery experience. He achieved this with the sophistication of his technique and the probing nature of his subject matter. (Caravaggio and Manet did something similar in their days.)

Note how he turned the impersonality of the comic-book image into something very personal. He organized, redefined, and exaggerated his images with the skill and knowledge of an Old Master. He had a meticulous technique: a highly controlled use of black outline; the use of Ben Day dot, and intense colour. He was deeply interested in life, love, and death (traditional high-art subjects) and in modern American society. He parodied other artists and (like Manet) played with art history.

KEY WORKS: *Drowning Girl*, 1963 (New York: Museum of Modern Art); *Whaam!* 1963 (London: Tate Collection); *As I Opened Fire*, 1964 (Amsterdam: Stedelijk Museum); *M-Maybe (A Girl's Picture)*, 1965 (Cologne: Museum Ludwig)

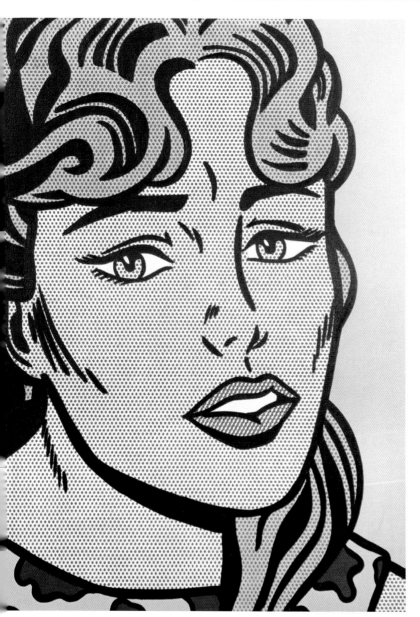

◁ *Anxious Girl Roy Lichtenstein, 1964, oil on canvas, private collection.* Lichtenstein first showed in New York in 1962 with the brilliant Leo Castelli whose gallery first promoted Pop Art in the US.

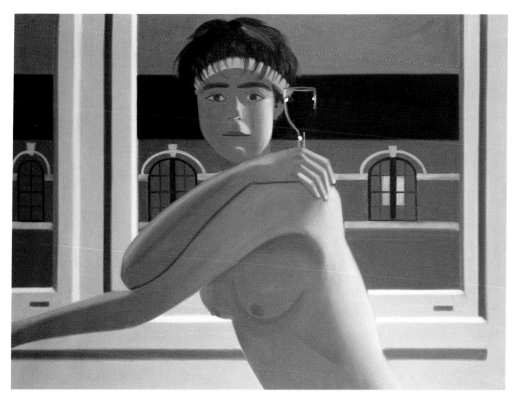

⊗ **Dusk** *Alex Katz, 1986, 137.2 x 183 cm (54 x 72 in), oil on canvas, private collection.* The artist's flat style and lean technique harks back to his early experiences as a designer of stage sets and costume.

Edward **Ruscha**

● 1937– ⚲ AMERICAN ⌗ OILS; ACRYLICS; PRINTS

Ruscha is an Oklahoma boy who went LA hip in 1956. His early work is Pop – icily perfect images of gasoline stations and billboards, plus booklets of photos of similar subjects. His recent work plays with images and words; for instance, a painting of water may have that word spelt out in a *trompe-l'oeil* spill of water. He uses unconventional media, such as fruit juice instead of watercolour.

KEY WORKS: *Lisp*, 1968 (Washington DC: National Gallery of Art); *Accordion Fold W/Vaseline Stains*, 1973 (New York: UBS Art Collection)

Alex **Katz**

● 1927– ⚲ AMERICAN ⌗ OILS; DRAWINGS

Katz is a very visual American figurative painter who reruns traditional themes and techniques in a contemporary American idiom.

He replays, with genuine inventiveness, themes and ideas beloved of the French Impressionists and Post-Impressionists (Manet, Monet, and Seurat especially): airy landscapes, the middle class at play, and a fascination with recording the effects of light. He uses direct wet-in-wet oil technique, colour harmonies and dissonances, and open brushwork that jumps into a focused image at a distance. Look for the self-absorbed faces, gestures, and intriguing psychology that you find in Manet's work.

He is to French art what Californian Cabernet Sauvignon wine is to French Bordeaux – not necessarily better or worse, but noticeably different: on a bigger scale, more direct, less complex. Enjoy his works for what they are: a refreshing, eye-filling pleasure with a distinguished, recognizable pedigree. Try to view the paintings by daylight, and look out for the sketches done from life, which he works up into large scale in the studio.

KEY WORKS: *Ada and Alex*, 1980 (Waterville, Maine: Colby College Museum of Art); *Rudy*, 1980 (Waterville, Maine: Colby College Museum of Art); *Tracy on the Raft at 7:30*, 1982 (Waterville, Maine: Colby College Museum of Art); *Varick*, 1988 (London: Saatchi Collection)

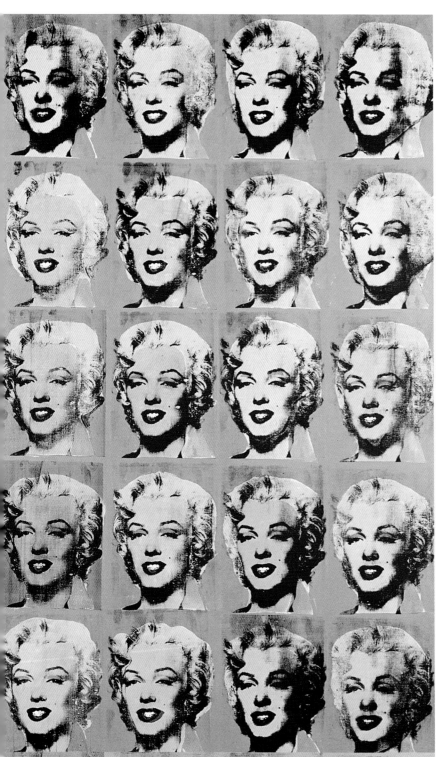

Andy **Warhol**

● 1928–87 🏴 AMERICAN ✍ OILS; ACRYLICS; PRINTS; SCULPTURE; VIDEO

A neurotic surrounded by drug addicts, Warhol was a key figure: his work represents one of art's turning points, changing the role of the artist and his or her way of seeing and doing things, as Leonardo did in the 16th century and Courbet in the 19th century. He was a great voyeur.

Look for instantly recognizable, talented work. Warhol's images were drawn from the world of Hollywood, films, TV, glamour, mass media, and advertising (Marilyn Monroe, Chairman Mao, Coca-Cola bottles, Campbell's soups). He deliberately recalled and exploited the values of consumer society by using its visual language: bright colours, silkscreen printing, repetition, commercial simplification, and compelling (sometimes shocking) images. He was also a (mediocre) fashion designer and film-maker.

He set up a new role model for the artist (much aspired to by today's young stars): no longer the solitary genius expressing intense personal emotion (as Picasso and Pollock did), but the artist as businessman – the equal of Hollywood film stars and directors and Madison Avenue advertising executives. The son of Slovakian immigrants, Warhol acted out an American dream cycle – pursuing a driving need to be famous and rich, like his subjects, and ending up destroying himself.

KEY WORKS: *Campbell's Soup Can* (see page 359); *Green Disaster Ten Times*, 1963 (Frankfurt: Museum für Moderne Kunst); *Suicide*, 1963 (New York: Leo Castelli Gallery); *Jacqueline Kennedy No.3*, 1965 (London: Hayward Gallery)

⟪ *Twenty Marilyns 1962, 197 x 116 cm (77 ½ x 45 ⅔ in), silk screen, private collection.* At about the time he produced this famous work, Warhol directed his assistant friends and hangers-on into an organization which he called The Factory.

Jasper **Johns**

● 1930– **▥** AMERICAN **✍** OILS; ENCAUSTIC PAINTS; SCULPTURE; PRINTS

Johns was a key figure in postwar American art and a founding father
of Pop Art. He was very influential and much admired. He is (and will be)
to American 20th-century art what Poussin is to 17th-century French art.

His art is intellectual, philosophical, closed, and
self-referential. He loves polarities – works that are
simultaneously cerebral and sensual, light-hearted
and serious, simple and complex, beautiful and
banal, realistic and illusionistic.

The classic Johns are his early American flag
paintings. They caused excitement because no
one could work out whether they were paintings or
objects, abstract works of art
or literal reproductions of the flag, banal or deeply
emotional – he enjoys riddles about definitions. He
can work on a small scale (the ale cans), or a large
scale (through canvases with objects attached). He
used encaustic (wax) technique for his early work.

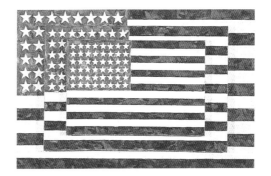

⏶ Three Flags *1958, 784 x 115.6 cm (308 ¾ x 45 in),
encaustic on canvas, New York: Whitney Museum of
American Art*. A teasing play on reality and illusion.

KEY WORKS: *Target with Plaster Casts*, 1955
(New York: Leo Castelli Gallery); *White Flag*,
1955 (New York: Leo Castelli Gallery); *0 through 9*,
1961 (London: Tate Collection)

The use of bronze and the
solid base raise expectations
that it is traditional sculpture

The use of two tins side
by side is artistic and
sculptural, yet the
subject is a disposable
object from everyday life

The large oval labels are
carefully painted, raising
the question, "Is it a
painting rather than
a sculpture?"

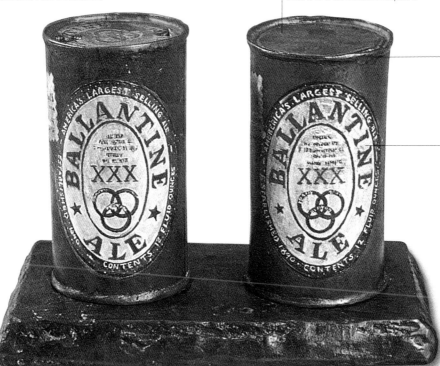

◀ Ale Cans *c.1964,
14 x 20.3 x 12 cm (5 ½ x
8 x 4 ¾ in), painted bronze,
private collection*. Cast in
bronze and painstakingly
painted, this sculpture is
key not just in the evolution
of Pop Art but of modern
art as a whole. It plays
a sophisticated game
with notions about the
perception of a work of art.

Philip **Guston**

● 1913–80 ▥ AMERICAN ✍ OILS

Guston was a well-regarded and influential artist whose work had several distinct and different phases.

His early work was figurative. In about 1950, he became an Abstract Expressionist, producing shimmering, nervously painted, high-minded abstract paintings. Around 1970, he returned to figuration, with crude, but perversely poetic, cartoon-like imagery that conjures up a bizarre world of everyday junk remnants.

It is difficult to explain Guston's changes of direction other than as autobiographical. He was probably working out the consequences of a traumatic childhood (father's suicide, brother's death, memories of Ku Klux Klan). His crudity perhaps reflects an element of self-loathing?

KEY WORKS: *The Native's Return*, 1957 (London: Phillips Collection); *The Painter's Table*, 1973 (Washington DC: National Gallery of Art)

◤ **Legend** *Philip Guston, 1977, 175 x 200 cm (65 ¾ x 78 ¾ in), oil on canvas, Houston: Museum of Fine Arts*. Guston said of his works around this time: "You see, I look at my paintings, speculate about them, they baffle me too. That's all I'm painting for."

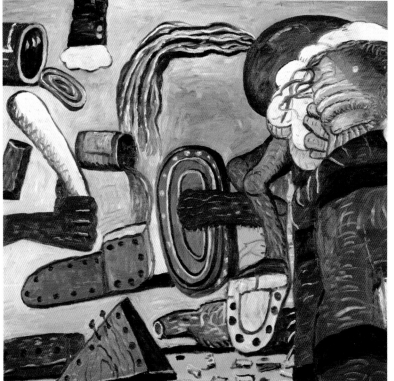

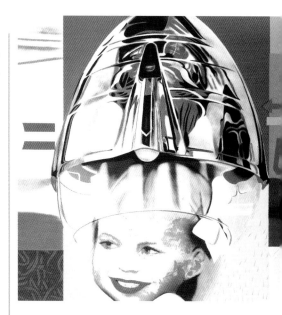

⬗ **F-111** (detail) *James Rosenquist, 1964–65, 3.05 x 26.21 metres (10 x 86 ft), oil on canvas and aluminium, New York: Museum of Modern Art*. A detail from a vast composition, which was a protest against the Vietnam War and American defence spending.

James **Rosenquist**

● 1933– ▥ AMERICAN ✍ OILS; PRINTS

One of the leading Pop artists, Rosenquist was initially trained, and became very successful, as a New York billboard painter and designer. He pieces together immaculately painted layers of commonplace imagery, which jump in scale and, because of their seeming disconnections, are resistant to (but demanding of) interpretation. In the 1960s, he created large-scale works that are chronicles of an era.

KEY WORKS: *Study for Marilyn*, 1962 (London: Mayor Gallery); *President Elect*, 1961–64 (Paris: Centre Pompidou)

Robert (John Clark) **Indiana**

● 1928– ▥ AMERICAN ✍ OILS; PRINTS

Indiana is remembered for the brief period when he created imagery of simple words and numbers painted on a large scale in blazing colour. His work is flat, razor-edged, and heraldic; it has effective, eye-bombarding, optical impact. He often uses a single, monosyllabic command – EAT; LOVE; DIE. He is influenced by billboard signs. His work is very Pop Art, very 1960s, and now very dated.

KEY WORKS: *The American Dream 1*, 1961 (New York: Museum of Modern Art); *LOVE*, 1967 (New York: Museum of Modern Art); *American Dream*, 1971 (Boston: Museum of Fine Arts)

Richard **Hamilton**

🌑 **1922–2011** 🅿️ **BRITISH** ✍️ **OILS; PRINTS; PHOTOMONTAGE**

The former intellectual guru of British Pop Art, Hamilton had an austere, rather self-conscious style, which can still come across as aloof and patronizing. He seemed to need to address his work to the adoring high priests of the art world rather than to the public at large (an odd attitude for one who claimed to be a true "pop", that is popular, artist).

KEY WORKS: *Chromatic Spiral*, 1950 (London: Tate Collection); *Just what is it that Makes Today's Homes so Different, so Appealing?* (see page 359)

Sir Eduardo **Paolozzi**

🌑 **1924–2005** 🅿️ **BRITISH** ✍️ **SCULPTURE; PRINTS; COLLAGE**

Born in Edinburgh, Paolozzi was the son of an Italian immigrant family who had settled in Scotland. Passionate, consistent, and generous, he was a founder of Pop Art and one of the great (though underrated) artists of the second half of the 20th century.

His sculptures, constructions, and prints (lithographs) are kaleidoscopes of images and ideas. At their heart is a dialogue about the human condition in the modern world. The fragmentation and unexpected juxtapositions of images are never arbitrary but part of a clearly thought-out strategy, commenting on questions such as: How do we fit into our fragmentary modern world? How do we use our powers over life and death? Can technology be poetic?

This is the art of a quick-firing, endlessly demanding imagination, which became more alert with age. To connect with it, be willing to be freely imaginative yourself, ready to see and revise all your familiar certainties. Look for the clues: the life and loves of Hollywood idols that equal those of Greek gods (we still need mythology); references to other fertile minds (for example, Burl Ives, who combined folk, band, and classical music); and to places of imagination (such as museums).

KEY WORKS: *I was a Rich Man's Plaything*, 1947 (London: Tate Collection); *Real Gold*, 1949 (London: Tate Collection); *Mosaics*, 1983–85 (London Underground: Tottenham Court Road Station)

Sir Peter **Blake**

🌑 **1932–** 🅿️ **BRITISH** ✍️ **OILS; PRINTS; MIXED MEDIA**

Blake was one of the founders of British Pop Art in the 1960s. He produces finely crafted work that is rather fey and increasingly has more to do with a nostalgic and often witty longing for a world that was the stuff of schoolboy dreams – comics, badges, pop and film stars, girls and wrestlers, corner shops – rather than anything modern. Blake is something of a Peter Pan figure.

KEY WORKS: *Self-Portrait with Badges*, 1961 (London: Tate Collection); *LP cover for Sgt. Pepper's Lonely Hearts Club Band*, 1967 (London: Victoria & Albert Museum)

Patrick **Caulfield**

🌑 **1936–2005** 🅿️ **BRITISH** ✍️ **OILS; PRINTS**

Caulfield was a pioneering Pop artist whose work was very recognizable in a once sought-after 1960s style using mass media images and spare, simple shapes and bright and flat colours with a strong, black outline. Somehow, he got stuck and never moved on.

KEY WORKS: *Black and White Flower Piece*, 1963 (London: Tate Collection); *Still Life with Dagger*, 1963 (London: Tate Collection)

Allen **Jones**

● 1937– 📖 BRITISH ✍ OILS; PRINTS; SCULPTURE

One of the founders of Pop Art, Jones uses simple, figurative imagery, often with an erotic charge (he likes fetish symbolism – high heels, body-clinging garments, and so on), combined with bright, bold, "modern" abstract colour. He was a product of the swinging London of the 1960s and was not ashamed to continue the theme.

KEY WORKS: *Wet Seal*, 1966 (London: Tate Collection); *What do you Mean, What do I Mean?*, 1968 (Private Collection)

David **Hockney**

● 1937– 📖 BRITISH ✍ ACRYLICS; OILS; PRINTS; PHOTOGRAPHY

Hockney is a genuinely gifted artist with an acute eye and fertile imagination. Once the bad boy of British art, he is now a respected elder statesman.

A truly great draughtsman (in the same league as Degas) – focused, precise, observant, free, who has a brilliant ability to extract only the essentials.

He has a stunning technique with pencil, pen, and crayon and an immaculate sense of colour. He can make the commonplace memorable and moving. Hockney has always chosen autobiographical subjects. Picasso has been an inspiration.

He is a brilliant observer and re-creator of light, space, and character in portraits, but not as convincing (though never uninteresting) when he tries to work solely from the imagination or to be a painterly painter (from the 1980s onwards). He is an inspired designer of sets for theatre, opera, ballet. His recent large-scale works have the eye-catching splashy paint techniques and simplified designs of the stage backdrop, although he is probably at his best when working on a small and intimate scale.

Always an insatiable experimenter, Hockney began exploring innovative uses of photography in the 1980s, and has recently enthusiastically embraced the possibilities offered by the iPad. Refreshingly impervious to the siren songs of money, celebrity status, or political correctness, delighted to celebrate his humble provincial roots and patriotism, he is a refreshing reminder that one of the principal purposes of art is to celebrate the joy of human existence and the thrill of uninhibited looking and creating.

KEY WORKS: *Peter C*, 1961 (Manchester: City Art Gallery); *California Bank*, 1964 (London: Mayor Gallery); *Rampant*, 1991 (London: Tate Collection); *Winter Timber*, 2009 (Private Collection); *The Arrival of Spring on Woldgate, East Yorkshire in 2011 (twenty eleven)* (New York: Pace Gallery)

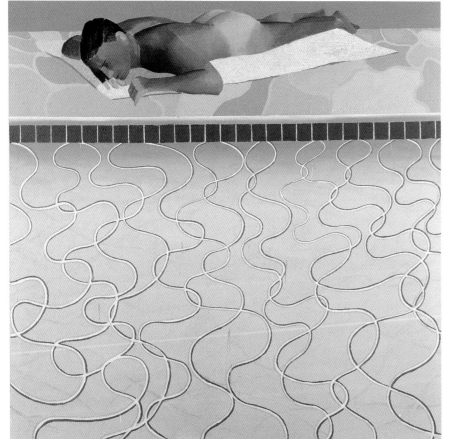

✉ *Sunbather* David Hockney, 1966, 183 x 183 cm (72 x 72 in), acrylic on canvas, Cologne: Ludwig Museum. 1966 was the era of the Beatles, Rolling Stones, and the Beach Boys. Homosexuality was legalized in the UK in July 1967.

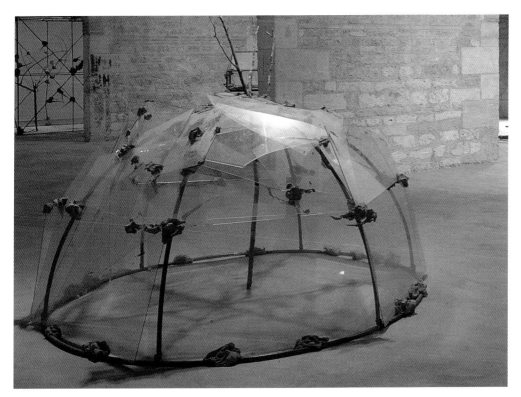

« What's to be Done?
*Mario Merz, 1969, shown
here in an exhibition in
1991, mixed media,
Bordeaux: CAPC Musée
d'Art Contemporain.*
One of Merz's "igloos",
part of a larger
installation involving
painting and sculpture.

Mario **Merz**

● 1925–2003 ⊓ ITALIAN ✍ INSTALLATIONS;
SCULPTURE; CONCEPTUAL ART

Merz was a leading member of Arte Povera who in
the 1960s and 1970s created works that addressed
geographical and environmental issues – notably
metal-framed "igloos" covered with clay, wax
branches, broken glass, etc. He produced transient,
temporary work to reveal art as a process of change
(like nature itself) and the artist as nomad. There
are references to Fibonacci numbers (an infinite
sequence of numbers in which each number equals
the sum of the previous two).

KEY WORKS: *Crocodile in the Night*, 1979
(Toronto: Art Gallery of Ontario); *Igloo*, 1983
(London: Courtauld Institute of Art); *Unreal City,
Nineteen Hundred Eighty-Nine*, 1989 (New York:
Guggenheim Museum)

»» **ARTE POVERA** 1960s–1970s

An Italian phrase meaning "Poor Art" or
"Impoverished Art". It was coined by an Italian
art critic to describe works much in evidence in
the 1960s and 1970s, which became – and still is –
a commonplace in contemporary art. Arte Povera
objects were made from basic or cheap and tacky
materials and carried a strong political agenda,
including the proposition that the elevation of
humble materials as art corresponded with a
wish for the elevation of poor social classes.
It also hoped to defy any possibility of being
commercially exploited.

Michelangelo **Pistoletto**

● 1933– ⊓ ITALIAN ✍ CONCEPTUAL ART;
SCULPTURE; PERFORMANCE; VIDEO

Pistoletto is a conceptual artist best known for work
using mirrors arranged so that the spectator keeps
on seeing him/herself. This is often achieved by
means of polished steel sheets on which life-size
photographed images of people are overlaid,
thereby creating a relationship between image
and spectator. His work is effective, puzzling, and
amusing, but not as profound as claimed.

KEY WORKS:
*Architecture of
the Mirror*, 1990
(Turin: Castello
di Rivoli Museum
of Contemporary
Art); *In the First Place*,
1997 (Turin: Castello di
Rivoli Museum of
Contemporary Art)

Jannis **Kounellis**

⬤ 1936– 🏛 GREEK/ITALIAN ✍ SCULPTURE

A leading member of Arte Povera, Kounellis creates strange objects and constructions out of materials such as blankets, mattresses, sacks, and blood, and likes to show evidence or traces of flames and smoke. His intention is to draw attention to, and make one think about, the dark side of 20th-century experience, especially social deprivation and spiritual starvation.

KEY WORKS: *Carboniera*, 1967 (London: Courtauld Institute of Art); *Untitled*, 1987 (New York: Guggenheim Museum)

Piero **Manzoni**

⬤ 1933–63 🏛 ITALIAN ✍ CONCEPTUAL ART; SCULPTURE; MIXED MEDIA

Manzoni was a short-lived (due to cirrhosis of the liver), experimental artist at the forefront of releasing art from traditional ideas, processes, and forms. He created objects and ideas that are now the commonplace of mainstream official art, but were genuinely cutting-edge in the late 1950s and

1960s: strange white objects with no specific meaning that were made by dipping material in kaolin or plaster; devices or strategies to preserve the evanescent (like the artist's breath) and challenge the idea of art as a tradable commodity; incorporating the public and the environment into a work of art. His work was provocative, but he was blessed with delicacy and humour.

KEY WORKS: *Artist's Breath*, 1960 (London: Tate Collection); *Declaration of Authenticity No. 025*, 1961 (Boston: Museum of Fine Arts)

Luciano **Fabro**

⬤ 1936–2007 🏛 ITALIAN ✍ SCULPTURE

Fabro created elegant, refined, carved sculptures using traditional materials, such as marble. He took delight in the visual and physical properties of material and was interested in craftsmanship and aesthetics – a contemporary interpretation of a tradition that goes back to Classical Greece. His work needs sunlight to bring it to life.

Enjoy his work for what it is. Let it play freely on your imagination through your own eyes. Close your ears to the prolix jargon of those

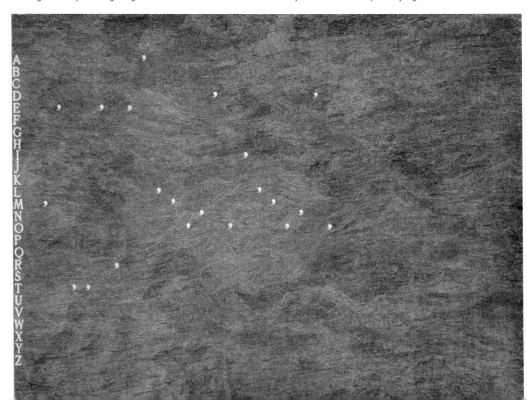

cataloguers and curators who spend more time looking at their computer keyboards and playing with words than looking at works of art. These works have all the gloriously refined qualities of haute couture: they are an open invitation for the eye and imagination to have a truly fulfilling private feast.

KEY WORKS: *Road Map of Italy*, 1969 (Turin: Private Collection); *Italia d'Oro (Golden Italy)*, 1971 (Los Angeles: Museum of Contemporary Arts); *Iconografia*, 1975 (Private Collection);

Alighiero **Boetti**

● 1940–94 🏴 ITALIAN ✍ SCULPTURE; CONCEPTUAL ART; MIXED MEDIA

A leading member of Arte Povera, Boetti specialized in coloured-wood creations. He created bits and pieces (such as assemblages, embroideries, and drawings) that scratch away at attempting to make sense of a "fragmented but all embracing world" (so what's new?). He created naïve systems, which the viewer is supposed to decode. His work is fashionable and not trivial, but ultimately insignificant. He was untrained (it shows).

Boetti is a useful reminder that the appearance, ideas, and agenda of the young, cutting-edge art of the 1990s have been in play for a good 40 years.

KEY WORKS: *The Thousand Longest Rivers in the World*, 1977–85 (New York: Museum of Modern Art); *Aerei*, 1984 (New York: Gagosian Gallery); *Map*, 1993–94 (Private Collection)

Mimmo **Paladino**

● 1948– 🏴 ITALIAN ✍ OILS; PRINTS; SCULPTURE

Paladino creates consciously individual, showy, expressively painted, colourful, large-scale figurative work made up of dislocated parts of animals, death masks, and bodies. He has a personal, mythical, and mystical agenda, which is probably (and deliberately?) impenetrable and was a leading member of the Italian Transavanguardia movement, which included Sandro Chia and Francesco Clemente.

KEY WORKS: *Canto Guerriero*, 1981 (Indiana: Ball State Museum of Art); *Untitled*, 1985 (New York: Metropolitan Museum of Art); *Sette*, 1991 (Buffalo: Albright-Knox Art Gallery)

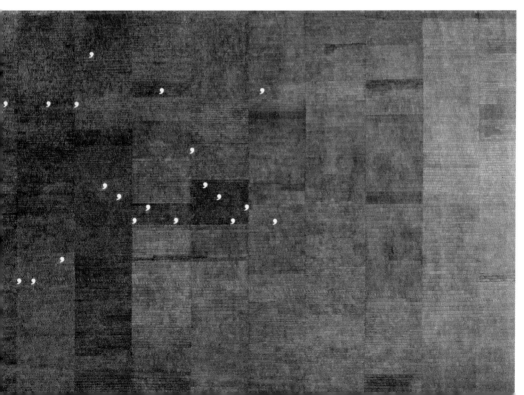

◀ *Bringing the World into the World* "Mettere al Mondo il Mondo", Alighiero Boetti, 1973–79, 135 x 178 cm and 132 x 201 cm (53 ¼ x 70 in and 53 ¼ x 80 in); ballpoint pen on paper mounted on linen, private collection. The commas indicate the letters of the original Italian title in horizontal sequence.

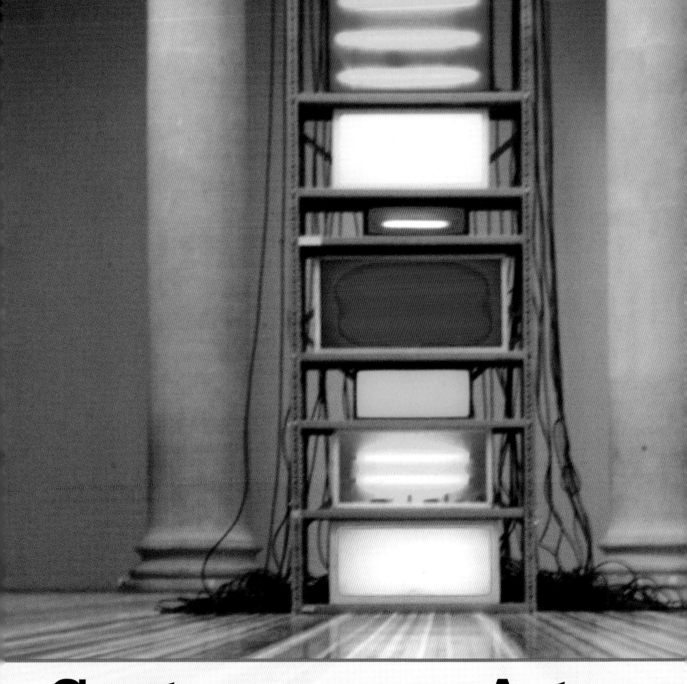

Contemporary Art
1970 onwards

Contemporary art cannot be evaluated in the same way as the art of the past. The historic events and works of art that are remembered as significant have been sieved by time. Often, what seems important in contemporary terms turns out, in the long run, to have been a dead end, or of no lasting relevance.

Art and artists

Every age has its popular obsessions. An artist of limited talent who plays up to these will receive more critical acclaim and exposure than a talented artist whose interests lie elsewhere. Only the truly great are able to say something meaningful for their own generation and for the future, and the future is, of course, unknown. Rather than try to predict who will be remembered in the years to come, it might be more pertinent to try to list the current fashions in art. In many respects it is a complete reverse of half a century ago. For example: today's most exhibited art is often large-scale with an emphasis on headline-grabbing social issues or personal revelations about an artist's life. Art which supposedly pushes the boundaries of what art is, is very much "in". Shock, gritty realism, almost any sort of confrontation, and artworks that play with concepts and words are exhibited more frequently than those concerned with looking and seeing, or aesthetic experience. Celebrity status,

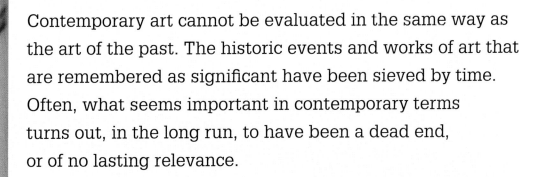

⟪ The Spectrum of Brick Lane *David Batchelor, 2003, mixed media*. Post Modernism often uses technology combined with installations and plays to an audience for whom presentation is a greater priority than content.

producing something which will draw in the crowds, and, above all, making money are promoted as desirable goals; modesty, self-doubt, the quiet commentary on the dignity or absurdity of humanity, or the wish to create a better world for mankind, do not offer a promising route to fame and fortune. Whereas half a century ago Picasso and his disciples were the prophets to follow, today it is Marcel Duchamp and his followers. Detachment and irony are widely praised as virtues; lip service is paid to personal manual skill but the slipshod is commonly applauded as spontaneity. Frequently the artist assumes the role of "manager", that is, one who controls or directs others to create a preconceived end product. Does art follow life, or life follow art? There are times when the visual arts have played a major role in leading society forward: in the Italian Renaissance and the first half of the 20th century artists believed that art had a crucial transformative role to play in the betterment of society. At other times art has been regarded as a diversion or entertainment, more prized for its populist and monetary possibilities than its spiritual values.

Patrons and collectors

Mainstream collecting and museum patronage is currently dominated by an international elite who are unashamed in their pursuit of conspicuous consumption, and who have driven the price of works of art, regardless of intrinsic merit, to unprecedented heights. Historical precedent shows that those whose self-esteem is based principally on how much money they have made tend to collect things which are a flattering reflection of themselves, offer quick undemanding gratification, and are ubiquitous and reassuringly expensive. Consequently, for such patrons and collectors, mainstream contemporary art fulfils most of their needs, and consummates Andy Warhol's prediction that the experiences of aesthetic appreciation and shopping would become indistinguishable. Artworks that are expensive trophy assets, produced by a limited circle of international artists with an easily recognizable "brand" who have themselves become rich celebrities, are now commonplace. Similarly, international corporations now customarily use art to bring some interest to soulless modern office buildings, and as public relations exercises to create a more benign environment and corporate image for employees and customers.

Lasting Values

To the artists, prelates, monarchs, and merchant princes of the Renaissance, most of this contemporary activity and outcome would be entirely familiar and laudable. So, if they lived in a world which had many of the material and corporate

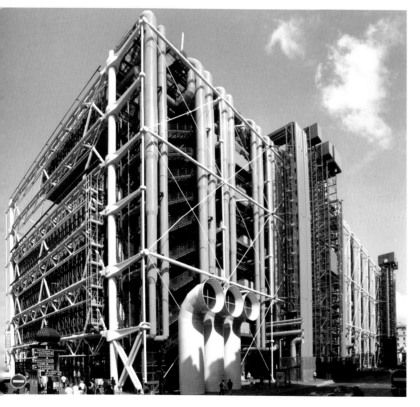

▽ **The Pompidou Centre (Beaubourg), Paris** Completed in 1978, this pioneering art centre brought modern and contemporary art to a mass audience for the fist time.

TIMELINE: 1970 onwards

1973 USA withdraws from Vietnam; Yom Kippur War in Middle East

1975 Khmer Rouge impose Marxist rule of terror in Cambodia

1980–88 Iran–Iraq War

1987 Palestinian protests (intifada) begin

1989–91 Collapse of Soviet communism in Eastern Europe, followed by collapse of the USSR in 1991

1970

1980

1974 President Nixon forced to resign after Watergate scandal

1976 Death of Chairman Mao

1979 Islamic Revolution in Iran; Soviet invasion of Afghanistan

1988 Gorbachev initiates reforms (*perestroika* and *glasnost*) in Soviet Union

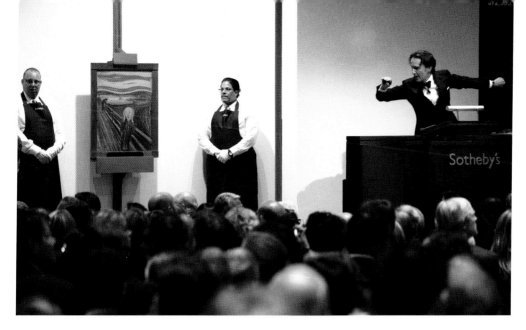

Collectors and investors have driven the price of artworks to unprecedented heights. In 2012, one of five versions of Edvard Munch's *The Scream* sold for a record £75 million pounds ($119.9 million dollars).

values which are a feature of today's society, how is it that artists then created works of art which have continued to speak so profoundly about the human spirit? Ultimately, it perhaps comes down to belief and aspiration. Any human activity that is concerned only with its own ends and means is, however accomplished, ultimately hollow. It is only when it strives to be a revelation of, or to be a means of reaching towards, something greater than itself, that it can hope to have a life and meaning beyond its own contemporary context and existence.

» ART AND TECHNOLOGY

The place of new technologies in contemporary art is ambiguous. We might be witnessing a breakout as significant as that of the early Renaissance, with the PC playing a role akin to Gutenberg's movable type (see page 33); but it may be that what is lauded currently as a period of profound artistic innovation will turn out to be a mannered and short-lived extravagance similar to that which followed the High Renaissance (see page 64). What is more certain is that contemporary art is currently ubiquitous as a recreational and consumer activity not experienced since the high point of Academic art in the latter half of the 19th century.

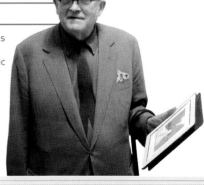

» British artist David Hockney has embraced new technologies like a sketch pad and palette.

1990 Iraqi invasion of Kuwait: first Gulf War

1998 India and Pakistan test nuclear weapons

2003 Second Gulf War: USA invades Iraq, overthrows Saddam Hussein

1990

2000

1993 Oslo Accords: limited Palestinian self-rule

1999 NATO bombing campaign to halt Serbian persecution of Albanians in Kosovo

2001 USA's "War against Terror" declared after al-Qaeda terror attacks; USA overthrows Taliban regime in Afghanistan

2005 French and Dutch electorates reject proposed EU constitution

Louise **Bourgeois**

● 1911–2010 FRENCH/AMERICAN
✍ SCULPTURE ; OILS; ENGRAVINGS

A current heroine of feminists, Bourgeois was unknown until she was in her 60s. The daughter of an emotionally dysfunctional family, she worked out the consequent trauma through her art.

Her eclectic work uses many materials and forms – sculpture, constructions, installations; images of bodily experiences, such as pregnancy, birth, breast-feeding; images of the house. She played on notions of desire, attraction, repulsion, and male–female relationships. There are references to her mother's activities of sewing and tapestry. She was not trying to illustrate anything, but to recreate her own feelings of anxiety, loneliness, defencelessness, vulnerability, aggression, sex, and death.

Her womanizing father installed a young mistress in the family home who was hated by her mother; Louise was caught in the middle. Like many from Van Gogh onwards, she turned to artistic activity to relieve her pain and find a role. Is she among those who have the ability to communicate to someone with completely different experiences? Or is she among those whose very insistence and predictability eventually kills the emotion or message?

KEY WORKS: *Dagger Child*, 1947–49 (New York: Guggenheim Museum); *Winged Figure*, 1948 (Washington DC: National Gallery of Art); *Mortise*, 1950 (Washington DC: National Gallery of Art); *Eyes*, 1982 (New York: Metropolitan Museum of Art)

◀ *Quarantania* Louise Bourgeois, 1947–53, cast 1984, 200 x 68.5 x 74.2 cm (78 ¾ x 30 x 29 ¼ in) bronze, Houston: Museum of Fine Arts. An early work suggestive of crowds and phalluses.

Agnes **Martin**

● 1912–2004 AMERICAN/CANADIAN
✍ ACRYLICS; OILS

Martin was a much-admired painter of gentle, lyrical abstracts, which reflect her search for spiritual purity and her rejection of material encumbrances and cares. She lived a simple life in New Mexico.

Her largish, square-shaped canvases of pure, pale colours and simple design were intended to reflect the qualities she valued. They are beautiful, with a haunting luminosity, and should be experienced as much as looked at. Let your mind go free, as when contemplating the ocean. Notice the soothing delicacy with which they are made: paint gently stroked on, precise pencil marks creating something close to those organic traces, webs, and honeycomb structures found in nature; subtle colour gradations like sunlight on early-morning mist or snow; horizontal lines suggestive of landscape spaces.

KEY WORKS: *White Flower*, 1960 (New York: Guggenheim Museum); *Little Sister*, 1962 (New York: Guggenheim Museum); *Leaf in the Wind*, 1963 (Pasadena: Norton Simon Museum); *With My Back to the World*, 1997 (New York: Museum of Modern Art)

Tony **Smith**

● 1912–80 AMERICAN
✍ SCULPTURE; OILS

Smith was an architect (until the 1950s), a sculptor (from the 1960s), and a painter. He created simple, satisfying, engineered structures (he designed and created the models, others built the end products). They are of varying size and scale but always with human proportions – romantic rather than minimal. Sleek black surfaces add a stylish, sophisticated presence. In his work, space is as important as form.

KEY WORKS: *Moondog*, model 1964, fabricated 1998–99 (Washington DC: National Gallery of Art); *Wandering Rocks*, 1967 (Washington DC: National Gallery of Art)

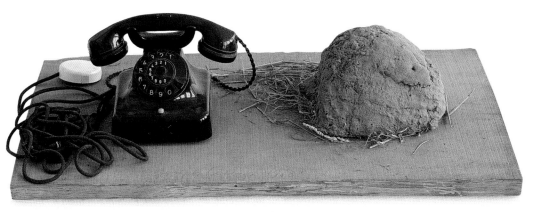

◀ Earth Telephone
*Joseph Beuys, 1968, 220
x 47 x 76 cm (8 x 18 ½ x
30 in), telephone, earth
and grass, connecting
cable on wooden board,
Hamburg: Kunsthalle.*
Beuys saw himself
as part witchdoctor,
part magician.

Joseph **Beuys**

● 1921–86 GERMAN SCULPTURE;
PERFORMANCE ART

A star of the 1980s, Beuys was highly regarded
by intellectuals and lionized by ambitious
curators and dealers. He was a serious, gentle,
mystic, and charismatic figure who sought to
comment on his own times, and was also
(paradoxically) a victim of them.

To establish a connection with these works you
have to establish a rapport with the whole Beuys
phenomenon – the man, his appearance, his
lifestyle, his biography, and his beliefs. Thus
the lumps of fat, fur, or felt that you find in the
museum showcases are like fragments of
a total work; or, they are like the traces that a
wild animal makes to establish its presence
or the extent of its territory.

Only by accepting the Beuys phenomenon
can you begin to "see" the energy of the world
references, harmony with nature, the dilemmas
of modern Germany, Beuys's early childhood
experiences, and so on. If you don't want to
or can't cross this threshold, don't worry – it
may all be self-deception anyway. The Beuys
phenomenon is an unexpected alliance of the
artist's ego with museum and commercial
interests, looking for instant history.

KEY WORKS: *How to Explain Pictures to a Dead
Hare*, 1965 (performance); *Felt Suit*, 1970 (London:
Tate Collection); *Four Blackboards*, 1972
(London: Tate Collection); *I Like America and America
Likes Me*, 1974 (performance); *Encounter with Beuys*,
1974–84 (New York: Guggenheim Museum)

Jules **Olitski**

● 1922–2007 RUSSIAN/AMERICAN
 ACRYLICS; SCULPTURE

Born in Russia, Olitski trained in Old-Master
painting techniques. He was the creator of
large-scale, decorative abstract paintings and used
a stain and spray-gun technique, which created a
field of atmospheric colour that seemed to dissolve
the picture surface. There is often a band of rich
pigment along one edge or at a corner. His work
is sensual, slightly precious, and self-conscious.

KEY WORKS: *Ino Delight*, 1962 (Saskatchewan,
Canada: Mackenzie Art Gallery); *Prince Patutsky's
Command*, 1966 (Canberra: National Gallery
of Australia)

Kenneth **Noland**

● 1924–2010 AMERICAN ACRYLICS;
SCULPTURE

Noland created simple, direct works in which the
impact is purely visual, coming solely from colour
on the canvas – there is no "meaning", drawn line,
or spatial depth. He played with colour variations
and simple, dynamic shapes (such as a bull's
eye or a chevron) and their relationship to the
shape or edge of canvas. He also played with
irregular-shaped canvases. His work is very
American and very good.

KEY WORKS: *Song*, 1958 (New York: Whitney Museum
of American Art); *Half*, 1959 (Houston: Museum of Fine
Arts); *Hade*, 1973 (Private Collection)

George **Segal**

● 1924-2000 🏳 AMERICAN ✍ SCULPTURE

Segal was a creator of environments that are like banal settings with real objects from everyday life, but in which the people are replaced by white plaster figures. He made casts from real live people, wrapping them in plaster-soaked gauze bandages like a mummy. These form a powerful and sensitive evocation of the lonely anonymity of everyday life. His work is highly distinctive and original.

KEY WORKS: *Cinema*, 1963 (Buffalo: Albright-Knox Art Gallery); *The Gas Station*, 1963 (Ottawa: National Gallery of Canada)

Duane **Hanson**

● 1925-96 🏳 AMERICAN ✍ ACRYLICS; OILS

Hanson was the maker of hyperrealistic sculptures (since 1967) – a modern reworking of the "everyday life" realism much loved by Victorian middle classes. His early work was strongly political.

He created unnervingly lifelike, life-size sculptures of people who are almost indistinguishable from the gallery-goers who look at them. His subjects are tourists, shoppers, construction workers, children – middle America at work and play. He took moulds from live models, which were then cast in polyester resin or bronze, and painted; he then added real accessories, such as shoes and clothes. Hanson's stated aim was to ennoble the commonplace and ordinary by turning it and its inhabitants into art.

Hanson was a slow worker – a single figure could take a year to complete. Note the realism of flesh textures, such as bruises, varicose veins, and hair on forearms or legs. His figures are often in movement, but always self-absorbed and introspective (even when in a group); sometimes they are asleep. The impact comes in part from his astonishing technical skill, in part from his contemporaneity. How powerful will these works be when they eventually look like historical figures, not part of the here and now?

KEY WORKS: *Tourist*, 1970 (Edinburgh: National Gallery of Modern Art); *Salesman*, 1992 (Missouri: Kemper Museum of Contemporary Art)

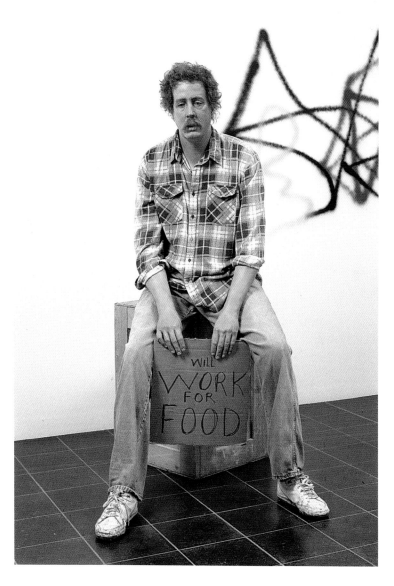

« **Homeless Person** Duane Hanson, 1991, height 168 cm (66 ¼ in), mixed media, Hamburg: Kunsthalle. Hanson often quoted Henry David Thoreau: "... men lead lives of quiet desperation..."

John **Chamberlain**

◉ 1927–2011 〔ᵁ〕 AMERICAN ✍ SCULPTURE

Influenced by David Smith in his early work, Chamberlain was famous for sculptures (freestanding and wall reliefs) made from welded-together car parts. They are carefully planned and painted for aesthetic effect (look for the inclusion of chrome parts). Many of his compositions are designed to be hung on walls, rather than stood on the ground. Don't look for a social comment on car-obsessed consumer society – his later work used non-car materials, such as aluminium foil, polyurethane foam, and paper bags.

KEY WORKS: *Essex*, 1960 (New York: Museum of Modern Art); *Dolores James*, 1962 (New York: Guggenheim Museum); *Koko-Nor II*, 1967 (London: Tate Collection)

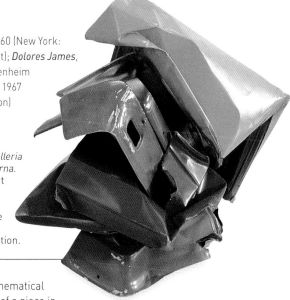

≫ Untitled John Chamberlain, c.1960s, sheet metal, Rome: Galleria Nazionale d'Arte Moderna. Chamberlain taught at the famous Black Mountain College, North Carolina, where visual art was central in a liberal arts education.

Donald (Don) **Judd**

◉ 1928–94 〔ᵁ〕 AMERICAN ✍ SCULPTURE; INSTALLATIONS; OILS

Judd created sculptures by giving instructions for the industrial production of modular (often large) box-shaped objects in polished metal and Plexiglas, which are often stacked and cantilevered. They are simple, minimal, with proportions and spaces based on mathematical progressions, and all of a piece in shape, colour, and surface. The works are detached and cool, with no human presence or reference.

KEY WORKS: *Untitled*, 1969 (New York: Guggenheim Museum); *Untitled*, 1970 (New York: Guggenheim Museum); *Untitled (Six Boxes)*, 1974 (Canberra: National Gallery of Australia)

Sol **Lewitt**

◉ 1928–2007 〔ᵁ〕 AMERICAN ✍ SCULPTURE; CONCEPTUAL ART; PRINTS

Lewitt was a pioneering Minimalist and one of the movement's "Grand Old Men". At first sight his structures and wall drawings look as if they are merely mechanical applications of established mathematical systems, but they are not.

He created a type of pure beauty that came out of an order that was logical but not rigid or predictable. He started with a system, ratio, or formula, which could be quite arbitrarily chosen, and employed assistants to make the modular structure or wall drawing that follows from it. His works can be on a large or small scale, but the bigger and more complex the better; they are completely self-referential and self-contained.

You can take the works intellectually and try to unravel the system, or you can take them visually for what they are and enjoy their unexpected, peaceful beauty and the way in which they generate light as well as space, thus creating a sense of emotional openness and purity. His wall drawings are created for each new location and then whitewashed out. His early work was in monochrome or white; he gradually introduced colour and his last work is richly colourful (and less pure and less effective as a result?).

KEY WORKS: *Floor Structure Black*, 1965 (Washington DC: National Gallery of Art); *A Wall Divided Vertically into Fifteen Equal Parts, Each with a Different Line Direction and Colour, and All Combinations*, 1970 (London: Tate Collection); *Steel Structure (formerly Untitled)*, 1975–76 (San Francisco: Museum of Modern Art); *Wavy Brushstrokes*, 1996 (Washington DC: National Gallery of Art)

≛ 49 Three-Part Variations of the Three Different Kinds of Cubes Sol Lewitt, 1967–71, 49 units, each 60 x 20 x 20 cm (24 x 8 x 8 in), enamel on steel, Hamburg: Kunsthalle. Lewitt was a leading exponent of Minimalism, a reaction against Abstract Expressionism and Pop.

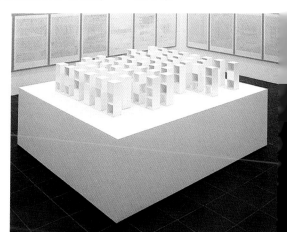

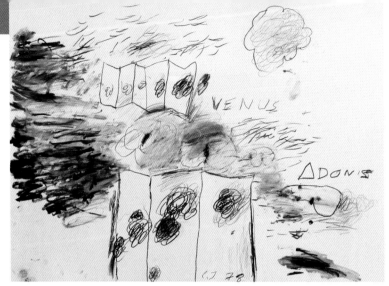

⟰ Untitled (Venus + Adonis) *Cy Twombly 1978, 70 × 100 cm (27 ²/₄ x 39 ³/₈ in), Ölfarbe, Kreide, Bleistift auf Zeichenkarton.* In 1957 Twombly settled permanently in Italy and began to create works influenced by classical mythology.

Cy **Twombly**

● 1928–2011 ⚑ AMERICAN ✍ OILS; DRAWINGS

Twombly was much admired for his highly personal abstract style consisting of apparently random scribbles and marks, sometimes incorporating bits of text and diagram. If you require order, clarity, structure, and specific meaning you will hate it; if you like improvisation, hints, whispers, and teases, you will love it.

KEY WORKS: *Vengeance of Achilles*, 1962 (Zurich: Kunsthaus); *Quattro Stagioni (a painting in four parts)*, 1993–94 (London: Tate Collection)

Robert **Ryman**

● 1930- ⚑ AMERICAN ✍ OILS; MIXED MEDIA

A self-taught abstract painter from Nashville, Tennessee, Ryman has a limited but highly visual theme. He is a musical enthusiast (Charlie Parker and Thelonius Monk). His works should be seen by daylight.

His paintings are about what paintings are made from, what paint can do, and what they look like (and why not?). So don't look for subjects, concepts, and spirituality, look instead at the way he uses oil paint (thick, thin, shiny, flat); his use of textured canvases, paper, metal surfaces, and so on; and how he fixes these works to the wall. It sounds banal, but actually they are beautiful to look at if you don't expect too much. Is it a dead end or a new beginning?

Ryman wants his work to be shown by daylight so that the textured surfaces will look different and interesting as the light changes (white attracts light). Look at his different choices of brush marks and surface, and the way they change in the same work; also notice what he does with canvas (stretched or unstretched, for instance). Look also at the edges and the way he incorporates his signature. The choice of frame, or lack of one, is also his.

KEY WORKS: *Classico IV*, 1968 (New York: Guggenheim Museum); *Surface Veil*, 1970–71 (San Francisco: Museum of Modern Art); *Monitor*, 1978 (Amsterdam: Stedelijk Museum)

Robert **Morris**

● 1931- ⚑ AMERICAN ✍ SCULPTURE; CONCEPTUAL ART; LAND ART; PERFORMANCE ART

Morris produces large-scale simple forms, either geometric and hard-edge, or curvilinear and soft-edge (such as mounds of hanging felt). He creates the blueprint, others make the pieces. He wants you to focus on an analysis of an activity of your perception and/or the decision-making process by which he arrives at final form – this is the classic agenda for Minimal art, of which he was a pioneer.

KEY WORKS: *Untitled (Corner Piece)*, 1964 (New York: Guggenheim Museum); *House of Vetti I*, 1983 (Hamburg: Deichtorhallen)

✉ Untitled (Felt Tangle) *Robert Morris, 1967, 190 x 400 x 220 cm (74 ⁴/₅ x 157 ¹/₂ x 86 ³/₅ in), felt and metal eyes, Hamburg: Kunsthalle.* Morris started making his felt constructions in 1967 after moving to a studio in Colorado, which used to be an old felt factory, and where remnants were still lying to hand.

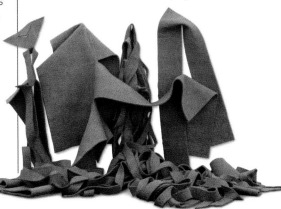

Richard **Estes**

● 1932- ᴾᴵ AMERICAN ✍ OILS; PRINTS

The king of photorealism, Estes uses many of the same techniques as Canaletto, but his images are not place-specific. His views could be of any modern city.

His fine, detailed paintings of the modern urban streetscape look at first sight as though they are merely enlarged photographs – but they are not. He paints from photographs to create a highly complex, composite view that heightens reality in a way that is impossible in a single photograph, but it gives the illusion of freezing a split second, as does a photo.

He produces carefully organized compositions that divide the scene into distinct areas – for example, he might create a diptych. Estes uses a multipoint perspective or viewpoint and reflecting windows to show what is happening outside the picture frame, behind the back of the viewer. Note the absence of human figures and activity. Look for rich, intense colour harmonies. Within his self-imposed limitations, he creates haunting, moody images that have beauty and detachment.

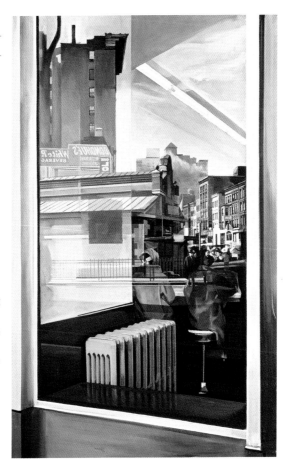

◀ *Donohue's Richard Estes*, 1967–68, 234 ½ x 134 cm (93 ¾ x 53 ½ in), *oil on masonite, private collection*. Estes was initially much influenced by Degas, Hopper, and Eakins, and worked in advertising.

KEY WORKS: *Parking Lot*, undated (New York: National Academy of Design); *Nedicks*, 1970 (Madrid: Museo Thyssen-Bornemisza); *Diner*, 1971 (Washington DC: Hirshhorn Museum)

Fernando **Botero**

● 1932- ᴾᴵ COLOMBIAN ✍ OILS; PRINTS

Botero is a creator of immediately recognizable paintings and sculptures that are wholly out of the mainstream of "serious" contemporary art. Tubby, cheerful, over-inflated (literally and metaphorically)

figures, meticulously painted in bright colours, through which he ridicules the pomposities of life, art, and officialdom. His work is a breath of fresh air.

KEY WORKS: *Our Lady Fatima*, 1963 (Bogota: Museo de Arte Moderno); *Dancing in Colombia*, 1980 (New York: Metropolitan Museum of Art)

Nam June **Paik**

● 1921–2006 ᴾᴵ FRENCH ✍ SCULPTURE; INSTALLATIONS; PERFORMANCE ART

Once a young "bad boy" with an instinct for public scandal, Paik eventually acquired a "grand old man" status. His first interest was music (that of John Cage). From the 1960s, he wanted to turn TV from a medium for passive

mass audiences into an individual and dynamic medium, like painting. He used the TV screen like collage and created large-scale installations with banks of screens. His work is pioneering and impressive.

KEY WORKS: *Global Groove*, 1973 (Pittsburgh: Carnegie Museum of Art); *Video Flag*, 1985–96 (Washington DC: Hirshhorn Museum

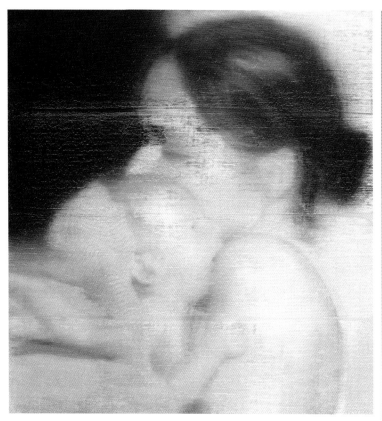

⊠ S. with Child
*Gerhard Richter,
c.1995, oil on canvas,
Hamburg: Kunsthalle.*
One of a series of eight
paintings Richter made
of his wife with their
newborn child, showing
his characteristic
blurred Photorealistic
technique. The
compositions revisit
the religious motif
of the Madonna
and Child.

KEY WORKS: *Passage*,
1968 (New York:
Guggenheim Museum);
Korn, 1982 (New York:
Guggenheim Museum);
St John, 1988 (London:
Tate Collection); *Abstract
Painting (726)*, 1990
(London: Tate Collection)

Gerhard **Richter**

● 1932– 🏴 GERMAN ✍ OILS; PRINTS

A refugee from Communist East Germany (1961),
and trained as an orthodox Communist *trompe-
l'oeil* social realist, Richter then had to assimilate
Western Modernism. He is often pigeonholed with
cutting-edge artists now in their 30s and 40s, but
he is in fact old enough to be their father.

   He produces three different types of work:
schematic Minimalist abstracts; splashy,
messy abstracts; but most typically, finely painted,
soft-focus photographic imagery. What is not in
doubt is his technical ability and high critical
esteem. What is less clear is his meaning (he
seems to deny any). Supporters say the deadpan
blurriness shows his "dialectical tension" and
virtuous ambivalence. Detractors ask how is
it that such "important" work can be so boring?

George **Deem**

● 1932–2008 🏴 AMERICAN ✍ OILS

New York-based Deem was famous for his "School
of" paintings. He took elements from well-known
works by famous artists, such as Vermeer, and
arranged them in a schoolroom setting – which is
itself borrowed from a painting by Winslow Homer.
Witty, perceptive, and inventive, he used subtle
brushwork, which reproduced the techniques of
the Old Masters. He makes you look and think twice.

KEY WORKS: *Visitation*, 1978 (Private Collection);
Vermeer's Chair, 1994 (New York: Nancy
Hoffman Gallery)

Dan **Flavin**

● 1933–96 🏴 AMERICAN ✍ INSTALLATIONS

Flavin was noted for constructions using
fluorescent tubes and neons, usually arranged
across a corner of a darkened empty room. He
claimed to be playing with the space of the room;
illuminating dull corners (of life?) and expressing
mystical notions about light. There are early
nostalgic references to Russian Constructivism.

KEY WORKS: *The Nominal Three (to William of
Ockham)*, 1963 (New York: Guggenheim Museum);
*Greens Crossing Greens (to Piet Mondrian, Who
Lacked Green)*, 1966 (New York: Guggenheim Museum)

Carl **André**

● 1935– 🏴 AMERICAN ✍ SCULPTURE

One of the first exponents of Minimal art, André's
work reflects his boyhood in a Massachusetts
shipyard town and his early job on the Pennsylvania
railroad – surrounded by metal plates, girders,
railway lines, industry, and quarries.

   He is notorious for the *Pile of Bricks*, which hit
the headlines in the 1970s (the Tate Gallery and
André were ridiculed in the popular press). His
most successful work is typically of industrially
made components (such as bricks or metal plates),
which are arranged in mathematical order; also
chunky, rough-cut wood constructions made from

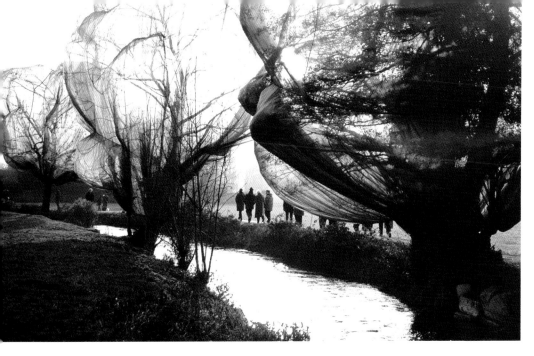

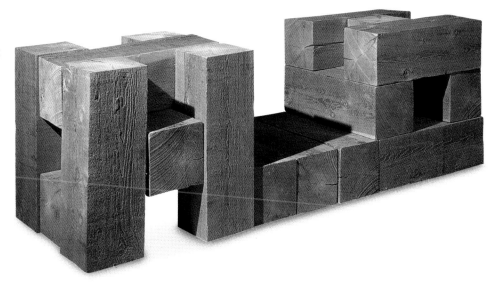

◄ Wrapped Trees
Christo and Jeanne-Claude, 1997–98, Fondation Beyeler and Berower Park, Basel, Switzerland. For this installation, 178 trees were wrapped in 55,000 sq m (592,000 sq ft) of woven polyester fabric and ropes.

Christo & Jeanne-Claude

● 1935– AND 1935–2009 ⚑ AMERICAN
✍ SCULPTURE; ENVIRONMENTAL ART

Christo and Jeanne-Claude – a husband and wife partnership based in New York – travelled the world to create highly original, memorable projects.

They wrapped objects. They started in 1958 with small items and moved on to very large ones in 1961, including wrapping the Pont Neuf in Paris and the Reichstag in Berlin, in fabric and ropes, which both suggest and conceal the thing wrapped. They also created landscape projects, such as a 40-km (24-mile)-long curtain (literally) running across open countryside. The big projects were deliberately temporary, so one only has a limited opportunity of seeing them.

Their underlying purpose wasn't social but aesthetic – the transformation of the well-known into the unfamiliar or disquieting, while at the same time touching and involving everyone in the creative process.

KEY WORKS: *Wrapped Coast*, 1968–69 (New South Wales, Australia: Little Bay); *Surrounded Islands*, 1983 (Florida: Biscayne Bay)

▼ Tomb of the Golden Engenderers *Carl André, c.1976, 91.4 x 274.3 x 91.4 cm (36 x 108 x 36 in), western red cedar wood, private collection.* André was a leading Minimalist, also writing in the tradition of concrete poetry.

pre-cut units. In the 1970s, he genuinely challenged the gallery-goer to question what is, and what is supposed to be, art. In 1985 he was charged with the murder of his wife (who fell from a window), but was later acquitted.

KEY WORKS: *Equivalent VIII*, 1966 (London: Tate Collection); *Venus Forge*, 1980 (London: Tate Collection); *Bandolin*, 2003 (New York: Paula Cooper Gallery); *Carbon Quarry*, 2004 (Düsseldorf: Konrad Fischer Galerie)

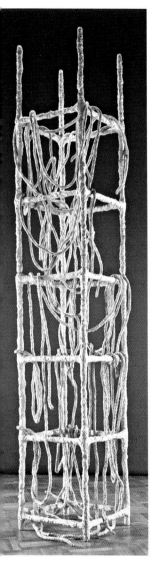

 Laocoon Eva Hesse, 1966, 330 x 59 x 59 cm (22 ¾ x 22 ¾ in), plastic tubing, rope, wire, papier-mache, cloth, and paint), Oberlin College, Ohio: Allen Memorial Art Museum. Although referencing the famous Hellenistic sculpture (see p. 17) the inspiration for this work was a ladder and piping in the artist's studio.

Eva **Hesse**

● 1936–70 ⃝ GERMAN/AMERICAN
✍ SCULPTURE; CONCEPTUAL ART; OILS

Hesse was a short-lived, deeply sensitive artist whose work was informed by her complicated biography. Born in Germany, she emigrated to New York with her family in 1938 to escape Nazi persecution, and lost her mother to suicide at age 10. She died of a brain tumour, aged 34. The decade before her death was a period of prodigious output and originality.

During her short career, Hesse was one of the first artists to question the austere exactitude of Minimalism, imbuing it with a capacity to move, change, and vary. She trained as a painter, but turned to sculpture in 1965 and began exploring processes outside the standard modes of carving, modelling, and bronze casting. She was committed to the handmade, and employed sculptural materials such as rope, latex, fibreglass, and cheesecloth, often looped and knotted in repetitive bindings or hanging loose like slack membranes.

Hesse's mature work abounds in contradictions. Her goal, she explained, was to portray the essential absurdity of life. Notice how this is conveyed though Hesse's use of materials – aging, discolouring, dripping, and sagging.

KEY WORKS: *Hang Up*, 1966 (Art Institute of Chicago); *Repetition Nineteen III*, 1968 (New York: Museum of Modern Art); *Contingent*, 1969 (Canberra: National Gallery of Australia)

Frank **Stella**

● 1936– ⃝ GERMAN/AMERICAN ✍ OILS; ACRYLICS; MIXED MEDIA

One of today's leading abstract painters, Stella is prolific and very varied – but a constant theme is investigating what paintings are and what they can or ought to look like.

His early work reduced painting to all but its most pure, minimal, and indispensable properties: simple, flat, shaped, and monochrome. He then introduced pure, bright, hard-edge colour with increasing complexity. After the early 1970s, he started to investigate how impure a painting could be and yet still remain a painting, by making constructions that are rich, interlocking clusters of shape and colour. He uses varied materials.

He likes to work on a large scale, borrowing ideas and techniques from sculpture and architecture, but always creates "pictures" – his creations have a back to the wall and are viewed from the front.

KEY WORKS: *Six Mile Bottom*, 1960 (London: Tate Collection); *Agbatana II*, 1968 (St Étienne: Musée de l'Art et de l'Industrie); *Harran II*, 1967 (New York: Guggenheim Museum)

Georg **Baselitz**

● 1938– ⃝ GERMAN ✍ OILS; SCULPTURE; MIXED MEDIA

Baselitz is the creator of big, lively, colourful, energetically painted, not very original paintings (neither in technique nor subject), in which bodies are often portrayed upside down. His work is acclaimed in official art circles. He also makes large-scale, crudely hewn sculptures out of wood.

Baselitz claims (perhaps honestly?) that his works have no particular meaning, although this does not deter the art establishment from endowing them with deep significance and cheerfully paying enormous prices for them. Notice the direction of the paint drips – at least they prove the figures were painted upside down and that he hasn't just up-ended his canvases.

KEY WORKS: *Studio Corner*, 1973 (Hamburg: Kunsthalle); *Three-legged Nude*, 1977 (Hamburg: Kunsthalle)

✉ *Picture-Eleven* Georg Baselitz, 1992, 289 x 461 cm (113 ¾ x 181 ½ in), oil on canvas, Hamburg: Kunsthalle. Baselitz was one of a number of artists born and trained in East Germany who escaped to the West.

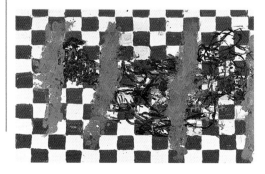

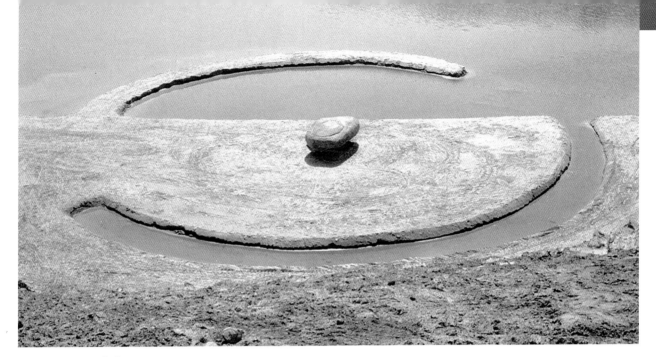

Robert **Smithson**

🌑 1938-73 🏳 AMERICAN ✍ LAND ART; CONCEPTUAL ART; SCULPTURE

Smithson was a pioneer land artist, who was tragically killed in his 30s. He had a pessimistic view of the world: he foresaw it ending in a new ice age, not a golden age, reduced to self-destructive banality by the anonymity of urban developments and indifference to the environment. He reacted against this by offering his workings on the land (and the documentation of the process) as works of art.

KEY WORKS: *Yucatan Mirror Displacements (1–9)*, 1969 (New York: Guggenheim Museum); *Spiral Jetty*, 1970 (situated at Great Salt Lake, Utah)

Brice **Marden**

🌑 1938– 🏳 AMERICAN ✍ OILS

Marden is a leading American abstract painter who is not easy to pigeonhole and who has not got stuck in a rut like many of his contemporaries.

His earlier works are either single spreads of voluptuous colour or combinations of rectangular forms (panels) playing on the rectangular nature of his canvas. He uses velvety, textured paint (also beeswax and encaustic) for these. The titles of his pieces often refer to art history.

His more recent works take a new direction. At first sight they look just like other examples of over-praised, messily painted abstracts. But linger on and let them be what they are: the lines become like the rhythmic, moving patterns on the surface of clear deep water; the colours have the hues of autumn leaves. He reminisces about landscape.

KEY WORKS: *Blonde*, 1970 (Boston: Museum of Fine Arts); *Green (Earth)*, 1983–84 (New York: Mary Boone Gallery); *Corpus*, 1991–93 (New York: Matthew Marks Gallery)

Judy **Chicago**

🌑 1939– 🏳 AMERICAN ✍ INSTALLATIONS; CONCEPTUAL ART

Chicago is best known for the collaborative venture *Dinner Party* (1973–79), a room-size installation of a triangular table, and elaborate named place settings for 39 key historic and mythological females. Although Chicago's activities are a celebration of sisterhood, they are more popular with the public than with feminists.

KEY WORKS: *Dinner Party*, 1973–79 (New York: Brooklyn Museum of Art); *The Rejection Quartet*, 1974 (San Francisco: Museum of Modern Art)

🔼 *Broken Circle*
Robert Smithson, 1971, diameter 42.7 m (140 ft), green water, white and yellow sand flats, Emmen (Holland). Smithson was interested in historic man-made environments, such as burial grounds and pyramids.

A. R. **Penck**

⬤ 1939– 🏳 GERMAN ✍ OILS; PRINTS; WOODCUTS

Born Ralf Winckler in East Germany (his earliest memory is of the fire bombing of his home town of Dresden in 1945), Penck creates highly individual works that have a consciously primitive and crude appearance. His hallmarks are his stylized, spindly, silhouetted figures; archaic symbols; and fragmented writing. He has a personal political agenda, which is not always easy to fathom.

KEY WORKS: *View of the World, Psychotronic-Strategic-Art*, 1966–71 (Frankfurt: Städel Museum); *Standart-Bild*, 1971 (Basel, Switzerland: Kunstmuseum)

Richard **Serra**

⬤ 1939– 🏳 AMERICAN ✍ SCULPTURE

Serra is the foremost American creator of sculpture for public spaces. He produces huge works, which have a commanding presence and are held together only by gravity.

Look for giant, minimal, monumental slabs of metal, often exhibited in open urban spaces. They are unmissable and unavoidable – and often seem to be unstable, as though the pieces could fall over. Take pleasure in his interest in massive weight and the way he likes to play with the sense and appearance of it: propped, balanced, rotated, moving, about to move, added to, subtracted from, towering, ground-hugging. He loves playing with the force and direction of weight.

Serra is also interested in the psychology of weight, in two ways: 1) observing the impact that his massive, apparently unstable or dangerous objects have on the viewers' own space and on their bodily and mental reactions to them; 2) as a metaphor for social realities, such as the weight of government control or personal tragedy. Legal actions have been taken to have some of his works removed.

KEY WORKS: *Strike: To Roberta and Rudy*, 1969–71 (New York: Guggenheim Museum); *Five Plates, Two Poles*, 1971 (Washington DC: National Gallery of Art); *Balance*, 1972 (Washington DC: Hirshhorn Museum)

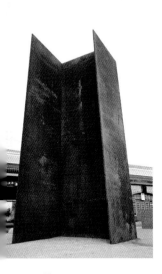

⌃ *T.W.U.*
Richard Serra, 1979–80, weathered steel, Hamburg, Germany: Deichtorhallen. Each plate weighs 72 tons. In 1980–81 the work was on public display on a street corner in Tribeca, New York.

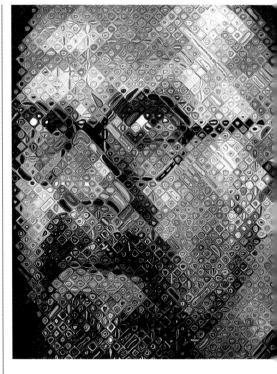

⌃ *Self-Portrait Chuck Close, 1997, 259.1 x 213.4 cm (102 x 84 in), oil on canvas, New York: Museum of Modern Art.* Close was paralyzed in 1988 but continues to work with brushes strapped to his wrists.

Chuck **Close**

⬤ 1940– 🏳 AMERICAN ✍ OILS; ACRYLICS; PRINTS

Close produces huge portraits of himself and his friends, always from the neck up. He works from photographs, which are squared up and the final images created tiny square by tiny square, according to a complex, time-consuming, and mechanical procedure. The end result is compelling. He used colour after 1971.

KEY WORKS: *Frank*, 1969 (Minnesota: Minneapolis Institute of Arts); *Big Self-Portrait*, 1977–79 (Minnesota: Minneapolis Institute of Arts); *Georgia*, 1984 (Youngstown, Ohio: Butler Institute of American Art)

Jan **Dibbets**

● 1941– 🏳 DUTCH ✍ PHOTOGRAPHY;
INSTALLATIONS

Dibbets is a photographer (black-and-white and colour) as well as a maker of installations.

His photographs are to be admired for their rigorous and meticulous qualities – formal and dry – and their limited experiments with perspective and space. He also produces installations that are strong sociological or political observations and critiques of capitalism.

His photo experiments are said to be part of a traditional Dutch interest in perspective and order that goes back to Saenredam via Mondrian. Maybe, but Dibbets does not have their feel for the poetry of space and light.

KEY WORKS: *Spoleto Floor*, 1981 (Turin: Castello di Rivioli Museum of Contemporary Art); *Four Windows*, 1991 (Tilburg, Netherlands: De Pont Foundation for Contemporary Art)

Bruce **Nauman**

● 1941– 🏳 AMERICAN ✍ INSTALLATIONS;
PERFORMANCE ART; SCULPTURE;
CONCEPTUAL ART; VIDEO

Regarded as one of the gurus of the official art world, Nauman aims to examine, document, and involve the viewer in experiences of pointless activity, humiliation, stress, and frustration.

He works in many media – video, performance, conventional sculpture, neon, you name it. He claims to be communicating his observations of human nature and examining our perceptions of it, but focuses on activities that are pointless, repetitive, and deliberately inept. Fair enough, but does it result in anything of significance, or merely the trivial and banal? If the answer is "that's the point", then isn't it just an exercise in perversity?

To answer the above, trust your own judgment; ignore museum labels and their over-anxious insistence on significance (translation: we have committed significant money and professional credibility to this; if it isn't deemed to be significant and profound we will look like complete idiots). Better still, as this is overtly public art, study the reactions of gallery goers. Are they engaged and interested? Or are they dismissive and disinterested? They will tell you if his strategies amount to meaningful art.

KEY WORKS: *Shelf Sinking into the Wall with Copper-Painted Plaster Casts of the Spaces Underneath*, 1966 (London: Tate Collection); *True Artist Helps the World by Revealing Mystic Truths (Window or Wall Sign)*, 1967 (Canberra: National Gallery of Australia)

Sigmar **Polke**

● 1941–2010 🏳 GERMAN ✍ PHOTOGRAPHY;
OILS; MIXED MEDIA

Polke's family migrated from East to West Germany in 1953. He produced large-scale work, which often appears to be a chaotic appropriation of images from consumer society, painted onto unorthodox grounds (such as woollen blankets or furs). He claimed to be attacking cliché-ridden banalities of current society, and aspired to make contact with a higher spiritual level of consciousness.

KEY WORKS: *Paganini*, 1982 (London: Saatchi Collection); *Saturn*, 1990 (San Francisco: Fine Arts Museums)

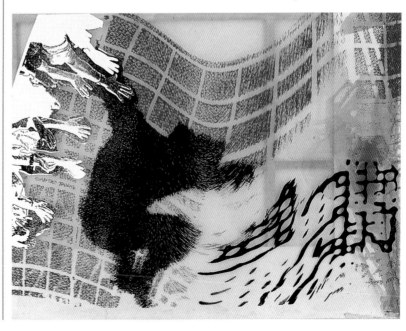

🗨 *Flight – Black, Red, and Gold* Sigmar Polke, 1997, 300 x 400 cm (118 ¼ x 157 ½ in), mixed media, polyester fabric, private collection, Hamburg: Kunsthalle. Polke's most recent works reflect an interest in exploring the relationship of abstract and figurative art.

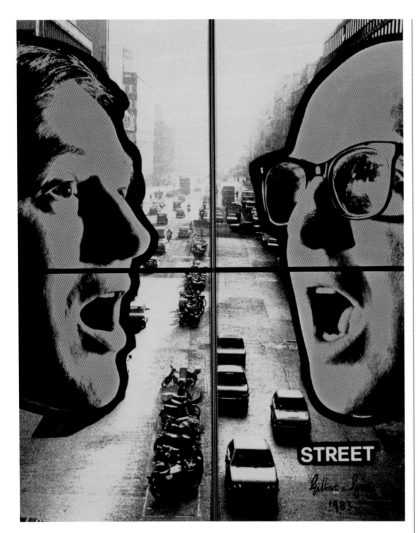

⌂ **Street** Gilbert and George, c.1983, 121 x 100 cm (47 ⅔ x 39 ⅓ in), mixed media, private collection. Gilbert and George were among the first artists to move to the East End of London, attracted by its affordability and roughness. The area is now a fashionable art Mecca, acting as a shop window for dealers and collectors.

Gilbert and George

◔ 1943– AND 1942– ⁂ BRITISH ✍ PERFORMANCE ART; PHOTOMONTAGE; VIDEO; MIXED MEDIA

Gilbert Proesch and George Passmore are a highly successful, narcissistic couple who regularly appear in their own work as two cheap-suited "nerds". They have a big international following and started as real-life "living sculptures".

Their large "photopieces" (produced since 1974) are made by an unknown process and are technically very impressive. Their subject matter comes out of inner-city decay and is often deliberately "in-yer-face" and offensive to all sides: to liberals (racist overtones, admiration for Thatcherism, swastikas, crude Little Englander nationalism) as much as to old-school conservatives (overt homosexuality with young men, turds, ridicule of religion and the monarchy).

Their work unquestionably reflects something significant about British society and its art world (1970s to the 1990s), but what? Are they criticizing the physical, moral, social, and educational decay of society (the period when Britain became "a nation state equivalent of Woolworths")? Are they praising it? Exploiting it? Or pandering to chattering-class voyeurism? Their work may rapidly begin to look very dated. Are they Hogarth's successors? Do they have a true message, or is their inability to set an agenda a comment in itself on the state of British society?

KEY WORKS: *Balls: the Evening Before the Morning After – Drinking Sculpture*, 1972 (London: Tate Collection); *Dream*, 1984 (New York: Guggenheim Museum); *Here*, 1987 (New York: Metropolitan Museum of Art)

Blinky **Palermo**

◔ 1943–77 ⁂ GERMAN ✍ SCULPTURE; OILS; MIXED MEDIA

Palermo's real name was Peter Heisterkamp. He was a short-lived refugee from Communist East Germany to Düsseldorf (1954) and a disciple of Beuys. He had a charismatic personality and adopted the pseudonym (Palermo) of a notorious boxer and Mafioso. He made objects, fabric works, and abstract paintings. His utopian dream was to use art as a means of modern salvation. This is perhaps another case where ambition ran too far ahead of the achievement.

KEY WORKS: *Staircase*, 1970 (London: Tate Collection); *Untitled (Fabric Painting)*, 1970 (Frankfurt: Städel Museum); *To the People of New York City*, 1976–77 (New York: Dia:Beacon)

James **Turrell**

● 1943- 🏳 AMERICAN ✍ INSTALLATIONS; LAND ART

Turrell produces gallery installations and land-art creations that are light-filled spaces. He wants to capture the physical reality (rather than the illuminating quality) of light (natural and artificial). You, the viewer, are to move about and become so involved and absorbed that you experience a different level of consciousness (spiritual or cosmic).

KEY WORKS: *Lunette*, 1974 (New York: Guggenheim Museum); *Night Passage*, 1987 (New York: Guggenheim Museum)

Rebecca **Horn**

● 1944- 🏳 GERMAN ✍ INSTALLATIONS; VIDEO

Horn is the creator of highly original installations incorporating machines that move, click, whirr, flick paint, or flap wings, and are generally surprising or unpredictable. Her work is compulsive viewing, entertaining and unnerving, and has the ability to set off odd and possibly alarming or subversive trains of thought (which is what she is after). Her machines need perfecting – there are too many breakdowns.

KEY WORKS: *The Hydra-Forest Performing Oscar Wilde*, 1988 (San Francisco: Museum of Modern Art); *Concert for Anarchy*, 1990 (London: Tate Collection)

Christian **Boltanski**

● 1944- 🏳 FRENCH ✍ SCULPTURE; INSTALLATIONS; PHOTOGRAPHY

Boltanski is a Frenchman who produces disturbing installations that are gloomy, dimly lit, labyrinthine, and claustrophobic. He collects items such as photographs, old clothes, and personal relics to address his central themes

of lost childhood, death, anonymity, and the Holocaust. Boltanski attempts to create a visual requiem for all innocent victims. He uses familiar war subject matter, to which he brings a new twist.

KEY WORKS: *The Reserve of Dead Swiss*, 1990 (London: Tate Collection); *Gymnasium Chases*, 1991 (San Francisco: De Young Museum)

☑ *Monuments: The Children of Dijon*
Christian Boltanski, 1986, 700 x 400 cm (275 ¾ x 157 ½ in), installation, Hamburg: Kunsthalle. Displaying photographs of anonymous French children, Boltanski has described his work as a monument to the glory of childhood.

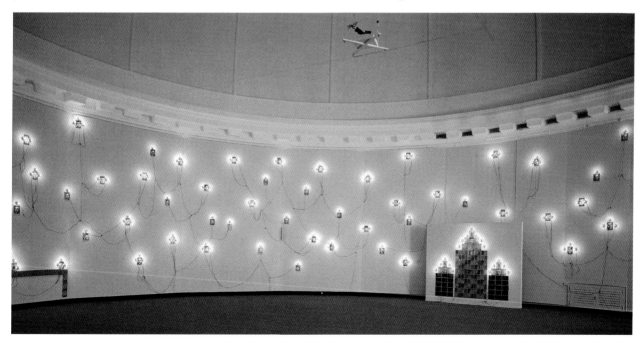

Sean **Scully**

● 1945- ℙ IRISH/AMERICAN ✍ OILS; PASTELS

Scully is noted for his high-minded abstract art (he believes in pure painting as high art). The favoured form is large, simple, horizontal and vertical stripes, and the technique emphasizes the qualities of paint through earthy grey colours and the subtle interplay of two and three dimensions. His works are sometimes made from separate panels. An "art for art's sake" of great refinement.

KEY WORKS: *Paul*, 1984 (London: Tate Collection); *Pale Fire*, 1988 (Texas: Modern Art Museum of Fort Worth)

Anselm **Kiefer**

● 1945- ℙ GERMAN ✍ OILS; ACRYLICS; MIXED MEDIA; SCULPTURE; PHOTOGRAPHY

A brilliant, charismatic, talented, dictatorial fanatic, Kiefer conceives on an apocalyptic scale. His energy for creating vast artistic schemes is manic. Very much in fashion and enthralls many who regard any criticism of him as impertinent, and ordinary praise as insufficient. He claims to be concerned with all the major issues of our day, especially Germany's place in history.

KEY WORKS: *Parsifal I*, 1973 (London: Tate Collection); *Margarethe*, 1981 (New York: Marion Goodman Gallery); *Osiris and Isis*, 1985-87 (San Francisco Museum of Modern Art); *Interior*, 1981 (Amsterdam: Stedelijk Museum)

Susan **Rothenberg**

● 1945- ℙ AMERICAN ✍ OILS; ACRYLICS; PRINTS; DRAWINGS

Rothenberg is a former dancer who came to prominence as a painter in the mid-1970s, whose work is now much displayed. Her large-scale works usually contain a human or animal form, emerging from a hazy background on the point of mutating into something else. Her work is weird, vaguely disturbing, and symptomatic of the American love of anxious self-analysis.

KEY WORKS: *Bone Man*, 1986 (New York: Museum of Modern Art); *Vertical Spin*, 1986–87 (London: Tate Collection)

>> *Red Banner* Susan Rothenberg, 1979, 228.6 x 314.6 cm (90 x 123 ¾ in), acrylic on canvas, Houston: Museum of Fine Arts. During this decade, Rothenberg explored themes based on horses, regarding the activity and investigation as akin to painting a self-portrait.

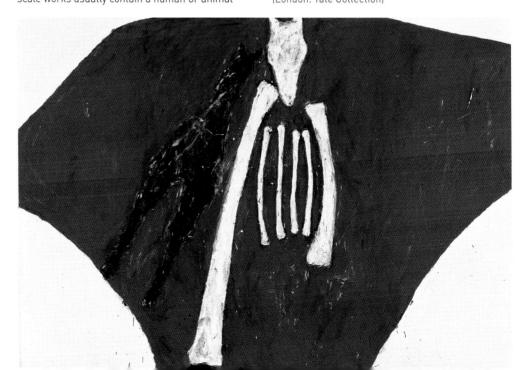

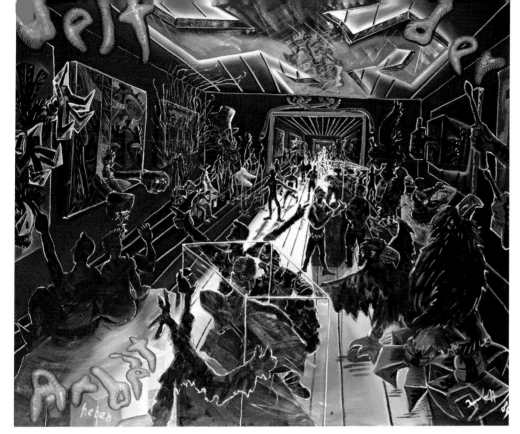

◀◀ **World of Work** *Jörg Immendorff, 1984, 284 x 330 cm (111 ¾ x 130 in), oil on canvas, Hamburg: Kunsthalle.* Never shy of publicity, Immendorf opened a bar in Hamburg's red light district in 1984.

Jörg **Immendorff**

● 1945–2007 ⚐ GERMAN ✍ OILS; SCULPTURE

Immendorff produced heavily painted Expressionist work that is essentially traditional and derivative (of Beckmann and 1920s German Expressionism). He addressed political issues such as the divided Germany or the environment.

Typical imagery within his work is a café interior with an anonymous crowd, and symbolism of watchtowers, uniforms, barbed wire, and eagles.

KEY WORKS: *The Rake's Progress*, 1992 (New Jersey: World House Gallery); *Untitled*, 1993 (New York: Philip Isles Collection)

Richard **Long**

● 1945– ⚐ BRITISH ✍ LAND ART; CONCEPTUAL ART; SCULPTURE; PHOTOGRAPHY

Long is a leading British land artist who achieved much early success. He won awards and attained international recognition in his 30s, but since the age of 50 has gone rather quiet.

He is an artist with very serious intentions. He works with the land, assembling bits of it (rocks, sticks, mud) in aesthetic configurations (typically, large-scale stone arrangements in a circle or line, or walls "painted" with the mud). His earlier work is in photographic form, recording marks made by him on and in the landscape he walked over.

Is he, as some claim, a development of the Constable-Wordsworth tradition (man's harmony with nature) or is he the opposite? Does he perhaps represent the modern city dweller's incomprehension of, and puzzlement at, nature – seeking to cover it in urban developments, transform it into municipal parks (however sensitively done), and bring it back to the city art gallery in chunks and buckets?

KEY WORKS: *A Square of Ground*, 1966 (London: Tate Collection); *A Line Made by Walking*, 1967 (London: Tate Collection); *Red Slate Circle*, 1980 (New York: Guggenheim Museum); *Wessex Flint Line*, 1987 (Southampton: City Art Gallery)

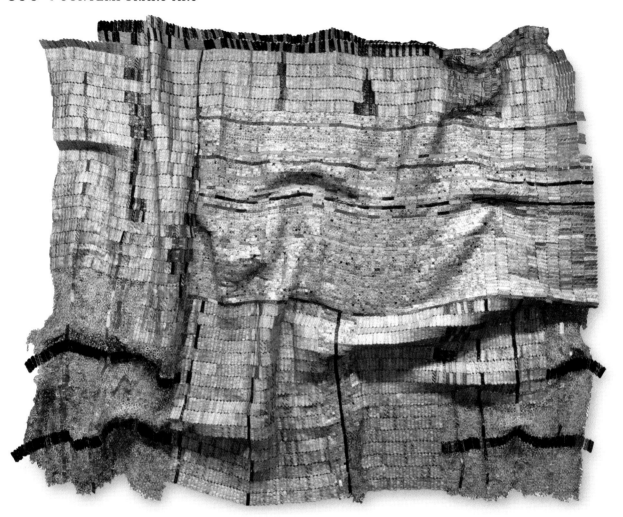

⚶ *Duvor Cloth*
El Anatsui, 2007,
aluminium and
copper wire, 296.2
x 518.2 cm (118 x
204 in), Indianapolis
Museum of Art, USA.

El **Anatsui**

● 1944– ᴾᵁ AFRICAN ✍ SCULPTURE; MIXED
MEDIA

Anatsui was born in Ghana and works in Africa.
He is best known for creating large-scale works
composed of thousands of small folded and
crumpled pieces of metal – sourced from local
recycling stations – which are connected together
with copper wires. These highly original works,
which are flexible and shimmering, assume
different forms each time they are installed,
and are created by teams of local workers.

KEY WORKS: *Flag for a New World Power*, 2005
(Artist's Collection); *Gravity and Grace*, 2010
(New York: Jack Shainman Gallery)

Jeff **Wall**

● 1946– ᴾᵁ CANADIAN ✍ PHOTOGRAPHY;
CONCEPTUAL ART

Wall produces immaculate cibachrome
photographs presented in steel frames and
illuminated from behind by fluorescent tubes.
The expectation created by their detailed
photographic realism is that they are "from
life". In fact, they are carefully selected and
posed artificial tableaux, maybe using actors.
His work is a neat play on what is reality and
what is art.

KEY WORKS: *A Sudden Gust of Wind (After Hokusai)*,
1993 (London: Tate Collection); *Citizen*, 1996 (Basel,
Switzerland: Kunstmuseum)

Anthony **Gormley**

● 1950- 🏛 BRITISH ✍ SCULPTURE; INSTALLATIONS

Gormley is an artist of increasing stature who has never been afraid to go against the grain of fashion.

His characteristically (but not exclusively) life-size human figures have no specific features and are made of metal, visibly soldered together in static poses. They are casts of the artist's own body. He is wrapped in clingfilm, then cloth, then coated with wet plaster, which dries. He is then cut out of the resulting mould, which is reassembled, and lead or other metal is pressed into the void, or beaten to take his form, and the pieces are welded together.

Gormley studied Buddhism in India, and there can be little doubt that he is an artist trying to say something (in which he may or may not succeed) rather than to play to a market. His 20-metre (65-ft)-high *Angel of the North* dominates the main A1 road on the approach to Tyneside.

KEY WORKS: *Three Ways: Mould, Hole, and Passage*, 1981 (London: Tate Collection); *Maquette for Leeds Brick Man*, 1986 (Leeds: City Art Gallery)

Bill **Viola**

● 1951- 🏛 AMERICAN ✍ VIDEO; INSTALLATIONS; PHOTOGRAPHY

Viola is one of a very small minority that uses video to genuinely creative effect. He tackles age-old subjects, such as birth, death, and human relationships with experience and understanding, and builds up imagery in ways analogous to the processes of painting. He also uses the technology to involve the viewer in creating the final image. His work is moving, perhaps even profound. One of the reasons why he is so successful and convincing is that he does not use the video medium and technology as an end or phenomenon in itself. He has something he wishes to say about the human condition and uses video technology to express it. Like all the best artists, he is totally in control of his chosen medium and can take it to the edge of its limitations.

KEY WORKS: *Nantes Triptych*, 1992 (London: Tate Collection); *The Crossing*, 1996 (New York: Guggenheim Museum)

🔽 *Angel of the North*
Anthony Gormley, 1997–98, height 20 m (65 ft), steel sculpture, Gateshead, UK. The work has a poetic significance as a memorial to the area's now defunct coal mining industry.

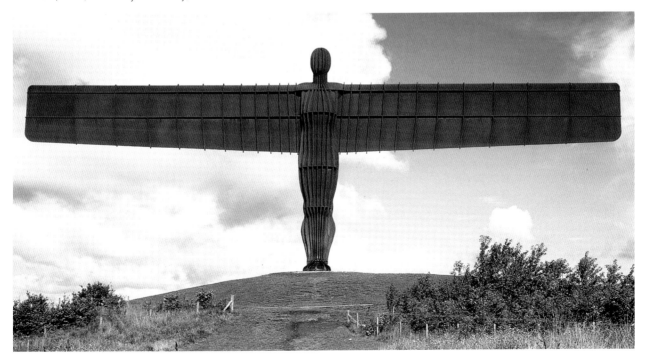

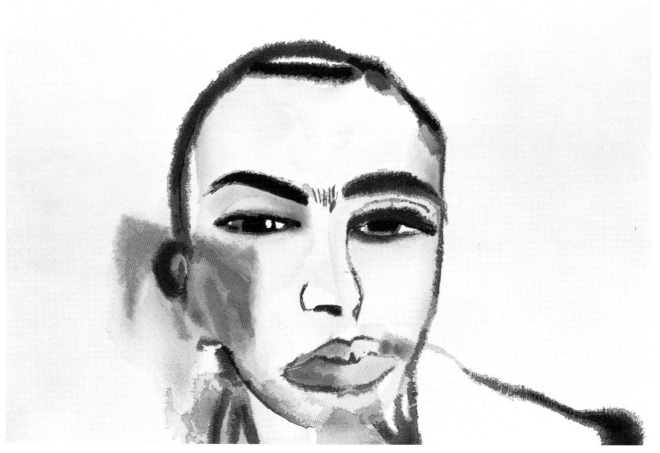

Head *Francesco Clemente, 1984, 93 ¾ x 53 ½ in, watercolour (London: Victoria & Albert Museum).* Clemente stated "My portraits are half what I see and the other half is invented".

Francesco **Clemente**

● 1952– Ⅺ ITALIAN/AMERICAN ✍ TEMPERA; WATERCOLOURS; OILS

Born in Naples, Clemente now lives in New York. He is one of the most respected members of the current art establishment. He is prolific, multifaceted, multinational – multi-everything. His work is the epitome of official contemporary artistic acceptability.

Clemente creates both large-scale works and smaller ones. He explores dual themes that are the meat of political correctness, such as the relationship between the past and present, the human and the animal, Europe and America, man and woman, East and West. He uses a wide variety of impeccable source material (Italian Renaissance, Indian art). Clemente is technically very sound and intellectually complex, with much symbolism to unravel.

With such correct, self-assured, firmly controlled agendas, technique, and subject matter, it is difficult to find fault. But why are the faces, eyes, and imagery in general so sad and lonely? Any art that takes itself so deadly seriously risks becoming passionless. Why the obsession with genitalia? It seems like joyless self-obsession: subjects are often sexual but not erotic. Yet it is the sort of art that public institutions want.

KEY WORKS: *Tondo*, 1981 (New York: Museum of Modern Art); *Fire*, 1982 (Zurich: Thomas Ammann Fine Art)

Mona **Hatoum**

◔ 1952– ⁍ LEBANESE ✍ VIDEO; INSTALLATIONS; PERFORMANCE ART; SCULPTURE

Hatoum is an involuntary refugee working in London. She creates installations and videos whose subjects are about exile, loneliness, and authoritarian politics, which she interweaves and interlinks with an examination of the undemocratic boundaries of traditional art practices.

KEY WORKS: *Measures of Distance*, 1988 (London: Tate Collection); *Corps Étranger*, 1994 (Paris: Pompidou Centre)

David **Salle**

◔ 1952– ⁍ AMERICAN ✍ OILS; ACRYLICS; PRINTS

Salle creates large-scale figurative paintings, which are a ragbag of familiar, not very taxing, images culled from art history, adverts, design, porn, and so on. Facile and technically feeble when examined closely at first hand, they, fortunately for him, look quite convincing as small-scale reproductions in books or catalogues. If you find this – or any other – artist's work awful or incomprehensible, but don't want to to say so or alienate yourself at private views, say "He (or she) has a style that is distinctly his own" (which is always true); "he neutralizes and subverts narrative and artistic conventions" (no one will dare disagree); "he appropriates art and images and simultaneously critiques them in his work" (people will be impressed, especially if you or they have no idea what you actually mean).

KEY WORKS: *Sextant in Dogtown*, 1987 (New York: Whitney Museum of American Art); *Walking the Dog*, 1992 (London: Tate Collection)

Sophie **Calle**

◔ 1953– ⁍ FRENCH ✍ PHOTOGRAPHY

Calle makes gallery displays with photographs and texts. She acts as a recorder and chronicler of society – spying on strangers, photographing them, recording what they say, involving them in her own deliberate role play. She is fascinated by the interplay of public and private, fiction and reality, exhibitionism and secrecy.

KEY WORKS: *The Birthday Ceremony*, 1981 (Chicago: Donald Young Gallery); *The Bronx*, 1991 (Boston: Barbara Krakow Gallery)

Nan **Goldin**

◔ 1953– ⁍ AMERICAN ✍ PHOTOGRAPHY

Goldin takes large-scale photographs, often in series, that create a visual diary of her social circle, travels, and emotional crises. She is especially concerned with so-called taboo (gay, lesbian, or transvestite) relationships and public awareness of their intimacies. Her work is honest, often moving, and beautifully crafted.

KEY WORKS: *Nan One Month after Being Battered*, 1984 (London: Tate Collection); *Siobhan in my Bathtub*, Berlin, 1992 (Winterthur, Switzerland: Fotomuseum)

Jaume **Plensa**

◔ 1955– ⁍ SPANISH ✍ CONCEPTUAL ART; INSTALLATIONS; SCULPTURE

The Spaniard Jaume Plensa is a good example of the new academic modern orthodoxy that is heavily promoted by the official art establishment.

He works with large-scale industrially made objects made to look significant, portentous, and profound, by being displayed in isolation or attached to big white walls in large official spaces. He "uses" steel, glass, and neon light, but the artist is only the designer: the physical creation is done anonymously, presumably in a factory.

If you remove the words that embellish the pieces ("Rembrandt", "womb", "desire", "Giotto", "a fool sees not the same tree a wise man sees"), what do they amount to? Profundity or banality? Is this art with deep meaning, or a clever exercise in marketing and packaging? Is this a good example of the way art establishments become mesmerized by big, slick productions?

KEY WORKS: *Knock, Knock, Knock*, 1999 (Kirishima, Japan: Kirishima Open-Air Museum); *Crown Fountain*, 2004 (Chicago: Millennium Park)

Martin **Kippenberger**

◒ 1953–97 ▥ GERMAN ✎ OILS; INSTALLATIONS; PERFORMANCE ART; PRINTS

Kippenberger created drawings, paintings, installations, and performances. Provocative, cynical, and anti-authority, he attempted to raise the trivial and "sub-cultural" to the status of high art (a mainstream activity of artists since 1900). His last work, *MetroNet*, is of an imaginary, underground railway world.

KEY WORKS: *Das Ende des Alphabets (ZYX)*, 1990 (Ghent: Stedelijk Museum voor Actuele Kunst); *The Raft of the Medusa*, 1996 (San Francisco: Museum of Modern Art)

Cindy **Sherman**

◒ 1954– ▥ AMERICAN ✎ PHOTOGRAPHY

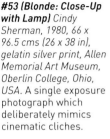

☑ *Untitled Film Still #53 (Blonde: Close-Up with Lamp)* Cindy Sherman, 1980, 66 x 96.5 cms (26 x 38 in), gelatin silver print, Allen Memorial Art Museum, Oberlin College, Ohio, USA. A single exposure photograph which deliberately mimics cinematic cliches.

Sherman is a leading New York artist beloved by art critics who swoon over the powerful manner in which she deconstructs and comments on women's role in a male-dominated consumer society.

She produces very large-scale photographs, often in high-key colour. Her works are in series. She acts the parts, makes the sets, and takes the photographs herself. There is no other (and no male) involvement. In the early series she depicted herself as media stereotypes and as ordinary girls and women. From 1985, she has produced series of grotesque images – teddy bears, dolls, or toys in a stew of vomit or slime; dehumanized medical dummies; also parodies of Old-Master portraits. She seems to have less of a specific agenda than most commentators wish on her. She claims to have discovered this style of work almost by accident. Her grotesque images are said to be a commentary on consumerism's excessive binges and purges. Try identifying with the stereotypes that Sherman portrays – career girl, runaway teenager, Ingres portrait, and so on.

KEY WORKS: *Untitled A–D*, 1975 (London: Tate Collection); *Untitled Film Stills (series)*, 1977–80 (New York: Museum of Modern Art); *Nr. 261*, 1992 (Hamburg: Kunsthalle)

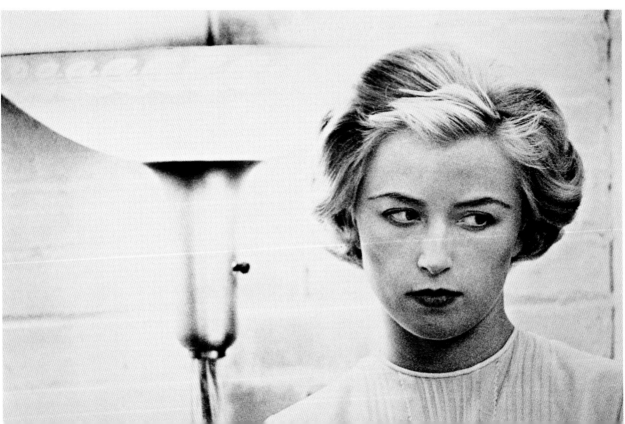

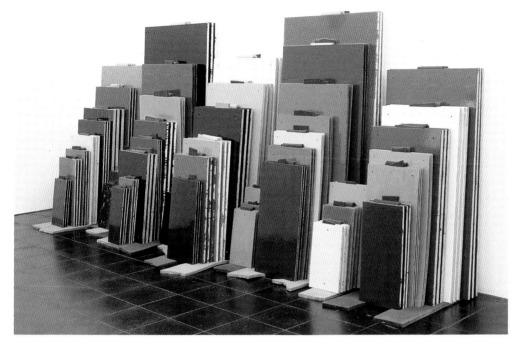

◀ *Lager (Store)* Thomas Schütte, 1978, 150 pieces, wood and varnish, personal collection

Thomas **Schütte**

● 1954– ⬛ GERMAN ✍ SCULPTURE; MIXED MEDIA; DRAWINGS

Schütte uses techniques and ideas from several disciplines in his work. He makes sculptures, which range from small, doll-like models to large pieces, drawings, and architectural models in wood similar to doll's houses. The human figure, scale, and presence are always apparent. His work encourages an open-ended, imaginative, non-aggressive questioning of the human condition and experience.

KEY WORKS: *Weinende Frau*, 1989 (Ghent: Stedelijk Museum voor Actuele Kunst); *Belgian Blues*, 1990 (Ghent: Stedelijk Museum voor Actuele Kunst)

Anish **Kapoor**

● 1954– ⬛ BRITISH/INDIAN ✍ SCULPTURE

Born in Bombay, Kapoor settled in the UK. He creates 3-D objects in which colour, space, and the interplay between the visible and invisible predominate – high-quality toys for adults, in the best sense.

His strange-looking objects are made from materials such as steel, fibreglass, or stone. They have highly polished or intensely pigmented surfaces, often on a large scale. Be prepared to suspend disbelief – stop seeing them as man-made objects and allow them to act freely on your perception and imagination. Go on, play with them.

If you let go and allow your mind and eye to follow their own course – rather as you may have been able to do as a child, looking at the sky and clouds – there is a lot there. Enjoy thrilling and strange spaces to sink into, colourful "magic kingdoms" to explore, the familiar made strange. Lots of simple, unthreatening, genuinely "out of this world" experiences. A fresh, inspiring affirmation of art's role in celebrating and creating some *joie de vivre*.

Kiki **Smith**

● 1954– ⬛ AMERICAN ✍ SCULPTURE; SCREENPRINTS; BODY ART; DRAWINGS

The daughter of sculptor Tony Smith, Kiki Smith trained briefly as a medical technician. She is obsessed with bodily fluids and parts, such as blood and saliva. She either displays these in jars or makes paper cutouts that suggest skin, and wax figures that seem to drip secretions. The underlying agenda for this need to play with the repellent is not clear.

KEY WORKS: *Ribs*, 1987 (New York: Guggenheim Museum); *Untitled (Train)*, 1994 (Santa Barbara, California: Museum of Art)

KEY WORKS: *As if to Celebrate, I Discovered a Mountain Blooming with Red Flowers*, 1981 (London: Tate Collection); *Untitled*, 1983 (London: Tate Collection); *Void Stone*, 1990 (Leeds: City Art Gallery)

Robert **Gober**

⬤ 1954– 🏳 AMERICAN ✍ SCULPTURE;
INSTALLATIONS; OILS; MIXED MEDIA

A maker of objects and installations, Gober is well regarded and much exhibited on the international circuit.

He explores various fashionable ideas, such as subversion of conventions and social norms (the happy family as oppressive rather than beneficial), gay politics, and green and conservation issues. Some of his objects look like found objects but are in fact made by Gober; others are everyday objects that overtly don't work (like an unconnected sink).

Does the work at times risk becoming too humourless, oblique, obscure, and overly didactic? Does he sometimes seem to say: "Today, students of mine, we are going to consider issues of normality and abnormality in contemporary society and strategies of how we might debate those issues by creating objects that will subvert our normal expectations"? Which interests him more: his strategies or the human issues? Aren't some of his chosen social issues very parochial?

KEY WORKS: *The Subconscious Sink*, 1985 (Minneapolis, Minnesota: Walker Art Center); *Prison Window*, 1992 (San Francisco: Museum of Modern Art)

Jeff **Koons**

⬤ 1955– 🏳 AMERICAN ✍ SCULPTURE;
CONCEPTUAL ART; OILS; PHOTOGRAPHY

Koons is good-looking, clever, witty, articulate, popular, good at self-publicity, and successful. A former salesman and Wall Street commodity broker, he is now one of the darlings of the contemporary art world. He is married to La Cicciolina (a famous Italian porn star and politician).

He glorifies and deifies the banal consumer object as a work of art. For instance, he presented pristine vacuum cleaners in the airtight, fluorescent-lit museum cases usually reserved for precious objects; he cast an inflatable toy rabbit as a polished sculpture like a Brancusi; he presented a kitsch life-size Michael Jackson model like a giant Meissen figurine; and he filmed himself and his wife making love in a sanitized, Disney-like setting. He has an obsession with newness.

His work displays layers of clever, deliberate symbolism: the pristine vacuum cleaner = phallic (male) + sucking (female) + cleaning (purity or goodness) + brand new (virginity and immortality). He comments on consumer society's relentless promotion of success and the luxury lifestyle – and also how the art market functions, since commodities can be turned into high art, and art into commodities.

KEY WORKS: *Lifeboat*, 1985 (Hamburg: Kunsthalle); *Three Balls Total Equilibrium Tank*, 1985 (London: Tate Collection); *Pink Panther*, 1988 (New York: Sonnabend Gallery); *Blue Poles*, 2000 (New York: Guggenheim Museum)

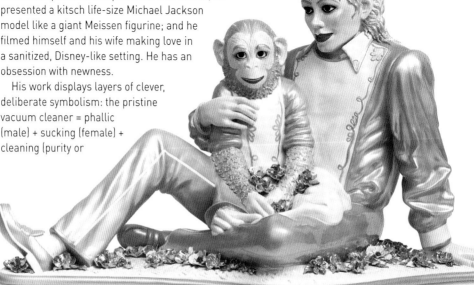

⏩ *Michael Jackson and Bubbles* Jeff Koons, 1988, porcelain, 234 ½ x 134 cm) 93 ¾ x 53 ½ in. The sculpture was made at the high point of the singer's career. Bubbles was his domestic pet.

Andreas **Gursky**

● 1955– 🏳 GERMAN ✍ PHOTOGRAPHY

Gursky is a commercially and critically successful capturer of the high-tech, fast-paced, modern world. He produces large-scale highly coloured photographs capturing various aspects of late capitalist society. Since the late 1980s, the scope of his images has expanded in size and subject matter (looking outside his native Germany to an increasingly global stimulus). He is particularly interested in the exchange mechanisms of capitalist societies. He produces highly formalized photos of North American and East Asian stock exchanges, where the crowds are colour-coordinated in an almost Abstract Expressionist way.

Gursky can be seen as a modern descendant of history painting, cataloguing our cultural mythologies. But don't expect documentation: his interest lies in the collective and anonymous, not the individual and personal.

KEY WORKS: *Schiphol*, 1994 (New York: Metropolitan Museum of Art); *Singapore Stock Exchange*, 1997 (New York: Guggenheim Museum); *99 Cent*, 1999 (New York: Metropolitan Museum of Art)

Felix **Gonzalez-Torres**

● 1957–96 🏳 CUBAN/AMERICAN ✍ CONCEPTUAL ART; INSTALLATIONS; MIXED MEDIA

Gonzalez-Torres was the acme of political correctness: Cuban, gay, and urban with a sad, untimely death (AIDS). His work is conceptual, featuring e.g. piles of sweets or paper, photographs, light bulbs. He is said to explore issues of illness, death, love, loss – life's sadness and transience – with a poetic aura.

Maybe his works don't achieve their stated ends unless accompanied by curatorial handouts, catalogues, or didactic writings? Who is creating the art work: the artist or the curator? Is it an example of art that is sincerely intentioned, but in the end amounts to very little?

KEY WORKS: *Untitled (Death by Gun)*, started 1990 (ongoing) (New York: Museum of Modern Art); *Untitled (Public Opinion)*, 1991 (New York: Guggenheim Museum)

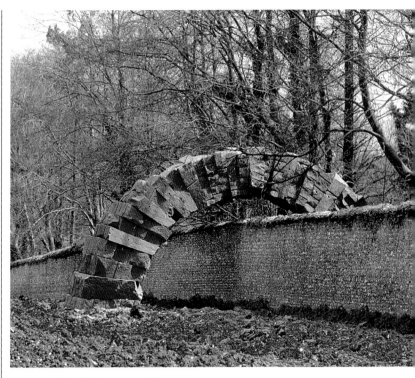

Andy **Goldsworthy**

● 1956– 🏳 BRITISH ✍ SCULPTURE; MIXED MEDIA; PHOTOGRAPHY

Goldsworthy works mostly in the open air with, and in response to, natural materials and particular places. He creates art with leaves, ice, trees, or stones.

His deeply sensitive response to nature, places, and seasons is in the English Romantic landscape tradition (like Constable or Palmer) but he offers new forms and interpretations. He weaves together the materials he uses in ways that rival nature's own ingenuity and beauty. Most works are made for, or left, out of doors where, as he intends, they eventually melt, fall over, or disintegrate.

He makes photographic records of these outdoor works, which he presents in book form as beautiful images and objects in themselves. He also produces work for gallery spaces and urban settings, though these tend to be less successful.

KEY WORKS: *Conch Shell Leafwork*, 1988 (Leeds: City Art Gallery); *Red Pool, Scaur River, Dumfriesshire*, 1994–95 (Virginia: Sweet Briar College Art Gallery)

🔼 *Arch at Goodwood*
Andy Goldsworthy, 2002, sandstone, Goodwood: Cass Sculpture Foundation. The pink quarried slabs of sandstone deliberately contrasts with the old grey flint wall which was built by French prisoners during the Napoleonic Wars.

>> *Portfolio of 5 Artists in Support of Bill T. Jones / Arnie Zane and Company*, Keith Haring, 1986, 229 ½ x 134 cm (93 ¾ x 53 ½ in). A set of prints inspired by Haring printing directly onto the body of choreographer Bill T. Jones.

KEY WORKS: *Subway Drawing*, 1980–81 (New York: Hyde Collection Art Museum); *Self-Portrait*, 1989 (Florence: Galleria degli Uffizi)

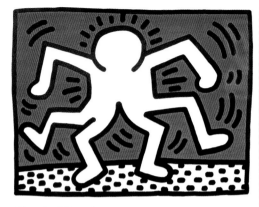

Keith **Haring**

● 1958–90 Ⓟ AMERICAN ✍ DRAWINGS; OILS; MIXED MEDIA; SCULPTURE

Haring was formally trained and first made his mark as a graffiti artist in the New York subway. In later life he was principally interested in marketing his easily recognizable images (simplistic pin men depicted with thick black outlines, participating in various inconsequential activities) via T-shirts, badges, and so on. The epitome of art and the artist as a brand image. He died of AIDS in 1990.

✉ *Profit I* Jean Michel Basquiat, 1982, 229 ½ x 134 cm (93 ¾ x 53 ½ in), acrylic & spray paint on canvas. Sold in 2002 for $5.5 million by drummer Lars Ulrich of heavy metal band Metallica.

Francis **Alys**

● 1959– Ⓟ BELGIAN ✍ CONCEPTUAL ART; OILS; PERFORMANCE ART; MIXED MEDIA

Alys is a painter, and conceptual and performance artist. He is active principally in Mexico City, where he sets up elaborate projects that are said to catalogue the (banal or surreal?) urban experience. Some of his works involve other people, such as advertisement painters. On one occasion, Alys dragged through the city a small magnetic dog that attracted metal debris.

KEY WORKS: *The Last Clown*, 1995–2000 (London: Lisson Gallery); *61 out of 60*, 1999 (London: Lisson Gallery)

Jean-Michel **Basquiat**

● 1960–88 Ⓟ AMERICAN ✍ ACRYLICS; MIXED MEDIA; COLLAGE

Basquiat was a young, black, middle-class New Yorker, who died of a drug overdose aged 28. He was a frenzied and prolific self-taught artist whose work powerfully reflected the obsessions and conflicts of his city and his decade. Basquiat's large-scale work has the

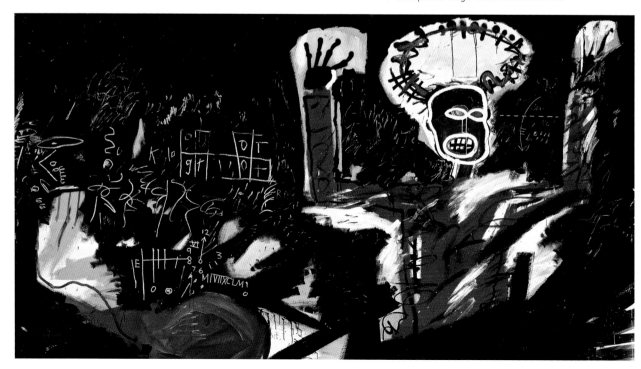

appearance, content, and crudity of graffiti on buildings (he began his career by secretly and illegally painting on public buildings). Their sheer energy, size, number, and consistency indicate an intelligence seeking release or crying for help. Shocking, controversial, ugly, drug-crazed they may be – boring and dismissable they are not.

His words, images, and collaged materials reflect the street life in which he grew up and lived, notably: racism, money (the art market took him up and his works sold for high prices), exploitation, Third World cultures, comics, TV and films, rap music, break-dancing, junk food, black heroes, urban ghettos, and sex.

KEY WORKS: *Untitled (Skull)*, 1981 (Santa Monica: Broad Art Foundation); *Saint*, 1982 (Zurich: Galerie Bruno Bischofberger)

Grayson **Perry**

◉ 1960– 🏛 **BRITISH** ✍ **MIXED MEDIA; CERAMICS; TEXTILES; METALWORK; DRAWINGS; ART**

Perry is one of the most intelligent artists working today. Realising the necessity of establishing a persona which would interest the media, he presented himself as a transvestite. Having satisfied the media's agenda, he now makes it pay attention to his. Deeply interested in his fellow human beings he explores what makes them tick in most subtle ways. Although known for his ceramic pots, these are not his forte (Perry has no real feel for the medium). Where he is truly inventive is with metalwork, fabrics, and stitching.

KEY WORKS: *Mother of All Battles*, 1996 (Kanazawa: 21st Century Museum of Contemporary Art); *Comfort Blanket*, 2014 (London: Victoria Miro)

Tracey **Emin**

◉ 1963– 🏛 **BRITISH** ✍ **INSTALLATIONS; CONCEPTUAL ART; SCULPTURE; VIDEO**

Emin is one of the great troopers in the art world. She is deeply and admirably loyal to her friends, colleagues, the students she teaches, the Royal Academy, and many worthy charitable causes.

But what of her art? It is by this that she will ultimately be remembered, or not. In her signature piece *My Bed* she laid bare her tragically unhappy youth (raped at 13; endless promiscuity; transient relationships, abortion). This public revelation was brave, but what she creates seems to be more about documenting her existence in a manner which is almost curatorial. The need to create things/installations/ so-called works of art as self explanation and self-justification now forms a significant part of what passes for art. How valid is the proposition that the celebrity/artist can by him/herself be a work of art?

KEY WORKS: *Just Love Me*, 1998 (Bergen, Norway: Kunstmuseum); *Hate and Power Can Be a Terrible Thing*, 2004 (London: Tate Collection)

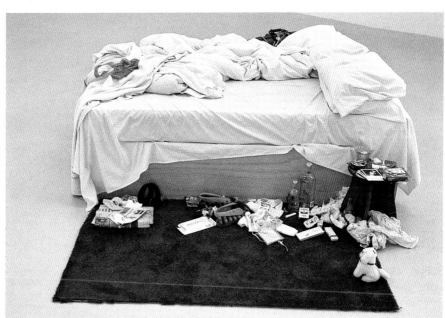

☒ *My Bed* Tracey Emin 1998, Mattress, linens, pillows, objects, 79 x 211 x 234 cm (31 x 83 x 92 in). Shortlisted for the Turner Prize in 1999, it was sold in 2014 for 2.2 million.

Rachel **Whiteread**

⬤ 1963– ◫ BRITISH ✍ SCULPTURE; DRAWINGS; PRINTS

Once one of the most fashionable of the young British artists who gained international attention, Whiteread was once much featured in the media.

She creates single-minded work of very serious, austere appearance. She makes physical casts in e.g. concrete, resin, rubber, of everyday objects and spaces (yes, spaces), such as the inside of a bath, spaces under chairs, and, most famously, the inside of complete rooms of a Victorian house (the house was then demolished by the local authority). The rationale behind her compositions is that she makes concrete the ordinary, banal spaces we inhabit and on which we leave the imprint of our existence.

Her most significant work is the Judenplatz Holocaust Memorial in Vienna, completed in 2000 – Whiteread's proposal was the unanimous choice in an international competition. Looking like a strange concrete bunker, the outer surfaces are casts of the vertical inner edges of identical books whose hidden titles are unknowable. In the centre of the main façade are double doors without handles, cast inside out, which cannot be opened. It is a consciously brutal presence amid the elegantly refined historic architecture of the City, and its potent symbolism is direct and unmistakeable.

KEY WORKS: *Untitled (Freestanding Bed)*, 1991 (Southampton: City Art Gallery); *Untitled (Air Bed II)*, 1992 (London: Tate Collection); *Untitled (Floor/Ceiling)*, 1993 (London: Tate Collection); **Monument (resin sculpture on a plinth)**, 2001 (London: Trafalgar Square)

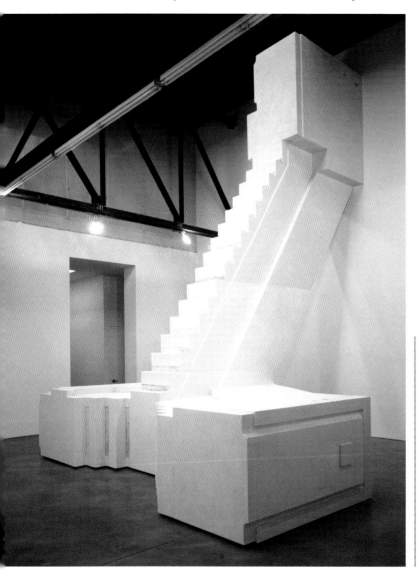

◖ *Untitled (Fire Escape)* Rachel Whiteread, 2002, 736 x 547.1 x 600.4 cm (290 x 215 x 236 in), plaster, fibreglass resin, and wood, Museum of Fine Arts, Houston, Texas, USA. Here the artist made a cast of ambient rather than enclosed space, but then reconfigured the separate parts to create a balanced abstract form.

Damien **Hirst**

⬤ 1965– ◫ BRITISH ✍ CONCEPTUAL ART; INSTALLATIONS; SCULPTURE; MIXED MEDIA; VIDEO

There is nothing shameful about making money out of works of art and some of the greatest artists have been shrewd businessman (Titian, Rubens). However, those who become artists principally to make money (there have been many) have nearly all disappeared without trace.

Damien Hirst has always been blatant about his desire for money and he has, together with his dealer, been phenomenally successful. Using assistants he has created a production line to supply the art market with what it is looking for. He claims to comment on life and death and current social obsessions such as genetic engineering, anxieties over health and becoming old and infirm. Famous for his animals preserved in formaldehyde he has made "art" from almost anything: carcases, cigarette butts, paint, and video. Once the biggest young name in the UK he is now middle-aged, and doubts are beginning to be expressed about the quality and originality of his work, and for how long he can continue to manipulate the market.

KEY WORKS: *Forms Without Life*, 1991 (London: Tate Collection); *In and Out of Love*, 1991 (London: Saatchi Gallery); *Prodigal Son*, 1994 (London: White Cube Gallery)

Matthew **Barney**

● 1967– 🏴 AMERICAN ✍ CONCEPTUAL ART; INSTALLATIONS; VIDEO; MULTIMEDIA

Barney is a former medical student, well known for creating events of interlinked film performances, installations, videos, and art books with a common narrative or theme. He is attracted by the repellent – strange, nightmarish forms made from horrible synthetic materials, slime made from Vaseline, mutants padded with cushions, bizarrely made-up models, and so on.

The underlying message is unclear: is he trying to make a meaningful comment on, or critique of, Western consumer society? Even if he is, is he merely pandering to that society's inherent voyeurism and narcissism – its love of looking at itself even (especially?) when it is particularly distorted, repellent, or violent?

KEY WORKS: *Metabolism of the Hubris Pill*, 1992 (Ghent: Stedelijk Museum voor Actuele Kunst); *The Cremaster Cycle*, 1994–2002 (New York: Guggenheim Museum); *Transexualis and Repressia*, 1996 (San Francisco: Museum of Modern Art)

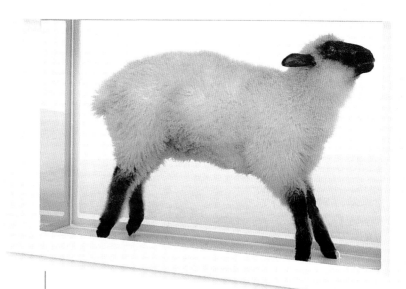

Mariko **Mori**

● 1967– 🏴 JAPANESE/AMERICAN ✍ VIDEO; PHOTOGRAPHY

Mori is the creator of strange, technically immaculate cibachrome or video images, which project a fantasy world that is a cocktail of futuristic science fiction, retro, Barbie dolls, kitsch, fashion, realism, and West and East. Her own extravagantly dressed image is central. She claims to be projecting an image of Utopia and the necessity of believing in utopias and optimism.

Can Utopia be so anodyne? This is not the vision of Utopia that sets out to reform the key moral, social, political, and environmental issues. It is the dream world of the global mega-shopper whose ambition is the latest "must have" brand. It is effective, but deeply narcissistic.

Chris **Ofili**

● 1968– 🏴 BRITISH ✍ MIXED MEDIA; COLLAGE

Ofili produces largish-scale technically complex works – layers of paint, resin, glitter, and collage. Famously uses elephant dung in the painted surface, or under the picture as a support (the result of a trip to his cultural homeland, Zimbabwe, in 1992). Addresses issues of black identity and experience via cultural references to the Bible, jazz, and porn. Has potential, but as yet undeveloped.

🖼 *Away From the Flock (second version)* Damien Hirst, 1994, 96 x 149 x 51 cm (37 ¾ x 58 ⅔ x 20 in), steel, glass, formaldehyde solution, and lamb, London: White Cube Gallery. A replica replacing the vandalized original.

KEY WORKS:
Empty Dream, 1995 (Chicago: Museum of Contemporary Art); *Birth of a Star*, 1995 (Chicago: Museum of Contemporary Art)

KEY WORKS: *Monkey Magic*, 1995 (Los Angeles: Museum of Contemporary Art); *No Woman No Cry*, 1998 (London: Tate Collection)

GLOSSARY

ABSTRACT ART A work of art with intellectual or emotional meaning (or both) that does not represent or imitate any visible object or figure.

ABSTRACT EXPRESSIONISM The avant-garde of the New York School, which flourished after Word War II: big, challenging, personal, emotional, painterly, and influential.

ABSTRACTION The word used when talking about an artist whose work distils natural forms or appearances into simpler forms, but who stops short of creating abstract art.

ACADEMIC STYLE The highly polished, finely detailed style that was promoted by the conservative 19th-century academies of art.

ACADEMICISM The clever but laborious reworking of established models. It exists in every age.

ACADEMIES The official institutions set up in many European countries to organize and promote exhibitions, art education, and aesthetic rules and standards.

ACTION PAINTING Painting produced by the emphatic physical activity of the artist; for instance, throwing the paint or dripping it onto canvas.

AERIAL PERSPECTIVE The illusion of receding space created by the use of warm colours (such as reds and oranges) in the foreground and cool colours (such as blues) in the distance.

AESTHETICISM, AESTHETIC MOVEMENT *See* Art for art's sake.

ALLEGORY A work of art in which symbols or symbolic messages are used to convey the "meaning". Thus it alludes to more than is apparent at first sight. Allegory and realism were combined with notable success by the Dutch 17th-century masters, and by 19th-century realists such as Winslow Homer.

ALTARPIECE The picture or sculpture made to go behind or on an altar and so enhance its part in the act of Christian worship.

ANALYTICAL CUBISM The works of Picasso and Braque from c.1901 to 1911, in which they fragmented form but still used conventional painting techniques.

ANTIQUE, ANTIQUITY Terms used to describe the art of ancient Greece and Rome.

ART FOR ART'S SAKE The idea that art is not concerned with storytelling, morality, religion, spiritual or intellectual enlightenment and suchlike, but only with its own aesthetic properties of colour, form, and so on.

ARTE POVERA Describes the work of the group of Italian avant-garde 1960s artists with a strong political agenda who created arte povera (poor art) objects from cheap materials.

ASHCAN SCHOOL An important group of late 19th-century American painters and illustrators who believed that art should portray the day-to-day hash realities of life and that artists should be seen to get their hands (and clothes) dirty.

ASSEMBLAGE A 3-D picture made from different everyday materials.

ATTRIBUTE The symbol associated with a figure that identifies it as a particular saint or god; thus Juno always has a peacock, St Catherine the wheel on which she was nearly martyred, and so on.

AVANT-GARDE Art that is so innovative it is ahead of the mainstream art of its time and is rejected as unacceptable by the official institutions.

BARBIZON SCHOOL A group of progressive mid-19th-century French landscape painters who worked in and around the village called Barbizon in the Forest of Fontainebleau near Paris.

BAROQUE The dominant artistic style of the 17th century. Look for illusion, movement in space, drama, love of rich colour and materials, heaviness, seriousness, and pomposity.

BAS RELIEF *See* Relief

BAUHAUS A famous modern art school that opened in Germany in 1919 and was closed by the Nazis in 1933. It was highly influential in the fields of architecture and design.

BEAUX ARTS The fine arts.

BIEDERMEIER The predominant style in Austria and Germany in the first half of the 19th century. Plain, bourgeois, modest, conservative, well made.

BIOMORPHIC FORMS Softly contoured organic (rather than geometric) forms used in abstract art.

BLAUE REITER, DER (THE BLUE RIDER) An important group of avant-garde German expressionists based in Munich c.1911. They wanted to put spiritual values into art and used abstraction, simplification, and the power of colour as a means of doing this.

BODY ART Art that takes the body as its subject or object (or both). Refers to such use in performance art, contemporary sculpture, or video.

BOLOGNESE SCHOOL An important 17th-century Italian school of artists based in and around Bologna, who successfully combined classicism and theatricality.

BOOK OF HOURS A prayer book used by laymen for private devotions. The hours refer to the times of day when prayers are said.

BRUCKE, DIE (THE BRIDGE) An important avant-garde group of German expressionists based in Dresden 1905–13 with radical political and social views expressed through modern, urban subject matter or landscapes and figures.

BYZANTINE ART The artistic tradition that flourished in Byzantium (Constantinople), the capital of the Eastern Roman Empire from c.330CE to the mid-15th century. Notable for stylized depictions of Christianity and Imperial Rome in mosaics, frescoes, and relief sculpture.

CALLIGRAPHY The art of fine handwriting.

CAMERA OBSCURA Latin for "dark chamber". A boxlike device that projects an image through a small hole or lens onto a sheet of paper or other material so that its outline can be traced. It works on the same principle as a simple photographic camera.

CAPRICCIO A fantasy townscape that combines both real and imaginary buildings. Used to good advantage by decorative 18th-century artists.

CARAVAGGISTI Followers of Caravaggio from all over Europe, who were influenced by his subjects, realism, and dramatic lighting.

CARICATURE An exaggerated, ludicrous, or satirical portrait.

CAROLINGIAN ART Art produced in the 8th and 9th centuries during the reign of Charlemagne and his successors.

CARTOON A full-sized drawing used as the design for a painting or tapestry.

CLASSICAL Belonging to or deriving from ancient Greece and Rome.

COLOUR FIELD PAINTING A type of Abstract Expressionism painting whose principal feature is a large expanse of colour with no obvious point of focus or attention.

COMPOSITION The arrangement of the shapes and areas of a picture, considered as surface pattern only.

CONCEPTUAL ART Works of art in which the only thing that matters is the idea or concept. No value or merit is given to materials or to physical or technical skill.

CONSTRUCTIVISM A very important avant-garde movement that originated in Russia (1917–21), concerned with abstraction, space, new materials, 3-D form, and social reform.

CONTRE-JOUR "Against the light" – looking at things that are strongly lit from behind, and so almost silhouetted.

CUBISM The most significant art and design innovation of the 20th century, Cubism overturned conventional systems of perspective and ways of perceiving form.

DADA The first of the modern anti-art movements. It deliberately used the absurd, banal, offensive, and shabby to shock and to challenge all existing ideas about art, life, and society.

DECONSTRUCTION The idea that the true meaning of a work of art is found not by examining what an artist professed to mean or tried to say, but by analysing the way he or she expressed it.

DIPTYCH A picture made in two parts. An altarpiece that is a diptych usually has the two parts hinged together.

DIVISIONISM A way of painting, in which colour effects are obtained optically, by separating them into individual dots or patches, for example, rather than by mixing colours on a palette. Seurat was the originator of Divisionism.

ELEVATION View of a building from one vantage point.

ENGRAVING A print technique, in which a sharp, V-shaped tool is pushed across a metal plate, producing precise, clear-cut lines. Widely used since the early Renaissance.

ENVIRONMENTAL ART Creating an environment (such as a room, but can be outside) so that the presence of the visitor in it becomes an integral part of the experience or event. Developed in the 1960s.

ETCHING A print technique widely used since the 17th century. The line is first drawn by hand, then acid is used to make the line eat into a metal plate. It produces a delicate, free-flowing line with a soft outline.

EUSTON ROAD SCHOOL An English group founded in the 1930s that promoted realism à la Cézanne.

EXPRESSIONISM A style conveying heightened sensibility through distortion of colour, drawing, space, scale, form, or intense subject matter, or a combination of these. One of the principal strands of 20th-century German art.

FAUVES, LES A French avant-garde movement that originated in 1905. One of the key early movements in Modern art. Decorative and expressive works full of bright colour and flat patterns, loosely painted.

FÊTE CHAMPÊTRE French for "outdoor feast". A group of elegant ladies and gents having a relaxed and happy time in a landscape setting and evidently absorbed with each other, love, and music. Much in vogue in 18th-century France.

FIGURATIVE ART Art that represents recognizable nature and objects. The opposite of abstract art.

FIN DE SIÈCLE Refers to the jaded, decadent attitudes in vogue at the end of the 19th century.

FINE ARTS Painting, sculpture, and architecture.

FORESHORTENING A perspective trick. An extreme example is a painting that gives the illusion of an arm pointing directly at the spectator, in fact only the hand is shown, the arm being hidden behind the hand.

FRESCO Italian for "fresh". Painting on the wet plaster of a wall so that when it dries, the painting is the plaster. This has to be done rapidly and with absolute certainty as there is no possibility for correction other than hacking off the plaster and starting again. Michelangelo's ceiling of the Sistine Chapel is fresco painting at its most magnificent.

FUTURISM One of the most important early avant-garde art movements. Originated in Italy in 1909–15, it was widely influential. Noisily promoted a worship of machinery, modernity, speed, and revolutionary change, using the latest avant-garde styles such as cubism.

GENRE A particular category of subject matter – such as portrait, landscape, marine, or history painting.

GENRE PAINTING A type of picture that purports to show a reassuring glimpse of everyday life. Usually small scale and intimate. Invented in 17th-century Holland and much in vogue in other prosperous bourgeois circles, such as 18th-century France, Biedermeier Germany, and 19th-century Britain.

GESSO A white absorbent ground for painting in tempera or oil. Made from chalk or gypsum mixed with glue.

GESTALT A one-word way of saying that the mind tries to turn chaos into order. It organizes what it perceives and senses, and tends to make the final result greater than the sum of individual parts.

GESTURE PAINTING *See* Action painting

GILDING Covering a surface with gold leaf.

GLAZING Old-Master technique of covering a layer of already-dried oil paint with a transparent layer of a different colour. One of the reasons for the rich, resonant, and subtle colour effects in Old Masters.

GOTHIC The principal European style in the arts (especially architecture) before the Renaissance, from the 12th to 15th centuries. Characterized by the soaring vertical and the pointed arch. The underlying message is spiritual uplift and devotion.

GOTHIC REVIVAL The reawakened interest in medieval art in the 18th and 19th centuries. Called *style troubadour* by the French.

GRAFFITO Strictly speaking "graffito" (or "sgraffito") describes any design scratched through a layer of paint or other material, to reveal a different ground underneath.

GRAND TOUR Rite-of-passage tour around Europe to see the major sights and works of art, and to experience life – very much the done thing in the 18th and 19th centuries.

GRAPHIC ART Art primarily dependent of the use of line, not colour, such as drawing, illustration, engraving, and printmaking.

GROTESQUE Decorative design incorporating fanciful human, animal, and plant features. The inspiration was the designs found in excavated crypts and grottoes (hence the name) in Rome in the early 16th century, notably the Golden House of Nero. In the 18th century the word came to mean something ridiculous and unnatural.

HALF-TONE Any tone or shade that lies between the extremes of light and dark.

HISTORY PAINTING Subjects of classical mythology, history, and biblical themes. Until the end of the 19th century any seriously ambitious painter had to succeed as a history painter or settle as an also-ran.

HUDSON RIVER SCHOOL Loosely organized group of American painters who established a new tradition for landscape painting in the US.

HUE Commonly described as colour.

ICON A sacred image – especially the images of Christ, the Virgin, and the saints produced for the Greek and Russian Orthodox churches.

ILLUMINATED MANUSCRIPT A handwritten text decorated with paintings and ornaments.

ILLUMINATION The embellishment of a written text with gold, silver, or colour.

IMPRESSION A print made by pressing a plate or block onto a piece of paper.

IMPRESSIONISM The famous progressive movement that started the dethronement of Academic art. The Impressionists went back to nature with the intention of painting only landscapes, portraits, and still lifes, freely and directly painted en plein air (outdoors).

INSTALLATION A work of art that integrates the exhibition space into its content. Currently the most pervasive form of official or museum art.

INTERNATIONAL GOTHIC A style of painting in favour in the late 14th and early 15th centuries. Colourful, very decorative, and rather artificial, with lots of realistic detail in costumes, animals, and landscapes.

ITALIANATE Strictly speaking, a work of art that recalls the Italian Renaissance, but sometimes used to describe a work with an Italian character, especially a golden light.

LAND ART Fashioning land into a work of art. Cannot be exhibited in a museum or gallery but photographs of land art projects are shown. Developed in the late 1960s.

LANDSCAPE A painting in which natural scenery is the principal subject and the motivating idea. Began to come into its own in the 17th century, and by the end of the 19th century replaced history painting as the main arm of any ambitious young artist.

LITHOGRAPHY This complicated printmaking process produces an image that looks as if it has been made with a soft or greasy crayon.

MANNERISM The predominant style c.1520–1600; elongated figures, artificial poses, complicated or obscure subject matter, vivid colour, unreal textures, deliberate lack of harmony and proportion. Seen at its best in Italy and France.

MARINE PAINTING A seascape with a narrative action, such as a naval battle.

MATT, MATTE Not shiny or glossy.

MEDIUM (PL. MEDIA) The material worked with and manipulated to make a work of art – such as oil paint, watercolour, charcoal, or clay.

METALPOINT A means of drawing using a fine needle of pure metal to make a mark on specially prepared paper.

MINIMAL ART A type of art that first became fashionable in the 1960s, designed for gallery and museum exhibition. Usually three-dimensional, large scale, and geometric, with the slick, anonymous precision qualities of manufactured or machine-made objects and little obvious visual significance or personal craftsmanship.

MIXED MEDIA Describes a work of art made with a variety of materials and techniques.

MOBILE A hanging sculpture with shapes of solids hung from wires of strings so that they move freely.

MODERN ART The great flowering of modern art occurred between 1880 and 1960 and it embraces all the avant-garde works produced at that time.

MONTAGE Use of cut-up, ready-made photographic and printed images (such as magazine advertisements) arranged and stuck down to make a work of art.

MOTIF A recurring or dominant theme, pattern, or subject.

MURAL A painting on a wall or ceiling

NABIS Group of progressive artists working in France c.1892–99. Believed in art for art's sake, decoration, simplification, emotion, and poetry. The name means "prophets" in Hebrew.

NAÏVE ART Art that looks as if it was done by someone who has had no professional training – with childish subject matter, bright local colours, wonky perspective, and unsophisticated enthusiasm.

NARRATIVE ART Art that tells a story.

NATURALISM The representation of nature with the least possible formal distortion or subjective interpretation.

NATURE MORTE French for "still life".

NAZARENES A group of progressive young Germans who formed a group in 1809 to revive the spirit and techniques of early Christian and Renaissance art.

NEOCLASSICISM The predominant fashionable style from about 1770 to 1830, emphasizing the spirit and appearance of Classical Greece and Rome. Tends to be severe, didactic, well made, and architectural (prefers straight lines).

NEUE SACHLICHKEIT German word meaning "New Objectivity". A stern, precise and detailed style often socially critical in content, fashionable in Germany in the 1920s.

NEW YORK SCHOOL *See* Abstract Expressionism

NON-OBJECTIVE ART *See* Abstract art

NORWICH SCHOOL Important group of landscape and seascape painters based in Norfolk c.1805–25. Inspired by the flat Norfolk landscape, and big skies, and by the Dutch masters.

ODALISQUE From the Turkish word *odalik* (*oda* = chamber; *lik* = function). An oriental female slave, usually painted half-naked and reclining. Ingres and Matisse both favoured the subject.

OEUVRE An artist's entire output.

OLD MASTER Strictly speaking describes any artist from the early Renaissance to roughly the mid-19th century. Popularly speaking describes any such artist whose reputation has stood the test of time, although reassessments and rediscoveries do occur. For example, Vermeer was rediscovered at the end of the 19th century. Georges de la Tour is currently being reassessed.

OP ART (OPTICAL ART) A type of abstract art that was at the forefront in the 1960s. Typified by hard-edge paintings, often in black and white, which bombard the eyes and cause them to "see" colours that are not actually there.

PALETTE The flat surface on which artists lay out their paints. Traditionally it is oval in shape with a hole for the thumb. The term also refers to the range of colours that an artists uses.

PASTORAL A scene portraying the life of shepherds and country people in an idealized way. The general atmosphere is usually sunny, fertile, peaceful, innocent, and carefree.

PATRON Somebody who commissions works of art from living artists – and so often influences the content or appearance of the work.

PEDESTAL The base on which a statue is placed.

PERSPECTIVE The basic rules of linear or geometric perspective were established in the Renaissance and are: a fixed, single viewpoint with lines that meet at a vanishing point, so creating the illusion of 3-D space on a flat white surface.

PHILISTINE Someone with a complete lack of interest in art or culture of any sort.

PHOTOREALISM Paintings that look like large, colour photographs but are in fact meticulously executed paintings.

PLEIN AIR A painting begun and completed in the open air, or one that conveys the qualities and sensations of open-air painting.

POINTILLISM Divisionism as practiced by Seurat, Signac, and Camille Pissaro.

POLYCHROME Many coloured. Used especially in reference to painted sculpture.

POP ART Predominant movement of the 1950s and the 1960s, especially in the US and UK. Played about with the popular fetishes of consumer society (such as advertisements, comics, and well known brand images like Coca-Cola). Often used quick and inexpensive commercial art techniques.

POST-IMPRESSIONISM Catchy phrase that doesn't mean very much, except that it includes all the more or less progressive artists from about 1885 to 1905.

PREDELLA In an altarpiece, the strip of small-size paintings set in the frame at the bottom of the main painting. They are usually narrative scenes related to the subject of the main painting.

PRE-RAPHAELITES Small influential group of young British artists who came together in 1848 and aimed to challenge conventional views by championing the artists who came before Raphael.

RAYONISM Avant-garde Russian movement of c.1913, which came near to abstraction. Its subject was light and rays of light.

REALISM Every generation defines realism in its own way. Renaissance artists thought their art was real because they opened a "window on the world" showing 3-D space and human emotion with an accuracy and intensity not seen before. On the other hand, modern abstract painters thought realism was showing that a picture is just paint on a flat surface. Some contemporary artists regard themselves as realists because they confront current social, green, or gender issues.

RELIEF From the Italian *rilevare* "to raise". Sculpture carved from a flat or curved surface so that part of the image projects. If the image projects slightly it is known as bas relief (low relief). If it projects more boldly, it is known as *alto rilievo* (high relief).

RELIEF PRINT A print made from a block or plate in which the area not to be printed is cut away, leaving the part to be inked standing in relief.

RENAISSANCE French, lit. "rebirth". The flowering of new ideas in Italian art between 1300 and 1550 which has influenced the subsequent development of all Western art.

ROCOCO The predominant style of the first half of the 18th century. Look for curves, pretty colours, playfulness, youth, elegance, fine craftsmanship, extravagance, carefree attitudes, and references to real and fanciful nature (flowers, leaves, rocks, birds, monkeys, or dragons).

ROMANESQUE The main style of Christian Europe in the 11th and 12th centuries, seen mostly in architecture and recognizable by the thick walls, small windows, and rounded arches. Look also for wall paintings, tapestries (such as the Bayeux tapestry), stained glass, and illuminated manuscripts.

SALON The French official annual public art exhibition, controlled by the Academie. Immensely influential, especially in the 19th century, when it was the bastion of conservative attitudes.

SCHOOL Group of artists whose work shows some similarities. A useful but often very imprecise term.

SCHOOL OF BOLOGNA Term encompassing 16th-century artists working in Bologna, fusing Venetian and Florentine influences into a distinctive Bolognese style.

SCHOOL OF FONTAINEBLEAU Group of 16th century Italian, French, and Flemish painters who decorated the Palace of Fontainebleau for Henri IV.

SCHOOL OF PARIS A useful term embracing the various artists, schools, and movements who pioneered new ideas in Paris in the first half of the 20th century.

SCULPTURE Three-dimensional work of art made by carving, modelling, or constructing. Like a picture, it has no useful function in itself.

SEASCAPE A picture that takes the sea as its subject. If the subject is ships, it is called a marine painting.

SECESSION Groups of progressive German and Austrian artists who challenged the ideals and authority of the academies in the 1890s. In Vienna, Gustav Klimt, a leading member of the Secession, explored the themes of love and sexuality that obsessed both the conservatives and the radical modernizers.

SECULAR Belonging to the everyday world, not to the spiritual or religious world.

SILHOUETTE Black paper cutout of the profile of a face, invented by a French Minister of finance called M. de Silhouette in the 18th century.

SILVERPOINT A method of drawing using an instrument with a fine silver tip, which makes a fine grey line on a specially prepared paper.

SKETCH A rapidly executed work in any medium. Used by artists to sort out general ideas for a painting (or sculpture) or to note the essential features of it.

SOCIAL REALISM Describes works of art showing everyday life, often in its harsher aspects.

ST IVES GROUP Group of British artists working in St Ives, Cornwall in the 1940s, 1950s, and 1960s.

STIJL, DE Dutch for "the style". The most influential avant-garde art magazine in the 1920s, founded and promoted by a group of Dutch artists. It was also the name of their movement, which advocated a geometrical type of abstract art, simplification, and social and spiritual forms.

STURM, DER German for "the storm". Name of a magazine and art gallery in Berlin, which was a major influence in promoting German and foreign modern art in Germany between 1912 and 1932.

SUBLIME A feeling of grandeur or awe induced by a work of art or nature – an aesthetic concept much discussed in the 18th century, reaching its fullest expression in the 18th and 19th centuries.

SUPERREALISM *See* Photorealism

SUPPORT A painting needs a support, which may be canvas, a wood panel, a copper sheet, paper, etc., The artist needs to prepare the support by painting on to it a primer and then a ground, to create a suitable smooth surface on which the picture can be painted.

SUPREMATISM Russian avant-garde movement pre-World War I, that strove to create a new spiritual awareness by developing an abstract art based on simplified geometric form, simple colour, and floating spatial relationships, unlike anything found in the material world.

SURREALISM The leading avant-garde movement of the 1930s. It sought to reach a new "super reality" by defying logic and accessing the unconscious (it was strongly influenced by Freud's theories).

SYMBOLISM Started as a progressive movement in 19th-century French poetry (Rimbaud, Baudelaire, Mallarmé, Verlaine), which influenced a number of painters interested in the mystical and spiritual. Look for strange, enigmatic and allegorical subjects designed to play on the emotions and come close to the power of dreams.

SYNTHETIC CUBISM The works done by Picasso, Braque, and Gris c.1912-15, featuring fragments of newspapers, tickets, and so on, incorporated into paintings.

TONE The lightness or darkness of a colour. Also described by referring to the lightness, value, intensity, or brilliance of a colour.

TOPOGRAPHY The detailed depiction of an actual place.

TROMPE L'OEIL French lit. "deceives the eye". A trompe l'oeil painting is designed to trick viewers into thinking that what they see is the real thing.

UTRECHT SCHOOL A group of 17th-century Dutch artists who visited Rome and were strongly influenced by the works of Caravaggio.

VANISHING POINT *See* Perspective

VANITAS A still life containing symbolic references (such as a skull or extinguished candles) to death and the transitory nature of life.

VELLUM Fine parchment made from the skin of a calf. (Same derivation as "veal".)

VIGNETTE Either a small, usually figurative, design, such as a portrait or a still life without a border and shading off at the edges, or a scene describing a brief, often domestic, narrative incident. Originally it meant a design of leaves and tendrils.

VORTICISM Avant-garde British art movement, 1913–15. Took up Cubist and Futurist ideas and aimed to shake up the stuffy British art world and art generally.

WOODCUT One of the most basic printing techniques, whereby the design to be printed is cut into a block of wood. Most 15th- and 16th-century prints, especially for book illustration, used the technique. It was replaced by metal engraving, and was revived at the end of the 19th century.

INDEX

Page numbers in **bold** refer to main entries.

PICTURE CREDITS

The publisher would like to thank the following for their kind permission to reproduce their photographs.

b = below; c = centre; l = left; r = right; t = top; BAL = Bridgeman Art Library.

1 BAL/Louvre, Paris; 2–3 BAL/Nasjonalgalleriet, Oslo, Norway/ © Munch Museum/Munch-Ellingsen Group, BONO, Oslo, DACS, London 2005; 4 Christie's Images Ltd © Successió Miró/ADAGP, Paris and DACS London 2015; 4–5 Corbis/D. Hudson; 5 Empics Ltd/Gorassini Giancarlo/ABACA; 6–7 Corbis/Sandro Vannini; 7 BAL/Naturhistorisches Museum, Vienna, Austria; 8 Getty Images/National Geographic/Sissie Brimberg; 9 BAL/Iraq Museum, Baghdad, Iraq, Giraudon; 10 BAL/Egyptian National Museum, Cairo, Egypt (tl); 10–11 Dorling Kindersley: Peter Hayman/The Trustees of the British Museum; 11 BAL (tr); BAL/Egyptian National Museum, Cairo, Egypt (br); 12 BAL/ Giraudon; 12–13 BAL; 13 Giraudon (tr); Peter Willi (br); 14 Corbis/Charles O'Rear (cl); BAL/British Museum, London (b); 15 Giraudon/Louvre, Paris (t); akg-images/Nimatallah (br); 16 BAL/Alinari /Museo Archeologico Nazionale, Naples; 17 Corbis/Gianni Dagli Orti (tr); akg-images/Nimatallah (b); 18 BAL/ Lauros/Giraudon (tr); Art Archive: Museo Capitolino Rome/Dagli Orti (bl); 19 Corbis/Sandro Vannini; 20 BAL/Giraudon/Louvre, Paris (t); 21 BAL/Castello Sforzesco, Milan; 22 Art Archive/Dagli Orti (A) (cl); BAL/San Vitale, Ravenna (b); 23 Art Archive/Dagli Orti (t); Cathedral of St Just Trieste (br); 24 BAL/British Museum, London/Boltin Picture Library (t); Corbis/Werner Forman (bl); 25 BAL/MS 58 fol.34r Chi-rho (initials of Christ's name) Gospel of St. Matthew, chap. 1 v. 18, Irish (vellum)/Board of Trinity College, Dublin, Ireland; 26 Dagli Orti/Bibliothèque Municipale Abbeville; 27 akg-images/Erich Lessing (tl); Art Archive/Dagli Orti (A)/Archaeological Museum Cividale Friuli (tr); Dagli Orti/Musée Condé Chantilly (b); 28 Alamy Images/Hideo Kurihara (t); 29 BAL/ Chartres Cathedral, Chartres, France (tr); BAL/Chartres Cathedral, Chartres, France, Peter Willi (b); 30–31 Corbis/Massimo Listri; 33 akg-images/Erich Lessing (cl); Alamy Images/AA World Travel Library (cr); 34 BAL/Samuel Courtauld Trust, Courtauld Institute of Art Gallery; 35 BAL/Musée Conde, Chantilly, France (c); Museo di San Marco dell'Angelico, Florence (bc); 36 BAL/ Galleria degli Uffizi, Florence; 37 BAL/Palazzo Pubblico, Siena; 38 Alamy Images/One World Images; 39 BAL/San Francesco, Upper Church, Assisi (t); Scrovegni (Arena) Chapel, Padua (b); 40 BAL/Fitzwilliam Museum, University of Cambridge; 41 BAL/Louvre, Paris; 42 BAL/Louvre, Paris; 43 Wallrat Richarts Museum, Cologne, Germany (t); BAL/Chartreuse de Champmol, Dijon (br); 44 BAL/Alinari/Bargello, Florence (tl); Palazzo Medici-Riccardi, Florence (b); 45 BAL/Galleria Nazionale delle Marche, Urbino; 46 BAL/Santa Maria Novella, Florence; 47 BAL/Louvre, Paris; 48 BAL/Bargello, Florence; 49 BAL/Museo dell'Opera del Duomo, Florence (tr); BAL/Ashmolean Museum, Oxford (b); 50 Louvre, Paris (tl); BAL/Campo Santi Giovanni e' Paolo, Venice (bl); 51 Photo Scala, Florence/Gabinetto dei Disegni e delle Stampe degli Uffizi, Florence; 52–53 BAL/Galleria degli Uffizi, Florence; 53 BAL/National Gallery of Art, Washington DC, US (cr); 54 BAL/Louvre, Paris; 55 BAL/Hermitage, St Petersburg, Russia (tr); Piccolomini Library, Duomo, Siena (bl); 56 BAL/ Palazzo Piccolomini, Siena; 57 Pushkin Museum, Moscow (tc); BAL/Pinacoteca, Sansepolero; 58 Louvre, Paris (tl); 58–59 BAL/Galleria dell'Accademia, Venice; 59 BAL/National Gallery, London (tr); 60 BAL/Musée de Picardie, Amiens, France; 61 Santi Giovanni e Paolo, Venice (tc); BAL/National Gallery, London (br); 62 BAL/Walker Art Gallery, Liverpool (b); Alamy Images/Norma Joseph (br); 63 BAL/Pinacoteca di Brera, Milan; 64 BAL/Gemaldegalerie, Berlin (tl); National Gallery, London (b); 65 BAL/National Gallery, London; 66 BAL/National Gallery, London; 67 BAL/Galleria degli Uffizi, Florence (tr); Musée des Beaux-Arts, Lille, France (bl); 68–69 BAL/Prado, Madrid; 70 BAL/ Louvre, Paris; 71 BAL/Galleria degli Uffizi, Florence; 72 BAL/Louvre, Paris; 73 BAL/Prado, Madrid (bl); BAL/Bibliothèque Nationale, Paris, France (br); 74 BAL/Musée Royaux des Beaux-Arts de Belgique, Brussels; 76 BAL/Musée d'Unterlinden, Colmar, France; 77 BAL/Musée d'Unterlinden, Colmar, France; 78 BAL/Walker Art Gallery, Liverpool; 79 BAL/Alte Pinakothek, Munich, Germany; 80–81 akg-images/Erich Lessing; 82 Corbis/Archivo Iconografico, S.A. (t); BAL/Lambeth Palace Library, London (b); 83 Alamy Images/ nagelestock.com; 84 BAL/Louvre, Paris (tl); Prado, Madrid (cr); 85 BAL/ Giraudon/Vatican Museums and Galleries, Vatican City; 86–87 BAL/Santa

Maria della Grazie, Milan (t); 86 BAL/Fitzwilliam Museum, University of Cambridge (bl); 87 BAL/National Gallery, London (tr); 88 Gemaldegalerie, Dresden, Germany (cl); BAL/Galleria degli Uffizi, Florence (br); 89 BAL/ Palazzo Pitri, Florence; 90 Bridgeman Images: Ashmolean Museum, University of Oxford, UK (tl); Museums and Galleries, Vatican City (b); 91 BAL/St Peter's Vatican, Rome; 92 BAL/Kunsthistoriches Museum, Vienna; 93 Galleria dell' Accademia, Venice; 94 Bridgeman Images: Louvre, Paris, France; 95 BAL/ Louvre, Paris; 96 BAL/Prado, Madrid; 97 Corbis/Trustees of the National Gallery, London; 98 Kunsthistoriches Museum, Vienna, Austria (tl); BAL/ Galleria degli Uffizi, Florence (bl); 99 BAL/Galleria degli Uffizi, Florence (tl); Louvre, Paris, France (br); 100 BAL/National Gallery, London; 101 BAL/ Bargello, Florence; 102 BAL/Galleria degli Uffizi, Florence; 103 BAL/Louvre, Paris; 104 BAL/Kunsthistorisches Museum, Vienna, Austria (tc); National Gallery, London (bl); 105 BAL/Giraudon/Château de Fontainebleau, Seine-et-Marne, France, Lauros; 106 BAL/Kunsthistorisches Museum, Vienna, Austria; 107 BAL/Prado, Madrid; Toledo, S. Tome (cl); 108 BAL/Gemaldegalerie, Kassel (tl); Private Collection (b); 109 BAL/Kunsthistorisches Museum, Vienna, Austria (tc), (cr); 110 BAL/Kunsthistorisches Museum, Vienna, Austria; 111 BAL/Kunsthistorisches Museum, Vienna, Austria; 112 National Gallery, London (t); BAL/Chatsworth House, Derbyshire (br); 113 Society of Antiquaries, London (cl); BAL/Beauchamp Collection (br); 114–115 Alamy Images/BL Images Ltd; 116 BAL/Giraudon/Musée Bargoin, Clermont-Ferrand, France, Lauros (t); Corbis/Massimo Listri (b); 117 Art Archive/Royal Society/Eileen Tweedy (t); Corbis/Bettmann (b); 118 BAL/Piazza Navona, Rome; 119 BAL/Palazzo Farnese, Rome (c, bl, br); 120 BAL/Prado, Madrid; 121 BAL/Hermitage, St Petersburg, Russia (tl); Louvre, Paris (br); 122 Vatican Museums and Galleries, Vatican City (tl); BAL/Ashmolean Museum, University of Oxford (b); 123 BAL/Birmingham Museums and Art Gallery; 124–125 BAL/National Gallery, London; 125 Palazzo Barberini, Rome (tr); BAL/Galleria Borghese, Rome (br); 126 BAL/Palazzo Pitti, Florence; 127 BAL/National Gallery, London; 128 BAL/Giraudon/Galleria Borghese, Rome, Lauros; 129 BAL/Santa Maria della Vittoria, Rome; 130 BAL/Louvre, Paris (tl); Louvre, Paris, Giraudon (b); BAL/Louvre, Paris (br); 131 BAL/National Gallery, London; 133 BAL/Louvre, Paris; 134 BAL/Apsley House, Wellington Museum, London (bl); Prado, Madrid (cr); 135 BAL/Prado, Madrid; 136 BAL/Louvre, Paris; 137 BAL/Bonhams, London; 138 BAL/Alte Pinakothek, Munich (bl); Kunsthistorisches Museum, Vienna, Austria (r); 139 BAL/National Gallery, London; 140 BAL/Wallace Collection, London (tr); BAL/Fitzwilliam Museum, University of Cambridge (cl); 141 BAL/Giraudon/Louvre, Paris, Lauros; 142 Private Collection (cl); BAL/Alte Pinakothek, Munich (bl); 143 Getty Images: Hulton Archive/Art Media/Print Collector (t, bc, br); 144 BAL/Wallace Collection, London; 145 BAL/Hamburg Kunsthalle, Hamburg (t); Townley Hall Art Gallery & Museum, Burnley, Lancashire (cr); 146 BAL/Barber Institute of fine Arts, University of Birmingham (tl); BAL/Gemaldegalerie, Kassel (b); 147 National Gallery, London (t); BAL/Fitzwilliam Museum, University of Cambridge (b); 148 BAL/ Louvre, Paris (tl); Giraudon/Louvre, Paris (b); 149 BAL/Harold Samuel Collection, Corporation of London; 150 BAL/Galleria degli Uffizi, Florence; 151 BAL/Private Collection (tr); Yale Centre for British Art, Paul Mellon Collection, US (bl); 152 BAL/British Museum, London; 153 BAL/National Gallery of Scotland, Edinburgh, Scotland (bl); BAL/Mauritshuis, The Hague, The Netherlands (br); 154 BAL/National Gallery, London; 155 BAL/National Gallery, London; 156 BAL/Wallace Collection, London; 157 BAL/Leeds Museums and Galleries (City Art Gallery); 158 BAL/Mauritshuis, The Hague (tl, b); 159 BAL/ Kunsthistorisches Museum, Vienna; 160 BAL/Scottish National Portrait Gallery, Edinburgh; 161 BAL/V&A Museum, London; 162–163 Alamy Images/Bildarchiv Monheim GmbH; 163 BAL/Musée de la Ville de Paris, Musée Carnavalet, Paris, France/Giraudon; 164 Dorling Kindersley: The Science Museum, London; 165 akg-images; 166 BAL/Louvre, Paris (tl); BAL/Louvre, Paris (cr); BAL/ British Museum, London (bl); 167 BAL/Giraudon/Louvre, Paris/Lauros; 168 Wieskirche, Wies, Germany (cl); BAL (bl); 169 BAL/Wallace Collection, London; 170 BAL/Worcester Art Museum, Massachusetts, US; 171 BAL/ Wallace Collection, London; 172 BAL/Louvre, Paris; 173 Detroit Institute of Arts (bl); BAL/Ca' Rezzonico, Museo di Settecento (tr); 174 Scuola Grande di San Rocco, Venice; 174–175 BAL/Residenz, Wurzburg; 176 BAL/Collection of the Earl of Pembroke, Wilton House, Wiltshire; 176–177 BAL/National Gallery, London; 178 BAL/Christies Images, London; 179 V&A Museum, London (t); BAL/Museum Narodowe, Warsaw, Poland (br); 180 Private Collection, Ken Welsh (t); BAL/National Gallery, London (b); 181 BAL/Hermitage, St Petersburg, Russia; 182 BAL/National Gallery London (t), (bl); 183 BAL/Yale Center for British Art, Paul Mellon Collection, US; 184 BAL/Scottish National Portrait Gallery, Edinburgh; 185 Private Collection; 186 BAL/Private Collection; 187 New Walk Museum, Leicester City Museum Service (cr); BAL/Charles

Young Fine Paintings, London (b);**188** BAL/Walker Art Gallery, Liverpool, Merseyside; **189** Fitzwilliam Museum, University of Cambridge (t); BAL/Christie's Images (br); **190** BAL/Detroit Institute of Arts (t); Whitworth Art Gallery, University of Manchester (b); **191** BAL/On Loan to Hamburg Kunsthalle, Hamburg; **192** BAL/Galleria Borghese, Rome (cl); John Bethell (br); **193** BAL/Louvre, Paris; **194** BAL/Château de Versailles, France; **195** BAL/Louvre, Paris (tr); Museum of Fine Arts, Boston, Massachusetts, US (bl); **196** BAL/Private Collection, Phillips, Fine Art Auctioneers, New York, US; **198–199** BAL/Giraudon/Louvre, Paris/Lauros; **199** BAL/Giraudon/Château de Versailles, France/Lauros; **200** Science & Society Picture Library/NMPFT (cl); Science Photo Library/Eadweard Muybridge Collection/Kingston Museum (cr); **201** BAL/Guildhall Library, Corporation of London; **202** BAL/Giraudon/Prado, Madrid (t); BAL/Index/Private Collection (bl); **203** BAL/Louvre, Paris, **204** BAL/Fitzwilliam Museum, University of Cambridge (tl); Staatliche Museen, Berlin (b); **205** BAL/Louvre, Paris, **206** BAL/Louvre, Paris, **206–207** BAL/Louvre, Paris; **208** BAL/Louvre, Paris (t); BAL/Castle Museum and Art Gallery, Nottingham (b); **209** BAL/Museum der Bildenden Kunste, Leipzig (tr); BAL/Hamburg Kunsthalle, Hamburg (bc); **210** BAL/White House, Washington DC; **211** BAL/Metropolitan Museum of Art, New York; **212** BAL/John Constable; **212–213** BAL/National Gallery, London; **214** V&A Museum, London (tl); BAL/Norwich Castle Museum (cr); **215** BAL/Apsley House, Wellington Museum, London; **216–217** BAL/National Gallery, London; **217** BAL/National Gallery, London; **218** Musée de la Ville de Paris, Musée du Petit-Palais, France Lauros/Giraudon (t); BAL/Giraudon/Château de Compiegne, Oise, France (b); **219** Private Collection (t); BAL/Musée d'Orsay, Paris (b); **220** BAL/Apsley House, Wellington Museum, London (t); Lady Lever Art gallery, Port Sunlight, Merseyside (b); **221** BAL/Lady Lever Art Gallery, Port Sunlight, Merseyside; **222** Whitworth Art Gallery, University of Manchester (cl); BAL/Louvre, Paris (b); **223** BAL/New York Historical Society; **224** BAL/Detroit Institute of Arts, US; **225** BAL/National Museum of American Art, Smithsonian Institute, US; **226** BAL/Museum of Fine Arts, Houston, Texas (tl); BAL/Private Collection (b); **227** BAL/Butler Institute of American Art (t); Bridgeman Images: Metropolitan Museum of Art, New York, US (bl); **228** BAL/Manchester Art Gallery; **229** BAL/Delaware Art Museum, Wilmington, (cl); National Gallery of Victoria, Melbourne, Australia (cr); **231** BAL/William Morris Gallery, Walthamstow; **232** Bridgeman Images: Musee d'Orsay, Paris, France; **233** BAL/Giraudon/Musée d'Orsay, Paris; **234** BAL/Musée d'Orsay, Paris; **235** BAL/Musée d'Orsay, Paris/© DACS 2005; **236** BAL/Louvre, Paris (tl); BAL/Walters Art Museum, Baltimore (b); **237** BAL/Musée d'Orsay, Paris; **238** BAL/Courtauld Institute Gallery, Somerset House, London; **238–239** BAL/Musée d'Orsay, Paris; **240** BAL/Musée Marmottan, Paris (tl); Private Collection, Christie's Images (bl); **241** BAL/Phillips Collection, Washington DC; **242** National Gallery, London (tl); BAL/Musée Marmottan, Paris (b); **243** BAL/National Gallery of Art, Washington DC; **244** BAL/Musée d'Orsay, Paris; **245** BAL/Musée d'Orsay, Paris (cr); National Gallery, London (bl); **246** BAL/Detroit Institute of Arts; **247** BAL/National Gallery of Art, Washington DC; **248** BAL/Hirshhorn Museum, Washington DC; **249** BAL/Musée Rodin, Paris; **250** BAL/Art Institute of Chicago; **251** BAL/V&A Museum, London; **252** BAL/Rijksmuseum Kröller-Müller, Otterlo, Netherlands (cr); V&A Museum, London (bl); **253** BAL/Detroit Institute of Arts; **254** Bridgeman Images: Musée d'Orsay, Paris, France; **255** akg-images (tr); **256** BAL/Museum of Fine Arts, Boston, Massachusetts; **257** BAL/Nationalmuseum, Stockholm, Sweden; **258** Private Collection (cl); BAL/Art Institute of Chicago (b); **259** BAL/Courtauld Gallery, London (t); Musée d'Orsay, Paris, France (b); **260** National Gallery, London; **261** BAL/Musée d'Orsay, Paris, France (t); Museum of Modern Art, New York (b); **262** Solomon R. Guggenheim Museum, New York (tl); BAL/Musée d'Orsay, Paris (br); **263** BAL/Bibliothèque Nationale, Paris, France; **264** Musée d'Orsay, Paris (tl); Philadelphia Museum of Art, Pennsylvania (cr); BAL/Musée d'Orsay, Paris (b); **265** BAL/Museum of Modern Art of the West, Moscow, Russia; **266** BAL/Musée National d'Art Moderne, Paris, France/© ADAGP, Paris and DACS, London 2005 (tl); Private Collection/© ADAGP, Paris and DACS, London 2005 (br); **268** BAL/© Mucha Trust (b); **269** BAL/Österreichische Galerie, Vienna, Austria; **270–271** Powerstock/Superstock/Richard Cummins © 2015 Calder Foundation, New York/DACS London; **272** Alamy Images/Petr Svarc; **273** Alamy Images/Ambient Images Inc (cl); Corbis/Rykoff Collection (tr); **274** DACS, London 2015: © Succession H. Matisse / DACS, London 2015 (cl); DACS, London 2015: © Succession H.Matisse / DACS 2015 (br); **275** The Baltimore Museum Of Art/ Cone Collection formed by Dr Claribel Cone and Miss Etta Cone of Baltimore, Maryland, BMA 1950.258. Mitro Hood/© Succession H. Matisse / DACS 2015; **276** BAL/National Gallery of Art, Washington DC/© ADAGP, Paris and DACS, London 2015 (t); Private Collection/© ADAGP, Paris and DACS, London 2015 (bl); **277** BAL/Private Collection/© ADAGP, Paris and DACS, London 2015; **278** Hamburg Kunsthalle, Hamburg/

© Fondation Oskar Kokoschka/DACS 2015 (c); BAL/Hamburg Kunsthalle, Hamburg (bl); **279** BAL/Musée National d'Art Moderne, Paris, France/© ADAGP, Paris and DACS, London 2005; **280** BAL/Nasjonalgalleriet, Oslo, Norway/© Munch Museum/Munch–Ellingsen Group, BONO, Oslo, DACS, London 2005, **281** BAL/Graphische Sammlung Albertina, Vienna, Austria (tl); BAL/Staatsgalerie, Stuttgart/© Nolde–Stiftung Seebull (br); **282** BAL/Brücke Museum, Berlin/© Ingeborg & Dr Wolfgang Henze–Ketter, Wichtrach, Bern; **283** BAL/Musée National d'Art Moderne, Centre Pompidou, Paris/© ADAGP, Paris and DACS, London 2005; **284** BAL/Saarland Museum, Saarbrucken/© DACS 2015 (bl); BAL/Stadtische Galerie im Lenbachhaus, Munich/© DACS 2015 (tr); **285** Art Archive/Dagli Orti/© DACS 2015 (t); BAL/J. Paul Getty Museum, Los Angeles/© DACS 2005 (b); **286** BAL/Musée Picasso, Paris France/© Succession Picasso/DACS, London 2015 (tl); National Gallery of Victoria, Melbourne Australia/© Succession Picasso/DACS, London 2015 (b); **287** BAL/Museum of Modern Art, New York/© Succession Picasso/DACS, London 2015; **288** Museum of Modern Art, New York/© Succession Picasso/DACS, London 2015 (cl); BAL/Art Institute of Chicago (br); **289** BAL/Giraudon/Lauros/Private Collection/© ADAGP, Paris and DACS, London 2015; **290** BAL/Christie's Images, London/© ADAGP, Paris and DACS, London 2015; **291** BAL/Private Collection/© ADAGP, Paris and DACS, London 2015; **293** BAL/Private Collection/Chagall ®/© ADAGP, Paris and DACS, London 2015; **294** BAL/Butler Institute for American Art; **295** Detroit Institute of Arts (t); BAL/Museum of Fine Arts, Houston, Texas (b); **296** BAL/Museum of Fine Arts, Houston, Texas; **298** BAL/© ADAGP, Paris and DACS, London 2015; **299** BAL/Solomon R. Guggenheim Museum, New York; **300** BAL/Albright Knox Art Gallery, Buffalo, New York/© DACS 2015 (tl); Private Collection (br); **301** BAL/Mattioli collection, Milan/© DACS 2015; **302** Stapleton Collection/© Wyndham Lewis and the estate of the late Mrs G.A. Wyndham Lewis by kind permission of the Wyndham Lewis Memorial Trust (a registered charity) (tr); BAL/Imperial War Museum, London/© Wyndham Lewis and the estate of the late Mrs G.A. Wyndham Lewis by kind permission of the Wyndham Lewis Memorial Trust (a registered charity) (b); **303** BAL/Coventry Cathedral, Warwickshire © Estate of Jacob Epstein/Tate, London 2005; **304** BAL/Private Collection, Lefevre Fine Art Ltd, London; **305** © Tate, London 2005; **306** Réunion Des Musées Nationaux Agence Photographique/Christian Bahier/Philippe Migeat/© Succession Marcel Duchamp/ADAGP, Paris and DACS, London 2015; **307** BAL/Abbot Hall Art Gallery, Kendal, Cumbria/© DACS 2015 (bl); Private Collection/© DACS 2015 (cr); **308** BAL/Scottish National Gallery of Modern Art, Edinburgh/© DACS 2005; **309** BAL/State Russian Museum, St Petersburg; **310** BAL/Kettle's Yard, University of Cambridge/The Works of Naum Gabo © Nina Williams (tc); Private Collection (cr); Musée Nationale d'Art Moderne, Centre Pompidou, Paris/© ADAGP, Paris and DACS, London 2015 (bl); **311** BAL/State Russian Museum, St Peterburg, Russia/© DACS 2005; **312** BAL/Detroit Institute of Arts/© DACS 2015 (t); Corbis © Succession Picasso/DACS, London 2015 (b); **313** BAL/© Christian Schad Stiftung Aschaffenburg/VG Bild–Kunst, Bonn and DACS, London 2015; **314** BAL/Hamburg Kunsthalle, Hamburg/© DACS; **315** Art Archive/Dagli Orti (cl); BAL/Museum of Fine Arts, Houston, Texas/© Hattula Moholy–Nagy/DACS 2015 (br); **316** akg-images/Erich Lessing/© DACS 2014; **317** Photo Scala, Florence/© Digital image, Museum of Modern Art, New York/© 2005 Mondrian/Holtzman Trust c/o HCR International, Warrenton, Virginia, US; **318** Kobal Collection/Buñuel–Dalí © Salvador Dalí, Fundació Gala–Salvador Dalí, DACS, 2015 (t); Photo Scala, Florence/© DACS 2015 (b); **319** BAL/Collection of Claude Herraint, Paris/© ADAGP, Paris and DACS, London 2015; **320** BAL/Philadelphia Museum of Art, Pennsylvania PA/© Salvador Dalí, Fundació Gala–Salvador Dalí, DACS, 2015 (tl); BAL/Kunsthaus, Zürich, Switzerland/© ADAGP, Paris and DACS, London 2015 (br); **321** BAL/Albright Knox Art Gallery, Buffalo, New York/© Successió Miró/ADAGP, Paris and DACS London 2015; **322** Photo Scala, Florence: White Images/© Man Ray Trust/ADAGP, Paris and DACS, London 2015; **323** Bridgeman Images: National Gallery of Art, Washington DC, US; **324** BAL/Imperial War Museum, London (cl); **324–325** Bridgeman Images: Wakefield Museums and Galleries, West Yorkshire, UK/Reproduced by permission of The Henry Moore Foundation; **326** Corbis/Andy Keate; Edifice (cr); BAL/Private Collection © Angela Verren Taunt 2015. All rights reserved, DACS (b); **327** BAL/Private Collection/Bowness, Hepworth Estate; **328** BAL/Mexico City, Mexico/Ian Mursell/Mexicolore/© DACS 2015; **329** BAL/Phoenix Art Museum, Arizona/© 2015. Banco de México Diego Rivera Frida Kahlo Museums Trust, Mexico, D.F./DACS (t); BAL/Private Collection/© DACS 2015 (b); **330** BAL/© Museum of Fine Arts, Houston, Texas, US, Gift of Meredith J. and Cornelia Long; **331** BAL/© Museum of Fine Arts, Houston, Texas, US/© ARS, NY and DACS, London 2015 (t); BAL/© Butler Institute of American Art, Youngstown, OH, US, Museum Purchase 1950 (br); **332** BAL/

AUTHOR ACKNOWLEDGEMENTS

Catalogue descriptions of Old Master paintings sometimes contain a caveat to the effect that although the work of art is principally by the hand of the artist in question, it is possible to detect other hands at work. I am very grateful to those who contributed, and whose hands can at times be detected. In particular I would like to thank Thomas Cussans who contributed the text on early art, and Reagan Upshaw. Nonetheless I take responsibility for what is written, and I hope that the fresh ideas outnumber the errors. Paintings also reveal influences and here I would like to acknowledge a few of many: Bernard Berenson, Kenneth Clark, Umberto Morra, Robert Hughes, John Updike, Virginia Spate, Norbert Lynton, Erika Langmuir, many generations of students, and, above all, my wife Carolyn.